SAMS
Teach Yourself
PL/SQL™

in 21 Days

SECOND EDITION

SAMS

A Division of Macmillan USA
201 West 103rd St., Indianapolis, Indiana, 46290 USA

Sams Teach Yourself PL/SQL™ in 21 Days, Second Edition

Copyright ©2000 by Sams Publishing

International Standard Book Number: 0-672-31798-2

Library of Congress Catalog Card Number: 99-65434

Printed in the United States of America

First Printing: December 1999

01   00   99   4   3   2   1

Trademarks

Warning and Disclaimer

ASSOCIATE PUBLISHER
Bradley L. Jones

ACQUISITIONS EDITOR
Chris Webb

DEVELOPMENT EDITOR
Steve Rowe

MANAGING EDITOR
Lisa Wilson

PROJECT EDITOR
Heather Talbot

COPY EDITOR
Kitty Jarrett

INDEXER
Chris Wilcox

PROOFREADER
Megan Wade

TECHNICAL EDITOR
Jeff Shockley

TEAM COORDINATOR
Meggo Barthlow

MEDIA DEVELOPER
Dave Carson

INTERIOR DESIGN
Gary Adair

COVER DESIGN
Aren Howell

COPY WRITER
Eric Borgert

PRODUCTION
Cyndi Davis-Hubler

Contents at a Glance

Contents

About the Authors

Jonathan Gennick is a manager in KPMG Consulting's Public Services practice, where he specializes in Oracle technologies. He got his start with relational database systems in 1990, first working with Ingres, and then later with Digital's Rdb software. In 1994 he made the leap to Oracle, and hasn't looked back yet. Much of his time is spent providing database administration services, as well as server-side PL/SQL support, to clients and internal project teams.

When he is not working with Oracle, Jonathan can often be found writing about it. Since 1997 he has been involved with a number of writing projects. He coauthored the first edition of this book, *Sams Teach Yourself PL/SQL in 21 Days*. He was the technical editor for *Oracle8 Server Unleashed* (Sams, 1998), and the development editor for *Sams Teach Yourself Access 2000 in 24 Hours* (Sams, 1999). His second book, *SQL*Plus, The Definitive Guide*, was published in 1999 by O'Reilly & Associates. In addition to coauthoring the second edition of this book, Jonathan continues to be involved in various other writing and editing projects.

Writing has given Jonathan the opportunity to pursue several interests outside his normal day-to-day work. He is a member of the technology committee for the Greater Lansing Adventist School, where he is currently helping to set up both a LAN and an Internet connection. This satisfies his gnawing need to learn new things, and also his desire to help others learn.

Jonathan is a member of MENSA, and he holds a bachelor of arts degree in information and computer science from Andrews University in Berrien Springs, Michigan. Jonathan resides in Lansing, Michigan, with his wife, Donna, and their two children, Jenny and Jeff. Jonathan can be contacted by email at jonathan@gennick.com.

Tom Luers, PMP, is a principle consultant with a leading international information technology consulting firm. Over the past 16 years, he has worked with clients and business partners in Europe, North America, and Asia. Tom specializes in Project Management, Oracle technologies, and implementing IT solutions to meet business, manufacturing, and engineering needs. He is also the author of Sams Publishing's *Essential Oracle7*.

Dedication

To my daughter, Jenny. You suffered without me while I wrote the first edition of this book, and now you've suffered again while I've written the second edition. Thanks for being so patient. I love you. I'm very proud of you, and now I owe you another "daddy-day."

—Jonathan Gennick

To my wife, Cathy, and children, Jon, Sarah, and Matthew.

—Tom Luers

Acknowledgments

First, I would like to thank Tom Luers for helping me to coauthor this second edition of *Sams Teach Yourself PL/SQL in 21 Days*. Both of us have worked hard on this revision. Tom is a pleasure to work with, and with his client-side PL/SQL experience, he brings a valuable perspective to the book.

I would also like to thank Chris Webb of Macmillan USA for working so hard on his end to make this project a reality. Steve Rowe, also of Macmillan, put a lot of effort into editing this book, and deserves a big piece of the credit for the final result. I've always felt that editors' names should go on the front cover with the authors'. My appreciation also goes out to Jeff Shockley and Meggo Barthlow. Jeff Shockley was the technical editor on this book. He not only tested all the scripts to be sure that they worked on systems other than our own, but also provided valuable feedback on the clarity of our explanations. Meggo Barthlow, of Macmillan, handled the large number of administrative details that go with the writing of any book.

Finally, I don't want to forget my family and my readers. To all the readers of the first edition who took the time to write in with questions, corrections, and other observations, I say thanks! Your emails helped shape this revision. Please keep the emails coming—I enjoy hearing from you. To my family also, I must say thanks. In fact, that just doesn't cut it, but I don't know what else to say. My wife Donna has been incredibly patient and supportive while I've worked on this project. There were many days when all I did from dawn to dusk was sit in my room and write. Thanks, Donna! To my son Jeff: Thanks for always running in and interrupting me with a hug whenever you were in trouble with Donna. To my daughter Jenny: Thanks for all those times that you let me drive you back and forth to school. I'll miss that when you're older.

—Jonathan Gennick

I wish to thank my great wife, Cathy, and my great kids, Jon, Sarah, and Matthew. Without their support, patience, and dedication, this project would not have been possible. I also wish to acknowledge the LSO sports organization, Thunderhawks, friends and family, and KI for providing many hours of relief for me and my family while working on this project. I wish to also thank Dad, Sis, Dee, and others for the special memories of them, which helped motivate me to complete this project.

—*Tom Luers*

Tell Us What You Think!

As the reader of this book, *you* are our most important critic and commentator. We value your opinion and want to know what we're doing right, what we could do better, what areas you'd like to see us publish in, and any other words of wisdom you're willing to pass our way.

As an associate publisher for Sams, I welcome your comments. You can fax, email, or write me directly to let me know what you did or didn't like about this book—as well as what we can do to make our books stronger.

Please note that I cannot help you with technical problems related to the topic of this book, and that due to the high volume of mail I receive, I might not be able to reply to every message.

When you write, please be sure to include this book's title and authors as well as your name and phone or fax number. I will carefully review your comments and share them with the authors and editors who worked on the book.

Fax: 317-581-4770

Email: adv_prog@mcp.com

Mail: Associate Publisher
          Sams Publishing
          201 West 103rd Street
          Indianapolis, IN 46290 USA

Introduction

Welcome to *Sams Teach Yourself PL/SQL in 21 Days, Second Edition*. The fact that you purchased this book indicates that you have an interest in learning the PL/SQL language, which is Oracle's relational database procedural programming language. It allows you to develop powerful and complex programs to access and manipulate data in the Oracle8i database. We have attempted to include as many examples of PL/SQL code as possible to illustrate PL/SQL features.

This book is organized to teach you the major components of Oracle's procedural language in 21 days, a chapter per day. Each chapter covers a specific topic in PL/SQL and should take approximately three to five hours to complete. (Of course, this time depends on your own pace.) This book introduces you to concepts and practical applications of them in PL/SQL programs. We strongly encourage you to practice what you read. Go ahead and type in the listings in your local Oracle database and experience PL/SQL for yourself. You will gain a much deeper understanding of PL/SQL by practicing as you go along. Feel free to experiment on your own with any concepts presented because this will reinforce what you learn.

We have made several assumptions about you, the reader. We have assumed that you are at least somewhat familiar with SQL and the Oracle database. You should understand how to write simple `SELECT`, `INSERT`, `UPDATE`, and `DELETE` statements. Additionally, you should have some knowledge about Oracle database objects such as tables, as well as other schema objects such as sequences and views. If needed, you might want to read *Sams Teach Yourself SQL in 21 Days* prior to reading this book. We have also assumed that you want to learn some practical applications of PL/SQL and not just the syntax of the language. Therefore, we have incorporated examples and notes to meet this goal.

What This Book Is About

The beginning of this book lays the foundation on which you will build PL/SQL programs. In the first week, you will discover the building blocks of PL/SQL, such as expressions, various iterations, built-in functions, procedures, and error-handling routines. After this foundation is built, in the second week, you will move directly to learning about more advanced PL/SQL topics, such as how to build PL/SQL programs with cursors processing, collections, triggers, composite database structures, debugging processing, and large object data types. Finally, the third week covers transaction management, dynamic SQL, the Java engine, and advanced queuing. When you complete this book, you will be able to develop your own PL/SQL programs. You will have the knowledge to store these programs in the database and execute them.

Many of the chapters build on each other. As the book progresses from chapter to chapter, topics are covered in more detail and complexity, so it is advisable to start at the beginning and work through all 21 days. If you are already familiar with PL/SQL, however, you might prefer to go to the chapters of specific interest to you.

You should be aware of your own version of Oracle in regard to the code that is used here. Although Oracle8i has been used in the development of this book, most of the code here is backward compatible with earlier versions of Oracle. We also mention new features of Oracle8i so that those of you who are using that can learn about, and take advantage of, these enhancements.

Finally, all source code listings used in this book's sample code can be accessed at www.samspublishing.com. Simply search the Web site to find this book and download the files.

Who This Book Is For

This book is developed for beginning to intermediate programmers. This book is beneficial as a resource to more experienced developers as well. The details covered in this book allow the novice to get up to speed quickly and start developing PL/SQL applications immediately.

A Note About the Listings

All the listings in this book have been generated by SQL*Plus. All the listings also have line numbers so that the analysis following each listing can easily refer to specific lines of code. When you type PL/SQL blocks into SQL*Plus, SQL*Plus generates its own line numbers as part of the prompt. To avoid confusion between the SQL*Plus generated line numbers and the listing line numbers, the listings have been edited to show only one set of line numbers.

For example, when typing in a simple PL/SQL block, SQL*Plus would generate line numbers as shown here:

```
SQL>BEGIN
  2    NULL;
  3 END;
  4 /
```

In the book, a listing such as the above will usually be shown as

```
1: BEGIN
2:    NULL;
3: END;
4: /
```

In cases where a listing consists of more than one PL/SQL block, the SQL*Plus line numbers and the listing line numbers will not match up. By not showing both sets of line numbers, we hope to avoid confusion.

What's New

This is the second edition of *Sams Teach Yourself PL/SQL in 21 Days*. Our primary goal in bringing out a new edition now was to add coverage for some significant new features that were added to the language when Oracle8i (release 8.1.5) was released. A second goal was to rearrange some content that, based on emails received from readers, seemed to be causing some confusion. We believe that we've succeeded on both counts.

The new PL/SQL features introduced in Oracle8i, which you will read about in this book, include the following:

- Use of invoker's rights when executing stored code
- PL/SQL bulk binds
- Embedded dynamic SQL within PL/SQL
- Parameter passing by reference
- Autonomous PL/SQL blocks
- Calling Java from PL/SQL, and vice versa
- Advanced queuing

Advanced queuing is a robust messaging system, suitable for use in distributed computing environments. It was actually introduced in Oracle8, but has been significantly enhanced for Oracle8i. It provides a publish/subscribe messaging system with functionality that far exceeds that provided by dbms_pipes.

Oracle8i implements a Java engine within the database. Oracle has been making a lot of noise in the marketplace about this. It is now possible for PL/SQL code to make calls to Java code, and vice versa. This book won't teach you how to code in Java, but it will show you how you can load Java classes into Oracle, and how you can package the methods in those classes so that they can be called from PL/SQL.

Autonomous PL/SQL blocks support autonomous transactions. These are independent transactions that may be executed and committed within the context of a larger transaction. This feature was added to make it easier for developers to write reusable components, and is something that I've wanted in a language for years. Finally, with Oracle8i, it has arrived.

Parameter passing by reference is a relatively minor enhancement. It provides a safer way to pass parameters to functions when you know that the function is not supposed to change anything.

Embedded dynamic SQL is Oracle's new syntax for writing dynamic SQL code from PL/SQL. It provides functionality similar to the DBMS_SQL package, but is much easier to use.

PL/SQL bulk binding is a mechanism used to pass large chunks of data back and forth between the client and the server. Instead of retrieving 50 rows one at a time, you get all 50 rows in one shot. This gives you a large performance boost because you have eliminated a lot of network overhead.

The Oracle definer's rights model for stored code is one that always seems to confuse developers who are new to the Oracle environment. Oracle8i now allows you to choose between a definer's rights model and an invoker's rights model when you deploy stored code. This allows you to publicly deploy a generic procedure that accesses data without compromising data security.

Oracle8i is an exciting new product. PL/SQL is an excellent language to use for database programming. We hope that you enjoy learning about both as you read this book.

WEEK 1

At a Glance

Get ready! You are about to embark on a three-week journey to learn Oracle's PL/SQL programming language. PL/SQL is at the core of several Oracle products, including Developer/2000 and the Oracle 8i database itself. During the first week, you will cover the basics of the PL/SQL language. During the second week, you will learn some of the more advanced features, and you will also learn how to use PL/SQL in conjunction with the database. Week 2 also explores some of Oracle8i's object-oriented features. The third week takes you into the world of Oracle's built-in packages.

Where You Are Going

Day 1 starts the week with an introduction to PL/SQL, a discussion of how it relates to other Oracle products, and an example of a stored function written in PL/SQL. On Days 2 and 3, you will move on to learn the basics of the PL/SQL language. You will learn about the datatypes available in PL/SQL and what they can be used for; how to write PL/SQL expressions; and about the block structure used to write PL/SQL code and what that means to you as a developer. Days 4 and 5 teach you about the various control structures, such as loops and IF statements, that are available. Day 6 includes a discussion of PL/SQL's built-in functions. The week finishes with Day 7, which discusses the major building structures of PL/SQL (procedures, packages, errors, and exceptions) gives you some tips for experimenting with them, and provides examples showing how you can use the more commonly used functions. Good luck and have fun!

1

2

3

4

5

6

7

WEEK 1

DAY 1

Learning the Basics of PL/SQL

by Jonathan Gennick

Congratulations on your decision to read this book, *Sams Teach Yourself PL/SQL in 21 Days, Second Edition*! If you are new to the Oracle environment, this book will help you learn and master Oracle's built-in procedural language quickly. Knowledge of PL/SQL (Procedural Language/Structured Query Language) is becoming a fundamental necessity no matter which of Oracle's many products you use.

Today, on your first day, you will accomplish these tasks:

- Learn what PL/SQL is and why you should master it
- Learn how PL/SQL relates to other Oracle products
- Learn what resources you need to finish this book
- Write your first PL/SQL function

Over the remaining 20 days, you'll delve deeper into the power and capabilities of this language and learn how to leverage its power in your applications regardless of whether you are doing client/server programming with Oracle's tools (such as Developer/2000), using other front-end tools (such as PowerBuilder), or simply writing some batch jobs that run on the server.

What Is PL/SQL?

PL/SQL is a procedural language that Oracle developed as an extension to standard SQL to provide a way to execute procedural logic on the database.

NEW TERM   If you have worked with relational databases in the past, you are no doubt familiar with SQL, which stands for *Structured Query Language*. SQL itself is a powerful declarative language. It is *declarative* in the sense that you describe the results that you want but not how they are obtained. This is good because you can insulate an application from the specifics of how the data is physically stored. A competent SQL programmer can also push a great deal of processing work back to the server level through the creative use of SQL.

There are limits, though, to what you can accomplish with a single declarative query. The real world is seldom as neat and clean as we would like it to be. Developers often find themselves needing to execute several queries in succession and process the specific results of one query before going on to the next. This leads to two problems in a client/server environment:

- The procedural logic, that is, the definition of the process, resides on client machines.
- The need to look at the data from one query and use it as the basis for the next query results in an increased amount of network traffic.

Why are these problems? The procedural logic on client machines can quickly become out of sync if the software is upgraded. It can also be implemented incorrectly, resulting in a loss of database integrity. The need to pull down large amounts of intermediate data to a client results in a long wait for the end users who must sit there staring at the hourglass while the data is transferred to their machines. The cumulative effects of a number of clients pulling large amounts of data across the network further decrease performance.

PL/SQL provides a mechanism for developers to add a procedural component at the server level. It has been enhanced to the point where developers now have access to all the features of a full-featured procedural language at the server level. It also forms the basis for programming in Oracle's continually evolving set of client/server development tools, most notably Developer/2000.

Why Learn PL/SQL?

1

If you are developing with Oracle products, Developer/2000 for example, the answer to this question is simple. You need to know PL/SQL because those products use PL/SQL for any procedural code. But what if you don't develop with Oracle's products? What if all you use is Oracle's database engine? Is PL/SQL of any use to you? Absolutely, it is!

Regardless of the front-end tool that you are using, you can use PL/SQL to perform processing on the server rather than the client. You can use PL/SQL to encapsulate business rules and other complicated logic. It provides for modularity and abstraction. You can use it in database triggers to code complex constraints, which enforce database integrity; to log changes; and to replicate data. PL/SQL can also be used with stored procedures and functions to provide enhanced database security. Finally, it provides you with a level of platform independence. Oracle is implemented on many hardware platforms, but PL/SQL is the same on all of them. It makes no difference whether you are running Personal Oracle on a laptop or Oracle8i Enterprise on UNIX.

Regardless of what development tools you use, if you are developing in an Oracle environment, your knowledge of PL/SQL and your ability to apply it will give you a competitive advantage against those who do not. With PL/SQL you have the power to make your applications more robust, more efficient, and more secure.

SQL, SQL*Plus, PL/SQL: What's the Difference?

This question has bedeviled many people new to Oracle. There are several products with the letters "SQL" in the title, and these three, SQL*Plus, SQL, and PL/SQL, are often used together. Because of this, it's easy to become confused as to which product is doing the work and where the work is being done. This section briefly describes each of these three products.

SQL

SQL stands for Structured Query Language. This has become the *lingua franca* of database access languages. It has been adopted by the International Standards Organization (ISO) and has also been adopted by the American National Standards Institute (ANSI). When you code statements such as SELECT, INSERT, UPDATE, and DELETE, SQL is the language you are using. It is a declarative language and is always executed on the database server. Often you will find yourself coding SQL statements in a development tool, such as PowerBuilder or Visual Basic, but at runtime those statements are sent to the server for execution.

PL/SQL

PL/SQL is Oracle's *Procedural Language* extension to SQL. It, too, usually runs on the database server, but some Oracle products such as Developer/2000 also contain a PL/SQL engine that resides on the client. Thus, you can run your PL/SQL code on either the client or the server depending on which is more appropriate for the task at hand. Unlike SQL, PL/SQL is *procedural*, not declarative. This means that your code specifies exactly how things get done. As in SQL, however, you need some way to send your PL/SQL code up to the server for execution. PL/SQL also enables you to embed SQL statements within its procedural code. This tight-knit relationship between PL/SQL, SQL, and SQL*Plus is the cause for some of the confusion between the products.

SQL*Plus

SQL*Plus is an interactive program that allows you to type in and execute SQL statements. It also enables you to type in PL/SQL code and send it to the server to be executed. SQL*Plus is one of the most common front ends used to develop and create stored PL/SQL procedures and functions.

What happens when you run SQL*Plus and type in a SQL statement? Where does the processing take place? What exactly does SQL*Plus do, and what does the database do? If you are in a Windows environment and you have a database server somewhere on the network, the following things happen:

1. SQL*Plus transmits your SQL query over the network to the database server.
2. SQL*Plus waits for a reply from the database server.
3. The database server executes the query and transmits the results back to SQL*Plus.
4. SQL*Plus displays the query results on your computer screen.

Even if you're not running in a networked Windows environment, the same things happen. The only difference might be that the database server and SQL*Plus are running on the same physical machine. This would be true, for example, if you were running Personal Oracle on a single PC.

PL/SQL is executed in much the same manner. Type a PL/SQL block into SQL*Plus, and it is transmitted to the database server for execution. If there are any SQL statements in the PL/SQL code, they are sent to the server's SQL engine for execution, and the results are returned back to the PL/SQL program.

The important thing is that SQL*Plus does not execute your SQL queries. SQL*Plus also does not execute your PL/SQL code. SQL*Plus simply serves as your window into the Oracle database, which is where the real action takes place. Figure 1.1 illustrates this relationship.

FIGURE 1.1

*Relationship of
SQL*Plus, PL/SQL,
and Oracle.*

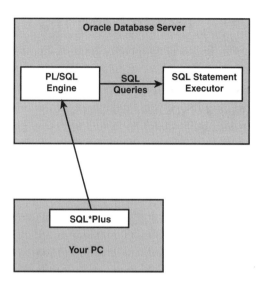

Several other tools besides SQL*Plus can serve as your window to the database. Server Manager, which has an interface similar to SQL*Plus, is one such tool, although Oracle plans to stop supporting it sometime in the future. If you have Oracle Enterprise Manager installed, you should take a look at SQLPlus Worksheet. SQLPlus Worksheet is a GUI tool that is fully compatible with SQL*Plus but is much easier to use. If you are a Developer 2000 programmer, you'll have access to Oracle's Procedure Builder—a tool designed for developing and debugging PL/SQL code. You'll read more about SQLPlus Worksheet and Procedure Builder later in this chapter.

SQL*Plus is used for most of the examples in this book because of its universal availability to developers. It is perhaps still the most widely used tool to develop, test, and create PL/SQL stored subprograms and SQL queries.

Note

In addition to Oracle's tools, several third-party vendors also have tools that can be used to develop PL/SQL code. Some of the major products in this space are

- *SQL-Programmer* by Sylvain Faust Inc. Web address: www.sfi-software.com
- *SQL-Station* by Platinum Technology Inc. Web address: www.platinum.com
- *SQL-Navigator* by Quest Software. Web address: www.quest.com
- *Tool for Oracle Application Developers* (TOAD) by Quest Software. Web address: www.quest.com

What You Need to Finish This Book

In order totry the examples and complete the exercises in this book, you will need access to

- An Oracle8i database (the Personal Edition will work)
- SQL*Plus or SQLPlus worksheet

Note

> Where possible, the exercises and examples in this book have been designed to run equally well under both Oracle8 and Oracle8i. Many, especially those in the first nine days, will even run under Oracle7. However, Oracle8i contains many new features that are not available in previous releases. Days 10, 11, 12, 20, and 21, in particular, are heavily focused on the new 8i features.

If you do not currently have access to an Oracle database, there are at least two ways to get your hands on one. For a nominal cost, you can visit Oracle's online store and purchase a 30-day evaluation version of almost any Oracle product, including the database. You can get to the online Oracle Store from Oracle's home page, `http://www.oracle.com`. Another option is to join the Oracle Technology Network (OTN). OTN members can download developer-licensed copies of Oracle's database software at no charge. OTN members also have the option of subscribing to various technology tracks in order to get regular shipments of Oracle software CDs. You can register as an OTN member at no cost. The URL to visit is `http://technet.oracle.com`.

You will need these database privileges roles:

- `CREATE PROCEDURE`
- `CREATE SEQUENCE`
- `CREATE SESSION`
- `CREATE TABLE`
- `CREATE TRIGGER`
- `CREATE VIEW`
- `CREATE TYPE`

The following Oracle-supplied packages should be available:

- `DBMS_OUTPUT`
- `DBMS_SQL`
- `UTL_FILE`

- DBMS_PIPE

- DBMS_ALERT

Your database administrator can help you verify that these packages are available to you.

If you are using Oracle8i Personal Edition, you can verify the existence of these packages by logging on as the user SYSTEM and issuing the following query:

```
SELECT object_name
FROM dba_objects
WHERE owner='SYS'
AND object_type = 'PACKAGE';
```

The resulting list will show you all packages in the database owned by the user SYS. The packages named in this chapter should be in that list. Of those, the DBMS_OUTPUT is the most essential and is used throughout most of the exercises and examples to display results. The other packages are discussed only in specific chapters.

| Caution | I recommend that you do not use a production database and that you create the sample tables in a schema that is not shared with other users. If you are using Personal Oracle on your own PC, you won't have a problem with this. If you are using an employer's facilities, you might want to discuss use of the database with your employer's database administrator, or DBA, as they are often called. There is nothing inherently dangerous in any of the exercises or examples, but there is always the risk that a coding mistake, such as an infinite loop, might tie up CPU or I/O resources. It's always good etiquette to minimize the potential impact of your mistakes on other developers and end users. |

Getting Started with PL/SQL

By now you should have a basic understanding of what PL/SQL is and how it relates to other Oracle products. You should have access to an Oracle database environment either at work or at home. During the rest of this chapter, you will learn some of the basics of PL/SQL, and you will write your first Oracle stored function.

PL/SQL Is Block Structured

NEW TERM PL/SQL is referred to as a *block structured* language A PL/SQL block is a syntactical unit that might contain program code, variable declarations, error handlers, procedures, functions, and even other PL/SQL blocks.

The Syntax for a PL/SQL Block

```
DECLARE
  variable_declarations
BEGIN
  program_code
EXCEPTION
  exception_handlers
END;
```

In this syntax, `variable_declarations` are any variables that you might want to define. Cursor definitions and nested PL/SQL procedures and functions are also defined here. `program_code` refers to the PL/SQL statements that make up the block. `exception_handlers` refers to program code that gets triggered in the event of a runtime error or exception.

The declaration section of a PL/SQL block is optional, although in practice it is unusual not to have any declarations at all. The exception handler portion of a PL/SQL block is also optional, and you won't see much of it until Day 7, "Procedures, Packages, Errors, and Exceptions."

▲

> **Note**
>
> When you're defining PL/SQL functions, procedures, and triggers, the keyword DECLARE is not used. When defining a function, the function specification, or function header as it is sometimes called, begins the block. Similarly, procedure and trigger specifications begin procedure and trigger blocks. Function, procedure, and trigger blocks are covered in more detail on Day 2, "Writing Declarations and Blocks."

NEW TERM Any variable declarations must immediately follow DECLARE and come before BEGIN. The BEGIN and END keywords delimit the procedural portion of the block. This is where the code goes. The EXCEPTION keyword signifies the end of the main body of code, and begins the section containing exception handling code. The semicolon at the end of the block, and at the end of each statement, is the PL/SQL statement *terminator*, and signifies the end of the block.

> **Tip**
>
> Omitting the semicolon at the end of a block is a common oversight. Leave it off, and you'll get a syntax error. Remember to include it and you will save yourself lots of aggravation.

Blocks such as the one shown in "The Syntax for a PL/SQL Block" form the basis for all PL/SQL programming. An Oracle stored procedure consists of one PL/SQL block. An Oracle stored function consists of one PL/SQL block. An Oracle database trigger consists of one PL/SQL block. It is not possible to execute PL/SQL code except as part of a block.

PL/SQL blocks can be *nested*. One block can contain another block as in the following example:

```
DECLARE
  variable declarations go here
BEGIN
  some program code
  BEGIN
    code in a nested block
  EXCEPTION
    exception_handling_code
  END;
  more program code
END;
```

Nesting of blocks is often done for error-handling purposes. You will read more about error handling on Day 7.

Compiling and Executing a Simple Block

Are you ready to try writing your first PL/SQL code? Good. Remember that for this and all other examples in this book, you will be using SQL*Plus to send the PL/SQL code to the Oracle database for execution.

1. Begin by running SQL*Plus and connecting to your Oracle database. Your initial SQL*Plus screen should look like the one shown in Figure 1.2.

2. Next, type in the following lines of code from Listing 1.1 exactly as shown. Notice the slash at the end. It must be typed in as well, exactly as shown.

INPUT   **LISTING 1.1**   Your First PL/SQL Block

```
DECLARE
  x      NUMBER;
BEGIN
  x := 72600;
END;
/
```

FIGURE **1.2**

*Initial SQL*Plus
screen.*

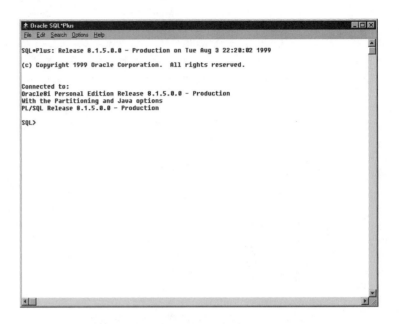

Note	The slash at the end tells SQL*Plus that you are done typing PL/SQL code. SQL*Plus will then transmit that code to the Oracle database for execution. The slash has meaning to SQL*Plus only, not to PL/SQL.

Tip	The slash character must be typed on a line by itself, and it must be the first character on that line; otherwise, it will get sent to the database and generate an error message.

After you type the slash, SQL*Plus transmits your code to Oracle for execution. After
your code executes, your output should look like the following:

INPUT

```
declare
  x    integer;
begin
  x := 65400;
end;
/
```

OUTPUT `PL/SQL procedure successfully completed`

ANALYSIS The code you just executed was probably not very exciting, possibly because there was no output. PL/SQL does have some limited output facilities, and next you will learn how to produce some simple screen output.

What About Some Output?

When it was originally designed, PL/SQL had no output facilities at all. Remember that PL/SQL is not a standalone language. It is almost always used in conjunction with some other program or tool that handles the input, output, and other user interaction.

Oracle now includes the DBMS_OUTPUT package with PL/SQL, which provides you with some limited output capabilities. You will learn more about packages during Day 8, "Using SQL," but for now it's enough to know that you can use the dbms_output.put_line procedure as shown in Listing 1.2.

INPUT **LISTING 1.2** PL/SQL Block Showing the Use of the `dbms_output.put_line` Procedure

```
DECLARE
  x      NUMBER;
BEGIN
  x := 72600;
  dbms_output.put_line('The variable  X = ');
  dbms_output.put_line(x);
END;
/
```

ANALYSIS The dbms_output.put_line() procedure takes exactly one argument and generates a line of text as output from the database server. In order for you to see that line of text, you must tell SQL*Plus to display it. This is done with the SQL*Plus command:

`SQL> SET SERVEROUTPUT ON`

1. Type the preceding command now. It needs to be executed only once per session, so you won't need to reissue it unless you exit SQL*Plus and get back in again.

2. Next, type in the PL/SQL code from Listing 1.2. The resulting output from SQL*Plus should look like that shown below.

OUTPUT
```
The variable x=
72600
```

Note

> It is SQL*Plus that prints the server output on the screen for you to see. You must remember to execute the SET SERVEROUTPUT ON command, or you won't see any output. You also can use the SET SERVEROUTPUT OFF command to turn off output when you don't want to see it.

Alternatives to Retyping

Until now, you have been retyping each PL/SQL block as you tried it. If you made a mistake, you had to type the code all over again. There are some alternatives to typing PL/SQL straight into SQL*Plus. Depending on your personal preferences, and on what you are trying to do, there are three basic ways to go about this:

- Cut and paste from Notepad.
- Execute a text file using the SQL*Plus @ command.
- Use the SQL*Plus EDIT command.

The first method involves running Windows Notepad, typing your PL/SQL code (or SQL queries) into it, and then copying and pasting from Notepad into SQL*Plus to execute the desired code. This method is ideal for experimenting with short snippets of PL/SQL code and SQL queries. You can keep several related items in the same text file where you can easily call them up when you want to work on them.

The second method makes use of a SQL*Plus command to execute a file. For example, if you have a text file named test.sql with the code from Listing 1.2, you could execute that file by typing this command:

INPUT
```
SQL> @c:\a\test
```

The resulting output would look like:

OUTPUT
```
The variable X =
65400
```

> **Note**
>
> When you're executing a file, the default file extension is .SQL. SQL*Plus looks for the file first in the default directory and then follows a search path that you can define. How you define this path is operating system–specific and outside the scope of this book. For details, you should consult the *SQL*Plus User's Guide* and also your operating system documentation.

Executing commands from a file like this is most useful in cases where you are re-creating a stored procedure, function, or database trigger and you have the definition already stored in its own text file.

The third option involves using the SQL*Plus EDIT command to invoke your system's text editor. Under Windows, this will be Notepad unless you have specifically defined a different editor. When you issue the EDIT command, SQL*Plus will launch Notepad and automatically place in it the text of the most recently executed PL/SQL block or SQL statement. See Figure 1.3 for an example of this.

FIGURE 1.3

*Using the SQL*Plus EDIT command.*

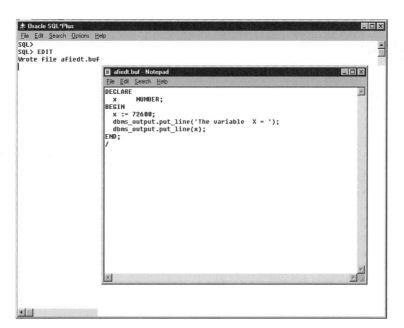

After you've brought up Notepad, you can edit the PL/SQL block to your satisfaction and then exit from Notepad, being sure to save the file. When you save your file, SQL*Plus will not immediately reexecute it. It is merely placed in an internal buffer. You must use the / command, by typing / on a line by itself, in order to execute the code you just edited.

Using the EDIT command works well as long as you keep in mind one important thing. SQL*Plus remembers only the most recent SQL statement or PL/SQL block. If you have been working on a PL/SQL block, and you execute just one SQL statement, that statement will replace the PL/SQL block you have been editing.

Caution

> Do not allow the SQL*Plus buffer to contain your only copy of a long procedure. It's too easy to enter a SQL command without thinking and wipe out the much longer PL/SQL procedure you have been developing.

Which of these three methods you choose is up to you, and depends in part on your personal preferences. You are likely to find the first method, copying and pasting between Notepad and SQL*Plus, most useful during the first few chapters of this book. As you write larger PL/SQL functions and procedures, you will find yourself gravitating toward keeping each in its own file.

Writing Your First Function

Perhaps one of the most useful things you can do with your knowledge of PL/SQL is to use it to write stored functions and stored procedures. Encapsulating the code you wrote earlier into a stored function enables you to compile it once and store it in the database for future use. The next time you want to run that PL/SQL block, all you need to do is invoke the function. Using SQL*Plus, type in the input code shown in bold in Listing 1.3, which will create a PL/SQL function to return the value that was output by Listing 1.2.

INPUT   **LISTING 1.3**   The SS_THRESH Function

```
1: CREATE OR REPLACE FUNCTION ss_thresh
2: RETURN NUMBER AS
3:   x      NUMBER;
4: BEGIN
5:   x := 72600;
6:   RETURN x;
7: END;
8: /
```

OUTPUT   Function created

ANALYSIS Compare the code in Listing 1.3 to that in Listing 1.2. Notice that the keyword DECLARE has been replaced in lines 1 and 2 by the words CREATE OR REPLACE FUNCTION ss_thresh RETURN NUMBER AS. This will be explained further in Day 3. Also notice that the calls to dbms_output.put_line() have been replaced by the RETURN command (line 6), which returns the value of the variable X to the caller. The only output from Listing 1.3 is a confirmation that the function has been successfully created, which is shown in line 9.

Notice that Oracle has created the function. SQL*Plus indicates this by displaying the words Function created.

Finding Compilation Errors

You probably were able to type in the code from Listing 1.3 and create the SS_THRESH function with no errors. However, that might not have been the case. To show you how to deal with an error, Listing 1.4 contains the same code as Listing 1.3, but with one small error.

INPUT **LISTING 1.4** The SS_THRESH Function with an Error

```
1: CREATE OR REPLACE FUNCTION ss_thresh
2: RETURN NUMBER AS
3:    x      NUMBER;
4: BEGIN
5:    x = 72600;
6:    RETURN x;
7: END;
8: /
```

OUTPUT Warning: Function created with compilation errors.

ANALYSIS Unlike most compilers, which will display a listing of errors found in source code, Oracle stores any errors it finds in a database table named USER_ERRORS. If you want to see the specific details, and you may well, you need to retrieve the error listing yourself. Use the SQL*Plus command SHOW ERRORS, as shown in Listing 1.5, to do this.

INPUT   **LISTING 1.5**   The SHOW ERRORS Command

1: SHOW ERRORS

OUTPUT   Errors for FUNCTION SS_THRESH:

LINE/COL ERROR
-------- --
5/5   PLS-00103: Encountered the symbol "=" when expecting one of the
          following:
          := . (@ % ;
          The symbol ":= was inserted before "=" to continue.

ANALYSIS   As you can see, the error listing has two columns of output. The first column
            contains the line number where the error occurred and also the character position
within that line. The second column contains the specific error message. In this example,
the error occurred in line 5 at the fifth character position. The error message tells you that
Oracle encountered an equal sign when it was really expecting something else. That
"something else," in this case, is the assignment operator, represented by :=.

Figure 1.4 shows the SQL*Plus screen as it would look after executing Listings 1.4
and 1.5.

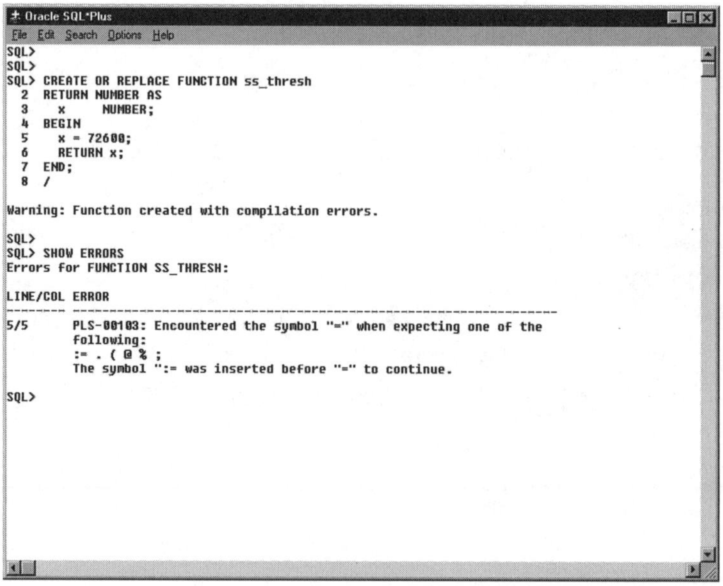

FIGURE 1.4

*Error listing for
SS_THRESH.*

Tip

> Typing = instead of : = is a common mistake to make, especially if you also
> program in other languages that do use = for assignment.

Displaying the Function's Return Value

Now that you have written and compiled the function, it's time to execute it and see the results. The easiest way to do this using SQL*Plus is to issue the following SQL command:

INPUT
```
SELECT SS_THRESH FROM DUAL;
```

OUTPUT
```
SS_THRESH
----------
     72600
```

ANALYSIS The SS_THRESH function does not have any parameters, so be sure not to add any parentheses when you call it. In other words, don't use SS_THRESH( ) because Oracle will return an error. The table DUAL is a special Oracle table that always exists, always has exactly one row, and always has exactly one column. It's the perfect table to use when experimenting with functions. Selecting the function from the DUAL table causes the function result to be displayed.

Can Even This Simple Function Be Useful?

The SS_THRESH function is a very simple function, and you might rightly wonder if something so absurdly simple can be useful. The value this function returns is the Social Security Contribution and Benefit Base, a value that changes from year to year. If you were a programmer working on a payroll system and needed to write several queries using this value, you could use a function like this to *encapsulate* this information. To encapsulate information means to embed it within a function so that values like this don't need to be replicated all through your code, and so that any changes can be made in one central place. There's another benefit to this approach. Your queries become more self-documenting. It's a bit easier to remember six months later what you meant when you see

```
SELECT * FROM employee_table
 WHERE emp_salary > SS_THRESH;
```

than if you had simply hard-coded the value

```
SELECT * FROM employee_table
 WHERE emp_salary > 72600;
```

Executing PL/SQL Using Developer 2000's Procedure Builder

Procedure Builder is part of Oracle's Developer 2000 development environment. It allows you to develop and debug PL/SQL program units for use in Developer 2000 applications. With Developer 2000, PL/SQL is used on the client to program the behavior behind the forms, reports, and menus that you develop. You end up with a PL/SQL engine on the client as well as on the server. A nice benefit of this is that Procedure Builder can be used to execute PL/SQL code without having to be connected to a database.

 Note

Many of the advanced features discussed later in this book are available only when executing PL/SQL code in the database.

Starting Procedure Builder

If you have Developer 2000 installed, you start Procedure Builder by selecting Start, Programs, Developer 2000 R2.0, Procedure Builder. The opening screen is shown in Figure 1.5 and is divided into three sections.

As you can see, the Procedure Builder window is divided into three major parts. The Object Navigator window allows you to navigate through the various program units, PL/SQL libraries, and database objects to which you have access. The other two parts of the display combine to make up the PL/SQL Interpreter window. The top pane is used when debugging PL/SQL code and shows the code being debugged. The bottom pane is where you can type in and execute ad-hoc PL/SQL blocks.

 PL/SQL may be used to write procedures, functions, package bodies, package types, and triggers. These constructs are referred to as *program units*.

PL/SQL Interpreter's
Debugger Pane

FIGURE 1.5

*Procedure Builder's
opening screen.*

Object Navigator

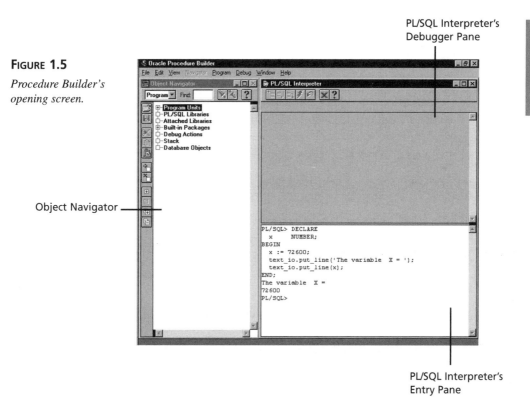

PL/SQL Interpreter's
Entry Pane

Using Interactive PL/SQL

The PL/SQL interpreter allows you to enter a PL/SQL anonymous block and have it executed. The small block in Listing 1.2, that you typed in earlier, is one such anonymous block. You can type that block into Procedure Builder and execute it, but first you need to make one small change. The code shown in Listing 1.2 contains the following two calls to DBMS_OUTPUT:

```
dbms_output.put_line('The variable  X = ');
dbms_output.put_line(x);
```

DBMS_OUTPUT is a package that only exists within the database server. Procedure Builder will return errors if you try to execute the code as it stands now. Fortunately, Oracle has a package similar to DBMS_OUTPUT that can be used in its place when you are executing code on a client. The name of that package is TEXT_IO, and it also contains an entry point named PUT_LINE. Take the code shown in Listing 1.2, replace the calls to DBMS_OUTPUT.PUT_LINE with TEXT_IO.PUT_LINE, and you have the code shown in Listing 1.6. This code will run from Procedure Builder.

INPUT **LISTING 1.6** A PL/SQL Block Using TEXT_IO That Will Run from Procedure Builder

```
DECLARE
  x      INTEGER;
BEGIN
  x := 72600;
  text_io.put_line('The variable  X = ');
  text_io.put_line(x);
END;
```

Now, you can take this code and type it into Procedure Builder's PL/SQL Interpreter. The interpreter will automatically execute the block when you finish entering the last line. The results will look like the following:

OUTPUT
```
The variable X =
72600
```

ANALYSIS Procedure Builder has been written specifically to work with PL/SQL. Unlike SQL*Plus, you do not need to enter a forward-slash to tell Procedure Builder that you are done entering a block of PL/SQL.

Creating the SS_THRESH Function

Creating a function (or any other program unit such as a procedure or package) using Procedure Builder requires a bit more than just typing the CREATE FUNCTION statement into the interpreter. To create a function, you need to tell Procedure Builder that you want to create a new program unit. Do this by selecting the File, New, Program Unit menu option. You will see the dialog box shown in Figure 1.6.

This dialog contains radio buttons allowing you to choose the type of program unit that you are creating and also contains a textbox for the program unit's name. Choose Function, type the name SS_THRESH into the textbox, and click OK. You will see a screen similar to that shown in Figure 1.7.

Figure 1.7 shows the function with the code already written. Of course, Procedure Builder does not write the code for you. When Procedure Builder opens this window, it places a skeleton function in the textbox. You have to fill in the details. When you get the code entered the way that you want it, click the Compile button to compile it, and then click the Close button to close the window.

To execute the function that you just created, type the following statement into the PL/SQL interpreter:

FIGURE 1.6

*Creating a New
Program Unit.*

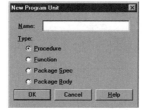

FIGURE 1.7

*Entering the code for
SS_THRESH.*

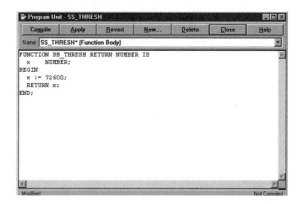

INPUT   `TEXT_IO.PUT_LINE(SS_THRESH);`

When you execute this statement, Procedure Builder will execute the function and display the following results:

OUTPUT   `72600`

Connecting to a Database

In addition to creating PL/SQL program units on the client, Procedure Builder can also be used to create and execute program units in a database. To do this, you first need to connect to a database. Use the File, Connect menu option to connect to a database. Once you've logged in, you will be able to browse database program units using the Object Navigator. Figure 1.8 shows the program units owned by the user named JEFF.

FIGURE **1.8**

Program units in the
JEFF schema.

The Create
Toolbar button

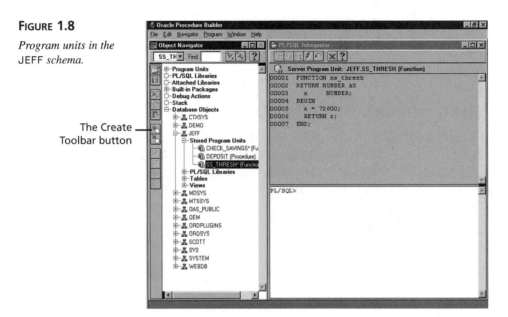

FIGURE **1.8**

Program units in the
JEFF schema.

To create a stored function or other program unit in the database, follow these steps:

1. Click to highlight the *Stored Program Units* entry under the user's name.

2. Click the Create Toolbar button.

3. Proceed as you would when creating a local program unit.

Except for having to choose the schema, the process for creating a PL/SQL function in
the database is the same as for creating one locally.

Using SQLPlus Worksheet

If you have Enterprise Manager available, consider using SQLPlus Worksheet for the
examples in this book. SQLPlus Worksheet is completely compatible with SQL*Plus,
and can be used for all the examples in this book. The advantage that SQL*Plus worksheet has over SQL*Plus is in the interface. Rather than type in large blocks of code one
line at a time, you can use a text editor-like interface. After you get the code entered the
way that you want it, you can click a toolbar button to execute it.

Executing a PL/SQL Block Using SQLPlus Worksheet

Figure 1.9 shows the SQLPlus Worksheet.

1

FIGURE 1.9

The SQLPlus Worksheet.

The Execute Button

The Entry Pane

The Output Pane

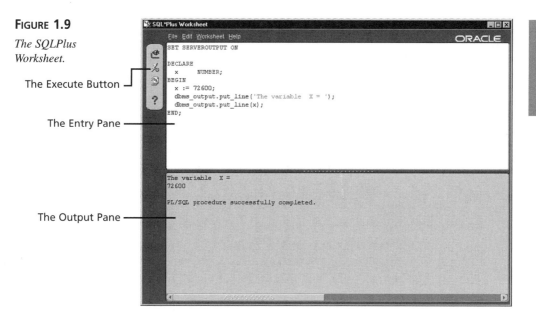

As you can see, the SQLPlus Worksheet screen is divided into two halves. The upper half is used for the entry and editing of SQL statements and PL/SQL blocks. The lower half is used to display output. The execute toolbar button, the one with the lightning bolt, is used to execute the statements that you have entered in the upper pane.

There are two ways to use SQLPlus Worksheet to execute commands from a file. One way is to use the File, Open menu option to load the contents of a file into the upper pane, and then click the lightning bolt button. The other way is to use the Worksheet, Run Local Script menu option.

Summary

In this chapter you learned a little about PL/SQL, what it is, and why it is used. You know that PL/SQL is Oracle's procedural language extension to SQL, and that you can use it to write procedures and functions that execute on the server.

This chapter also explains the relationship between PL/SQL, SQL, and SQL*Plus. This should give you a good grasp of how PL/SQL fits into the larger Oracle picture.

You wrote your first PL/SQL stored function, which should give you a good feel for the mechanics of programming with PL/SQL.

SQL*Plus is the tool used throughout this book for PL/SQL code examples. SQLPlus Worksheet and Procedure Builder are two other tools that may also be used to write and execute PL/SQL code.

Q&A

Q Where does PL/SQL code execution take place?

A Usually, execution takes place at the server level. For the examples in this book, that will always be the case. Some Oracle products, such as Developer/2000, also have the capability to execute PL/SQL blocks locally on the client machine.

Q Can I write a complete application with PL/SQL?

A Generally speaking you cannot, at least not as most people envision an application. For an end-user application, you would still need a tool, such as PowerBuilder or Developer/2000, in order to design screens and generate reports.

Q I executed some PL/SQL code which used `dbms_output.put_line()` to print some data, but I didn't see anything. How come?

A You probably forgot to enable the server output option. Use this SQL*Plus command:

```
SET SERVEROUTPUT ON
```

If you forget that, your PL/SQL output goes to oblivion.

Q I am using Procedure Builder, and I get errors when I try to execute code that contains calls to `dbms_output.put_line()`. Why?

A When you use Procedure Builder to execute code locally, you must use `text_io.put_line` rather than `dbms_output.put_line()`. If you are using Procedure Builder, and you have connected to a database, you will be able to execute calls to `dbms_output.put_line()`, but you won't see the results.

Workshop

Use the following workshop to test your comprehension of this chapter and put what you've learned into practice. You'll find the answers to the quiz and exercises in Appendix A, "Answers."

Quiz

1. What tells SQL*Plus to send your PL/SQL code to the Oracle database for execution?

2. What is the fundamental basis of all PL/SQL code?

3. List an advantage of pushing program logic up to the server level.

4. Name three Oracle products that use PL/SQL.

5. What command tells SQL*Plus to display PL/SQL output?

6. Name at least two options for managing your PL/SQL source code.

Exercises

1. If you didn't encounter any errors when compiling your first function, try putting some in on purpose. Then try out the SHOW ERRORS command.

2. Try each of the three ways mentioned in the chapter for managing your source code. Become familiar with the SQL*Plus EDIT command. Try using the @ command or the START command to execute your PL/SQL code from a text file.

WEEK 1

DAY 2

Writing Declarations and Blocks

by Jonathan Gennick

The *block* is the fundamental unit of PL/SQL programming. Blocks contain both program code and variable declarations. Understanding the various datatypes available to you when declaring variables is crucial when programming in any language, and PL/SQL is no exception. It's also important to understand PL/SQL's block structure, its use, and its impact on the scope of variable declarations. Today you are going to learn more about

- PL/SQL datatypes
- PL/SQL blocks
- Scoping rules

Exploring Datatypes

PL/SQL provides a number of datatypes for your use, and they can be grouped into several categories: *scalar* datatypes, large object datatypes, records, and pointers. This chapter focuses on the scalar types, which are listed in Table 2.1. Later in the book, you'll learn about the other categories.

NEW TERM   A *scalar variable* is a variable that is not made up of some combination of other variables. Scalar variables don't have internal components that you can manipulate individually. They are often used to build up more complex datatypes such as records and arrays.

TABLE 2.1   PL/SQL Datatypes

Datatype	Usage
VARCHAR2	Variable-length character strings
CHAR	Fixed-length character strings
NUMBER	Fixed or floating-point numbers
BINARY_INTEGER	Integer values
PLS_INTEGER	New in version 2.3; used for fast integer computations
DATE	Dates
BOOLEAN	true/false values
NVARCHAR2	Variable-length character strings using the national character set
NCHAR	Fixed-length character strings using the national character set
ROWID	Used to store physical rowids (obsolete, use UROWID instead)
UROWID	Used to store both physical and logical rowids
LONG	Used to store long character strings (obsolete)
LONG RAW	Used to store large amounts of binary data (obsolete)
RAW	Used to store binary data (obsolete)

These datatypes can be used for creating simple scalar variables, or they can be combined into structures such as records or PL/SQL tables. You will learn more about records and tables during Day 8, "Using SQL." The LONG, LONG RAW, and RAW datatypes are obsolete. If you're dealing with large objects, you should use the new large object types instead. Those are covered in Day 14, "Leveraging Large Object Types."

You might notice that some of the datatype names match those used by Oracle for defining database columns. In most cases the definitions are the same for both the database and PL/SQL, but there are a few differences. These differences are noted later in this chapter when each datatype is discussed in detail.

NEW TERM PL/SQL also provides *subtypes* of some datatypes. A subtype represents a special case of a datatype, usually representing a narrower range of values than the parent type. For example, POSITIVE is a subtype of BINARY_INTEGER that holds only positive values. In some cases, the subtypes exist only to provide alternative names for compatibility with the SQL standard or other popular database brands on the market.

2

Variable Naming Rules

Before you go on to learn about each of the datatypes in detail, you should first consider some basic rules and conventions for naming variables. Oracle has some simple rules for variable naming. Variable names can be composed of letters, dollar signs, underscores, and number signs. No other characters can be used. A variable name must start with a letter, after which any combination of the allowed characters can be used. The maximum length for a variable name is 30 characters. Variable names, like those of keywords and other identifiers, are not case-sensitive.

In addition to the preceding rules, it is often helpful to follow some sort of naming convention for variables and to make their names as descriptive as possible. For example, although empyersal is a legal variable name, your code might be easier to read if you used emp_yearly_salary. Another option, which uses capital letters to highlight each word in order to dispense with the underscores, is EmpYearlySalary. Many programmers also capitalize language keywords in order to more easily distinguish them from variable, function, and procedure names.

The naming rules for variables also apply to function and procedure names. The importance of a consistent naming convention for all identifiers is discussed in more detail in Day 13, "Debugging Your Code and Preventing Errors."

In the next few sections, you'll learn about each of the PL/SQL datatypes. You'll learn the type of data that each one holds, what the range of possible values is, and any subtypes that are defined for it.

VARCHAR2

The VARCHAR2 datatype is used to hold variable-length character string data. It typically uses 1 byte per character and has a maximum length of 32767 bytes.

SYNTAX

The Syntax for the VARCHAR2 Datatype

```
variable_name VARCHAR2(size);
```

In this syntax, *variable_name* is whatever name you want to give to the variable, and *size* is the maximum length, in bytes, of the string.

Here are some examples:

```
employee_name VARCHAR2(32);
employee_comments VARCHAR2(10000);
```

 Note   Even though PL/SQL allows a maximum of 32767 bytes for a VARCHAR2 variable, the Oracle database does not. The Oracle database itself only allows
VARCHAR2 columns to be a maximum of 4000 bytes long. You can use longer
strings in PL/SQL, but 4000 is the limit (2000 if you are using any release of
Oracle7) if you want to store the string in the database.

Referring to the example declaration of employee_name, here are some sample assignment statements showing values that could be assigned to this variable:

```
employee_name := 'Jenny Gennick';
employee_name := 'Jonathan Gennick';
```

VARCHAR2 Subtypes

Oracle has two subtypes defined for VARCHAR2, which are

- VARCHAR
- STRING

These subtypes exist for compatibility with other database brands and also with the SQL
standard. Both have the exact same meaning as VARCHAR2. However, Oracle currently recommends against using the VARCHAR datatype because its definition is expected to change
as the SQL standards evolve.

CHAR

The CHAR datatype is used to hold fixed-length character string data. Unlike VARCHAR2
strings, a CHAR string always contains the maximum number of characters. Strings shorter
than the maximum length are padded with spaces. Like VARCHAR2, the CHAR datatype typically uses 1 byte per character and has a maximum length of 32767 bytes.

The Syntax for the CHAR Datatype

variable_name CHAR(*size*);

In this syntax, *variable_name* is whatever you want to call the variable, and *size* is the
size, in bytes, of the string.

Here are some examples:

```
employee_name CHAR(32);
employee_comments CHAR(10000);
```

Note The Oracle database only allows CHAR columns to be 2000 bytes long (255 if you are using any release of Oracle7). Even though PL/SQL allows a maximum of 32767 bytes for a CHAR variable, 2000 is the limit if you want to store the string in the database.

2

Referring to the example declaration of employee_name, here are some sample assignment statements showing values that could be assigned to this variable:

```
employee_name := 'Jenny Gennick';
employee_name := 'Jeff Gennick';
```

Because CHAR variables are fixed length and the preceding strings are each less than 32 characters long, they will be right-padded with spaces. In other words, enough spaces will be appended to make them 32 characters long. Thus, the actual values in employee_name would be

```
'Jenny Gennick                  '
```

and

```
'Jeff Gennick                   '
```

This point is important to remember, especially when doing string comparisons, because the trailing spaces count as part of the string. Listing 2.1 illustrates the impact those trailing spaces have when comparing different types of strings.

Note Before executing the code shown in Listing 2.1 and most of the other listings in this chapter, make sure that you have first executed the following command at least once during the session:

SET SERVEROUTPUT ON

If you omit this command, SQL*Plus won't display the output generated by the calls to DBMS_OUTPUT.PUT_LINE. You need to execute this command only once each time you start SQL*Plus.

INPUT   **LISTING 2.1**   Comparison of CHAR with VARCHAR2

```
 1: DECLARE
 2:   employee_name_c CHAR(32);
 3:   employee_name_v VARCHAR2(32);
 4: BEGIN
 5:   --Assign the same value to each string.
 6:   employee_name_c := 'Jenny Gennick';
 7:   employee_name_v := 'Jenny Gennick';
 8:
 9:   --Test the strings for equality.
10:   IF employee_name_c = employee_name_v THEN
11:     DBMS_OUTPUT.PUT_LINE('The names are the same');
12:   ELSE
13:     DBMS_OUTPUT.PUT_LINE('The names are NOT the same');
14:   END IF;
15: END;
16: /
```

OUTPUT
```
17: The names are NOT the same
18:
19: PL/SQL procedure successfully completed.
```

ANALYSIS   What happened here? The same value was assigned to both strings (lines 6 and 7), yet they did not test as being equal (line 10). This occurred because the CHAR string contains a number of trailing spaces, whereas the VARCHAR2 string does not. Day 3, "Writing PL/SQL Expressions," talks about the issue in detail.

> **Tip**
>
> When comparing CHAR strings against VARCHAR2 strings, use the rtrim function to eliminate trailing spaces, as in the following example:
>
>   IF RTRIM(employee_name_c) = employee_name_v THEN...

The RTRIM function is one you will learn more about on Day 6, "Using Oracle's Built-in Functions."

CHAR Subtypes

Oracle has one subtype defined for the CHAR datatype, and it is called CHARACTER. It has exactly the same meaning as CHAR.

NUMBER

The NUMBER datatype is used for declaring both fixed-point and floating-point numbers. It can be used to represent numbers in the range 1.0E-123 through 9.99E125, and it allows for up to 38 decimal digits of precision. It is very commonly used and is a bit more complicated than the character datatypes discussed earlier.

The Syntax for the NUMBER Datatype

```
variable_name NUMBER [(precision[,scale])]
```

In this syntax, *variable_name* is whatever name you want to give this variable. *precision* specifies the number of decimal digits used to represent the value internally. The range is 1 to 38, and the default is 38. *scale* indicates where the decimal point is and where rounding occurs. The range is -84 to 127, and the default is zero.

Here are some examples:

```
dollar_amount number (5,2);
no_cents number (3);
big_floating number;
shares_traded number (5,-2);
microns number (1,6)
```

The easiest way to understand precision and scale is to think of `precision` as telling you how many digits are used to represent the number. Then the `scale` tells you where the decimal point is.

The `dollar_amount` variable, defined in the preceding example as `NUMBER(5,2)`, would then be precise to five digits, two of which would be to the right of the decimal. All amounts would be rounded to the nearest hundredth. It could store values such as `123.45`, `-999.99`, and so on. Assigning it a value of `123.456` would result in the value being rounded off to `123.46`.

> **Note**
>
> Trying to assign any number a value greater than its precision, for example, assigning `dollar_amount` a value of `1000`, will result in an error.

The `no_cents` variable, defined in the preceding example as `NUMBER(3)`, would take the default scale of zero. Thus it could store no digits to the right of the decimal, and all values will be rounded to the nearest whole number. Assigning it a value of `-123.45` would result in it being rounded off to `-123`.

The `big_floating` variable, defined only as `NUMBER`, has no `precision` and `scale` specified in its declaration. Use this to define a floating-point value.

The shares_traded variable is interesting because the example declared it with a negative scale, that is, as NUMBER(5,-2). It stores five digits of precision, but all values are in hundreds. It could store values ranging from 0 to 9,999,900, but all values would be rounded to the nearest hundred. Assign it a value of 100, and it will store 100. Assign it a value of 327, and it will be rounded off to 300. Why use a variable like this? It saves a bit of space and allows you to use the 38 digits to represent some very large numbers without making excessive demands on memory. For a real-world example, take a look at the stock market listings in almost any newspaper, and you will see that the number of shares traded is usually reported in blocks of 100.

The microns variable is also a bit unusual because the example specified a scale that is larger than the precision. This is perfectly legitimate and is really the reverse of what was done with shares_traded. It will store values of one millionth, two millionths, and so on up to nine millionths. All values will be rounded to the nearest millionth, so if you assigned it a value of 0.00000016, you would get 0.0000002. Because the precision is only one, trying to assign a value of 0.000001 would result in an error. 0.000001 is 10 millionths, which in this case requires two digits of precision to store.

The NUMBER datatype is the only numeric datatype that is available both at the database level and in PL/SQL. It is stored using a hardware-independent representation and manipulated using hardware-independent code. Oracle guarantees portability of this datatype across the various platforms supported by Oracle.

NUMBER Subtypes

Oracle has defined several subtypes of NUMBER. Most of these have exactly the same meaning as, and can be used interchangeably with, the keyword NUMBER. Table 2.2 shows a complete list of NUMBER subtypes and describes their use.

TABLE 2.2 Subtypes of the NUMBER Datatype

Subtype	Usage
DECIMAL	Same as NUMBER.
DEC	Same as DECIMAL.
DOUBLE PRECISION	Same as NUMBER.
NUMERIC	Same as NUMBER.
REAL	Same as NUMBER.
INTEGER	Equivalent to NUMBER(38).
INT	Same as INTEGER.
SMALLINT	Same as NUMBER(38).
FLOAT	Same as NUMBER.
FLOAT(prec)	Same as NUMBER(prec), but the precision is expressed in terms of binary bits, not decimal digits. Binary precision can range from 1 through 126.

> **Restrictions on Subtypes**
>
> With the release of Oracle8i, Oracle has tightened up the rules a bit regarding these subtypes. It used to be, because NUMBER was the underlying datatype, that you could get away using a declaration such as DOUBLE PRECISION (5,2). In other words, you could specify a specific number of decimal digits for a floating point number. You can no longer do this. You can declare a floating-point variable as DOUBLE PRECISION (5), but you can't specify a scale.
>
> Things are different however, with the INTEGER subtype. Strange as it may seem, it's entirely possible to declare an integer variable and use it to store non-integer values. For example, you can declare a variable as INTEGER (5,2), and use it to store non-integer values such as 123.45. In this respect, INTEGER is more like a synonym for NUMBER than a subtype of NUMBER. Please don't use it that way though. If you're going to use the INTEGER subtype, use it only to declare integer variables.

2

BINARY_INTEGER

The BINARY_INTEGER datatype is used for declaring signed integer variables. Compared to the NUMBER datatype, BINARY_INTEGER variables are stored in binary format, which takes less space. Calculations on binary integers can also run slightly faster because the values are already in a binary format.

SYNTAX

The Syntax for the BINARY_INTEGER Datatype

```
variable_name BINARY_INTEGER;
```

In this syntax, *variable_name* is whatever you want to name the variable.

Here is a sample declaration:

```
my_integer BINARY_INTEGER;
```

A BINARY_INTEGER variable can store any integer value in the range -2,147,483,647 through 2,147,483,647.

Tip

> If you are running PL/SQL version 2.3 or later, you have access to the new PLS_INTEGER datatype, which is optimized for fast calculations. For new applications, use PLS_INTEGER instead of BINARY_INTEGER.

BINARY_INTEGER Subtypes

Oracle has defined four subtypes for the BINARY_INTEGER datatype, as explained in Table 2.3.

TABLE 2.3 Subtypes of BINARY_INTEGER

Subtype	Usage
POSITIVE	Allows only positive integers to be stored, up to the maximum of 2,147,483,647. Zero is not considered a positive number, and so is not an allowed value.
NATURAL	Allows only natural numbers to be stored, which includes zero. Allowed values are 0, 1, 2, 3, and so on up to the maximum of 2,147,483,647.
POSITIVEN	Like POSITIVE but cannot be null.
NATURALN	Like NATURAL but cannot be null.
SIGNTYPE	Restricts a variable to only the values -1, 0, and 1. Oracle's built-in sign() function returns values in this range depending on whether its argument is negative, zero, or positive. (New for Oracle8.)

Note

The BINARY_INTEGER subtypes are constraining. There is no way, for example, to define a POSITIVE in such a way as to still allow negative values.

Why would you want to use these subtypes? One reason might be for purposes of documentation. A subtype might be more descriptive of the type of data you intend to store in a variable, which can help prevent mistakes by other programmers who later work on the code. Another reason might be for error detection. If the code is later modified to assign the wrong type of value to a variable, a VALUE_ERROR exception will be generated alerting the programmer to the mistake. Listing 2.2 shows an example of this.

INPUT

LISTING 2.2 An Attempt to Assign a Negative Value to a POSITIVE Variable

```
 1: --Assign a negative value to a POSITIVE variable
 2: DECLARE
 3:    age     POSITIVE;
 4:
 5:    current_year  NATURAL;     --a year of 00 is valid.
 6:    current_month POSITIVE;
 7:    current_day   POSITIVE;
 8:
 9:    birth_year    NATURAL;     --a year of 00 is valid.
10:    birth_month   POSITIVE;
11:    birth_day     POSITIVE;
12:
13:    birth_date    DATE := TO_DATE('11-15-1961','mm-dd-yyyy');
14:    current_date  DATE;
15: BEGIN
16:    --Set the current date.  Normally we would do "current_date := sysdate",
```

```
17:    --but let's pretend it's the year 2000.
18:    current_date := TO_DATE ('12-1-2000','mm-dd-yyyy');
19:
20:    --Show the effect of trying to set a negative age.
21:    --Pretend it's the year 2000 and we forgot to convert this code.
22:    --Note that only the two digit year is retrieved.
23:    current_year := TO_NUMBER(TO_CHAR(current_date,'yy'));
24:    current_month := TO_NUMBER(TO_CHAR(current_date,'mm'));
25:    current_day := TO_NUMBER(TO_CHAR(current_date,'dd'));
26:
27:    --Oops! Only two digits allowed for birth year.
28:    birth_year := TO_NUMBER(TO_CHAR(birth_date,'yy'));
29:    birth_month := TO_NUMBER(TO_CHAR(birth_date,'mm'));
30:    birth_day := TO_NUMBER(TO_CHAR(birth_date,'dd'));
31:
32:    --Now make the actual computation.
33:    IF current_month > birth_month THEN
34:       age := current_year - birth_year;
35:    ELSIF (current_month = birth_month) and (current_day >= birth_day) THEN
36:       age := current_year - birth_year;
37:    ELSE
38:       age := current_year - birth_year - 1;
39:    END IF;
40: END;
41: /
```

OUTPUT

```
DECLARE
*
ERROR at line 1:
ORA-06502: PL/SQL: numeric or value error
ORA-06512: at line 33
```

ANALYSIS   Had the variable age been declared as a BINARY_INTEGER, it would have been assigned a negative value and the result of the "Year 2000" error might show up in a manner far removed from the problem code. Because of the use of the subtype POSITIVE, you know instantly when an error occurs.

PLS_INTEGER

The PLS_INTEGER datatype is new in release 2.3 of PL/SQL and is used for declaring signed integer variables. Like the BINARY_INTEGER datatype, it also stores values in the range –2,147,483,647 through 2,147,483,647. How is it different from a BINARY_INTEGER? The PLS_INTEGER datatype uses the native machine instructions for performing computations. Thus, PLS_INTEGER calculations are much faster than BINARY_INTEGER calculations, which use library functions to perform arithmetic.

SYNTAX
The Syntax for the PLS_INTEGER Datatype

variable_name PLS_INTEGER;

In this syntax, *variable_name* is whatever name you want to give to the variable.

Here is a sample declaration:

```
my_integer PLS_INTEGER;
```

> **Note**
>
> Because of the performance advantage, Oracle recommends use of the PLS_INTEGER datatype over the BINARY_INTEGER datatype in all new applications.

DATE

The DATE datatype is used to store date and time values. A better name might perhaps be DATETIME because the time component is always there whether you use it or not. The range for date variables is from 1 Jan 4712 BC through 31 Dec 4712 AD. If you do not specify a time when assigning a value to a variable of type DATE, it will default to midnight (12:00:00 a.m.).

SYNTAX
The Syntax for the DATE Datatype

variable_name DATE;

In this syntax, *variable_name* is the name that you want to give the variable.

Here are some examples:

```
hire_date DATE;
emp_birthdate DATE;
```

The following example shows a date being declared, and then being initialized using the TO_DATE function:

INPUT
```
DECLARE
  a_date DATE;
BEGIN
  a_date := TO_DATE('29-DEC-1988','DD-MON-YYYY');
END;
/
```

This code won't produce any output, but it does shown how date variables are declared and initialized. The TO_CHAR function converts a text string into a date. You can read more about it on Day 6.

Be careful when comparing dates—the time value can trip you up. Values in a database that are intended to contain only dates sometimes mistakenly have a time value stored with them, and this can cause comparisons for equality to fail. To be safe, if you really don't care about the time of day, you can use the TRUNC() function. For example, instead of

```
    IF hire_date = fire_date then...
```
use
```
    if TRUNC(hire_date) = TRUNC(fire_date) then...
```
Use of the TRUNC() function will truncate any time value so that you are truly comparing only dates. This function will be discussed in more detail on Day 6.

BOOLEAN

The BOOLEAN datatype is used to store true/false values. Its range is only the two values, true or false.

The Syntax for the BOOLEAN Datatype

```
variable_name BOOLEAN;
```

In this syntax, *variable_name* is the name that you want to give this variable.

Here are some examples:

```
hired_fired_same_day BOOLEAN;
birthday_is_today BOOLEAN;
print_this_record BOOLEAN;
```

Boolean variables are often used as flag variables, and are also used to store the results of logical calculations. For example, if you needed to know if an employee's birthday was today, you could write this code:

```
birthday_is_today := (emp_birthdate = trunc(sysdate))
```

Then you could reference birthday_is_today anywhere in your code where you need to know this information. You would not have to compare again each time.

Using Boolean variables to store the results of comparisons can be a powerful construct. If you code a comparison only once, you can go back and change the calculation later without having to find and change several occurrences in your program. It can also add to readability. With a variable named birthday_is_today, you know why the comparison was made.

LONG

The LONG datatype in PL/SQL is just like VARCHAR2 except that it can store a maximum of 32760 bytes instead of 32767, which is actually 7 bytes less than the VARCHAR2 type. For this reason, you should usually use VARCHAR2 instead.

The Syntax for the LONG Datatype

```
variable_name LONG(size);
```

In this syntax, *variable_name* is the name that you want to give this variable, and *size* is the size, in bytes, of the variable. This must be a number between 1 and 32760.

Here are some sample declarations:

```
emp_comment LONG(32760);
work_history LONG(10000);
```

In PL/SQL, you can treat LONG values as character strings, for example:

```
DECLARE
    emp_comment LONG(32760);
BEGIN
    emp_comment := 'Jenny is a great employee.';
END;
/
```

Here, a LONG value was assigned a character string value just as if it were a CHAR or a VARCHAR.

> **Note**
>
> The PL/SQL LONG differs from the database version of a LONG in that a LONG database column can store 2 gigabytes of data, whereas the PL/SQL version can store only 32760 bytes.

RAW

The RAW datatype is used to store strings of byte-oriented data. The difference between a RAW and a VARCHAR2 string is that Oracle does no character set translation on raw data. Thus, if you are retrieving raw data from an Oracle server using ASCII to a machine using the EBCDIC character set, no translation would be done.

The Syntax for the RAW Datatype

```
variable_name RAW(size);
```

In this syntax, *variable_name* is the name you want to give the variable, and *size* is the size, in bytes, of the variable. This must be a number between 1 and 32767.

Here are some sample declarations:

```
sound_bytes RAW(32767);
some_data RAW(255);
```

Like VARCHAR2, the maximum length of a RAW variable is 32767 bytes.

> **Note** The database version of RAW allows only 255 bytes.

LONG RAW

The LONG RAW datatype is just like RAW except that the maximum length is 32760 bytes. That's not a misprint. In PL/SQL, the maximum length of a LONG RAW really is 7 bytes less than the maximum length of a RAW.

The Syntax for the LONG RAW Datatype

```
variable_name LONG RAW(size);
```

In this syntax, *variable_name* is the name you want to give this variable, and *size* is the size, in bytes, of the variable. This must be a number between 1 and 32760.

Here are some examples:

```
sound_byte LONG RAW(20000);
a_picture LONG RAW(30000);
```

As with a RAW, no character set conversion is performed.

> **Note** The database version of LONG RAW allows up to 2 gigabytes of data.

ROWID

ROWID is a special datatype used to store the physical rowids of rows stored in a table.

The Syntax for the ROWID Datatype

```
variable_name ROWID;
```

In this syntax, *variable_name* is the name that you want to give the variable.

The ROWID type is supported for purposes of backward compatibility with earlier releases of Oracle. If you are writing new code, you should use UROWID instead.

UROWID

UROWID is a special datatype that enables you to store Oracle's internal key for database records. The UROWID datatype works for both logical and physical rowids.

The Syntax for the UROWID Datatype

```
variable_name UROWID;
```

In this syntax, *variable_name* is the name that you want to give the variable.

Here is an example:

```
employee_row_id UOWID;
```

Each row in an Oracle table has a unique internal key associated with it. This key can be useful if you are planning to access the same record multiple times. For example, you might use a cursor to retrieve a number of rows, including the UROWID for each row, and then use that UROWID in a DELETE statement to delete some of the rows. Using the UROWID results in better performance because it tells Oracle exactly where to find the record so no index searches or table scans are necessary.

MSLABEL

The MSLABEL datatype is used with *Trusted Oracle*, which is a version of Oracle designed for use in high security environments such as those dealing with classified data.

The Syntax for the MSLABEL Datatype

```
variable_name MSLABEL;
```

In this syntax, *variable_name* is the name you want to give this variable.

Here is an example:

```
binary_label MSLABEL;
```

In a Trusted Oracle system, this datatype is used to store binary operating system labels. Standard Oracle allows the datatype to be declared, but only null values can be assigned to it.

Using Block Structure

On Day 1, "Learning the Basics of PL/SQL," you saw that the fundamental programming structure in PL/SQL is referred to as a block. In order to master PL/SQL, it is essential to understand the block structure, the various types of blocks, and how blocks are used. In the rest of this chapter, you will learn about anonymous blocks, trigger blocks, function blocks, and procedure blocks. You will also learn that blocks can be nested and what the implications are in terms of scoping.

2

Anonymous Blocks

 An *anonymous block* is one that is unnamed and that does not form the body of a procedure, function, or trigger. Remember the examples and exercises from Day 1? They were all anonymous blocks.

Anonymous blocks can be used inline as part of a SQL*Plus script, and can also be nested inside procedure and function blocks for purposes of error handling.

The Syntax for PL/SQL Anonymous Blocks

```
[DECLARE
  variable declarations]
BEGIN
  program code
[EXCEPTION
  error handling code]
END;
```

In this syntax, `variable_declarations` is where you declare your variables. `program_code` is where you write your PL/SQL program statements. `error_handling_code` is an optional section to which control branches in the event of an error.

As you can see, the keyword DECLARE is used to begin the block. Any variable declarations must follow this and precede the next keyword, which is BEGIN.

The keyword BEGIN signifies the beginning of the procedural section of the block. The program code goes here.

The keyword EXCEPTION begins the portion of the block that contains exception-handling code. The exception-handling portion of a block is optional and you might not always use it. If the exception-handling portion is present, any runtime error or exception will cause program control to branch to this part of the block. The word *exception* is used to connote something that is outside the normal flow of events. It is used rather than *error*

▼ because an exception does not always imply that something is wrong. For example, issuing a SELECT statement and not getting any data back might be an exception to what you would normally expect, but it does not necessarily mean that an error occurred. Day 7, "Procedures, Packages, Errors, and Exceptions," shows you how to use PL/SQL's

▲ exception handling features.

Listing 2.3 shows an example of an anonymous block. Note especially the declaration used for the hundreds_counter variable.

INPUT   **LISTING 2.3**   An Example of an Anonymous Block

```
 1: --An example of an
 2: --anonymous block.
 3: --Count up by hundreds until we get an error.
 4: DECLARE
 5:    --Note that with a scale of -2 this variable can only
 6:    --hold values like 100,200,300... up to 900.
 7:    hundreds_counter  NUMBER(1,-2);
 8: BEGIN
 9:    hundreds_counter := 100;
10:    LOOP
11:      DBMS_OUTPUT.PUT_LINE(hundreds_counter);
12:      hundreds_counter := hundreds_counter + 100;
13:    END LOOP;
14: EXCEPTION
15: WHEN OTHERS THEN
16:    DBMS_OUTPUT.PUT_LINE('That is as high as we can go.');
17: END;
18: /
```

OUTPUT
```
:
: 100
: 200
: 300
: 400
: 500
: 600
: 700
: 800
: 900
```

That is as high as we can go.

ANALYSIS In Listing 2.3, a counter variable named `hundreds_counter` is declared in line 7. Because it is defined with a precision of one, it is only using one digit to represent the value. The scale of -2 tells you that you are using that one digit to represent hundreds. Lines 10 through 13 contain a loop that prints the value of the counter and then increments it by one hundred. Because the counter's precision is only one digit and the two zeros are assumed, the program can only count up to 900. When you try to go past 900 to 1,000, the variable won't be able to hold the value and an exception will be triggered.

Look at the output from Listing 2.3. You can see that the code indeed works as described. It successfully counted up to 900. When the variable was incremented to 1,000, an exception was generated, control passed to the EXCEPTION portion of the block, and a message was displayed.

Function and Procedure Blocks

PL/SQL allows you to define functions and procedures. These are similar to functions and procedures defined in any other language, and are always defined as one PL/SQL block.

The Syntax for Defining a Function

SYNTAX ▼

```
FUNCTION name [( argument_list )] RETURN datatype {IS,AS}
  variable declarations
BEGIN
  program code
[EXCEPTION
  error handling code]
END;
```

In this syntax, the placeholders are as follows:

- *name*—The name you want to give the function.
- *argument_list*—A list of input and output parameters for the function.
- *datatype*—The datatype of the function's return value.
- *variable_declarations*—Where you declare any variables that are local to the function.
- *program_code*—Where you write the PL/SQL statements that make up the function.
- *error_handling_code*—Where you write any error-handling code.

Notice that the keyword DECLARE has been replaced by the function header, which names the function, describes the parameters, and indicates the return type. Except for this, the function block looks just like the declarations for the anonymous blocks that you have seen so far.

▲

You will learn more about functions on Day 4, "Using Functions, IF Statements, and Loops." Listing 2.4 shows an example of a function.

INPUT   **LISTING 2.4**   A Function Block

```
 1: FUNCTION iifn(boolean_expression in BOOLEAN,
 2:                 true_number IN NUMBER,
 3:                 false_number IN NUMBER)
 4: RETURN NUMBER IS
 5: BEGIN
 6:   IF boolean_expression THEN
 7:     RETURN true_number;
 8:   ELSIF NOT boolean_expression THEN
 9:     RETURN false_number;
10:   ELSE
11:     --nulls propagate, i.e. null input yields null output.
12:     RETURN NULL;
13:   END IF;
14: END;
```

ANALYSIS   To execute the function shown in Listing 2.4, you need to declare it and execute from within a PL/SQL block. The section "Nesting Functions and Procedures," later in this chapter, shows how this is done.

The declaration for a procedure is almost identical to that of a function.

The Syntax for Declaring a Procedure

▼ SYNTAX

```
PROCEDURE name [( argument_list )] {IS,AS}
  variable declarations
BEGIN
  program code
[EXCEPTION
  error handling code]
END;
```

In this syntax, the placeholders are as follows:

- *name*—The name you want to give the procedure.

- *argument_list*—A list of input and output parameters for the procedure.

- *variable_declarations*—Where you declare any variables that are local to the procedure.

- *program_code*—Where you write the PL/SQL statements that make up the procedure.

▼   - *error_handling_code*—Where you write any error-handling code.

▼ As you can see, the procedure declaration resembles a function declaration except that there is no return datatype and the keyword PROCEDURE is used instead of FUNCTION.

▲ Listing 2.5 shows an example of a procedure.

INPUT **LISTING 2.5** A Procedure Block

```
1: PROCEDURE swapn (num_one IN OUT NUMBER, num_two IN OUT NUMBER) IS
2:     temp_num    NUMBER;
3:   BEGIN
4:     temp_num := num_one;
5:     num_one := num_two;
6:     num_two := temp_num ;
7:   END;
```

ANALYSIS You will see how this function is executed later in this chapter in the section titled "Nesting Functions and Procedures."

Procedures and functions are both useful constructs that promote modularity, allow you to hide complexity, and facilitate reuse of code. During Day 6, you will read about many of the built-in functions provided by Oracle, and on Day 4, you will learn more about creating your own functions.

Trigger Blocks

PL/SQL can also be used to write database triggers. Triggers are used to define code that is executed when certain actions or events occur. At the database level, triggers can be defined for events such as inserting a record into a table, deleting a record, and updating a record.

The following syntax for creating a database trigger is much more complex than that for a function or a procedure.

The Syntax for Creating a Database Trigger

SYNTAX

```
CREATE [OR REPLACE] TRIGGER trigger_name
  {BEFORE¦AFTER} verb_list ON table_name
  [[REFERENCING correlation_names] FOR EACH ROW [WHEN (condition)]]
DECLARE
  declarations
BEGIN
  pl/sql_code
END;
```

In this syntax, the placeholders are as follows:

- *trigger_name*—The name you want to give the trigger.
- *verb_list*—The SQL verbs that fire the trigger.
- *table_name*—The table on which the trigger is defined.
- *correlation_names*—Allows you to specify correlation names other than the default of OLD and NEW.
- *condition*—An optional condition placed on the execution of the trigger.
- *declarations*—Consists of any variable, record, or cursor declarations needed by this PL/SQL block.
- *pl/sql_code*—The PL/SQL code that gets executed when the trigger fires.

As you can see, even though the specification for a trigger is much more complex than that of a procedure or a function, the basic PL/SQL block structure is still present. The first three lines of the declaration tell Oracle the type of trigger, the table it is associated with, and when it should be fired. The remainder is simply the PL/SQL block that executes when the trigger fires. Don't worry if this doesn't all make sense now. Triggers are complex, and you need to learn more about PL/SQL before you can write them. Triggers are discussed in detail on Day 11, "Writing Database Triggers."

Nested Blocks

PL/SQL blocks can be nested, one inside the other. This is often done for purposes of error handling, and also for purposes of modularity. Listing 2.6 shows a nested anonymous block.

LISTING 2.6 A Nested Anonymous Block

```
 1: --A PL/SQL block
 2: --showing an example
 3: --of a nested anonymous blocks.
 4: DECLARE
 5:   error_flag  BOOLEAN := false;  --true if an error occurs while counting.
 6:
 7: BEGIN
 8:   DBMS_OUTPUT.PUT_LINE('We are going to count from 100 to 1000.');
 9:
10:   --Execute the nested block to do the actual counting.
11:   --Any errors will be trapped within this block.
12:   DECLARE
13:     hundreds_counter  NUMBER(1,-2);
14:   BEGIN
15:     hundreds_counter := 100;
```

```
16:      LOOP
17:        DBMS_OUTPUT.PUT_LINE(hundreds_counter);
18:        hundreds_counter := hundreds_counter + 100;
19:        IF hundreds_counter > 1000 THEN
20:          EXIT;
21:        END IF;
22:      END LOOP;
23:    EXCEPTION
24:    WHEN OTHERS THEN
25:      --set the error flag if we can't finish counting.
26:      error_flag := true;
27:    END;
28:
29:    --We are done. Were we successful?
30:    IF error_flag THEN
31:      DBMS_OUTPUT.PUT_LINE('Sorry, I cannot count that high.');
32:    ELSE
33:      DBMS_OUTPUT.PUT_LINE('Done.');
34:    END IF;
35: END;
36: /
```

OUTPUT

```
We are going to count from 100 to 1000.
100
200
300
400
500
600
700
800
900
Sorry, I cannot count that high.
PL/SQL procedure successfully completed.
```

ANALYSIS The exception handler on the inner block, lines 23 through 26, sets the error_flag variable to true if any error occurs while counting. This allows the outer block to detect the error and display an appropriate message.

Nesting Functions and Procedures

Functions and procedures can be declared and executed from within other PL/SQL blocks. Remember the iifn function shown in Listing 2.4? That function takes three arguments: one Boolean and two numbers. It functions as an inline IF statement. If the first argument is true, the first number is returned. If the first argument is false, the second number is returned. You can see how the function works by writing a simple PL/SQL block to declare and execute it, as shown in Listing 2.7.

INPUT   **LISTING 2.7**   Executing the `iifn` Function

```
1:--This is a pl/sql wrapper
2:--that exercise the
3: -- function shown in listing 2.4.
4: --
5: DECLARE
6: temp  NUMBER;
7:
8:   FUNCTION iifn(boolean_expression IN BOOLEAN,
9:                true_number IN NUMBER,
10:                false_number IN NUMBER)
11:   RETURN NUMBER IS
12:   BEGIN
13:     IF boolean_expression THEN
14:       RETURN true_number;
15:     ELSIF NOT boolean_expression THEN
16:       RETURN false_number;
17:     ELSE
18:       --nulls propagate, i.e. null input yields null output.
19:       RETURN NULL;
20:     END IF;
21:   END;
22: BEGIN
23:     DBMS_OUTPUT.PUT_LINE(iifn(2 > 1,1,0));
24:     DBMS_OUTPUT.PUT_LINE(iifn(2 > 3,1,0));
25:     --
26:     --The next few lines verify that a null input yields a null output.
27:     temp := iifn(null,1,0);
28:     IF temp IS NULL THEN
29:       DBMS_OUTPUT.PUT_LINE('NULL');
30:     ELSE
31:       DBMS_OUTPUT.PUT_LINE(temp);
32:     END IF;
33: END;
34: /
```

OUTPUT
```
1
0
NULL

PL/SQL procedure successfully completed.
```

ANALYSIS   Line 5 begins a PL/SQL anonymous block. The `iifn` function is declared within the scope of this outer block (see lines 8 through 21). The keyword BEGIN in line 22 marks the start of the procedural section of the outer block. Because the `iifn` function is declared within the outer block, it can also be called from the procedural section of the outer block.

Line 23 calls the iifn function with a Boolean expression that evaluates as true. It then prints the value returned, which in this case is the second argument.

Line 24 calls the iifn function with a Boolean expression that evaluates as false, so the third argument is returned.

Finally, in lines 26–32, a null expression is passed to the function. A null input should result in a null output, and you can see that the function properly handles this case by returning a null value.

A procedure can be nested in the same manner as a function. Listing 2.8 shows a simple PL/SQL block illustrating the use of the swapn procedure you saw earlier in Listing 2.5.

INPUT **LISTING 2.8** Executing the swapn Procedure

```
 1: --
 2:-- This is a  PL/SQL wrapper
 3:- that executes the procedure shown in listing 2.5
 4: --Demonstration of a nested procedure block.
 5: DECLARE
 6:   first_number     NUMBER;
 7:   second_number    NUMBER;
 8:
 9:   PROCEDURE swapn (num_one IN OUT NUMBER, num_two IN OUT NUMBER) IS
10:     temp_num    NUMBER;
11:   BEGIN
12:     temp_num := num_one;
13:     num_one := num_two;
14:     num_two := temp_num ;
15:   END;
16:
17: BEGIN
18:   --Set some initial values, and display them.
19:   first_number := 10;
20:   second_number := 20;
21:   DBMS_OUTPUT.PUT_LINE('First Number = ' || TO_CHAR (first_number));
22:   DBMS_OUTPUT.PUT_LINE('Second Number = ' || TO_CHAR (second_number));
23:
24:   --Swap the values
25:   DBMS_OUTPUT.PUT_LINE('Swapping the two values now.');
26:   swapn(first_number, second_number);
27:
28:   --Display the results
29:   DBMS_OUTPUT.PUT_LINE('First Number = ' || to_CHAR (first_number));
30:   DBMS_OUTPUT.PUT_LINE('Second Number = ' || to_CHAR (second_number));
31: END;
32: /
```

OUTPUT

```
First Number = 10
Second Number = 20
Swapping the two values now.
First Number = 20
Second Number = 10

PL/SQL procedure successfully completed.
```

ANALYSIS The swapn procedure simply swaps two numeric values. You can see in lines 12 through 14 that it does just that, using the temp_num variable to hold the value of num_one until it can be assigned to num_two, after num_two has been assigned to num_one.

Scope Rules

With any language, and PL/SQL is no exception, it is important to have an understanding of the *scope* of the various variables, procedures, and functions which you declare. Scope means the range of code within which a given identifier can be referenced.

In PL/SQL the general rule is that an identifier (that is, variable name, procedure name, function name) can be referenced only by code executing inside the block in which the identifier was declared. This includes code inside any nested blocks, procedures, or functions.

Take a look at the code in Listing 2.9, which has been carefully constructed to illustrate this point.

INPUT **LISTING 2.9** Illustrates the Scope of Various Identifiers

```
 1: --
 2: --3: DECLARE
 4:   a_name  VARCHAR2(30) := 'Jeff Gennick';
 5:
 6: PROCEDURE name_print IS
 7: BEGIN
 8:   DBMS_OUTPUT.PUT_LINE(a_name);
 9: END;
10:
11: BEGIN
12:   DBMS_OUTPUT.PUT_LINE(a_name);
13:
14:   DECLARE
15:     b_name  VARCHAR2(30) := 'Jenny Gennick';
16:   BEGIN
17:     DBMS_OUTPUT.PUT_LINE('Inside nested block');
18:     DBMS_OUTPUT.PUT_LINE(a_name);
19:     DBMS_OUTPUT.PUT_LINE(b_name);
20:     name_print;
21:   END;
```

```
22:
23:    DBMS_OUTPUT.PUT_LINE('Back in the main block');
24:
25:    --But we cannot compile the following line because b_name
26:    --is not defined in this block.
27:    --DBMS_OUTPUT.PUT_LINE(b_name);
28:
29:    --Our procedure, however, can access the value of a_name.
30:    name_print;
31: END;
32: /
```

2

OUTPUT
```
Jeff Gennick
Inside nested block
Jeff Gennick
Jenny Gennick
Jeff Gennick
Back in the main block
Jeff Gennick
```

ANALYSIS The code shown in Listing 2.9 consists of two nested anonymous blocks and one procedure definition. The outermost block begins at line 3 and ends on line 31. A nested anonymous block begins on line 14 and ends on line 21. Lines 6 through 9 define the name_print procedure.

The variable a_name is declared in the outermost block (see line 4), thus any nested block, procedure, or function has access to it. To demonstrate this, the outer block displays the value of a_name in line 12, the nested block displays the value of a_name in line 18, and in line 30 of the outer block, the nested procedure name_print is called to also print the value of a_name. The name_print procedure has access to all other identifiers declared at that same level because it is defined within the outer block.

The variable b_name is declared in the inner block (see line 15) and can only be referenced within that block. If you were to uncomment line 27 and try to execute the code shown in the listing, you would receive an error because b_name would not be recognized.

Summary

In this chapter, you learned about the many datatypes that are available to you when programming in PL/SQL. You learned about the several nuances and variations of the NUMBER datatype, which are important to understand as you continue to work with PL/SQL.

This chapter also discusses the PL/SQL block structure in detail and illustrates several different types of blocks; that is, functions, procedures, triggers, and anonymous blocks.

No discussion of PL/SQL blocks is complete without addressing the issue of scope. You should now feel comfortable that when you declare an identifier, whether it be a variable, function, or procedure, you fully understand from where it can be referenced.

Q&A

Q Why shouldn't I use the VARCHAR datatype?

A Oracle warns against it because the definition of that datatype might be changed in the near future, and any change might have adverse ramifications on your code.

Q What is a subtype?

A A subtype allows you to declare variables of a particular data type that hold only a subset of the possible values that are normally handled by that datatype.

Q What is the difference between the BINARY_INTEGER type and the PLS_INTEGER type?

A Both use binary representations to store values. However, operations on PLS_INTEGERS use native machine instructions, whereas operations on BINARY_INTEGERS use internal library functions, which are slower.

Q What is the difference between a function and a procedure?

A A function returns a value and can be used in an expression. A procedure does not return a value and cannot be used in an expression.

Workshop

Use the following workshop to test your comprehension of this chapter and put what you've learned into practice. You'll find the answers to the quiz and exercises in Appendix A, "Answers."

Quiz

1. What are three benefits of using functions and procedures?
2. What values can a variable declared as NUMBER(6,2) hold? What will be the maximum value?
3. What values can a variable declared as NUMBER(2,2) hold? Where will rounding occur?
4. What is the maximum length of a VARCHAR2 variable in PL/SQL? In the Oracle database?

5. What can you do to ignore the time portion of a DATE variable?

6. When comparing a VARCHAR2 and a CHAR variable, how can you eliminate any trailing spaces?

Exercises

1. Try writing an anonymous block that declares a variable and displays the value. Then add a nested block that declares a variable of the same name and displays its value. What happens and why?

2. Write a function that computes a person's age in years. Hint: To get started on this, look at Listing 2.2.

2

DAY 3

Writing PL/SQL Expressions

by Jonathan Gennick

Today's lesson is about expressions. Expressions enable you to manipulate data inside your PL/SQL routines. They combine values and operators and are used to perform calculations and compare data. Today you will read and learn about the following:

- The various PL/SQL operators at your disposal
- How to understand and control the precedence of operations in an expression
- Issues involved when comparing fixed-length to variable-length strings
- The effects of nulls on expressions
- How to work with nulls
- How to convert values from one datatype to another

Understanding Operators, Expressions, and Conversions

NEW TERM   PL/SQL expressions are composed of *operands* and *operators*. *Operands* represent values. An *operand* is often a variable, but can also be a literal, a constant, or a function call. *Operators* specify actions, such as addition, multiplication, and so on, which can be performed using one or two *operands*. Here is a typical expression:

```
total_wages := hourly_rate * hours_worked
```

The three variables, `total_wages`, `hourly_rate`, and `hours_worked`, are all examples of operands. The * is the multiplication operator, and the := is the assignment operator.

Yesterday you learned about datatypes and variable declarations. Today you will read about the operators you can use to manipulate those variables. You'll see how to build simple expressions, such as the one just shown that multiplies two numbers together. You'll see how to build much more complex expressions that consist of function calls and relational comparisons. You'll also learn how to control the order in which an expression is evaluated.

Expressions often contain operands of multiple datatypes. It's not unusual, for example, to want to subtract a number of years from a date. In cases like this, you must first convert one of the values being operated on to a datatype that is compatible with the other. Only then can the necessary calculation be performed. In many cases, when the conversion is obvious, PL/SQL will handle this for you. You'll learn how and when PL/SQL does this. You'll also learn how you can explicitly specify the conversion, when you should do it, and why.

Building Expressions with PL/SQL Operators

Operators are the glue that hold expressions together. A very simple expression could consist of just one variable or value, but to accomplish anything useful, you need more than that. Operators enable you to take one or two values, perform an operation that uses those values, and return a result. The operation could be as simple as adding two numbers together and returning the total, or it could be a complex logical expression used in an `if` statement. PL/SQL operators can be divided into the following categories:

- Arithmetic operators
- Comparison operators
- Logical operators
- String operators

NEW TERM PL/SQL operators are either *unary* or *binary*. Most are binary operators, which means that they act on two values. An example is the addition operator, which adds two numbers together. A few, such as the negation operator, are unary. Unary operators only operate on one value.

Each of these types of operators are described in the following sections. There is nothing unusual about the operators in PL/SQL, and if you have any other programming experience, you will see that the operators and the order of evaluation are pretty much the same as any other language.

Arithmetic Operators

Arithmetic operators are used for mathematical computations, such as addition and subtraction. Table 3.1 shows the arithmetic functions supported by PL/SQL.

TABLE 3.1 Arithmetic Operators

Operator	Example	Usage
**	10**5	The exponentiation operator. It raises one number to the power of another. In the example shown, it raises 10 to the fifth power, resulting in a value of 100,000.
*	2*3	The multiplication operator. The example shown, 2 times 3, results in a value of 6.
/	6/2	The division operator. In the example, 6 divided by 2, the result would be 3.
+	2+2	The addition operator, which is used to add two values together. The example evaluates to 4.
-	4-2	The subtraction operator, which is used to subtract one number from another. The example subtracts 2 from 4, resulting in a value of 2.
-	-5	The negation operator. Used by itself, the minus sign negates the operand. The expression shown evaluates to a negative 5.
+	+5	Used by itself, the plus sign is the identity operator. It complements the negation operator, and the result of the expression is simply the value of the operand. In the example shown, the result is 5.

3

Addition, Subtraction, Multiplication, and Division

The basic four arithmetic operators (addition, subtraction, multiplication, and division) probably need no further explanation. Listing 3.1 shows some sample expressions and their resulting values.

> **Note**
>
> If you are executing these listings from SQL*Plus, you will need to issue the SET SERVEROUTPUT ON command at least once after you connect to your database, otherwise you won't see any output.

INPUT   **LISTING 3.1**   The Basic Four Arithmetic Operators in Action

```
1: --
2: --The basic arithmetic operators in action.
3: BEGIN
4:    DBMS_OUTPUT.PUT_LINE(4 * 2);   --multiplication
5:    DBMS_OUTPUT.PUT_LINE(24 / 3);  --division
6:    DBMS_OUTPUT.PUT_LINE(4 + 4);   --addition
7:    DBMS_OUTPUT.PUT_LINE(16 - 8);  --subtraction
8: END;
9: /
```

OUTPUT
```
8
8
8
8
PL/SQL procedure successfully completed.
```

ANALYSIS As you can see, the DBMS_OUTPUT.PUT_LINE procedure was used to display the values of four simple expressions, all of which evaluated to eight.

Exponentiation

Exponentiation, or raising a number to a power, is simply the act of multiplying a number by itself a specified number of times. Table 3.2 shows a few examples of exponentiation together with equivalent expressions using multiplication and the resulting values.

TABLE 3.2   Examples of Exponentiation

Example	Equivalent to	Result
10**5	10*10*10*10*10	100,000
2**3	2*2*2	8
6**2	6*6	36

Negation and Identity

You are familiar with negation, in its simplest form, when you use it to write a negative value such as −242.24. One way to look at it would be to say that the − preceding the number indicates that the value is negative. Another way to look at this is that you wrote a positive number, in other words 242.24, and applied the negation operator to it, thus yielding a negative value. Take the latter approach, and you will quickly realize that the target of the negation operator could just as well be a variable or an expression.

The identity operator, represented by the plus sign, doesn't do much at all. It's the opposite of the negation operator and simply returns the value of its operand.

Listing 3.2 shows some examples of how you can use these two operators.

INPUT   **LISTING 3.2**   The Negation and Identity Operators in Action

```
 1: --The negation and
 2: --identity operators in action.
 3: DECLARE
 4:    x    NUMBER;
 5: BEGIN
 6:    DBMS_OUTPUT.PUT_LINE(-242.24);
 7:    --You can also negate a variable.
 8:    x := 5;
 9:    DBMS_OUTPUT.PUT_LINE(-x);
10:    --Negating a negative number yields a positive value.
11:    x := -5;
12:    DBMS_OUTPUT.PUT_LINE(-x);
13:    --The identity operator simply returns the value of its operand.
14:    DBMS_OUTPUT.PUT_LINE(+10);
15:    DBMS_OUTPUT.PUT_LINE(+x);
16: END;
17: /
```

OUTPUT
```
-242.24
-5
5
10
-5
PL/SQL procedure successfully completed.
```

ANALYSIS   In line 6, the negation operator is used to simply write a negative number. In lines 7 through 9, the negation operator is used to negate the value of a variable. In line 12, it is used again, but this time the variable contains a negative number to start with, so the resulting value is positive. The remaining lines show the identity operator returning the operand's value unchanged.

Comparison Operators

Comparison operators are used to compare one value or expression to another. You can use them in your code to ask questions such as "Are these two values equal?" and then make decisions based on the result. Table 3.3 lists all the comparison operators supported by PL/SQL.

TABLE 3.3 Comparison Operators

Operator	Example	Usage
=	IF A = B THEN	The equality operator. This compares two values to see if they are identical.
<>	IF A <> B THEN	The inequality operator. This compares two values to see if they are *not* identical.
!=	IF A != B THEN	Another inequality operator, synonymous with <>.
~=	IF A ~= B THEN	Another inequality operator, synonymous with <>.
<	IF A < B THEN	The less than operator. Checks to see if one value is less than another.
>	IF A > B THEN	The greater than operator. Checks to see if one value is greater than another.
<=	IF A <= B THEN	The less than or equal to operator. Checks to see if one value is less than or equal to another.
>=	IF A >= B THEN	The greater than or equal to operator. Checks to see if one value is greater than or equal to another.
LIKE	IF A like B THEN	The pattern-matching operator. Checks to see if a character string matches a specified pattern.
BETWEEN	IF A BETWEEN B AND C THEN	Checks to see if a value lies within a specified range of values.
IN	IF A IN (B,C,D) THEN	Checks to see if a value lies within a specified list of values.
IS NULL	IF A IS NULL THEN	Checks to see if a value is null.

The first eight operators shown in Table 3.3 are referred to as *relational opera-tors*. These operators are very common and are present in almost any program-ming language.

All comparison operators return a Boolean result. They either represent a true statement or do not. This true/false, or Boolean, result can be used in a branching statement such as an IF...THEN statement, or it can be assigned to a Boolean variable for later reference.

With the exception of the LIKE operator, you can use all comparison operators with any of the *scalar* datatypes discussed on Day 2, "Writing Declarations and Blocks." The LIKE operator is only valid for character strings.

The Relational Operators: =, <>, !=, ~=, <, >, <=, >=

Like the basic arithmetic operators, the relational operators are commonly used in almost every programming language, and there is probably no need to elaborate much on the explanations in Table 3.3.

The relational operators test values for equality, inequality, and to see if one value is less than or greater than another. You can use these operators to compare two values belong-ing to any of the scalar datatypes. Table 3.4 gives some sample true and false expres-sions.

TABLE 3.4 Relational Operator Examples

True Expressions	False Expressions
5 = 5	5 = 3
'Jonathan' = 'Jonathan'	'Jonathan ' = 'Jonathan'
5 != 3	5 <> 5
'Jonathan ' ~= 'Jonathan'	'Jonathan ' ~= 'Jonathan'
10 < 200	10.1 < 10.05
'Jeff' < 'Jenny'	'jeff' < 'Jeff'
TO_DATE('15-Nov-61' < '15-Nov-97')	TO_DATE('1-Jan-97' < '1-Jan-96')
10.1 <= 10.1	10 <= 20
'A' <= 'B'	'B' <= 'A'
TO_DATE('1-Jan-97') <= TO_DATE('1-Jan-97')	TO_DATE('15-Nov-61') <= TO_DATE ('15-Nov-60)

You should be aware of some considerations when comparing dates and character strings. Oracle dates contain a time component, and it's important to remember that when comparing two dates for equality. String comparisons are case-sensitive, dependent on the character set being used, and affected by the underlying datatype. Comparing two values as CHAR strings might yield different results than the same values compared as VARCHAR2 strings. These issues are discussed later in this lesson in the section "Using Comparison Operators with Strings."

LIKE

LIKE is PL/SQL's pattern-matching operator and is used to compare a character string against a pattern. It's especially useful for performing wildcard searches when you need to retrieve data from the database and you aren't exactly sure of the spelling of your search criteria. Unlike the other comparison operators, LIKE can only be used with character strings.

The Syntax for LIKE

string_variable LIKE *pattern*

In this syntax, *string_variable* represents any character string variable, whether VARCHAR2, CHAR, LONG, and so on. *pattern* represents a pattern. This can also be a string variable, or it can be a string literal.

The LIKE operator checks to see if the contents of *string_variable* match the pattern definition. If the string matches the pattern, a result of true is returned; otherwise, the expression evaluates to false.

NEW TERM Two *wildcard* characters are defined for use with LIKE, the percent sign (%) and the underscore (_).The percent sign matches any number of characters in a string, and the underscore matches exactly one. For example, the pattern 'New %' will match 'New York', 'New Jersey', 'New Buffalo', and any other string beginning with the word 'New '. Another example is the pattern '___day'. It is looking for a six-letter word ending with the letters 'day', and would match 'Monday', 'Friday', and 'Sunday'. It would not match 'Tuesday', 'Wednesday', 'Thursday', or 'Saturday' because those names have more than three letters preceding 'day'.

Listing 3.3 shows a short function that makes use of the LIKE operator to return the area code from a phone number. Figure 3.1 shows how the function works.

LISTING 3.3 A Function Using the LIKE Operator to Return a Phone

INPUT Number's Area Code

```
 1: CREATE OR REPLACE FUNCTION area_code (phone_number IN VARCHAR2)
 2: RETURN VARCHAR2 AS
 3: BEGIN
 4:   IF phone_number LIKE '___-___-____' THEN
 5:     --we have a phone number with an area code.
 6:     RETURN SUBSTR(phone_number,1,3);
 7:   ELSE
 8:     --there is no area code
 9:     RETURN 'none';
10:   END IF;
11: END;
12: /
```

OUTPUT
```
Function created.
SQL>
```

ANALYSIS The preceding code simply creates a stored function. Type it into SQL*Plus exactly as it is shown. The LIKE operator is used in line 4 to see if the phone number matches the standard XXX-XXX-XXXX format, which would indicate that an area code is part of the number. Figure 3.1 demonstrates the use of this area_code function.

FIGURE 3.1

The area_code *function in action.*

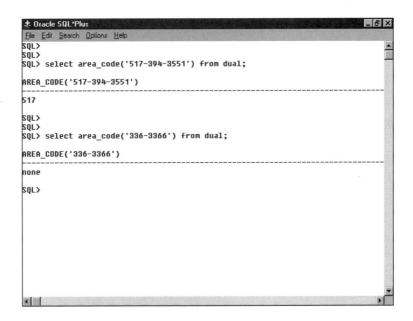

BETWEEN

The BETWEEN operator tests to see if a value falls within a given range of values.

The Syntax for BETWEEN

```
the_value [NOT] BETWEEN low_end AND high_end
```

In this syntax, `the_value` is the value you are testing, `low_end` represents the low end of the range, and `high_end` represents the high end of the range.

A result of `true` is returned if the value in question is greater than or equal to the low end of the range and less than or equal to the high end of the range.

You might have already guessed that the BETWEEN operator is somewhat redundant. You could easily replace any expression using BETWEEN with one that used <= and >=. The equivalent expression would look like this:

```
(the_value >= low_end) AND (the_value <= high_end)
```

Table 3.5 shows some expressions using BETWEEN and the equivalent expressions using <= and >=.

TABLE 3.5   Expressions Using the BETWEEN Operator

Expression	Result	Equivalent Expression
5 BETWEEN -5 AND 5	true	(5 >= -5) AND (5 <= 5)
4 BETWEEN 0 AND 3	false	(4 >= 0) AND (4 <= 3)
4 BETWEEN 3 AND 5	true	(4 >= 3) AND (4 <= 5)
4 NOT BETWEEN 3 AND 4	false	(4 >= 3) AND (4 <= 4)

> **Tip**
>
> Even though the BETWEEN operator is redundant, using it can add clarity to your code, making it more readable.

IN

The IN operator checks to see if a value is contained in a specified list of values. A `true` result is returned if the value is contained in the list; otherwise, the expression evaluates to `false`.

SYNTAX

The Syntax for IN

```
the_value [NOT] IN (value1, value2, value3,...)
```

In this syntax, *the_value* is the value you are testing, and *value1*, *value2*, *value3*, ... represents a list of comma-delimited values.

A result of true is returned if the value in question matches one of the values in the list.

Table 3.6 shows some examples of the IN operator in use.

TABLE 3.6 Expressions Using the IN Operator

Expression	Result
3 IN (0,1,2,3,4,5,6,7,8,9)	true
'Sun' IN ('Mon','Tue','Wed','Thu','Fri')	false
'Sun' IN ('Sat','Sun')	true
3 NOT IN (0,1,2,3,4,5,6,7,8,9)	false

Listing 3.4 shows a short sample of code that uses the IN operator to see if a holiday will result in a three-day weekend.

INPUT   **LISTING 3.4**   The IN Operator Used to Test for Long Weekends

```
 1: --Demonstrate the IN operator
 2: DECLARE
 3:   test_date      DATE;
 4:   day_of_week    VARCHAR2(3);
 5:   years_ahead    INTEGER;
 6: BEGIN
 7:   --Assign a date value to test_date.
 8:   --Let's use Independence Day.
 9:   test_date := TO_DATE('4-Jul-1997','dd-mon-yyyy');
10:   --Now let's look ahead ten years and see how many
11:   --three day July 4 weekends we can expect.
12:   FOR years_ahead IN 1..10 LOOP
13:     --get the name for the day of the week.
14:     day_of_week := TO_CHAR(test_date,'Dy');
15:     --most employers give an extra day if July 4 falls on a weekend.
16:     IF day_of_week IN ('Mon','Fri','Sat','Sun') THEN
17:       DBMS_OUTPUT.PUT_LINE(TO_CHAR(test_date,'dd-Mon-yyyy')
18:                            || '     A long weekend!');
19:     ELSE
20:       DBMS_OUTPUT.PUT_LINE(TO_CHAR(test_date,'dd-Mon-yyyy')
21:                            || ' Not a long weekend.');
22:     END IF;
```

continues

LISTING 3.4   continued

```
23:     --advance one year (12 months)
24:     test_date := ADD_MONTHS(test_date,12);
25:   END LOOP;  —for each year
26: END;
27: /
```

OUTPUT
```
04-Jul-1997     A long weekend!
04-Jul-1998     A long weekend!
04-Jul-1999     A long weekend!
04-Jul-2000 Not a long weekend.
04-Jul-2001 Not a long weekend.
04-Jul-2002 Not a long weekend.
04-Jul-2003     A long weekend!
04-Jul-2004     A long weekend!
04-Jul-2005     A long weekend!
04-Jul-2006 Not a long weekend.
PL/SQL procedure successfully completed.
```

ANALYSIS   The preceding code checks the date for Independence Day over a 10-year period and tells you whether or not it will result in a long weekend. Line 9 is where the starting date of 4 July 1997 is set. A FOR loop is used in lines 12 through 25 to check the July 4 day for a 10-year period. In line 14, the TO_CHAR function is used to retrieve the day of the week on which July 4 falls during the year in question. Line 16 uses the IN operator to test for a long weekend. The obvious cases to check for are when Independence Day falls on a Monday or a Friday, resulting in a three-day weekend. The test in line 16 also includes Saturday and Sunday because many employers still give employees a day off, resulting in a three-day weekend. Line 24 uses PL/SQL's ADD_MONTHS function to advance the date 12 months, which is one year. You will read more about ADD_MONTHS on Day 6, "Using Oracle's Built-in Functions." It is also covered in Appendix B, "Oracle Functions Reference."

IS NULL

The IS NULL operator is used to test a variable for the absence of a value. Variables that have no value are referred to as being *null* and are most commonly encountered when retrieving data from a database. Variables you declare in a PL/SQL block are also initially null, or have no value, and remain null until your code specifically assigns a value to them.

SYNTAX

The Syntax for IS NULL

the_value IS [NOT] NULL

In this syntax, *the_value* is a variable, or another expression, that you are testing.

If the value you are testing is null, the IS NULL operator returns true. You can also reverse the test by using IS NOT NULL, in which case true is returned if the variable or expression in question contains a value.

Listing 3.5 shows an example of using the IS NULL operator to demonstrate that a variable has no value until one is specifically assigned.

INPUT   **LISTING 3.5**   The IS NULL Operator in Action

```
 1: --Demonstrate the IS NULL operator
 2: DECLARE
 3:   test  INTEGER;
 4: BEGIN
 5:   --The variable TEST is currently null because
 6:   --a value hasn't been assigned to it yet.
 7:   IF test IS NULL THEN
 8:     DBMS_OUTPUT.PUT_LINE('The variable TEST is null.');
 9:   END IF;
10:   --Assign a value to TEST and display it.
11:   test := 1;
12:   DBMS_OUTPUT.PUT_LINE('TEST = ' || TO_CHAR(test));
13:   --Test is no longer null because a value has been assigned to it.
14:   IF test IS NOT NULL THEN
15:     DBMS_OUTPUT.PUT_LINE('The variable TEST is NOT null.');
16:   END IF;
17: END;
18: /
```

OUTPUT
```
The variable TEST is null.
TEST = 1
The variable TEST is NOT null.
PL/SQL procedure successfully completed.
```

ANALYSIS   The variable test is declared in line 3. Initially it has no value and is considered to be null. The IS NULL operator is used in line 7 to check for this. Because no value has yet been assigned, the comparison evaluates to true and the message is printed. In line 11, a value is assigned to the variable test, and it is no longer considered to be null. The IS NOT NULL test in line 14 proves this.

> **Tip**
>
> It is extremely important to understand the effects of null values on expressions, especially comparison expressions. The rule about comparison expressions being either `true` or `false` flies right out the window when nulls are introduced into the equation, and nulls are often encountered when retrieving data from databases. Be sure to read the section titled "Null Values in Expressions" later in this lesson.

Logical Operators

PL/SQL implements three logical operators: AND, OR, and NOT. The NOT operator is typically used to negate the result of a comparison expression, whereas the AND and OR operators are typically used to link together multiple comparisons.

NOT

Use the NOT operator when you are interested in the case in which a comparison is not true.

The Syntax for the NOT Operator

```
NOT boolean_expression
```

In this syntax, *boolean_expression* can be any expression resulting in a Boolean, or `true`/`false`, value. This is often a comparison expression such as `(a = b)`, but can also be a variable of the BOOLEAN datatype.

Applying the NOT operator to an expression causes the expression to evaluate to the opposite of what it normally would. For example, the following expression evaluates to `true`:

```
(8 = 8)
```

Applying the NOT operator to that same expression results in a value of `false` being returned, for example:

```
NOT (8 = 8)
```

It is possible to write the preceding expression without using the NOT operator. For example, the two expressions shown next are equivalent:

```
NOT (8 = 8)
(8 <> 8)
```

In a simple case like the preceding example, using the second expression will probably result in clearer code. With more complex expressions, that decision becomes a judgment call. Sometimes it is easier to define the case you aren't interested in and then negate it.

AND

The AND operator is used to join two comparison expressions when you are interested in testing whether both expressions are true. It can also be used for the same purpose with two Boolean variables—to check to see whether both are equal to true.

SYNTAX

The Syntax for the AND Operator

boolean_expression AND *boolean_expression*

In this syntax, *boolean_expression* can be any expression resulting in a Boolean, or true/false, value. This is often a comparison expression such as (a = b), but can also be a variable of the BOOLEAN datatype.

The AND operator returns a value of true if both expressions each evaluate to true; otherwise, a value of false is returned. Use AND when you need to test several conditions and execute some code only when they are all true. Table 3.7 shows some sample expressions using the AND operator.

TABLE 3.7   Expressions Using the AND Operator

Expression	Result
(5 = 5) AND (4 < 100) AND (2 >= 2)	true
(5 = 4) AND (5 = 5)	false
'Mon' IN ('Sun','Sat') AND (2 = 2)	false

OR

The OR operator is used to join two comparison expressions when you are interested in testing whether at least one of them is true. It can also be used with two Boolean variables to see whether at least one is set to true.

SYNTAX

The Syntax for the OR Operator

boolean_expression OR *boolean_expression*

In this syntax, *boolean_expression* can be any expression resulting in a Boolean, or true/false, value. This is often a comparison expression such as (a = b), but can also be a variable of the BOOLEAN datatype.

The OR operator returns a value of true if any one of the expressions evaluates to true. A value of false is returned only if both the expressions evaluate to false. Table 3.8 shows some sample expressions using the OR operator.

TABLE 3.8 Expressions Using the OR Operator

Expression	Result
(5 <> 5) OR (4 >= 100) OR (2 < 2)	false
(5 = 4) OR (5 = 5)	true
'Mon' IN ('Sun','Sat') OR (2 = 2)	true

String Operators

PL/SQL has two operators specifically designed to operate only on character string data. These are the LIKE operator and the concatenation (¦¦) operator. The LIKE operator is a comparison operator used for pattern matching and was described earlier in the section titled "Comparison Operators," so only the concatenation operator is described here.

The Syntax for the Concatenation Operator

SYNTAX

string_1 ¦¦ *string_2*

In this syntax, *string_1* and *string_2* are both character strings and can be either string constants, string variables, or a string expression. The concatenation operator returns a result consisting of all the characters in *string_1* followed by all the characters in *string_2*.

Listing 3.6 shows several ways in which you can use the concatenation operator.

INPUT   **LISTING 3.6** Use of the Concatenation Operator

```
 1: --Demonstrate the concatenation operator
 2: DECLARE
 3:    a      VARCHAR2(30);
 4:    b      VARCHAR2(30);
 5:    c      VARCHAR2(30);
 6: BEGIN
 7:    --Concatenate several string constants.
 8:    c := 'Jack' ¦¦ ' AND ' ¦¦ 'Jill';
 9:    DBMS_OUTPUT.PUT_LINE(c);
10:    --Concatenate both string variables and constants.
11:    a := 'went up';
12:    b := 'the hill';
13:    DBMS_OUTPUT.PUT_LINE(a ¦¦ ' ' ¦¦ b ¦¦ ',');
14:    --Concatenate two string variables.
15:    a := 'to fetch a ';
16:    b := 'pail of water.';
17:    c := a ¦¦ b;
18:    DBMS_OUTPUT.PUT_LINE(c);
19: END;
20: /
```

OUTPUT

```
Jack and Jill
went up the hill,
to fetch a pail of water.
PL/SQL procedure successfully completed.
```

ANALYSIS The preceding code shows the concatenation operator used in several different ways. Notice that you do not always have to assign the result directly to a string variable. For example, in line 13, the concatenation operator is used to create a string expression that is passed as input to the PUT_LINE procedure.

Using Comparison Operators with Strings

You can use any of the PL/SQL comparison operators to compare one character string to another. Strings can be compared for equality, for inequality, to see if one string is less than another, to see if one string matches a given pattern, and so on. When using character strings in comparison expressions, the result depends on several things:

- Character set
- Datatype
- Case (upper versus lower)

The Effect of Character Set on String Comparisons

When comparing two strings to see if one is greater or less than another, the result depends on the sort order of the underlying character set being used. In the typical ASCII environment, all lowercase letters are greater than all uppercase letters, digits are less than all letters, and the other characters fall in various places depending on their corresponding ASCII codes. However, if you were working in an EBCDIC environment, you would find that all the digits were greater than the letters and all lowercase letters are less than all uppercase letters, so be careful.

The Datatype's Effect on String Comparisons

NEW TERM The underlying datatype has an effect when comparing two string variables, or when comparing a string variable with a constant. Remember that variables of the CHAR datatype are fixed-length and padded with spaces. Variables of the VARCHAR2 datatype are variable-length and are not automatically padded with spaces. When comparing two CHAR datatypes, Oracle uses *blank-padded comparison semantics*. This means that Oracle conceptually adds enough trailing spaces to the shorter string to make it equal in length to the longer string and then does the comparison. Trailing spaces alone will not result in any differences being found between two springs. Oracle also does the same thing when comparing two string constants. However, when one of the values in a comparison is a variable-length string, Oracle uses *non-padded comparison semantics*. The use of *non-padded comparison semantics* means that Oracle does not pad either of the values with spaces, and any trailing spaces will affect the result. Listing 3.7 shows several string comparisons that illustrate this point.

INPUT   **LISTING 3.7**   Demonstration of String Comparison Semantics

```
 1: --Demonstrate string comparision semantics
 2: DECLARE
 3:    fixed_length_10  CHAR(10);
 4:    fixed_length_20  CHAR(20);
 5:    var_length_10    VARCHAR2(10);
 6:    var_length_20    VARCHAR2(20);
 7: BEGIN
 8:    --Constants are compared using blank-padded comparison semantics,
 9:    --so the trailing spaces won't affect the result.
10:    IF 'Jonathan' = 'Jonathan         ' THEN
11:       DBMS_OUTPUT.PUT_LINE
12:       ('Constant: ''Jonathan'' = ''Jonathan          ''');
13:    END IF;
14:    --Fixed length strings are also compared with blank-padded
15:    --comparison semantic, so the fact that one is longer doesn't matter.
16:    fixed_length_10 := 'Donna';
17:    fixed_length_20 := 'Donna';
18:    IF fixed_length_20 = fixed_length_10 THEN
19:       DBMS_OUTPUT.PUT_LINE('Char: ''' || fixed_length_10 || ''' = '''
20:                          || fixed_length_20 || '''');
21:    END IF;
22:    --Comparison of a fixed length string and a literal also
23:    --results is the use of blank-padded comparison semantics.
24:     IF fixed_length_10 = 'Donna' THEN
25:       DBMS_OUTPUT.PUT_LINE('Char and constant: '''
26:         || fixed_length_10 || ''' = ''' || 'Donna' || '''');
27:    END IF;
28:    --But compare a variable length string
29:     --against a fixed length, and the
30:    --trailing spaces do matter.
31:    var_length_10 := 'Donna';
32:    IF fixed_length_10 = var_length_10 THEN
33:       DBMS_OUTPUT.PUT_LINE('Char and Varchar2: '''
34:         || fixed_length_10 || ''' = '''
35:         || var_length_10 || '''');
36:    ELSE
37:       DBMS_OUTPUT.PUT_LINE('Char and Varchar2: '''
38:         || fixed_length_10 || ''' NOT = '''
39:         || var_length_10 || '''');
40:    END IF;
41:    --The maximum lengths of varchar2 strings do not matter,
42:    --only the assigned values.
```

```
43:   var_length_10 := 'Donna';
44:   var_length_20 := 'Donna';
45:   IF var_length_20 = var_length_10 THEN
46:     DBMS_OUTPUT.PUT_LINE('Both Varchar2: '''
47:       || var_length_20 || ''' = '''
48:       || var_length_10 || '''');
49:   ELSE
50:     DBMS_OUTPUT.PUT_LINE('Both Varchar2: '''
51:       || var_length_20 || ''' NOT = '''
52:       || var_length_10 || '''');
53:   END IF;
54: END;
55: /
```

OUTPUT

```
Constant: 'Jonathan' = 'Jonathan        '
Char: 'Donna        ' = 'Donna           '
Char and constant: 'Donna        ' = 'Donna'
Char and Varchar2: 'Donna        ' NOT = 'Donna'
Both Varchar2: 'Donna' = 'Donna'
PL/SQL procedure successfully completed.
```

ANALYSIS You can see from the output that the first three comparisons in Listing 3.7 use blank-padded comparison semantics. The strings being compared are considered to be equal even though the number of trailing spaces differs in each case. The fourth comparison, however, compares a VARCHAR2 variable against a CHAR variable. Because one of the strings in question is variable-length, the trailing spaces count, and the two strings are not considered to be equal.

The Effect of Case on String Comparisons

PL/SQL string comparisons are always case-sensitive. The obvious ramification of this is that a lowercase string such as 'aaa' is not considered equal to its uppercase equivalent of 'AAA'. But case also makes a difference when comparing two strings to see which is greater. In an ASCII environment, the letter 'A' will be less than the letter 'B'. However, the letter 'a' will not only be greater than 'B'; it will be greater than 'Z'.

> **Tip**
>
> If you need to perform case-insensitive string comparisons, use PL/SQL's built-in UPPER() function. For example:
>
> ```
> IF UPPER('a') < UPPER('B') THEN...
> ```
>
> You can use the LOWER() function in the same manner.

Use of Comparison Operators with Dates

Date comparison works pretty much as you might expect and has fewer complexities than string comparisons do. Earlier dates are considered to be less than later dates, and it follows that more recent dates are greater than earlier dates. The only complication arises from the fact that PL/SQL date variables also contain a time component. Listing 3.8 illustrates this and another potential problem to be aware of when comparing date values against each other.

INPUT   **LISTING 3.8**   Date Comparison Example

```
 1: --Demonstrate date comparisions
 2: DECLARE
 3:   payment_due_date  DATE;
 4: BEGIN
 5:   --In real life the payment_due date might be read from
 6:   --a database or calculated based on information from a database.
 7:   payment_due_date := TRUNC(SYSDATE);
 8:   --Display the current date and the payment date.
 9:   DBMS_OUTPUT.PUT_LINE('Today is ' || TO_CHAR(SYSDATE,'dd-Mon-yyyy'));
10:   DBMS_OUTPUT.PUT_LINE('Payment is due on '
11:     || TO_CHAR(payment_due_date,'dd-Mon-yyyy'));
12:   IF payment_due_date = SYSDATE THEN
13:     DBMS_OUTPUT.PUT_LINE('Payment is due today.');
14:   ELSE
15:     DBMS_OUTPUT.PUT_LINE('Payment can wait a while.');
16:   END IF;
17:   --In reality, the time does not matter when speaking of a due date.
18:   IF TRUNC(payment_due_date) = TRUNC(SYSDATE) THEN
19:     DBMS_OUTPUT.PUT_LINE('Wrong! Payment is due today!');
20:   ELSE
21:     DBMS_OUTPUT.PUT_LINE('Wrong! Payment can wait a while.');
22:   END IF;
23: END;
24: /
```

OUTPUT
```
Today is 01-Jun-1997
Payment is due on 01-Jun-1997
Payment can wait a while.
Wrong! Payment is due today!
PL/SQL procedure successfully completed.
```

ANALYSIS   Today's date and the payment due date both match, yet the IF statement in line 12 failed to detect this. Why? Because SYSDATE is a function that returns the current date and time, with the time resolved down to the second. The payment_due_date variable will contain a time of midnight because the TRUNC function was used when the due date was set. See line 7. The only time that line 12 would function correctly would be for one second at midnight each day. In line 18, the TRUNC function is used to truncate the time values from the two dates, resulting in a comparison that works as desired in this case. Admittedly this is a contrived example, but it does illustrate the problem.

Tip   Be especially careful comparing dates read from the database. Sometimes they have time components that you don't expect. Even if programmers aren't supposed to store a time, it's a pretty easy mistake to make.

Having the time as part of a date variable is not necessarily a bad thing. It's just something you need to be aware of, especially when comparing dates with each other.

Exploring Expressions

When you combine values and operators to produce a result, you have an expression. You have already learned about the various datatypes available in PL/SQL and PL/SQL's extensive collection of operators. In addition, in order to use expressions effectively in your code, you also need to understand

- Operator precedence
- Use of parentheses
- Types of expressions
- The effects of null values in an expression
- Conversion between datatypes

Understanding the effects of a null value on an expression is particularly important, especially when you move into retrieving data from a database. The remainder of this chapter discusses each of these items in detail.

Expressions Defined

Simply put, an expression is some combination of variables, operators, literals, and functions that returns a single value. Operators are the glue that hold an expression together and are almost always present. The other elements might not all be present in every expression.

In its very simplest form, an expression might simply consist of a literal value, a variable name, or a function call. The first few entries in Table 3.9 are examples of this type of expression. More typical expressions involve two values and an operator, with the operator defining the action to be taken and the result to be returned. Complex expressions can be built up by stringing several simple expressions together with various operators and function calls. Finally, the unary operators can be applied to any expression or value.

TABLE 3.9 Sample Expressions

Expression	Comments
`1000`	Evaluates to one thousand
`some_variable_name`	Evaluates to the contents of the variable
`SYSDATE`	An Oracle function that returns the current date
`1000 + 2000`	A typical expression using a binary operator
`-1000`	An expression using a unary operator
`10 * 20 + 30 / 2`	Two expressions joined together
`LENGTH('Lansing ' ¦¦ 'MI')`	A function call evaluating a sub-expression is itself an expression
`1-5**2<=10*4-20`	Two expressions, each containing sub-expressions, joined together

Take a look at the last example in Table 3.9. The comment notes that it is actually two expressions joined together, but which two? What value should Oracle return for this expression? The answer to both these questions can be found in the rules governing operator precedence.

Operator Precedence

When evaluating an expression consisting of different values, datatypes, and operators, Oracle follows a specific set of rules that determine which operations are done first. Each operator has an assigned precedence. Operators with a higher precedence are evaluated first. Operators of the same precedence level are evaluated from left to right. Table 3.10 shows these precedence levels for each of the various operators.

TABLE 3.10   Operator Precedence

Precedence	Operators	Operation
First	`**`, `NOT`	Exponentiation and logical negation
Second	`+`, `-`	Arithmetic identity and negation (+ and - used as unary operators)
Third	`*`, `/`	Multiplication and division
Fourth	`+`, `-`, `¦¦`	Addition, subtraction, and string concatenation
Fifth	`=`, `<>`, `!=`, `~=`, `<`, `>`, `<=`, `>=`, `LIKE`, `BETWEEN`, `IN`, `IS NULL`	Comparison
Sixth	`AND`	Logical conjunction
Seventh	`OR`	Logical inclusion

Take another look at the expression referred to in the previous section. The following list shows the steps Oracle would take to evaluate it:

1. `1-5**2<=10*4-20`
2. `1-25<=10*4-20`
3. `1-25<=40-20`
4. `-24<=20`
5. `true`

You can control the order in which Oracle evaluates an expression by using parentheses. Oracle will evaluate any part of an expression in parentheses first. If parentheses are nested, Oracle will always evaluate the innermost expression first and then move outwards. Here is what happens to the preceding expression if you add some parentheses:

1. `(1-5)**2<=10*(4-20)`
2. `(-4)**2<=10*(-16)`
3. `16<=-160`
4. `false`

Tip

Use parentheses in complex expressions, even when they are not strictly necessary, in order to make the intended order of evaluation clear to other programmers.

Types of Expressions

One way of classifying expressions is by the datatype of the resulting value. Using this scheme, expressions can be classified as one of these types:

- Arithmetic or numeric
- Boolean
- String
- Date

Any expression returning a numeric value is referred to as an *arithmetic expression*, or sometimes as a *numeric expression*.

A Boolean expression is any expression that returns a `true` or `false` value. Comparison expressions are really special cases of this type, but they are not the only way to get a `true/false` value. A Boolean variable—or several Boolean variables linked together with the logical operators `AND`, `OR`, and `NOT`—will also return a Boolean result.

String expressions are those that return character strings as results, and date expressions are those that result in a date-time value.

Generally speaking, you can use an expression of the appropriate datatype anywhere in your PL/SQL code where a value is required. The exception to this would be in function and procedure calls that modify their arguments.

Null Values in Expressions

Until now, the discussion has ignored the effect of nulls in expressions. This was done in order to concentrate on the normal function of each of the operators and also because nulls pretty much have the same effect regardless of the operation being done.

What is a null? The term is best understood as referring to an unknown value. Any variable or expression is considered *null* when the value of that variable or expression is unknown. This situation can occur if you declare a variable and use it in an expression without first assigning a value. Because the variable has no assigned value, the result of the expression can't be known. More commonly, nulls are encountered when reading data from a database. Oracle, like any other relational database, does not force you to store a value for each column in a table. When no specific value is stored, the contents of that column are considered unknown, and the column is referred to as being null.

New Term The effects of nulls are particularly insidious when writing Boolean expressions, such as the WHERE clause in a SQL SELECT statement. SQL uses what is called *three-valued logic*. Three-valued logic says that the result of a Boolean expression can be either true, false, or NULL. Many a programmer has felt the sting of an IF statement gone awry because of an unexpected null value, and some consider three-valued logic to be more of a three-pronged pitchfork prodding them in the behind. The code in Listing 3.9 shows why nulls can cause so much grief.

INPUT **LISTING 3.9** Effects of Nulls on Boolean Expressions

```
 1: --Demonstrate the effects of null values on boolean expressions.
 2: DECLARE
 3:   a       INTEGER;
 4:   b       BOOLEAN;
 5:   n       INTEGER;      --this will be our null value.
 6: BEGIN
 7:   --Assign a value to the variable A, but leave N null.
 8:   a := 2;
 9:   --Note that the test for A=N fails.
10:   IF a = n THEN
11:     DBMS_OUTPUT.PUT_LINE('a = n is true');
12:   ELSE
13:     DBMS_OUTPUT.PUT_LINE('a = n is not true');
14:   END IF;
15:   --But also note that the test for a <> n fails.
16:   IF a <> n THEN
17:     DBMS_OUTPUT.PUT_LINE('a <> n is true');
18:   ELSE
19:     DBMS_OUTPUT.PUT_LINE('a <> n is not true');
20:   END IF;
21:   --Here is an expression that many people first
22:   --expect to always be true.
23:   IF (a = n) OR (a <> n) THEN
24:     DBMS_OUTPUT.PUT_LINE('(a = n) or (a <> n) is true');
25:   ELSE
26:     DBMS_OUTPUT.PUT_LINE('(a = n) or (a <> n) is not true');
27:   END IF;
28:   --TRUE and NULL = NULL
29:   IF (a = 2) AND (a <> n) THEN
30:     DBMS_OUTPUT.PUT_LINE('TRUE and NULL = TRUE');
31:   ELSE
32:     DBMS_OUTPUT.PUT_LINE('TRUE and NULL = NULL');
33:   END IF;
```

continues

LISTING 3.9   continued

```
34:    --TRUE or NULL = TRUE
35:    IF (a = 2) OR (a <> n) THEN
36:      DBMS_OUTPUT.PUT_LINE('TRUE or NULL = TRUE');
37:    ELSE
38:      DBMS_OUTPUT.PUT_LINE('TRUE or NULL = NULL');
39:    END IF;
40:    --NOT NULL = NULL
41:    IF (NOT (a = n)) IS NULL THEN
42:      DBMS_OUTPUT.PUT_LINE('NOT NULL = NULL');
43:    END IF;
44:    --TIP: try this if you want a null value to be
45:     --considered "not equal".
46:    --Be careful though, if BOTH A and N are NULL
47:    --NVL will still return TRUE.
48:    IF NVL((a <> n),true) THEN
49:      DBMS_OUTPUT.PUT_LINE('The values are not equal.');
50:    ELSE
51:      DBMS_OUTPUT.PUT_LINE('The values are equal.');
52:    END IF;
53:    --TIP: a three-valued if construct.
54:    b := (a <> n);
55:    IF b THEN
56:      DBMS_OUTPUT.PUT_LINE('a <> n is TRUE');
57:    ELSIF NOT b THEN
58:      DBMS_OUTPUT.PUT_LINE('a <> n is FALSE');
59:    ELSE
60:      DBMS_OUTPUT.PUT_LINE('a <> n is NULL');
61:    END IF;
62: END;
63: /
```

OUTPUT

```
a = n is not true
a <> n is not true
(a = n) or (a <> n) is not true
TRUE and NULL = NULL
TRUE or NULL = TRUE
NOT NULL = NULL
The values are not equal.
a <> n is NULL
PL/SQL procedure successfully completed.
```

ANALYSIS   Listing 3.9 is a somewhat contrived example, but it illustrates very well the effects of nulls on comparison expressions. Take a close look at what is going on here. The first IF statement in line 10 tests for a = n. As you might expect, this is not true, but it is important to understand that it is not false either. The second IF statement in line 16 proves this. The test there is for a <> n, the exact opposite of the previous comparison, and it also is not `true`. Line 23 shows an extreme case, an expression which many people at first glance would expect to always be `true`. However, because the value of n is unknown, the truth of this expression is also unknown and it evaluates to `null`.

There are three basic things to understand when dealing with nulls:

- How nulls propagate in expressions
- How the logical operators `AND`, `OR`, and `NOT` handle nulls
- How the `IF` statement deals with nulls

In an expression, null values propagate. For the most part, any arithmetic, date, string, or Boolean expression containing even one `null` value will also evaluate to `null`. There are some exceptions to this rule, which are described shortly.

 Note

Where strings are concerned, Oracle considers an empty string ('' for example) to be a null. A string of spaces, however, is not the same as an empty string, and is not null.

3

The logical operators `AND`, `OR`, and `NOT` are often used to link together comparison expressions. Table 3.11 shows how these operators function in expressions with null values.

TABLE 3.11 Three-Valued Logic Truth Table

Operator	Expression	Result
AND	TRUE AND TRUE	TRUE
	TRUE AND FALSE	FALSE
	TRUE AND NULL	NULL
	FALSE AND NULL	FALSE
	NULL AND NULL	NULL
OR	TRUE OR TRUE	TRUE
	TRUE OR FALSE	TRUE
	TRUE OR NULL	TRUE
	FALSE OR NULL	FALSE
	NULL OR NULL	NULL
NOT	NOT TRUE	FALSE
	NOT FALSE	TRUE
	NOT NULL	NULL

Lines 28 through 43 in Listing 3.9 contain some IF statements that demonstrate how each of the logical operators operate on null values.

The IF statement is the fundamental decision-making structure of PL/SQL. Give it a Boolean expression, and it evaluates that expression and makes a decision as to which piece of code to execute. However, Boolean expressions can have three values: TRUE, FALSE, and NULL. An IF statement has only two parts: the code to be executed when an expression is TRUE, and the code to be executed when it isn't. There is a mismatch here, and it's very important to keep in mind that the ELSE portion will be executed when the result of an expression is unknown, or in other words, when the expression is null.

Tip

Lines 53 through 61 of Listing 3.9 show a way to construct an IF statement that has separate execution paths for TRUE, FALSE, and NULL.

There are some exceptions to the general rule that nulls propagate in expressions. Null character strings are sometimes handled as if they were zero-length strings, and PL/SQL does have some functions and operators that have been specifically designed to help you work with nulls.

You can concatenate strings, even if one is null, and get the results you would expect. This is because the concatenation operator simply ignores any null strings. However, if all the strings are null, the result will be null. Also bear in mind that PL/SQL treats a zero-length VARCHAR2 string as a null value.

Note

Treating a zero-length string as a null value is an Oracle-specific behavior that is not specified in the ANSI standard for SQL.

You can use the IS NULL operator to see whether or not a particular variable or expression is null. It allows your code to detect and act on null values. You saw an example of this earlier in Listing 3.5. The IS NULL operator returns only a true or false value, never a NULL.

Caution

Always use the IS NULL operator when checking for null values. Do not use the equality or inequality operators to compare a variable to null. You can code a statement such as IF some_var = NULL, but you won't get the results you might expect. Use IF some_var IS NULL instead.

The built-in NVL function allows you to specify an alternate value to be used when its argument is null. Briefly, the syntax for NVL looks like this:

The Syntax for the NVL Function

NVL(expression, value_if_expression_is_null)

Usually, when people use NVL, they simply supply a variable for the expression. However, that doesn't have to be the case. When you invoke NVL, the result of the first expression is computed. If that result is not null, then it will be returned as the result of NVL. If the result of the expression does happen to be null, then NVL will return the value of the second argument as its result. The end result is that the value_if_expression_is_null argument becomes an alternate value for expression, to be used if expression is null.

Lines 44 through 52 of Listing 3.9 show an interesting use of the NVL function to account for the possibility of the variable n being null. You can read more about NVL in Appendix B.

The built-in SQL DECODE function actually treats null as a specific value instead of an unknown value. It might seem contradictory, but it's useful. DECODE is also described in Appendix B.

Do	**Don't**
Do initialize all your variables in order to eliminate the possibility of null values. **Do** use NVL where feasible when retrieving values from that database in order to replace null values with an acceptable alternative.	**Don't** forget to think through the possible implications of null values in every expression you write, especially the Boolean, including comparison and expressions.

Converting Datatypes

Sometimes you need to convert a value of one datatype to another. This is frequently true with dates and numbers, which are often converted to and from character strings. You might want to display a date, for example, so you must first convert it to a character string in the desired format. There are two ways of approaching the issue of conversion. One is to rely on Oracle to implicitly convert datatypes, which it will do automatically when it makes sense. The second and more preferred method is to code your conversions explicitly.

Implicit Conversion

NEW TERM
When you mix different datatypes in an expression, Oracle will convert them for you when it makes sense to do so. This is referred to as *implicit conversion*. Listing 3.10 shows several examples of implicit conversion.

INPUT   **LISTING 3.10**   Implicit Conversion Examples

```
 1: --Demonstrate implicit conversion
 2: DECLARE
 3:    d1      DATE;
 4:    cd1     VARCHAR2(10);
 5:    cd2     VARCHAR2(10);
 6:    n1      NUMBER;
 7:    cn1     VARCHAR2(10);
 8:    cn2     VARCHAR2(10);
 9: BEGIN
10:    --Assign a value to this string which represents a date.
11:    cd1 := '15-Nov-61';
12:    --Now assign the string to a date variable.
13:    --The conversion is implicit.
14:    d1 := cd1;
15:    --Now assign that date variable to another string.
16:     --Again the conversion
17:    --is implicit, but this time the conversion is
18:     --from a date to a string.
19:    cd2 := d1;
20:    --Display the two character strings to show that they are the same.
21:    DBMS_OUTPUT.PUT_LINE('CD1 = ' || cd1);
22:    DBMS_OUTPUT.PUT_LINE('CD2 = ' || cd2);
23:    --Repeat the same example as above, but with numbers.
24:    cn1 := '995';
25:    n1 := cn1 + .99 ;
26:    cn2 := n1;
27:    DBMS_OUTPUT.PUT_LINE('CN1 = ' || cn1);
28:    DBMS_OUTPUT.PUT_LINE('CN2 = ' || cn2);
29: END;
30: /
```

OUTPUT
```
CD1 = 15-Nov-61
CD2 = 15-NOV-61
CN1 = 995
CN2 = 995.99
PL/SQL procedure successfully completed.
```

ANALYSIS The code in Listing 3.10 illustrates some common implicit conversions. The first assignment, in line 11, causes no conversion at all because a string is assigned to a string variable. The assignment statement in line 14, however, does represent an implicit conversion because it must convert the string representation of the date to Oracle's internal format before it can assign the value to d1. In line 19, that date is again converted back to a string format. Lines 23 through 28 repeat the same process, but this time with a number.

Implicit conversions are convenient, but can sometimes cause problems. In relying on them, you are relying on Oracle's built-in assumptions and on default settings you might not even be aware of, and which might change from one release to another. The format of a date leads to some good examples. Did you know that Oracle's default date format varies depending on the language setting? That it can also be installation-dependent? And that it can vary between a client PC executing a Developer/2000 script and a database server? In fact, the date format can even be changed for the duration of a particular session. Figure 3.2 illustrates this by showing the same PL/SQL code succeeding once and then failing after the date format has been changed.

FIGURE 3.2

The default date format is changed.

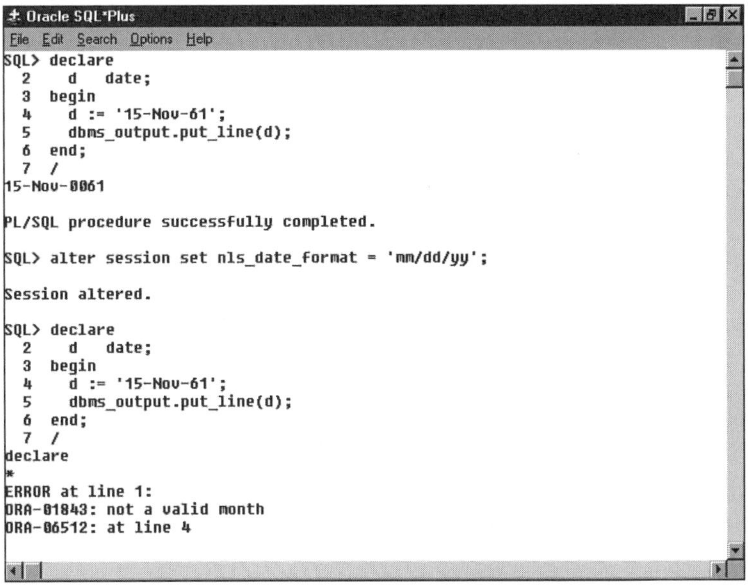

```
± Oracle SQL*Plus                                                    _ 8 X
File  Edit  Search  Options  Help
SQL> declare
  2     d    date;
  3   begin
  4     d := '15-Nov-61';
  5     dbms_output.put_line(d);
  6   end;
  7   /
15-Nov-0061

PL/SQL procedure successfully completed.

SQL> alter session set nls_date_format = 'mm/dd/yy';

Session altered.

SQL> declare
  2     d    date;
  3   begin
  4     d := '15-Nov-61';
  5     dbms_output.put_line(d);
  6   end;
  7   /
declare
*
ERROR at line 1:
ORA-01843: not a valid month
ORA-06512: at line 4
```

For the reasons just listed, it is often safer to code conversions explicitly. Explicit conversions also better document your code by making it clear to other programmers exactly what is happening.

Explicit Conversion

Oracle has several built-in functions that are designed to convert information from one datatype to another. These are shown in Table 3.12.

TABLE 3.12 Conversion Functions

Function	Purpose
TO_DATE	Converts a character string to a date
TO_NUMBER	Converts a character string to a number
TO_CHAR	Converts either a number or a date to a character string

Each of these functions takes three arguments: the value to be converted, a format string specifying how that conversion is to take place, and optionally a string containing language-specific parameters. These functions are described in detail on Day 6, but Listing 3.11 gives some common examples of how you can use them.

INPUT   **LISTING 3.11**   Examples of the Conversion Functions

```
 1: --Demonstrate conversion functions
 2: DECLARE
 3:    d1    DATE;
 4:    d2    DATE;
 5:    d3    DATE;
 6:    d4    DATE;
 7:    n1    NUMBER;
 8:    n2    NUMBER;
 9:    n3    NUMBER;
10: BEGIN
11:    --Here are some common date formats which you might encounter.
12:    d1 := TO_DATE('1/1/02','mm/dd/yy');
13:    d2 := TO_DATE('1-1-1998','mm-dd-yyyy');
14:    d3 := TO_DATE('Jan 1, 2000','mon dd, yyyy');
15:    --Year 2000 problems? Note the effect of using rr instead of yy.
16:    d4 := TO_DATE('1/1/02','mm/dd/rr');
17:    DBMS_OUTPUT.PUT_LINE('d1 = ' || TO_CHAR(d1,'dd-Mon-yyyy'));
18:    DBMS_OUTPUT.PUT_LINE('d2 = ' || TO_CHAR(d2,'mm/dd/yyyy'));
19:    DBMS_OUTPUT.PUT_LINE('d3 = ' || TO_CHAR(d3,'Day, Month dd, yyyy'));
20:    DBMS_OUTPUT.PUT_LINE('d4 = ' || TO_CHAR(d4,'Dy, Mon dd, yyyy'));
21:    --Here are some examples of numeric conversions.
22:    n1 := TO_NUMBER ('123.99','999D99');
```

```
23:     n2 := TO_NUMBER ('$1,235.95','$9G999D99');
24:     DBMS_OUTPUT.PUT_LINE('n1 = ' || TO_CHAR(n1,'999D99'));
25:     DBMS_OUTPUT.PUT_LINE('n2 = ' || TO_CHAR(n2,'$9G999D99'));
26: END;
27: /
```

OUTPUT

```
d1 = 01-Jan-1902
d2 = 01/01/1998
d3 = Saturday , January   01, 2000
d4 = Tue, Jan 01, 2002
n1 =  123.99
n2 = $1,235.95
PL/SQL procedure successfully completed.
```

ANALYSIS Lines 12 through 16 show the TO_DATE function being used to convert some common date formats to a date variable. Lines 17 through 20 display these dates and show some more formatting possibilities. Lines 22 through 25 show some examples of conversions between numeric and character datatypes.

Summary

Today you have learned about writing PL/SQL expressions. You have read descriptions of each of the PL/SQL operators and seen examples of these operators in action. You have also seen how to write complex expressions and how the rules of operator precedence govern Oracle's evaluation of these expressions. Remember that you can use parentheses when you need to exercise control over a calculation. Most important to remember are the effects of null, or unknown, values on expressions. This is a particularly important subject to keep in mind when writing comparisons for use with if statements. Mastering this one area will save you untold grief as you write code in the future.

Q&A

Q Why does the expression TRUE AND NULL evaluate to NULL, but the expression TRUE OR NULL evaluates to true?

A This is a good question. To understand the answer, it might help to think in terms of null being an unknown value. The AND operator requires that *both* its operands be true in order to return a true result. If one of the operands is unknown, you can't be sure that if it were known it would be true, so AND must evaluate to false in this case. Things are different, however, for the expression TRUE OR NULL. The OR operator only requires one of its operands to be true in order to return a true result. In the case of TRUE OR NULL, you do know that one operand is true.

Whether the other operand is true, false, or unknown doesn't matter at this point because you have one you know is true, and one is all you need.

Q Does the IN operator let me do anything that I couldn't do otherwise?

A No, not really, but it does make your code more readable and easier to maintain. The expression x IN (1,3,4,10,30,30,40,100) is equivalent to x=1 OR x=3 OR x=4 OR x=10 OR x=30 OR x=40 OR x=100, but you will probably find the first version a bit easier to read and understand.

Q You said that a statement like IF X = NULL THEN... would not work as expected, and that IF X IS NULL THEN ... should be used instead. Why?

A The first expression will never be true. It will always evaluate to null because one of the operands is null, and it can never be known if two values are equal when one of the values is unknown. The second expression uses the IS NULL operator, which is designed to check for nulls. It specifically checks to see if the value of X is unknown and evaluates to true if that is the case.

Q When I am comparing strings, especially when comparing a CHAR string to a VARCHAR2 string, is there a convenient way to tell PL/SQL to ignore any trailing spaces in the CHAR string?

A Yes. Use the built-in RTRIM function. For example: IF RTRIM(char_string) = varchar2_string then...

Q I'm comparing two dates and only want to know if they are in the same year. Can I use the TRUNC function to accomplish this?

A Yes. By default, the TRUNC function truncates the time portion of a date, but the optional second argument enables you to specify a different point of truncation. To compare only the years, you can write: IF TRUNC(date_1,'yyyy') = TRUNC(date_2,'yyyy') THEN...

Q Sometimes you capitalize your date format strings. Why?

A When converting a date to a character string for display purposes, capitalizing parts of the format string controls whether that part of the date is capitalized. Suppose the current month is January. The expression TO_CHAR(SYSDATE,'mon') would result in a value of 'jan', the expression TO_CHAR(SYSDATE,'Mon') would result in a value of 'Jan', and the expression TO_CHAR(SYSDATE,'MON') would result in a value of 'JAN'.

Q Is there any way to prevent Oracle from implicitly converting data from one type to another?

A No, there is not. The only way that you can prevent implicit conversions from happening is to watch what you're doing and code all conversions explicitly.

Workshop

Use the following section to test your comprehension of this chapter and put what you've learned into practice. You'll find the answers to the quiz and exercises in Appendix A, "Answers."

Quiz

1. What is the difference between a unary operator and a binary operator?

2. What are the results of each of the following expressions?

    a. `(5-4)-(3-1)`

    b. `4*2**3-2`

    c. `4*2**(3-2)`

    d. `4=4 AND 5=6 or 3=3`

3. Using the `NOT` operator, write equivalent expressions for each of the following:

    a. `A <> B`

    b. `A < B`

    c. `(A <= B) AND (B <= C)`

4. Match the patterns and strings shown following. Hint: Not every string or pattern has a match, and one pattern matches more than one string.

    `'123-45-6789'` `'___-__-____'`

    `'Boom'` `'John%'`

    `'Johnson'` `'_oo_'`

    `'517-555-1212'`

    `'Broom'`

    `'Jonson'`

    `'Johnston'`

5. When does PL/SQL not pad strings with spaces, in order to make them of equal length, when doing comparisons?

Exercise

Write a function to compute wages based on an hourly rate and the number of hours worked. Have it use a minimum wage of $5 per hour if the rate is unknown. Have it also use the minimum wage if the rate is too low.

3

DAY 4

Using Functions, IF Statements, and Loops

by Tom Luers

Functions, IF statements, and loops are simple yet powerful features of PL/SQL. Functions allow you to compartmentalize your code to be more manageable and easily executed, while the IF statement and loop constructs allow you to execute program logic repeatedly. Today's lesson covers the following topics:

- Functions
- The NOCOPY hint
- The NULL statement
- The IF statement
- Nested IFs
- The ELSIF statement
- FOR loops

Exploring PL/SQL Functions

As you saw in Day 1, "Learning the Basics of PL/SQL," functions are similar to PL/SQL procedures except for the following differences:

- Functions return a value.
- Functions are used as part of an expression.

Why should you write functions? You have many reasons. The main reason is to reduce the total lines of coding and take a modular approach to writing code. You can retype in each PL/SQL block the same repetitive lines of code, or you can write a function. Then, you can call that function repeatedly as needed. What if you had to change all those blocks of code for one small reason? Just trying to find and change all those blocks would make a COBOL programmer shudder when contemplating Year 2000 changes! With functions, you simply make the change in one location. (Keep in mind that if the parameters to be passed to the function change, you still have some editing to do within the PL/SQL blocks.)

Even if you do not write your own functions, don't forget that Oracle provides you a vast array of powerful built-in functions. However, if you do not get the opportunity to write your own functions, you miss out on a powerful feature of PL/SQL.

In Day 1, you created a function called SS_THRESH, which is shown in Listing 4.1. This function simply returns a value formatted as a number with nine total digits, two of which are allocated to the decimal place. Your values range from -9999999.99 to 9999999.99.

INPUT   **LISTING 4.1**   The SS_THRESH Function

```
CREATE OR REPLACE FUNCTION ss_thresh
RETURN NUMBER AS
  x      NUMBER(9,2);
BEGIN
  x := 65400;
  RETURN x;
END ss_thresh;
  /
```

The Syntax for Declaring a Function

A function is declared as follows:

```
FUNCTION function_name [(parameters {IN¦OUT¦IN OUT})]
    RETURN return_data_type
IS¦AS
    <declaration statements>
BEGIN
    <executable statements>
[EXCEPTION]
    <exception handler statements>
END function_name;
/
```

This syntax has the following statements and parameters:

- *function_name*—The function name follows the keyword FUNCTION and follows the standard naming convention, which is covered in Day 2, "Writing Declarations and Blocks."

- *parameters*—Functions let you pass parameters in and out. The brackets [] indicate it is optional to include parameters because the SS_THRESH function does not require them.

- RETURN—This is the type of data returned. You can have more than one RETURN statement in a function, but only one is executed. One RETURN statement is required even if you return nothing or ignore what is returned.

- IS¦AS—These parameters allow you to set up variables local to the function. These variables can hold values passed from the parameters or values assigned in the function. The variables can't be seen outside of the function.

- BEGIN—This statement starts the execution of statements pertinent to the function.

- EXCEPTION—Again, this statement is optional, but it allows you to handle the PL/SQL block properly when an error occurs. If you do not address this up front, when an error occurs, control is passed back to the PL/SQL block with the original values instead of the values that should have been returned.

- END—This statement denotes the end of the function. Errors will occur if you omit the END statement. The function name may follow the END statement. If the name is included, it must match the name exactly as the name of the function.

4

Listing 4.2 shows an example of a full function.

```
CREATE OR REPLACE FUNCTION emptype (paytype CHAR)
    RETURN VARCHAR2 IS
BEGIN
    IF paytype = 'H' THEN
        RETURN 'Hourly';
    ELSIF paytype = 'S' THEN
        RETURN 'Salaried';
    ELSIF paytype = 'E' THEN
        RETURN 'Executive';
    ELSE
        RETURN 'Invalid Type';
    END IF;
EXCEPTION
    WHEN OTHERS THEN
        RETURN 'Error Encountered';
END emptype;
```

The function in Listing 4.2 is titled emptype. It uses parameters passed from a procedure called paytype of type CHAR. You then return a value of type VARCHAR2, which is Hourly, Salaried, Executive, Invalid Type, or Error Encountered. When you begin the function's statements, you use IF...ELSIF to determine the text to return. (IF statements are covered later in the lesson in the section "The IF Statement.") If an exception occurs, the function stops processing and returns the value Error Encountered. The function is then terminated by calling the END statement followed by the function name.

Defining Parameters: Formal and Actual

Parameters are a key feature of PL/SQL. A parameter is a value that you can pass from a block of statements to a function. The function then performs calculations, checks, and so on and might or might not return a value based upon the conditions in the function. This concept is similar to functions in other third-generation languages such as C. You want to make sure that you code your functions to accept parameters that can be used from other areas of your PL/SQL code.

When a subprogram calls a function using variables or expressions referenced in a parameter list, then the parameters are called *actual*. In this case, the parameter actually holds the parameter value in memory. If the variables or expressions are declared in the subprogram specification and referenced in the subprogram body, the parameters are considered *formal*. In this case, a pointer to the real parameter value resides in memory.

The Syntax for Defining a Parameter

parameter_name [MODE] *parameter_type* [:= *value* ¦ DEFAULT *value*]

In this syntax, *parameter_name* is the name you assign to the parameter, and the *parameter_type* is the variable type you assign.

The simplest parameter can be coded as

(p_squared NUMBER)

p_squared is the *parameter_name*, and NUMBER is the *parameter_type*.

What if you want to accept a parameter from a table, and you do not want to hard-code a parameter type because it might change in the future? You can simply add a %TYPE after the parameter to pick up the field type from the table. For instance, the following line sets the parameter p_emptype to the field definition of pay_type in the table employee:

(p_emptype employee.pay_type%TYPE)

Using TYPE% is a common method when referencing tables, and it is highly recommended. You encounter much less rework if the type in the database changes from CHAR to VARCHAR2 than if you hard-code the type in the function and then go back and change the function, too. You can see how good functions and good coding can reduce the effort required to develop an application!

MODE

The optional MODE statement gives you complete control over your incoming parameters. Table 4.1 lists the three types of modes along with how the MODE statement operates.

TABLE 4.1 Types of Modes

MODE	Handling of Parameter	Description
IN [NOCOPY]	Read-only	When you specify IN, you state that the parameter is read-only and completely protected from being changed.
OUT [NOCOPY]	Write-only	When you specify OUT, you are ignoring any parameters passed from the calling statement and assigning values to this parameter from within the function; therefore, it is write-only.
IN OUT [NOCOPY]	Read or write	This gives you full control over the parameter. You read in the parameter as passed; if you like, you can change the value of the parameter from within the function; and upon exit, the values are assigned to the values written inside the function. This method allows you to return more than one value.

4

The following segment includes some examples of the MODE statement:

```
FUNCTION addemployee(
    p_hiredate_in IN DATE,
    p_employeeID_out OUT NUMBER,
    p_hourlyrate_in_out IN OUT NUMBER,
    p_empname_in_out IN OUT varchar2)
```

In addemployee, you are unable to change the hire date because it is read-only. You assign an employee ID in the function and write it out to this parameter. You can change the hourly rate if the initial rate was too low, and you can change the employee name if the employee gets married before being added to your database.

The NOCOPY Hint

As mentioned earlier, the actual parameter shows the value in memory, but the formal parameter holds a pointer to the real value in memory. There are pros and cons to each kind of parameter. I want to briefly discuss the effect of the parameter type on performance.

Performance can take a serious hit when your parameters contain large values, expressions, or records. It takes time to copy these data structures into the parameters. One way a programmer can help performance is to use the NOCOPY hint in the parameter mode statement.

When you use the NOCOPY hint, you give instructions, not directives, to the compiler to pass parameters by reference and not by value.

 Note   NOCOPY is a hint and not a directive. Therefore, the PL/SQL engine can choose to ignore your request and do what it thinks is the correct behavior.

One thing to consider when using the NOCOPY hint is the resulting value of the parameter after an unhandled exception. Remember that there is some uncertainty about whether the value of a parameter is a value or a reference when using the NOCOPY hint. When an unhandled exception occurs, you cannot rely on the parameter values. If the parameters are copied as actual, they are not rolled back to their original values when your program hits an unhandled exception. However, the formal parameters retain their referenced values when an unhandled exception occurs.

Assigning Values to Parameters

Sometimes, you might want to assign values to parameters either by using := or DEFAULT. When you use a default value, the function uses the DEFAULT assignment if no parameter is passed. If a value is passed, that value is used. The following code has an example of assignment with both DEFAULT and :=:

```
p_emptype CHAR DEFAULT 'H'
p_hourlyrate NUMBER := 7.25 --minimum rate
```

Return Types

In a function, you must declare a return data type. The return data type can be any data type allowed by Oracle, such as

- CHAR
- VARCHAR2
- NUMBER
- INTEGER
- DATE
- BOOLEAN (true/false values)
- TABLE
- RECORD

As you see, you have complete flexibility in the way you process and return data from the function to the PL/SQL statements.

Function Violations

As with any stored program unit, the calling program assumes several things about the function. First, it assumes the syntax is correct. It also makes an assumption that the function will not disrupt the flow or logic of the calling program. Therefore, PL/SQL mandates that the function cannot

- Execute any DDL statement when called from a select or DML statement
- Execute a query or DML statement that modify the same objects when called from a DML statement
- Execute any transaction-control or system-control statements when called from a DML statement

Your function generates an error statement if you include any of these mistakes. You will learn more about DDL, DML, transaction-control statements, and system control statements on Day 8, "Using SQL to Manipulate Data and Control Transactions."

Exception Handling

You saw that Listing 4.2 included the EXCEPTION statement. This statement tells Oracle what to do if some error occurs while processing the function or procedure.

The Syntax for Exceptions

```
EXCEPTION
    WHEN OTHERS THEN
        <statements>
```

In this syntax, statements is one or more statements that will be processed when the exception occurs.

You can always code a NULL statement if no action is to be taken. This helps clarify your intent in the PL/SQL code to let others know you considered all conditions. NULL statements are covered later in this lesson in the section "The NULL Statement."

Creating a Stored Function

A *stored function* is a function saved to the database that can be called by any PL/SQL code. The only difference between a function and a stored function is the addition of the CREATE [OR REPLACE] keywords before the keyword FUNCTION. Refer to "The Syntax for Declaring a Function" earlier in this lesson for an explanation of the parameters.

The Syntax for Creating a Stored Function

```
CREATE [OR REPLACE]FUNCTION function_name [(parameters {IN¦OUT¦IN OUT})]
    RETURN return_data_type
IS¦AS
    <declaration statements>
BEGIN
    <executable statements>
[EXCEPTION]
    <exception handler statements>
END function_name;
```

You are now going to write your first stored function in PL/SQL. You will create a function that simply returns the shortened value of pi (3.14) and calls the function mypi.

The first line you need identifies the stored function:

```
CREATE OR REPLACE FUNCTION mypi
```

Notice that you did not have to put parentheses after the function name mypi because you do not need to pass parameters to the function. If you were calculating the diameter of a circle, you would then pass the value of the radius.

The next line requires the return type. In this case, you are returning a NUMBER. The next line to enter is

```
RETURN NUMBER IS
```

You now need to start the body of your function by typing the keyword **BEGIN**:

```
BEGIN
```

Because you are not performing anything in this function except returning a value, you will code a NULL statement, which is discussed later in this lesson in the section "The NULL Statement," and the RETURN statement to pass the value of pi:

```
NULL;
RETURN 3.14;
```

You can now end the function by typing the keyword **END** followed by the function name:

```
END mypi;
```

Listing 4.3 contains the entire function that you enter. Review the listing to make sure you have typed the lines correctly.

INPUT   **LISTING 4.3**   The mypi Function

```
CREATE OR REPLACE FUNCTION mypi
    RETURN NUMBER IS
BEGIN
    NULL;
    RETURN 3.14;
END mypi; --end of mypi function
```

OUTPUT   When you type / to execute the code, you should see the following Oracle output:

```
PL/SQL procedure successfully completed.
```

You can now call the function mypi from any PL/SQL statement.

To prove that the process worked, you can write a miniprocedure to see the value of pi. Enter the code in Listing 4.4 and type / to execute the PL/SQL block.

Note   Before you continue, make sure that you enter **SET SERVEROUTPUT ON** at the SQL*Plus prompt. This allows you to see output to the screen as the PL/SQL code executes.

INPUT   **LISTING 4.4**   Verifying the `mypi` Function

```
BEGIN
     DBMS_OUTPUT.PUT_LINE('value of pi is ' || mypi);
END;
/
```

By using the SET SERVEROUTPUT ON statement with the DBMS_OUTPUT.PUT_LINE, you can send variables to the console (screen). Your output should have been

OUTPUT   value of pi is 3.14

Finding Errors

In Day 1, you learned how to use the EDIT command directly from Oracle. Instead of entering the code line by line, you can now practice using the EDIT command. To show you how to debug compilation errors, I am going to make extensive use of the built-in editor. If you haven't done so already, you are going to enter the `mypi` function into the editor, including planned errors.

To start the process, simply type **EDIT mypi** and press Enter. Because the SQL code does not exist, Oracle prompts you to create a new file. Click Yes. When the edit screen appears, enter the code exactly as it appears in Listing 4.5.

INPUT   **LISTING 4.5**   A Poorly Written Function

```
CREATE OR REPLACE FUNCTION mypi
     RETIRN NUMBER IS
BEGIN
     NULL;
     RETURN 3.14
END;
```

Tip

> After you type the last END; statement, make sure that you press the Enter key to insert a blank line when using the built-in editor. If you do not do this, you receive a compiler error because Oracle does not recognize the semicolon in the last END statement.

After you have entered the function, click File and then Exit, and when the editor asks you whether you want to save changes, click Yes. You are now ready to execute this poorly written function.

Type the command **GET mypi** and press Enter. The function is loaded to your buffer and listed on the screen. Type / to execute this function. You should see the following error message:

```
Warning: Function created with compilation errors.
```

Where do you go from here? Simply type **SHOW ERRORS** and press Enter. Your screen should contain the same errors as the following output:

```
LINE/COL ERROR
-------- --------------------------------------------------------------
2/5      PLS-00103: Encountered the symbol "RETIRN" when expecting one of
         the following:
         ( return compress compiled wrapped
         The symbol "return was inserted before "RETIRN" to continue.

6/1      PLS-00103: Encountered the symbol "END" when expecting one of the
         following:
         * & = - + ; < / > in mod not rem an exponent (**)
         <> or != or ~= >= <= <> and or like between is null is not ¦¦
```

What does this tell you? You can consult Oracle help, but the error code PLS-00103 only states that there is a syntax error when parsing the PL/SQL code. However, you can go immediately to the line and column in question.

Edit mypi by typing **EDIT mypi** and pressing Enter. Now, go to row 2, column 5. The error is at the keyword RETURN. You can see that it expected a RETURN statement but could not find any. Make the spelling correction.

Now, go to column 6, line 1. The error message states that it encountered the END statement before finding required punctuation. When looking for errors, start working your way from the error to the top of the code. In line 5, you should see that the required ; is missing. Make that correction, save the function, and exit.

Type **GET mypi** and press Enter. You always have to reload the code back into the buffer after it has been changed. Now, execute the PL/SQL code to create the function by typing / and pressing Enter. If the function was successfully created, you should see

```
Function created.
```

The NULL Statement

The NULL statement is simply a statement that does nothing. Its format is

NULL;

Why Use the NULL Statement?

There are many reasons to use the NULL statement. You can improve readability, especially if you have a block of code that does absolutely nothing. Another good reason is to use it as a placeholder. As you saw in the mypi function, you used the NULL statement to indicate that the function had no procedures but simply returned a value.

How to Call a Function from PL/SQL with or Without Parameters

You can call a function from PL/SQL in many ways. If there are no parameters to pass, you can simply call the function without the parentheses as you did in verifying the mypi function.

The second way is to pass actual values, using commas as placeholders for parameters that you do not want to pass. (In this case, DEFAULT becomes the new value of the parameter.) Go ahead and create the stored function squareme from Listing 4.6. This function simply multiplies a number by itself.

INPUT   LISTING 4.6   The Stored Function squareme

```
CREATE OR REPLACE FUNCTION squareme(thenum number)
     RETURN NUMBER IS
BEGIN
     RETURN thenum * thenum;
END squareme;
```

After you have entered the function, execute. You can troubleshoot if there are any errors by typing the SQL command SHOW ERRORS at the SQL*Plus prompt.

You are now ready to enter a block of PL/SQL code to see actual output and the passing of parameters. Enter and then execute the code in Listing 4.7.

`INPUT`   **LISTING 4.7**   Passing Parameters to `squareme`

```
BEGIN
    DBMS_OUTPUT.PUT_LINE('9 squared is ' || squareme(9) );
END;
```

Your output should be

`OUTPUT`   `9 squared is 81`

One last word on passing values to a function: Values can either be constants or variables. Remember, if no parameters are passed, make sure that you have a DEFAULT or that your code prohibits passing parameters to a function.

Invoker and Definer Rights

By default, a function executes with the same privileges as the function definer, not the function invoker. These definer rights are bound to the schema where it resides. You can fully qualify the object names in the PL/SQL statements to enable you to modify tables in other schemas. However, be aware that this limits the portability of your code.

Oracle allows you to call functions with invoker rights. In this case, you are not bound to one schema; rather, you are bound by the privileges of the caller. You can use invoker rights via the AUTHID clause. The example in Listing 4.8 illustrates the use of the AUTHID clause. In this example, the function is executed with the rights of the invoker and not the function definer.

LISTING 4.8   AUTHID Clause

```
CREATE OR REPLACE FUNCTION mypi
    AUTHID CURRENT_USER AS
BEGIN
    NULL;
    RETURN 3.14
END;
```

Using PL/SQL Statements

The two statements I cover today are the IF statement and the FOR loop. These statements help you control the execution of PL/SQL blocks. Tomorrow's lesson covers additional statements and loops.

The IF Statement

The IF statement allows you to evaluate one or more conditions. Some examples of IF statements are

- IF the salary is more than $500,000 per year, grant the officer $2,000 in stock options.
- IF the pay_type equals Salaried, then the total hours paid is equal to 40.
- If the pay_rate is between $9.00 to $10.00 and the pay_type is Hourly, then the pay grade is level 9.

The Syntax for the IF Statement

▼ SYNTAX

The format of a simple IF statement is as follows:

```
IF <some condition evaluates to true>
THEN
<perform statements>
END IF;
```

In this syntax, the first parameter *some condition evaluates to true* is the BOOLEAN condition you want to check. If the BOOLEAN condition evaluates to true, then the parameter *perform statements* executes, which contains one or more statements.

▲

Suppose you want to calculate for an hourly employee how many hours of overtime he worked during the week. Type the IF statement from Listing 4.9.

INPUT **LISTING 4.9** Calculating Overtime Hours with IF

```
set echo on
DECLARE
  v_HoursWorked Number := 50 ; --Number of hours worked by hourly employee
  v_OverTime Number := 0 ; --Storage of Overtime Hours
BEGIN
  IF v_HoursWorked > 40 THEN
    v_OverTime := v_HoursWorked - 40;
      DBMS_OUTPUT.PUT_LINE('Hours overtime worked = ' || v_OverTime);
  END IF;
END;
/
```

By previously typing SETSERVEROUTPUT ON, you tell Oracle to run the DBMS_OUTPUT package, which aids in the debugging process by allowing you to display output to the screen. This step, combined with executing the DBMS_OUTPUT.PUT_LINE statement, shows you the calculated values of the variable v_OverTime.

OUTPUT   Your output should be

```
Hours overtime worked = 10
```

ANALYSIS   You set up two variables—V_HoursWorked and v_OverTime—to store the actual number of hours worked and the calculated number of overtime hours. These two variables are defined as a NUMBER to allow calculations on these values:

```
v_HoursWorked NUMBER := 50 ; --Number of hours worked by hourly employee
v_OverTime NUMBER := 0 ; --Storage of Overtime Hours
```

PL/SQL then starts evaluating the IF statement. Because you initialized v_HoursWorked to a value of 50, 50 is greater than 40, so the IF statement is evaluated to true. Because the condition is true, you process all statements under the THEN keyword:

```
IF v_HoursWorked > 40 THEN
```

You can calculate the hours of overtime by simply subtracting 40 from v_HoursWorked. You then display the output to the screen using the DBMS_OUTPUT.PUT_LINE command:

```
v_OverTime := v_HoursWorked - 40;
        DBMS_OUTPUT.PUT_LINE('Hours overtime worked = ' ¦¦ v_OverTime);
```

Finally, the ending / tells Oracle to execute the statements entered.

The IF...THEN...ELSE Statement

In the preceding example, you did not care about the results if the hours were under 40 because you were only trying to determine the total hours of overtime worked. However, what if you did not initialize v_OverTime to a value of zero? The IF...THEN...ELSE statement allows you to process a series of statements under ELSE if the condition is false.

The Syntax for the IF...THEN...ELSE Statement

```
IF <some condition evaluates to true>
THEN
<perform statements_condition_true>
    ELSE
    <perform statements_condition_false>
END IF;
```

In this syntax, the first parameter, *some condition evaluates to true*, tests a BOOLEAN condition that you provide. If the condition is true, the second parameter, *perform statements_condition_true*, executes. If the condition is false, the parameter *perform statements_condition_false* executes.

You can alter your original IF statement to reflect what to do if the condition is false (see Listing 4.10).

Tip

> Adding the ELSE statement is good programming practice not only to make sure that you know what happens for all possible conditions, but also to make your logic easy to follow and understand for another Oracle programmer.

INPUT   **LISTING 4.10**   Adding ELSE to the IF Block

```
set echo on
DECLARE
   v_HoursWorked Number := 50 ; --Number of hours worked by hourly employee
   v_OverTime Number ; --Storage of Overtime Hours
BEGIN
   IF v_HoursWorked > 40 THEN
     v_OverTime := v_HoursWorked - 40;
       DBMS_OUTPUT.PUT_LINE('Hours overtime worked = ' ¦¦ v_OverTime);
     ELSE
          v_OverTime := 0;
   END IF;
END;
/
```

The only change was to remove the initialization of variables in the declaration area and to set the value of v_OverTime to zero if there was no overtime under the ELSE statement.

ANALYSIS   In this listing, your program had to determine if the hours worked was over 40 or not. If the hours worked is over 40, then the processing of the logic takes you into the first IF statement. If the hours worked was less than 40, then the processing is passed to the statement under the ELSE thereby by-passing the code directly under the IF statement.

Note

> You can still initialize v_OverTime to a value of zero in the declaration section, and under the ELSE statement, you can make good use of the NULL statement as discussed earlier in this lesson.

Nested IF Statements

By nesting IF statements, you can check for many complex conditions before executing a series of statements. This allows you to defer executing inner IF statements unless the outer IF conditions apply.

> **Tip**
>
> To improve processing time and decrease costly CPU time, always make sure the outermost loop is the loop that narrows down your search criteria the most so that you do not have to execute statements in the inner loops. For instance, if you query a database of employees who are mainly hourly, but only a few of them worked overtime, your outermost condition should look for Total Hours Worked over 40, and the next condition should check to make sure the employee is hourly, not salaried. This arrangement produces a lot less checking because you easily filter the population of employees to a small group by the time you hit the next condition, instead of the other way around!

The Syntax for Nested IF Statements

SYNTAX ▼

```
IF <condition1 evaluates to true>
THEN
      IF <condition2 evaluates to true>
      THEN
            <perform statements>
      ELSE <both conditions have been evaluated to false>
            IF <condition3 evaluates to true>
            THEN
                  <perform statements>
            ELSE
                  <perform statements>
            END IF;
      END IF;
END IF;
```

▲

4

Did you notice that even on the ELSE statements you can keep adding IF statements? As you can see, it is possible to continue to nest loops for as long as you need, but nesting too much will most likely cause you grief in the debugging stage. Imagine only four levels of IF statements and sorting through all the possible conditions to make sure you produce the desired outcome.

In the overtime example, you first determine how many people worked more than 40 hours. If the employee is hourly, overtime hours are calculated. If the employee paytype is set to 'S', then the employee is salaried with no overtime. If the employee paytype is set to 'E', then the employee is an executive manager who gets no overtime (but a lot of options!). See the code in Listing 4.11.

INPUT   **LISTING 4.11**   Using Nested IF Statements

```
DECLARE
    v_HoursWorked Number := 80 ; --Number of hours worked by hourly employee
    v_OverTime Number := 0 ; --Storage of Overtime Hours
    v_PayType char(1) := 'E'; --Classification of employee, E,S, or H

BEGIN
IF v_HoursWorked > 40 THEN
    IF v_PayType = 'H' THEN
        v_OverTime := v_HoursWorked - 40;
        DBMS_OUTPUT.PUT_LINE('Hours overtime worked = ' ¦¦ v_OverTime);
    ELSE
        IF v_PayType = 'S' THEN
            DBMS_OUTPUT.PUT_LINE('Employee is Salaried');
        ELSE
            DBMS_OUTPUT.PUT_LINE('Employee is Executive Management');
        END IF;
    END IF;
END IF;
END;
/
```

ANALYSIS   In Listing 4.11, the first IF statement evaluates to true. Notice that because most employees do not work more than 40 hours, you can avoid all the inner logic. The second statement evaluates to false because the paytype is set to 'E' for executive management. Control passes to the ELSE statement where another IF statement is evaluated. Again, the condition is evaluated to false because the value of paytype is set to 'E'. The final ELSE statement then defaults to executive management because there are only three types of workers. Therefore the output from this listing would create the statement "Employee is Executive Management".

Note   Instead of nested IF statements, consider the use of the Boolean AND. For instance, you can easily change the preceding code to
```
IF v_HoursWorked > 40 AND
    v_PayType =l 'H' THEN
```

This example of nested IF statements is a poor programming choice. What happens if another classification of paytype is added? The user of nested IF statements is better suited to reading data from a form or creating a user-defined function to handle scenarios such as new pay types.

> **Tip**
>
> If you do use logical AND, make sure that the first condition narrows down the population as extensively as possible because Oracle evaluates from left to right.

Using IF...ELSIF

In all the examples so far, you coded IF statements in an AND environment. You might often want to check a value against a series of conditions that have distinct boundaries. In a third-generation language, you use a CASE statement, or in Boolean logic, you separate the conditions with a logical OR.

The Syntax for IF...ELSIF

▼ SYNTAX

```
IF <condition1 evaluates to true>
THEN
    <perform statements>
ELSIF <condition2 evaluates to true>
THEN
     <perform statements>
ELSIF <condition3 evaluates to true>
THEN
    <perform statements>
...
ELSE —this is always optional as the default value
    <perform statements>
END IF;
```

In this syntax, the IF...ELSIF statement acts like a logical OR statement. The first parameter, condition1 evaluates to true, is a BOOLEAN condition. If it evaluates to true, then one or more statements are executed at the perform statements parameter. You keep adding as many ELSIF statements as required to include all the conditions. Notice that only one END IF statement is required, unlike the other IF...THEN...ELSE statements. Also, note that the ELSE statement is optional, and it acts as a default value if none of the other values is true.

▲

> **Tip**
>
> When using ELSIF, do not allow any overlapping of values to evaluate because you will not get the desired result. If you are checking for grades, you do not want to check for values between 70 and 80 for a C and then check for values of 80 to 90 for a B. The person who scores 80 percent would be upset with a grade of C, instead of the letter grade B she deserves!

4

Listing 4.12 is an example of using ELSIF to determine the grade letter for a student. You have several approaches. One is to check a range using BETWEEN; another method is to use > or < for evaluation; and finally, you can use a default letter 'E' or include it as part of the conditional criteria. To ensure no overlapping, the following example uses the < sign and, to practice a default, uses the letter 'E' for failure.

INPUT   **LISTING 4.12**   Using IF...ELSIF to Determine a Grade

```
DECLARE
v_Score Number := 85; --Percentage
v_LetterGrade Char(1);
BEGIN
IF v_Score >= 90 THEN
    v_LetterGrade := 'A';
ELSIF v_Score >= 80 THEN
    v_LetterGrade := 'B';
ELSIF v_Score >= 70 THEN
    v_LetterGrade := 'C';
ELSIF v_Score >= 60 THEN
    v_LetterGrade := 'D';
ELSE
    v_LetterGrade := 'E';
END IF;
    DBMS_OUTPUT.PUT_LINE('Your Letter Grade is: ' || v_LetterGrade);
END;
/
```

OUTPUT   When you execute the code from Listing 4.12, your output is

```
Your Letter Grade is B
```

ANALYSIS   Remember, IF...ELSIF continues through all cases until the first true evaluation, and then the rest of the statements are ignored. If you start out with v_Score >= 60, 85 is evaluated to true and the student receives a v_LetterGrade of 'D'.

Nested IF Versus ELSIF

You can think of nested IF statements as performing a logical AND but ELSIF performing a logical OR. The nice feature about using ELSIF instead of nested IFs is that it is much easier to follow the logic in the ELSIF statement because you can easily identify which statements occur under which logical conditions.

Formatting IF Statements

Although no specific rules apply to the placement of IF...THEN...ELSIF, and so forth, following some general rules will help make your code more readable and easier to follow. See Listing 4.13 for an example of proper formatting.

- When using multiple IF statements, indent the next IF statement five spaces inward. See line 2 of Listing 4.13 for an example.

- Always match the END IF in the same column in which the IF statement occurs. See line 11 of Listing 4.13 for an example.

- It is helpful to put comments after the END IF statement, especially when nesting IFs, to state the end of a condition. I abbreviate and use -- for comments instead of multiple lines of /* ... */. See line 12 of Listing 4.13.

- Always indent the blocks of statements five spaces inward from the IF statement. See line 3 of Listing 4.13.

- If any conditions or statements "wrap" around, meaning they are too long for one line, simply indent an additional five spaces on the next line. See line 5 of Listing 4.13.

- Always match ELSE underneath the IF statement associated with the ELSE. See line 6 of Listing 4.13.

LISTING 4.13   Formatting IF Statements

```
 1: IF v_HoursWorked > 40 THEN
 2:      IF v_PayType = 'H' THEN
 3:          v_OverTime := v_HoursWorked - 40;
 4:          DBMS_OUTPUT.PUT_LINE('The many Hours which have been worked
 5:               overtime= ' ¦¦ v_OverTime);
 6:      ELSE
 7:          IF v_PayType = 'S' THEN
 8:              DBMS_OUTPUT.PUT_LINE('Employee is Salaried');
 9:          ELSE
10:              DBMS_OUTPUT.PUT_LINE('Employee is Executive Management');
11:          END IF;
12:      END IF; — End check for PayType = H
13: END IF;
14: END;
15: /
```

4

Avoiding Common Mistakes When Using IF

You can avoid some common pitfalls when using IF statements by keeping this list in mind.

Do	Don't
Do make sure that every IF statement has a matching END IF statement. **Do** make sure that you spell ELSIF without the extra E (as in ELSEIF). **Do** make sure that you place a space in the END IF statement instead of using no space or a dash.	**Don't** make nested loops too complex. Complexity makes it harder to follow and debug if problems or changes occur. Evaluate your logic to see whether a function might accomplish the same task. **Don't** forget your punctuation. You do need semicolons after END IF and after each of the statements, but not after the keyword THEN.

Looping Statements

This section discusses one form of looping by using the FOR statement. Looping allows you to execute a block of code repeatedly until some condition occurs. Day 5, "Implementing Loops and GOTOs," demonstrates a similar use with recursion; recursion calls the same function repeatedly until some condition occurs.

The Syntax for FOR Loops

```
FOR loop_index IN [REVERSE] low_value..high_value LOOP
     Statements to execute
END LOOP;
```

The *loop_index* is defined by Oracle as a local variable of type INTEGER. REVERSE allows you to execute the loop in reverse order. The *low_value..high_value* is the range of how many times to execute the loop. These values can be constants, or they can be variables. The line must be terminated with LOOP with no semicolon at the end. You can list the statements to be executed until the LOOP is evaluated to false.

> **Note**
>
> You can use the EXIT statement to terminate a loop prematurely based upon some Boolean condition; however, you should avoid this practice because the purpose of the FOR loop is to execute from the beginning to the end of the predetermined range. Day 5 discusses the EXIT statement.

Enter and then execute the code in Listing 4.14 for your first FOR loop.

INPUT   **LISTING 4.14**   Your First FOR Loop

```
set echo on
BEGIN
    FOR v_loopcounter IN 1..5 LOOP
        DBMS_OUTPUT.PUT_LINE('Loop counter is ' || v_loopcounter);
    END LOOP;
END;
/
```

When you execute the preceding loop, your output should be

OUTPUT
```
Loop counter is 1
Loop counter is 2
Loop counter is 3
Loop counter is 4
Loop counter is 5
```

You can start to get more complex by nesting FOR loops. When you nest FOR loops, the outer loop is executed once, the inner loop is executed as many times as the range indicates, and then control is returned to the outer loop until its range expires. Type and then execute the loop from Listing 4.15.

INPUT   **LISTING 4.15**   Nesting FOR Loops

```
BEGIN
    FOR v_outerloopcounter IN 1..2 LOOP
        FOR v_innerloopcounter IN 1..4 LOOP
            DBMS_OUTPUT.PUT_LINE('Outer Loop counter is ' ||
                    v_outerloopcounter ||
                    ' Inner Loop counter is ' || v_innerloopcounter);
        END LOOP;
    END LOOP;
END;
/
```

When you execute the preceding code, your output looks like

OUTPUT
```
Outer Loop counter is 1 Inner Loop counter is 1
Outer Loop counter is 1 Inner Loop counter is 2
Outer Loop counter is 1 Inner Loop counter is 3
Outer Loop counter is 1 Inner Loop counter is 4
Outer Loop counter is 2 Inner Loop counter is 1
Outer Loop counter is 2 Inner Loop counter is 2
Outer Loop counter is 2 Inner Loop counter is 3
Outer Loop counter is 2 Inner Loop counter is 4
```

ANALYSIS The order of nested loops is important, depending on what you want to accomplish. In the preceding example, the outer loop executes once which in turn causes the inner loop to execute four times. Once the inner loop completes its 4 loops, the outer loop executes the second and final time. Again the inner loop will execute 4 times when the outer loop executes its second time.

Reversing the Loop

By adding the keyword REVERSE after IN, you tell Oracle to process the loop in reverse. You still must list the range from low to high values; otherwise, the loop does not execute. The test of REVERSE also demonstrates using variables instead of fixed constants, as shown in Listing 4.16.

INPUT **LISTING 4.16** Reversing the Loop

```
DECLARE
    v_Start Integer := 1;
BEGIN
    FOR v_loopcounter IN REVERSE v_Start..5 LOOP
        DBMS_OUTPUT.PUT_LINE('Loop counter is ' ¦¦ v_loopcounter);
    END LOOP;
END;
/
```

Your output should appear as follows:

OUTPUT
```
Loop counter is 5
Loop counter is 4
Loop counter is 3
Loop counter is 2
Loop counter is 1
```

Tip

> The example in Listing 4.16 has the starting counter as a variable, but it is always good practice to make all the LOOP parameters variables as well. Following this guideline makes it easier to understand your code and make changes, including assigning dynamic values to the LOOP parameters.

Incrementing Through a Loop Differently

As you can see, Oracle provides no option to step through a loop with an increment other than one. You can write loops that execute with a different increment by only executing statements if a certain condition is true. The example from Listing 4.17 demonstrates how to increment by a value of 2.

LISTING 4.17   Changing the Loop Increment

```
BEGIN
    FOR v_loopcounter IN 1..6 LOOP
        IF MOD(v_loopcounter,2) = 0 THEN
            DBMS_OUTPUT.PUT_LINE('Loop counter is ' || v_loopcounter);
        END IF; -- End execution of statements for even counter
    END LOOP;
END;
/
```

After the loop has executed, your output should appear as

```
Loop counter is 2
Loop counter is 4
Loop counter is 6
```

This example shows just one of many ways in which you could increment a loop. The MOD function in this case simply tests to make sure the number is divisible evenly by a value of 2. You can easily change this to 3, 5, or whatever you want to increment. To decrement, simply add the keyword REVERSE.

Final Programming Tips on Loops

Just like IF statements, FOR loop syntax must be coded properly. Some common pitfalls follow:

- Not putting a space in END LOOP;.
- Forgetting semicolons after the END LOOP;.
- Entering the counter from high to low when using REVERSE or setting the range from high to low and forgetting to use REVERSE.
- Setting variables in a loop so the lower boundary has a value greater than the upper boundary.
- Variables for the boundaries winding up with NULL values.
- When nesting loops, make sure that the statements follow the intended logic. (When in doubt, use the DBMS_OUTPUT package, which is discussed on Day 17, "Writing to Files and the Display.")

4

Summary

You accomplished a lot in Day 4! First, you took a closer look at how to create your own functions. The reduction of code and ease of use are two major reasons to write functions. If you work in a corporate environment and you share code, creating functions is a must.

NULL statements are simply that. They do nothing but act as a placeholder.

IF statements can take many forms. IF statements are always evaluated from left to right (unless the order is overridden by parentheses), and if one of the conditions becomes false, the whole statement is invalid. This order is important to know because the largest room for error is not syntax, but rather the logical errors, which are harder to debug. Formatting the IF statement blocks is important not only from a coding perspective, but also from a readability perspective. Regular IF and nested IF statements operate similar to AND, but IF...ELSIF statements act similar to an OR, which allows you to create the equivalent of CASE statements as long as none of the conditions overlap.

Finally, loops allow you to repeat a series of PL/SQL code until either a condition is met or you break out of the loop using EXIT. It is important to know the order of execution of the loops to reduce logic errors. You also saw a neat trick on how to increment loops by values other than one, an option that is not provided by Oracle.

Q&A

Q Does Oracle allow you to create your own functions?

A Yes! This is what makes Oracle so powerful. It allows you to reduce the amount of PL/SQL coding.

Q Can you call functions from any PL/SQL code?

A Yes, but this is only a recent development to include stored functions as part of the Oracle product.

Q Is there any reason to use the NULL statement?

A The NULL statement acts as a placeholder to make your code more readable. You can also use it when no action is required.

Q What is the difference between nested IFs and IF...ELSIF?

A Nested IFs allow you to do logical AND checking. In addition, you do not always have to execute nested IF statements further in the block if the first IF statement evaluates to false. IF...ELSIF blocks allow you to check through a series of mutually exclusive choices.

Q What is the order of execution of nested loops?

A The outer loop executes first. The inner loop then executes in full from low to high values before it returns control to the outer loop. All looping ends when the outer loop has been completed or an EXIT statement is encountered.

Workshop

Review your knowledge of functions and conditional branching with a quick quiz, followed by some challenging exercises. You can find the answers to both in Appendix A, "Answers."

Quiz

1. What parts of the function are required for coding?
2. If a function takes parameters, is it always necessary to pass these parameters from the calling statement?
3. If an error occurs, and you have not coded the EXCEPTION statement, what gets returned from the function?
4. Is there a way to return more than one value from a function?
5. If you code an IF...ELSE statement, and you do not have any conditions to execute if the statement is false, how do you code the ELSE statement?
6. What are some of the common pitfalls in coding IF statements?
7. How can you determine what is wrong with your code when it compiles?
8. When coding a loop in reverse, how must you code the beginning and ending values?

Exercises

1. Rewrite the Grade example from Listing 4.12 as a stored function that passes the parameter of the score and returns a value of a grade letter.
2. Rewrite the Grade example from Listing 4.12 and use between for the ranges. Make sure that there is no overlapping of ranges.
3. Write a loop that increments by a value of 3 and then multiplies this counter by the returned value of the function mypi. The range should be 1 to 9. Output the values with DBMS_OUTPUT. Make sure that you enter SET SERVEROUTPUT ON to see the output.
4. Write a loop to calculate a factorial. In other words, 6! is 6 * 5 * 4 * 3 * 2 * 1. Allow the high boundary to be a variable that can change. Use an initial value of 3 for testing.

4

DAY 5

Implementing Loops and GOTOs

by Tom Luers

Day 4, "Using Functions, IF Statements, and Loops," demonstrates ways to change the order of execution with PL/SQL. Today's lesson covers several additional methods of changing the order of execution. Today's material covers the following topics:

- Statement labels
- The GOTO statement
- The WHILE loop
- The simple LOOP
- Emulating a REPEAT...UNTIL loop
- Recursion

Exploring Labels and the GOTO Statement

The GOTO statement allows for unconditional branching to a statement label. You will first learn about statement labels, which are necessary to include before you can even use the GOTO statement.

Statement Labels

Statement labels are identifiers of a block of code that is similar to a function, but they are not actual PL/SQL statements. The GOTO statement can directly access these labels. In addition, these labels can be accessed by loops, which are covered in the section "The EXIT and EXIT WHEN Statements." The format of a label is

<<*label_name*>>

Notice two things about the label:

- The label is surrounded by double brackets (<<).
- The label must not have a semicolon after the label name.

The label name does not contain a semicolon because it is not a PL/SQL statement, but rather an identifier of a block of PL/SQL code.

Caution

Labels can't take the place of required statements therefore you must have at least one statement after the label or an error results. If your intention is to execute the code after a label, you should re-evaluate your code decisions and choose an alternate method such as a function.

The GOTO Statement

The GOTO statement enables you to immediately transfer control to another labeled PL/SQL block without the need for conditional checking. As soon as the GOTO statement is encountered, all control is transferred to the code following the matching *label_name*. This target label can appear anywhere in the same block of code.

The Syntax for the GOTO Statement

SYNTAX

GOTO *label_name*;

The *label_name* is the matching *label_name* that must be contained within the same PL/SQL block of code.

Scoping Rules for the GOTO Statement

The GOTO destination must be in the same block, at the same level as, or higher than the GOTO statement itself. This means that the label must be within the same scope as the GOTO statement itself. Conditions that cause Oracle to not compile the PL/SQL code include

- Jumping into a subblock
- Jumping into a loop
- Jumping into an IF statement
- Using GOTO to jump from one part of an IF statement to another
- Jumping from an exception handler back to a current block of PL/SQL code

You encounter the following error message if you do not follow the proper coding of GOTO statements and their labels:

```
PLS-00375:  illegal GOTO statement; this GOTO cannot branch to label
```

If you want a more global approach, using stored functions is one appropriate method.

Jumping into a Lower-Level Block

You can't jump from an outer block of PL/SQL code back to an inner block of PL/SQL code. Listing 5.1 is an example of an illegal GOTO call.

 Caution

> The following listing, and the next few after it, is for illustration purposes only. Due to the errors they generate, you might not want to enter and execute them. However, if you do enter and execute these listings, they will not destroy anything, and they might help you to troubleshoot errors in your code in the future because you can see what errors these listings generate.

5

INPUT   **LISTING 5.1**   Illegal GOTO Call to an Inner Block

```
 1: DECLARE
 2:      v_Emergency_Warning VARCHAR2(50);
 3:      v_Status NUMBER = 0;
 4: BEGIN
 5:      GOTO Emergency_Check;
 6:      BEGIN
 7:          <<Emergency_Check>>
 8:              IF v_Status = 1 THEN
 9:                  PANIC();
10:              END IF;
11:      END;
12: END;
```

In Listing 5.1, you see the first block of PL/SQL code noted by a BEGIN statement. The block then calls the PL/SQL GOTO statement, which attempts to transfer control to the <<Emergency Check>> label. Because the label is within a separate block of PL/SQL code noted by another BEGIN statement, it is out of the required scope of the GOTO statement. If, instead of the keyword BEGIN, an <<Emergency_Check>> label appeared within the first block, everything would compile and execute properly (barring errors in the logic of the code).

Jumping into a Loop

The scope of the loop is not complete until the entire range of the loop has completed. Therefore, attempting to jump into the middle of the loop is illegal. Listing 5.2 shows an attempt to make an illegal call into a FOR loop.

> **Caution**
>
> The following listing is another that serves illustration purposes only because it generates several errors. You might or might not want to enter and execute this listing, depending on whether you want to see what kinds of errors it generates.

INPUT **LISTING 5.2** Illegal GOTO Call to a Loop

```
1: BEGIN
2: GOTO insideloop;
3:     FOR v_loopcounter IN 1..5 LOOP
4:         <<insideloop>
5:         DBMS_OUTPUT.PUT_LINE('Loop counter is ' || v_loopcounter);
6:     END LOOP;
7: END;
```

OUTPUT
```
Error at Line 2
ORA-06550 Line 2
PLS-00201: Identifier 'insideloop' must be declared
```

ANALYSIS As you can see, although the loop and the GOTO statement are within the same block of PL/SQL code, Oracle does not know how to handle the jump inside the loop. The obvious question is "What is the value of the loop counter?" Because there is no answer, any attempt to implement this logic results in a compile error.

Jumping into an IF Statement

Another illegal attempt to use the GOTO statement is to jump inside an IF statement. Listing 5.3 provides an example of another illegal call.

Caution

The following listing serves illustration purposes only because it generates several errors. You might or might not want to enter and execute this listing, depending on whether you want to see what kinds of errors it generates.

INPUT **LISTING 5.3** Illegal GOTO Call Inside an IF Statement

```
 1: DECLARE
 2:     v_Emergency_Warning VARCHAR2(50);
 3:     v_Status NUMBER = 0;
 4:     v_ReactorStatus VARCHAR2(10);
 5: BEGIN
 6:     GOTO Emergency_Check;
 7:     IF v_ReactorStatus = 'Very Hot' THEN
 8:         <<Emergency_Check>>
 9:             PANIC();
10:     END IF;
11:  END;
```

ANALYSIS From the GOTO call in Listing 5.3, if this block of PL/SQL code were allowed to actually execute, it would never check to see whether v_ReactorStatus = 'Very Hot'. There might not even be an emergency because v_ReactorStatus could have a value of 'Cool'. Because the value is never evaluated, the program always goes into crisis mode. Fortunately, this improper use of GOTO is not allowed!

Jumping from One Part of an IF Statement to Another

Although you can call a label from an IF statement, it is illegal for the jump to go from the IF clause to the THEN clause. Listing 5.4 is yet another example of a label not being within the same scope as the GOTO.

5

Caution

> The following listing is another that serves illustration purposes only because it generates several errors. You might or might not want to enter and execute this listing, depending on whether you want to see what kinds of errors it generates.

INPUT

LISTING 5.4 Illegal GOTO Call from One Clause of an IF Statement to Another Clause

```
 1: DECLARE
 2:     v_Emergency_Warning VARCHAR2(50);
 3:     v_Status NUMBER = 0;
 4:     v_ReactorStatus VARCHAR2(10);
 5: BEGIN
 6:     IF v_ReactorStatus = 'Very Hot' THEN
 7:         GOTO Emergency_Check;
 8:     ELSE
 9:         <<Emergency_Check>>
10:             PANIC();
11:     END IF;
12: END;
```

As Listing 5.4 suggests, the program jumps from an evaluation of the IF statement as true to executing code as if the entire statement were false. This is a definite misuse of the GOTO statement, and the code in this case probably does not require a GOTO statement.

From Listing 5.5, it should be apparent that you can't raise an error and then return to the original block of code where the error was generated from the exception handler.

Caution

> The following listing is another that serves illustration purposes only because it generates several errors. You might or might not want to enter and execute this listing, depending on whether you want to see what kinds of errors it generates.

INPUT   **LISTING 5.5** Illegal GOTO Call from an Exception Handler

```
 1: DECLARE
 2:     v_Emergency_Warning VARCHAR2(50);
 3:     v_Status NUMBER = 0;
 4:     v_ReactorStatus VARCHAR2(10);
 5: BEGIN
 6:     <<Emergency_Check>>
 7:         PANIC();
 8: EXCEPTION
```

```
 9:      WHEN e_TOOHOT THEN
10:           GOTO Emergency_Check;
11:  END;
```

An Example of the GOTO Statement in Action

So far, you have seen conditions that exceed the scope of the GOTO statement. Now, how about an example of a legitimate block of PL/SQL code? See Listing 5.6 for a proper GOTO.

INPUT   **LISTING 5.6**   Example of a Proper GOTO Statement

```
 1: DECLARE
 2:      v_Status NUMBER := 1;
 3: BEGIN
 4:      IF v_Status = 1 THEN
 5:           GOTO mybranch;
 6:      ELSE
 7:           v_Status := 1;
 8:      END IF;
 9: <<mybranch>>
10:      NULL;
11: END;
```

ANALYSIS   In the GOTO example from Listing 5.6, the program checks the value of v_Status. If the value is equal to 1, then the program goes immediately to the block <<mybranch>>; if the value is false, the program changes the value of v_Status to equal 1.

Why Use the GOTO Statement?

As in any procedural language, the use of GOTO statements is highly discouraged. As you saw from the listings earlier in the lesson, GOTO statements are easy to code improperly. In almost all cases, your code can and should be written to avoid the use of GOTO. There are several reasons not to use the GOTO statement:

- It is easy to make logic errors when using GOTO.
- It is easy to make coding errors even when you are trying to make the process work.

- If you use multiple GOTO statements, your code jumps all over the place out of sequence, which is known as spaghetti code. Using multiple GOTOs not only causes longer execution times, but also leads to confusion when you review your code and make changes.
- Almost all cases in which you use the GOTO statement can be written with other Oracle constructs.

Perhaps the only proper use of GOTO statements is to immediately stop all other execution of statements and branch to a section of code to handle an emergency situation.

WHILE Loops

The WHILE loop enables you to evaluate a condition before a sequence of statements is executed. In fact, if the condition is false, the code is never executed. This situation is different from the FOR loop where you must execute the loop at least once.

The Syntax for the WHILE Loop

The syntax of the WHILE loop is

```
WHILE <condition is true> LOOP
     <statements>
END LOOP;
```

The WHILE loop requires the keywords LOOP and END LOOP to designate the statements to
▲ execute.

> **Note**
> WHILE loops are invaluable because the program does not have to ever execute the code within the LOOP parameters. This is one fact I cannot stress enough!

Examples of WHILE Loops

All the WHILE loop examples are meant to be entered and executed so that you can get some experience coding WHILE loops.

> **Note**
> When you first sign on to the database, it is a good idea to create a login script—or else you can make a habit of typing and executing the statement SET SERVEROUTPUT ON. When you learn about the DBMS_OUTPUT package on Day 17, "Writing to Files and the Display," using this statement allows you to see the actual output as the PL/SQL code executes to make PL/SQL easier to understand.

You can enter the loops directly or use the EDIT command to save a file, which can be executed at any time. Listing 5.7 demonstrates how the conditions for a WHILE loop can cause the loop to never execute.

INPUT   **LISTING 5.7**   Example of a WHILE Loop That Never Executes

```
1: DECLARE
2:        v_Calc NUMBER := 0;
3: BEGIN
4:      WHILE v_Calc >= 10 LOOP
5:            v_Calc := v_Calc + 1;
6:            DBMS_OUTPUT.PUT_LINE('The value of v_Calc is ' ¦¦ v_Calc);
7:      END LOOP;
8: END;
9: /
```

ANALYSIS   In Listing 5.7, the condition is never evaluated to true. The condition v_Calc
>= 10 from line 4 is never true because v_Calc is initialized at line 2 to a value of 0, which is less, not greater, than 10. When Listing 5.7 is executed, no output is sent to the screen.

Listing 5.8 shows the corrected version of this WHILE loop.

INPUT   **LISTING 5.8**   Corrected WHILE Loop That Executes

```
1: DECLARE
2:        v_Calc NUMBER := 0;
3: BEGIN
4:      WHILE v_Calc <= 10 LOOP
5:            v_Calc := v_Calc + 1;
6:            DBMS_OUTPUT.PUT_LINE('The value of v_Calc is ' ¦¦ v_Calc);
7:      END LOOP;
8: END;
9: /
```

5

OUTPUT
```
The value of v_Calc is 1
The value of v_Calc is 2
The value of v_Calc is 3
The value of v_Calc is 4
The value of v_Calc is 5
The value of v_Calc is 6
The value of v_Calc is 7
The value of v_Calc is 8
The value of v_Calc is 9
The value of v_Calc is 10
The value of v_Calc is 11
```

ANALYSIS To make the WHILE loop execute, I simply changed the >= to <= in line 4. The
loop executes at least once because v_Calc <= 10.

It is important to understand that the loop continues to execute until v_Calc <= 10. This
is a potential source of logic error flaws if the intent was to enter the loop until v_Calc
had a value of 10 and not 11.

> **Tip** When debugging loops, in general it is a good idea to use Oracle's
> DBMS_OUTPUT package to track the flow of the logic. It is a great help when
> testing all possible outcomes to make sure that the logic portion is working
> properly. A full discussion of this package occurs on Day 17.

Listing 5.9 illustrates how to step through a WHILE loop in increments other than one.

INPUT **LISTING 5.9** Stepping Through a WHILE Loop

```
 1: DECLARE
 2:     v_Radius NUMBER := 2;
 3: BEGIN
 4:     WHILE v_Radius <=10 LOOP
 5:         DBMS_OUTPUT.PUT_LINE('The Area is ' ¦¦
 6:             mypi * v_Radius * v_Radius);
 7:         v_Radius := v_Radius + 2 ; — Calculates Area for Even Radius
 8:     END LOOP;
 9: END;
10: /
```

OUTPUT
```
The Area is 12.56
The Area is 50.24
The Area is 113.04
The Area is 200.96
The Area is 314
```

ANALYSIS On Day 4, you created a method to trick Oracle into stepping through a FOR loop.
The WHILE loop gives you more flexibility in looping, whether you are stepping
through a loop or even executing a loop. Listing 5.9 demonstrates stepping through the
loop. This sequence increments v_Radius by a value of 2 from line 7 until it is equal to
10 from the condition specified in line 4.

> **Note**
>
> Did you even need the <= Boolean operators? You could easily have set the condition to exit if v_Radius != 12. You could have then incremented, decremented, or had fun doing both with the value of v_Radius.

The next WHILE loop is contained in a function. This arrangement allows you to review functions from Day 4. If you run into any problems, it doesn't hurt to review the previous lesson. Create the stored function from Listing 5.10.

INPUT   **LISTING 5.10**   The WHILE Loop as Part of a Function

```
 1: CREATE OR REPLACE function dontcountsp(p_pass_string VARCHAR2)
 2:      RETURN NUMBER IS
 3:          v_MYCOUNTER INTEGER := 1;
 4:          v_COUNTNOSP NUMBER := 0;
 5: BEGIN
 6:      WHILE v_MYCOUNTER <= LENGTH(p_PASS_STRING) LOOP
 7:          IF SUBSTR(p_PASS_STRING,v_MYCOUNTER,1) != ' ' THEN
 8:              v_COUNTNOSP := v_COUNTNOSP + 1;
 9:          ELSE
10:              NULL;
11:          END IF;
12:          v_MYCOUNTER := v_MYCOUNTER + 1;
13:      END LOOP;
14:      RETURN v_COUNTNOSP ;
15: END dontcountsp;
16: /
```

ANALYSIS   You create a function called dontcountsp from Listing 5.10, which counts all characters except spaces from a variable-length string up to 20 characters long. The function is passed a string from p_PASS_STRING called from the procedure. The return type in line 14 is simply a number telling you how many characters are actually contained in the string.

Of the two variables, v_MYCOUNTER holds the positional location for the current location in the string. V_COUNTNOSP holds the total count of characters that are not spaces.

The program finally enters the WHILE loop. The loop continues to execute as long as v_MYCOUNTER is less than the total LENGTH of the string. In the body of the loop, the program checks each character, beginning at position one all the way to the length of the string, and checks for the value of a space, defined by ' '. If the value in a position is not a space, the program increments v_COUNTNOSP by 1. If the value is a space, the program does nothing, as indicated by the NULL statement. The placeholder in the string

5

v_MYCOUNTER is then incremented by 1, and the loop continues to execute until it reaches the end of the string. To see the function in action, type the procedure in Listing 5.11 and then execute it.

INPUT   **LISTING 5.11**   Executing the WHILE Loop Function

```
1: DECLARE
2:       v_MYTEXT VARCHAR2(20) := 'THIS IS A TEST';
3: BEGIN
4:       DBMS_OUTPUT.PUT_LINE('Total count is ' ¦¦ dontcountsp(v_MYTEXT));
5: END;
6: /
```

ANALYSIS   The code in Listing 5.11 creates a variable called v_MYTEXT and assigns it a value of 'THIS IS A TEST' in line 2. It then outputs to the screen the total count of characters not including spaces in line 4.

Note

> Both the SUBSTR() function and the LENGTH() function are covered on Day 6, "Using Oracle's Built-In Functions."

The EXIT and EXIT WHEN Statements

The EXIT and EXIT WHEN statements enable you to escape out of the control of a loop. When an EXIT statement is encountered, the loop completes immediately and control is passed to the next statement. The format of the EXIT loop is

EXIT;

To terminate a loop, simply follow your condition with the EXIT statement. This method is common in IF statements.

The Syntax for the EXIT WHEN Loop

SYNTAX

The syntax of the EXIT WHEN loop is

EXIT WHEN <condition is true>;

The EXIT WHEN statement enables you to specify the condition required to exit the execution of the loop. In this case, no IF statement is required. When this statement is encountered, the condition of the when clause is evaluated. If the clause equates to true, then the loop exits; otherwise, the looping continues.

Examples Using EXIT and EXIT WHEN

In this lesson, you created a WHILE loop that incremented by a value of 2 to calculate the area of a circle. You will change this code so that the program exits when the value of the radius is 10 after you have calculated the area. Enter and execute the code in Listing 5.12.

INPUT **LISTING 5.12** Using EXIT with a WHILE Loop

```
1: DECLARE
2:      v_Radius NUMBER := 2;
3: BEGIN
4:      WHILE TRUE LOOP
5:          DBMS_OUTPUT.PUT_LINE('The Area is ' ||
6:              mypi * v_Radius * v_Radius);
7:          IF v_Radius = 10 THEN
8:              EXIT;
9:          END IF;
10:          v_Radius := v_Radius + 2 ; — Calculates Area for Even Radius
11:      END LOOP;
12: END;
13: /
```

Notice that the output is the same as the WHILE loop output from Listing 5.9.

5

Switching the output statements with the IF statement from Listing 5.12, which alters your output, is illustrated in the following code:

```
IF v_Radius = 10 THEN
    EXIT;
END IF;
DBMS_OUTPUT.PUT_LINE('The Area is ' || mypi * v_Radius * v_Radius);
```

Logic errors cause the most problems in any coding situation and can be difficult to resolve. Next, you will see how to code EXIT WHEN instead of EXIT in Listing 5.13 to achieve the same results.

INPUT   **LISTING 5.13**   Using EXIT WHEN with a WHILE Loop

```
 1: DECLARE
 2:     v_Radius NUMBER := 2;
 3: BEGIN
 4:     WHILE TRUE LOOP
 5:         DBMS_OUTPUT.PUT_LINE('The Area is ' ||
 6:             mypi * v_Radius * v_Radius);
 7:         EXIT WHEN v_RADIUS = 10;
 8:         v_Radius := v_Radius + 2 ; — Calculates Area for Even Radius
 9:     END LOOP;
10: END;
11: /
```

ANALYSIS   Listing 5.13 performs the same function as Listing 5.12 but uses the EXIT WHEN statement on one line, instead of the multiple lines of IF...THEN...EXIT statements from Listing 5.12. This version is easier to read and understand.

If you can exit from a WHILE loop, you should be able to exit from a FOR loop. The code from Listing 5.14 performs the same function as the code from Listings 5.9, 5.12, and 5.13 to calculate the area of a circle but this time uses a FOR loop.

INPUT   **LISTING 5.14**   Using EXIT with a FOR Loop

```
 1: BEGIN
 2:     FOR v_loopcounter IN 1..20 LOOP
 3:         IF MOD(v_loopcounter,2) = 0 THEN
 4:             DBMS_OUTPUT.PUT_LINE('The AREA of the circle is ' ||
 5:                 v_loopcounter*v_loopcounter * mypi);
 6:         END IF; — End execution of statements for even counter
 7:         IF v_loopcounter = 10 THEN
 8:             EXIT;
 9:         END IF;
10:     END LOOP;
11: END;
12: /
```

ANALYSIS The loop terminates after the area has been calculated for a radius of 10 from line 7. Notice that the IF condition from line 7 fully terminates the loop prematurely before the loop can increment to a value of 20.

If you exit out of a loop in the middle of the function, what happens? To see the outcome, first enter the code in Listing 5.15 to create the function called exitfunc.

INPUT **LISTING 5.15** Impact of EXIT in a Function

```
 1: CREATE OR REPLACE function exitfunc(p_pass_string VARCHAR2)
 2:     RETURN NUMBER IS
 3:         v_MYCOUNTER INTEGER := 1;
 4:         v_COUNTNOSP NUMBER := 0;
 5: BEGIN
 6:     WHILE v_MYCOUNTER <= LENGTH(p_PASS_STRING) LOOP
 7:         IF SUBSTR(p_PASS_STRING,v_MYCOUNTER,1) != ' ' THEN
 8:             v_COUNTNOSP := v_COUNTNOSP + 1;
 9:         ELSE
10:             NULL;
11:         END IF;
12:         v_MYCOUNTER := v_MYCOUNTER + 1;
13:         EXIT WHEN SUBSTR(p_PASS_STRING,v_MYCOUNTER,1) = ' ';
14:     END LOOP;
15:     RETURN v_COUNTNOSP ;
16: END exitfunc;
17: /
```

ANALYSIS Notice the addition of only one statement that tells the program to exit the loop if it encounters a space. To test and execute the function, enter the code from Listing 5.16.

INPUT **LISTING 5.16** Executing EXIT Within a Function

```
1: DECLARE
2:     v_MYTEXT VARCHAR2(20) := 'THIS IS A TEST';
3: BEGIN
4:     DBMS_OUTPUT.PUT_LINE('Total count is ' ¦¦ exitfunc(v_MYTEXT));
5: END;
6: /
```

OUTPUT The output when executed should be

```
Total count is 4
```

5

ANALYSIS The effect of breaking out of a loop in the function is that it still returns the value of the variable when the EXIT statement has been executed. Instead of counting all the characters in the line, it stops when it hits the first space and properly returns the value of 4 for the word 'Test'.

> **Tip**
>
> If you do use the EXIT or EXIT WHEN statement in a loop, make sure to always initialize the parameters. This way, some value always returns even if the loop never executes.

Using Labels and EXIT Statements with Loops

You can use labels within loops to identify a loop. When you're nesting loops, labels help to document the code.

The Syntax for Using Labels with Loops

▼ SYNTAX

```
<<label_name1>>
LOOP (FOR, WHILE, LOOP)
     <<label_name2>>
     LOOP (FOR, WHILE, LOOP)
         ...
     END LOOP <<label_name2>>
END LOOP <<label_name1>>
```

▲

You will use the example of nested FOR loops from Day 4 (Listing 4.15) and modify it with label names, as shown in Listing 5.17.

INPUT   **LISTING 5.17**   Using Labels with Loops

```
 1: BEGIN
 2:     <<outerloop>>
 3:     FOR v_outerloopcounter IN 1..2 LOOP
 4:         <<innerloop>>
 5:         FOR v_innerloopcounter IN 1..4 LOOP
 6:             DBMS_OUTPUT.PUT_LINE('Outer Loop counter is ' ||
 7:                     v_outerloopcounter ||
 8:                     ' Inner Loop counter is ' || v_innerloopcounter);
 9:         END LOOP innerloop;
10:     END LOOP outerloop;
11: END;
12: /
```

ANALYSIS The only difference between Listing 4.15 in Day 4 and Listing 5.17 is the use of the label names outerloop and innerloop. Otherwise, there is no difference in execution, output, and so on, but it is much easier to follow the logic.

You can even change the order of execution of a loop by using the EXIT and EXIT WHEN statements, as shown in Listing 5.18.

INPUT   **LISTING 5.18**   Changing Labeled Loop Execution with EXIT Statements

```
 1: BEGIN
 2:      <<outerloop>>
 3:      FOR v_outerloopcounter IN 1..2 LOOP
 4:          <<innerloop>>
 5:          FOR v_innerloopcounter IN 1..4 LOOP
 6:              DBMS_OUTPUT.PUT_LINE('Outer Loop counter is '
 7:                   ¦¦ v_outerloopcounter ¦¦
 8:                    ' Inner Loop counter is ' ¦¦ v_innerloopcounter);
 9:              EXIT outerloop WHEN v_innerloopcounter = 3;
10:          END LOOP innerloop;
11:      END LOOP outerloop;
12: END;
13: /
```

OUTPUT   When you run the code in Listing 5.18, you should see the following output:

```
Outer Loop counter is 1 Inner Loop counter is 1
Outer Loop counter is 1 Inner Loop counter is 2
Outer Loop counter is 1 Inner Loop counter is 3
```

ANALYSIS   The EXIT WHEN statement directs the program to exit the outer loop when the inner loop reaches a value of 3. Notice that this completely aborts the execution of both loops.

Simple LOOPs

The final loop to discuss today is the simple LOOP. This type of loop is the simplest to use and understand out of all the loops. The Simple Loop is a simple variation of the other loops presented.

The Syntax for a Simple LOOP

SYNTAX

The syntax of the simple LOOP is

```
LOOP
    <statement(s)>
END LOOP;
```

If you do not have an EXIT or EXIT WHEN statement located in the loop, you have an infinite loop.

> **Tip**
>
> When using EXIT or EXIT WHEN, always place these commands either at the beginning of the LOOP block or at the end of the LOOP block. This way, you can avoid many logic errors.

Sample Simple LOOPs

> **Caution**
>
> The following is an example of an infinite loop. You probably do *not* want to execute this example. As you can see, the loop never ends and never does anything!

```
BEGIN
    LOOP
          NULL;
    END LOOP;
END;
/
```

You can properly exit out of a loop by simply adding the word EXIT after the NULL statement. Execute the code in Listing 5.19.

 LISTING 5.19   Using EXIT with a Simple LOOP

```
1: BEGIN
2:     LOOP
3:            NULL;
4:            EXIT;
5:     END LOOP;
6: END;
```

Creating a REPEAT...UNTIL Loop

Oracle does not have a built-in REPEAT *<statements>* UNTIL *<condition is true>* loop. However, you can simulate one by using the simple LOOP and the EXIT or EXIT WHEN statements.

The Syntax for a Simulated REPEAT...UNTIL Loop

```
LOOP
  <statements>
    IF <condition is true>
        EXIT;
    END IF;
END LOOP;
```

Alternatively, you can use the preferable method of

```
LOOP
  <statements>
    EXIT WHEN <condition is true>;
END LOOP;
```

> **Tip**
>
> You will find as a programmer that using the EXIT WHEN statement will save your time. This statement requires less coding that the other looping statements. One typical reason you use nested IF statements is for fine-tuning Oracle to speed up the process.

An Example of a Simulated REPEAT...UNTIL Loop

Enter the code in Listing 5.20. You are still calculating the area of a circle as you did in Listings 5.9, 5.12, 5.13, and 5.14, but this time, you use a simulated REPEAT...UNTIL loop.

INPUT   **LISTING 5.20**   Demonstrating a REPEAT...UNTIL Loop

```
 1: DECLARE
 2:     v_Radius NUMBER := 2;
 3: BEGIN
 4:     LOOP
 5:         DBMS_OUTPUT.PUT_LINE('The AREA of the circle is '
 6:             || v_RADIUS*v_RADIUS * mypi);
 7:         v_Radius := v_Radius + 2;
 8:         EXIT WHEN v_Radius > 10;
 9:     END LOOP;
10: END;
```

5

Notice that the code in Listing 5.20 creates the same five output lines computing the area of the circle that were produced by Listing 5.12. This simulated REPEAT...UNTIL loop simply starts the loop, outputs the area of the loop to the screen, increments the radius, and then exits when the radius is greater than 10. This arrangement allows you to use the values 2, 4, 6, 8, and 10 as in the other examples.

What Loop Should I Use?

All of these loop options can get confusing! As you saw in the examples, you can use the FOR, WHILE, and LOOP statements to create the same output. However, Table 5.1 shows some general guidelines about when to use what type of loop.

TABLE 5.1   When to Use Which Loop

Loop	When to Use It
FOR	Always use the FOR loop if you know specifically how many times the loop should execute. If you have to code an EXIT or EXIT WHEN statement in a FOR loop, you might want to reconsider your code and go with a different loop or different approach.
WHILE	Use this if you might never even want to execute the loop one time. Although you can duplicate this result in a FOR loop using EXIT or EXIT WHEN, this situation is best left for the WHILE loop. The WHILE loop is the most commonly used loop because it provides the most flexibility.
LOOP	You can use the simple LOOP if you want to create a REPEAT <statements> UNTIL <condition is true> type of loop. The simple LOOP is perfect for performing this task.

Loop Guidelines

Some loop guidelines you should follow appear in the following Do/Don't box.

Do	**Don't**
Do make sure when you are using a LOOP with an EXIT or EXIT WHEN statement that the condition will be met at least once; otherwise, you'll have an infinite loop.	**Don't** ever create an infinite loop.
Do always use label names with loops. This makes the code much easier to follow, plus it gives you flexibility.	**Don't** use a RETURN statement within a loop when using loops in a function. Although it might work, this is poor programming practice that could have some unwanted results and is the improper termination of a loop.
Do make sure when you're using label names that the label name follows the END LOOP statement.	
Do code label names to the far left when you use them with the GOTO statement; otherwise, Oracle does not see the label name.	
Do use EXIT WHEN instead of EXIT. EXIT WHEN is much easier to follow and requires less coding.	
Do refer to Table 5.1 for some general guidelines if you don't know which loop to use.	
Do make sure that you have proper punctuation in your loops.	
Do choose which type of loop to use with increments. You can handle any type of increment with any loop. Refer to the examples in Day 4 and in this lesson.	
Do make variables out of the lower and upper boundaries in FOR loops if either of the boundaries can potentially change in the future. You can assign these on-the-fly in your code. In reality, you will most likely not have a fixed boundary, so you should follow this advice automatically.	

5

Style Tips for Loops

Two last items I want to mention concerning loops are label names and proper indentation. Always use label names when creating any type of nested loop or when nesting FOR loops to make the index counter more meaningful.

Proper spacing should include aligning the END LOOP with the LOOP statement and the usual indent of five spaces for statements within the loop. Listing 5.21 contains an example in which the spacing is proper, but the loop itself appears confusing because the code doesn't follow these tips. After Listing 5.21, you will see the same example with a better style of coding in Listings 5.22 and 5.23.

INPUT   **LISTING 5.21**   A Confusing FOR Loop

```
 1: BEGIN
 2:      FOR I = 1995 to 1997
 3:      LOOP
 4:          FOR J = 1 to 31
 5:          LOOP
 6:              FOR K = 1 to 12
 7:              LOOP
 8:                  <statements>
 9:              END LOOP;
10:          END LOOP;
11:      END LOOP;
12: END;
```

A programmer might take an initial look at the code in Listing 5.21 and say "Huh?" A better approach is shown in Listing 5.22.

INPUT   **LISTING 5.22**   Making the FOR Loop More Meaningful

```
 1: BEGIN
 2:      FOR year = 1995 to 1997
 3:      LOOP
 4:          FOR day = 1 to 31
 5:          LOOP
 6:              FOR month = 1 to 12
 7:              LOOP
 8:                  <statement(s)>
 9:              END LOOP; —end month
10:          END LOOP; —end day
11:      END LOOP; —end year
12: END;
```

ANALYSIS As you can see, not only does this example clarify the counters, but it also clarifies the END LOOP statements. You can further clarify the loop by adding label names as shown in Listing 5.23.

INPUT **LISTING 5.23**   Further Clarifying the FOR Loop

```
 1: BEGIN
 2:     <<year_loop>>
 3:     FOR year = v_START_YEAR to v_END_YEAR
 4:     LOOP
 5:         <<day_loop>>
 6:         FOR day = 1 to v_last_day_of_month
 7:         LOOP
 8:             <<month_loop>>
 9:             FOR month = 1 to 12
10:             LOOP
11:                 <statements>
12:             END LOOP month_loop;
13:         END LOOP day_loop;
14:     END LOOP year_loop;
15: END;
```

ANALYSIS The code in Listing 5.23 is the ideal way to code this nested FOR loop. The label names are concise and easy to follow. In addition, I changed the outer boundary of the day loop to a variable called v_last_day_of_month. Because this value is truly a variable, you should code it as such. I also made the beginning and ending years variables because the analysis period might change some time down the road.

Recursion

Earlier in this book, you learned how to use Oracle's built-in functions, as well as how to create your own functions. Functions allow you to create reusable code, which is also easier to test and debug when broken into smaller components. In PL/SQL, functions can easily call other functions. A *recursive* function is one that calls itself until some exit condition occurs. One problem with coding recursion is making sure that the exit condition is met.

Guidelines

It is important to realize that each time your code goes into recursion, a new instance is created of any items declared in the subprogram, including parameters, variables, cursors, and exceptions. Be careful where you place a recursive call. If you place it inside a cursor FOR loop or between OPEN and CLOSE statements, another cursor is opened at each call. As a result, your program might exceed the limit set by the Oracle initialization parameter OPEN_CURSORS.

A good guideline is to make sure that if you use recursion, your code has at least two paths. One path takes the control through the recursive code, and the other path takes you out of or around the recursive code.

Practicing Recursion

As with any third-generation programming language, you have to code the functions as recursive because recursion is not already built into PL/SQL. The classic example of using recursion is to calculate the factorial of a number. To compute the factorial of the number, you multiply the number by the number [ms]1 (n*(n[ms]1)) until n equals the value of 1. Table 5.2 shows factorial calculations for the numbers 1 through 6. Factorial in math textbooks uses the punctuation !, so 3! means three factorial, which is 3 * 2 * 1 = 6.

TABLE 5.2 Factorial Calculations

Factorial	Calculation	Result
1!	1	1
2!	2 * 1	2
3!	3 * 2 * 1	6
4!	4 * 3 * 2 * 1	24
5!	5 * 4 * 3 * 2 * 1	120
6!	6 * 5 *4 * 3 * 2 * 1	720

Now, try using recursion to calculate the factorial of an integer. First, you need to create the function FACTORIAL by executing the code in Listing 5.24.

INPUT   **LISTING 5.24**   Creating the FACTORIAL Recursive Function

```
CREATE OR REPLACE FUNCTION Factorial(p_MyNum INTEGER)

/* Creates a recursive function that simply calculates
   the factorial of a number. The function starts with
   the number and then calls the function with n-1
   until n = 1, which returns a value of 1.  Without this
   statement, the function never ends.        */

    RETURN NUMBER AS
BEGIN -- Start of Factorial Function
```

```
        IF p_MyNum = 1 THEN -- Checking for last value to process of n-1
            RETURN 1;
        ELSE
            RETURN(p_MyNum * Factorial(p_MyNum-1)); -- Recursive
        END IF;
END; — End of Factorial Function
```

OUTPUT After you execute the code in Listing 5.24, you should see the following output to the screen:

```
function created
```

ANALYSIS This function FACTORIAL continues to call itself until n[ms]1, where n is the factorial processed, equals a value of one. After this value is reached, the return value is equal to the running factorial multiplied by the value of calling the same function submitting the running factorial number less one. As you can see, this is a short, brief function that is easy to read but difficult to follow.

To see a demonstration of all factorial values from 1 to 10, first make sure that you have typed SET SERVEROUTPUT ON at the SQL*Plus prompt. Then, execute the code in Listing 5.25.

INPUT **LISTING 5.25** Testing the Recursive Function with an Anonymous PL/SQL Block

```
DECLARE
    v_test NUMBER := 10;
    v_Counter INTEGER ; -- Counter for For Loop
BEGIN
    FOR v_Counter IN 1..v_test LOOP
        DBMS_OUTPUT.PUT_LINE('The factorial of ' ||
            v_Counter || ' is ' || factorial(v_Counter));
    END LOOP;
END;
```

5

Your output should look like the following:

OUTPUT
```
The factorial of 1 is 1
The factorial of 2 is 2
The factorial of 3 is 6
The factorial of 4 is 24
The factorial of 5 is 120
The factorial of 6 is 720
The factorial of 7 is 5040
The factorial of 8 is 40320
The factorial of 9 is 362880
The factorial of 10 is 3628800
```

In this example, you can see that the code is executed iteratively to produce the factorial of the numbers 1 through 10. These numbers happen to also be the counter used to control the execution of the loop.

Why Use Recursion?

When the need to call a function by itself does not occur more than 10 to 15 times, recursion provides an elegant, and sometimes simple, solution to a problem. However, there are many reasons why you will probably never use recursion:

- All recursion problems can be solved by a different method, such as writing custom functions, using FOR loops, or using IF statements, all of which are discussed on Day 4. You can also use WHILE or LOOP statements, covered earlier in this lesson.
- The more complex the calculation, or the more times the function calls itself, the slower the execution of the PL/SQL code.
- Recursion can be difficult for other programmers to follow.

Summary

Congratulations on completing another day! You learned how to branch by using the GOTO statement followed by the appropriate label name. You also learned that the label name must appear in the same block and within the same scope as the GOTO statement.

This day continued with more ways to loop PL/SQL code. You started with the WHILE loop, which might not even execute the loop once because it checks for a condition first. This concept is important because the other loops must execute at least once (unless you use EXIT or EXIT WHEN statements at the beginning of the other loop types, which is probably not the best way to code the loop). You continued with learning ways to exit loops and ways to change the execution of nested loops by using the EXIT or EXIT WHEN statements in conjunction with label names. You then learned about the simple LOOP and how to create a REPEAT...UNTIL loop. To clear up the loop options, you reviewed the loop types and the best times to use which loop. This day closed with a discussion of recursion.

Q&A

Q **What is the scope of the label called by the GOTO statement?**

A The *label_name* must be within the same PL/SQL block of code that was called by the corresponding GOTO statement.

Q **How many times must the WHILE loop execute?**

A Depending upon the condition, the WHILE loop might never have to execute. This is one of the great features of this type of loop.

Q **What is the syntax and purpose of the EXIT statement?**

A The EXIT statement is simply coded as EXIT. It gives you a means to abort out of a loop without executing the loop in its entirety.

Q **Can you exit out of loops contained in a function and still return a value?**

A Yes. However, the returned value is the value assigned to the variable at the time the EXIT statement is called.

Q **Can you change the execution order of nested loops with EXIT or EXIT WHEN?**

A Yes. You can abort both loops with the use of EXIT and EXIT WHEN if you use label names with loops.

Q **What statement must be present in a simple LOOP so that it does not become an infinite loop?**

A The EXIT or EXIT WHEN statement is required. Although these statements are not part of the syntax, not using them makes a loop infinite, which you should avoid at all costs.

Workshop

Use the following workshop to review and practice the GOTO statement, WHILE loops, and the simple LOOP statement. The answers to the quiz and exercises appear in Appendix A, "Answers."

Quiz

1. True or False: The label name must be within the same PL/SQL block of code as the GOTO statement calling the label name.

2. When should you use GOTO?

3. WHILE loops must end with a(n) _____ statement.

4. Can you potentially write a WHILE loop that never ends?

5. What statement(s) allow you to abort the processing of a loop?

6. To change the execution of nested loops, you can use the EXIT and EXIT WHEN statement in conjunction with _____.

7. Must you have EXIT or EXIT WHEN as part of a simple LOOP?

8. Does Oracle have a REPEAT...UNTIL loop?

9. In a simple LOOP, where is the best location for the EXIT or EXIT WHEN statements?

Exercises

1. Create an example using GOTO that checks some variable for a value of 10 and then branches off to a NULL statement.

2. Create a WHILE loop to calculate a factorial. In other words, 6! is 6 * 5 * 4 * 3 * 2 * 1. Use an initial value of 4! for testing. Make sure to issue the command SET SERVEROUTPUT ON and use DBMS_OUTPUT.

3. Create the same factorial calculation as you do in Exercise 2, but use the simple LOOP statement instead.

DAY 6

Using Oracle's Built-In Functions

by Tom Luers

Day 4, "Using Functions, IF Statements, and Loops," demonstrates how to create functions within the code and stored functions. However, the Oracle RDBMS already comes complete with many excellent prewritten functions. With so many of these functions, it is unlikely that even the best Oracle guru has them all memorized. Today's lesson covers the most frequently used functions. I highly recommend that you review Appendix B, "Oracle Functions Reference," and keep it near you while you work. Appendix B contains a complete list of Oracle functions, their purpose, and their syntax. In this lesson you will learn the following:

- Categories of functions
- Using Conversion functions
- Using Date functions

Tip

The best way to learn a programming language, whether it is a third-generation language or a database management language, is to always initially review all the commands and functions, their syntax, and their usage. Any time you need to use any of these functions, you can then refer to this lesson for the syntax and definition. Otherwise, you might miss some powerful features, never knowing that they even exist. This methodology also helps you easily understand and learn competing vendor's products and makes you a more valuable programmer.

Comparing SQL Functions and PL/SQL Functions

As with any database, you can use SQL within PL/SQL to take advantage of all the features of PL/SQL. Almost all the functions work within PL/SQL except those functions that operate on rows such as MAX, MIN, or any other "grouping or summary" type functions, as well as special functions such as DUMP.

The Major Categories of Functions

Tables 6.1 through 6.6 summarize Oracle's functions within the categories character functions, number functions, date functions, conversion functions, group functions, and miscellaneous functions.

TABLE 6.1 Character Functions

Function Name	Function Description
ASCII	Returns the ASCII code of the character.
CHR	Returns a character when given its ASCII value.
CONCAT	Joins (concatenates) two strings together. (It's the same as using the ¦¦ operator, which you might have noticed on Day 4 and Day 5, "Implementing Loops and GOTOs.")
INITCAP	Returns a string in which the first letter in each word is capitalized and all remaining characters are converted to lowercase. Does not affect any non-alphabetic characters.
INSTR	Returns the location of a string within another string.

Function Name	Function Description
INSTRB	Returns the location of a string within another string but returns the value in bytes for a single-byte character system.
LENGTH	Returns the length of a character string, including pads. Returns NULL if the value is NULL.
LENGTHB	Returns the length of a character string in bytes, except that the return value is in bytes for single-byte character sets.
LOWER	Converts the entire character string to lowercase. Does not affect any non-alphabetic characters.
LPAD	Pads a string on the left side with any string specified.
LTRIM	Trims a character string on the left side.
NLS_INITCAP	Same as the INITCAP function except that it can use a different sort method as specified by NLSSORT.
NLS_LOWER	Same as the LOWER function except that it can use a different sort method as specified by NLSSORT.
NLS_UPPER	Same as the UPPER function except that it can use a different sort method as specified by NLSSORT.
NLSSORT	Changes the method of sorting the characters. Must be specified before any NLS function; otherwise, the default sort is used.
REPLACE	Replaces every occurrence of one string with another string.
RPAD	Pads a string on the right side with any string specified.
RTRIM	Trims a character string on the right side.
SOUNDEX	Returns the phonetic representation of a string. Useful for words that are spelled differently but sound alike.
SUBSTR	Returns a portion of a string from within a string.
SUBSTRB	Same as SUBSTR except the parameters are expressed in bytes instead of characters to handle single-byte character systems.
TRIM	Combines the functionality of the LTRIM and RTRIM functions. Trims leading and trailing characters from a string.
TRANSLATE	Same as REPLACE except operates at a character-level basis instead of a string-level basis.
UPPER	Converts the entire character string to uppercase. Does not affect any non-alphabetic characters.

6

TABLE 6.2 Number Functions

Function Name	Function Description
ABS	Returns the absolute value of a number.
ACOS	Returns the arc (inverse) cosine of a number, expressed in radians.
ASIN	Returns the arc (inverse) sine of a number, expressed in radians.
ATAN	Returns the arc (inverse) tangent of a number (x), expressed in radians.
ATAN2	Returns the arc (inverse) tangent of a number (y/x), expressed in radians.
CEIL	Returns the value representing the smallest integer that is greater than or equal to a specified number.
COS	Returns the cosine of a number, expressed in radians.
COSH	Returns the hyperbolic cosine of a number, expressed in radians.
EXP	Returns the exponentiation of e raised to the power of some number, where e = 2.7182818….
FLOOR	Returns the value representing the largest integer that is greater than or equal to a specified number.
LN	Returns the natural logarithm of some number x.
LOG	Returns the logarithm of some base x of some number y.
MOD	Returns the remainder of some number x divided by some number y.
POWER	Returns some number x to the power of some number y.
ROUND	Returns x rounded to y places.
SIGN	Determines whether a number is negative, zero, or positive by the following rules: If x is negative, it returns a value of -1. If x is zero, it returns zero. If x is positive, it returns a value of 1.
SIN	Returns the sine of some number x in radians.
SINH	Returns the hyperbolic sine of some number x in radians.
SQRT	Returns the square root of some number x. The value of x can't be an imaginary number; x must never be negative.
TAN	Returns the tangent of some number x in radians.
TANH	Returns the hyperbolic tangent of some number x in radians.
TRUNC	Returns some number x, truncated to y places. Does not round; just cuts off at the location specified.

TABLE 6.3 Date Functions

Function Name	Function Description
ADD_MONTHS	Adds one month to the date specified. It does not add 30 or 31 days but simply adds one to the month. If the resulting month has fewer days, it returns the last day of that month instead.
LAST_DAY	Returns the last day of the given month. A useful function, especially for programming in accounting departments.
MONTHS_BETWEEN	Computes the months between two dates. Returns an integer if both dates are the last days of the month; otherwise, it returns the fractional portion of a 31-day month.
NEW_TIME	Returns the time/day value from a time zone specified by the user.
NEXT_DAY	Returns the date of the first day of the week specified in a string after the beginning date.
ROUND	Gives you full flexibility to round to the nearest date parameter of your choice, such as month, year, century, and so on.
SYSDATE	Simply returns the system date and time in type DATE format.
TRUNC	Truncates up to the specified date parameter, such as day, month, and so on.

TABLE 6.4 Conversion Functions

Function Name	Function Description
CHARTOROWID	Converts a CHAR or VARCHAR2 from an external format provided by Oracle to its internal binary format.
CONVERT	Converts from one character set to another character set.
HEXTORAW	Converts hex string values to internal raw values.
RAWTOHEX	Converts internal raw values to an external hex string.
ROWIDTOCHAR	Converts the ROW ID into its external 18-character string representation.
TO_CHAR	Converts DATES, MLSLABELS, and NUMBERS to a VARCHAR2 string.
TO_DATE	Converts a CHAR or VARCHAR2 string into a DATE value.
TO_LABEL	Converts a CHAR or VARCHAR2 string into a MLSLABEL.
TO_MULTI_BYTE	Converts any single-byte string of characters into a multibyte string.
TO_NUMBER	Converts a CHAR or VARCHAR2 string into a NUMBER value.
TO_SINGLE_BYTE	Converts any multibyte string of characters into a single-byte string.

6

TABLE 6.5 Grouping Functions

Function Name	Function Description
AVG	Average of a column of values.
COUNT	Total count of rows returned in a query.
GLC	Greatest lower bound of a MLSLABEL.
LUB	Least upper bound of a MLSLABEL.
MAX	Returns the largest value of a row in a column from a query.
MIN	Returns the smallest value of a row in a column from a query.
STDDEV	Returns the standard deviation of a selected column in a query.
SUM	Returns the SUM of a selected column in a query.
VARIANCE	Returns the statistical VARIANCE of a selected column in a query.

TABLE 6.6 Miscellaneous Functions

Function Name	Function Description
BFILENAME	Similar to C language. Returns a pointer, which is referred to as a *locator* in Oracle, to the associated physical LOB binary file where the file is stored.
DECODE	Acts as a nested IF...THEN...ELSE statement from a list of values.
DUMP	Provides a dump of values in a string VARCH2 to show the representation in many different formats.
EMPTY_BLOB	Used to initialize a BLOB variable or column that contains no data.
EMPTY_CLOB	Used to initialize a CLOB variable or column that contains no data.
GREATEST	Takes a list of values or expressions and returns the largest evaluated value.
GREATEST_LB	Takes a list of MLSLABELS and returns the greatest lower bound.
LEAST	Takes a list of values or expressions and returns the smallest evaluated value.
LEAST_LB	Takes a list of MLSLABELS and returns the least lower bound.
NLS_CHARSET_ID	Returns the NLS character set ID number associated with the NLS character set name.
NLS_CHARSET_NAME	Returns the NLS character set name associated with the ID passed to the function.
NVL	Selects the first non-null value from a list of values or expressions.
UID	Returns the user ID assigned to the user in Oracle.
USER	Returns the name of the current user in a VARCHAR2 string.
USERENV	Returns information about your current working environment.
SQLCODE	Returns an error code based upon the current error.
SQLERRM	Returns the error message associated with the Oracle error code.
VSIZE	Returns the number of bytes in some value.

Experimenting with Functions

The best way to understand functions in Oracle is to test all of them with your own data. However, the easiest way is to use SQL*Plus and the SQL command `SELECT FUNCTION(arguments,column_headings)` from DUAL to test these functions. The examples in today's lesson use this method.

> The DUAL table is simply a standard Oracle table that is used as a dummy table to evaluate a condition to true. When you are testing your functions while selecting from DUAL, the table allows you to return one result. Use DUAL only when data itself is irrelevant.

Using Conversion Functions

Some of the most important and widely used functions are the conversion functions. These functions allow you to convert from one data type to another data type. This section discusses two major types of conversions: going from a CHAR or VARCHAR2 data type to either a NUMBER or a DATE or converting from a DATE or a NUMBER data type to a VARCHAR2.

Using TO_DATE

The TO_DATE function converts a character string (a CHAR or VARCHAR2), as denoted by the apostrophe (`'`) surrounding the character string, to an actual DATE value. The syntax for the TO_DATE function is as follows.

```
TO_DATE(character string, format, NLS_DATE_LANGUAGE)
```

The *format* parameter is optional, and if you do not use it, the default DATE format DD-MMM-YY applies. The format must be the representation of the character date you are supplying to convert.

> Always make sure you specify the proper format for the date you are supplying; otherwise, you will get to know the Oracle error messages very well. For instance, if you forget to use the format option and pass `'061167'`, Oracle returns an error message stating that the month is invalid. Considering that the default format is DD-MMM-YY, it's easy to see that the day is 06, but the month is not correct at 116.

6

The TO_DATE function has some limitations:

- You can pass no more than 220 characters into the function for conversion.
- You are limited to the format masks listed in Table 6.7.
- You can't mix and match formats such as specifying 24-hour time and also requesting AM or PM because you want either 24-hour time or 12-hour time.
- You can't specify the same element twice in the conversion such as YYYY-MM-MMM-DD. The MM-MMM are duplicate elements. The function has problems attempting to decode the intent and always causes an error.

Refer to Table 6.7 for the available format masks you can pass when using the TO_DATE function.

TABLE 6.7 Date Format Elements

Format Element	Description
BC, B.C.	BC indicator, which you can use with or without the periods.
AD, A.D.	AD indicator, which you can use with or without the periods.
CC, SCC	Century code. Returns a negative value if you use BC with the SCC format.
SYYYY, YYYY	Four-digit year. Returns a negative value if you use BC with the SYYYY format.
IYYY	Four-digit ISO year.
Y,YYY	Four-digit year with a comma inserted.
YYY, YY, Y	The last three, two, or one digits of the year. The default is the current century.
IYY, IY, I	The last three, two, or one digits of the ISO year. The default is the current century.
YEAR, SYEAR	Returns the year spelled out. SYEAR returns a negative value if you use BC dates.
RR	Last two digits of the relative year.
Q	Quarter of the year, values 1 to 4.
MM	The month number from 01 to 12: January=01, February=02, and so on.
MONTH	The month name always allocated to nine characters, right-padded with blanks.
MON	The month name abbreviated to three characters.
RM	Roman numeral representation of the month, values I to XII.
WW	The week in the year, values 1 to 53.
IW	The ISO week in the year, values 1 to 52 or 1 to 53.

Format Element	Description
W	The week in the month, values 1 to 5. Week 1 begins on the first day of the month.
D	The day of the week, values 1 to 7.
DD	The day of the month, values 1 to 31.
DDD	The day of the year, values 1 to 366.
DAY	The name of the day spelled out, always occupying nine characters, right-space padded.
DY	Abbreviated name of the day to two characters.
J	Julian day counted since January 1, 4712 BC.
HH, HH12	The hour of the day, values 1 to 12.
HH24	The hour of the day, values 0 to 23.
MI	The minute of the hour, values 0 to 59.
SS	The second of the minute, values 0 to 59.
SSSS	How many seconds past midnight, values 0 to 86399. (60 minutes/hr * 60 seconds/minute * 24 hours = 86,400 seconds.)
AM, A.M.	The ante meridian indicator for morning, with or without the periods.
PM, P.M.	The post meridian indicator for evening, with or without the periods.
Punctuation	All punctuation is passed through to a maximum of 220 characters.
Text	All text is passed through to a maximum of 220 characters.
TH	Suffix to convert numbers to ordinal format, so 1 is 1st, 2 is 2nd, and so on. Always returns value in English language only.
SP	Converts a number to its spelled format, so 109 becomes one hundred nine. Always returns value in English language only.
SPTH	Spells out numbers converted to ordinal format, so 1 is FIRST, 2 is SECOND, and so on. Always returns value in English language only.
FX	Uses exact pattern matching between data element and the format.
FM	Fill mode: Toggles suppression of blanks in output from conversion.

Finally, the last part of the TO_DATE function is NLS_DATE_LANGUAGE. For all you network gurus, this is simply the language you want returned, such as English, Spanish, and so on. Remember, certain functions only return values in the English language, such as SPTH, SP, and so forth.

To confuse you even further, take a look at the syntax of the TO_DATE function using Julian days. This is the number of days that has elapsed since January 1, 4712 BC:

TO_DATE(*number*, *format*, *NLS_Params*)

The syntax is not much different from the previous syntax for normal character-based dates, except that you pass to the function a number value that represents the Julian days.

As you can see, you can format this simple function in many different ways. The best way is to type all the following listings to see your output. These examples use SQL*Plus as a quick method for testing, but you can easily use them in your PL/SQL code except where specified as SQL only. Enter and execute Listings 6.1 and 6.2.

INPUT **LISTING 6.1** Converting a Number Representation to DATE Format

```
SELECT TO_DATE('031092','MMDDYY') "Birthday" from DUAL;
```

The output appears as

OUTPUT
```
Birthday
..........
10-MAR-92
```

INPUT **LISTING 6.2** Converting a Spelled Date to DATE Format

```
SELECT TO_DATE('April 21','MONTH DD') "Sample" from DUAL;
```

Your output should appear similar to the following:

OUTPUT
```
Sample
..........
21-APR-99
```

ANALYSIS Notice that even though the example did not specify the century or the year, the output shows the default system century and year.

What are some of the possible errors that you can encounter with TO_DATE? What if you leave off the mask or incorrectly specify the mask? Listing 6.3 reflects a sample error.

INPUT **LISTING 6.3** Errors with TO_DATE

```
SELECT TO_DATE('031092') "Error" from DUAL;
```

You should get the error message

OUTPUT
```
ERROR at line 1:
ORA-01861:Literal does not match format string
```

Because you did not apply a mask, the standard date mask was applied from the format DD-MMM-YY. Because 03 is a valid day, Oracle has no problems with handling the day. However, the program expects the month to use the default three-letter abbreviation. The value it takes next, 109, is not a valid abbreviation for a month. Listing 6.4 shows an instance when you can use the default date.

INPUT   **LISTING 6.4**   Proper Use of the Default Format Mask

```
SELECT TO_DATE('03-MAR-92') "Correct" from DUAL;
```

The output appears as

OUTPUT
```
Correct
.........
10-MAR-92
```

As you can see, making sure that you pass the format mask in the same manner as the character string is highly important.

The next example demonstrates using TO_DATE as part of PL/SQL code for practice. Enter the code in Listing 6.5.

Note | Before you continue, make sure that you enter SET SERVEROUTPUT ON at the SQL*Plus prompt. This allows you to see the output onscreen as the PL/SQL code executes.

INPUT   **LISTING 6.5**   Using TO_DATE Within PL/SQL

```
1: DECLARE
2:     v_Convert_Date DATE;
3: BEGIN
4:     v_Convert_Date := TO_DATE('031092','MMDDYY');
5:     DBMS_OUTPUT.PUT_LINE('The converted date is: ' ¦¦ v_Convert_Date);
6: END;
7: /
```

6

The output should be

OUTPUT
```
The converted date is: 03-MAR-92

PL/SQL procedure successfully completed.
```

ANALYSIS All the PL/SQL code does is create a variable of type DATE in line 2 and assign it to the converted character date in line 4. How many people know another foreign language? How do you convert to the Oracle built-in DATE from another language?

Remember to use the NLS_DATE_LANGUAGE parameter to specify the language. Listing 6.6 is an example of converting a German date to an Oracle DATE.

INPUT   **LISTING 6.6**   Converting a German Date to DATE Format

```
SELECT TO_DATE('april-21','MONTH-DD','NLS_DATE_LANGUAGE=german')
    "Converted" from DUAL;
```

The output appears in the default Oracle format as

OUTPUT
```
Converted
----------
21-APR-99
```

How about some calculations on that date just returned? Listing 6.7 reflects adding 5 days to the converted date.

INPUT   **LISTING 6.7**   Performing Calculations on a Converted Date

```
1: DECLARE
2:      v_Convert_Date DATE;
3: BEGIN
4:      v_Convert_Date := TO_DATE('042199','MMDDYY') + 5;
5:      DBMS_OUTPUT.PUT_LINE('The converted date is: ' ¦¦ v_Convert_Date);
6: END;
7: /
```

Your output should appear as follows:

OUTPUT
```
The converted date is: 26-APR-99

PL/SQL procedure successfully completed.
```

You have taken a converted date of 04/21/99 and added 5 days in line 4, which brings you to the proper result of 26-APR-99.

You should be starting to grasp how Oracle converts characters to dates. Experiment with some of the other formats in the rest of this section.

Using TO_CHAR for Dates

If you can turn character strings into dates, you should be able to reverse this process. Oracle's answer is the TO_CHAR function.

SYNTAX

TO_CHAR(*date*, *format*, *NLS_Params*)

Remember to refer to Table 6.7 for allowable mask formats. The best way to demonstrate TO_CHAR is through many examples, especially with format varieties. The first example takes the current system date and time from the SYSDATE function and formats it to a spelled-out date in Listing 6.8.

> **Note**
>
> Some of these listings allow you to enter the code directly at the SQL*Plus prompt, or you can enter it directly into the editor. If you use the editor, do not use the ending semicolon for the one-line SQL listings. If you are entering at the prompt, the semicolon performs the SQL statement, similar to using a / to execute the code.

INPUT **LISTING 6.8** Converting DATE to a Spelled-Out Character Format

```
SELECT TO_CHAR(SYSDATE,'MONTH DDTH YYYY') "Today" from DUAL;
```

Your output should appear as follows:

OUTPUT
```
Today
-------------------
SEPTEMBER 29TH 1999
```

ANALYSIS In this example, we selected the current date from the Oracle system and formatted it in the Month-Day-Year format. We also added a output label which explains that the date is the current day.

How about using this example as a PL/SQL procedure and returning to the good old days of BC? Listing 6.9 shows another example of using TO_CHAR with converting and formatting dates.

INPUT **LISTING 6.9** Converting DATE to a Spelled-Out Character Format

```
1: DECLARE
2:     v_Convert_Date DATE := TO_DATE('06112067BC','MMDDYYYYBC');
3:     v_Hold_Date VARCHAR2(100);
4: BEGIN
5:     v_Hold_Date := TO_CHAR(v_Convert_Date,'MMDDSYYYY');
6:     DBMS_OUTPUT.PUT_LINE('The converted date is: ' ¦¦ v_Hold_Date);
7: END;
8: /
```

6

There are several items to note here. First, to assign a date to a DATE value, you need to convert a character date to a DATE data type by using the TO_DATE function, as shown in line 2. If you simply enter or assign a date as in the following example, you generate an error:

```
v_Convert_Date DATE := 11-JUN-67;
```

The second item to notice is how Oracle displays dates for BC. When you run the code from Listing 6.9, your output appears as follows:

```
The converted date is: 0611-2067
```

```
PL/SQL procedure successfully completed.
```

As you can see, a negative sign before the year value represents BC.

Finally, you can have some fun with using another language for your output. Enter and execute the code in Listing 6.10 for an example of German output.

 LISTING 6.10   Converting a DATE to Another Language

```
SELECT TO_CHAR(SYSDATE,'MONTH DD YY','NLS_DATE_LANGUAGE=german')
       "German Date" from dual;
```

Your output should appear as

```
German Date
-----------------
JUNI      21 99
```

> **Note**   Make sure when you are displaying your output that you specify such mask formats as Month or MONTH because the output displays in the same case-sensitive format of either all uppercase, all lowercase, or proper case (that is, JUNE, june, or June).

Using TO_NUMBER

The TO_NUMBER function is similar to the TO_DATE function. This function converts a character string of type CHAR or VARCHAR2 into a number. As with TO_DATE, the format mask is important for a proper conversion.

SYNTAX

TO_NUMBER(*character_string*, *format*, *NLS_Params*)

There are many reasons to convert from a character to a number value. For instance, you decide to store data of type VARCHAR2 for the age when hired. Suppose you want to perform some calculations on the age to determine retirement income and information. Simply use the TO_NUMBER function to change the value to a NUMBER data type and then perform the calculation. It's more efficient to store a number in the CHAR or VARCHAR2 format because most systems store it as a single byte (instead of two bytes with a NUMBER data type), and you do not often perform calculations on this data.

Tip

> If you frequently use a field to perform calculations, never store it as a VARCHAR2 or CHAR because the process to convert it to a number really slows down the system, and other end users will not be too happy!

See Table 6.8 for the available format masks you can pass when using the TO_NUMBER function.

TABLE 6.8 Number Format Elements

Format Element	Samples	Description
9	9999	Each nine is considered a significant digit. Any leading zeros are treated as blanks.
0	09999 or 99990	By adding the 0 as a prefix or suffix to the number, all leading or trailing zeros are treated and displayed as zeros instead of drawing a blank (pun intended). Think of this display type as NUMERIC values, such as 00109.
$	$9999	Prefix of currency symbol printed in the first position.
B	B9999	Returns any portion of the integer as blanks if the integer is 0. This overrides the leading zeros by using a 0 for the format.
MI	9999MI	Automatically adds a space at the end to hold either a minus sign if the value is negative or a placeholder space if the value is positive.
S	S9999 or 9999S	Displays a leading or trailing sign of + if the value is positive and a leading or trailing sign of - if the value is negative.

6

TABLE 6.8 continued

Format Element	Samples	Description
PR	9999PR	If the value is negative, angle brackets (<>) are placed around the number; placeholder spaces are used if the number is positive.
D	99D99	Decimal point location. The nines on both sides reflect the maximum number of digits allowed.
G	9G999G999	Specifies a group separator such as a comma.
C	C99	Returns the ISO currency symbol in the specified position.
L	L9999	Specifies the location of the local currency symbol (such as $).
,	9,999,999	Places a comma in the specified position, regardless of the group separator.
.	99.99	Specifies the location of the decimal point, regardless of the decimal separator.
V	999V99	Returns the number multiplied to the 10n power, where n is the number of nines after the V.
EEEE	9.99EEEE	Returns the value in scientific notation.
RM, rm	RM, rm	Returns the value as uppercase or lowercase Roman numerals.
FM	FM9,999.99	Fill mode: Removes leading and trailing blanks.

After the format mask are several possible NLS parameters:

- NLS_NUMERIC_CHARACTERS—Specifies characters to use for group separators and the decimal point.
- NLS_CURRENCY—Specifies the local currency.
- NLS_ISO_CURRENCY—Characters to represent the ISO currency symbol.

In the examples in this section, you can practice some of these conversions. First, you'll perform a simple character-to-number conversion. Execute the code in Listing 6.11.

INPUT **LISTING 6.11** Converting a Character to an Integer Value

```
1: DECLARE
2:     v_Convert_Number VARCHAR2(20) := '1999';
3:     v_Hold_Number NUMBER ;
4: BEGIN
5:     v_Hold_Number := TO_Number(v_Convert_Number,'9999');
```

```
6:     DBMS_OUTPUT.PUT_LINE('The converted number is: ' || v_Hold_Number);
7:     DBMS_OUTPUT.PUT_LINE('The converted number plus 10 is: ' ||
8:                          (v_Hold_Number+10));
9: END;
```

After executing the PL/SQL block, your output should be

OUTPUT
```
The converted number is: 1999
The converted number plus 10 is: 2009
```

ANALYSIS This block of code simply converts a character integer with a value of 1999 to a number in line 6 and then additionally performs a mathematical calculation to add 10 to the integer in line 7. Without the TO_NUMBER function, you are not able to perform any calculations on characters.

You often need to convert a field in a table from one data type to another. For instance, a real estate company uses Oracle to track its listings. Unfortunately, the house prices were declared as a type VARCHAR2(20). The format entered was always the currency symbol ($) followed by the price, offset in commas. The range of prices can be from $.01 to $999,999,999.99. You can write a function to update a column added to the table, change the data type, and delete the extra column no longer needed. For now, you only need to calculate your commission for some property you just sold. The going commission rate for agents in the area is 6 percent. Listing 6.12 shows the conversion of a VARCHAR2 to a NUMBER and then calculates your commission.

INPUT **LISTING 6.12** Converting a Character Formatted as Currency to an Integer Value

```
1: DECLARE
2:     v_Convert_Number VARCHAR2(20) := '$119,252.75';
3:     v_Hold_Number NUMBER ;
4: BEGIN
5:     v_Hold_Number := TO_Number(v_Convert_Number,'$999,999,999.99');
6:     DBMS_OUTPUT.PUT_LINE('The converted number is: ' || v_Hold_Number);
7:     DBMS_OUTPUT.PUT_LINE('Your commission at 6% is: ' ||
8:                          (v_Hold_Number*.06));
9: END;
10: /
```

6

When you execute this code, your output appears as

OUTPUT
```
The converted number is: 119252.75
Your commission at 6% is: 7155.165
```

ANALYSIS This PL/SQL block has an unusually long format mask. When you convert a number, the format mask must be equal to or greater than the length of the number of characters to convert. Remember, the largest value can be $999,999,999.99, so you should create the format for the largest possible value as demonstrated in line 5. What happens if you break this rule? Enter and then execute the code in Listing 6.13.

INPUT **LISTING 6.13** Errors with the Format Mask

```
 1: DECLARE
 2:     v_Convert_Number VARCHAR2(20) := '$119,252.75';
 3:     v_Hold_Number NUMBER ;
 4: BEGIN
 5:     v_Hold_Number := TO_Number(v_Convert_Number,'$99,999.99');
 6:     DBMS_OUTPUT.PUT_LINE('The converted number is: ' || v_Hold_Number);
 7:     DBMS_OUTPUT.PUT_LINE('Your commission at 6% is: ' ||
 8:                          (v_Hold_Number*.06));
 9: END;
10: /
```

Immediately upon execution of this code, you receive the following errors:

OUTPUT
```
declare
*
ERROR at line 1:
ORA-06502: PL/SQL: numeric or value error
ORA-06512: at line 5
```

How do you handle these errors? Simply look up these errors in the program Oracle Messages and Codes. Then find the ORA-06502 error in the book. The help you receive from Oracle is

```
ORA-06502 PL/SQL: numeric or value errorstring
```

Cause: An arithmetic, numeric, string, conversion, or constraint error occurred. For example, this error occurs if an attempt is made to assign the value NULL to a variable declared NOT NULL, or if an attempt is made to assign an integer larger than 88 to a variable declared NUMBER(2).
Action: Change the data, how it is manipulated, or how it is declared so that values do not violate constraints.

You're probably wondering, "What does all that error code mean?" When you get help on the second error message, you see

```
ORA-06512  at str line num
```

```
Cause:  This is usually the last of a message stack and indicates where
 a problem occurred in the PL/SQL code.
Action:  Fix the problem causing the exception or write an exception
```

handler for this condition. It may be necessary to contact the
application or database administrator.

Copyright (C) 1995, Oracle Corporation

> **Note**
>
> When you look up error messages, make sure that you type the code in the
> same exact manner as displayed. For example, do not type ORA-06502 as
> ORA-6502 because Oracle will never find the match for the error in the help
> file.

When Oracle compiles, it looks for all possible errors. The first error message indicates
that the number assigned to the variable is too large for the mask. Remember, Oracle has
no clue as to your intent. In the case of the error messages, you could have made an
incorrect declaration, or according to the second error message, you did not create a large
enough mask for the function TO_NUMBER.

The last example is a store, which stores all the sales percentages as a VARCHAR2(4) field
in the format 33.33. You need to convert these numbers to their decimal equivalents. Run
the code in Listing 6.14.

INPUT   **LISTING 6.14**   Converting VARCHAR2 Percentage Data to a Decimal Equivalent

```
1: DECLARE
2:      v_Convert_Number VARCHAR2(20) := '33.33';
3:      v_Hold_Number NUMBER ;
4: BEGIN
5:      v_Hold_Number := TO_Number(v_Convert_Number,'999.999999');
6:      DBMS_OUTPUT.PUT_LINE('The converted number is: ' || v_Hold_Number);
7:      DBMS_OUTPUT.PUT_LINE('Your decimal equivalent is: ' ||
8:                          (v_Hold_Number/100));
9: END;
10: /
```

When you execute the code in Listing 6.14, your output should appear as

OUTPUT
```
The converted number is: 33.33
Your decimal equivalent is: .3333
```

ANALYSIS The PL/SQL code in Listing 6.14 is simply a repeat, except that you now divide
the converted number by 100 with the statement in lines 7 and 8 to arrive at the
decimal point.

Always use the TO_NUMBER function if you need to convert characters to numbers for
computations or for changing data types. The next section explains the inverse function
TO_CHAR.

6

Using TO_CHAR for Numbers

Once again, if you can change characters to numbers, you should also be able to change numbers to characters by using the function TO_CHAR.

SYNTAX

TO_CHAR(*number*, *format*, *NLS_Params*)

The format mask and the NLS parameters are identical to those in the TO_NUMBER function. You can review the format masks in Table 6.8. The NLS parameters again are

- NLS_NUMERIC_CHARACTERS—Specifies characters to use for group separators and the decimal point.
- NLS_CURRENCY—Specifies the local currency.
- NLS_ISO_CURRENCY—Characters to represent the ISO currency symbol.

You can make some decent format attempts for numbers in a column. You will print an employee ID number with leading zeros and a total length of 10 characters. Go ahead and try the PL/SQL code in Listing 6.15.

INPUT **LISTING 6.15** Converting Numbers to Characters Formatted as a Numeric String

```
1: DECLARE
2:     v_Convert_Number NUMBER := 90210;
3:     v_Hold_Char VARCHAR2(21) ;
4: BEGIN
5:     v_Hold_Char := TO_CHAR(v_Convert_Number,'0000000000');
6:     DBMS_OUTPUT.PUT_LINE('The employee ID is: ' ¦¦ v_Hold_Char);
7: END;
8: /
```

After executing the PL/SQL code block, your output should appear as

OUTPUT   The employee ID is: 0000090210

ANALYSIS You were able to take a five-digit number, or any NUMBER with a value of 10 digits as specified by the mask in line 5, and pad the number to the left with zeros. The number 90210 becomes 0000090210 because you use 0s for the format mask, which means that zeros should be output instead of blanks.

You can look at some other types of NUMBER formatting. Suppose you are asked to do some work for engineers or scientists. They require you to express the results in scientific notation. This is simply the number converted to however many significant digits to the nth power of 10. The number 1000 is 1.00E+03 because you shift the decimal point to the left three places. You can practice this in Listing 6.16.

LISTING 6.16   Expressing Your Work in Scientific Notation

```
1: DECLARE
2:      v_Convert_Number NUMBER := 90210;
3:      v_Hold_Char VARCHAR2(21) ;
4: BEGIN
5:      v_Hold_Char := TO_CHAR(v_Convert_Number,'9.99EEEE');
6:      DBMS_OUTPUT.PUT_LINE('The Scientific Notation is: ' ¦¦ v_Hold_Char);
7: END;
8: /
```

Your output would appear as

OUTPUT   `The Scientific Notation is: 9.02E+04`

ANALYSIS   Again, 90210 allows you to shift the decimal point to the left four spaces. Because you are taking only two significant digits after the decimal point, the result is `9.02E+04`. Practice formatting numbers. When you are finished, you can continue with performing calculations on dates.

DATE Functions

Oracle provides several built-in date functions to perform many complex date calculations. Oracle holds the true system DATE in the format DD-MM-YYYY to handle all dates from January 1, 4712 BC to December 31, 4712 AD. By that time, you will be working with Oracle version 5000! In addition, Oracle holds the true system TIME in the format HH-MM-SS in 24-hour military format.

SYSDATE

The SYSDATE function returns the current date and time in the Oracle server. Note the distinction that it is the *server* and not the *client's* date and time that is returned. The format for the SYSDATE function is

SYSDATE

That's it! Not only can you get the system DATE and TIME from Oracle, but you also can format it in any way possible, and you can perform calculations on the system DATE and TIME. Refer to Table 6.7 for possible formats. You can begin with the standard output from using SYSDATE from Listing 6.17.

6

LISTING 6.17   Default Output of SYSDATE

```
SELECT SYSDATE from DUAL;
```

Your output should appear similar to

```
SYSDATE
. . . . . . . . . .
21-JUN-99
```

Don't forget that SYSDATE is not a variable but a function that retrieves the date and time from the server. You can add the TO_CHAR function to format the system date and time to something you are more familiar with, as shown in Listing 6.18.

LISTING 6.18   Combining TO_CHAR to Format SYSDATE

```
SELECT TO_CHAR(SYSDATE,'MM/DD/YYYY HH:MM:SS AM')
       "Today's Date and Time" from DUAL;
```

A similar output should look like

```
Today's Date and Time
. . . . . . . . . . . . . . . . . . . . . . . . . . . . . . .
06/21/1999 11:06:21 PM
```

As you can see from the time, the standard programming time of all hours of the night still exists! In the rest of this section, you can practice some of the other built-in DATE functions.

The TRUNC Function

The TRUNC function is useful for returning a truncated DATE or TIME to a specified mask. For instance, you can truncate to the nearest day, month, quarter, century, and so on. The main use of TRUNC is to simply eliminate the time from the SYSDATE by setting all time values for all dates to 12:00 AM.

```
TRUNC(date_passed,truncate mask)
```

To understand the TRUNC function, see Table 6.9, which provides a list of possible values to use with the TRUNC and ROUND functions.

TABLE 6.9 Masks Used with the ROUND and TRUNC Functions

Mask Options	Description
CC, SCC	Rounds or truncates to the century
YYYY, SYYYY, YEAR, SYEAR, YYY, YY, Y	Truncates to the year or rounds up to the next year after July 1st
IYYY, IYY, IY, I	ISO year
Q	Truncates to the quarter or rounds up to the nearest quarter on or after the 16th day of the second month of the quarter
MM, MON, MONTH, RM	Truncates the month or rounds up to the next month on or after the 16th day
DD, DDD, J	Truncates or rounds to the day
WW	Same day of the week as the first day of the year
IW	Same day of the week as the first day of the ISO year
W	Same day of the week as the first day of the month
Day, Dy, D	Truncates or rounds to the first day of the week
HH24, HH12, HH	Truncates to the hour or rounds up to the next hour on or after 30 minutes
MI	Truncates to the minute or rounds up on or after 30 seconds

Now that you have seen all the possible masking options, try the TRUNC function by testing it with different examples. You will first truncate the time from the system date. Remember, you still see the time displayed, but if you use TRUNC on all dates, the time is always 12:10 AM. instead of the time the date was assigned; therefore, all dates can be calculated properly regardless of time. Go ahead and execute the SQL code in Listing 6.19.

INPUT **LISTING 6.19** Removing the Time from SYSDATE

```
1: SELECT TO_CHAR(TRUNC(SYSDATE),'MM/DD/YYYY HH:MM:SS AM')
2:    "Today's Date and Time"
3:    from DUAL;
```

6

Your output appears similar to

OUTPUT
```
Today's Date and Time
---------------------
06/21/1999 12:10:00 AM
```

ANALYSIS Notice that the time element is still displayed, but if you were to subtract two truncated dates with the same time, you get an even number of days. One more observation is that the default for TRUNC is the same as a format mask of DD, which simply eliminates the need to worry about the time in your calculations.

You can test the TRUNC function by truncating the SYSDATE to the nearest quarter by executing the code in Listing 6.20.

INPUT   **LISTING 6.20**   Truncating to the Quarter

```
1: SELECT TO_CHAR(TRUNC(SYSDATE,'Q'),'MM/DD/YYYY HH:MM:SS AM')
2:    "Today's Date and Time"
3:  from DUAL
```

Assuming today's date is 06/01/99, you get the following output:

OUTPUT
```
Today's Date and Time
. . . . . . . . . . . . . . . . . . . . .
04/01/1999 12:10:00 AM
```

ANALYSIS   This result makes sense because June is in the second quarter, and the quarter ranges from 04/01/99 to 06/30/99. Truncating to the quarter gives the beginning date for the applicable quarter. You'll get the opportunity to test this function in the exercises at the end of the lesson.

The ADD_MONTHS Function

The ADD_MONTHS function adds or subtracts months from a date. Because this function is *overloaded*, which means that you can pass different data types to the same function or change the order of the parameters, you can specify the parameters in any order.

SYNTAX

The syntax can be expressed in two ways:

```
ADD_MONTHS(date_passed, months_to_add)
ADD_MONTHS(months_to_add, date_passed)
```

If *months_to_add* is positive, it adds months into the future. If the *months_to_add* number is negative, it subtracts months from *date_passed*. You can specify *months_to_add* as a fraction, but Oracle completely ignores the fraction. You can indicate the day level by using other Oracle functions. Another caution is that Oracle returns the same day in the resulting calculation except when the last day in one month (for example, March 31st) and the resulting month do not have as many days. (For example, April 30th is the answer to adding one month.) The following three examples in Listing 6.21 provide the same result.

INPUT   **LISTING 6.21**   Adding Two Months to SYSDATE

```
1: SELECT ADD_MONTHS(SYSDATE,2) from DUAL;
2: SELECT ADD_MONTHS(SYSDATE,2.654) from DUAL;
```

All of these (assuming the date is 06/02/99) produce the following output:

OUTPUT
```
ADD_MONTH
- - - - - - - - -
02-AUG-99
```

You can see what happens for the last day of the month by adding one month to March
31st, as shown in Listing 6.22.

INPUT   **LISTING 6.22** Adding One Month

```
SELECT ADD_MONTHS(TO_DATE('31-MAR-99'),1) from DUAL;
```

This example has the output

OUTPUT
```
ADD_MONTH
- - - - - - - - -
30-APR-99
```

Oracle could not output April 31st because no such date exists.

The NEXT_DAY Function

The NEXT_DAY function returns the next date in the week for the day of the week specified after the input date. The time returned is the time specified by the input date when
called.

SYNTAX
```
NEXT_DAY(input_date_passed, day_name)
```

ANALYSIS   The NEXT_DAY function offers a lot of possibilities. You can calculate anything
from the first Monday of every month to each payday in a calendar year. You'll
start by testing the NEXT_DAY function on the SYSDATE function to find the next Monday.
Assume the SYSDATE is June 3, 1999. Your own results will differ when you execute the
code in Listing 6.23.

6

INPUT   **LISTING 6.23** Finding the First Monday After the Current Date and Time

```
1: SELECT TO_CHAR(NEXT_DAY(SYSDATE,'Monday'),'MM/DD/YYYY HH:MM:SS AM')
2:      "Next_Day"
3:  from DUAL;
```

The result returned for the SYSDATE of June 3, 1999 is

OUTPUT
```
Next_Day
.......................
06/07/1999 07:06:38 AM
```

ANALYSIS The first Monday after the date is June 7, 1999. Because you are using the SYSDATE, the corresponding time value is returned when the function is called.

You can find the first Monday for August 1999 by executing the code in Listing 6.24.

INPUT **LISTING 6.24** Finding the First Monday in the Month of August

```
1: SELECT TO_CHAR(NEXT_DAY('01-AUG-99','Monday'),'MM/DD/YYYY HH:MM:SS AM')
2:      "Next_Day"
3:   from DUAL;
```

Your output is

OUTPUT
```
Next_Day
.......................
08/02/1999 12:00:00 AM
```

ANALYSIS Although the first Monday in August *is* 08/02/99, is there a logic problem here? If you repeat the example but use a month in which Monday is the first day of the month, what happens? Execute the code in Listing 6.25.

INPUT **LISTING 6.25** Finding the First Monday in the Month of September

```
1: SELECT TO_CHAR(NEXT_DAY('01-SEP-99','Monday'),'MM/DD/YYYY HH:MM:SS AM')
2:      "Next_Day"
3:   from DUAL;
```

Your output is

OUTPUT
```
Next_Day
.......................
09/06/1999 12:00:00 AM
```

ANALYSIS The result is definitely not what you had in mind! The NEXT_DAY function returns the next day of the day specified. If the day of the week specified matches the input date, it adds one week to the input date. If you want to calculate the first occurrence of any day in the month, always use the end date of the previous month. Review the proper code in Listing 6.26.

INPUT **LISTING 6.26**   The Proper Method to Find the First Monday in a Given
Month

```
1: SELECT TO_CHAR(NEXT_DAY('31-AUG-99','Monday'),'MM/DD/YYYY HH:MM:SS AM')
2:      "Next_Day"
3:  from DUAL;
```

Your output is

OUTPUT
```
Next_Day
---------------------
09/01/1999 12:00:00 AM
```

You finally have the proper logic for what you intended to find.

The LAST_DAY Function

The LAST_DAY function provides the last day of the given month. A useful purpose is to
determine how many days are left in the given month.

SYNTAX

LAST_DAY(*input_date_passed*)

You will compute the last days in the month when summer officially starts from 1999.
Execute the code in Listing 6.27.

INPUT   **LISTING 6.27**   Finding the Last Day of the Month Starting Summer

```
1: SELECT TO_CHAR(LAST_DAY('30-JUN-99'),'MM/DD/YYYY HH:MM:SS AM') "Last_Day"
2:  from DUAL;
```

Your output is

OUTPUT
```
Last_Day
---------------------
06/30/1999 12:06:00 AM
```

ANALYSIS   I purposefully used the last day of the month to illustrate an important fact.
Unlike NEXT_DAY, which adds one week if the day of the week specified is the
same as the input date, the LAST_DAY function always returns the last day of the month
even if the input date is the same.

You can take this one step further and see how many days of summer exist in the month
of June by subtracting the last day of the month by the start date of summer. Execute
Listing 6.28 to see the result.

6

INPUT   **LISTING 6.28**   Calculating the Number of Days of Summer in June

```
1: SELECT LAST_DAY('20-JUN-99') "Last_Day",
2:            LAST_DAY('20-JUN-99') - TO_DATE('20-JUN-99') "Days_Summer"
3:      from DUAL;
```

Your output is

OUTPUT
```
Last_Day  Days_Summer
--------------------
30-JUN-99           10
```

The MONTHS_BETWEEN Function

The MONTHS_BETWEEN function returns the number of months between two given dates. If the day is the same in both months, you get an integer value returned. If the day is different, you get a fractional result based upon a 31-day month. If the second date is prior to the first date, the result is negative.

```
MONTHS_BETWEEN(input_date1,input_date2)
```

You can see all the possible returned values by executing the code in Listing 6.29.

INPUT   **LISTING 6.29**   Experimenting with MONTHS_BETWEEN

```
1: SELECT MONTHS_BETWEEN('25-DEC-99','02-JUN-99') "Fractional",
2:            MONTHS_BETWEEN('02-FEB-99','02-JUN-99') "Integer"
3:      from DUAL;
```

Your output is

OUTPUT
```
Fractional   Integer
----------  --------
6.7419355        -4
```

Tip

Who cares about seeing the fractional part of a 31-day month? To convert the fraction to days, simply multiply the TRUNC value of the fractional part by 31. If you want to display the month, use TRUNC on this value.

The NEW_TIME Function

Have you ever wondered what time it is in Germany? Would your phone call wake up your friend in the middle of the night? The NEW_TIME function enables you to find out the time in the time zones listed in Table 6.10 by simply passing the date and time of the first zone and specifying the second zone.

```
NEW_TIME(input_date and time, time_zone1, time_zone2)
```

See Table 6.10 for the valid time zones.

TABLE 6.10 Time Zones

Time Zone Abbreviation	Time Zone Description
AST	Atlantic Standard Time
ADT	Atlantic Daylight Savings Time
BST	Bering Standard Time
BDT	Bering Daylight Savings Time
CST	Central Standard Time
CDT	Central Daylight Savings Time
EST	Eastern Standard Time
EDT	Eastern Daylight Savings Time
GMT	Greenwich Mean Time (the date line!)
HST	Alaska-Hawaii Standard Time
HDT	Alaska-Hawaii Daylight Savings Time
MST	Mountain Standard Time
MDT	Mountain Daylight Savings Time
NST	Newfoundland Standard Time
PST	Pacific Standard Time
PDT	Pacific Daylight Savings Time
YST	Yukon Standard Time
YDT	Yukon Daylight Savings Time

You can compute the date and time difference between Chicago and Los Angeles by specifying Central Daylight Time to Pacific Daylight Time. Enter and execute the code in Listing 6.30.

INPUT   **LISTING 6.30**   Time Change from Chicago to Los Angeles

```
1: SELECT TO_CHAR(NEW_TIME(TO_DATE('060299 01:00:00 AM',
2:            'MMDDYY HH:MI:SS AM'),
3:            'CDT','PDT'), 'DD-MON-YY HH:MI:SS AM') "Central to Pacific"
4:    from DUAL;
```

Tip | Remember, minutes are expressed as MI, not MM. This is a common mistake!

Your output is

OUTPUT
```
Central to Pacific
---------------------
01-JUN-99 11:00:00 PM
```

ANALYSIS   Because there is a two-hour time difference, you not only see the revised time, but also the revised date. I guess you truly can go back in time!

Tip | In a database that traverses time zones, you might want to store the time and date for all entries in one standardized time zone, along with the time zone abbreviation from the original time zone. This arrangement saves you a lot of time and coding when designing the database.

The ROUND Function

ROUND is similar to the TRUNC function. In fact, it uses the same format mask as TRUNC in Table 6.9. This function enables you to round up or down based upon the format mask. The default mask when specifying a DATE value is DD. Some useful purposes for this are

- Rounding to the nearest minute for billing cellular-based calls
- Rounding to closest month to determine a pay period

SYNTAX

ROUND(*input_date and time or number*, *rounding_specification*)

You can practice rounding to the nearest minute to charge people who use cellular phones by entering the code in Listing 6.31.

INPUT   **LISTING 6.31**   Rounding to the Nearest Minute

```
1: SELECT TO_CHAR(ROUND(TO_DATE('060299 01:00:35 AM',
2:           'MMDDYY HH:MI:SS AM'),
3:           'MI'), 'DD-MON-YY HH:MI:SS AM') "Rounded to nearest Minute"
4:      from DUAL;
```

Your output is

OUTPUT
```
Rounded to nearest Minute
-------------------------
02-JUN-99 01:01:00 AM  10
```

ANALYSIS   Because the seconds were 30 or greater, this example rounded to the next minute at 1:01 from 1:00. Had the number of seconds been 22, the return value would be 1:00. You should test this code on your own.

The TRIM Function

The TRIM function truncates leading and trailing characters from a specified string. This is equivalent to using the LTRIM and RTRIM functions simultaneously.

SYNTAX

TRIM (*trim location*, *trim character* FROM *trim source*)

You can practice the TRIM function to remove leading and trailing zeroes from a specified number by entering the code in Listing 6.32.

INPUT   **LISTING 6.32**   TRIM Leading and Trailing Zeroes

```
SELECT TRIM (0 FROM 067270676800) "TRIM Example"
FROM DUAL;
```

Your output is

OUTPUT
```
TRIM Example
------------
672706768
```

6

ANALYSIS   The TRIM function lets us remove all unwanted leading and trailing zeroes from the specified number.

Summary

Today, you discovered only a fraction of Oracle's powerful built-in functions. Today's lesson stressed the importance of converting data and working with dates. I highly recommend that you refer to Appendix B to review the rest of the functions. A final tip: Punctuation is important!

Q&A

Q Are all the functions available within PL/SQL?

A No. Several functions can be used in SQL only. Refer to Appendix B.

Q Must I use Oracle's built-in functions?

A No. You can always create your own similar functions, but when speed is of the essence, why reinvent the wheel? Use the built-in functions whenever possible.

Q What date does the Julian system start counting from?

A January 1, 4712 BC.

Q When using TO_DATE, is the format mask important?

A Not just a little bit important, but very important and required! Without the proper format mask, you will most certainly get an Oracle error message.

Q How long should the number format mask be?

A At least equal to or greater than the length of the largest value.

Q What function allows you to perform mathematical computations on character strings?

A TO_NUMBER converts character strings to numbers so that you can perform any mathematical calculations you want.

Q Where does the SYSDATE date and time originate?

A If you are using Personal Oracle, the system date and time come from the PC's internal clock. If you are in a client/server environment, the system date and time are pulled from the server.

Workshop

Use the following workshop to test your ability to understand and use several of Oracle's built-in functions. The answers to the quiz and exercises appear in Appendix A, "Answers."

Quiz

1. True or False: All functions are accessible within PL/SQL.
2. What function do I use to combine two strings together?
3. What function converts '11/28/99' to an Oracle DATE?
4. In a VARCHAR2 string, each string can be a variable length. What function do you use to determine the length so that you can search through the entire string?

5. How do you get rid of padded spaces to the right of a string in Oracle?

6. To determine the remainder, you use the _____ function.

7. To determine how many months a customer is delinquent, you can use the _____ function.

8. You can use the TRUNC and ROUND functions with what data types?

Exercises

1. Create a PL/SQL block that reads in the month of a date and displays the month in a Roman numeral format. Use a date of 06/11/67. This allows you to practice the TO_CHAR function. When printing the Roman numeral equivalent, use LTRIM to remove any spaces padded to the left of the Roman numeral. If you are really ambitious, on your own you can create the same RM-type function by using IF...THEN...ELSE statements for practice from Day 4. Remember, practice helps to solidify your knowledge through repetition and understanding.

2. Use the TRUNC function on the SYSDATE to round to the nearest century.

3. Use CONCAT to link two strings together. Repeat the same line by using ¦¦ instead of CONCAT.

4. Calculate the number of days between 01/01/97 to 03/31/97. Remember to use the TRUNC function to eliminate the TIME dependency.

5. Convert the CHARACTER string '06/11/67' to a date, and subtract from 06/11/97 to see how old your author is (and holding).

6. Calculate how many months are between 05/15/97 and 08/22/97.

7. Round the SYSDATE to the nearest century.

8. Calculate the time in Newfoundland from Central Standard Time from 02-22-97, 05:00 AM.

9. From Listing 6.22, subtract one month and explain the answer.

10. Calculate the number of days until Christmas from the last day of the month of today's date. (We don't get paid until the end of the month!)

6

DAY 7

Procedures, Packages, Errors, and Exceptions

by Tom Luers

Procedures and packages enable you to organize your program code into logical groups for easier maintenance and implementation. Additionally, these groups have built-in error trapping to prevent the code from abnormally stopping during processing. In today's lesson on procedures, packages, errors, and exceptions, you will learn about

- Creating procedures
- Invoking stored procedures
- Invoking rights for procedure
- Creating packages
- Trapping errors and exceptions

Using Procedures

NEW TERM   A *procedure* is a logically grouped set of SQL and PL/SQL statements that perform a specific task. It's a miniature self-contained program. A *stored procedure*
is a procedure that has been compiled and stored inside the database. Once stored the
procedure is a *schema* object (that is, a specific database object).

Procedures have several parts. The declarative part contains declarations of types, cursors,
constants, variables, exceptions, and nested subprograms. Procedures can be declared in
PL/SQL blocks, packages, and other procedures. The executable part contains statements
that control execution and manipulate data. Occasionally, the procedure might contain an
exception-handling part to deal with exceptions raised during execution. Procedures can be
defined and executed by using any Oracle tool that supports PL/SQL, such as SQL*Plus.

Why Use Procedures?

Procedures are created to solve a specific problem or task. PL/SQL procedures offer the
following advantages:

- In PL/SQL, you can tailor a procedure to suit your specific requirements.
- Procedures are modular, which means they let you break a program down into
  manageable, well-defined units.
- Because procedures are stored in a database, they are reusable. After a procedure
  has been validated, it can be used over and over, without being recompiled or distributed over the network.
- Procedures improve database security. You can restrict database access by allowing
  users to access data only through stored procedures.
- Procedures take advantage of shared memory resources.

Procedures Versus Functions

Procedures and functions are PL/SQL subprograms that are stored in the database. The
significant difference between the two is simply the types of output the two objects generate. A function returns a single value, whereas a procedure is used to perform complicated processing when you want a substantial amount of information back.

Creating Procedures

The CREATE PROCEDURE command creates a procedure. The following syntax box shows
the proper form of the CREATE PROCEDURE command.

The Syntax for the CREATE PROCEDURE Command

SYNTAX

```
CREATE OR REPLACE PROCEDURE procedure_name
(arguments)
AS
[pl/sql body code]
```

In this syntax, the keywords and parameters are as follows:

- OR REPLACE—An optional keyword. I strongly suggest you always use this keyword because it re-creates the procedure if it already exists. You can use this keyword to change an existing procedure without having to drop and re-create the procedure.
- procedure_name—The name you assign to the procedure being created.
- arguments—The arguments in the procedure, which can be the following:
    - in—Specifies that you must pass a value to the subprogram being called. The in parameter might not be assigned a value because it acts like a constant. The actual value that corresponds to the parameter can be a constant, a literal, an initialized variable, or an expression.
    - out—Specifies that the procedure returns a value to the calling program. This parameter acts like an uninitialized parameter; therefore, its value cannot be assigned to another variable. The actual value that corresponds to the parameter must be a variable. It cannot be a literal, a constant, or an expression. Within your subprogram, the out parameter must be assigned a value.
        - inout—Specifies that you must pass a value to the procedure and that the procedure returns a value to its calling environment after execution.
- pl/sql body code—The logic of the procedure. There must be at least one PL/SQL statement, or an error occurs.

The code shown in Listing 7.1 creates a simple stored procedure named emp_change_s. This procedure accepts one argument, the emp_id parameter.

INPUT **LISTING 7.1** Creating a Stored Procedure

```
CREATE OR REPLACE PROCEDURE emp_change_s (i_emp_id IN integer)

AS BEGIN
UPDATE employee
set pay_type = "S"
WHERE emp_id =  i_emp_id;
END emp_change_s;
```

7

In this sample code, you have created a procedure that is stored in the database. This procedure is named `emp_change_s` and can accept one parameter, `emp_id`. When this procedure is stored in the database, you can invoke the program via any other PL/SQL block. To see the effect of this procedure, first select the rows from the employee table prior to running this procedure. Then run the procedure and re-select the rows from the table. The records are now updated.

Normally, procedures are created as standalone schema objects. However, you can create a procedure as part of a package; this topic is discussed later in this lesson, in the section "Exploring Packages."

The RETURN Statement

The RETURN statement causes a subprogram to immediately complete its execution and return to the calling program. Execution in the calling program resumes with the statement following the procedure call.

In procedures, the RETURN statement cannot contain an expression. Its sole purpose is to return control to the calling program before the end of the procedure is reached.

Procedure Dependencies

One of the inherent features of Oracle is that it checks the database to make sure that the operations of a procedure, function, or package are possible based on the objects the user has access to. For example, if you have a procedure that requires access to several tables and views, Oracle checks during compilation time to see if those tables and views are present and available to the user. The procedure is said to be *dependent* on these tables and views.

 Caution

Oracle automatically recompiles all dependent objects when you explicitly recompile the parent object. This automatic recompilation of dependent objects happens when the dependent object is called. Therefore, you should not recompile a parent module in a production system: It causes all dependent objects to recompile and consequently can cause performance problems for your production system.

You can discover object dependencies in several different ways. You can examine the procedure or function code and determine which database objects it depends on. Or you can talk with the database administrator (DBA) and examine the schema to identify dependencies. Finally, you can run the Oracle `utldtree.sql` script, which generates a temporary table and a view that lets you see the objects that are dependent on a given object. This script generates a listing only for the objects to which you have access.

Recompiling Stored Procedures

To explicitly recompile a stored procedure, issue the ALTER PROCEDURE command. This command must be used only on standalone stored procedures and not on procedures that are part of the package.

Recompiling a procedure does not change the procedure's declaration or definition. You must use CREATE PROCEDURE with the OR REPLACE clause to do these things. If Oracle successfully recompiles a procedure, then the procedure becomes a valid procedure that can be executed without runtime compilation. If compilation fails, the procedure becomes invalid and must be debugged.

You can use the ALTER PROCEDURE command to explicitly recompile a procedure that is invalid. After a procedure is compiled, it does not need to be recompiled implicitly during runtime processes. This leads to reduced overhead and elimination of runtime compilation errors.

You can produce debugging information from within an application by issuing the PUT or PUT_LINE commands. These commands place the debugging information into a buffer that was created by the DBMS_OUTPUT package. To display the contents of the buffer, type the SET SERVEROUTPUT ON command at the SQL*Plus prompt.

The code in Listing 7.2 illustrates the PUT_LINE command line that you can include inside a procedure.

INPUT   **LISTING 7.2**   The PUT_LINE Command Within a Procedure

```
CREATE OR REPLACE PROCEDURE emp_change_s (i_emp_id IN integer)

AS BEGIN
UPDATE employee
set pay_type = "S"
WHERE emp_id =  i_emp_id;
PUT_LINE ('New Pay Type = ' ¦¦ pay_type);            -- debug Line
END emp_change_s;
```

The following statements are issued at the SQL*Plus command line to execute the parts procedure and to display the debugging information:

INPUT
```
SQL> execute user_01.emp_change_s
SQL> execute user_01.emp_change_s
```

The following are the results of these statements being executed. This information is generated from the dba_output buffer area:

OUTPUT   New Pay Type = S

ANALYSIS In this example, the `emp_change_s` procedure was created and then executed. During its invocation, one parameter was passed. During its execution, this procedure simply displayed the current `Pay Type` value, created the new `Pay Type` value, and displayed it.

Re-creating and Modifying Procedures

A valid standalone procedure cannot be altered; it must be either replaced with a new definition or dropped and re-created. For example, you cannot just slightly alter one of the PL/SQL statements in the procedure. Instead, you must re-create the procedure with the modification.

When replacing a procedure, you must include the `OR REPLACE` clause in the `CREATE PROCEDURE` statement. The `OR REPLACE` clause is used to replace an older version of a procedure with a newer version of the procedure. This replacement keeps all grants in place; therefore, you do not have to re-create the grants. *Grants* are statements which when executed allow certain privileges to be given to the object of the grant. However, if you drop the procedure and re-create it, the grants are dropped and consequently have to be rebuilt. If you attempt a `CREATE PROCEDURE` command for a procedure that already exists, Oracle generates an error message.

Listing 7.3 re-creates the procedure named `parts`.

INPUT **LISTING 7.3** Re-creating a Procedure By Using `OR REPLACE`

```
CREATE OR REPLACE PROCEDURE emp_change_s (i_emp_id IN integer)
AS BEGIN
UPDATE employee
set pay_type = "S"
WHERE emp_id =  i_emp_id;
END emp_change_s;
```

Invoking Stored Procedures

You can invoke procedures from many different environments, including SQL*Plus and Oracle*Forms. Also, you can invoke procedures from within another procedure or trigger.

For example, the procedure `parts_sum` can be called from another procedure or trigger, with the following statement:

INPUT
```
DECLARE
    qty        number;
    wip_nbr    number;
    ...                         -- other PL/SQL block code
    ...
    BEGIN
```

```
        emp_change_s(2);        --calls the emp_change_s procedure
    ...                         -- remainder of PL/SQL block
```

ANALYSIS This example is an illustration of how you can call a stored procedure and pass parameters. In this case, the stored procedure sum is called with parameters qty and wip_nbr. You can see this in the line of code immediately after the BEGIN statement. When the stored procedure is invoked and successfully runs, control of the program is returned to the next line of code immediately following the procedure invocation line.

Another example of the same procedure being executed from within SQL*Plus is the following:

INPUT `SQL> execute emp_change_s (2);`

The following example shows a procedure being called from within a precompiler program:

OUTPUT
```
exec sql execute
BEGIN
parts_sum(qty, :wip_nbr)
END
END-exec
```

ANALYSIS This is a fairly common and simple method for executing a stored procedure. You will probably use this approach frequently during your developments efforts.

Using Parameters

  Procedures use *parameters* (that is, variables or expressions) to pass information. When a parameter is being passed to a procedure, it is known as an *actual parameter*. Parameters declared internal to a procedure are known as *internal,* or *formal,* parameters.

The actual parameter and its corresponding formal parameter must belong to compatible datatypes. For example, PL/SQL cannot convert an actual parameter with the datatype DATE to a formal parameter with the datatype LONG. In this case, Oracle would return an error message. This compatibility issue also applies to the return values.

Parameter Definitions

When you invoke a procedure, you must pass it a value for each of the procedure's parameters. If you pass values to the parameter, they are positional and must appear in the same order as they appear in the procedure declaration. If you pass argument names, they can appear in any order. You can have a combination of values and names in the argument values. If this is the case, the values identified in order must precede the argument names.

Listing Stored Procedure Information

Oracle provides several data dictionary views that provide information about procedures that are currently stored in a schema:

7

- `all_errors`—A list of current errors on all objects accessible to the user
- `all_source`—The text source of all stored objects accessible to the user
- `user_objects`—A list of all the objects the current user has access to
- `dba_errors`—Current errors on all stored objects in the database
- `dba_object_size`—All PL/SQL objects in the database
- `dba_source`—The text source of all stored objects in the database
- `user_errors`—The current errors on all a user's stored objects
- `user_source`—The text source of all stored objects belonging to the user
- `user_object_size`—The user's PL/SQL objects

The code in Listing 7.4 queries the `user_errors` view to obtain information about the current errors on a procedure owned by `user_01`.

INPUT/ OUTPUT   **LISTING 7.4**   Viewing Errors in a Database

```
SELECT LINE, TYPE, NAME, TEXT from user_errors

LINE  TYPE   NAME    TEXT
----- ------ ------- ------------------------------------
   4  PROC   PST_QTY PL/SQL-00387: into variable cannot be a database object
                     PL/SQL: SQL statement ignored
```

ANALYSIS   The `user_errors` database table is a great debugging tool. In this example, you can see that the stored procedure has an error in line 4 and more specifically with the variable `PST_QTY`.

Additionally, you can select from the `user_objects` table and interrogate which objects are invalid and need to be recompiled. `User_objects` is a database table which comes by default with your database. It contains information about all objects owned by a specific user. Executing the following piece of code via SQL*PLUS produces the object names and their types for the database objects that need to be evaluated for recompilation:

INPUT
```
SELECT object_name, object_type
from user_objects
WHERE status = 'INVALID';
```

OUTPUT
```
Object_Name       Object_Type

Emp_change_h      Procedure
```

   In this example, the procedure named `emp_change_h` is listed in the `user_objects` table as invalid. `Emp_change_h` is a procedure that I have made up to illustrate this table. It will not show up in your exercise. Now the developer knows which object is invalid and can correct it. For other databases, you may see other objects listed as well.

Dropping a Stored Procedure

You can issue the SQL statement DROP procedure to drop a procedure object.

NEW TERM   In the Oracle environment, the term *drop* means to delete that object from the database.

The following statement drops the procedure emp_change_s:

INPUT

```
DROP PROCEDURE emp_change_s;
```

OUTPUT

```
Procedure dropped.
```

ANALYSIS   In this example, the DROP command deletes the procedure named emp_change_s from the database. This is a permanent move and can not be undone. The only way to bring this procedure back is to re-create it with the create procedure command.

Overloading Procedures

NEW TERM   Oracle permits you to call the same procedure name in a package but with different arguments. This is known as *overloading*. This technique is very useful, especially when you want to execute the same procedure several times, but with arguments that have different datatypes. One example of using procedure overloading is with the package DBMS_OUTPUT, in which the PUT_LINE procedure is called numerous times to produce output lines of different datatypes.

The following example illustrates the definition of two overloaded local procedures:

```
DECLARE
PROCEDURE compute_sales (begin_date in date) RETURN boolean   -- 1st example of
procedure is
BEGIN
RETURN begin_date > :start_date;
END;

PROCEDURE compute_sales (sales_in in date) RETURN boolean     -- overloaded
example of procedure is
BEGIN
RETURN sales_in > :sales_target;
END;
```

When the PL/SQL engine encounters a call to compute_sales, the compiler executes the module in the body that has the correct and matching module header.

Using Recursive Procedures

NEW TERM   A *recursive procedure* is a procedure that calls itself. Each recursive call creates a new instance of any object declared in the procedure, including parameters, variables, cursors, and exceptions. Also, new instances of SQL statements are created at each level in the recursive procedure.

7

With recursive logic, the procedure must be able to terminate itself at some pre-defined point, or the recursion would last forever. This point of termination is defined in a *terminating condition*.

The following code example uses a conditional statement to terminate the recursive cycle:

```
FUNCTION inv_calc
BEGIN
IF qty = > :max_qty THEN                    -- terminating condition;
RETURN 1;
ELSE
RETURN qty * inv_calc (qty * :part_qty); -- recursive call
...
END IF
END inv_calc;
```

ANALYSIS In this example, the function inv_calc calls itself continuously until max_qty is reached. When max-qty is reached, recursion stops and the function returns 1.

It's important to be careful with recursion and where you place the recursive call. If you place the recursive call inside a cursor FOR loop or between OPEN and CLOSE statements, a cursor is opened at each call. This can open enough cursors to violate the maximum allowable open cursors permitted by the OPEN_CURSOR initialization parameter.

Procedure Invocation Security

When executing a stored procedure, Oracle verifies that you have the necessary privileges to do so. If you do not have the appropriate execution permissions, an error occurs. The primary way you grant execution privileges to a user is via the Oracle Role. Oracle evaluates and uses roles in different ways, depending the type of PL/SQL block (named or anonymous) and the type of rights of the user (invoker or definer).

As you learned on Day 2, "Writing Declarations and Blocks," an anonymous block is one that is not part of a formal block, such as a procedure or function, and a named block is one that is part of a formal block.

Like functions, definer and invoker rights dictate the security of procedure invocation. By default, the function executes with the same privileges as the function definer, not the function invoker. These definer rights are bound to the schema in which it resides. You can fully qualify the object names in the PL/SQL statements so that you can modify tables in other schemas. However, be aware that this limits the portability of your code. Oracle allows you to call functions with invoker rights. In this case, you are not bound to one schema, but you are bound by the privileges of the caller. You can use the INVOKER rights via the AUTHID clause.

All roles are disabled in any named PL/SQL block (that is, stored procedure, function, or trigger) that executes with definer rights. Roles are not used for privilege checking and you cannot set roles within a definer-rights procedure. The SESSION_ROLES view shows all roles that are currently enabled. If a named PL/SQL block that executes with definer rights queries SESSION_ROLES, the query does not return any rows.

Named PL/SQL blocks that execute with invoker rights and anonymous PL/SQL blocks are executed based on privileges granted through enabled roles. Current roles are used for privilege checking within an invoker-rights PL/SQL block, and you can use dynamic SQL to set a role in the session.

Exploring Packages

New Term A *package* is an encapsulated collection of related schema objects. These objects can include procedures, functions, variables, constants, cursors, and exceptions. A package is compiled and then stored in the database's data dictionary as a schema object. A common use for packages is to package together all procedures, functions, and other related objects that perform similar tasks. For example, you might want to group all account billable objects in one package and accounts receivable objects in a different package.

New Term The packages contain stored subprograms, or standalone programs, which are called the package's *subprograms*. These subprograms can be called from another stored program, triggers, precompiler programs, or any of the interactive Oracle programs, such as SQL*Plus. Unlike the stored subprograms, the package itself cannot be called or nested, and parameters cannot be passed to it.

New Term A package usually has two components to it: a specification and a body. The *specification* declares the types, variables, constants, exceptions, cursors, and subprograms that are available for use. The *body* fully defines cursors, functions, and procedures and so implements the specification.

Why Use Packages?

Packages offer the following advantages:

- They enable you to organize your application development more efficiently into modules. Each package is easily understood, and the interfaces between packages are simple, clear, and well defined.
- They allow you to grant privileges efficiently.
- A package's public variables and cursors persist for the duration of the session. Therefore, all cursors and procedures that execute in this environment can share them.
- They enable you to perform overloading on procedures and functions.

7

- They improve performance by loading multiple objects into memory at once. Therefore, subsequent calls to related subprograms in the package require no input/output.
- They promote code reuse through the use of libraries that contain stored procedures and functions, thereby eliminating redundant coding.

Do	Don't
DO keep packages simple and general to promote their reuse in future applications. **DO** design the package body after you design the application. Place only those objects that you want visible to all users in the package specification.	**DON'T** write packages that replicate existing Oracle functionality. **DON'T** place too many items in the package specification; specifically, avoid placing in the package specification items that need to be compiled. Changes to a package body do not require Oracle to recompile dependent procedures. However, changes to the specification of a package require Oracle to recompile every stored subprogram that references the package.

The Package Specification

The package specification contains public declarations of the name of the package and the names and datatypes of any arguments. This declaration is local to the database and global to the package. This means that the declared objects in the package are accessible from anywhere in the package. Therefore, all the information the application needs to execute a stored subprogram is contained in the package specification.

The Syntax for the CREATE PACKAGE Specification Command

▼ SYNTAX

```
CREATE [OR REPLACE] PACKAGE package_name
[AUTHID {CURRENT_USER | DEFINER}] {IS | AS}
[package body object declaration]
END [package_name];
```

In this syntax, the keywords and parameters are as follows:

- *package name* is the name of the package the creator defines. It is important to give it a name that is meaningful and represents the contents of the package.
- AUTHID represents the type of rights you want invoked when the package is executed. The rights may be those of the *CURRENT_USER* or of those of the package *DEFINER* (creator).
- *package body object declaration* is where you list the objects that will be created within the package.

▲

The following is an example of a package declaration. In this example, the specification declares a function and two procedures. Then the package body contains the actual logic for the items declared in the specification:

INPUT
```
CREATE PACKAGE employee_maint
AS
Procedure emp_change_s (I_emp_id IN intger);
Procedure emp_change_h (I_emp_id IN integer);
Function emp_rate (rate number)
RETURN number;
End employee_maint;
```

ANALYSIS The package `employee_maint` is first defined in the package declaration. This declaration makes the existence of the package known to the domain of the database instance. Hence it can be called by any program in the instance that also has the appropriate access rights.

Sometimes a specification declares only variables, constants, and exceptions, and therefore, a package body is not necessary. This is a great method to use when defining global variables that you want to be persistent during a session.

The following example is a package specification for a package that does not have a package body:

INPUT
```
CREATE PACKAGE inv_costings         -- package specification header
AUTHID DEFINER                      -- invokes definer rights when executed
is

type inv_rec is record
(part_name varchar2(30),
part_price number,
part_cost number);

price number;
qty   number;
no_cost exception;
cost_or exception;
```

ANALYSIS This package header declares the package. When executed, this package runs with the privileges of the invoker and not with the privileges of the creator. Additionally, this package simply creates variables for use in other parts of the package and does not have any package body. This is a common technique when you want to create and control variables in a single and central location.

The Package Body

The body of a package contains the definition of the public objects you declare in the specification. The body also contains other object declarations that are private to the package. The objects declared privately in the package body are not accessible to other objects outside the package. Unlike the package specification, the declaration portion of the package body can contain subprogram bodies.

> **Note**
>
> Remember that if the specification declares only constants and variables, the package body is not necessary.

After the package is written, applications can reference its types, call its subprograms, use its cursor, or raise its exceptions. After the package is created, it is stored in the database for general use.

Creating Packages

The first step to creating a package is to create its specification. The specification publicly declares the schema objects that are continued in the body of the package.

The Syntax for the CREATE PACKAGE Body Command

```
CREATE [OR REPLACE] PACKAGE BODY package_name   {IS ¦ AS}
[package body object declaration]
BEGIN
programming statements
END [package_name];
```

In this syntax, the keywords and parameters are as follows:

- *package name* is the name of the package the creator defines. It is important to give it a name that is meaningful and represents the contents of the package body.

- *package body object declaration* is where you list the objects that will be created within the package.

- *programming statements* represents the logic for a particular package body.

In the following examples, I will illustrate the entire process to create the package specification and body. To create a specification, issue the CREATE PROCEDURE command:

INPUT
```
CREATE PACKAGE employee_maint
AS
Procedure emp_change_s (I_emp_id IN intger);
Procedure emp_change_h (I_emp_id IN integer);
End employee_maint;
```

ANALYSIS Note that the OR REPLACE clause is used here. This clause re-creates the package specification without losing any grants that already exist.

After the specification is created, you create the body of the package, which is a collection of schema objects declared in the specification. These objects, or package subprograms, are accessible outside the package only if their specifications are included in the package specification.

In addition to the object definitions for the declaration, the package body can also contain private declarations. These private objects are for the internal workings of the package and are local in scope. External objects cannot reference or call internal declarations to another package.

If you perform any initialization in the package body, it is executed once, when the package is initially referenced.

The following is an example of the body of the package from the previous example's specification:

INPUT

```
CREATE OR REPLACE PACKAGE BODY employee_maint
AS
Procedure emp_change_s (I_emp_id IN integer)
BEGIN
UPDATE employee
set pay_type = "S"
WHERE emp_id =  i_emp_id;
END emp_change_s;

Procedure emp_change_h (I_emp_id IN integer)
BEGIN
UPDATE employee
set pay_type = "H"
WHERE emp_id =  i_emp_id;
END emp_change_h;

END employee_maint;
```

ANALYSIS   The final part of the procedure body in this example is the package initialization. By definition, this runs only once, when the procedure is referenced the first time.

Calling Package Subprograms

When a package is invoked, Oracle performs three steps to execute it:

1. Verify user access—Confirms that the user has the execute system privilege grant for the subprogram.
2. Verify procedure validity—Checks with the data dictionary to determine whether the subprogram is valid. If the object is invalid, it is automatically recompiled before being executed.
3. Execute—The package subprogram is executed.

To reference the package's subprograms and objects, you must use dot notation.

NEW TERM   *Dot Notation* is a method to fully qualify an object name based on the object's owner.

7

The Syntax for Dot Notation

▲ SYNTAX

```
package_name.type_name
package_name.object_name
package_name.subprogram_name
```

In this syntax, the parameters are as follows:

- *package_name* is the name of the declared package.
- *type_name* is the name of the type that you define, such as record.
- *object_name* is the name of the constant or variable you declare.
- *subprogram_name* is the name of the procedure or function contained in the package body.

▲

To reference the procedure emp_change_s in the package employee_maint, the referencing statement would be

```
Declare
Begin
If employee_maint.emp_change_s(3)
Then ….
End if;
End;
```

This example is a fairly typical approach to variable referencing. The dot notation allows this PL/SQL block to reference the emp_change_s procedure in the package named employee_maint.

When Oracle executes a package subprogram, an implicit savepoint is created. If the subprogram fails with an unhandled exception, before returning to the host environment, Oracle rolls back to the savepoint, thereby undoing any changes made by the package subprogram.

Recompiling Packages

To recompile a package, you use the ALTER PACKAGE command with the compile keyword. This explicit recompilation eliminates the need for any implicit runtime recompilation and prevents any associated runtime compilation errors and performance overhead. It is common to explicitly recompile a package after modifications to the package.

When you recompile a package, you also recompile all objects defined within the package. Recompiling does not change the definition of the package or any of its objects.

The following examples recompile just the body of a package. The second statement recompiles the entire package, including the body and specification:

```
ALTER PACKAGE employee_maintcompile body

ALTER PACKAGE employee_maint compile package
```

All packages can be recompiled by using the Oracle utility `dbms_utility`:

```
execute dbms_utility.compile_all
```

Private Versus Public Package Objects

Within the body of a package, you can define subprograms, cursors, and private declarations for types and objects. Objects that are declared inside the package body can be used only within that package. Therefore, PL/SQL code outside the package cannot reference any of the variables that are privately declared within the package.

NEW TERM — Any items declared inside the package specification are visible outside the package. This enables PL/SQL code outside the package to reference objects from within the package. These objects declared in the package specification are called *public*.

NEW TERM — *Private* declarations allow items to be seen only within the package and not to the entire database. This is a good technique to use to increase security around sensitive topics such as accounting information.

Package Invocation Security

As for functions and procedures, the security necessary to execute a package subprogram is determined by the user's rights. The AUTHID clause determines whether all the packaged subprograms execute with the privileges of their definer (the default) or their invoker, and whether their unqualified references to schema objects are resolved in the schema of the definer or invoker.

Variables, Cursors, and Constant Persistence

Variables, cursors, and constants can change their value over time and have a specific life span. This life duration can vary, depending on where the declaration is located. For standalone procedures, variables, cursors, and constants persist only for the duration of the procedure call and are lost when the procedure execution terminates.

If the variable, constant, or cursor was declared in a package specification or body, their values persist for the duration of the user's session. The values are lost when the current user's session terminates or the package is recompiled.

Package States

A package is always either valid or invalid. A package is considered valid if none of its source code or the objects it references have been dropped, replaced, or altered since the package specification was last recompiled.

The package is considered invalid if its source code or any object that it references have been dropped, altered, or replaced since the package specification was last recompiled.

7

When a package becomes invalid, Oracle also makes invalid any object that references the package.

Package Dependency

During the process of recompiling a package, Oracle invalidates all dependent objects. These objects include standalone or package subprograms that call or reference objects declared in the recompiled specification. If another user's program calls or references a dependent object before it is recompiled, Oracle automatically recompiles it at runtime.

During package recompilation, Oracle determines whether objects on which the package body depends are valid. If any of these objects are invalid, Oracle recompiles them before recompiling the package body. If recompilation is successful, then the package body becomes valid. If any errors are detected, the appropriate error messages are generated and the package body remains invalid.

Trapping Errors and Exceptions

NEW TERM   Sometimes the Oracle server or the user's application causes an error to occur during runtime processing. Such errors can arise from hardware or network failures, application logic errors, data integrity errors, and many other sources. These errors are known as *exceptions*; that is, these unwanted events are exceptions to the normal processing that is expected.

NEW TERM   Typically, when an error occurs, processing of the PL/SQL block terminates immediately. Hence, the application stops processing and the task at hand goes unfinished. Oracle enables you to be prepared for these errors and write logic into programs to handle errors gracefully and allow processing to carry on. This logic written to manage errors is known as *exception-handling code*. With Oracle exception handling, when an error is detected, control is passed to the exception-handling portion of the program, and processing completes normally. Handling errors also provides valuable information for debugging applications and for better bulletproofing the application against future errors.

Without a means to handle exceptions, a program must check for execution errors after each statement, as the following example shows:

```
SELECT....
IF error-- check for error associated with SELECT statement
THEN....
INSERT ....
IF error-- check for error associated with INSERT statement
THEN...
UPDATE....
IF error-- check for error associated with UPDATE statement
THEN...
```

As you can see, this increases the processing overhead because you have to explicitly check for errors after each statement. There is always a risk that you might overlook a statement and fail to check for errors, thereby leaving open the potential for an abnormal termination to the application.

With exception handling incorporated into the application, the same statement would be transformed to look like this:

```
BEGIN
SELECT....
INSERT....
UPDATE....
exception
-- check for and process errors here
END
```

This way of handling errors removes all the added processing required to explicitly handle errors and improves the readability of the program.

Exception-Handling Structures

In PL/SQL, the user can anticipate and trap for certain runtime errors. Exceptions can be internally defined by Oracle or the user.

There are three types of exceptions:

- Predefined Oracle errors
- Undefined Oracle errors
- User-defined errors

These types of exceptions are covered in the following sections.

Predefined Oracle Errors

To build the exception-handling portion of a program, you start the block of code with the keyword exception, followed by the when clause.

The Syntax for the exception Command

SYNTAX

```
exception
when exception 1 THEN
statements
when exception 2 THEN
statements
...
```

In this syntax, the parameters are as follows:

- *exception 1* and *exception 2* are the names of the predefined exceptions.
- *statements* is the PL/SQL code that will be executed if the exception name is satisfied.

7

The Oracle server defines several errors with standard names. Although every Oracle error has a number, an error must be referenced by name. PL/SQL has predefined some common Oracle errors and exceptions, including the following:

- no_data_found—The single-row SELECT returned no data.
- too_many_rows—The single-row SELECT returned more than one row.
- invalid_cursor—An illegal cursor operation was attempted.
- value_error—An arithmetic, a conversion, a truncation, or a constraint error occurred.
- invalid_number—The conversion of a number to a character string failed.
- zero_divide—An attempt to divide by zero occurred.
- dup_val_on_index—An attempt was made to insert a duplicate value into a column that has a unique index.
- cursor_already_open—An attempt was made to open a cursor that was previously opened.
- not_logged_on—A database call was made without the user being logged into Oracle.
- transaction_backed_out—A remote portion of a transaction is rolled back.
- login_denied—A login to Oracle failed because of an invalid username and password.
- program_error—PL/SQL encounters an internal problem.
- storage_error—PL/SQL runs out of memory or if memory is corrupted.
- timeout_on_resource—A timeout occurred while Oracle was waiting for a resource.
- value_error—An arithmetic, a conversion, a truncation, or a constraint error occurred.
- others—A catchall statement that traps an error that was not trapped in the preceding exception traps.

Oracle declares predefined exceptions globally in the database as a standard option. Specifically, these exceptions are defined in the package named *standard*. Therefore, you do not need to declare them yourself.

The following is an example of a PL/SQL exception-handling block:

```
...
SELECT * from employees
WHERE name like 'Bluekers%';
...                        -- additionbal logic can go here
exception                          -- Exceptions block beginning
when no_data_found                 -- first exceptions trap
CREATE_employee ('new','Bluekers');
COMMIT;
```

```
when others THEN                -- second exceptions trap
ROLLBACK;
COMMIT;
END                             -- end of exceptions handling
```

This snippet of code illustrates the use of two common predefined Oracle exceptions. The first exception, no_data_found, is used to trap any occurrence when no data is returned from a query. In this case you don't want execution to stop, so you trap it and address what execution should do next. In this example, a new record is created when the exception no_data_found is encountered. The second exception used here is the catchall others exception. That is, when an exception is not trapped by any previous line of code, processing is transferred to this section of the block. Specifically in this example, the code rolls back and commits all transaction to date and terminates itself cleanly.

Undefined Oracle Errors

As you saw in the previous section's example of exception-handling blocks, the others exception is used as a catchall exception handler. others is normally used when the exact nature of the exception isn't important, when the exception is unnamed, or even when it's unpredictable. Fortunately, Oracle allows use to add meaning to these mysterious errors via the pragma directive.

NEW TERM   A *pragma* is a compiler directive, which can be thought of as a parenthetical remark to the compiler. Pragmas (also called *pseudoinstructions*) are processed at compile time, not at runtime.

A different way to handle an error that is unnamed is with the pragma exception_init compiler directive. This directive simply transfers information to the compiler. The pragma tells the compiler to associate an exception name with an Oracle error number. In this way, you can refer to any internal exception by name and write a specific handler for it.

Declaration of the exception_init

The declaration of the pragma exception_init must appear in the declarative portion of the PL/SQL block, packages, or subprogram. The following is the syntax for this declaration:

```
pragma exception_init (exception_name, error_number);
```

Where:

- *exception_name* is the name the programmer assigns to the error
- *error_number* is the arbitrary number the programmer assigns to the specific error

7

The exception name is a previously declared execution. The pragma declaration must appear somewhere after the appearance of the exception declaration. The following example shows the exception and pragma declarations and the exception-handling block for the exception:

```
insufficient_funds  exception;
pragma exception_init (insufficient _funds, -2019);
BEGIN
...
exception
when insufficient_funds THEN
ROLLBACK;
END;
```

User-Defined Errors

A user can explicitly raise an exception by using the RAISE command. This procedure should be used only when Oracle does not raise its own exception or when processing is undesirable or impossible to complete.

The steps for trapping a user-defined error are as follows:

1. Declare the name for the user exception within the declaration section of the block.

2. Raise the exception explicitly within the executable portion of the block, by using the RAISE command.

3. Reference the declared exception with an error-handling routine.

The following example illustrates the use of the user-defined exception:

INPUT
```
DECLARE
invalid_pay_type        exception;              -- user-defined exception
pay_type_code varchar2(2);

BEGIN
...
IF pay_type_code not in ('H','S') THEN  -- error trap
RAISE invalid_pay_type;                     -- raise user defined exception
END IF;
exception                                 -- handle user define exception
when invalid_pay_type THEN
ROLLBACK;
END
```

ANALYSIS This program first declares an exception variable, and then defines that any pay code other than H or S should be considered invalid. If the program encounters one of these invalid pay types, then the transactions are rolled back and the program terminates cleanly.

NEW TERM Exceptions can be raised in declarations when declarations and initializations are done incorrectly. When this happens, the exception handler must reside in the enclosing block. This is called *exception propagation*, and is discussed in more detail later in this lesson, in the section "Propagating Exceptions."

SQLCODE and SQLERRM

In the exception-handling part of the program, you can use the functions SQLCODE and
SQLERRM to obtain information about the most recent error that has occurred. This is
especially useful when the exception is trapped with the when others clause, which is
used to trap unanticipated or unknown exceptions.

You cannot use SQLCODE and SQLERRM directly in a SQL statement. Instead, you must
assign their values to local variables and then use these variables in the SQL statement.

The SQLCODE function returns the error code for the exception. SQLERRM returns the corresponding error message. The following are the valid values from the SQLCODE function:

- 0—No exception has been raised.
- 1—A user-defined exception has been raised.
- +1403—A no_data_found exception has been raised.
- -###—The remaining negative values correspond to the actual error codes, as
  defined in the *Oracle Server Messages and Codes* manual.

The following example traps and records the error code and message of the offending
exception and stores it in a table for access at a later time:

INPUT

```
DECLARE
error_code   number;
error_msg    varchar2(250);

BEGIN
...
exception
...
when others THEN
error_code := SQLCODE;
error_msg := SQLERRM;
INSERT into user_exceptions_table (error_message)
values (to_char(error_code) || ': ' || error_msg)
COMMIT;
END;
```

ANALYSIS This example illustrates ways to record and preserve errors that occur in processing. There may be times, such as in batch processing, when you do not want
program execution to stop at any time. You might be willing to let processing continue
even when errors occur—especially on applications that are not mission critical. In this
case, for example, you might want to check the status of last night's processing when
you get into the office in the morning. This example is a typical method to achieve this
concept. As processing occurs, all errors are stored in a table named user_exceptions,
which holds the Oracle error code number and its corresponding error message.

7

You can now perform a SELECT on user_exceptions_table to view the exception error code and message.

If PL/SQL cannot find an exception handler for an error, it turns the exception over to the host environment for handling.

Continuing Processing After an Exception

Exception handlers let you handle errors that would normally be fatal to an application. However, exception handlers as described so far in this chapter create a logic processing problem.

Look at the following PL/SQL block:

```
DECLARE
invalid_fam_code        exception;      -- user-defined exception
part_fam_code varchar2(2);
BEGIN
...
IF part_fam_code not in ('AU','UC','BG') THEN  -- error trap
RAISE invalid_fam_code;                  -- raise user- defined exception
END IF;
INSERT....
UPDATE....
....
exception                    -- handle user-defined exception
when invalid_fam_code THEN
ROLLBACK;
END
```

When the invalid_fam_code exception occurs, process control is transferred to the handler. The INSERT and UPDATE commands are never executed in this scenario, which could pose a problem for your application.

To get around the problem of code being bypassed due to exceptions, embed the exception handler in its own subblock, as shown in the following example:

```
DECLARE
invalid_fam_code        exception;              -- user-defined exception
part_fam_code varchar2(2);
BEGIN
...
BEGIN                                    -- subblock begin
IF part_fam_code not in ('AU','UC','BG') THEN  -- error trap
exception                          -- handle user-defined exception
when invalid_fam_code THEN
ROLLBACK;
END IF;
END;                              -- subblock end
INSERT...
UPDATE...
...
END;
```

In this example, the exception `invalid_fam_code` is handled locally in its own subblock. This arrangement allows the INSERT, UPDATE, and any other following statements to be executed.

Retrying After an Exception

Sometimes you might want to retry a transaction after some exception. For example, say you are creating new identification numbers for parts coming out of the factory. You make an attempt to create a new part number, but receive a message stating that that particular part number already exists. What would you do? Normally, you create a different part number and retry the task, as shown in the following example. You would not want to cease transaction processing when you get a duplicate part number message. Fortunately, you know enough about the causes of the problem to add corrective logic to the program.

The following example illustrates the use of programming logic to resolve exceptions:

INPUT

```
DECLARE
max_count        integer;
part_number      integer := 1;

BEGIN
SELECT count(*) into max_count from new_parts
LOOP  FOR I in 1..max_count loop

BEGIN                          -- create a subblock
savepoint top_loop;            -- establish rollback point
part_number :=part_number+1;   -- create new part number
INSERT into inventory value (part_number);
COMMIT;
EXIT;

exception
when dup_val_on_index THEN
part_number :=part_number+1;   -- create a newer part number
ROLLBACK to top_loop;          -- force us to top of loop
END;                           -- end subblock

END LOOP;                      -- end loop
END;                           -- end block
```

ANALYSIS As mentioned previously, you can programmatically code yourself out of exceptions in some cases. In this example, when a duplicate part number is encountered, the program creates a new part number and assigns it to the new part. Hence, the problem is identified and resolved at the same time.

Re-raising Exceptions

At times, you might want to handle an exception locally and pass the exception to an enclosed block. The following example raises the exception `out_of_stock` in the subblock and passes the exception handling to the enclosed block:

7

```
· DECLARE
out_of_stock     exception;     -- declare exception

BEGIN     -- beginning of subblock to check qty of order
IF qty_ordered > qty_on_hand THEN
RAISE out_of_stock;              -- raise the exception
END IF;

exception
-- for exception indicated that order_qty is invalid
when out_of_stock THEN
...
RAISE;                           -- reraise the current exception
...
END;

--  end of subblock
exception
-- handle the exception differently than earlier.
when out_of_stock THEN
...
END;
```

Exception Scope Rules

You should be aware of the following guidelines with regard to the scope of exception declarations:

- An exception cannot be declared twice in the same block, but the same exception can be declared in two different blocks.

- Exceptions are local to the block where they were declared and global to all of the block's subblocks. Enclosing blocks cannot reference exceptions that were declared in any of their subblocks.

- Global declarations can be redeclared at the local subblock level. If this occurs, the local declaration takes precedence over the global declaration.

Propagating Exceptions

NEW TERM When an error is encountered, PL/SQL looks in the current block for the appropriate exception handler. If no handler is present, then PL/SQL *propagates* the error to the enclosing block. PL/SQL searches the enclosing block for the correct error handler. If no handler is found there, the error is propagated to the enclosing blocks until a handler is found. This process can continue until the host environment receives and handles the error. For example, if SQL*Plus received an unhandled error from a PL/SQL block, SQL*Plus handles this error by displaying the error code and message on the user's screen.

Summary

This lesson covers a lot of material, including Oracle procedures, packages, and error- and exception-handling capabilities. Procedures and packages offer the programmer powerful constructs for PL/SQL blocks. An Oracle procedure is a concise and logically grouped set of statements to perform a specific task. A package is an encapsulated collection of related schema objects such as functions and procedures that achieve a common purpose. Runtime errors should be anticipated and planned for in your application, using exception-handling code to prevent the unwanted termination of an application.

Q&A

Q Do I have to use a package when I have only one function in an application?

A No, you do not have to use a package when you have only one function. You should think seriously about the future growth of your application. If you think the application will grow and include additional functions and procedure, then you should start by using a package from the beginning.

Q Why do I need to write extra code to process errors detected by Oracle?

A If your code does not explicitly trap for any and all exceptions, your PL/SQL processing will halt when the error is detected.

Q Can I build my procedure before building my database?

A Not usually. Because of dependency issues, you might have to have the tables and views (or other schema objects) in place before compiling your procedure.

Q What if I don't know what error to anticipate from Oracle?

A Fortunately, Oracle provides the when others clause to handle this exception by trapping all exceptions.

Workshop

You can use this workshop to test your comprehension of this lesson and put what you've learned into practice. You'll find the answers to the quiz and exercises in Appendix A, "Answers."

Quiz

1. What statement do you use to recompile a procedure?
2. How do you invoke a procedure?
3. Name at least four predefined Oracle exception errors.
4. How do you call a module of a package?

7

Exercises

1. Write a package specification for the functions written in previous lessons. Additionally, include in the specification one or two of the procedures used in this lesson.

2. Write an exception-handling piece of code to trap the error of receiving more rows than you expected as well as an unknown error.

WEEK 1

In Review

Here you are at the end of Week 1. By now you should have a good grasp of the basics of PL/SQL. On the first day, you read about the relationship of PL/SQL to other Oracle products, and you also saw your first example of a short, but useful, PL/SQL function. On the second day, you learned about the various PL/SQL datatypes and saw examples of how they are used. During the following day, Day 3, you went over PL/SQL expressions and operators. You learned how operator precedence affects an expression's order of evaluation and how you can control that by using parentheses. You learned about three-valued logic and the effect of null values on an expression's evaluation, and you learned how data is converted from one type to another. Days 4 and 5 covered the PL/SQL statements that control program flow and execution, including IF statements, FOR loops, and WHILE loops. On Day 6 you learned about the many powerful, built-in functions that Oracle provides as part of PL/SQL. The week concluded with Day 7, which covered packages, procedures, errors, and exceptions.

1

2

3

4

5

5

6

WEEK 2

At a Glance

Congratulations! You have completed Week 1 and are now
ready to take on Week 2. During Week 1, you learned many of
the building blocks and core features of PL/SQL.

Where You Are Going

During Week 2 you will take some of the features you learned
in Week 1 and learn more complex methods of using them. In
this second week, you will begin to integrate your PL/SQL
code with the Oracle database. You will create some sample
tables and then use your PL/SQL code to manipulate data in
these tables. By the end of the week, you will know how to
perform multiple row queries and process the rows one at a
time, all within PL/SQL. On Day 13, you will be introduced
to techniques you can use to debug your PL/SQL programs.
Finally, you learn about the datatypes to handle very large
data objects, and you will learn how to manipulate those
objects from PL/SQL. Additionally, this week you will learn
how to code your programs to anticipate and handle the many
different runtime errors that can occur in PL/SQL code.

WEEK 2

DAY 8

Using SQL

by Tom Luers

By definition, PL/SQL is SQL's procedural language extension. PL/SQL supports all SQL's data manipulation commands (except for EXPLAIN PLAN), transaction control commands, functions, pseudocolumns, and operators. Additional information relevant to today's lessons is contained in Appendix B, "Oracle Functions Reference," which provides comprehensive coverage of SQL functions and Day 4, "Using Functions, IF Statements, and Loops," which covers SQL Operators. Today you will learn about the following:

- Using SQL's Data Manipulation Language (DML)
- Using Transaction control statements
- Using pseudocolumns

NEW TERM *Data Manipulation Language* (DML) commands enable the user to query a database and to manipulate data in an existing database. The execution of a DML statement does not implicitly commit the current transaction. The user has an opportunity to roll back or save the transaction.

NEW TERM *Transaction Control* commands enable the user and Oracle to ensure data integrity within the database. Transaction control statements are used by the developer to make permanent or remove the effects of DML statements.

When a PL/SQL block executes a SQL DML command, the block passes the SQL command to the Oracle database for processing in its own SQL engine. Figure 8.1 illustrates this concept.

FIGURE 8.1

*The Oracle PL/SQL
server engine.*

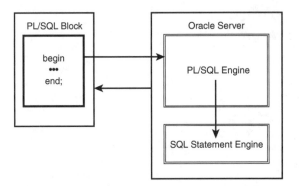

Because PL/SQL passes the DML statements to the RDBMS, the PL/SQL statements must conform to the required SQL syntax standards. This is one of the few times that you must be aware of the syntax differences between SQL and PL/SQL.

PL/SQL allows the use of SQL DML statements in order to provide an easy, safe, and flexible environment to manipulate data. In a simple program, SQL statements are processed one statement at a time, as diagrammed in Figure 8.2. If you have four separate SQL statements, Oracle would process these in four independent actions and return four different results. Through the use of PL/SQL, you can group these same SQL statements into a PL/SQL block and have them processed at one time, hence improving your overall performance.

FIGURE 8.2

*SQL versus PL/SQL
code processing.*

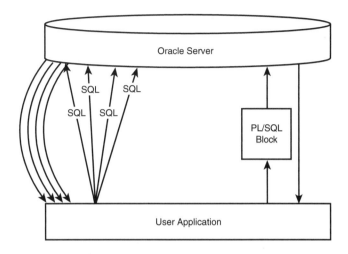

Types of SQL DML Statements

PL/SQL allows you to use five different DML commands: INSERT, DELETE, UPDATE, SELECT, and LOCK TABLE. This chapter discusses each one of these and their use within PL/SQL. The INSERT statement adds new data to the database. The DELETE command removes data from the database. The UPDATE command modifies existing data in the database, and the SELECT statement retrieves data from the database.

This chapter covers the five basic statements just described: INSERT, SELECT, UPDATE, DELETE, and LOCK TABLE. This chapter does not teach the use or syntax of SQL itself. Only the most basic SQL statements and queries are included to illustrate the use of SQL within PL/SQL. Refer to the book *Sams Teach Yourself SQL in 21 Days* for more in-depth knowledge of SQL queries.

Creating Some Oracle Tables

You now need to create several Oracle tables to use in the remainder of the book. In order to create these tables, you must have the CREATE TABLE system privilege. You will create three tables in this chapter. These are the Employee table, Department table, and the Emp_Dept tables. Figure 8.3 shows an Entity Relationship Diagram (ERD) for these three tables. This diagram also shows a physical layout of these tables.

Figure 8.3

ERD and physical data model for the three tables.

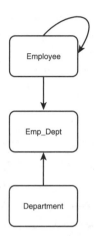

Employee

emp_id	integer	unique key
emp_name	varchar2 (32)	
supervised_by	integer	
pay_rate	number (9,2)	
pay_type	char	
emp_dept_id	integer	

Emp_Dept

emp_id	integer	composite unique key	
dept_id	integer		

Department

dept_id	integer	unique key
dept_name	varchar2 (32)	

The first table you need to create is the Employee table. This table will hold information about the employees. Specifically, for each employee, it will hold the employee's name, supervisor's name, pay rate, pay type, and a key that indicates which department the employee belongs to. The syntax for the CREATE TABLE command is as follows.

SYNTAX

```
CREATE TABLE table_name
(column_name column_datatype);
```

In this syntax, *table_name* is the name you assign to the table. *column_name* is the name of the column you assign, and *column_datatype* is the datatype for that column.

Go ahead and execute the code shown in Listing 8.1 to create this table.

INPUT **LISTING 8.1** Creating the Employee Table

```
CREATE TABLE employee
      (emp_id              INTEGER,
       emp_name        VARCHAR2(32),
       supervised_by       INTEGER,
       pay_rate              NUMBER(9,2),
       pay_type              CHAR);

ALTER TABLE employee
ADD CONSTRAINT pk_emp primary key (emp_id);
```

ANALYSIS Take a look at some of the fields in the table you just created. The `emp_id` field will hold a unique numeric value that guarantees uniqueness across all rows of the table. For example, the `emp_id` field would be the only way to pick the correct row when you have two employees with the exact same name.

The `supervised_by` field will hold the value of the `emp_id` for that person's supervisors, as shown in the following example:

emp_id	emp_name	supervised_by	pay_rate	pay_type
1	Jack Richards	3	100.50	H
2	Melinda Williams	1	6.50	H
3	Jenny Catherines	5	2,000.00	S
4	David Madison	5	1,500.00	S

You can see that Jenny is the supervisor of Jack. This is indicated by the `supervised_by` value of 3 in Jack's record. This 3 represents the `emp_id` of the person who is Jack's supervisor. In this case, it is Jenny.

The next table you will create is the Department table. This table will contain information about the department in which the employees work. It will hold the department's ID, department name, and the number of employees. Execute the code shown in Listing 8.2 to create this table.

INPUT **LISTING 8.2** Creating the Department Table

```
CREATE TABLE department
       (dept_id          INTEGER,
        dept_name     VARCHAR2(32));

ALTER TABLE department
ADD CONSTRAINT pk_dept PRIMARY KEY (dept_id);
```

ANALYSIS With this sample code, you just created a table named `department`. In this table there are two columns: an ID number column and a department name column.

The final table you need to create is the Emp_Dept table. This table tells you which employees work in which departments. Execute the code shown in Listing 8.3 to create the emp_dept table.

INPUT   **LISTING 8.3**   Creating the Emp_Dept Table

```
CREATE TABLE emp_dept
   (emp_id            INTEGER,
    dept_id           INTEGER,
    CONSTRAINT unq_1 unique (emp_id, dept_id))
```

ANALYSIS   This table contains two columns. The purpose of this table is to define which employees work in which departments. This table does not hold actual employee or department specific data, but rather pointers back to the Employee and Department tables. Pointers, or rather referential ID numbers, are used so data does not become replicated. It's best to keep and manage one set of data and not have to worry about managing multiple copies of data floating around the database.

Now that your base tables are created, go ahead and use them. First you will insert data into the tables, and then you will retrieve that same data.

Using the INSERT Statement

The INSERT command is used to add new rows to an existing Oracle table or view. In this case, you will only be inserting data into a table. The following example displays the proper INSERT command syntax.

SYNTAX

```
INSERT into table_name  [column_name]  values (values)
```

In this syntax, *table_name* is the name of the table into which you're inserting data. *column_name* is the name of the column being inserted into the table, and *values* is the data that will be placed in the column.

Try working through two examples to illustrate the usage of the INSERT command. You might want to refer back to Figure 8.3 to refresh your memory on the Employee table layout.

The first example is

INPUT

```
INSERT into employee values
     ( 1, ' Jessica Loraine', 2, '8.50', 'H',
  2, ' Kurt Roberts', 5, 100.00, 'S');
```

ANALYSIS   When this statement is executed, the Employee table will have two rows in it and look like Table 8.1:

TABLE 8.1 The Employee Table After Inserting

emp_id	emp_name	supervised_by	pay_rate	pay_type
1	Jessica Loraine	2	8.50	H
2	Kurt Roberts	5	100.00	S

This insert statement simply created two records in the employee table. The statement provided the data to be used in the record creations.

Note that there were no *column_name* references in the INSERT statement. The reason is that SQL will make a one-to-one match of the *column_name* to the data included in the INSERT statement. If you want, you can insert data into selected columns as shown in the second example.

> It is advisable to always include the column list to ensure clarity to others. The column list will come in handy whenever you have to debug your code. Likewise it is advisable to use a sequence number for any of the table's primary key values.

Here's the second example:

```
INSERT into employee (emp_id, emp_name) values
        ( 1, ' Jessica Loraine',
          2, ' Kurt Roberts');
```

In the second example, you only placed data in the emp_id and emp_name columns. All other columns would be blank, as seen in Table 8.2.

TABLE 8.2 Inserting with Named Columns

emp_id	emp_name	supervised_by	pay_rate	pay_type
1	Jessica Loraine			
2	Kurt Roberts			

Inserting Some Data

You will now insert data into the employee table for use in the remainder of the book. Type in the PL/SQL block shown in Listing 8.4, and then compile and execute it. When you run this block of code, it will ask you for an employee's name and related information and in turn insert this data into the Employee table. Run this anonymous PL/SQL block multiple times in order to end up with roughly 10 employees' worth of data loaded. Your goal here is to input data that represents the typical organizational chart shown in Figure 8.4. You want data loaded for all levels of the organizational chart. While inserting data, feel free to use any names you like.

FIGURE 8.4

Organization chart.

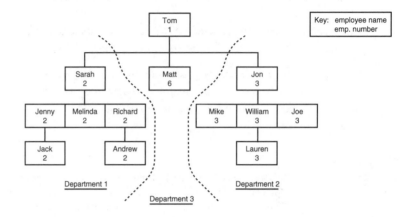

Listing 8.4 shows the PL/SQL anonymous block that you can run to insert the necessary data.

INPUT   **LISTING 8.4**   Inserting Records with PL/SQL Code

```
DECLARE                  -- insert department data first
i_dept_id  INTEGER,
i_dept_name,
BEGIN
INSERT into department values
(&i_dept_id,'&dept_name');
END;
/

COMMIT;            -- save the department data

DECLARE            -- insert employee and emp_dept data
i_id   INTEGER;
e_id   INTEGER;
i_name  VARCHAR2(32);
i_super  INTEGER;
i_rate    NUMBER(9,2);
i_type   CHAR;
i_emp_dept INTEGER;
```

```
e_emp_dept INTEGER;
BEGIN
e_id:=&employee_id;
e_emp_dept:=&employee_department_id;

INSERT into employee values
(e_id, '&i_name',&i_super,&i_rate,'&i_type');
INSERT into emp_dept values (e_id,e_emp_dept);
END;
/

COMMIT;          -- save employee  and emp_dept datadata
```

ANALYSIS The code in Listing 8.4 is used to insert data first into the Department table, and then the Employee table, and finally the `Emp_Dept` table.

Singleton SELECT Statement

The `SELECT` statement is one of the ways to get data out of the database. In order to use the `SELECT` statement, you must have `SELECT` system privileges. Depending on how you design and use the `SELECT` statement, you can retrieve a single (singleton) row or multiple rows of data from the database. Sometimes you'll only want a single row returned; otherwise, you want your PL/SQL block to handle the multiple rows without terminating. The syntax for the `SELECT` statement is as follows.

```
SELECT column_name
from table_name
WHERE condition
ORDER BY expression
```

In this syntax, `column_name` is the name of the column or columns from which you want data. `table_name` is the name of the table or tables in which the previous columns belong. The `condition` statement is used to specify the criteria to retrieve specific rows. The `ORDER BY` clause enables you to define the order in which to display the retrieved rows. For example, you might want to display the rows in alphabetical order or in numeric sequence. Both the `WHERE` and the `ORDER BY` clauses are optional.

Some SELECT Command Examples

 The first example is a simple `SELECT` statement to retrieve all the rows from the Employee table:

```
SELECT emp_id, emp_name, supervised_by, pay_rate, pay_type
from employee
ORDER BY emp_name
```

ANALYSIS This statement will return all rows from the Employee table sorted in ascending order by the employee name. Because this statement grabs all columns and rows from the table, you could use the wildcard * to achieve the same result.

The following example is synonymous with the previous example as it will select all rows and columns from the Employee table.

INPUT `SELECT * from employee ORDER BY emp_name`

A more complex, but realistic, example would be

```
SELECT * from employee
WHERE pay_type = 'S'
ORDER BY pay_rate desc
```

ANALYSIS This SELECT statement will return all rows from the table that have the pay_type equal to 'S'. The returned rows will be in pay_rate descending order.

Finally, Listing 8.5 is an example of a singleton SELECT. An assumption is made here that you only have one employee with the name of Jack Richards. You might want your program to indicate to you if you have multiple occurrences of a specific employee. The bottom line is that you don't want processing to halt if this happens.

INPUT **LISTING 8.5** Multiple-Row SELECT Command

```
DECLARE
v_emp_id        INTEGER;
BEGIN
SELECT emp_id              -- select statement
into v_emp_id
from employee
WHERE emp_name = 'Jack Richards';    -- where clause
exception
when too_many_rows THEN        -- type of exception
Null;    --exception logic can go here as needed
END;
```

ANALYSIS In this example, an exception is raised when more than one row is returned by the SELECT statement.

Exploring the UPDATE and DELETE Statements

The next two SQL DML statements to cover are the UPDATE and the DELETE statements. You can use these in any PL/SQL block as necessary. The purpose of these commands is synonymous with their names. The UPDATE command enables the user to change the values of an existing row. The DELETE command provides the means to remove or delete a row from a table.

The Syntax for the UPDATE Command

SYNTAX

```
UPDATE table_name
set (column_name = value)
WHERE statement
```

In this syntax, *table_name* is the table containing the row you want to update, *column_name* is the column you want to update, and the WHERE statement identifies the row in the table to be identified.

The following is an example of the UPDATE command to change the values of the Employee table. This statement will change the value of the employee name to Tim Brandon for the table row which has the EMP_ID equal to 2.

```
UPDATE employee
SET (emp_name = 'Timothy Brandon')
WHERE emp_id = 2;
```

The Syntax for the DELETE Command

SYNTAX

```
DELETE from table_name
WHERE statement
```

In this syntax, *table_name* is the table containing the row to be deleted, and the WHERE statement identifies the row to be deleted.

The following example will delete all records from the Department table where the department name is equal to Accounting.

```
DELETE FROM department
WHERE dept_name = 'ACCOUNTING';
```

The example illustrates the deletion of all records from the Department table where the department name is Accounting. All other records with department names other than Accounting will remain in the table and untouched.

> **Caution** Once records are deleted from a table they remain unusable until a COMMIT or a ROLLBACK command is issued. The COMMIT command will permanently delete the records while the ROLLBACK command will restore the records.

Refer to the *Oracle SQL Language Reference Manual* for a more comprehensive syntax diagram for these last two commands.

Handling Types of Exceptions

Exceptions are errors that occur during runtime processing. These exceptions can arise due to different situations. Normally, PL/SQL processing will terminate as soon as it encounters an exception. Fortunately, PL/SQL gives you several tools to handle these exceptions so that processing does not terminate. After an exception is detected, processing is transferred to your handling routine within the PL/SQL block. Refer to Day 7, "Procedures, Packages, Errors, and Exceptions," for additional information about Oracle's exception-handling capabilities.

The following are the more commonly used predefined exceptions that you can trap in your exception-handling section of your PL/SQL block:

- no_data_found—Singleton SELECT statement returned no data.
- too_many_rows—Singleton SELECT statement returned more than one row of data.
- invalid_cursor—Illegal cursor operation occurred.
- value_error—Arithmetic, conversion, or truncation error occurred.
- when others—Used when no other exception is explicitly listed.

Listing 8.6 offers an enhancement to the code in Listing 8.5. In this example, I added another exception to handle the case when no rows are returned from the database.

INPUT   **LISTING 8.6**   Multiple-Row SELECT Command with Several Exception-Handling Routines

```
DECLARE
v_emp_id        INTEGER;
BEGIN
SELECT  emp_id
into v_emp_id
from employee
WHERE emp_name = 'Jack Richards';
exception
when no_data_found THEN
v_emp_id := 888;  -- 888 is just an example of any code you can use
➥ to indicate a specific error
when too_many_rows THEN
v_emp_id := 999;  -- 999 is just an example of any code you can use
➥ to indicate a specific error
END;
```

ANALYSIS   In the example in Listing 8.6, one of several exceptions can be raised. An exception is raised when no rows are returned by the SELECT statement as well as when more than one row is returned by the SELECT statement.

Using the LOCK TABLE Statement

The final DML statement covered in this chapter is the LOCK TABLE statement. This SQL statement will lock one or more tables during the execution of your session. Although not typically thought of as a DML statement, it is indeed one. It is used primarily to enhance the effects of the other four DML statements. The syntax for the LOCK TABLE statement is as follows.

SYNTAX

```
LOCK TABLE table_name
IN lockmode MODE
{NOWAIT};
```

In this syntax,

- *table_name* is the name of the table to be locked

- *lockmode* represents the nature or extent of the lock. The following are the possible values for the *lockmode*:

  - ROW SHARE allows concurrent access to the locked table, but prohibits users from locking the entire table for exclusive access. ROW SHARE is synonymous with SHARE UPDATE, which is included for compatibility with earlier versions of Oracle.

  - ROW EXCLUSIVE is the same as ROW SHARE, but also prohibits locking in SHARE mode. Row Exclusive locks are automatically obtained when updating, inserting, or deleting.

  - SHARE UPDATE allows concurrent access to the locked table, but prohibits users from locking the entire table for exclusive access.

  - SHARE allows concurrent queries but prohibits updates to the locked table.

  - SHARE ROW EXCLUSIVE is used to look at a whole table and to allow others to look at rows in the table, but to prohibit others from locking the table in SHARE mode or updating rows.

  - EXCLUSIVE allows queries on the locked table but prohibits any other activity on it.

- *nowait* option is an optional parameter. This specifies that Oracle returns control to you immediately if the specified table is already locked by another user. In this case, Oracle returns a message indicating that the table, partition, or subpartition is already locked by another user. If you omit this clause, Oracle waits until the table is available, locks it, and returns control to you.

The following is an example of using the LOCK TABLE statement to lock the Department table in exclusive mode, which means the lock command does not have to wait for other locks to dissipate.

```
LOCK TABLE department
IN EXCLUSIVE MODE
NOWAIT;
```

The sample code will place a lock on the Department table. This lock will prevent others from modifying the table while you have the lock on it.

Transaction Control Statements

Transaction control statements are the last set of SQL statement we will discuss in this chapter. Transaction control statements help you manage the changes made by any of the other DML statements. The four transaction control statements are

- COMMIT—makes permanent any changes to the database during this session.
- ROLLBACK—used to remove any changes since the last commit during this session. This command will restore the data to where it was at the last commit.
- SAVEPOINT—a bookmark within or at the boundaries of a transaction. This bookmark is referenced in other parts of your PL/SQL program when needed to roll-back.
- SET TRANSACTION—defines the nature of the transaction and its behavior during rollback processes.

Using Records

A record is a collection of individual values that are related somehow. Most often, records are used to represent a row in a table, and thus the relationship is based on all the values being from the same row. Each field in a record is unique and has its own values. A record as a whole does not have a value.

By using records, you can group like data into one structure and then manipulate this structure as one entity or logical unit. This helps reduce coding and keeps the code easier to maintain and understand.

Declaring a Record Variable

In order to use a record, you must define the record by declaring a record type. Then, you must declare one or more PL/SQL variables to be of that type.

You declare a record type in the declaration portion of a PL/SQL block, subprogram, or package. The following example declares a record type named emp_pay_info:

```
TYPE emp_pay_info IS RECORD        --record declaration
(emp_id        INTEGER,
 emp_name      VARCHAR2(32),
 pay_rate      NUMBER(9,2),
 pay_type      CHAR(1)
);
```

With the record type defined, you can then declare variables of that type, as in the following example:

```
DECLARE
...
emp emp_pay_info;
...
BEGIN
...
```

After you have a record variable declared, you can use dot notation to reference the individual fields within the record. In the following example, the pay_type field in the emp record is referenced in an IF statement:

```
IF emp.pay_type = 'S' THEN...
```

Having related fields grouped together in a record allows you to more easily keep things together when you are passing those values as parameters to other program units. This example shows the declaration for a procedure that takes a record of type emp_pay_info as a parameter:

```
procedure calculate_check (emp IN emp_pay_info) IS
...
```

Passing related values as a record not only makes your code more readable, but it makes it more maintainable as well. If you need to add another field to the emp_pay_info record, you only need to change the record definition, and that new value will be passed around everywhere that the record goes. If you were dealing with separate variables, you would have to change the header for every procedure and function that used the record.

Using the %TYPE Attribute

If you're declaring a record, and you want some of the field definitions to match definitions of columns in a database table, you can use the %TYPE attribute.

Note   %TYPE can be used in any variable declaration, not just with records.

To declare a variable to match a column definition, place an entry such as this in the declaration section of the PL/SQL block:

```
variable_name table_name.column_name%TYPE;
```

The %TYPE following the table and column name tells Oracle that you want the variable being declared to inherit its datatype and length from the definition of the named column. The following example shows another way to define the emp_pay_info record shown in the previous section:

```
TYPE emp_pay_info IS RECORD
(emp_id         employee.emp_id%TYPE,
 emp_name       employee.emp_name%TYPE,
 pay_rate       employee.pay_rate%TYPE,
 pay_type       employee.pay_type%TYPE
);
```

Using %TYPE like this helps insulate your PL/SQL code from changes in the underlying database columns. In the next section you'll learn an even easier technique, using %ROWTYPE, that you can use when you want the record to contain fields for all columns in a table.

Using Record Variables Based on Database Tables

If a record type variable is based on a table, it means that the fields in the record have the exact same name and datatype as the columns in the specified table. You use the %ROWTYPE attribute to declare a record based on a table.

To declare a record variable that exactly matches the definition of a table—that is, that contains one field for each column in the table—use the following syntax for the record type:

```
table_name%ROWTYPE;
```

where table_name is the name of the table. %ROWTYPE is a keyword that tells Oracle that the record should have one field for each column in the table, and that the datatypes of the fields should exactly match the datatypes of the columns. The following example declares the variable dept so that it matches the definition of the Department table:

```
DECLARE
   dept department%ROWTYPE;
   ...
```

8

The beauty of this is that a change to the table definition automatically ripples through to your PL/SQL code. You don't need to manually hunt down and change record definitions.

Note
> Adding a column to a table would be transparent to your PL/SQL code, as would certain types of datatype changes. However, if you drop a table column that your code is using, you need to visit that code and make some changes.

As with any other record, you use dot notation to reference a specific field. As far as PL/SQL is concerned, using department%ROWTYPE has the same effect as if you had declared the record like this:

```
DECLARE
    TYPE dept_type IS RECORD
        (
        dept_id department.dept_id%type,
        dept_name department.dept_name%type,
        no_of_emps department.no_of_emps%type
        );

    dept dept_type;
```

If you're working with all or most of the fields in a table, use %ROWTYPE to declare your records. You'll save typing, and you'll insulate your code somewhat from changes to the table.

Using Record Variables and SELECT Statements

If you have a record where all the fields in the record correspond exactly to the fields being returned from a SELECT statement, you can retrieve the values directly into that record. Here's an example:

```
DECLARE
    dept department%ROWTYPE;
BEGIN
    SELECT * INTO dept
    FROM department
    WHERE dept_id = 502;
    ...
END;
/
```

You don't have to use %ROWTYPE when you do this, and you don't have to use SELECT *
either. Listing 8.7 shows the dept record being declared without the use of %ROWTYPE,
and Listing 8.8 shows a SELECT statement other than SELECT *.

> **Note**
>
> Listing 8.7 selects for department 502. If you don't have that department,
> replace 502 with a valid number for your database.

INPUT   **LISTING 8.7**   Selecting Directly into a Record

```
 1: DECLARE
 2:     TYPE dept_type IS RECORD
 3:         (
 4:         dept_id department.dept_id%type,
 5:         dept_name department.dept_name%type,
 6:         no_of_emps department.no_of_emps%type
 7:         );
 8:
 9:     dept dept_type;
10: BEGIN
11:     SELECT * INTO dept
12:     FROM department
13:     WHERE dept_id = 502;
14: END;
15: /
```

ANALYSIS   A record type named dept_type is defined in lines 2–7. The declaration in line 9
declares a variable named dept to be of type dept_type. Because the fields in the
dept_type record match exactly the fields in the Department table, the SELECT statement
in lines 11–13 will work.

INPUT   **LISTING 8.8**   Selecting a Specific List of Fields into a Record

```
 1: DECLARE
 2:     TYPE dept_type IS RECORD
 3:         (
 4:         dept_id department.dept_id%type,
 5:         dept_name department.dept_name%type,
 6:         no_of_emps department.no_of_emps%type
 7:         );
 8:
 9:     dept dept_type;
10: BEGIN
11:     SELECT dept_id, dept_name, no_of_emps INTO dept
12:     FROM department
13:     WHERE dept_id = 502;
```

```
14: END;
15: /
```

ANALYSIS The three fields in the Department table are enumerated in the SELECT list. Because the number of fields (and their datatypes) corresponds with the definition of the dept_type record, you are able to retrieve the data directly into a variable of type dept_type.

The key thing to keep in mind when selecting data directly into a record is that the columns and datatypes represented in the SELECT list must correspond exactly to the fields and datatypes in the record definition. The column names and field names do not need to match, as Oracle assigns column values to fields in a record based on position, but the datatypes must match. If you are using SELECT * to retrieve values from a table, you are safest using %ROWTYPE when declaring the record.

Using Record Variables Based on Cursor Definitions

Just as you can base a record on a table, you can also base a record definition on a cursor. Records that are based on an Oracle cursor draw their structure from the SELECT statement used for the cursor. This type of record has the same number of columns, with the same names and datatypes, as those in the cursor. The %ROWTYPE keyword is used to declare the record that is based on a cursor. Listing 8.9 shows a cursor named all_depts, and a record named dept that is based on that cursor.

INPUT   **LISTING 8.9**   Declaring a Record to Match a Cursor

```
 1: DECLARE
 2:     CURSOR all_depts is
 3:         SELECT dept_id, dept_name
 4:         FROM department
 5:         ORDER BY dept_name;
 6:
 7:     dept all_depts%ROWTYPE;
 8: BEGIN
 9:     OPEN all_depts;
10:
11:     LOOP
12:         EXIT WHEN all_depts%NOTFOUND;
13:         FETCH all_depts INTO dept;
14:         DBMS_OUTPUT.PUT_LINE(dept.dept_name);
15:     END LOOP;
16:
17:     CLOSE all_depts;
18: END;
19: /
```

BOTTLING
BUILDING MAINTENANCE
DISTILLATION
EMPLOYEE NEWSLETTERS
FERMENTATION
FLEET REPAIR
GUTTING
PAYROLL
SCALE PROCESSING
SEWAGE
TECHNICAL WRITING
UNLOADING
UNLOADING

ANALYSIS The cursor `all_depts` is declared in lines 2–5. In line 7, a record variable named `dept` is declared based on the definition of the cursor. Because the variable `dept` matches the cursor exactly, the `FETCH` statement in line 13 can fetch the results of the `SELECT` statement directly into the record. If at some point in the future you need to add columns to the select list, that change will automatically ripple through to the record definition, and the `FETCH` statement will continue to operate.

Declarations at the Package Level

Declaring a package has two parts: the package specification and the package body. The package body defines all the functions, procedures, and other constructs that are declared in the package specification. The package specification declares all variables, constants, cursors, procedures, and functions. This section reviews the declarations of variables in the package specification.

The package specification contains the declaration of all objects that will be used in the package body. The following are several examples of a package specification that declares a cursor, variable, constant, and record.

INPUT

```
package emp_data is      -- package specification

pay_raise     constant real := 1.25;
high_rate     INTEGER;
CURSOR salary_cur (emp_id INTEGER, pay_rate NUMBER (9,2));
TYPE sal_rec is record (emp_name VARCHAR2(32), pay_rate NUMBER (9,2));
emp_rec   salary_cur%rowtype;

END emp_data;
```

ANALYSIS One of the advantages of declaring items in a package is that they are global in nature and accessible by all. This means that any program in your application can use the variables, cursors, constants, and records declared in the package specification. You treat these items (except constants) as if they were declared locally in that you can

8

change their values as needed. This global nature of the data is only within a session and is not available across multiple sessions. This means, for example, that the variables running in one user's applications are not accessible to a different user's application unless the DBMS_PIPE package is used.

Pseudocolumns

Pseudocolumns are not really columns in a table; they just have characteristics of columns. These pseudocolumns will return values when referenced just like real table columns. However, you cannot do any other DML or DDL statements on these pseudocolumns. Pseudocolumns are primarily used to give the programmer more tools to use in his code. They provide a convenient way to obtain information about different aspects of the database. The following are the Pseudocolumns we will discuss: CURRVAL, NEXTVAL, ROWID, and ROWNUM.

CURRVAL and NEXTVAL Pseudocolumns

The CURRVAL and NEXTVAL pseudocolumns are used in conjunction with sequences. The CURRVAL pseudocolumn returns the current value of the referenced sequence. The NEXTVAL pseudocolumn, when referenced, will increment the sequence value and then return the new sequence value.

Note

These pseudocolumns may only be used in the SELECT VALUE clause, and SET clause statements.

To reference the CURRVAL and NEXTVAL pseudocolumns, the SQL dot notation must be used. For example, the following statement will insert a new record into the Employee table.

This insert statement will use the next increment of the emp_id_seq sequence for the value to be inserted into the emp_id column.

INPUT

```
INSERT into employee
VALUES (emp_id_seq.NEXTVAL,'Stanton Bernard');
```

ANALYSIS
This sample code inserts a single record into the Employee table. The employee id is created and provide by the emp_id_seq sequence number. The employee name is hard coded and provide in the insert statement.

ROWID Pseudocolumns

The ROWID pseudocolumn represents the binary address of a row in a table. You can use variables of type UROWID to store rowids in a readable format. In the following example, you declare a variable named emp_row_id for that purpose:

```
DECLARE
    emp_row_id UROWID;
```

When you select or fetch a rowid into a UROWID variable, you can use the function ROWIDTOCHAR, which converts the binary value to an 18-byte character string. Then, you can compare the UROWID variable to the ROWID pseudocolumn in the WHERE clause of an UPDATE or DELETE statement to identify the latest row fetched from a cursor.

ROWNUM Pseudocolumns

The ROWNUM pseudocolumn refers to the order in which data was retrieved from a table. For example, ROWNUM of 1 indicates that row was the first row retrieved from the table. Likewise, ROWNUM of 2333 refers to 2333rd row retrieved from the table. ROWNUM values are assigned when the fetch occurs and are not affected by the ORDER BY clause.

The most common usage of the ROWNUM pseudocolumn is in the WHERE clause statement. For example, you may want to do an interactive select on a table until the ROWNUM is equal to some constant.

In this example, the interaction will continue until the ROWNUM is greater than 100.

```
DECLARE
CURSOR c1 IS SELECT sal
FROM employee
WHERE sal > 500 AND ROWNUM < 100;
```

The above cursor declaration code uses the ROWNUM pseudocolumn in the WHERE clause. The ROWNUM is used to limit the number of records processed to the first 99 records in the table.

Summary

Today's lesson presents you with a quick overview of using SQL statements within a PL/SQL block. You learned how to insert and retrieve data from tables that you created and how to prepare for runtime errors. You also learned about PL/SQL variables—how to declare them; how to use them; and how to base them on other objects such as database tables, columns, constants, and even other variables. The %type attribute enables you to keep the variable declaration in synch with the datatypes in the database.

Q&A

Q **What happens if my SQL statement fails inside the PL/SQL block?**

A The processing of your PL/SQL block will terminate unless you have code in place to trap and handle the exception. PL/SQL allows for numerous predefined exceptions that make your coding easier.

Q **What is a PL/SQL record?**

A A PL/SQL record is a variable with the type record. It is a composite structure containing fields with its own datatypes. Records can help the developer by reducing the volume of code necessary. Records allow similar fields to be grouped and treated as one logical entity.

Q **What is the difference between Data Manipulation Language statements and Transaction control statements?**

A The Transaction control statements ensure the integrity of the data while using Data Manipulation Language statements. That is, while you use the SELECT, UPDATE, INSERT, and DELETE statements, the programmer will insert the appropriate transaction control statements to ensure the data is accurate and does not become corrupted.

Workshop

The following workshop will test your comprehension of this chapter and give you an opportunity to practice what you have just learned. The answers to the quiz and exercises are provided in Appendix A, "Answers."

Quiz

1. Name some of the database objects that you can base a variable declaration on.

2. Name at least two of the exception types discussed in this chapter.

3. Do you need to list the table column names while inserting data into that table?

4. What are the five SQL DML statements permitted in a PL/SQL block?

Exercises

Evaluate each of the following three declarations and determine which ones are legal or not legal. Explain your answer for those that are not legal.

1. Legal or not legal:
```
DECLARE
emp_rec        emp_rec_type;
```

2. Legal or not legal:

```
DECLARE
emp_last_name          %type;
```

3. Legal or not legal:

```
LOCK TABLE department
IN EXCLUSIVE MODE;
```

DAY 9

Manipulating Data with Cursors

by Tom Luers

PL/SQL cursors provide a way for your program to select multiple rows of data from the database and then process each row individually. Specifically, a *cursor* is a name assigned by Oracle to every SQL statement processed. This name provides Oracle a means to direct and control all phases of the SQL processing. Today, you will learn

- Cursor creation
- Cursor processing
- Defining and using cursor attributes

What Is a Cursor?

 Oracle uses two kinds of *cursors*: *implicit* and *explicit*. PL/SQL implicitly declares a cursor for every SQL statement used, regardless of the number of rows returned by the statement. It needs to do this to manage the processing of the SQL statement. Implicit cursors are declared by Oracle for each UPDATE, DELETE, and INSERT SQL command. The user declares and uses explicit cursors to process multiple rows returned by a SELECT statement. Explicitly defined cursors are constructs that enable the user to name an area of memory to hold a specific statement for access at a later time.

As you recall from earlier in this book, SELECT statements can return zero, one, or many rows of data. When a PL/SQL cursor query returns multiple rows of data, the resulting group of rows is called the *active set*. This active set is stored by Oracle in the explicitly defined and named cursor that you create. The Oracle cursor is a mechanism used to process multiple rows of data easily. Without cursors, the Oracle developer would have to explicitly fetch and manage each individual row that is selected by the cursor query.

Another feature of the cursor is that it contains a pointer that keeps track of the current row being accessed, which enables your program to process the rows one at a time. Figure 9.1 illustrates an Oracle cursor: It shows the active set, which is the row returned by the cursor's SELECT statement and the pointer indicating the latest row fetched from the active set.

FIGURE 9.1

An Oracle multirow cursor.

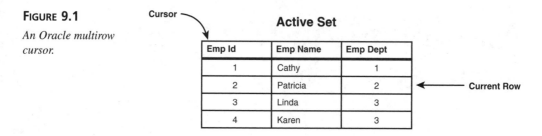

Explicit Cursors

Explicit cursors are defined by the programmer to process a multiple-row active set one record at a time. The following are the steps for using explicitly defined cursors within PL/SQL:

1. Declare the cursor.
2. Open the cursor.
3. Fetch data from the cursor.
4. Close the cursor.

Declaring a Cursor

The first step is to declare the cursor for PL/SQL to reference the returned data. You must do this in the declaration portion of your PL/SQL block. Declaring a cursor accomplishes two goals:

- It names the cursor.
- It associates a query with the cursor.

The name you assign to a cursor is an undeclared identifier, not a PL/SQL variable. You cannot assign values to a cursor name or use it in an expression. This name is used in the PL/SQL block to reference the cursor query.

SYNTAX ▲

```
DECLARE cursor_name
is
SELECT statement
```

In this syntax, cursor_name is the name you assign to the cursor. SELECT statement is the query that returns rows to the cursor active set.

In the following example, the cursors named c_names_salary and c_names_hourly are defined with a SELECT statement that queries the employee table:

```
DECLARE
CURSOR c_names_salary
  is
     SELECT emp_name from employee
     WHERE pay_type = 'S';
CURSOR c_names_hourly
  is
     SELECT emp.name from employee
     WHERE pay_type = 'H';
```

The only constraint that can limit the number of cursors is the availability of memory to manage the cursors. Oracle system administrators use the OPEN_CURSOR parameter in the init.ora file to help manage this memory use.

You can also use a subquery in your cursor declaration:

```
DECLARE
    CURSOR c_names_landscapers
    IS SELECT emp_name from employee
    Where area_name IN (SELECT area_name from dept
    Where street_name <> 'MINGO WAY');
```

Passing Parameters to Cursors

In PL/SQL, you can pass parameters into cursors just as you do with functions and procedures. (Cursors cannot pass parameters out of the cursors.) For example, you can establish the value of a parameter depending on your logic and then pass this parameter into the cursor for processing. These parameters make your code more modular and maintainable. You no longer have to hard-code values in the query statement.

Declaring Cursor Parameters

To declare cursor parameters, place the parameters in the cursor definition statement enclosed in parentheses. In Oracle, you can use as many parameters as you need.

```
CURSOR name (parameter_1 data_type, parameter_2 data_type...)
IS SELECT statement...
```

In this syntax, *name* is the name you assign to the cursor. *parameter_1* and *parameter_2* are the parameters that you pass into the cursor. The *data_types* correspond to the parameters. Finally, the SELECT *statement* is the statement that defines the cursor contents.

Here is an example of a cursor that is to receive two parameters. One of the parameters is used in the SELECT statement:

```
DECLARE
CURSOR emp_cur
(emp_nbr  number,  emp_name varchar2(32))
IS SELECT pay_rate FROM employee WHERE emp_id = emp_nbr;
                                -- parameter is used here
```

You can also initialize cursor parameters in the declaration statement. This is a convenient method for passing default values to the cursor. Likewise, you can override these default values with different, explicitly defined values. The following example passes two different parameters to the cursor in a stock-purchasing scenario:

```
DECLARE
CURSOR stock_cur
(buy_price    number  default 23.50,
sell_price    number  default 38.33) IS SELECT ...
```

Using the preceding declaration, you can pass actual values to the two parameters in the OPEN cursor statement, thereby overriding the specified default values. The following example causes the cursor to be declared with a buy_price of $24.25 and a sell_price of $44.67:

```
OPEN stock_cur (24.25, 44.67);
```

If you pass no values to the cursor in the OPEN statement, the default values take effect. Hence, the following two OPEN statements are equivalent:

```
OPEN stock_cur;
OPEN stock_cur (23.50,38.33);
```

Opening the Cursor

Opening the cursor activates the query and identifies the active set. When the OPEN command is executed, the cursor identifies only the rows that satisfy the query. The rows are not actually retrieved until the cursor fetch is issued. OPEN also initializes the cursor pointer to just before the first row of the active set.

SYNTAX

```
OPEN cursor_name;
```

In this syntax, *cursor_name* is the name of the cursor that you have previously defined.

After the OPEN command is issued, the cursor looks like Figure 9.2, which shows that the active set has retrieved its data from the database. The cursor establishes its pointer at the top of the active set; the pointer is before the first row because the FETCH command has not been issued yet.

FIGURE 9.2

View of the opened cursor.

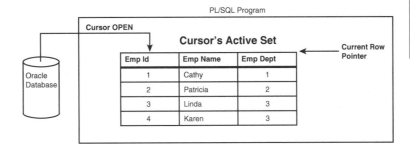

Note

After a cursor is opened, until the moment you close the cursor, all fetched data in the active set remains static. This means that the cursor ignores all SQL DML commands (INSERT, UPDATE, DELETE, and SELECT) performed on that data after the cursor was opened. Hence, you should only open the cursor when you need it. To refresh the active set, simply close and reopen the cursor.

If you try to open a cursor that is already open, you receive the following error:

```
ORA-06511: PL/SQL: cursor already open
```

If this error occurs, check your logic or close the cursor earlier in the block and reopen it when needed. You can check the status of the cursor by using the cursor %isopen attribute. Later in the lesson, additional cursor attributes are covered in the section "Explicit Cursor Attributes." The following example demonstrates the %isopen attribute:

```
IF not employee%isopen
THEN
OPEN employee;
END IF;
```

Oracle 8i also lets you pass parameters to the cursor via the OPEN clause. Using parameters in the OPEN clause allows you to override the default values for each formal parameter. The following code segment illustrates that there needs to be a formal parameter defined in the cursor OPEN clause for each parameter declared:

```
DECLARE
    Stock_listing_name stock.sname%TYPE;
    Stock_listing_price stock.sprice%TYPE;
CURSOR stock_listing_cur (stock_name VARCHAR2(15), stock_price NUMBER)
Is SELECT …
```

With this code, you cannot open the cursor with parameters containing any of the following:

```
OPEN stock_listing_cur (stock_listing.name, 'ABCDEFG');
OPEN stock)listing_cur (stock_listing_name, stock_listing_price);
```

Fetching Data in a Cursor

You get data into the cursor with the FETCH command. The FETCH command retrieves the rows in the active set one row at a time. You usually use the FETCH command in conjunction with some type of iterative process. The first FETCH statement sorts the active set as necessary. In the iterative processes, the cursor advances to the next row in the active set each time the FETCH command is executed. The FETCH command is the only means to navigate through the active set.

SYNTAX

FETCH cursor_name INTO record_list;

In this syntax, cursor_name is the name of the previously defined cursor from which you are now retrieving rows—one at a time. record_list is a list of variables that will receive the columns from the active set. The FETCH command places the results of the active set into these variables.

▲

After a FETCH has been issued, the cursor looks like Figure 9.3, which shows that the results in the active set are fetched into the PL/SQL variables for use within that PL/SQL block. After each fetch, the cursor pointer moves to the next row in the active set.

FIGURE 9.3

View of the opened cursor after the FETCH command is issued.

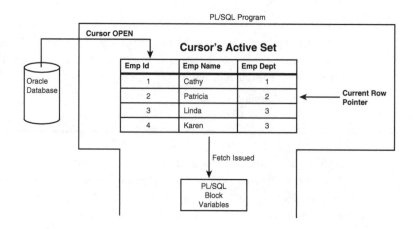

The *record list*, or variable list, is the PL/SQL structure that receives the fetched rows of data. Each column value retrieved by the cursor's query must have a corresponding variable in the INTO list. Additionally, their data types must be compatible. If you fetch into a record, the number of columns in the record must match the number of expressions in the select list in the cursor.

If you want to revisit a previously fetched row, you must close and reopen the cursor and then fetch each row in turn. If you want to change the active set, you must assign new values to the input variables in the cursor query and reopen the cursor. This re-creates the active set with the results of the revised query statement.

Note

> The cursor's active set is limited in size to the number of rows returned. Therefore, when the FETCH is looping throughout the cursor, it is bound to fail when there are no more rows to fetch. With cursors, no exceptions are raised when the FETCH reaches the end of the active set. You must use cursor attributes to detect when this condition occurs.

Closing the Cursor

The CLOSE statement closes or deactivates the previously opened cursor and makes the active set undefined. Oracle implicitly closes a cursor when the user's program or session is terminated. After the cursor is closed, you cannot perform any operation on it, or you receive an invalid_cursor exception.

```
CLOSE cursor_name;
```

In this syntax, *cursor_name* is the name of the previously opened cursor.

Explicit Cursor Attributes

Each cursor, whether it is explicitly or implicitly defined, carries with it attributes that provide useful data regarding the results of a multirow SELECT. The four cursor attributes are %isopen, %found, %notfound, and %rowcount. You can use these attributes in any PL/SQL statement. You cannot use cursor attributes against closed cursors; an invalid_cursor error is issued if you attempt it.

The %isopen Attribute

The %isopen attribute indicates whether a cursor is open. If the named cursor is open, this attribute equates to true; otherwise, it is false. The following example uses the %isopen attribute to open a cursor if it is not already open:

```
IF c_names%isopen THEN
      process_data_procedure;
ELSE
```

```
      OPEN  c_names;
END IF;
```

The %found Attribute

The %found attribute equates to true if the last FETCH statement affects one or more rows. Therefore, the %found attribute is the logical opposite of the %notfound attribute. The %found attribute equates to false when no rows are fetched. Like %notfound, this attribute also equates to NULL prior to the first fetch.

The following example illustrates a practical use of the %found attribute:

```
LOOP
FETCH c_names INTO record_names;
IF c_names%found THEN
process_names_function;
ELSE
EXIT;
END IF;
END LOOP;
```

The %notfound Attribute

The %notfound attribute is useful in telling you whether a cursor has any rows left in it to be fetched. The %notfound attribute equates to false when there are rows remaining in the cursor. It equates to true when there are no more rows remaining. After the fetching has started, until and including the fetch on the last row, %notfound is false. Prior to the first fetch, this attribute equates to NULL. An error is returned if you evaluate %notfound on a cursor that is not open.

The following example illustrates a practical use of the %notfound attribute:

```
LOOP
 FETCH c_names INTO record_names;
  EXIT when c_names%notfound;
END LOOP;
```

The %rowcount Attribute

The %rowcount attribute returns the number of rows fetched so far for the cursor. Prior to the first fetch, %rowcount is zero. There are many practical applications of the %rowcount attribute. The following example performs a commit after the first 250 employees' salaries are processed:

```
LOOP
FETCH c_names INTO record_names;
IF c_names%rowcount = 250;
COMMIT;
ELSE
EXIT;
END IF;
END LOOP;
```

Explicit Cursor Example

The following example illustrates the use of all four components of a PL/SQL cursor:

```
DECLARE

v_emp_name     VARCHAR2(32);
v_salary_rate   NUMBER(9,2);
v_payroll_total  NUMBER(9,2);
v_pay_type      CHAR;

CURSOR c_emp is                                    -- cursor declaration
SELECT emp_name, pay_rate, pay_type from employee
WHERE emp_dept_id = 3;

BEGIN

OPEN c_emp;                                        -- opening cursor
LOOP
FETCH  c_emp INTO v_emp_name, v_salary_rate, v_pay_type;    -- FETCH command
EXIT when c_emp%notfound;

IF v_pay_type = 'S' THEN
v_payroll_total := (v_salary_rate *  1.25);
ELSE
v_payroll_total := (v_salary_rate * 40);
END IF;
INSERT INTO weekly_salary values (v_payroll_total);
END LOOP;

CLOSE c_emp;                                       -- closing cursor
END;
```

Automated Explicit Cursors

The previous section illustrates the basic mechanics of declaring and using cursors. In many programming situations, there is more than one way to code your logic. This also applies to PL/SQL cursors; you have opportunities to streamline or simplify their coding and usage. One such way is to place the cursor within a FOR loop, which is known as a CURSOR FOR loop. A CURSOR FOR loop implicitly

- Declares the loop index
- Opens the cursor
- Fetches the next row from the cursor for each loop iteration
- Closes the cursor when all rows are processed or when the loop exits

CURSOR FOR loops are ideal when you want to loop through all the records returned by the cursor. With CURSOR FOR loops, you should not declare the record that controls the loop. Likewise, you should not use CURSOR FOR loops when the cursor operations must be handled manually. Listing 9.1 illustrates the use of CURSOR FOR loops.

INPUT   **LISTING 9.1** Using CURSOR FOR Loops

```
DECLARE
CURSOR c_employees is
     SELECT * from employees
     WHERE pay_type = 'H';

BEGIN                                  -- implicit cursor open
  FOR emp_record  in c_employees loop  -- implicit cursor fetch
       process_monthly_hourly_checks
 END LOOP;                             -- implicit cursor close
 COMMIT;
END;
```

Implicit Cursors

As mentioned earlier in this lesson, Oracle creates and opens a cursor for every SQL statement that is not part of an explicitly declared cursor. The most recent implicit cursor can be referred to as the SQL cursor. You cannot use the OPEN, CLOSE, and FETCH commands with an implicit cursor. However, you can use the cursor attributes to access information about the most recently executed SQL statement through the SQL cursor.

In the following example, PL/SQL creates an implicit cursor to identify the set of rows that are affected by the UPDATE command:

```
UPDATE employee
set pay_rate=pay_rate*1.08
WHERE pay-type='S'
```

Implicit Cursor Attributes

Like explicit cursors, implicit cursors use attributes as well. The implicit cursor attributes are named %isopen, %found, %notfound, and %rowcount. Because implicit cursors have no name, you must append SQL to the attributes. The implicit cursor contains information concerning the processing of the last SQL statement (INSERT, UPDATE, DELETE, and SELECT INTO) that was not associated with an explicit cursor. You can only use implicit cursor attributes in PL/SQL statements, not in SQL statements. The following sections briefly describe each attribute.

The %isopen Attribute

After the execution of the SQL statement, the associated SQL cursor is always closed automatically by Oracle. Hence, the %isopen attribute always evaluates to false.

The %found Attribute

The %found attribute equates to true if an INSERT, UPDATE, or DELETE affects one or more rows or a SELECT INTO returns one or more rows. Otherwise, it evaluates to false. %found equates to NULL until a SQL DML statement is executed. The following is an example using the implicit %found attribute:

```
UPDATE employees
set pay_type = 'S'
WHERE name = 'Bernard' or name = 'Stanton';

IF sql%found THEN
      COMMIT;
ELSE
     employee_not_found_procedure;
END IF;
```

The %notfound Attribute

The %notfound attribute evaluates to true if the most recent SQL statement does not affect any rows. Otherwise, it evaluates to false. The following example illustrates the implicit %notfound attribute:

```
UPDATE employees
set pay_type = 'S'
WHERE name = 'Bernard' or name = 'Stanton';

IF sql%notfound THEN
     employee_not_found_procedure;
ELSE
     COMMIT;
END IF;
```

You must design your code carefully with the SELECT INTO statements. You cannot use the %notfound attribute immediately after the SELECT INTO statement when no records are retrieved. The no_data_found exception is raised before the %notfound attribute is set. The following example illustrates this point:

```
/* The exception %notfound used with no exception handler in place.*/
/* Hence, proper processing might be inappropriately missed.*/
BEGIN
SELECT pay_type INTO hold_type
from employee WHERE name = 'Catherine';
    IF SQL%notfound THEN            -- processing may never reach here if
  employee_not_found_procedure;     -- the prior SELECT statement returns no
rows
    END IF;
```

```
exceptions
        ...
END;
```

The following shows the same example but adds an exception handler:

```
/* The exception %notfound is used with exception handler in place.*/
/* Hence proper processing takes place.*/
BEGIN
SELECT pay_type INTO hold_type
from employee WHERE name = 'Catherine';    -- processing goes to the exceptions
                                           -- area when no rows are returned.
when others THEN
    IF SQL%notfound THEN                    -- not found logic is executed here
            employee_not_found_procedure;
    END IF;
END;
```

The %rowcount Attribute

The %rowcount attribute equates to the total number of rows affected by the most recent SQL statement. An example of the %rowcount follows:

```
BEGIN
UPDATE employees
set pay_rate = pay_rate * 1.05
WHERE pay-type = 'S';
message('Total records updated are:'to_char(sql%rowcount));
END
```

Scope of Cursor Parameters

Cursor parameters are visible only to that cursor. You cannot reference a cursor parameter outside the context of the cursor. If you try to refer to a cursor parameter outside the cursor, Oracle returns an error indicating that the variable is undefined.

Cursor Return Clause and Packages

As you learned earlier in this lesson, you can declare and use cursors inside packages. Oracle does allow you to place the cursor declaration in the package specification and the cursor body in the package body. This separation of declaration and body gives the developer some level of design and programming flexibility. The programmer can alter the cursor body without having to alter the specification. Or better yet, the programmer only needs to know what the cursor returns and not how it is accomplished. The following example illustrates the separation of the cursor body from its declaration.

The package specification is

```
CREATE PACKAGE  stock_purchase as
CURSOR stock_cur RETURN stock%rowtype;
END stock_purchase;
```

The package body is

```
CREATE PACKAGE BODY stock_purchase as
CURSOR stock_cur return stock%rowtype
SELECT stock_type, stock_name, curr_prics
FROM stocks
WHERE stock_type = :stock_type;
```

Note that the preceding example uses the return clause. The return clause is mandatory when you elect to separate the cursor components. This clause creates the bridge between the two just as if they appear together in a typical cursor construct.

Cursor Variables

As you recall from the previous lesson, the PL/SQL cursor is a named area in the database. The cursor variable, by definition, is a reference to that named area. A cursor variable is like a pointer in a programming language such as C. Cursor variables point to a query's work area in which the query's result set is stored. A cursor variable is also dynamic in nature because it is not tied to a specific query. Oracle retains this work area as long as a cursor pointer is pointing to it. You can use a cursor variable for any type-compatible query.

One of the most significant features of the cursor variable is that Oracle allows you to pass a cursor variable as an argument to a procedure or function call. The cursor variable cannot accept variables to itself.

You can also declare cursor variables using programs such as Pro*C or OCI. After the cursor variable is declared there, you can pass it as a bind variable to your PL/SQL block. These variables can be declared in other Oracle products such as Forms. Additionally, you can pass cursor variables back and forth between servers and applications through Oracle's remote procedure calls.

The Cursor Variable Declaration

To create a cursor variable, you must first create a referenced cursor type and then declare a cursor variable on that type.

```
TYPE cursor_type_name IS REF CURSOR RETURN return_type;
```

In this syntax, REF stands for reference, *cursor_type_name* is the name of the type of cursor, and *return_type* is the data specification for the return cursor type. The return clause is optional.

Oracle makes a subtle distinction in cursor variables based upon whether a return clause is included in the cursor variable. If the return clause is present, then the cursor variable is known as a *strong* cursor variable. If the return clause is not present, the cursor variable is a *weak* cursor variable. Do not confuse the RETURN statement with the return clause, which specifies the data type of the result value in a stored program.

The following example illustrates this declaration:

```
DECLARE
TYPE stocks_cur_type IS REF CURSOR RETURN stocks%rowtype;
                          -- strong cursor type creation
TYPE stocks_cur_price IS REF CURSOR;
                             -- weak cursor type creation

stocks_cur  stocks_cur_type;
      -- creation of cursor variable based on cursor type

BEGIN
...
END;
```

Remember, the cursor variable declaration does not create a cursor object, but rather a pointer to a cursor object. As such, you cannot substitute a cursor variable where a proper cursor is expected and required.

Cursor Usage with Cursor Variables

After the cursor variable is declared, you can use the variable in three different statements: OPEN...FOR, FETCH, and CLOSE. You can assign a value to it through the OPEN...FOR cursor statement.

```
OPEN cursor_name FOR select_statement
```

In this syntax, *cursor_name* is the name of the cursor, the cursor variable, or the host cursor variable, and *select_statement* is the appropriate SQL statement. This statement cannot use the FOR UPDATE clause.

The OPEN...FOR statement executes the multirow query associated with the declared cursor variable. The OPEN...FOR statement also identifies the result set, which consists of all rows that meet the query search criteria. Other OPEN...FOR statements can open the same cursor variable for different queries as needed. The following is an example of opening a cursor variable that is a bind variable:

```
BEGIN
OPEN :stocks_quote FOR SELECT * FROM stocks;
END;
```

After the cursor is opened, you can perform a typical FETCH using the cursor variable. The syntax for the FETCH statement using a cursor variable is the same as for a normal static cursor.

SYNTAX

FETCH *cursor_variable_name* INTO *record_name* or *variable_name*

In this syntax, *cursor_variable_name* is the variable you declared in the local block, package specification, or host environment such as Pro*C, and *record_name* or *variable_name* is the object where the FETCH will place the data from the cursor.

PL/SQL makes sure the return type of the cursor variable is compatible with the INTO clause of the FETCH statement. Each column value returned by the query associated with the cursor variable must have a corresponding variable in the INTO clause. Also, the number of fields or variables must equal the number of column values.

The following example pulls together the concepts of declaring, opening, and fetching cursors:

```
DECLARE
TYPE stocks_cur_type IS REF cursor RETURN stocks%rowtype
stocks_cur   stocks_cur_type;

BEGIN
OPEN stocks_cur for
SELECT stock_name, stock_type, stock_quote from stocks;
FETCH stocks_cur INTO stocks_rec;
END;
```

After you are finished using the cursor variable in your logic, you need to close the variable. The syntax follows your normal cursor syntax:

```
CLOSE stocks_cur;
```

The following example illustrates the use of different INTO clauses on different fetches that happen to use the same cursor variable. Each of the fetches retrieves another row from the same result set:

```
BEGIN
...
FETCH stock_quote_cur INTO stock_rec1;
...
FETCH stock_quote_cur INTO stock_rec2:
...
END;
```

Cursor Variable Assignments

You can include the cursor variable in any assignment statement. This is a convenient and efficient method to share the cursor pointer.

▼ SYNTAX ▲

```
assignment statement := cursor variable name
```

In this syntax, *cursor variable name* is a PL/SQL cursor variable that has been previously defined and is in the scope of the *assignment statement*. It can also be a host cursor variable name. The host cursor variable name is declared in a PL/SQL host environment such as Pro*C. This variable is passed into the assignment statement as a bind variable.

An example of the assignment statement using a cursor variable (bind variable) is

```
current_stock_price := :host_cur_stock_quote;
```

Cursor Variables as Arguments

As mentioned earlier, Oracle allows you to pass Oracle cursor variables as arguments to procedures and functions. When your parameter list contains a cursor variable, the mode of the parameter and the data type must be specified. The data type for the cursor variable used as an argument is the REF cursor type.

The following example illustrates the use of the REF cursor syntax and the use of a cursor variable as a parameter:

```
DECLARE
TYPE cur_var_type IS REF CURSOR RETURN employee%rowtype;

PROCEDURE SELECT emp_query (cur_var_out  out cur_var_type) IS
BEGIN
...
END;
```

This example works well in local modules with a program. However, if you are creating a standalone procedure or function, then you must reference a pre-existing REF cursor type that exists in a package specification. As you recall from Day 7, "Procedures, Packages, Errors, and Exceptions," all variables declared in a package specification are global to the package body. You can reference a cursor type using the standard package dot notation.

To use a cursor variable in a package, you must first declare the REF cursor type in the specification:

```
PACKAGE stocks
IS
TYPE cur_var_type IS REF CURSOR RETURN stocks%rowtype;
END package;
```

To use the cursor variable declared in the preceding example, simply reference the REF cursor type using the dot notation:

```
PROCEDURE obtain_stock_quotes (cur_var_out in stocks.cur_var_type) IS
BEGIN
...
END;
```

You can use the preceding notation for any of the function and procedure calls within that package.

The cursor variable is a true variable, and it is global in nature to the package or local module. It does not reflect the state of the object but rather is the reference to the cursor object. To change the value of a cursor variable, you must change the cursor object to which the variable points.

The cursor variable argument can have one of three different modes:

- IN—The program can have read-only abilities with the parameter. In other words, the cursor argument is passed only to the procedure or function.
- OUT—The program can return values to the calling PL/SQL block.
- IN OUT—The program can read or write to the variable.

When you declare a cursor variable as a parameter of a procedure or function that fetches from the cursor variable, you must specify the IN or IN OUT mode. Likewise, if the procedure or function also opens the cursor variable, you must specify the IN OUT mode. Finally, you must use the IN OUT mode when you want the procedure or function to pass an open cursor back to the calling program.

The Current Row of Cursors

The current row of a cursor always refers to the latest row retrieved by the FETCH statement. Oracle allows you to delete and update this current row. To delete or update the fetched row, the cursor must be declared using the FOR UPDATE clause and must be open. The following example illustrates the update of the current row for the employee cursor:

```
DECLARE
CURSOR emp_cur IS                          -- cursor declared for update
SELECT emp_name, pay_type, pay_rate
FROM employee
WHERE pay_rate > 5000.00
FOR UPDATE of pay_type;                        -- FOR UPDATE clause

emp_rec   emp_cur%rowtype;

BEGIN
OPEN emp_cur;                                  -- cursor is opened
```

```
LOOP
FETCH emp_cur INTO emp_rec;
UPDATE employee                            -- updates current row
SET pay_type = 'H'
WHERE CURRENT OF emp_cur;
EXIT WHEN emp_cur%notfound;
END LOOP;
END;
```

Cursor Scoping

The scope of a cursor variable follows these rules:

- The cursor variable is available to the local module in which it is declared.
- The cursor variable is global in nature when declared in a package.
- The cursor variable can exist outside its original scope, as shown in Figure 9.4.

FIGURE 9.4

Cursor variable scope.

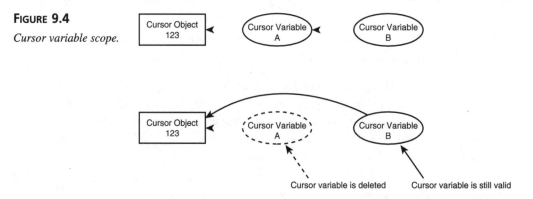

At the top of Figure 9.4, cursor variable B is assigned to cursor variable A. Cursor variable A is assigned to the cursor object 123. Both cursor variables are within the scope of cursor object 123. Cursor object 123 remains accessible to cursor variable B even when cursor variable A is deleted—as shown in the bottom half of Figure 9.4.

Remember that any variable, cursor or otherwise, is valid only in the scope of the loop. You cannot make any external reference to the cursor variable declared in a loop because it does not exist. Any cursor variable declared in an inner PL/SQL block is not accessible to the outer PL/SQL block. Likewise, you cannot refer to a cursor outside the declaring block unless the cursor is declared in a package specification.

Cursor Alias

As shown in Figure 9.4, you can have two cursor variables assigned to a single cursor object. Each of the variables is an alias to the cursor object. They both share the result set of the cursor object 123 query. Anything that one alias, or cursor variable, does that affects the cursor object is seen immediately in the other cursor variable. The following cursor pseudo-code illustrates this concept:

```
PROCEDURE obtain_stock_quotes (stock_cv_1  in out  stock_cur_type,
                                       stock_cv_2 in out stock_cur_type);
stock_rec     stocks%rowtype;

BEGIN
OPEN stock_cv_1 FOR SELECT * FROM stocks;      -- open the cursor

stock_cv_2 := stock_cv_1;                   -- cursor variable assignment
FETCH stock_cv_1 INTO stock_rec;         -- fetch first record from cursor
FETCH stock_cv_2 INTO stock_rec;        -- fetch second record from cursor
FETCH stock_cv_2 INTO stock_rec;         -- fetch third record from cursor

CLOSE stock_cv_1;                         -- closes cursor for both aliases
```

Because the cursor is closed at this point, you *cannot* fetch from the cursor using either of the stock_cv_1 or stock_cv_2 variables. If you do attempt a fetch at this point, an error occurs, stating that the cursor is closed.

Summary

Cursors are PL/SQL constructs that enable you to process, one row at a time, the results of a multirow query. Implicit cursors are created for each DML statement, whereas explicit cursors are created by users to process queries that return multiple rows. Furthermore, cursors improve code processing by reducing the need to parse code repeatedly. The ability to pass parameters to cursors increases the coding power of the developer.

Q&A

Q When do you use an explicit cursor instead of an implicit cursor?

A Explicit cursors must be declared and used when you want to process queries that return multiple rows and you want to handle these rows individually.

Q What are the four steps to using an explicit cursor?

A The four steps are

1. Declare the cursor.

2. Open the cursor.

3. Fetch the rows.

4. Close the cursor.

Q Is there any way to expedite or simplify the steps to using a cursor?

A Yes. The CURSOR FOR loop construct causes Oracle to implicitly open, fetch, and
close the cursor.

Workshop

The following workshop will test your understanding of PL/SQL cursors and their uses.
The answers to the quiz and exercise appear in Appendix A, "Answers."

Quiz

1. What are the cursor attributes and what is their purpose?

2. How many cursors can you use at a time?

3. Where is the cursor pointer when the cursor is first opened?

4. Name the different cursor variable parameter modes and their purpose.

Exercise

Create a PL/SQL block that determines the top five highest paid employees from your
employee table. Be sure to incorporate the usage of the appropriate cursor attributes.
Print these five employees to the screen.

DAY 10

Collections

by Jonathan Gennick

Collections in PL/SQL allow you to group together many occurrences of an object. PL/SQL now supports three types of collections:

- Index-by tables
- Nested tables
- Variable-sized arrays (varrays)

If you're familiar with other programming languages, you might think of a collection as being similar to an array. An *array* is a repeating series of elements, all of the same type. You'll learn later in this lesson that some of Oracle's collection types are more like traditional arrays than others.

Today, you will learn how to:

- Declare and use index-by tables
- Declare and use nested tables
- Declare and use varrays

Using PL/SQL Index-by Tables

Index-by tables are one of the three collection types supported by PL/SQL. In fact, they are the original collection type. If you are using PL/SQL release 2.3 or lower, then index-by tables are the only collection type you have.

NEW TERM An *index-by* table is a table of elements, held in memory, where each element is indexed by an integer value. Index-by tables function similarly to arrays, with a couple major differences:

- An index-by table can be sparsely populated.
- You don't set a maximum size for an index-by table.

The next few sections show you how to declare an index-by table, and insert data into that table. You will also learn how individual table elements are referenced, and how they can be modified.

Declaring an Index-by Table

You declare an index-by table by declaring a type, and then by declaring one or more variables of the type. When you declare the type, you specify a datatype for the collection and a datatype for the table's index. The datatype for the collection may be a scalar type such as NUMBER or VARCHAR2, or it may be a composite type such as a record. The datatype for the table's index must always be BINARY_INTEGER. The syntax for declaring an index-by table type follows.

▼ SYNTAX

```
TYPE type_name IS TABLE OF data_type [NOT NULL] INDEX BY BINARY_INTEGER;
```

In this syntax the parameters are as follows:

- *type_name* is the name of the type you are declaring. You use this to declare index-by table variables.
- *data_type* is the datatype of the collection. Each element of the table stores a value of this type.
- NOT NULL prohibits a table entry from being null.

▲

The datatype used for the elements in the table can be either a scalar type or a record type. A *scalar* variable is one that has a single value. A *record* variable is one that contains several related values. The following two examples declare types for a table of numeric values, and a table of employee records, respectively:

```
TYPE num_table IS TABLE OF NUMBER INDEX BY BINARY_INTEGER;
TYPE emp_table IS TABLE OF employee%ROWTYPE INDEX BY BINARY_INTEGER;
```

After you have defined the types, you can go ahead and declare variables, as in the following example:

```
salaries num_table;
emp emp_table;
```

It is not possible to declare a variable as an index-by table without first declaring a type. You can't combine the type declaration with the variable declaration. After you declare a table variable, you can proceed to use it much as you would an array.

Inserting Entries into an Index-by Table

The elements in an index-by table are each uniquely identified by an integer value, or index. Whenever you reference a value in the table, you must supply that value's index. To insert values into a PL/SQL table, you use an assignment statement that looks like this:

```
table_var (index) := value;
```

The *index* value can be any number between 1 and 2,147,483,647. Index values don't need to be consecutive. If you were to place only two entries into a table, you could use indexes 1 and 2, or you could use 1 and 2,147,483,647. Either way, you would have two entries. PL/SQL does not reserve space for entries that are not used.

Listing 10.1 shows the entire contents of the `employee` table being read into an index-by table named emp.

INPUT   **LISTING 10.1**   Placing Employee Records in an Index-by Table

```
 1: DECLARE
 2:     --Declare a cursor that returns all employee records.
 3:     CURSOR all_emps IS
 4:         SELECT *
 5:         FROM employee
 6:         ORDER BY emp_name;
 7:
 8:     --Define an index-by table type.
 9:     TYPE emp_table IS TABLE OF employee%ROWTYPE
10:                 INDEX BY BINARY_INTEGER;
11:
12:     --Declare an index-by table variable to
13:     --hold the employee records that we read in.
14:     emps emp_table;
15:     emps_max BINARY_INTEGER;
16: BEGIN
17:     emps_max := 0;
```

continues

LISTING **10.1**   continued

```
18:
19:      FOR emp IN all_emps LOOP
20:          emps_max := emps_max + 1;
21:
22:          emps(emps_max).emp_id := emp.emp_id;
23:          emps(emps_max).emp_name := emp.emp_name;
24:          emps(emps_max).supervised_by := emp.supervised_by;
25:          emps(emps_max).pay_rate := emp.pay_rate;
26:          emps(emps_max).pay_type := emp.pay_type;
27:      END LOOP;
28: END;
29: /
```

ANALYSIS   The table type is declared in lines 9–10. The table itself is defined in line 14. In line 15, a variable named emps_max is defined as BINARY_INTEGER. This variable will be used as the index to the table. The cursor FOR loop in lines 19–27 increments this index for each new row added to the table. In lines 22–26, you can see the values of the employee columns being assigned to an entry in the table. Notice the use of dot notation. Because this is a table of employee records, each entry has several fields. If you weren't assigning values to fields in a record, dot notation would be unnecessary.

The example in Listing 10.1 adds entries to the table by using sequentially ascending index values. That's not a requirement. Because the employee ID is a number, you could modify the assignments in Listing 10.1 to use that value as the index. The result would look like this:

```
emps(emp.emp_id).emp_id := emp.emp_id;
emps(emp.emp_id).emp_name := emp.emp_name;
emps(emp.emp_id).supervised_by := emp.supervised_by;
emps(emp.emp_id).pay_rate := emp.pay_rate;
emps(emp.emp_id).pay_type := emp.pay_type;
```

You should choose the indexing method that works best for what you are trying to do. If you just need to keep large amounts of data in memory, then a sequential index might be best. On the other hand, if you need to quickly find a record, then basing the index on that record's primary key might be the best choice.

Referencing Values in an Index-by Table

To reference a specific entry in an index-by table, you specify an index value, using the same array-like syntax you used when inserting the data. For example, to evaluate the 12th salary value from the salaries table declared previously, you could write an IF statement like this:

INPUT   `IF salaries(12) > 100000 THEN ...`

You can place a reference to an index-by table entry in an expression, or you can pass it as a parameter to a procedure or function.

Index-by tables are sparsely populated. This means that there might be index values for which there is no entry. If you try to reference one of those, you get a NO DATA FOUND exception. If you're not sure that you are referencing an entry that exists, you can either trap the exception, or you use the EXISTS method. Listing 10.2 demonstrates both approaches.

INPUT   **LISTING 10.2**   Referencing Table Entries That Don't Exist

```
 1: DECLARE
 2:     --Define an index-by table type.
 3:     TYPE num_table IS TABLE OF NUMBER
 4:                 INDEX BY BINARY_INTEGER;
 5:
 6:     --Declare an index-by table variable to
 7:     --hold the employee records that we read in.
 8:     nums num_table;
 9:     some_num NUMBER;
10: BEGIN
11:     --First, insert an entry into the table.
12:     nums(10) := 11;
13:
14:     --Now, reference a nonexistant entry.
15:     --Trap the exception if it occurs.
16:     BEGIN
17:         some_num := nums(11);
18:     EXCEPTION
19:     WHEN NO_DATA_FOUND THEN
20:         DBMS_OUTPUT.PUT_LINE('Element 11 does not exist.');
21:     END;
22:
23:     --Try again, this time using the EXISTS METHOD.
24:     IF nums.EXISTS(11) THEN
25:         some_num := nums(11);
26:     ELSE
27:         DBMS_OUTPUT.PUT_LINE('Element 11 still does not exist.');
28:     END IF;
29: END;
30: /
```

ANALYSIS   Line 12 places a value into the table associated with the index value 10. There are no other values in the table. Line 17, inside the nested PL/SQL block (lines 16–21), attempts to reference entry 11, which is a non-existent entry. That triggers a NO DATA FOUND exception, which is caught by the exception handler. In lines 24–28, another attempt is made to access entry 11. This time, the EXISTS method is used first to see if that is a valid entry.

Changing Table Entries

You update a PL/SQL table in a very similar way as you do for inserting data into a PL/SQL table. If you have already inserted a row number 102 in the emps table, then you can update that same row with a statement like this:

INPUT   `emps(102).emp_name := 'Joseph Lawhead';`

This statement updates the emp_name field for the record in table entry number 102 with the new value in the assignment statement.

Deleting Table Entries

You can delete entries in a table by invoking the DELETE method. A *method* is a function or procedure that is attached to an object. Here, the table is the object, and the DELETE procedure is the method. DELETE can be used to delete one entry, a range of entries, or all entries, from the table. The syntax for the DELETE method is as follows.

`table_name.DELETE[(first_entry[,last_entry])];`

In this syntax the parameters are as follows:

- `table_name` is the table variable name.
- `first_entry` is the index of the entry that you want to delete, or the index of the first entry in a range of entries that you want to delete.
- `last_entry` is the last index in a range that you want to delete.

Invoking the DELETE method by itself causes all data to be deleted from the table. So to clear the emps table, for example, you could use the following statement

`emps.DELETE;`

To erase just one entry (the 10th entry, for instance), you would use this:

`emps.DELETE(10);`

Finally, to delete entries 1 through 10, you would use this:

`emps.DELETE(1,10);`

If you're using an older release of PL/SQL (older than the 8.0 release), the DELETE method isn't available to you. The only way to delete the data from a table is to keep an empty table around, and to assign it to the table that you want to delete. Listing 103 provides an example.

LISTING 10.3 Using an Empty Table to Erase Data

```
 1: DECLARE
 2:     TYPE salary_table IS TABLE OF NUMBER INDEX BY BINARY_INTEGER;
 3:
 4:     salaries salary_table;
 5:     salaries_empty salary_table;
 6: BEGIN
 7:     --Place some values into the salaries table.
 8:     salaries(20) := 50550;
 9:     salaries(40) := 50550;
10:     salaries(60) := 50550;
11:
12:     --Now, clear the salaries table by assigning the
13:     --empty version to it.
14:     salaries := salaries_empty;
15: END;
16: /
```

ANALYSIS Two tables are defined in lines 4 and 5. One table, the salaries table, is the one that we are using to hold data. The other is kept empty purposely so that we can use it to erase the salaries table from time to time. Lines 8–10 create three entries in the salaries table. To delete those entries, you would use the DELETE method, but prior to the 8.0 release of PL/SQL, that wasn't available. Instead, to free up the space used by the entries in the salaries table, you would assign an empty table over the top of them. Line 14 does this. It assigns the salaries_empty table to the salaries table. This automatically releases the memory used by the three entries created earlier. Using this technique, it's possible to erase all entries in the table, but not to erase just one. To erase specific entries, you need to use the DELETE method.

Caution

If you invoke the DELETE method with no parameters, you will delete all data in the table. Be sure that you really intend to do that.

PL/SQL Table Methods

You've already learned about the DELETE and EXISTS methods. PL/SQL provides several other useful built-in methods for use with PL/SQL tables. The complete list is as follows:

- count — The count method returns the number of entries in the table. The following example shows it being used to return the number of rows in the emps table:

```
num_rows := emps.count;
```

The specification, or declaration, for the `count` method looks like this:

```
FUNCTION count RETURN INTEGER;
```

- `exists`—This function returns the value `true` if a specific table entry exists. Otherwise, it returns `false`. In the following example, `exists` returns `true` if the emps table contains an entry for the index value 11:

```
IF emps.exists(3) THEN...
```

The specification for the `exists` method looks like this:

```
FUNCTION exists (index in INTEGER) RETURN boolean;
```

- `limit`—This method returns the maximum number of elements that a collection can contain. Only variable-sized arrays, which you'll learn about later in this lesson, have an upper limit. When used with nested tables and index-by tables, the `limit` method returns `NULL`. The following example shows `limit` being used to avoid the use of an index value that is too high with a variable-sized array:

```
IF inx > emp_array.limit THEN
   ...
ELSE
   emp_array(inx) := emp_rec;
END IF;
```

The specification for the `limit` method looks like this:

```
FUNCTION limit RETURN INTEGER;
```

- `first`—This built-in method returns the lowest-used index value in a collection. The following example shows it being used to return the index value for the first entry in the emps table:

```
first_valid_index :=emps.first;
```

The specification for the `first` method looks like this:

```
FUNCTION first RETURN INTEGER;
```

- `last`—This function returns the value of the highest index in the PL/SQL table. The following example returns the value of the highest-used index in the emps table:

```
highest_valid_index := emps.last;
```

The specification for the `last` method looks like this:

```
FUNCTION last RETURN INTEGER;
```

- `next`—The next method returns the value of the next valid index that is higher than a value you supply. Take note of the syntax shown in the following example for the next built-in function:

```
next_index := emps.next (current_index);
```

The specification for the `next` method looks like this:

```
FUNCTION next RETURN INTEGER;
```

- `prior`—The `prior` method returns the value of the highest valid index preceding the index value you supply. Here's an example:

```
prior_index := emps.prior(current_index);
```

The specification for the `prior` method looks like this:

```
FUNCTION prior RETURN INTEGER;
```

- `delete`—The `delete` method allows you to delete entries from a collection. You can delete all entries by calling `DELETE` with no parameters, as in this example:

```
emps.delete;
```

You can also delete a specific entry, or a range of entries, by passing parameters to the method. The following two examples delete the 10th entry and entries 20–29, respectively

```
emps.delete(10);
emps.delete(20,29);
```

The `delete` method is a procedure, and does not return a value. The specification for `delete` looks like this:

```
PROCEDURE delete [(first_entry IN INTEGER[,
                   last_entry IN INTEGER])];
```

- `trim`—The `trim` method allows you to delete entries from the end of a collection. You can use `trim` on just one entry, or on several entries. The following two examples trim one and three entries, respectively, from the end of the `emps` collection:

```
emps.trim;
emps.trim(3);
```

The `trim` method is a procedure, and does not return a value. The specification for `trim` looks like this:

```
PROCEDURE trim [(number_to_trim IN INTEGER)];
```

The `trim` method can only be used with variable-sized arrays and with nested tables, both of which are described later in this lesson.

- `extend`—The `extend` method allows you to add entries to the end of a collection. You can add one entry or you can add multiple entries, by specifying the number to add as a parameter. The following two examples add 1 entry and 10 entries, respectively, to the `emps` table:

```
emps.extend;
emps.extend(10);
```

10

The extend function can also be used to clone existing entries. You clone an entry by passing the entry number as a second parameter to extend. The following example makes another copy of table entry 3, and adds it to the end of the table:

```
emps.extend(1,3);
```

The extend method is a procedure, and does not return a value. The specification for extend looks like this:

```
PROCEDURE extend [(entries_to_add IN INTEGER[, entry_to_clone IN
INTEGER])];
```

Like trim, extend can only be used with variable-sized arrays and with nested tables.

Using Nested Tables

Nested tables came into being with Oracle8. In the database, a nested table is an unordered collection of rows. Think of an order entry system where each order contains a number of line items. Traditionally, database designers would implement this by using two database tables, one for the orders and a second for the line items. Each line item record would contain a foreign key linking it to its parent order. With Oracle8 and Oracle8i, it's possible for each order to have its own line item table and for that table to be stored as a column in the order table.

PL/SQL supports nested tables because the database does. Nested tables are declared and used in a manner similar to index-by tables, but there are some differences you should to be aware of:

- When you retrieve a nested table from the database, the entries are indexed consecutively. Even when building a nested table within PL/SQL, you can't arbitrarily skip index values the way you can with index-by tables.
- Nested tables do not support PL/SQL-specific datatypes.
- You need to use a constructor method to initialize a nested table.
- The index range for nested tables is -2,147,483,647 through 2,147,483,647. Indexes for index-by tables cannot be 0 or negative.

When nested tables are in the database, the rows have no particular ordering associated with them. When you read a nested table into PL/SQL, each row is given an index. So in a sense, at that point, there is some ordering involved. However, the ordering is not preserved. If you select the same nested table twice, you might get a different row ordering each time.

Declaring a Nested Table

You declare a nested table by using the same two steps as you do in declaring a index-by table. First, you declare a type, and then you declare one or more variables of that type.

▼ SYNTAX

```
TYPE type_name IS TABLE OF data_type [NOT NULL];
```

In this syntax the parameters are as follows:

- `type_name` is the name of the type you are declaring.
- `data_type` is the datatype of the collection. The datatype for a nested table cannot be one of the following:

    BOOLEAN

    NCHAR

    NCLOB

    NVARCHAR2

    REF CURSOR

    TABLE

    VARRAY

- `NOT NULL` prohibits a table entry from being null.

The type declaration for a nested table is similar to that used for an index-by table, but the `INDEX BY` clause is not used. The presence or lack of an `INDEX BY` clause is what Oracle looks for to determine whether you are declaring an index-by table or a nested

▲ table.

After you've declared a nested table type, you can used that type to declare nested table variables.

Adding Entries to a Nested Table

NEW TERM Adding entries to a nested table is a bit different from adding them to an index-by table. Before you can add any entries, you have to use a special function called a *constructor* to initialize the table. The term constructor comes from the object-oriented world, where a constructor is the function that actually allocates memory to an

10

object, and initializes the data structures associated with that object. In the case of a nested table, the constructor function is what actually creates the collection and assigns it to the variable that you've declared.

After you initialize your nested table, if you want to increase the size, you need to call the extend method. See the section earlier in this lesson titled "PL/SQL Table Methods."

Initializing a Nested Table

When you declare a variable for a nested table, you get a variable that contains absolutely nothing. It's considered null. To make it a table, you need to call a constructor function to create that table, and then store the result of that function in the variable you are using. For example, say you used the following declarations to create a nested table named depts:

```
TYPE dept_table IS TABLE OF department%ROWTYPE;

depts dept_table;
```

To actually use depts as a nested table, you need to call a constructor function to initialize it. The constructor function always takes its name from the name of the type used to declare the table, so in this case, the constructor function would be named dept_table. You can call the constructor function without passing any arguments, and create an empty table, as in the following example:

```
depts := dept_table ();
```

You can also call the constructor function and pass in values for one or more entries. However, the values listed in the constructor must be of the same type as the table. That's a bit difficult to do where records are concerned. The following example shows how you would declare depts as a table of department records, and then initialize it with two departments:

INPUT

```
 1: DECLARE
 2:     TYPE dept_table IS TABLE OF department%ROWTYPE;
 3:     depts dept_table;
 4:     dept1 department%ROWTYPE;
 5:     dept2 department%ROWTYPE;
 6: BEGIN
 7:     dept1.dept_id := 1201;
 8:     dept1.dept_name := 'Sweeping Department';
 9:     dept2.dept_id := 1202;
10:     dept2.dept_name := 'Mopping Department';
11:
12:     depts := dept_table (dept1, dept2);
```

The key here is that the arguments to the constructor are dept1 and dept2. Both of those are records of type department%ROWTYPE, and so match the element type of the table. Obviously it's a bit cumbersome to set things up this way.

To add more entries to a table than those you created with the constructor, you need to extend the table, as discussed in the following section.

Extending a Nested Table

To extend a nested table so that you can add more entries to it, use the extend method. The extend method allows you to add one entry, or several entries. It also allows you to clone an existing entry one or more times. The syntax for the extend method is as follows.

```
collection.extend[(entries_to_add[, entry_to_clone])];
```

In this syntax the parameters are as follows:

- *collection* is the name of the nested table.
- *entries_to_add* is a variable or constant indicating the number of new entries you want to add.
- *entry_to_clone* is a variable or constant indicating which entry you want to clone.

Listing 10.4 shows the extend method being used and illustrates how constructors work.

INPUT **LISTING 10.4** The extend Method, Adding Entries to a Nested Table

```
 1: DECLARE
 2:     --Declare a cursor that returns all department records.
 3:     CURSOR all_depts IS
 4:         SELECT *
 5:         FROM department
 6:         ORDER BY dept_name;
 7:
 8:     --Define a nested table type.
 9:     TYPE dept_table IS TABLE OF department%ROWTYPE;
10:
11:     --Declare a nested table variable to
12:     --hold the employee records that we read in.
13:     depts dept_table;
14:     depts_max PLS_INTEGER;
15:     inx1 PLS_INTEGER;
16: BEGIN
17:     --Initialize the index into the table.
18:     depts_max := 0;
19:
```

continues

LISTING 10.4 continued

```
20:        --Initialize the table by creating one empty entry.
21:        depts := dept_table ();
22:
23:        FOR dept IN all_depts LOOP
24:            depts_max := depts_max + 1;
25:            depts.extend;
26:            depts(depts_max).dept_id := dept.dept_id;
27:            depts(depts_max).dept_name := dept.dept_name;
28:            depts(depts_max).no_of_emps := dept.no_of_emps;
29:        END LOOP;
30:
31:        --Clone the first entry five times.
32:        depts.extend(5,1);
33:
34:        --Display the results.
35:        FOR inx1 IN 1..depts_max+5 LOOP
36:            DBMS_OUTPUT.PUT_LINE (
37:                depts(inx1).dept_id ||
38:                ' ' || depts(inx1).dept_name);
39:        END LOOP;
40: END;
41: /
```

OUTPUT

```
403 BOTTLING
402 DISTILLATION
501 Employee Newsletters
401 FERMENTATION
405 GUTTING
404 SCALE PROCESSING
502 Technical Writing
406 UNLOADING
403 BOTTLING
403 BOTTLING
403 BOTTLING
403 BOTTLING
403 BOTTLING
```

ANALYSIS Line 8 declares the type for the nested table, and defines it to match the department table. In line 13, the variable depts is declared, and becomes the nested table. However, the table can't be used until it is initialized, which happens in line 21, with a call to the constructor. Because no values are passed to the constructor, the nested table is created with zero entries.

The FOR loop in lines 23–29 reads the department records, and inserts them into the table. Before each record is inserted, a call to extend is made in order to add space for the new entry. After all the data has been read, another call to extend is made in line 32 to clone the first entry five times. The last FOR loop, in lines 35–39, dumps the contents of the table to the screen (if you are using SQL*Plus) by using the DBMS_OUTPUT package. Sure enough, you can see that the first entry has been replicated five more times at the end of the table.

Removing Entries from a Nested Table

You can remove entries from a nested table by using the delete method, just as you do with index-by tables. The following example deletes entry 10 from the depts table:

```
depts.delete(10);
```

You can reuse entries after you delete them. The other entries in the table are not renumbered.

Another method of removing rows from a nested table is to invoke the trim method on the table. The trim method removes a specified number of entries from the end of the table.

```
nested_table.trim[(entries_to_trim)];
```

In this syntax the parameters are as follows:

- nested_table is the name of the nested table.
- entries_to_trim is the number of entries to remove from the end. The default is 1.

The trim method applies only to nested tables and variable-sized arrays. It cannot be applied to index-by tables.

Listing 10.5 is an extension of Listing 10.4. This time, after the new entries are added to the table and displayed, the trim method is used to remove them.

INPUT **LISTING 10.5** The trim Method

```
 1: DECLARE
 2:     --Declare a cursor that returns all department records.
 3:     CURSOR all_depts IS
 4:         SELECT *
 5:         FROM department
 6:         ORDER BY dept_name;
 7:
 8:     --Define a nested table type.
 9:     TYPE dept_table IS TABLE OF department%ROWTYPE;
10:
11:     --Declare a nested table variable to
```

continues

LISTING **10.5**   continued

```
12:        --hold the employee records that we read in.
13:        depts dept_table;
14:        depts_max PLS_INTEGER;
15:        inx1 PLS_INTEGER;
16: BEGIN
17:        --Initialize the index into the table.
18:        depts_max := 0;
19:
20:        --Initialize the table by creating one empty entry.
21:        depts := dept_table ();
22:
23:        FOR dept IN all_depts LOOP
24:            depts_max := depts_max + 1;
25:            depts.extend;
26:            depts(depts_max).dept_id := dept.dept_id;
27:            depts(depts_max).dept_name := dept.dept_name;
28:            depts(depts_max).no_of_emps := dept.no_of_emps;
29:        END LOOP;
30:
31:        --Clone the first entry five times.
32:        depts.extend(5,1);
33:
34:        --Display the results.
35:        FOR inx1 IN 1..depts_max+5 LOOP
36:            DBMS_OUTPUT.PUT_LINE (
37:                depts(inx1).dept_id ||
38:                ' ' || depts(inx1).dept_name);
39:        END LOOP;
40:        --Trim off the five clones of entry #1
41:        depts.trim(5);
42:
43:        --Delete the first entry.
44:        depts.delete(1);
45:
46:        --Display the new count.
47:        DBMS_OUTPUT.PUT_LINE(depts.count);
48:
49:        --Display the results.
50:        FOR inx1 IN 1..depts_max+5 LOOP
51:            IF depts.exists(inx1) THEN
52:                DBMS_OUTPUT.PUT_LINE (
53:                    depts(inx1).dept_id ||
54:                    ' ' || depts(inx1).dept_name);
55:            END IF;
56:        END LOOP;
57:
58: END;
59: /
```

OUTPUT

```
403 BOTTLING
402 DISTILLATION
501 Employee Newsletters
401 FERMENTATION
405 GUTTING
404 SCALE PROCESSING
502 Technical Writing
406 UNLOADING
403 BOTTLING
403 BOTTLING
403 BOTTLING
403 BOTTLING
403 BOTTLING
7
402 DISTILLATION
501 Employee Newsletters
401 FERMENTATION
405 GUTTING
404 SCALE PROCESSING
502 Technical Writing
406 UNLOADING
```

ANALYSIS Up through line 39, this listing is the same as Listing 10.4. Departments are read from the database, the first one is cloned, and the results are displayed. After that, in line 41, the `trim` method is used to remove the five clones of entry 1. Next, the `delete` method is called in line 44 to delete the first entry as well. Line 47 displays the new count, telling how many entries are now in the table. It also serves a more interesting purpose than that: PL/SQL doesn't seem to recognize that you trimmed and deleted entries until after you reference the table's count, so line 47 is really a bug workaround. Finally, lines 50–56 display the table entries that remain after the deleting and trimming.

Note
> If you remove line 47 (which invokes the `count` method) from Listing 10.5, and run it again, the second list of departments will match the first. In other words, the `exists` method won't recognize that you deleted some entries. This is true with Oracle release 8.1.5, and is almost certainly a bug. The workaround is to invoke the `count` method at least once.

Using Variable-Sized Arrays

NEW TERM Like nested tables, variable-sized arrays or varrays also came into existence with the release of Oracle8. *Varrays* are similar to nested tables, but they have a fixed maximum size. They differ from nested tables in that when you store a varray into a database column, the order of elements is preserved.

Note   You need the Enterprise Edition of Oracle8i in order to use varrays.

Declaring and Initializing a Varray

To create a varray, you use the VARRAY keyword in a type declaration to create an array type. Then you can use that type to declare one or more variables. The syntax for declaring a varray type is as follows.

```
TYPE type_name IS {VARRAY¦VARYING ARRAY} (size) OF entry_type [NOT NULL];
```

In this syntax the parameters are as follows:

- *type_name* is the name of the array type.
- *size* is the number of elements you want the array to hold.
- *entry_type* is the data type for elements of the array.
- NOT NULL prohibits array entries from being null.

Varrays need to be initialized just as nested tables do. Before you can use a varray, you need to call its constructor. You can pass values to the constructor, and those values are used to create array elements, or you can invoke the constructor with no parameters in order to create an empty array.

The code in Listing 10.6 shows a varray being declared, and the constructor being called to create the array with some initial data.

INPUT   **LISTING 10.6**   Declaring and Creating a Varray

```
 1: DECLARE
 2:      --Define an array type
 3:      TYPE dept_array IS VARRAY(100) OF VARCHAR2(30);
 4:
 5:      --Define the array variable and other variables.
 6:      depts dept_array;
 7:      inx1 PLS_INTEGER;
 8:
 9: BEGIN
10:      --Initialize the array and create two entries
11:      --using the constructor.
12:      depts := dept_array ('Dept One','Dept Two');
13:
14:      --Display the contents of the two entries.
15:      FOR inx1 IN 1..2 LOOP
16:          DBMS_OUTPUT.PUT_LINE(depts(inx1));
17:      END LOOP;
18: END;
19: /
```

OUTPUT
```
Dept One
Dept Two
```

ANALYSIS Line 3 declares a type that results in a 100-element array of VARCHAR2(30) values. The depts variable is declared in line 6 to be of this type. In line 12 the array is initialized by calling the constructor. In this example, two values are supplied to the constructor, so the array is created with those two elements. The size of the array is still 100 because that's what is specified in the type declaration. The elements created by the constructor are numbers 1 and 2, and elements 3 through 100 are empty.

Adding and Removing Data from a Varray

After you've initialized a varray, you can add data to and remove it from the varray just as you do with a nested table. If you want to add more elements to the array than you created when you initialized it, you can call the extend method. However, you can only extend an array up to the maximum size specified in the array type definition.

Listing 10.7 shows the contents of the department table being read into a varray.

INPUT **LISTING 10.7** Reading Data into a Varray

```
 1: DECLARE
 2:     --Declare a cursor that returns all department records.
 3:     CURSOR all_depts IS
 4:         SELECT *
 5:         FROM department
 6:         ORDER BY dept_name;
 7:
 8:     --Define a varray type.
 9:     TYPE dept_array IS VARRAY(100) OF department%ROWTYPE;
10:
11:     --Declare a varray variable to
12:     --hold the employee records that we read in.
13:     depts dept_array;
14:     inx1 PLS_INTEGER;
15:     inx2 PLS_INTEGER;
16: BEGIN
17:     --Initialize the index into the array.
18:     inx1 := 0;
19:
20:     --Initialize the array.
21:     depts := dept_array ();
22:
23:     FOR dept IN all_depts LOOP
24:         inx1 := inx1 + 1;
25:         depts.extend();
```

continues

10

LISTING 10.7 continued

```
26:         depts(inx1).dept_id := dept.dept_id;
27:         depts(inx1).dept_name := dept.dept_name;
28:         depts(inx1).no_of_emps := dept.no_of_emps;
29:     END LOOP;
30:
31:     --Display the results.
32:     FOR inx2 IN 1..depts.count LOOP
33:         DBMS_OUTPUT.PUT_LINE (
34:             depts(inx2).dept_id ||
35:             ' ' || depts(inx2).dept_name);
36:     END LOOP;
37: END;
38: /
```

ANALYSIS The array type is declared in line 9, with a maximum size of 100 entries. The actual array variable is declared in line 13. The call to the constructor in line 21 initializes the array. It now exists, but with zero entries. As each entry is added, the array must be extended in order to hold that entry. Line 25, inside the FOR loop, does this. Note that extend cannot be used to grow the array beyond the maximum specified size of 100 entries.

Taking Advantage of Bulk Binding

NEW TERM PL/SQL bulk binding is a new feature with Oracle8i. *Bulk binding* lets you code SQL statements that operate on all entries in a collection, without having to loop through that collection by using PL/SQL code. Several of the examples so far in this lesson have used a cursor FOR loop to load data from a database table into a PL/SQL table or array. The switch from SQL (for the fetch) to PL/SQL (to add the data to the array) is called a *context switch*, and consumes quite a bit of overhead. You can use the bulk binding feature to avoid much of that overhead.

Note If you are not using Oracle8i, you won't be able to execute any of the bulk binding examples shown in this chapter.

Two new keywords support binding. BULK COLLECT is used with SELECT statements to place all the data into a collection. FORALL is used with INSERT, UPDATE, and DELETE statements to execute those statements once for each element in a collection.

Using BULK COLLECT

You can use the BULK COLLECT keywords to have the results of a SELECT statement placed directly into a collection. You can use BULK COLLECT with SELECT INTO statements, and also with FETCH statements. For example, if dept_ids and dept_names were both nested tables, you could issue the following SELECT statement:

```
SELECT dept_id, dept_name
BULK COLLECT INTO dept_ids, dept_names
FROM department;
```

If you had a cursor named all_depts that returned the same data, you could write BULK COLLECT into the FETCH statement, like this:

```
OPEN all_depts;
FETCH all_depts BULK COLLECT INTO dept_ids, dept_names;
CLOSE all_depts;
```

For some reason, Oracle does not allow you to use BULK COLLECT in a collection of records. Thus, if you are selecting 10 columns, you need to declare 10 collections, one for each column.

Listing 10.8 shows an example of BULK COLLECT being used to load all department names and IDs into a nested table.

INPUT   **LISTING 10.8**   An Example Showing the Use of BULK COLLECT

```
 1: DECLARE
 2:     --Declare a cursor that returns all department records.
 3:     CURSOR all_depts IS
 4:         SELECT dept_id, dept_name
 5:         FROM department
 6:         ORDER BY dept_name;
 7:
 8:     --Define a nested table type for each column.
 9:     TYPE dept_id IS TABLE OF department.dept_id%TYPE;
10:     TYPE dept_name IS TABLE OF department.dept_name%TYPE;
11:
12:     --Declare a nested table variable for each column.
13:     dept_ids dept_id;
14:     dept_names dept_name;
15:     inx1 PLS_INTEGER;
16: BEGIN
17:     OPEN all_depts;
18:     FETCH all_depts BULK COLLECT INTO dept_ids, dept_names;
19:     CLOSE all_depts;
20:
21:     --Display the results.
22:     FOR inx1 IN 1..dept_ids.count LOOP
```

continues

LISTING 10.8 continued

```
23:           DBMS_OUTPUT.PUT_LINE (
24:               dept_ids(inx1) ||
25:               ' ' || dept_names(inx1));
26:      END LOOP;
27: END;
28: /
```

OUTPUT

```
403 BOTTLING
402 DISTILLATION
501 Employee Newsletters
401 FERMENTATION
405 GUTTING
404 SCALE PROCESSING
502 Technical Writing
406 UNLOADING
```

ANALYSIS The all_depts cursor declared in lines 3–6 returns two values: the department ID and name. Lines 9 and 10 declare nested table types for each of these columns. Corresponding nested table variables are declared in lines 13–14. The FETCH statement in line 18 then uses the BULK COLLECT keyword to read all the data selected directly into the arrays. This is much faster than fetching one row at a time using a PL/SQL loop.

Note that Listing 10.8 contain no call to the nested tables' constructor methods. The FETCH statement takes care of that for you.

The ability to do bulk binds is a great feature. The single annoying thing about it is that you cannot declare a nested table of department%rowtype, and use that as the target. BULK COLLECT won't handle tables of records.

Note

> I imagine that some future release of Oracle will remove the restriction against BULK COLLECT loading tables of records. At least I hope that happens.

Using FORALL

The FORALL keyword allows you to base a Data Manipulation Language (DML) statement (that is, INSERT, UPDATE, or DELETE) on the contents of a collection. When FORALL is used, the statement is executed once for each entry in the collection, but only one context switch is made from PL/SQL to SQL. The resulting performance is much faster than what you get when you code a loop in PL/SQL.

Looking back at Listing 10.8, let's say you wanted to set the employee count to null for each department. You could do that, after selecting the department information into the nested tables, by writing the following FORALL statement:

```
FORALL x IN dept_ids.first..dept_id.last
    UPDATE department
    SET no_of_emps := NULL
    WHERE dept_id = dept_ids(x);
```

In this case, index x ranges from the first entry in the dept_id table to the last. If you don't want the statement to apply to all entries in the table, you can specify a different range. The use of dept_ids(x) indicates that this is where you want nested table values substituted into the SQL statement when it executes.

Listing 10.9 shows a similar FORALL statement being used to change all the department names to uppercase.

10

INPUT   **LISTING 10.9**   An Example Showing the Use of FORALL

```
 1: DECLARE
 2:     --Declare a cursor that returns all department records.
 3:     CURSOR all_depts IS
 4:         SELECT dept_id, dept_name
 5:         FROM department
 6:         ORDER BY dept_name;
 7:
 8:     --Define a nested table type for each column.
 9:     TYPE dept_id IS TABLE OF department.dept_id%TYPE;
10:     TYPE dept_name IS TABLE OF department.dept_name%TYPE;
11:
12:     --Declare a nested table variable for each column.
13:     dept_ids dept_id;
14:     dept_names dept_name;
15:     inx1 PLS_INTEGER;
16: BEGIN
17:     OPEN all_depts;
18:     FETCH all_depts BULK COLLECT INTO dept_ids, dept_names;
19:     CLOSE all_depts;
20:
21:     --Uppercase the names and Display the results.
22:     FOR inx1 IN 1..dept_ids.count LOOP
23:         dept_names(inx1) := UPPER(dept_names(inx1));
24:
25:         DBMS_OUTPUT.PUT_LINE (
26:             dept_ids(inx1) ||
27:             ' ' || dept_names(inx1));
28:     END LOOP;
```

continues

LISTING 10.9 continued

```
29:
30:     FORALL x IN dept_ids.first..dept_ids.last
31:     UPDATE department
32:     SET dept_name = dept_names(x)
33:     WHERE dept_id = dept_ids(x);
34: END;
35: /
```

 ANALYSIS Aside from lines 30–33, this listing is almost exactly like Listing 10.8. One line
(line 23) has been added to the FOR loop to make each department name uppercase. The FORALL statement writes the new names back to the database by using an
UPDATE statement. FORALL causes a bulk bind to be used, which is much more efficient
than if you had updated each row individually inside of a PL/SQL loop.

> **Note** When you use FORALL, all the collection elements in the specified range must
> exist. If they don't, you get an error.

If you try to use FORALL on a range with missing elements, SQL stops executing the statement and raises an error. At this point, you have to decide whether to commit or roll back
the transaction. If you commit, any changes made prior to the single entry that caused the
error are saved. You don't, however, have any way to know how many array entries were
processed before the error occurred.

Exception Handling for Collections

Some PL/SQL exceptions are directly related to collections. These are listed in
Table 10.1.

TABLE 10.1 Collection-Related Exceptions

Exception	Cause
COLLECTION_IS_NULL	You tried to use the collection before initializing it with its constructor function.
NO_DATA_FOUND	You tried to access the value of an entry in a collection, and that entry doesn't exist.
SUBSCRIPT_BEYOND_COUNT	You used a subscript that exceeds the number of elements currently in the collection.

Exception	Cause
SUBSCRIPT_OUTSIDE_LIMIT	You used a subscript with a varray that was larger than the maximum supported by the varray's type declaration.
VALUE_ERROR	You used a subscript that couldn't be converted to an integer.

When writing code that deals with collections, you can either trap these exceptions or write code that avoids them. You can avoid NO_DATA_FOUND, for example, by testing the validity of each entry with the exists method before you attempt to access the value the entry. The following snippet of code shows how this is done:

```
IF dept_names.EXISTS(10) THEN
ELSE
    /* Element 10 does not exist */
    ...
END IF;
```

You can avoid subscript errors by careful coding. If you're working with varray, you should know how many elements you declared that varray to hold in the first place. If you're working with a nested table, and you aren't sure of the size anymore, you can use the count method to check and see how large the table is.

Summary

Today you've learned how to declare and use records. You have also had an opportunity to learn about all of PL/SQL's collection types, including index-by tables, nested tables, and variable-sized arrays. PL/SQL's bulk bind feature delivers some significant performance improvements. To use bulk binds, you need to be working with data stored in collections. You can then execute SQL statements that are automatically applied to each entry in a collection.

Q&A

Q How do I choose whether to use a variable-sized array in my code, a nested table, or an index-by table?

A If you're dealing with database columns, then you should first base your decision on the column type. For example, if you're reading a VARRAY column from a database table, don't read it into a PL/SQL nested table. Read it into a PL/SQL varray. If this issue doesn't apply to your situation, then base your decision on whether you will be working with a fixed number of elements. Varrays can only grow to the limit specified in their type declaration. Tables can grow to any size. If you can't easily conceive of a maximum size, then use a table.

10

Q Are nested tables the preferred choice for tables? Why would I ever want to use an index-by table?

A Had nested tables been created first, Oracle might never have developed the index-by type. However, both are available, and you must choose between them. If you need an array of a PL/SQL-specific datatype, such as a BOOLEAN, NATURAL, or INTEGER, then an index-by table is your only choice. The other thing to look at is the indexes you use. Nested tables require that your indexes are consecutive, such as 1, 2, 3, and so on. Index-by tables allow you to use any arbitrary index value for an entry, such as 1, 987234, 345, and so on.

Q Why are bulk binds so great?

A Bulk binds reduce the number of PL/SQL to SQL context switches. Each time your PL/SQL program executes an SQL statement, control switches to the SQL world, and a context switch occurs. Bulk binds allow you to operate on a large collection of records with only one context switch occurring. The result is less overhead and faster execution.

Q What is a PL/SQL record?

A A PL/SQL record is a variable that contains several related elements. The elements are not treated as an array, and they do not all have to have the same datatype. Records are commonly declared to match table definitions, or to match the columns returned by a cursor. They simplify code by allowing you to package related values, such as the columns in a row, into one unit.

Workshop

You can use this to test your comprehension of this chapter and put what you've learned into practice. You'll find the answers to the quiz and exercises in Appendix A, "Answers."

Quiz

1. Name the three collection types PL/SQL supports.
2. What declaration would you use to declare a variable named emp_name with a datatype and size that exactly match the definition of the employee.emp_name column in the database?
3. What declaration would you use to declare a record named emp that matches the definition of a row in the employee table?

4. What method can you call on to be sure that a collection element really exists?

5. What must you be sure to do before you can add data to a nested table or to a varray?

Exercise

Write the code necessary to generate a PL/SQL nested table with 10 new department IDs and names. Use department ID numbers that are not currently being used in the database. Make up the department names. Next, write a FORALL statement that inserts all the records by using a bulk bind.

10

WEEK 2

DAY 11

Writing Database Triggers

by Jonathan Gennick

Today's lesson discusses database triggers. A *trigger* is used to write procedural logic that is invoked in response to a specific event. Creative application of database triggers will enable you to accomplish many useful things that otherwise would be impossible. Examples of what you can do with triggers include replicating data, storing data redundantly to avoid frequent table joins, and enforcing complex business rules.

Today, you will learn how to:

- Differentiate among the several types of triggers.
- Create triggers that fire in response to specific DML statements that are issued against a table.
- Use triggers to modify data being inserted into a table.
- Use triggers to maintain a history of changes to a record.
- Use the new database and schema event triggers that were introduced with Oracle8i.

What Is a Trigger?

A trigger is a PL/SQL block that is associated with a specific event, stored in a database, and executed whenever that event occurs. Oracle8i now supports four fundamental types of triggers:

- Data manipulation language (DML) triggers
- Instead-of triggers
- Data definition language (DDL) triggers
- Database event triggers

DML triggers are the traditional INSERT, UPDATE, and DELETE triggers that Oracle has supported for years. Instead-of triggers were introduced with Oracle8 as a way to make it possible to update certain types of views. DDL triggers and Database event triggers are new with Oracle8i.

DML Triggers

DML triggers are the traditional triggers that can be defined on a table, and are executed, or *fired*, in response to the following events:

- A row is inserted into a table.
- A row in a table is updated.
- A row in a table is deleted.

It is not possible to define a trigger to fire when a row is selected.

A DML trigger definition consists of these basic parts:

- The event that fires the trigger
- The database table on which the event must occur
- An optional condition controlling when the trigger is executed
- A PL/SQL block containing the code to be executed when the trigger is fired, or a CALL statement to a stored procedure

A trigger is a database object, like a table or an index. When you define a trigger, it becomes part of the database and is always executed when the event for which it is defined occurs. It doesn't matter if the event is triggered by someone typing in an SQL statement using SQL*Plus, running a client-server program that updates the database, or running a utility like Oracle's SQL*Loader in order to bulk-load data. Because of this, a trigger serves as a choke point, allowing you to perform critical validation or computations in response to database changes, no matter what the source.

An Example of a DML Trigger

Suppose for a moment that you wanted to be sure that all department names were stored using uppercase letters. Perhaps you are doing this to facilitate searching on that field. Listing 11.1 shows one way to do this with a trigger.

INPUT **LISTING 11.1** Example of a Trigger

```
 1: CREATE OR REPLACE TRIGGER department_insert_update
 2:   BEFORE INSERT OR UPDATE ON department
 3:   FOR EACH ROW
 4: DECLARE
 5:   dup_flag  INTEGER;
 6: BEGIN
 7:   --Force all department names to uppercase.
 8: :NEW.dept_name := UPPER(:NEW.dept_name);
 9: END;
10: /
```

ANALYSIS Line 1 tells Oracle to create this trigger with the name
department_insert_update and to replace any existing trigger of the same
name if necessary. Line 2 says that it will be fired whenever a new row is inserted into
the department table or whenever a department record is changed. In line 8 there is one
line of code that uses the built-in UPPER function to force the department name to uppercase. Notice the reference to :NEW. This is the default alias for the new value of the
record. The alias :OLD can be used to refer to the old value of a field before an update
takes effect. Line 3 tells Oracle to fire this trigger once for each row modified. If you
were to issue an UPDATE statement to change the names of all departments in the table,
this trigger would be fired for each one of those records.

To demonstrate the effect of this trigger, try issuing the statements shown in Listing 11.2.

**INPUT/
OUTPUT** **LISTING 11.2** Testing the department_insert_update Trigger

```
 1: INSERT INTO department (dept_id, dept_name) VALUES (10,'payroll');
 2: 1 row created.
 3: INSERT INTO department (dept_id, dept_name) VALUES (11,'Sewage');
 4: 1 row created.
 5: UPDATE department SET dept_name = 'Payroll' WHERE dept_id = 10;
 6: 1 row updated.
 7: SELECT dept_id, dept_name FROM department WHERE dept_id BETWEEN 10 AND 11;
 8:   DEPT_ID DEPT_NAME
 9: -------- --------------------------------
10:        10 PAYROLL
11:        11 SEWAGE
```

11

Note that the trigger has forced all department names to uppercase regardless of whether the name was the result of a new record inserted or an existing record that was updated.

Types of DML Triggers

DML triggers can be classified in two different ways: by when they fire in relation to the triggering SQL statement, or by whether or not they fire for each row affected by the triggering SQL statement. This results in four basic trigger types.

 There are two choices when a trigger fires in relation to an SQL statement: either before or after. *Before triggers* are executed before the triggering SQL statement. *After triggers* are executed following the triggering SQL statement.

 A DML trigger is either a *row-level trigger* or a *statement-level trigger*. A row-level trigger executes once for each row affected by the triggering SQL statement, whereas a statement-level trigger is executed only once. Only row-level triggers have access to the data values in the affected records. Statement-level triggers do not. This is because SQL is a set-oriented language--SQL statements can affect many or even all rows in a table. Statement-level triggers are only fired once, so it would not be possible to resolve a column reference in such a trigger.

The possible combinations of the choices result in the four DML trigger types listed in Table 11.1.

TABLE 11.1   The Four Basic Trigger Types

When Fired	Level	Description
Before	Statement	Executed once for the triggering SQL statement before that statement is executed.
Before	Row	Executed once for each record affected by the triggering SQL statement before the record in question is changed, deleted, or inserted.
After	Row	Executed once for each record affected by the triggering SQL statement after the record in question has been changed, deleted, or inserted.
After	Statement	Executed once for the triggering SQL statement after that statement has been executed.

Triggers execute in response to an SQL statement and can be defined for the INSERT, UPDATE, and DELETE statements. These are often referred to as *insert triggers*, *update triggers*, and *delete triggers*, respectively. Together with the four types from Table 11.1, this gives a total of 12 possible triggers that you can define on a table. In addition, any one trigger may be defined to fire for more than one DML statement.

Note The SELECT statement is the only data manipulation statement for which no triggers can be defined.

Because there are four possible triggers that can be created for a specific SQL statement, it makes sense to ask about the execution order. Which trigger gets executed first? Which last? What if multiple triggers are defined identically? Figure 11.1 shows the order of execution of the various trigger types in relation to each other and in relation to the triggering SQL statement.

FIGURE 11.1

Trigger execution order.

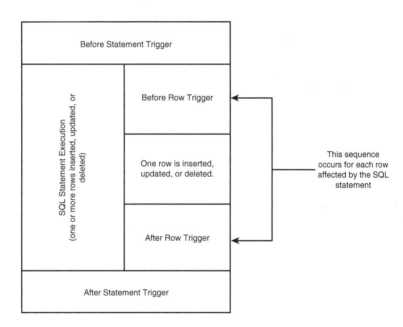

Triggers defined identically are executed in no particular order. If you write several that fire before a row is updated, you must ensure that the integrity of the database does not depend on the order of execution.

Do	Don't
Do use before-update row-level triggers for complex business rule enforcement, security checking, and performing complex calculations. You want to do all these things before the row is inserted. **Do** use after-update row-level triggers for data replication and logging of changes. **Do** use statement-level before triggers to enforce security rules where the rule is not dependent on any values in the records being affected.	**Don't** use before triggers for data replication and change logging because an integrity constraint or another trigger could prevent the SQL statement from completing. **Don't** use triggers to enforce referential integrity in cases where you can use a declarative constraint instead.

The Syntax for Defining a Database Trigger

This section shows the syntax used to define a traditional DML trigger on a database table. Parts of the syntax get somewhat complex, but don't be intimidated by that. There are plenty of examples in this chapter to give you a good feel for how triggers are used.

▼ SYNTAX

```
CREATE [OR REPLACE] TRIGGER [schema.]trigger_name
  {BEFORE¦AFTER} verb_list ON [schema.]table_name
  [[REFERENCING correlation_names] FOR EACH ROW [WHEN (condition)]]
DECLARE
  declarations
BEGIN
  pl/sql_code
END;
/
```

In this syntax, the parameters are as follows:

- *schema* refers to the owner of an object. When used before a trigger name, it refers to the owner of the trigger. When used before a table name, it refers to the owner of the table.

- *trigger_name* is the name you want to give the trigger.

- *verb_list* identifies the SQL verbs that fire the trigger. The syntax of the *verb_list* is as follows:

▼
```
{INSERT¦DELETE¦UPDATE [OF column_list]} [OR verb_list]
```

▼ The parameters in the verb list are

column_list	Causes an update trigger to fire only when one of the columns listed is changed. Otherwise, the trigger fires whenever any column in the table is changed.
verb_list	This is another iteration of the verb list. You can create a trigger that is fired by more than one SQL verb.

- *table_name* is the table on which the trigger is defined.
- *correlation_names* allows you to specify correlation names other than the default of OLD and NEW. This is useful if the table on which the trigger is defined happens to be named OLD or NEW, and can also be helpful in making the trigger code self-documenting. The referencing clause looks like this:

{OLD AS *old_alias*¦NEW AS *new_alias* [*correlation_names*]}

In the preceding syntax, the parameters are

old_alias	This is a name you want to use when referring to the value of a field before the SQL verb executes.
new_alias	This is a name you want to use when referring to the value of a field after the SQL verb executes.
correlation_names	This is another iteration of the alias list. You can specify an alias for both old and new values.

- *condition* is an optional condition placed on the execution of the trigger. This can only be used on row-level triggers. If *condition* is present, the trigger will only be fired when the condition is true. The condition can be any Boolean expression, cannot contain any queries, and must use correlation names, in other words NEW and OLD, to refer to column values in the row being changed.
- *declarations* consists of any variable, record, or cursor declarations needed by this PL/SQL block.
- *pl/sql_code* is the PL/SQL code that gets executed when the trigger fires.
- DECLARE...END; You can optionally replace the entire PL/SQL block with a CALL statement that looks like this:

```
CALL procedure_name;
```

The CALL statement is used to have the trigger consist of only a stored procedure
▲ call.

11

The *correlation names* : OLD and : NEW deserve some extra explanation. It is common when writing a trigger to need to reference the values in the record being inserted, updated, or deleted. Further, in the case of an update, it is often necessary to access both the before and after values of a given field. The correlation names : OLD and : NEW are provided for this purpose. These function much like a PL/SQL record. : OLD contains the field values before they are updated, and : NEW contains the field values after the update takes place. Use the standard dot notation, in other words : OLD. *field_name*, to refer to the value of a particular field. You will see examples of this in several of the listings in this chapter.

> **Note**
>
> Accessing both before and after versions of a record usually only makes sense in an update trigger. However, Oracle does allow you to reference both : OLD and : NEW in delete and insert triggers. In an insert trigger, the field values in : OLD will be null and : NEW will contain the data to be inserted. In a delete trigger, the situation is reversed. The field values in : OLD contain the data about to be deleted and the : NEW values will be null.

Uses for Triggers

The possible uses for database triggers are varied and are limited only by your imagination. Some common uses are

- Enforcing business rules
- Maintaining referential integrity
- Enforcing security
- Maintaining a historical log of changes
- Generating column values, including primary key values
- Replication of data

The next few sections show some examples of these uses.

Maintaining Data Integrity

A common use for triggers is to assist in maintaining the integrity of the data stored in the database. Suppose that you wanted to store a count of the number of employees in each department and that you wanted to store this count in the department table. You would first add an employee count field to the department table using a statement like this:

```
ALTER TABLE department
   ADD (no_of_emps     NUMBER(38));
```

The no_of_emps field is used to keep track of the number of employees in any given department. Think of how this employee count could be maintained. One possible solution would be to have any program that adds an employee, deletes an employee, or changes an employee's department assignment to update this value appropriately. This would work as long as the programs always worked correctly, and as long you never forgot that the value needed to be maintained. Unfortunately, as you add programmers to a project and as the number of programs that need to maintain this value increases, the likelihood of a mistake also increases. Triggers provide you with a mechanism to centralize the code to maintain a counter like this.

Because you have to deal with inserts, updates, and deletes, three triggers are needed to maintain the departmental employee count. These are listed in Table 11.2.

TABLE 11.2 Triggers Needed to Maintain Department Employee Counts

Trigger Type	What the Trigger Should Accomplish
Insert	When an employee is added, this trigger needs to increment the count for the appropriate department.
Update	When an employee's department is changed, this trigger needs to decrement the count for the previous department and increment the count for the new department.
Delete	When an employee is deleted, this trigger needs to decrement the count for the appropriate department.

Note

These triggers will all be implemented as after triggers because you are only interested in adjusting the counts after a successful change. You could implement them as before triggers, but if subsequent validation caused a transaction to be rolled back, the work the triggers had done would also need to be rolled back, resulting in extra work for the database engine.

Listing 11.3 shows the code to create the three triggers needed to maintain employee counts for each department.

INPUT **LISTING 11.3** Triggers to Maintain Departmental Employee Counts

```
1: CREATE OR REPLACE TRIGGER emp_dept_ins
2:   AFTER INSERT ON emp_dept
3:   FOR EACH ROW
```

continues

LISTING 11.3   continued

```
 4: BEGIN
 5:   --Increment the employee count for the department
 6:   --referenced by the record just inserted.
 7:   UPDATE department
 8:     SET no_of_emps = NVL(no_of_emps,0)+1
 9:   WHERE dept_id = :NEW.dept_id;
10: END;
11: /
12:
13:  CREATE OR REPLACE TRIGGER emp_dept_del
14:   AFTER DELETE ON emp_dept
15:   FOR EACH ROW
16: BEGIN
17:   --Decrement the employee count for the department
18:   --referenced by the record just deleted.
19:   UPDATE department
20:     SET no_of_emps = no_of_emps-1
21:   WHERE dept_id = :OLD.dept_id;
22: END;
23: /
24:
25: CREATE OR REPLACE TRIGGER emp_dept_upd
26:   AFTER UPDATE OF dept_id ON emp_dept
27:   FOR EACH ROW
28: BEGIN
29:   --Increment the employee count for the employee's new department
30:   UPDATE department
31:     SET no_of_emps = NVL(no_of_emps,0)+1
32:   WHERE dept_id = :NEW.dept_id;
33:
34:   --Decrement the employee count for the employee's
35:   --previous department.
36:   UPDATE department
37:     SET no_of_emps = no_of_emps - 1
38:   WHERE dept_id = :OLD.dept_id;
39: END;
40: /
```

ANALYSIS   The DDL, or data definition language, statements shown in Listing 11.3 create three triggers on the emp_dept table: one for inserts, one for updates, and one for deletes. Each trigger is very simple and simply increments or decrements the employee counter for the department(s) affected by the operation that fired the trigger.

Now that you have created the triggers, one more task remains. The triggers maintain the employee count; they do not initialize it to the correct value. You must initialize the counts yourself, which can be easily done by issuing this SQL statement:

```
UPDATE department
  SET no_of_emps = (SELECT COUNT(*)
                      FROM emp_dept
                     WHERE emp_dept.dept_id = department.dept_id);
```

> **Note**
>
> Be sure to commit this transaction. You do that by issuing the COMMIT state-
> ment. That tells Oracle to make the changes permanent.

Now that you have created the necessary triggers and initialized the counters, you might want to issue some queries to test your code. Listing 11.4 shows some examples of employee records being inserted, updated, and deleted, and also shows the effect on the no_of_emps field for the affected departments.

INPUT/ OUTPUT

LISTING 11.4 Testing the Employee Count Triggers

```
 1: --Create some departments.
 2: INSERT INTO department (dept_id, dept_name, no_of_emps)
 3:   VALUES (101,'Building Maintenance',0);
 4: 1 row created.
 5: INSERT INTO department (dept_id, dept_name, no_of_emps)
 6:   VALUES (102,'Fleet Repair',0);
 7: 1 row created.
 8: --Insert some employees.
 9: INSERT INTO employee (emp_id, emp_name, pay_rate, pay_type)
10:     VALUES (102,'Herman T Jugglehead',250000,'S');
11: 1 row created.
12: INSERT INTO employee (emp_id, emp_name, pay_rate, pay_type)
13:     VALUES (103,'Albert Foxtrot',23,'H');
14: 1 row created.
15: INSERT INTO employee (emp_id, emp_name, pay_rate, pay_type)
16:     VALUES (104,'Moncton Dequinder',19.95,'S');
17: 1 row created.
18: --Now, assign each employee to a department and then look at the counts.
19: INSERT INTO emp_dept (emp_id, dept_id) VALUES (102,101);
20: 1 row created.
21: INSERT INTO emp_dept (emp_id, dept_id) VALUES (103,101);
22: 1 row created.
23: INSERT INTO emp_dept (emp_id, dept_id) VALUES (104,102);
24: 1 row created.
25: SELECT * FROM department WHERE dept_id in (101,102);
26: DEPT_ID DEPT_NAME                          NO_OF_EMPS
27: -------- ---------------------------------- ----------
28:     102 FLEET REPAIR                                1
29:     101 BUILDING MAINTENANCE                        2
```

11

continues

LISTING **11.4** continued

```
30: --Delete one employee's department assignment and look again at the counts.
31: DELETE FROM emp_dept
32:  WHERE emp_id = 103 and dept_id = 101;
33: 1 row deleted.
34: SELECT * FROM department WHERE dept_id in (101,102);
35: DEPT_ID DEPT_NAME                          NO_OF_EMPS
36: --------- ------------------------------- ----------
37:       102 FLEET REPAIR                             1
38:       101 BUILDING MAINTENANCE                     1
39: --Reassign the other employee and take one last look at the counts.
40: UPDATE emp_dept
41:    SET dept_id = 101
42:  WHERE emp_id = 104 and dept_id = 102;
43: 1 row updated.
44: SELECT * FROM department WHERE dept_id in (101,102);
45:  DEPT_ID DEPT_NAME                          NO_OF_EMPS
46: --------- ------------------------------- ----------
47:       102 FLEET REPAIR                             0
48:       101 BUILDING MAINTENANCE                     2
49: COMMIT;
50: Commit complete.
```

The advantages of this set of triggers are twofold. They give you a central point of control for maintaining the number of employees in a department, and they relieve you from having to program and test this logic several places in your application.

Maintaining History

This last example concerning triggers will involve using them to maintain a historical record of changes made to the data in a table. The approach will be to create an audit trail table containing the data that we want to track, a timestamp, and a sequentially incremented number as a primary key. Listing 11.5 shows the DDL to create such a table. An Oracle *sequence* is also created. A sequence is a database object that returns incrementing numbers. Sequences are often used for the purpose of generating unique primary keys, especially where preserving the original order of events is important.

INPUT/
OUTPUT   LISTING **11.5** The Employee Pay History Table

```
1: CREATE TABLE emp_pay_history
2:   (emp_pay_history_pk   INTEGER,
3:    emp_id     INTEGER,
4:    as_of      DATE,
5:    emp_name   VARCHAR2(32),
6:    pay_type   CHAR(1),
```

```
 7:    pay_rate    NUMBER(9,2),
 8:    constraint emp_pay_history_pk
 9:      primary key (emp_pay_history_pk)
10:    );
11: Table created.
12: CREATE sequence emp_pay_history_key
13:    start with 1
14:    increment by 1
15:    nocycle;
16: Sequence created.
```

ANALYSIS The table created by the preceding listing resembles the employee table but has two added fields. One additional field, named as_of (line 4), is of type DATE and represents the date and time an employee's pay was changed. The other additional field, named emp_pay_history_pk (line 2), is used as the table's primary key. To ensure uniqueness and to ensure that you can always add to the log, this primary key is populated from an Oracle sequence (lines 12–15). To make querying and reporting easier, the employee's name will also be saved with each record (line 5).

Note The date/time field as_of is not used as part of the primary key because it might not always be unique. Oracle only resolves a date/time value down to the second, and it is possible to make two changes to a record within a one-second window.

11

As you might have already guessed, there is a downside to having the applications maintain this table. The code would need to be replicated in several places, resulting in several possible points of failure. Furthermore, if you weren't developing a new system from scratch, you might already have several applications written and in production. Changing these would be costly. The solution? You guessed it--write some triggers.

Listing 11.6 shows a trigger that will maintain a chronological salary history for employees in the sample database.

INPUT **LISTING 11.6** Trigger to Maintain Employee Pay History

```
1: CREATE OR REPLACE TRIGGER maintain_pay_history
2:   AFTER INSERT OR UPDATE OR DELETE ON employee
3:   FOR EACH ROW
4:   WHEN ((new.pay_rate <> old.pay_rate)
5:     OR (new.pay_rate IS NULL AND old.pay_rate IS NOT NULL)
6:     OR (new.pay_rate IS NOT NULL AND old.pay_rate IS NULL)
```

continues

LISTING 11.6 continued

```
 7:    OR  (new.pay_type <> old.pay_type)
 8:    OR  (new.pay_type IS NULL AND old.pay_type IS NOT NULL)
 9:    OR  (new.pay_type IS NOT NULL AND old.pay_type IS NULL)
10:    )
11: DECLARE
12:   log_sequence_num    INTEGER;
13: BEGIN
14:   --Get the next value from the sequence. This can only
15:   --be done by using a SELECT statement.
16:   SELECT emp_pay_history_key.NEXTVAL INTO log_sequence_num FROM dual;
17:
18:   --Log this change in the history table
19:   INSERT INTO emp_pay_history
20:     (emp_pay_history_pk, emp_id, as_of, emp_name, pay_type, pay_rate)
21:     VALUES (log_sequence_num
22:             ,NVL(:NEW.emp_id,:OLD.emp_id), SYSDATE
23:             ,NVL(:NEW.emp_name,:OLD.emp_name)
24:             ,:NEW.pay_type, :NEW.pay_rate);
25: END;
26: /
```

ANALYSIS This one trigger fires for inserts, updates, and deletes (line 2). The WHEN condition ensures (lines 4–10) that the trigger only fires in response to changes in the pay rate or pay type. It is rather long because either of those fields could be null; remember the three-valued logic issues from Day 3, "Writing PL/SQL Expressions." Notice in lines 22 and 23 that the NVL function is used on the emp_id and emp_name fields, and that if the new versions of these are null, the old versions are used. This is to accommodate deletes because in a trigger the new values of a deleted record are null. However, even when deleting, the new values for pay rate and pay type are always logged (line 24). The SELECT statement in line 16, against the table dual, is used to grab the next available sequence number for use as a primary key.

Listing 11.7 shows an employee record being inserted, the pay rate being updated, and the employee record then being deleted. The history table is shown before and after so that you can see the effect of the trigger.

INPUT/OUTPUT LISTING 11.7 Pay Rate History Example

```
1: SELECT * FROM emp_pay_history;
2: no rows selected
3: INSERT INTO employee
4:   (emp_id, emp_name, pay_rate, pay_type)
5:   VALUES (301,'Jerome Finkbeiner',2000,'H');
```

```
 6: 1 row created.
 7: UPDATE employee
 8:    SET pay_rate = 4000000,
 9:        pay_type = 'S'
10:  WHERE emp_id = 301;
11: 1 row updated.
12: DELETE FROM employee
13:    WHERE emp_id = 301;
14: 1 row deleted.
15: COLUMN as_of FORMAT a20
16: COLUMN emp_name FORMAT a20
17: SELECT   emp_pay_history_pk,
18:          emp_id,
19:          TO_CHAR(as_of,'dd-Mon-yyyy hh:mm pm') as_of,
20:          emp_name,
21:          pay_type,
22:          pay_rate
23:    FROM   emp_pay_history;
24: EMP_PAY_HISTORY_PK EMP_ID AS_OF                EMP_NAME           P PAY_RATE
25: ------------------ ------ -------------------- ------------------ - --------
26: 7                     301  18-Jun-1997 06:06 pm Jerome Finkbeiner  H     2000
27: 8                     301  18-Jun-1997 06:06 pm Jerome Finkbeiner  S  4000000
28: 9                     301  18-Jun-1997 06:06 pm Jerome Finkbeiner
```

ANALYSIS You can see from lines 1 and 2 that the history table is initially empty. A new employee is then inserted (lines 3–5), his pay rate is changed from hourly to salaried (lines 7–10), and finally the employee is deleted (lines 12–13). The COLUMN commands that you see in line 15 and 16 are SQL*Plus commands that limit the width of the AS_OF and EMP_NAME columns to 20 characters, so everything will fit on one line. The SELECT statement in line 17 displays the history table again, and this time it does have some data. There is one history record for each change made to Jerome Finkbeiner's pay rate. The last history record contains a null rate and type to reflect the fact that the employee record was deleted.

Managing Triggers

If you write database triggers, you need to be able to do several things in terms of managing the code:

- List triggers that already exist
- View code for triggers that already exist
- Enable and disable your triggers

The easiest way to do these things is to use a GUI-based tool such as Oracle Enterprise Manager (OEM). OEM's Database Administration Pack contains a program named Schema Manager that makes these tasks very easy. Developer 2000 also can be used to browse database triggers. However, if you don't have these tools, you can query Oracle's data dictionary views using SQL*Plus.

Listing Triggers

The ALL_TRIGGERS view returns one row for each trigger that you are allowed to see. This includes all triggers that you own, as well as those on other user's tables to which you have been granted access. You can easily query ALL_TRIGGERS to get a list of triggers that you own. The example in Listing 11.8 shows how.

INPUT/OUTPUT   **LISTING 11.8**   Listing Triggers That You Own

```
 1: COLUMN trigger_name FORMAT A26
 2: COLUMN table_owner FORMAT A12
 3: COLUMN trigger_type FORMAT A16
 4: COLUMN triggering_event FORMAT A8 WORD_WRAPPED HEADING Event
 5: SELECT trigger_name, table_owner, triggering_event, trigger_type
 6: FROM all_triggers
 7: WHERE owner='JEFF';
 8:
 9:
10: TRIGGER_NAME                     TABLE_OWNER  Event    TRIGGER_TYPE
11: --------------------------       ---------    ------   ----------------
12: DEPARTMENT_INSERT_UPDATE    JEFF              INSERT   BEFORE EACH ROW
13:                                                OR
14:                                                UPDATE
15:
16: EMP_DEPT_DEL                     JEFF              DELETE   AFTER EACH ROW
17: EMP_DEPT_INS                     JEFF              INSERT   AFTER EACH ROW
18: EMP_DEPT_UPD                     JEFF              UPDATE   AFTER EACH ROW
```

ANALYSIS   The COLUMN commands in lines 1 through 4 aren't part of the SQL query. They are there to format the output to fit the width of the screen. The SQL statement querying the ALL_TRIGGERS view is in lines 5 through 7. The owner name (line 7) in this example is JEFF. Be sure to substitute your own username here when you execute this query. The results, in lines 16–18, show three triggers defined on the emp_dept table. These are, of course, the three you created while reading this chapter.

Viewing Trigger Code

The PL/SQL code for a trigger is stored in the TRIGGER_BODY column of the USER_TRIGGERS view. To see the PL/SQL code for a trigger, you could just select the TRIGGER_BODY column for the trigger in which you are interested. Usually, though, it will be more meaningful to see the DDL statement used to create the trigger. The SQL*Plus code in Listing 11.9 will rebuild the CREATE TRIGGER statement for any DML trigger you specify.

INPUT   **LISTING 11.9**   Commands to Extract a Trigger Definition

```
 1: SET ECHO off
 2: SET MAXDATA 50000
 3: SET LONG 50000
 4: SET LONGCHUNKSIZE 1000
 5: SET PAGESIZE 0
 6: SET HEADING off
 7: SET VERIFY off
 8: SET TRIMSPOOL on
 9: SET TRIMOUT on
10: SET RECSEP OFF
11: ACCEPT trigger_name CHAR PROMPT 'What trigger do you want to see? '
12: ACCEPT trigger_owner CHAR PROMPT 'Who owns the trigger? '
13: ACCEPT file_name CHAR PROMPT 'Enter the output filename: '
14: SET TERMOUT off
15: SET FEEDBACK off
16: COLUMN when_clause FORMAT a60 WORD_WRAPPED
17: SPOOL &file_name
18: SELECT 'CREATE OR REPLACE TRIGGER ' || description
19: FROM ALL_TRIGGERS
20: WHERE trigger_name = UPPER('&trigger_name')
21: AND owner = UPPER('&trigger_owner');
22: SELECT 'WHEN (' || when_clause || ')'  when_clause
23: FROM ALL_TRIGGERS
24: WHERE trigger_name = UPPER('&trigger_name')
25: AND owner = UPPER('&trigger_owner')
26: AND when_clause IS NOT NULL;
27: SELECT trigger_body
28: FROM ALL_TRIGGERS
29: WHERE trigger_name = UPPER('&trigger_name')
30: AND owner = UPPER('&trigger_owner');
31: SELECT '/' FROM dual;
32: SPOOL off
33: SET TERMOUT on
34: SET FEEDBACK on
35: SET VERIFY on
36: SET HEADING on
37: SET PAGESIZE 24
```

11

ANALYSIS Lines 1 through 10 set several options that are necessary to get the entire trigger out of the view and into a file in a format that is usable. The COLUMN command in line 16 formats the when_clause column so that it will be word-wrapped. This is necessary because Oracle returns the WHEN clause as one long string. Any line breaks you might have had there when you created the trigger aren't preserved. The ACCEPT commands in lines 11–13 prompt you for the trigger to extract, and for the name of the file in which to place it. The SPOOL command in line 17 tells SQL*Plus to begin writing output to that file. The subsequent queries extract the trigger, and another SPOOL command is used in line 32 to close the file.

Of course, you don't want to actually type all the commands shown in Listing 11.9 into SQL*Plus each time you want to see a trigger definition. Instead, build a file containing these commands. Be sure to save it with the .SQL extension. You can then use the SQL*Plus @ command to execute the file whenever you like. Listing 11.10 shows this command file being used to extract the definition of the maintain_pay_history trigger.

INPUT/OUTPUT **LISTING 11.10** Extracting the Definition for the emp_dept_ins Trigger

```
1: SQL> @TYP11_9
2: What trigger do you want to see? emp_dept_ins
3: Who owns the trigger? jeff
4: Enter the output filename: c:\a\emp_dept_ins.sql
```

ANALYSIS Line 1 shows the command to execute the command file. Line 2 shows the user being prompted for a trigger name. In line 3, the user is prompted for the owner of the trigger, and line 4 shows the prompt for an output filename. In this example, the DDL to re-create the emp_dept_ins trigger will be put in the file named C:\A\EMP_DEPT_INS.SQL.

> **Tip** Consider saving the DDL you use to create a trigger in a file, which you can later edit and reexecute. You will find this easier than extracting the trigger definition from the database each time you need to change it.

Enabling and Disabling Triggers

Triggers can be temporarily disabled without having to go through the trouble of deleting and then re-creating them. This can be useful if you need to do some special processing such as loading data. The ALTER TRIGGER command is used to enable and disable triggers.

SYNTAX

The Syntax for the ALTER TRIGGER Command

```
ALTER TRIGGER name {ENABLED | DISABLED};
```

In this syntax, *name* is the name of the trigger you want to disable or enable.

If you want to temporarily disable the emp_dept_ins trigger for example, you could issue this command:

```
ALTER TRIGGER emp_dept_ins DISABLE;
```

Disabling this trigger might be a good thing to do if you were planning to load a large number of new records into the emp_dept table. The load would run faster if each insert didn't force an update of the department table. After the load was finished, you could reenable the trigger using this command:

```
ALTER TRIGGER emp_dept_ins ENABLE;
```

In this case, before reenabling the trigger, you would need to take steps to reinitialize the NO_OF_EMPS column in the department table.

Nontraditional Triggers

11

Oracle8i introduces the exciting new capability of creating triggers on certain database and data definition events. You can now, for example, write a trigger that is executed every time the database is started. Here is the complete list of events supported by Oracle8i:

- Database shutdown
- Database startup
- Logon
- Logoff
- The occurrence of a server error
- Object creation (the CREATE command)
- Object modification (the ALTER command)
- Object deletion (the DROP command)

Event triggers may be defined at the database level, or at the schema level. For example, a logon trigger may be defined such that it applies to all users when they log on to the database, or it may be applied to one specific user. Table 11.3 shows which triggers may be applied globally, and which must be applied to a particular schema. Table 11.3 also shows the keyword used with the CREATE TRIGGER command to create each type of trigger.

TABLE 11.3 Database Event Triggers

Event	Trigger Keyword	Schema Level	Database Level
Database startup	STARTUP	No	Yes
Database shutdown	SHUTDOWN	No	Yes
Server error	SERVERERROR	No	Yes
Logon	LOGON	Yes	Yes
Logoff	LOGOFF	Yes	Yes
Object creation	CREATE	Yes	No
Object modification	ALTER	Yes	No
Object deletion	DROP	Yes	No

In order to create triggers at the database level, you must have the ADMINISTER DATABASE TRIGGER system privilege. This privilege comes with the DBA role, and typically only database administrators will have that.

The Syntax for Defining a Trigger on a Database or Schema Event

The syntax used for creating a trigger on a database or schema event is only slightly different than that used for creating the traditional type of trigger on data manipulation language (DML) events. Because there are no tables involved, the REFERENCING clause goes away. Similarly, the WHEN condition goes away for the same reason.

▼ **SYNTAX**

```
CREATE [OR REPLACE] TRIGGER [schema.]trigger_name
  {BEFORE¦AFTER}
  {ddl_event [OR ddl_event...] ¦ database_event [OR database_event...]}
  ON {DATABASE ¦ [schema.]SCHEMA}
  [WHEN (condition)]]
DECLARE
  declarations
BEGIN
  pl/sql_code
END;
/
```

In this syntax, the parameters are as follows:

- *schema* is the owner of a trigger or other object.
- *trigger_name* is the name you want to give the trigger.
- *ddl_event* is either CREATE, ALTER, or DELETE.
▼
- *schema* is the name of the schema, or user, to which the trigger applies.

▼

- *condition* is an optional condition placed on the execution of the trigger. You can use the attributes shown in Table 11.4 as part of the condition.
- *declarations* consists of any variable, record, or cursor declarations needed by this PL/SQL block.
- *pl/sql_code* is the PL/SQL code that gets executed when the trigger fires.
- DECLARE...END; You can optionally replace the entire PL/SQL block with a call statement that looks like this:

  ```
  CALL procedure_name;
  ```

  The CALL statement is used to have the trigger consist of only a stored procedure call.

▲

Event Attributes

To help you make use of these triggers, Oracle provides you with several useful attributes that you can reference from with a trigger. When writing a logon trigger for example, you can determine the name of the user who just logged on from the sys.login_user attribute. Table 11.4 lists the available attributes and the trigger types where they are valid.

11

TABLE 11.4   Event Attributes

Attribute	Description	Valid In
sys.sysevent	Returns a 20-character string describing the event that caused the trigger to fire.	All types
sys.instance_num	Returns the Oracle instance number.	All types
sys.database_name	Returns the database brand name, usually "ORACLE".	All types
sys.server_error (stack_position)	Returns the error number from the indicated position in the error stack. Use sys.server_error(1) to find the most recent error.	SERVERERROR
is_servererror (error_number)	Returns TRUE if the given error number is found anywhere in the error stack. Otherwise this returns false.	SERVERERROR
sys.login_user	Returns the name of the user who caused the trigger to fire.	All types
sys.dictionary _obj_type	Returns the type of object involved when a DDL trigger fires.	CREATE ALTER DROP

continues

TABLE 11.4   continued

Attribute	Description	Valid In
sys.dictionary _obj_name	Returns the name of the object involved when a DDL trigger fires.	CREATE ALTER DROP
sys.dictionary _obj_name	Returns the name of the object's owner when a DDL trigger fires.	CREATE ALTER DROP
sys.des_encrypted _password	When a user is being created or modified, this returns the encrypted password for that user.	CREATE ALTER

When you write a trigger, you can use these attributes just as you would a variable. The following example references sys.login_user to find out the username and stores that value in a variable named logon_username:

```
logon_username := sys.login_user;
```

You'll see many of these attributes being used in the following two sections.

Writing a Trigger for a Database Event

One possible use of the STARTUP and SHUTDOWN triggers would be to keep track of when the database was up versus when it was down. To do this, you would need to do the following:

1. Create a table to hold log entries indicating when each startup and shutdown took place.
2. Create a database startup trigger to log the time of each startup.
3. Create a database shutdown trigger to log the time of each shutdown.

 Note

> Only privileged users can create database triggers. You will either have to log in as SYSTEM to create these, or you will have to grant ADMINISTER_DATABASE_TRIGGERS and CREATE TABLE privileges to some other user just for this purpose.

To hold the log entries, you might create a table such as that shown in Listing 11.11:

INPUT   **LISTING 11.11**   The UPTIME_LOG Table

```
CREATE TABLE uptime_log (
    database_name      VARCHAR2(30),
    event_name         VARCHAR2(20),
    event_time         DATE,
    triggered_by_user  VARCHAR2(30)
    );
```

ANALYSIS   This table contains one record for each shutdown or startup event. The event_name distinguishes between the two. The exact time of each startup and shutdown is recorded in the event_time field.

After you've created the table, in order to keep the uptime log maintained automatically you could code two triggers. One trigger would fire on SHUTDOWN, and the other would fire on STARTUP. These are shown in Listings 11.12 and 11.13.

INPUT   **LISTING 11.12**   The STARTUP Trigger

```
CREATE OR REPLACE TRIGGER log_startup
AFTER STARTUP ON DATABASE
BEGIN
    INSERT INTO uptime_log
        (database_name,
         event_name,
         event_time,
         triggered_by_user)
        VALUES (sys.database_name,
                sys.sysevent,
                sysdate,
                sys.login_user);
    COMMIT;
END;
/
```

11

INPUT   **LISTING 11.13**   The SHUTDOWN Trigger

```
CREATE OR REPLACE TRIGGER log_shutdown
BEFORE SHUTDOWN ON DATABASE
BEGIN
    INSERT INTO uptime_log
        (database_name,
         event_name,
```

continues

LISTING 11.13 continued

```
        event_time,
        triggered_by_user)
    VALUES (sys.database_name,
            sys.sysevent,
            sysdate,
            sys.login_user);
    COMMIT;
END;
/
```

ANALYSIS These two triggers fire on database startup and shutdown, respectively. In each case, they log the event by inserting a record with the event name and date (including the time) into the uptime_log table. Notice that these triggers use several of the sys. attributes listed in Table 11.4.

With the tables and triggers in place, you can get a history of when the database was started and stopped by querying the table. For example:

INPUT

```
SQL> SELECT * FROM uptime_log;
```

OUTPUT

```
DATABASE_NAME    EVENT_NAME  EVENT_TIME             TRIGGERED_BY_USER
--------------   ----------  -------------------    -----------------
ORACLE           STARTUP     01-Sep-1999 11:59:39   SYS
ORACLE           SHUTDOWN    01-Sep-1999 12:00:57   SYS
ORACLE           STARTUP     01-Sep-1999 12:01:18   SYS
ORACLE           SHUTDOWN    01-Sep-1999 12:04:05   SYS
ORACLE           STARTUP     01-Sep-1999 12:04:22   SYS
```

Writing a Trigger for a DDL Event

In addition to database events such as startup and shutdown, you can also write triggers that fire when users create or modify objects such as tables, views, and so forth. The trigger shown in Listing 11.14 will record an audit entry each time an object owned by the user JEFF is modified.

INPUT **LISTING 11.14** A Trigger to Audit Schema Changes

```
CREATE OR REPLACE TRIGGER audit_schema_changes
AFTER ALTER ON jeff.SCHEMA
BEGIN
    INSERT INTO alter_audit_trail
        (object_owner,
         object_name,
         object_type,
```

```
            altered_by_user,
            alteration_time
            )
        VALUES (sys.dictionary_obj_owner,
                sys.dictionary_obj_name,
                sys.dictionary_obj_type,
                sys.login_user,
                sysdate);
END;
/
```

ANALYSIS This trigger fires each time someone executes an ALTER statement for any object owned by the user named JEFF. It records the object being altered, the time at which it was altered, and the user who made the change. Notice that the ON clause refers to jeff.SCHEMA. This is the syntax that Oracle requires for this type of trigger. SCHEMA is a keyword indicating that the trigger applies to any object in the schema, which is currently your only choice.

Before you create the trigger shown in Listing 11.14, you must first create the alter_audit_trail table. The statement to do that is shown in Listing 11.15.

INPUT **LISTING 11.15** The ALTER_AUDIT_TRAIL Table

```
CREATE TABLE ALTER_AUDIT_TRAIL (
    object_owner        VARCHAR2(30),
    object_name         VARCHAR2(30),
    object_type         VARCHAR2(20),
    altered_by_user     VARCHAR2(30),
    alteration_time     DATE
    );
```

ANALYSIS The alter_audit_trail table must be in place before you can create the trigger shown in Listing 11.14. That's because Oracle validates references to schema objects such as tables when it compiles a trigger. If the trigger references a table that does not exist, the trigger will not compile, and you will receive an error.

Unlike with database event triggers, you do not need to be a database administrator to create a trigger on a DDL event. All you need is the CREATE TRIGGER privilege.

> **Note** Oracle's built-in auditing facility also allows you to audit changes to a user's objects. However, the viewing of audit records is usually restricted to the database administrator. Using DDL triggers allows a user who is not a DBA to accomplish the same thing on his own.

11

Using Instead-of Triggers

Instead-of triggers provide a way around the age-old problem of views that can't be updated. Instead-of triggers may be created only on views, and provide a block of PL/SQL SQL code that is executed instead of a DML statement such as INSERT or UPDATE.

The Syntax for Defining an Instead-of Trigger

Instead-of triggers are created using the CREATE TRIGGER statement, with the difference that the keywords INSTEAD-OF are used in place of BEFORE or AFTER.

> **Note**
>
> Instead-of triggers may be defined only for views.

▼ SYNTAX

```
CREATE [OR REPLACE] TRIGGER [schema.]trigger_name
  INSTEAD OF verb_list ON [schema.]view_name
  [[REFERENCING correlation_names] FOR EACH ROW [WHEN (condition)]]
DECLARE
  declarations
BEGIN
  pl/sql_code
END;
/
```

In this syntax, the parameters are as follows:

- *schema* represents the owner of the trigger or view.
- *trigger_name* is the name you want to give the trigger.
- *verb_list* identifies the SQL verbs that fire the trigger. The format of the verb list is the same as for regular DML triggers.
- *view_name* is the view on which the trigger is defined.
- *correlation_names* allows you to specify correlation names other than the default of OLD and NEW.
- *condition* is an optional condition placed on the execution of the trigger.
- *declarations* consists of any variable, record, or cursor declarations needed by this PL/SQL block.
- *pl/sql_code* is the PL/SQL code that gets executed when the trigger fires.

▼

▼
- DECLARE...END; You can optionally replace the entire PL/SQL block with a call statement that looks like this:

  ```
  CALL procedure_name;
  ```

  ▲ The CALL statement is used to have the trigger consist of only a stored procedure call.

Writing an Instead-of Trigger

When you write an instead-of trigger, you are basically writing your own code to update the table (or tables) that underlies a view. You do not need to provide for all the columns in the view. In fact, you can limit your trigger to just one column if you like. Say, for example, that you had defined the view shown in Listing 11.16.

INPUT   **LISTING 11.16**   The Public Data View

```
CREATE OR REPLACE VIEW emp_public_data AS
    SELECT e.emp_id,
           e.emp_name,
           NVL(s.emp_name,'Unsupervised') supervisor_name,
           d.dept_name
    FROM employee e,
         employee s,
         emp_dept ed,
         department d
    WHERE e.supervised_by = s.emp_id (+)
    AND e.emp_id = ed.emp_id
    AND d.dept_id = ed.dept_id;
```

ANALYSIS   This view joins together three tables and may return multiple rows for any one employee. Because of that, it is not a view that you can update directly.

While Oracle doesn't allow you to update a view like the EMP_PUBLIC_DATA view directly, you can write an instead-of trigger to provide code to handle an update. The trigger shown in Listing 11.17 handles updates to the employee name field:

INPUT   **LISTING 11.17**   An Instead-of Trigger

```
CREATE OR REPLACE TRIGGER emp_name_change
INSTEAD OF UPDATE ON emp_public_data
BEGIN
    --Only do something if the name was changed.
    --Changes from null are ok, but we don't allow
    --changing a name *to* null.
```

continues

11

LISTING 11.17 continued

```
        IF (:new.emp_name <> :old.emp_name)
        OR (:old.emp_name IS NULL AND :new.emp_name IS NOT NULL) THEN
            UPDATE employee
            SET emp_name = :new.emp_name
            WHERE emp_id = :new.emp_id;
        END IF;
    END;
    /
```

ANALYSIS Because this trigger is defined using INSTEAD OF UPDATE, it will be called as a result of any UPDATE statement issued against the view. The trigger only supports name changes. It checks the old and new values of the name. If they are different, an UPDATE is issued against the employee table.

Exploring Trigger Limitations

When writing code for triggers, there are a few limitations you have to keep in mind. Here is a list of some things you cannot do with a trigger:

- Query or modify a mutating table
- Execute data definition language statements
- Execute COMMIT, ROLLBACK, or SAVEPOINT statements

NEW TERM A *mutating table* is one that is in the process of being changed while the trigger is executing. For example, executing an UPDATE statement on a table makes that table a mutating table for the duration of the UPDATE statement. Any triggers fired as a result of the update are not allowed to query or modify the table being changed.

Data definition language statements, such as a CREATE TABLE statement, cannot be executed from within a trigger, nor can they be executed from within any function or procedure that is called by a trigger.

Triggers are also not allowed to execute any sort of transaction control statement such as COMMIT or ROLLBACK. If you think about it, this limitation makes a lot of sense. You would quickly lose control of your transactions and possibly compromise the integrity of your database if COMMITs and ROLLBACKs were sprinkled throughout various triggers.

Triggers and Mutating Tables

The problem of a trigger needing to query the table that is being changed by the triggering statement is one that sooner or later vexes every trigger writer. Oracle does not allow row triggers to query the table being modified. Doing so gives rise to an error message that looks like this:

```
ORA-04091: table MY_READER.EMP_DEPT is mutating,
►trigger/function may not see it
ORA-06512: at "MY_READER.ONLY_TWO_DEPARTMENTS", line 6
ORA-04088: error during execution of trigger
► 'MY_READER.ONLY_TWO_DEPARTMENTS'
```

Oracle refers to the table being changed as a mutating table.

Take a closer look at this issue. Suppose that you wanted to limit employees in the sample database to a maximum of two departments. The data model actually supports an infinite number of departments per employee, thus it is necessary to check each time you modify the emp_dept table to be sure that the two-department limit has not been exceeded. To do this, you might first think to write a trigger similar to the one shown in Listing 11.18.

INPUT **LISTING 11.18** A Trigger to Enforce the Two-Department Limit

```
 1: CREATE OR REPLACE TRIGGER only_two_departments
 2:   BEFORE UPDATE OR INSERT ON emp_dept
 3:   FOR EACH ROW
 4: DECLARE
 5:   dept_count  INTEGER;      --# of depts for this employee
 6:   max_depts   INTEGER := 2; --max number of depts per employee.
 7: BEGIN
 8:   --Get the current number of departments for this employee.
 9:   SELECT COUNT(*) INTO dept_count
10:     FROM emp_dept
11:    WHERE emp_id = :NEW.emp_id;
12:
13:   --On an update, when the old and new emp_id values are the same,
14:   --we do not need to recheck the count.
15:   IF :OLD.emp_id = :NEW.emp_id THEN
16:     RETURN;
17:   ELSE
18:     --if the employee already is at the max, don't allow him to
19:     --have another department.
20:     IF dept_count >= max_depts THEN
21:       RAISE_APPLICATION_ERROR (-20000,
22:           'Employees are limited to a max of two departments.');
23: END IF;
24:   END IF;
25: END;
26: /
```

11

ANALYSIS This trigger fires for each new record inserted into the emp_dept table and for each updated record in the same table. In either case, it checks to see if the employee in question already has been assigned to the maximum of two departments, and rejects any insert or update if that is the case. There is some special logic in lines 15 and 16 to account for the case where a department assignment is changed, but the employee ID is not changed.

The trigger shown in Listing 11.18 will almost work, but it will fail in certain cases. Listing 11.19 shows how the only_two_departments trigger functions when you insert and update data.

INPUT/OUTPUT **LISTING 11.19**   Testing the ONLY_TWO_DEPARTMENTS Trigger

```
 1: INSERT INTO employee
 2:   (emp_id,emp_name) VALUES (401,'Harvey Wallbanger');
 3: 1 row created.
 4: INSERT INTO employee
 5:   (emp_id,emp_name) VALUES (402,'Scarlet Tanninger');
 6: 1 row created.
 7: INSERT INTO department
 8:   (dept_id, dept_name) VALUES (401,'Fermentation');
 9: 1 row created.
10: INSERT INTO department
11:   (dept_id, dept_name) VALUES (402,'Distillation');
12: 1 row created.
13: INSERT INTO department
14:   (dept_id, dept_name) VALUES (403,'Bottling');
15: 1 row created.
16: INSERT INTO emp_dept
17:   (emp_id, dept_id) VALUES (401,401);
18: 1 row created.
19: INSERT INTO emp_dept
20:   (emp_id, dept_id) VALUES (401,402);
21: 1 row created.
22: INSERT INTO emp_dept
23:   (emp_id, dept_id) VALUES (402,402);
24: 1 row created.
25: INSERT INTO emp_dept
26:   (emp_id, dept_id) VALUES (402,403);
27: 1 row created.
28: INSERT INTO emp_dept
29:   (emp_id, dept_id) VALUES (401,403);
30: INSERT INTO emp_dept
31:            *
32: ERROR at line 1:
33: ORA-20000: Employees are limited to a max of two departments.
34: ORA-06512: at "MY_READER.ONLY_TWO_DEPARTMENTS", line 17
35: ORA-04088: error during execution of trigger
```

```
➥'MY_READER.ONLY_TWO_DEPARTMENTS'
36: UPDATE emp_dept
37:   SET dept_id = 403
38:  WHERE emp_id = 401 AND dept_id = 402;
39: UPDATE emp_dept
40:       *
41: ERROR at line 1:
42: ORA-04091: table MY_READER.EMP_DEPT is mutating,
➥trigger/function may not see it
43: ORA-06512: at "MY_READER.ONLY_TWO_DEPARTMENTS", line 6
44: ORA-04088: error during execution of trigger
Â'MY_READER.ONLY_TWO_DEPARTMENTS'
```

ANALYSIS   The first five inserts in Listing 11.19 merely set up some employee and department records for you to experiment with. The next four inserts assign each employee to two departments. So far, so good. However, the tenth INSERT statement (lines 28–29) attempts to assign employee number 401 to a third department. You can see that the trigger caught this and raised an error (lines 30–35), causing the insert to fail. The last statement (lines 36–38) is an update, and it gives rise to the mutating error (lines 39–44) because the trigger is querying the change in the table.

As you can see, this trigger will not serve the purpose of limiting each employee to a maximum of two departments. At this point, there are three options you can use to enforce this rule without redesigning the database:

- Enforce the rule in the application code.
- Take a different approach to the problem.
- Use a combination of table-level and row-level triggers, combined with a package to enforce the rule at the database level.

Enforcing the rule at the application level is possible but requires that the code to enforce the rule be replicated in each program that updates the emp_dept table. Sometimes you can take an entirely different approach to the problem. For example, in this case you could choose not to allow updates to the emp_dept table at all. Any changes to an employee's department assignment would then be done by first deleting the old record and then inserting a new one. The third, and most complicated, approach is to code the validation in a table-level trigger while using a row-level trigger to build a list of newly inserted or modified records. This solution takes advantage of the fact that variables in an Oracle stored package persist throughout a database session. To implement this approach, you will need to write

- A table-level before trigger on emp_dept to initialize the list of records being inserted/updated.

11

- A row-level trigger on emp_dept to add the primary key of each new or updated record to the list.
- A table-level after trigger on emp_dept to loop through the list and check to be sure that none of the updates or inserts violates the maximum of two departments per employee.
- A package implementing procedures to add to the list, initialize the list, and retrieve from the list, and which will also contain the list itself.

Why will the approach just described work? It works because a row-level trigger cannot query a mutating table, but a table-level trigger can. By the time the table-level after trigger fires, all the changes have been made and the table is in a consistent state.

Listing 11.20 shows the emp_dept_procs package, which will be part of the solution to enforce the two-department rule. Listing 11.21 shows the DDL to create the triggers that will enforce this rule. Notice that the triggers in Listing 11.21 each call procedures that are part of the emp_dept_procs package, and that emp_dept_procs contains package-level variables that are used to maintain a list of records that have been inserted or modified.

INPUT   **LISTING 11.20**   The emp_dept_procs Package

```
 1: CREATE OR REPLACE package emp_dept_procs AS
 2: PROCEDURE init_list;
 3: PROCEDURE add_to_list (emp_id IN emp_dept.emp_id%TYPE
 4:                       ,dept_id IN emp_dept.dept_id%TYPE);
 5: FUNCTION get_count RETURN NUMBER;
 6: PROCEDURE get_from_list (to_get IN BINARY_INTEGER
 7:                         ,emp_id OUT emp_dept.emp_id%TYPE
 8:                         ,dept_id OUT emp_dept.dept_id%TYPE);
 9: END emp_dept_procs;
10: /
11:
12: CREATE OR REPLACE package body emp_dept_procs AS
13: --These variables persist throughout a session.
14: listx   BINARY_INTEGER;   --current max index into the list.
15:
16: --Declare a record containing the table's primary key.
17: TYPE emp_dept_pk IS RECORD (
18:     emp_id  emp_dept.emp_id%TYPE,
19:     dept_id emp_dept.dept_id%TYPE);
20:
21: --This defines a pl/sql table which will store a list of all records
22: --"touched" by an insert or update statement.
23: TYPE emp_dept_list_type IS TABLE OF emp_dept_pk
24:     INDEX BY BINARY_INTEGER;
```

```
25:
26: --Declare the actual table which will contain our list.
27: emp_dept_list    emp_dept_list_type;
28:
29: PROCEDURE init_list is
30: BEGIN
31: --Initialize the list pointer to zero.
32: listx := 0;
33: END;
34:
35: PROCEDURE add_to_list (emp_id IN emp_dept.emp_id%TYPE
36:                        ,dept_id IN emp_dept.dept_id%TYPE) IS
37: BEGIN
38: --increment the list index and save the primary key values.
39: listx := listx + 1;
40: emp_dept_list(listx).emp_id := emp_id;
41: emp_dept_list(listx).dept_id := dept_id;
42: END;
43:
44: FUNCTION get_count RETURN NUMBER IS
45: BEGIN
46: --return the number of entries in the list.
47: RETURN listx;
48: END;
49:
50: PROCEDURE get_from_list (to_get IN BINARY_INTEGER
51:                          ,emp_id OUT emp_dept.emp_id%TYPE
52:                          ,dept_id OUT emp_dept.dept_id%TYPE) IS
53: BEGIN
54: emp_id := emp_dept_list(to_get).emp_id;
55: dept_id := emp_dept_list(to_get).dept_id;
56: END;
57:
58: END emp_dept_procs;
59: /
```

11

ANALYSIS Lines 1–10 create the package header, which defines the procedures and functions from this package that are available to external objects, such as a trigger. Lines 17–19 define a record containing the primary key fields for the emp_dept table. This record in turn is used to define a PL/SQL table type (lines 23–24). Finally, in line 27, a PL/SQL table is declared. This is the table that will hold the list of records inserted or updated--it must be validated by the table-level after trigger.

Listing 11.21 shows how you would drop the previous ONLY_TWO_DEPARTMENTS trigger, which didn't always work, and create a new one that uses the package created in Listing 11.20.

INPUT/
OUTPUT **LISTING 11.21** Triggers to Enforce the Two-Department Limit

```
 1: DROP TRIGGER only_two_departments;
 2: Trigger dropped.
 3: CREATE OR REPLACE TRIGGER only_two_departments_1
 4:   BEFORE UPDATE OR INSERT ON emp_dept
 5: BEGIN
 6:   --Reset the list counter before starting any insert/update.
 7:   emp_dept_procs.init_list;
 8: END;
 9: /
10: Trigger created.
11: CREATE OR REPLACE TRIGGER only_two_departments_2
12:   BEFORE UPDATE OR INSERT ON emp_dept
13:   FOR EACH ROW
14: BEGIN
15:   --Add this record to the list of those changed.
16:   --Validation is done after the STATEMENT is finished.
17:   emp_dept_procs.add_to_list(:NEW.emp_id, :NEW.dept_id);
18: END;
19: /
20: Trigger created.
21: CREATE OR REPLACE TRIGGER only_two_departments_3
22:   AFTER UPDATE OR INSERT ON emp_dept
23: DECLARE
24:   check_emp_id     emp_dept.emp_id%TYPE;
25:   check_dept_id    emp_dept.dept_id%TYPE;
26:
27:   listx     BINARY_INTEGER;
28:   list_max  BINARY_INTEGER;
29:
30:   dept_count  NUMBER;
31: BEGIN
32:   --Get the number of records we "touched".
33:   list_max := emp_dept_procs.get_count;
34:
35:   --We need to check each record to see if we have
36:   --violated the "only two departments" rule.
37:   FOR listx IN 1..list_max loop
38:     --Get the primary key for the record we are checking.
39:     emp_dept_procs.get_from_list (listx, check_emp_id, check_dept_id);
40:
41:     --Get the number of departments for this employee.
42:     SELECT COUNT(*) INTO dept_count
43:       FROM emp_dept
44:      WHERE emp_id = check_emp_id;
45:
46:     --Does the employee in question have more than two departments?
47:     IF dept_count > 2 THEN
48:       RAISE_APPLICATION_ERROR(-20000,
```

```
49:             'Employees are limited to a max of two departments.');
50: END IF;
51:   END LOOP;
52: END;
53: /
54: Trigger created.
```

ANALYSIS Notice in line 1 that the previous trigger is dropped. Be sure to do this. The table-level before trigger in lines 3–9 is fired at the beginning of an INSERT or UPDATE statement. It calls a package procedure that initializes the list counter. The row-level trigger, named only_two_departments_2 (defined in lines 11–19), is fired for each row added or changed. This trigger adds the primary key of each record to the list maintained in the package-level PL/SQL table. The third trigger, defined in lines 21–52, is the one that does the actual validation work. It is fired after the INSERT or UPDATE statement is complete. It loops through each new or changed record and checks to be sure that each employee in question has a maximum of two department assignments.

Now that you have created these triggers and the emp_dept_procs package, you can execute the SQL statements shown in Listing 11.22 in order to demonstrate that it works.

INPUT/ OUTPUT **LISTING 11.22** Testing the Triggers and Package That Enforce the Two-Department Rule

```
 1: INSERT INTO employee
 2:   (emp_id,emp_name) VALUES (403,'Freddie Fisher');
 3: 1 row created.
 4: INSERT INTO employee
 5:   (emp_id,emp_name) VALUES (404,'Charlie Tuna');
 6: 1 row created.
 7: INSERT INTO department
 8:   (dept_id, dept_name) VALUES (404,'Scale Processing');
 9: 1 row created.
10: INSERT INTO department
11:   (dept_id, dept_name) VALUES (405,'Gutting');
12: 1 row created.
13: INSERT INTO department
14:   (dept_id, dept_name) VALUES (406,'Unloading');
15: 1 row created.
16: INSERT INTO emp_dept
17:   (emp_id, dept_id) VALUES (403,404);
18: 1 row created.
19: INSERT INTO emp_dept
20:   (emp_id, dept_id) VALUES (403,405);
21: 1 row created.
22: INSERT INTO emp_dept
```

continues

11

LISTING **11.22** continued

```
23:    (emp_id, dept_id) VALUES (404,405);
24: 1 row created.
25: INSERT INTO emp_dept
26:    (emp_id, dept_id) VALUES (404,406);
27: 1 row created.
28: INSERT INTO emp_dept
29:    (emp_id, dept_id) VALUES (403,406);
30: INSERT INTO emp_dept
31: *
32: ERROR at line 1:
33: ORA-20000: Employees are limited to a max of two departments.
34: ORA-06512: at "MY_READER.ONLY_TWO_DEPARTMENTS_3", line 21
35: ORA-04088: error during execution of trigger
➥'MY_READER.ONLY_TWO_DEPARTMENTS_3'
36: UPDATE emp_dept
37:    SET dept_id = 406
38:  WHERE emp_id = 403 AND dept_id = 405;
39: 1 row updated.
40: UPDATE emp_dept
41:    SET emp_id = 403
42:  WHERE emp_id = 404
43:    AND dept_id = 405;
44: update emp_dept
45:         *
46: ERROR at line 1:
47: ORA-20000: Employees are limited to a max of two departments.
48: ORA-06512: at "MY_READER.ONLY_TWO_DEPARTMENTS_3", line 21
49: ORA-04088: error during execution of trigger
'MY_READER.ONLY_TWO_DEPARTMENTS_3'
```

ANALYSIS The first five inserts (lines 1–15) put some sample employees and departments in place for testing purposes. The next four inserts (lines 16–27) assign each of the two employees just inserted to two departments. The tenth insert (lines 28–29) attempts to assign employee number 403 to a third department. This violates the two-department rule, causing the insert to fail (lines 30–35). There are two UPDATE statements. The first update (lines 36–38) is allowed because it only changes a department assignment for employee number 403. That employee still has exactly two departments. The second update (lines 40–43) fails because it is changing the emp_id field in a record from 404 to 403, resulting in 403 having more than two department assignments.

Caution The solution shown in Listings 11.20 and 11.21 will work when triggers only need to query the mutating table. The problem gets more complex if you need to update those rows. Updating records in the mutating table from a trigger will fire off the very same set of triggers that will also try to use the very same package-level PL/SQL table to build a list of affected records, thus clobbering the data needed to validate the initial update.

Summary

This chapter has been complex, but it gave you the chance to see and experiment with triggers implementing several different types of functionality. To reiterate, some possible uses for triggers are to enforce business rules, generate column values (Listing 11.3), enhance security, and maintain a historical record (Listing 11.6). These are just the tip of the iceberg. The possibilities are limited only by your creativity and imagination. You have also learned about the mutating table error, the bane of many trigger writers, and should now have a good understanding of how to work around it.

Q&A

11

Q If I am using a trigger to enforce a business rule or a referential integrity rule, does this affect the records that predate creation of the trigger?

A No, it doesn't, and that's a good point to keep in mind. When you create a declarative constraint, you are really making a statement about the data that must always be true. You cannot create a constraint if data is present that violates that constraint. Triggers, on the other hand, affect only records that have been inserted, updated, or deleted after the trigger was created. For example, creating the triggers limiting an employee to only two department assignments will do nothing about preexisting cases where an employee has more than two assignments.

Q The inserts in Listing 11.18 (lines 16–27) did not generate a mutating table error message, yet they did query the table. Why is this?

A Single-row inserts are an exception to the rule about querying the underlying table. However, if the insert is one that could possibly create more than one row, for example an INSERT INTO emp_dept SELECT..., the rule about not querying the mutating table still applies.

Q **What's the difference between a statement-level trigger and a row-level trigger?**

A A statement-level trigger is executed only once, either before or after the triggering SQL statement executes. It cannot refer to any values in the rows affected by the statement. A row-level trigger fires once for each row affected by the triggering SQL statement and can reference the values for each of the rows.

Q **Why should I generally validate business rules in a before trigger rather than an after trigger?**

A It's potentially more efficient because you can prevent Oracle from doing the work involved in inserting, updating, or deleting a record. By validating in an after trigger, you are allowing Oracle to first update the table in question, update any indexes that might be affected by the change, and possibly fire off other triggers.

Q **The triggers in Listing 11.3 maintain employee counts for each department as records are inserted into, updated in, and deleted from the emp_dept table. What happens, however, if a department record is deleted and then reinserted? Won't the employee count be reset to zero in that case, making it incorrect?**

A Yes, this is absolutely true. Typically, in a production database, you would also have referential integrity constraints defined to prevent deletion of department records referenced by other tables.

Q **Can I define DDL triggers on a specific schema object such as a table?**

A No, you cannot. Oracle may have plans to change this. The syntax certainly leaves that possibility open. For now though, you may only define DDL triggers at the schema level.

Workshop

Use the following sections to test your comprehension of this chapter and put what you've learned into practice. You'll find the answers to the quiz and exercises in Appendix A, "Answers."

Quiz

1. Which data manipulation statements can support triggers?
2. What are the four basic parts of a trigger?
3. In a trigger, what are the correlation names :OLD and :NEW used for?

4. What is the name of the system view that can be used to retrieve trigger definitions?

5. What is a mutating table?

6. Name some possible uses for triggers.

Exercises

1. Write a set of triggers to maintain the emp_name and dept_name fields redundantly in the emp_dept table so that you do not have to join with the employee and department tables just to get a simple department listing.

2. Write the SQL statements necessary to populate the emp_name and dept_name fields for any existing emp_dept records.

11

WEEK 2

DAY 12

Using Oracle8i Objects for Object-Oriented Programming

by Jonathan Gennick

PL/SQL and Oracle contain a limited amount of support for object-oriented programming. Object-oriented features were first introduced in Oracle release 8.0, and make it possible to define object classes, instantiate, or to construct, objects, and save those objects in the database. Although it's not yet clear whether PL/SQL's object-oriented features are catching on with developers, you should certainly be aware of them. The potential benefits to you are increased opportunities for abstraction and for writing reusable code.

Today you will learn:

- How to define an Oracle object type.
- How to create an object table, and how to use PL/SQL to store objects in that table.

- How to create an object column in a regular table, and then access the data in that column from PL/SQL.
- How to write the ORDER and MAP methods used when comparing objects.

A Brief Primer on Object-Oriented Programming

Let's begin by reviewing the basics of object-oriented programming (OOP). There is really no magic to OOP: It's simply a way of organizing code and data within your programs, one that you can use to model your code to more closely match the real world. There are three pillars of good object-oriented design:

- Encapsulation
- Inheritance
- Polymorphism

Each of these is described in more detail in the following sections, using as examples some real-world objects that you interact with every day.

Encapsulation

NEW TERM   The term *encapsulation* refers to the fact that each object takes care of itself. A well-designed object has a clear and well-defined interface that is used to manipulate the object. All the program code necessary to perform any function on the object is contained within the object definition itself. Thus an object is completely self-contained and can be dropped in anywhere you need it.

A classic, and often used, real-world example of objects is audio/video components. Say you are setting up a home theater. You drive to the nearest appliance superstore and pick out whatever objects interest you—a big-screen TV, an FM tuner, an amplifier, and some speakers. All these components have well-defined interfaces, and each contains the internal electronics and software that are necessary to make them work. The FM tuner tunes in radio stations, regardless of whether you plug it in to the amplifier. The TV does not need any circuitry that might be present in the speakers. After integrating all these components, you might decide that you also want a subwoofer. Adding one is simple. You don't have to rebuild your stereo system—you just run back to the store, buy the desired component, come home, and plug it in.

It sounds pretty easy, but there are some gotchas. In real life, interfaces are not always compatible, and sometimes components have overlapping functionality. That amplifier, for example, might also have a built-in tuner, and how often have you had to buy an adapter to mate two incompatible connectors? Often it's easier to work with components that have all been built by the same manufacturer and that have been designed to work together. The same is true in OOP.

Inheritance

NEW TERM *Inheritance* refers to the fact that as you design new objects, you often build on objects that have been created previously. In other words, you can create new objects that *inherit* the functionality of previously created objects. When you do this, you might choose to modify some of the inherited functionality, or you might choose to add new functionality. The telephone is a good example of this. Originally it was a very simple device. You picked up the phone, listened for a dial tone, and dialed a number by using a rotary dial. When pushbutton phones came out, the original functionality was inherited, except for the dialing interface, which was replaced by buttons. Cordless phones inherited this functionality, added a radio to the implementation, and added an on/off switch to the handset interface so that the handset did not need to be returned to the cradle after each call.

One big advantage of inheritance in the OOP world, which is not present in the physical world, is that you can change the definition of a software object, and the change will propagate through all objects of that type, all objects inherited from those objects, and so forth. Imagine changing the definition of a telephone to include pushbutton dialing, and as a result having all the rotary phones in the world suddenly transform themselves into pushbutton phones. Of course that can't be done, but the software equivalent of it can.

Polymorphism

NEW TERM *Polymorphism* enables different objects to have methods of the same name that accomplish similar tasks but in different ways. Think back to the home entertainment system example for a moment. Each of the components—the TV, the FM tuner, the amplifier, and so forth—has an on button. Many components also have associated remotes, each also with an on button. Each of these buttons can invoke different processes inside each piece of equipment. A TV remote, for example, has to send an infrared beam of light to the TV set when the on button is pushed. Despite the fact that each on button invokes a different sequence of events, each button is still labeled *on*. It would be inconvenient if this were not the case. Consistent naming frees your mind from having to remember specifically for each device how to turn it on. You quickly become conditioned to pushing the on button, or flipping a switch to on, no matter what device you are using.

12

Polymorphism similarly enables your software objects to use method names that are consistent with the function being performed, even though the way in which that function is implemented can differ from object to object.

Classes, Objects, Attributes, and Methods

NEW TERM The term *class* refers to the definition for an object. Like a blueprint for a house, it tells you everything you need to build an object, and it tells you what that object will look like when it is built. An `employee` class, for example, might be created to contain all attributes of an employee. Examples of employee attributes would be pay rate, name, and address.

NEW TERM Many *objects* can be built from a class, just as one set of blueprints can be used to build numerous houses. If you were writing code to process employee records, you would use the `employee` class to *instantiate*, or construct, an `employee` object for each employee record.

NEW TERM Objects consist of attributes and methods. An *attribute* can be anything you need to know about an object. Name, phone number, Social Security number, pay rate, and pay type are all examples of attributes for an `employee` object. Attributes are implemented as variable declarations made within the object class definition. *Methods* are the functions and procedures used to perform functions related to the object. Like attributes, methods are implemented as functions and procedures in the object class definition. Anything you want to do to an object should be implemented as a method. If you want to compare two objects, you should implement a compare method. If you want to copy an object, you should implement a copy method. An `employee` object class, for example, might contain a method to calculate an employee's yearly bonus based on pay type, longevity with the firm, and so on.

Advantages of OOP Over Traditional Methods

Objects offer the opportunity for increased reliability because of their well-defined interfaces. Reuse is made easier because all necessary code and data are part of the object definition; thus object classes can easily be added to programs as new functionality is required. Because you can model real-world business objects, as well as encapsulate and hide the details behind an object's functionality, you can program at a higher level of abstraction, minimizing the amount of detail you need to remember, which makes your job as a developer much easier.

How Oracle8i Implements Objects

Oracle8i implements several constructs in support of object-oriented programming:

- *Object types*, with which you can define object classes.
- *Object tables*, with which you can store objects.
- *Object views*, which allow you to synthesize objects from the existing relational data.

Oracle also implements an object-relational database. The underpinnings are still relational, but the underlying relational model has been extended to include support for new datatypes, which in this case are object types. By doing this, Oracle has maintained compatibility with existing relational databases and provided a path for gradual migration to objects.

Object Types

To use an object, first you need to define it. To do this, you create an *object type,* which is a database-level definition and is equivalent to the term *class* as used in object-oriented languages such as Java and C++. It contains both the code and data definitions for an object. Object types are also treated as datatypes and can be used in PL/SQL programs for declaring variables that will contain objects.

Object Tables

Object tables are based on an object definition and essentially map each attribute of an object to a column in the table.

Object Views

An *object view* is the object analog of a view on a table. A full discussion of object views is beyond the scope of this book, but basically you should know that a database administrator can use them to define pseudo-objects based on existing relational data. Like a relational view, object views are based on a SQL statement that retrieves the data for the object.

Defining an Object Type

You should now have a good idea of what OOP is and how Oracle handles objects. It's time to get down to some practical examples. To begin, let's define an object type for employee addresses. Listing 12.1 shows one possible implementation.

LISTING 12.1   The address Object Type

```
 1: CREATE OR REPLACE TYPE address AS OBJECT (
 2: street_1 VARCHAR2(40),
 3: street_2 VARCHAR2(40),
 4: city          VARCHAR2(40),
 5: state_abbr       VARCHAR2(2),
 6: zip_code VARCHAR2(5),
 7: phone_number      VARCHAR2(10),
 8: MEMBER PROCEDURE ChangeAddress (
 9: st_1 IN VARCHAR2, st_2 IN VARCHAR2, cty IN VARCHAR2,
10: state IN VARCHAR2, zip IN VARCHAR2),
11: MEMBER FUNCTION getStreet (line_no IN number) RETURN VARCHAR2,
12: MEMBER FUNCTION getCity RETURN VARCHAR2,
13: MEMBER FUNCTION getStateAbbr RETURN VARCHAR2,
14: MEMBER FUNCTION getPostalCode RETURN VARCHAR2,
15: MEMBER FUNCTION getPhone RETURN VARCHAR2,
16: MEMBER PROCEDURE setPhone (newPhone IN VARCHAR2)
17: );
18: /
19
20: CREATE OR REPLACE TYPE BODY address AS
21: MEMBER PROCEDURE ChangeAddress (
22: st_1 IN VARCHAR2, st_2 IN VARCHAR2, cty IN VARCHAR2,
23: state IN VARCHAR2, zip IN VARCHAR2) IS
24: BEGIN
25: IF (st_1 IS NULL) OR (cty IS NULL) OR
26: (state IS NULL) OR (zip IS NULL)
27: OR (upper(state) NOT IN ('AK','AL','AR','AZ','CA','CO',
28:                           'CT','DC','DE','FL','GA','HI',
29:                           'IA','ID','IL','IN','KS','KY',
30:                           'LA','MA','MD','ME','MI','MN',
31:                           'MO','MS','MT','NC','ND','NE',
32:                           'NH','NJ','NM','NV','NY','OH',
33:                           'OK','OR','PA','RI','SC','SD',
34:                           'TN','TX','UT','VA','VT','WA',
35:                           'WI','WV','WY'))
36: OR (zip <> ltrim(to_char(to_number(zip),'09999'))) THEN
37: RAISE_application_error(-20001,'The new Address is invalid.');
38: ELSE
39: street_1 := st_1;
40: street_2 := st_2;
41: city := cty;
42: state_abbr := upper(state);
43: zip_code := zip;
44: END IF;
45: END;
46:
47: MEMBER FUNCTION getStreet (line_no IN number)
48: RETURN VARCHAR2 IS
```

```
49: BEGIN
50: IF line_no = 1 THEN
51: RETURN street_1;
52: ELSIF line_no = 2 THEN
53: RETURN street_2;
54: ELSE
55: RETURN ' ';     --send back a blank.
56: END IF;
57: END;
58:
59: MEMBER FUNCTION getCity RETURN VARCHAR2 IS
60: BEGIN
61: RETURN city;
62: END;
63:
64: MEMBER FUNCTION getStateAbbr RETURN VARCHAR2 IS
65: BEGIN
66: RETURN state_abbr;
67: END;
68:
69: MEMBER FUNCTION getPostalCode RETURN VARCHAR2 IS
70: BEGIN
71: RETURN zip_code;
72: END;
73:
74: MEMBER FUNCTION getPhone RETURN VARCHAR2 IS
75: BEGIN
76: RETURN phone_number;
77: END;
78:
79: MEMBER PROCEDURE setPhone (newPhone IN VARCHAR2) IS
80: BEGIN
81: phone_number := newPhone;
82: END;
83: END;
84: /
```

12

ANALYSIS   The statements in this listing show how to define an object type. Notice that the form of an object type declaration closely resembles that of a package definition. Like packages, object types have both a specification and a body. The specification, shown in lines 1 through 18, lists the object's attributes and member functions. The object body, lines 20 through 84, contains the actual code for the methods.

▼ SYNTAX

The Syntax for Defining an Object Type

```
CREATE TYPE type_name [IS ¦ AS] OBJECT (
  attribute_name    datatype,
  attribute_name    datatype,
  ...
  MEMBER [function_specification ¦ procedure_specification],
  MEMBER [function_specification ¦ procedure_specification],
  ...
  [MAP ¦ ORDER] MEMBER function_specification,
  pragma,
  pragma,
  ...
  );
CREATE TYPE BODY type_name [IS ¦ AS]
  MEMBER [function_definition ¦ procedure_definition];
  MEMBER [function_definition ¦ procedure_definition];
  ...
  [MAP ¦ ORDER] MEMBER function_definition;
END;
```

In this syntax, the parameters are as follows:

- *type_name*—The name of the object type that you are defining. This can be any name you choose, but it must conform to Oracle's naming rules. Names may be up to 30 characters long, must begin with a letter, and thereafter may contain letters, digits, underscores (_), pound signs (#), and dollar signs ($).

- *attribute_name*—The attribute can have any name you choose, and must conform to the rules for naming variables. An object must have at least one attribute.

- *datatype*—This can be another object type or an Oracle datatype. The Oracle datatypes LONG, LONG RAW, NCHAR, NCLOB, NVARCHAR2, and ROWID cannot be used here. PL/SQL-specific datatypes, such as BINARY_INTEGER and BOOLEAN, are also not allowed. That's because objects are stored in database tables, and the database does not recognize PL/SQL specific datatypes.

- *function_specification*—This is the same kind of PL/SQL function specification that would appear in a package definition.

- *procedure_specification*—This is the same kind of PL/SQL procedure specification that would appear in a package definition.

- *pragma*—This is any pragma, or compiler directive, such as those used to define exceptions or to tell Oracle whether a method modifies any database tables.

- *function_definition*—This contains the code for a function.

▲ - *procedure_definition*—This contains the code for a procedure.

An object must contain at least one attribute, and may contain as many as a thousand. Member functions and procedures are entirely optional, as are compiler directives (that is, pragmas). The definition of a MAP function or an ORDER function is also optional, but if present, only one type may be used. MAP and ORDER functions are discussed later in this lesson, in the section "Comparing Objects."

As mentioned previously, an object type is a database-level definition. After an object type is defined in the database, it can be used to create object tables, to define table columns that are themselves objects, or to declare object variables in PL/SQL blocks.

Constructor Methods

 Each Oracle object type has a built-in *constructor* method that is used to create an instance of that type. This method is responsible for initializing all the object's attributes and for doing any internal housekeeping necessary. You do not have to declare or define this method, and in fact you cannot—Oracle does it for you.

> **Note**
>
> The inability to declare and define your own constructor methods represents a serious weakness in Oracle's current implementation of objects. Your flexibility is limited, and your control is limited as well because you have nowhere to write validation code, which can prevent an object from being created with an invalid combination of attribute values.

The constructor method always has the same name as the object type, and has as its arguments each of the object's attributes, in the order in which you declared them. Thus the constructor method for the address object type would be

```
FUNCTION address (street_1 in VARCHAR2, street_2 in VARCHAR2,
                  city in VARCHAR2, state_abbr, zip_code,
                  phone_number) returns address
```

The constructor function always returns an object of the same type. In your code, you would reference address as a function, passing values for each argument, in order to create an object of the address type, such as the following:

```
address_variable := address('101 Oak','','Detroit','MI',
    '48223','3135358886');
```

You will see more examples of this later in the lesson, in the section "Instantiating and Using Objects."

Accessor Methods

 Accessor methods are used to return an object's attributes, and by convention, they usually begin with `get`. The implementation of the `address` object shown in Listing 12.1 contains five accessor methods:

- `getStreet`
- `getCity`
- `getStateAbbr`
- `getPostalCode`
- `getPhone`

In most cases, these simply return the attribute in question. The `getStreet` method does a bit more: It returns a blank if an invalid street address line is requested.

At first glance, it might seem silly to use a function like `getStreet` when you could just as easily reference the `street_1` and `street_2` attributes directly. However, accessor methods provide extra insulation between the underlying implementation of the objects and the programs that use them. Consider the implications if, for whatever reason, you decided to remove the `street_2` attribute from the `address` object. What impact would that have on existing programs? None if they are using `getStreet`. One small change to that function, and your programs wouldn't know the difference.

> **Caution**
>
> Most object-oriented languages allow you to force the use of accessor functions by letting you define attributes as *private*, meaning that they cannot be accessed directly. Oracle does not yet do this, so even though the accessor functions exist, there is no way to be completely sure that they are always used.

Mutator Methods

 A *mutator method* is the opposite of an accessor method. It lets you set attribute values without referencing them directly. The advantages are the same as for accessor methods. Mutator methods simply provide an extra level of insulation between a program and an object's underlying implementation. By convention, mutator method names typically start with `set`.

The `ChangeAddress` method of the `address` object described previously, for example, would be considered a mutator method. It could have been named `setAddress` to conform more closely to convention, but the name `ChangeAddress` was chosen because it is more descriptive of the real-world event for which this method exists, and because in a real-life situation, changing an address might involve more than just setting a few attributes.

Instantiating and Using Objects

After you have defined an object type, you probably want to do something with it. To use an object from within PL/SQL, you need to follow these steps:

1. Declare one or more variables in which the datatype is the object type you want to use.

2. Instantiate one or more of the objects.

3. Use the object's member methods to manipulate the objects.

4. Optionally, store the objects in a database.

This section discusses how to perform the first three of these four steps. There are two different approaches to storing objects, and those are discussed later in this lesson, in the section "Storing and Retrieving Objects."

Listing 12.2 shows some fairly simple code that uses the address object defined earlier. Several variables of the address object type are declared. A few address objects are instantiated, their values are manipulated, and the object's attributes are displayed.

INPUT   **LISTING 12.2**   Using the address Object

```
 1: --A PL/SQL block demonstrating the
 2: --use of the address object.
 3: DECLARE
 4:    address_1    address;
 5:    address_2    address;
 6:    address_3    address;
 7: BEGIN
 8:    --Instantiate a new address object named address_1,
 9:    --and assign a copy of it to address_2.
10:    address_1 := address ('2700 Peerless Road','Apt 1',
11:                    'Cleveland','TN','37312','4235551212');
12:    address_2 := address_1;
13:
14:    --Change address #1
15:    address_1.ChangeAddress ('2800 Peermore Road','Apt 99',
16:                    'Detroit','MI','48823');
17:
18:    --Instantiate a second object.
19:    address_3 := address ('2700 Eaton Rapids Road','Lot 98',
20:                    'Lansing','MI','48911','5173943551');
```

continues

12

LISTING 12.2   continued

```
21:
22:     --Now print out the attributes from each object.
23:     dbms_output.put_line('Attributes for address_1:');
24:     dbms_output.put_line(address_1.getStreet(1));
25:     dbms_output.put_line(address_1.getStreet(2));
26:     dbms_output.put_line(address_1.getCity
27:                            || ' ' || address_1.getStateAbbr
28:                            || ' ' || address_1.getPostalCode);
29:     dbms_output.put_line(address_1.getPhone);
30:
31:     dbms_output.put_line('-------------------------');
32:     dbms_output.put_line('Attributes for address_2:');
33:     dbms_output.put_line(address_2.getStreet(1));
34:     dbms_output.put_line(address_2.getStreet(2));
35:     dbms_output.put_line(address_2.getCity
36:                            || ' ' || address_2.getStateAbbr
37:                            || ' ' || address_2.getPostalCode);
38:     dbms_output.put_line(address_2.getPhone);
39:
40:     dbms_output.put_line('-------------------------');
41:     dbms_output.put_line('Attributes for address_3:');
42:     dbms_output.put_line(address_3.street_1);
43:     dbms_output.put_line(address_3.street_2);
44:     dbms_output.put_line(address_3.city
45:                            || ' ' || address_3.state_abbr
46:                            || ' ' || address_3.zip_code);
47:     dbms_output.put_line(address_3.phone_number);
48: END;
49: /
```

OUTPUT

```
Attributes for address_1:
2800 Peermore Road
Apt 99
Detroit MI 48823
4235551212
-------------------------
Attributes for address_2:
2700 Peerless Road
Apt 1
Cleveland TN 37312
4235551212
-------------------------
Attributes for address_3:
2700 Eaton Rapids Road
Lot 98
Lansing MI 48911
5173943551

PL/SQL procedure successfully completed.
```

ANALYSIS Notice that in lines 4–6, three object variables are defined. They are of type `address` and are used to contain `address` objects. When first created, these objects are considered to be null. Any calls to their member methods result in errors and any reference to their attributes evaluates to null.

The first `address` object is instantiated in line 10. This is done by calling the constructor function for the `address` object, and assigning the value returned to the object variable `address_1`. In line 12 a copy of this object is assigned to `address_2`. Then the value of `address_1` is changed. This is done with a call to the `ChangeAddress` method (lines 15–16), and is done in order to demonstrate that `address_1` and `address_2` are indeed separate objects. In line 19 a third `address` object is created.

The values of these three `address` objects are displayed by the code in lines 22–47. Notice that although the accessor methods are used to retrieve the attribute values from the first two objects, the attributes of the third object are accessed directly.

Storing and Retrieving Objects

There are two ways to store an object in an Oracle database. One is to store the object as a column within a table. (This is the approach this chapter takes to storing the `address` objects. This way, each employee record has one address associated with it.) The other approach to storing objects involves the use of an object table, which as you learned earlier in the chapter is a relational table that has been defined to store a particular type of object. Each row in the table represents one object, and each column represents one attribute in the object.

Storing Objects as Table Columns

Oracle's object-relational model allows an object to be stored as a column in a database table. In order to do this, a column of the appropriate object type must first be added to the table in question. To create an address column in the employee table, you must first execute the Data Definition Language (DDL) statement shown in Listing 12.3.

INPUT **LISTING 12.3** Creating a Column for the `address` Object

```
1: ALTER TABLE employee
2:    ADD (
3:       home_address     address
4:    );
```

12

ANALYSIS This statement simply adds a column, which is named `home_address`, to the employee table. The column type is given as `address`, which is a reference to the object type defined earlier in this chapter. For any existing employee records, the object is considered to be null.

Now that an address column exists in the employee table, you can create some employee records and store each employee's address, along with the other information. Listing 12.4 shows two different ways to do this.

INPUT/OUTPUT   **LISTING 12.4** Saving address Objects with Employee Records

```
 1: INSERT INTO employee
 2:   (emp_id, emp_name,pay_rate,pay_type,home_address)
 3:   VALUES (597,'Matthew Higgenbottom',120000,'S',
 4:           address('101 Maple','','Mio','MI','48640','5173943551'));
 5:
 6: 1 row created.
 7:
 8: COMMIT;
 9:
10: Commit complete.
11:
12: DECLARE
13:   emp_home_address    address;
14: BEGIN
15:   emp_home_address := address('911 Pearl','Apt 2','Lewiston',
16:                               'MI','48645','5173363366');
17:   INSERT INTO employee
18:     (emp_id, emp_name,pay_rate,pay_type,home_address)
19:     VALUES (598, 'Raymond Gennick',55,'H',emp_home_address);
20:   COMMIT;
21: END;
22: /

23: PL/SQL procedure successfully completed.
24:
25: SELECT emp_id, emp_name, home_address
26:   FROM employee
27:  WHERE home_address IS NOT null;
28:
   EMP_ID EMP_NAME
-------- --------------------------------
HOME_ADDRESS(STREET_1,STREET_2, CITY, STATE_ABBR, ZIP_CODE, PHONE_NUMBER)
---------------------------------------------------------------------------
      597 Matthew Higgenbottom
ADDRESS('101 Maple', NULL, 'Mio', 'MI', '48640', '5173943551')

      598 Raymond Gennick
ADDRESS('911 Pearl', 'Apt 2', 'Lewiston', 'MI', '48645', '5173363366')
```

ANALYSIS Lines 1–4 show how a constructor method can be referenced from within a SQL statement. In fact, the statement in question was executed from within SQL*Plus, although it could have been inside a PL/SQL block. Lines 12-22 show a PL/SQL block that first instantiates an `address` object, and then inserts that object into the employee table as part of an employee record. The `emp_home_address` variable is defined in line 13 as being of type `address`. Then in line 15 of the third segment, the `address` constructor is used to instantiate a new `address` object, which is assigned to the `emp_home_address` variable. Finally, in lines 17–19, an `INSERT` statement is executed, saving the employee record. The `emp_home_address` variable is included in the values list and is stored as a part of the record.

The `SELECT` statement (lines 1–3 of the fourth segment) retrieves the `address` objects that you have just inserted into the database. Notice how SQL*Plus uses the `address` type constructor in the resulting output to indicate that the addresses are from an embedded object.

Retrieving and Updating Objects in a Table Column

As with inserting, you can retrieve and update an object that is stored in a column, just as you would any other column value. Listing 12.5 shows a PL/SQL block that retrieves the address for employee number 597, changes the phone number, and then updates the table to contain the new value of the object.

INPUT/OUTPUT   **LISTING 12.5**   Retrieving and Updating the `address` Object

```
 1: DECLARE
 2:   emp_addr      address;
 3: BEGIN
 4:   --Retrieve the object from the table
 5:   SELECT home_address INTO emp_addr
 6:     FROM employee
 7:    WHERE emp_id = 597;
 8:
 9:   --Use a mutator method to change the phone number.
10:   emp_addr.setPhone('3139830301');
11:
12:   UPDATE employee
13:      SET home_address = emp_addr
14:    WHERE emp_id = 597;
15:
16:   COMMIT;
17: END;
18: /
19:
20: PL/SQL procedure successfully completed.
```

12

continues

LISTING 12.5   continued

```
21:
22: SELECT emp_id, emp_name, e.home_address.phone_number home_phone
23:   FROM employee e
24:  WHERE emp_id = 597;
```

```
   EMP_ID EMP_NAME                                HOME_PHONE
---------- ------------------------------------- ----------
      597 Matthew Higgenbottom                    3139830301
```

ANALYSIS Lines 5–7 retrieve the address object into the emp_addr variable for the employee whose phone number you want to change. In line 10, the setPhone method is used to update the phone number. At this point, only the object in memory has the updated phone number. Lines 12–14 update the employee's record, storing the new value of the address object.

It is also possible to update an employee's phone number by using only one update, rather than the three steps—retrieve, modify, and store—shown in Listing 12.5. This can be accomplished by creating an entirely new address object and assigning it to the employee's home_address field. Listing 12.6 shows the phone number for employee number 598 being modified, using this method.

INPUT/ OUTPUT   **LISTING 12.6**   Updating an address Object

```
 1: UPDATE employee e
 2:   SET e.home_address   = address(e.home_address.street_1,
 3:                   e.home_address.street_2, e.home_address.city,
 4:                   e.home_address.state_abbr, e.home_address.zip_code,
 5:                   '5173433333')
 6: WHERE emp_id = 598;
 7:
 8: 1 row updated.
 9:
10: SQL>
11: SQL> COMMIT;
12:
13: Commit complete.
```

Note   When you reference objects within a query like this, you must use a correlation name. In this example, the employee table is given the correlation name e, and e. has been prepended to each attribute reference.

ANALYSIS The SET clause of this UPDATE statement uses the information from the existing address object, plus a new phone number, to instantiate an entirely new address object. This is done in lines 2–5 by calling the object type's constructor and passing attributes of the original address as arguments. The home_address column is then set to the value of this new object.

Using Object Tables

NEW TERM As you learned earlier in the chapter, another way to store objects is in an object table in which each column of the table matches one of the attributes of the object. Consequently each row of the table is used to store one instance of an object. In addition to the columns for the object's attributes, an object table also has an additional column that is used to contain an *object identifier*, which is an Oracle-generated value that uniquely identifies each object in the database.

Take a look at Listing 12.7. It defines a building type for the sample database, and then creates an object table that can store instances of that type.

INPUT/OUTPUT   **LISTING 12.7**   The building Object

```
 1: CREATE OR REPLACE TYPE building AS OBJECT (
 2:    BldgName          VARCHAR2(40),
 3:    BldgAddress       address,
 4:    BldgMgr           INTEGER,
 5:    MEMBER PROCEDURE  ChangeMgr (NewMgr IN INTEGER),
 6:    ORDER MEMBER FUNCTION Compare (OtherBuilding IN building)
 7:       RETURN INTEGER
 8:    );
 9: /
10
11   Type created.
12
13: CREATE OR REPLACE TYPE BODY building AS
14:    MEMBER PROCEDURE  ChangeMgr(NewMgr IN INTEGER) IS
15:      BEGIN
16:        BldgMgr := NewMgr;
17:      END;
18:
19:    ORDER MEMBER FUNCTION Compare (OtherBuilding IN building)
20:    RETURN INTEGER IS
21:        BldgName1     VARCHAR2(40);
22:        BldgName2     building.BldgName%TYPE;
23:      BEGIN
24:        --Grab the two building names for comparison.
25:        --Make sure that we don't get messed up by leading/trailing
```

12

continues

LISTING **12.7**   continued

```
26:         --spaces or by case.
27:         BldgName1 := upper(ltrim(rtrim(BldgName)));
28:         BldgName2 := upper(ltrim(rtrim(OtherBuilding.BldgName)));
29:
30:         --Return the appropriate value to indicate the order of
31:         --this object vs OtherBuilding.
32:         IF BldgName1 = BldgName2 THEN
33:           RETURN 0;
34:         ELSIF BldgName1 < BldgName2 THEN
35:           RETURN -1;
36:         ELSE
37:           RETURN 1;
38:         END IF;
39:     END;
40: END;
41: /
```

```
Type body created.
```

CREATE TABLE buildings OF building;

```
Table created.
```

ANALYSIS Lines 1–9 contain the `building` object's type definition. As you can see, the `building` object has three attributes containing the building's name, the building's address, and the employee ID of the building manager. The second attribute is interesting because it is itself an object. Objects can be nested in this manner to any level.

The `ORDER` function, in line 6, enables you to compare two objects of type `building` for equality or to see which is greater. You decide what *equality* means when you write the function. The keyword `ORDER` tells Oracle which member function to call when doing comparisons. Comparing objects by using order functions is described later in this lesson, in the section "Comparing Objects."

Lines 13–40 define the object body, which contains the definitions for the two member functions `ChangeMgr` and `Compare`.

The last command in the listing, shown in the third segment, is very important. This is a new form of the `CREATE TABLE` statement, which creates an object table for objects of type `building`. (You will be using this table later in this chapter.) You can look at the table's structure by typing this command:

```
describe buildings
```

When you use an object table to store objects, they have visibility outside the table. Other objects can be linked to them, referencing them by their object identifiers. Another advantage of object tables is that they can be queried just like any other relational tables. This gives you some flexibility and enables you to mix and match relational and object-oriented methods in your software development projects.

Storing Objects in an Object Table

You can insert information about buildings into the object table you just created by using a SQL INSERT statement. Instead of a list containing separate values for each attribute, you can use the building object's constructor to create an object. This one object becomes the only value in the values list.

Type the statements shown in Listing 12.8 in order to insert a few building objects. These will be used in later examples that show how to update object tables and how to link objects in the database.

INPUT/OUTPUT **LISTING 12.8** Inserting Some building Objects

```
1: INSERT INTO buildings
2:    values (building('Victor Building',
3:            address('203 Washington Square',' ','Lansing',
4:                    'MI','48823',' '),
5:            597));

1 row created.

1: INSERT INTO buildings
2:    values (building('East Storage Shed',
3:            address('1400 Abbott Rd','','Lansing','MI','48823',''),
4:            598));

1 row created.

1: INSERT INTO buildings
2:    values (building('Headquarters Building',
3:            address('150 West Jefferson','','Detroit','MI','48226',''),
4:            599));

1 row created.

SELECT * from buildings;

BLDGNAME
-----------------------------------------
BLDGADDRESS(STREET_1, STREET_2, CITY, STATE_ABBR, ZIP_CODE, PHONE_NUMBER)
```

continues

12

LISTING 12.8   continued

```
---------------------------------------------------------------
   BLDGMGR
----------
Victor Building
ADDRESS('203 Washington Square', ' ', 'Lansing', 'MI', '48823', ' ')
       597

East Storage Shed
ADDRESS('1400 Abbott Rd', NULL, 'Lansing', 'MI', '48823', NULL)
       598

Headquarters Building
ADDRESS('150 West Jefferson', NULL, 'Detroit', 'MI', '48226', NULL)
       599

COMMIT;

Commit complete.
```

ANALYSIS   In each of these segments, the building constructor is called in order to instantiate a building object. Because one of the building attributes is an address
object, the address constructor is also called to create that object. The SELECT statement
at the end shows that the building data was inserted properly.

> **Note**
>
> When inserting objects into an object table, it is not absolutely necessary to
> call the object constructor for that table, so in the preceding example the
> reference to the building constructor could have been omitted. Oracle
> knows what object type is stored in the table, and Oracle also allows you to
> treat the table as a regular relational table. However, the call to the address
> constructor cannot be omitted because the address object is an embedded
> object.

Retrieving and Updating Objects in an Object Table

When retrieving and updating data in an object table, you can choose to treat the table as
a normal, relational table, and simply write conventional SELECT, UPDATE, and DELETE
queries against it. For example, if you simply wanted to retrieve a list of building names,
you could execute the query shown in Listing 12.9.

INPUT/OUTPUT   **LISTING 12.9**   A Simple SELECT Against the Building Table

```
SELECT BldgName
  FROM buildings
ORDER BY BldgName;

BLDGNAME
----------------------------------------
East Storage Shed
Headquarters Building
Victor Building
```

ANALYSIS   This query is simply a traditional, relational query against the building table. Even though the building table is a table of objects, you can still treat it as you would any other database table.

Being able to execute a traditional, non–object-oriented query against an object table can be handy if you have both object-oriented and non–object-oriented programs accessing the same database. A non–object-oriented program would simply treat the building table as if it were any other relational table. Also, if you were doing a mass update, it would be more efficient to write one SQL UPDATE statement than it would be to write a PL/SQL loop to retrieve each object, update it, and save it again.

Using the VALUE Operator to Retrieve from an Object Table

If you're using object tables, you're going to want to retrieve objects from those tables. With an embedded object, such as address, this was done by retrieving the object column into an object variable (refer to line 5 of Listing 12.5). However, the building object table has no column of type building. It simply has a column for each attribute. So what do you select in order to retrieve the building object? In order to retrieve building objects, you need to use Oracle8's new VALUE operator. The VALUE operator takes a correlation variable as its argument and returns the value of the object stored in the selected row(s) of the table. Take a look at Listing 12.10, which retrieves all the building objects from the database.

12

INPUT   **LISTING 12.10**   Retrieving an Object from an Object Table

```
1: --Retrieve an object from the building table.
2: DECLARE
3:   this_building   building;
4:
5:   CURSOR all_buildings IS
6:     SELECT value (b) AS bldg
7:       FROM buildings b
```

continues

LISTING **12.10** continued

```
 8:       ORDER BY b.BldgName;
 9:
10: BEGIN
11:   FOR one_building IN all_buildings LOOP
12:      --Grab a copy of the building object.
13:      this_building := one_building.bldg;
14:      dbms_output.put_line(this_building.BldgName || ' is located in '
15:                     || this_building.BldgAddress.city
16:                     || ' ' || this_building.BldgAddress.state_abbr);
17:   END LOOP;
18:
19:   COMMIT;
20: END;
21: /
```

OUTPUT

```
East Storage Shed is located in Lansing MI
Headquarters Building is located in Detroit MI
Victor Building is located in Lansing MI

PL/SQL procedure successfully completed.
```

ANALYSIS In this example, a cursor is declared (lines 5–8) based on a SQL statement that selects building objects. Notice in line 6 that the result column is given the alias bldg. This makes it easy to reference the object retrieved by the cursor, and is used in line 13. The remainder of the code consists of a simple CURSOR FOR loop that retrieves each building object and displays each building's name and location. Notice in lines 15 and 16 that dot notation is used to navigate from the building object, to the address object, and finally to the city name and state abbreviation.

Updating an Object Table

The SQL UPDATE statement is used to update object tables. There are two basic parts to an UPDATE statement. The first part contains the SET clause, and specifies which table and column you are updating. The second part contains the WHERE clause, and specifies the search condition used to identify the rows to update. Both of these now have object-oriented variations.

Consider the SET clause first. In order to update the building table, you could write an UPDATE statement that began like this:

```
UPDATE buildings
  SET BldgName = 'Some Name'
  ...
```

However, if you wanted to update an entire `building` object, you would want your `UPDATE` statement to look like this:

```
UPDATE buildings b
  SET b = building(...)
  ...
```

In this code snippet, the building table has been given the correlation name b. This correlation name is used to represent the object stored in each row of the table, and new `building` objects can be assigned to it. In the preceding example, the building constructor was used to generate a new `building` object.

In addition to setting the new values, there is also the question of the WHERE clause. A traditional WHERE clause for the building table might look like this:

```
WHERE BldgName = 'Victor Building'
```

In this case the building name is being used to identify the row to be changed. If you are writing a PL/SQL program, you have another option. You can use the object identifier to uniquely identify the row to be changed. This method makes use of the REF operator, which retrieves an object's unique identifier. Here is a short example:

```
UPDATE buildings b
...
WHERE REF(b) = SELECT REF(b2) FROM building b2
               WHERE BldgName = 'Victor Building'
```

This example is a bit contrived. Normally you would not use a subselect statement to retrieve the object identifier. If you were writing PL/SQL code, for example, you might already have the object identifier as a result of having retrieved that object. The use of the REF operator is described more fully in the section "Nesting and Sharing Objects."

The options you have just seen for updating can be mixed and matched, giving you at least four different ways to code UPDATE statements against an object table. The SQL statements in Listing 12.11 show two ways to update the building table.

INPUT/OUTPUT **LISTING 12.11** Updating an Object Table

```
1: --For the first update, treat building as a traditional table.
2:  UPDATE buildings
3:    SET BldgName = 'Software Research'
4:    WHERE BldgName = 'Headquarters Building';
5:
6: 1 row updated.
7:
```

continues

Listing 12.11 continued

```
 8:   --This update calls the constructor in the SET clause.
 9:   UPDATE buildings b
10:      SET b = building(BldgName,BldgAddress,598)
11:    WHERE BldgName = 'Victor Building';
12: 1 row updated.
13:
14: COMMIT;
15:
16: Commit complete.
```

ANALYSIS The first update, lines 1–4, treats the `building` object table as if it were a normal relational table. The second update, lines 8–11, is more interesting. It updates the entire `building` object and features a call to the `building` constructor in line 10. The first two arguments passed to the `building` constructor are actually attributes of the object being updated. The third argument, `598`, represents a new building manager assignment. Especially notice in line 10 that the correlation name of the table is used as the target of the `SET` clause. This tells Oracle8 that the entire `building` object is being updated.

Deleting Objects from an Object Table

Objects can be deleted from an object table through the use of the `DELETE` statement. The same issues apply to the `WHERE` clause of a `DELETE` statement as apply to the `WHERE` clause of an `UPDATE` statement. The `WHERE` clause of a `DELETE` can use the `REF` operator and an object identifier to delete a specific object, or it can specify conditions for one or more attributes of the object.

Nesting and Sharing Objects

Objects can be nested inside other objects. They can also be shared, or referenced, by one or more other objects. You have already seen two examples of nested objects. The `building` object, created in Listing 12.7, contains a nested `address` object. The employee table also contains an `address` object, added in Listing 12.3.

Dot Notation

When objects are nested, it is possible to navigate through them by using the standard *dot notation*. When you reference an attribute of an object, you separate the attribute name from the object name with a dot (.). You already know that in a SQL statement, you can refer to a specific field by using the following notation:

`TableName.FieldName`

The same notation can also be used to reference a specific object attribute, as in the following example:

```
ObjectVarName.AttributeName
```

You have already seen examples of this in Listing 12.2, lines 24–29, 33–38, and 42–47. When you have objects that themselves contain objects, you can use this dot notation to navigate your way down to a specific attribute. That's because the nested object is itself an attribute of the containing object, and also contains attributes of its own. So if you had a `building` object and wanted to know what city the building was in, you could reference the city like this:

```
BldgVar.BldgAddress.City
```

Listing 12.12 shows a brief example of using dot notation on a `building` object in order to print the city and state.

INPUT

LISTING 12.12   Using Dot Notation to Reference the Attribute of a Nested Object

```
 1: --Show dot notation in use.
 2: DECLARE
 3:   this_building      building;
 4: BEGIN
 5:   --Retrieve a building object so we can print the attribute values.
 6:   SELECT value(b) INTO this_building
 7:     FROM buildings b
 8:    WHERE BldgName = 'East Storage Shed';
 9:
10:   COMMIT;
11:
12:   dbms_output.put_line(this_building.BldgName
13:                     || ' ' || this_building.BldgAddress.city
14:                     || ' ' || this_building.BldgAddress.state_abbr);
15: END;
16: /
```

12

OUTPUT

```
East Storage Shed Lansing MI

PL/SQL procedure successfully completed.
```

ANALYSIS   Line 12 uses dot notation to reference the building name attribute, and lines 13 and 14 use it to navigate through the nested `address` object to get the city name and state abbreviation.

Object References

When you store an object as an attribute of another object, the nested object is said to have no *visibility* outside the parent. This means that it exists only within the context of the parent object, and that same object cannot be referenced or made part of any other object. It makes sense to nest objects when you are dealing with something like a building address because each building has its own unique address, not shared with any other building.

Consider the case, though, where you want to specify the building in which an employee works. You could modify the employee table and add a column of type `building`, for example:

```
ALTER TABLE employee
  ADD (EmpBldg    building);
```

This solution has a big problem. Each employee will have his or her own private `building` object. If you have 1,000 employees in a building, then there will be 1,000 separate `building` objects, 1 for each employee, all containing redundant information. There is another way to deal with this situation: You can store only a reference to a `building` object in each employee's record.

 Each object stored in an object table is identified by a unique, system-generated, *object identifier*. It isn't necessary to know the precise nature of this identifier, and in fact Oracle does not document it. What's important is that given an object identifier, you can easily retrieve the object in question from the database.

As stated earlier, the solution to the problem of relating employees to buildings is to create a reference to the `building` object in each employee record. The `REF` keyword is used to do this, and Listing 12.13 shows how.

 LISTING 12.13   Creating a Reference to `building`

```
ALTER TABLE employee
  ADD (emp_bldg    REF building);

Table altered.
```

ANALYSIS As you can see, this listing adds one column of type `REF building` to the employee record. The use of the keyword `REF` tells Oracle that the column will contain only a reference to a `building` object and not the `building` object itself.

The REF and DEREF Operators

Two SQL operators, REF and DEREF, help you deal with object identifiers. The REF operator can be used in a SQL statement to return the object identifier for an object. The DEREF operator does just the opposite. It is used in a SQL statement to retrieve the actual object referenced by an object identifier. Doing this is referred to as *dereferencing* an object identifier.

The REF operator is used in Listing 12.14 to retrieve a reference to a specific building so that it can be stored in an employee's record. The DEREF operator is used in Listing 12.15 to retrieve an employee's building name and display it.

To demonstrate the use of the REF operator, Listing 12.14 shows a simple procedure that, given an employee number and a building name, assigns the employee to a building.

INPUT/
OUTPUT
LISTING 12.14   Using the REF Operator

```
 1: CREATE OR REPLACE PROCEDURE AssignEmpToBldg (
 2:   EmpNumIn IN employee.emp_id%TYPE,
 3:   BldgNameIn IN buildings.BldgName%TYPE
 4:   ) AS
 5: BEGIN
 6:   UPDATE employee
 7:     SET emp_bldg = (SELECT REF(b)
 8:                       FROM buildings B
 9:                      WHERE BldgName = BldgNameIn)
10:   WHERE emp_id = EmpNumIn;
11:
12:   --Raise an error if either the employee number or
13:   --building name is invalid.
14:   IF SQL%NOTFOUND THEN
15:     RAISE_application_error(-20000,'Employee ' ¦¦ EmpNumIn
16:                                ¦¦ ' could not be assigned to building '
17:                                ¦¦ BldgNameIn);
18:   END IF;
19: END;
20: /
21:
22: Procedure created.
23:
24: BEGIN
25:   AssignEmpToBldg (598,'Victor Building');
26:   AssignEmpToBldg (597,'East Storage Shed');
27: END;
28: /

PL/SQL procedure successfully completed.
```

12

> **ANALYSIS** The first part of this listing, lines 1-20, contains the definition for the
> `AssignEmpToBldg` procedure. This procedure takes both an employee ID and a
> building name as arguments. An UPDATE statement (lines 6–10) uses the building name to
> retrieve the matching `building` object and stores a reference to that object in the employee table. The PL/SQL anonymous block in lines 24–27 calls this procedure to make
> some building assignments.

To show the use of the DEREF operator, Listing 12.15 shows a simple function that
retrieves the name of the building in which an employee works.

LISTING 12.15 Using the DEREF Operator

```
 1: CREATE OR REPLACE FUNCTION GetEmpBldgName (
 2:    EmpNumIn IN employee.emp_id%TYPE
 3:    ) RETURN VARCHAR2 AS
 4: TheBldg      building;
 5: BEGIN
 6:    --Select the building object reference from this employee's record.
 7:    SELECT DEREF(emp_bldg) INTO TheBldg
 8:      FROM employee
 9:     WHERE emp_id = EmpNumIn;
10:
11:    IF TheBldg IS NULL THEN
12:      RETURN 'No Building Assigned';
13:    ELSE
14:      RETURN TheBldg.BldgName;
15:    END IF;
16: END;
17: /
18:
19: Function created.
20:
21: BEGIN
22:    dbms_output.put_line(GetEmpBldgName(598));
23:    dbms_output.put_line(GetEmpBldgName(597));
24: END;
25: /

Victor Building
East Storage Shed

PL/SQL procedure successfully completed.
```

> **ANALYSIS** The `GetEmpBldgName` function takes an employee ID as an argument and returns
> the name of the building in which the employee works. The SELECT statement, in
> lines 7–9, retrieves the building information for the selected employee. It does this by
> using the DEREF operator (line 7) to dereference the `emp_bldg` pointer. The DEREF

operator causes Oracle to automatically retrieve the referenced `building` object from wherever it is stored, which in this case is the building table.

Note

> Notice that you did not need to tell Oracle in Listing 12.15 that the `building` object you were retrieving was stored in the building table. The object reference, used by the `DEREF` operator, contains all the information necessary for Oracle to find the object. This is in contrast to a relational join, in which you do need to specify the tables being accessed.

Exploring the SELF Parameter

Each object method you write has a default first parameter named `SELF`. This `SELF` parameter, which is normally not specified in the method's declaration, is used to reference the attributes of the object being called. By default, any unqualified attribute reference in a member function or member procedure is automatically qualified by `SELF`. Listing 12.16 shows how the `building` object type definition would look if you explicitly defined and used the `SELF` parameter.

Note

> You won't be able to execute this listing because you are using the building type in the employee table, the building table, and two stored program units. In order to re-create the type, you would need to delete all those dependencies.

12

INPUT **LISTING 12.16** Using the SELF Parameter

```
 1: CREATE OR REPLACE TYPE building AS OBJECT (
 2:   BldgName          VARCHAR2(40),
 3:   BldgAddress       address,
 4:   BldgMgr           INTEGER,
 5:   MEMBER PROCEDURE  ChangeMgr (SELF IN OUT building,
 6:                                NewMgr IN INTEGER),
 7:   ORDER MEMBER FUNCTION Compare (SELF IN building,
 8:                                OtherBuilding IN building)
 9:       RETURN INTEGER
10:   );
11: /
12: CREATE OR REPLACE TYPE BODY building AS
13:   MEMBER PROCEDURE  ChangeMgr(SELF IN OUT building,
14:                                NewMgr IN INTEGER) IS
15:     BEGIN
16:       SELF.BldgMgr := NewMgr;
```

continues

LISTING **12.16**   continued

```
17:    END;
18:
19:    ORDER MEMBER FUNCTION Compare (SELF IN building,
20:                                   OtherBuilding IN building)
21:    RETURN INTEGER IS
22:        BldgName1      VARCHAR2(40);
23:        BldgName2      building.BldgName%TYPE;
24:      BEGIN
25:        --Grab the two building names for comparison.
26:        --Make sure that we don't get messed up by leading/trailing
27:        --spaces or by case.
28:        BldgName1 := upper(ltrim(rtrim(SELF.BldgName)));
29:        BldgName2 := upper(ltrim(rtrim(OtherBuilding.BldgName)));
30:
31:        --Return the appropriate value to indicate the order of
32:        --this object vs OtherBuilding.
33:        IF BldgName1 = BldgName2 THEN
34:           RETURN 0;
35:        ELSIF BldgName1 < BldgName2 THEN
36:           RETURN -1;
37:        ELSE
38:           RETURN 1;
39:        END IF;
40:      END;
41: END;
42: /
```

ANALYSIS   All the member method definitions now include SELF as the first parameter. All attribute references in the preceding listing are explicitly prefaced with SELF. Oracle always treats any unqualified attribute references in member methods as if you had really written them this way.

The SELF parameter must always be the object type being defined. By default it is an input (IN) parameter for member functions and an input/output (IN OUT) parameter for member procedures. This is because functions usually return values without altering an object's attributes, whereas procedures frequently do alter an object's attributes.

Although you normally do not specify the SELF parameter, you might do so if you want to specify an input/output mode other than the default. For example, if you wanted a member function to be able to modify an object's attributes, you would explicitly define SELF as an IN OUT parameter.

Overloading

NEW TERM   The term *overloading* refers to the ability to have more than one function or procedure of the same name, but with a different number and types of parameters. This ability to overload function and procedure names is a key feature of object-oriented languages.

Consider the `building` object type defined in Listing 12.7. It has a method named `ChangeMgr`, which allows you to specify an employee who is the building manager for a building. This method takes one argument, the employee number. What if you also wanted the ability to specify the manager by name? One solution would be to write a method named `ChangeMgrName` to do this, but then you would have to constantly remember which method to call each time you wrote code to change a building manager. Worse, you might get confused about the naming convention and try writing a call to `ChangeMgrNo`, or perhaps to `ChangeMgrEmpNo`, neither of which exist. Instead you can simply declare another member function named `ChangeMgr`, but with a string argument instead of a number. This function would look up the employee by name, get the employee number, and store that number as an attribute. Oracle would know to call this new version of the method when you supplied a string argument, and would know to call the old version of the method when you supplied a numeric argument. The advantage to this is that when you are coding, you call `ChangeMgr` whenever you need to specify a new building manager, regardless of whether you are specifying the new manager by name or number.

Comparing Objects

Are two objects equal? Is one greater than another? How do they compare? Sooner or later you will want to write code to answer these questions. Before you can do that, you must decide on the comparison semantics. What is it about two `building` objects, for example, that makes one greater than another? This is often not as simple a question as it might seem. When dealing with numbers, common convention dictates that the number with the larger value is greater than the other. But when dealing with buildings, what attribute do you consider? You could, for example, look at how tall the building is. A taller building would be greater than a shorter building. Alternatively, you could look at the *footprint* of the building, basing your decision on the number of square feet of ground space that the building occupied. Another alternative would be to base the decision on the total square footage of the building's floor space.

12

As you can see, even with a type as simple as the building type, there are many alternatives to look at when considering how comparisons should be done. The choice might ultimately become somewhat arbitrary based on how you intend to use the object.

To help you compare objects, Oracle allows you to declare two special member function types. These are identified by the keywords MAP and ORDER. A MAP function enables you to specify a single numeric value that is used when comparing two objects of the same type. The greater than/less than/equal to decision is based on this value. An ORDER function enables you to write whatever code you want in order to compare two objects, the return value indicating equality or which of the two is greater.

> **Note**
>
> It is possible to write your own code to compare objects without defining a MAP or an ORDER method. When comparing building objects, for example, you could simply write the following:
>
> ```
> IF BldgObj1.BldgName = BldgObj2.BldgName THEN ...
> ```
>
> The disadvantages of this approach are that your comparison semantics are spread all through your code, they might not be consistent, and the intent of the comparison might not be obvious. From the preceding IF statement, it is not clear that you are inferring that two objects are equal because their names are the same. It might be that you are simply comparing the names.
>
> Using the MAP and ORDER methods provides a way to store the comparison rules along with the object type, thus ensuring consistency wherever comparisons are made. The intent of your IF statements will then be clear. People will know that you are comparing two objects for equality when you write the following
>
> ```
> IF BldgObj1 = BldgObj2 THEN ...
> ```
>
> They'll also know that you are simply comparing two object attributes when you write the following
>
> ```
> IF BldgObj1.BldgMgr = BldgObj2.BldgMgr THEN ...
> ```

The ORDER Method

You might have noticed back in Listing 12.7 that the keyword ORDER was used in front of one of the member functions for a building. The specification for that function looks like this:

```
ORDER MEMBER FUNCTION Compare (OtherBuilding IN building)
     RETURN INTEGER
```

The keyword ORDER tells Oracle that Compare is a specially written function that should be called whenever it is necessary to compare one building object with another. It takes one argument, which must be of the same type. In other words, because Compare is a method of the `building` object type, the argument to `Compare` must also be of the `building` object type.

Remember that every object method has a default first argument named SELF, and that the SELF argument represents the object whose method is called. An ORDER function is expected to compare SELF to its argument and return one of the values shown in Table 12.1.

TABLE 12.1 ORDER Function Return Values

Return Value	Meaning
-1	SELF is less than the argument.
0	SELF is equal to the argument.
1	SELF is greater than the argument.

After you have defined an ORDER function for an object type, you can then use any of the PL/SQL relational operators with objects of that type. Listing 12.17 instantiates some `building` objects and shows the result of some simple comparisons.

INPUT **LISTING 12.17** Comparing Objects by Using ORDER Functions

```
 1: --A demonstration of the ORDER function.
 2: DECLARE
 3:    bldg_a        building;    --will be less than bldg_b
 4:    bldg_b        building;
 5:    bldg_b2       building;
 6:    bldg_c        building;
 7: BEGIN
 8:    --First, create four building objects.
 9:    bldg_a := building('A Building',null,null);
10:    bldg_b := building('Another Building',null,null);
11:    bldg_b2 := building('Another Building',null,null);
12:    bldg_c := building('Cosmotology Research Lab',null,null);
13:
14:    --Now compare the building objects and display the results;
15:    IF bldg_a < bldg_b THEN
16:      dbms_output.put_line('bldg_a < bldg_b');
17:    END IF;
18:
19:    --These two have the same name, so should be equal.
20:    IF bldg_b = bldg_b2 THEN
21:      dbms_output.put_line('bldg_b = bldg_b2');
22:    END IF;
23:
```

12

continues

LISTING 12.17 continued

```
24:    IF bldg_c > bldg_b2 THEN
25:      dbms_output.put_line('bldg_c > bldg_b2');
26:    END IF;
27: END;
28: /
```

OUTPUT
```
bldg_a < bldg_b
bldg_b = bldg_b2
bldg_c > bldg_b2

PL/SQL procedure successfully completed.
```

ANALYSIS Lines 9–12 instantiate, or construct, four new building objects. The remainder of the PL/SQL block compares these building objects against each other; see lines 15, 20, and 24. In each of these cases a relational operator is used to compare one building object to another. When executing these comparisons, Oracle automatically calls the ORDER method defined for this object type. The ORDER method then determines the result of the comparison.

The MAP Method

MAP functions provide an alternate way to specify comparison semantics for an object type. A MAP function enables you to compute a single value, based on one or more of the object's attributes, which is then used to compare the object in question to other objects of the same type.

MAP functions have no parameter because their purpose is to return a value representing only the object whose MAP method was invoked. The result of a MAP function must be one of the following types:

- NUMBER
- DATE
- VARCHAR2

When comparing two objects with MAP methods defined, Oracle first calls the MAP function for each object, and then compares the two results.

Note
It is possible to write a MAP function for the building object type, which would return the building name for comparison purposes. This could be used instead of the ORDER function.

Limitations of Oracle's Implementation

Although the object features introduced in Oracle8 represent a significant step forward for Oracle, there are some limitations to keep in mind:

- Inheritance is not supported.
- Private attributes are not supported.
- There is no support for custom constructors.
- Object types must be declared at the database level and cannot be declared within a PL/SQL function or procedure.
- Certain datatypes cannot be used as attributes.
- Objects support a maximum of 1,000 attributes.

Some of these limitations are fairly significant. The lack of support for private attributes, for example, means that anyone using your objects is free to bypass whatever accessor and mutator methods you have defined. In more mature object-oriented languages, you can protect attributes, allowing them to be set only by member functions, which then contain code to validate the values being set. Another issue here is that you cannot separate implementation-specific attributes from those that you intend to be publicly referenced.

The inability to write your own constructor functions also limits your opportunities to validate attribute values. Validation at object creation is impossible because the default constructors simply set the attributes to the values you supply. If you were dealing with an employee object, for example, you could easily instantiate it with a negative salary.

Inheritance is a key feature of any object-oriented language, and it is a feature that Oracle does not yet support. The other limitations are not as significant as the first three. For example, the 1,000-attribute limit is probably not one you will often run up against. The datatype limitation is related to the fact that all object types must be declared at the database level, and although it might be convenient to be able to define object types local to a PL/SQL procedure, you wouldn't be able to store those objects permanently in the database.

12

Summary

The object-oriented features of Oracle8 described in this lesson represent a significant step forward in the effort to marry object-oriented and relational technologies, in the process providing Oracle developers with access to some of the same powerful object-oriented features developers using languages such as C++ and Java enjoy. Oracle now supports the definition and creation of objects, complete with methods and attributes. These objects can be stored in the database as attributes of other objects, as columns in a table, or as rows in an object table. In addition, you can still access your data by using standard, relational methods. This can ease your transition to OOP and lets you still use relational queries in cases where they are most efficient.

Q&A

Q Why is encapsulation so important?

A Encapsulation provides two benefits. It provides for reusability and lessens the amount of detail you need to remember about an object's implementation. When an object's functionality is exposed through a well-defined interface, you no longer have to worry about all the details behind that interface. You just call the methods and let the object do its work. Encapsulation also aids in reusability because all the necessary code is part of the object definition, making it easy to drop that definition into other programs.

Q When I create objects based on an object type, is the code for all the methods replicated for each instance of the object?

A No, the code for the member functions and procedures is not duplicated for each instance of an object type. The function and procedure code exists in one place; only the object's attributes are distinct. Oracle always passes the SELF parameter to each member function and procedure to ensure that the proper attributes are referenced. Usually this is done transparently, so conceptually it is easy to think of each object having its own methods.

Q When should I use an object table to store objects, and when should I store objects as a single column in a table?

A The answer to this depends on how you will use the objects in question. Generally, if an object has meaning only in the context of a parent object, you can store it as a column. Objects that stand alone and need to be referenced by several other objects must be stored in object tables.

Q When do I need to worry about the SELF parameter?

A Rarely. You only need to worry about the SELF parameter when you want to use an input/output mode different from the default. For example, the SELF parameter of a member function is by default input only. This means that by default a member function cannot change an object's attributes. To change this behavior, and allow a member function to update an attribute, you would need to explicitly declare the SELF parameter as an IN OUT parameter.

Workshop

You can use this workshop to test your comprehension of this chapter and put what you've learned into practice. You'll find the answers to the quiz and exercises in Appendix A, "Answers."

Quiz

1. What is the difference between a class and an object?

2. What are the allowed return values for an ORDER function?

3. An object table has one column for each attribute of an object, plus one additional column. What is this additional column used for?

4. How is an object reference different from an object?

5. How many attributes must an object have? How many methods?

6. What datatypes are allowed for the return value of a MAP function?

7. What are accessor and mutator methods?

Exercises

1. Write a stored function that creates and returns an object of type building. This function should accept as parameters the building's name, its address, and the manager's employee number. Have the function check the database before creating the new building object, to be sure that another building with the same name does not already exist. If another building with the same name does exist, the function should return null.

2. Modify the building object type definition to use a MAP function, instead of an ORDER function, for comparisons.

12

DAY **13**

Debugging Your Code and Preventing Errors

by Timothy Atwood and Jonathan Gennick

No matter how good a programmer you are, inevitably you will make some coding errors. Programming errors fall into two main camps: syntax errors and logic errors. Today's lesson talks about some things you can do to avoid making these types of errors, and also discusses some techniques to locate the mistakes you do make. The topics covered today include the following:

- Syntax errors
- Logic errors
- Debugging
- Preventing errors

Locating and Eliminating Syntax Errors

 Possibly the most common type of error is the syntax error. A *syntax error* is one that occurs because you did not follow the rules of the programming language being used.

Identifying Syntax Errors

Syntax errors are usually easy to spot. When you compile PL/SQL code, Oracle points out syntax errors by telling you the line number and the column at which the error appears to occur. If you are executing a PL/SQL anonymous block by using SQL*Plus, you see the error on the screen immediately after you submit the block. Here's an example:

INPUT/
OUTPUT
```
1: BEGIN
2:    X := 100;
3:  END;
4:  /
 X := 100;
  *
ERROR at line 2:
ORA-06550: line 2, column 3:
PLS-00201: identifier 'X' must be declared
ORA-06550: line 2, column 3:
PL/SQL: Statement ignored
```

If you are using SQL*Plus to compile a stored procedure, function, or trigger, you need to use the SHOW ERRORS command to see where the errors occurred. Here's an example:

INPUT/
OUTPUT
```
1: CREATE OR REPLACE PROCEDURE with_errors AS
2:   BEGIN
3:     X := 100;
4:   END;
5:   /

Warning: Procedure created with compilation errors.

1: SHOW ERRORS
Errors for PROCEDURE WITH_ERRORS:

LINE/COL ERROR
-------- -----------------------------------------------
3/3      PLS-00201: identifier 'X' must be declared
3/3      PL/SQL: Statement ignored
SQL>
```

The SQL*Plus SHOW ERRORS command queries a data dictionary view named USER_ERRORS. You can get the same information by selecting from the view yourself.

Tip
There are times when SHOW ERRORS does not work as expected. If you run into problems with SHOW ERRORS, try selecting from the USER_ERRORS data dictionary view instead.

As you become more experienced with writing PL/SQL, you'll quickly notice that when a syntax error occurs, Oracle does not always point to the correct location of the error. (This is a problem with any language.) Not only does Oracle not always point to the line with the problem, sometimes the error messages can be misleading.

Even though Oracle sometimes points you to the wrong place, you should always start by looking for the syntax error where Oracle says it is found. It might be there, or you might see something there that leads you to find the real error. Take the location with a grain of salt, though, and don't be afraid to look elsewhere for the problem. Take the error message with a grain of salt, too, but don't discount it entirely.

If you get really stumped looking for a syntax error, try the divide-and-conquer approach. Comment out all the code except for the BEGIN and END keywords. Add a NULL statement in place of the commented-out code, and try to compile that. If the error still occurs, you probably have a problem in the declarations. Otherwise, begin uncommenting the code one statement at a time, or one section at a time, until the syntax error recurs.

Tip
If you are using the DBMS_SQL package to write dynamic SQL, and you are executing anonymous blocks, don't overlook the possibility that a syntax error might be in the dynamically generated SQL code, and not in the PL/SQL block itself. This is especially true if Oracle reports the syntax error by pointing to the line containing the DBMS_SQL.PARSE call. I once spent a lot of time tracking down what I thought was a PL/SQL syntax error, only to find that it was caused because I had terminated a dynamic SQL statement with a semicolon.

13

An Example of Identifying Syntax Errors

Listing 13.1 contains a number of syntax errors, some of which are rather glaring. You can follow the examples to get a feel for what it's like to find and correct syntax errors.

LISTING 13.1   Practicing Correcting Syntax Errors

```
 1: DECLARE
 2:    v_MyChar VARCHAR2(20) := 'test';
 3:    v_NUMBER NUMBER;
 4:    Date DATE = SYSDATE;
 5:    v_counter INTEGER;
 6: NEGIN
 7:    DBMS_OUTPUT.PUT_LINE('This is a Test')
 8:    DBMS_OUT.PUTPUT_LINE('Of Syntax Error Debugging');
 9:    For v_COUNTER IN 1..5 LOOP
10:        DBMS_OUTPUT.PUTLINE('You are in loop: ¦¦ v_counter);
11:    END-LOOP;
12: END
13: /
```

OUTPUT   ERROR:
ORA-01756: quoted string not properly terminated

ANALYSIS   This code contains a syntax error. However, when you execute it, Oracle doesn't
even bother to tell you at which line the error occurred. All you know is that
Oracle found a quoted string that wasn't terminated properly. Actually, all you know is
that Oracle *appears* to have found a quoted string that wasn't terminated properly.
Always keep an open mind on these things. In this case, you have no line number to go
on, so you must search through the code, looking for misquoted strings. Sure enough, in
line 10, there is a string missing a single quote. That must be the culprit. Change the line
to the following:

INPUT   `DBMS_OUTPUT.PUTLINE('You are in loop: '¦¦ v_counter);`

> **Note**   You can find the successive iterations of Listing 13.1 in the script files that
> you can download from this book's Web site. Look in the files named
> TYP13_1B.SQL, TYP13_1C.SQL, and so forth.

After you have corrected the changes, re-execute the code. Your next error will look like
this:

OUTPUT
```
Date DATE = SYSDATE;
             *
ERROR at line 4:
ORA-06550: line 4, column 15:
PLS-00103: Encountered the symbol ""="" when expecting one of the
           ➡]following:
:= . ( @ % ; not null range renames default
The symbol ":= was inserted before "=" to continue.
```

```
ORA-06550: line 8, column 5:
PLS-00103: Encountered the symbol "DBMS_OUT" when expecting
     one of the following:
:= ; not null default
The symbol ":=" was substituted for "DBMS_OUT" to continue.
ORA-06550: line 9, column 5:
PLS-00103: Encountered the symbol "FOR" when expecting
     one of the following:
begin function package pragma procedure subtype type use
<an identifier> <a double-quoted delimited-identifier> cursor
form
The symbol "begin" was subst
ORA-06550: line 11, column 8:
PLS-00103: Encountered the symbol "-" when expecting one of the
          ➥following:
loop
```

ANALYSIS Just changing one line now affects several other lines. The first error states that you are trying to compare one variable to another in a declaration area. You can fix that by changing = to := because you are trying to make an initial assignment, not compare values. You can also correct a second problem. You have defined a variable named date, and of type DATE, but you should never use keywords in variable names. The line should read as follows:

```
v_Date DATE := SYSDATE;
```

Upon re-execution, the next set of errors is the following:

OUTPUT
```
DBMS_OUT.PUTPUT_LINE("Of Syntax Error Debugging");
    *
ERROR at line 8:
ORA-06550: line 8, column 5:
PLS-00103: Encountered the symbol "DBMS_OUT" when expecting one of the
          ➥]following:
:= ; not null default character
The symbol ":=" was substituted for "DBMS_OUT" to continue.
ORA-06550: line 9, column 5:
PLS-00103: Encountered the symbol "FOR" when expecting one of the
          ➥]following:
begin function package pragma procedure subtype type use
<an identifier> <a double-quoted delimited-identifier> cursor
form current
The symbol "begin" w
ORA-06550: line 11, column 8:
PLS-00103: Encountered the symbol "-" when expecting one of the
          ➥]following:
loop
```

13

ANALYSIS Oracle is complaining about a symbol named DBMS_OUT in line 8. If you look closely, you'll see that DBMS_OUTPUT was mistyped as DBMS_OUT.PUT. That's an easy one to correct, now that you've spotted it. Correct line 8 to read like this:

```
DBMS_OUTPUT.PUT_LINE('Of Syntax Error Debugging');
```

The error message for line 9 tells you that Oracle was expecting a BEGIN, or some other keyword related to a program unit, not a verb such as FOR. Why was Oracle expecting BEGIN? Was there something wrong with the BEGIN in the code? Sure enough, there is. The keyword BEGIN has been mistyped as NEGIN. Correct that error, and recompile the code once more. You should see output like this:

OUTPUT
```
DBMS_OUTPUT.PUT_LINE('Of Syntax Error Debugging');
        *
ERROR at line 8:
ORA-06550: line 8, column 5:
PLS-00103: Encountered the symbol "DBMS_OUTPUT" when expecting
        one of the following:
:= . ( % ;
The symbol ":=" was substituted for "DBMS_OUTPUT" to continue.
ORA-06550: line 11, column 8:
PLS-00103: Encountered the symbol "-" when expecting one of the
        ➥]following:
loop
```

ANALYSIS You still have an error on line 8. This is because the line above it is missing the semicolon. This is a good example of the need to take the line number that Oracle reports with a grain of salt. In addition to the error on line 8, you can also fix the error on line 11. The END-LOOP statement should be END LOOP. Fix both errors (add the semicolon at the end of line 7, and remove the dash from END-LOOP), and re-execute the code. Here is the output you then get:

OUTPUT
```
DECLARE
*
ERROR at line 1:
ORA-06550: line 13, column 0:
PLS-00103: Encountered the symbol "end-of-file" when expecting one of
the
        [icc:ccc]following:
; <an identifier> <a double-quoted delimited-identifier>
The symbol ";" was substituted for "end-of-file" to continue.
```

ANALYSIS Amazingly, you are back to having errors in the first line. This is a tough one to solve. Oracle claims to have unexpectedly hit the end of the file. So start by asking yourself what Oracle expected to see at the end. The forward slash on the last line looks okay, so what about the line before that? It contains the END statement. Aha! It doesn't have a trailing semicolon. Add the semicolon to the end of the last line, and re-execute the code once more. Your results should look like this:

INPUT

```
 1: DECLARE
 2:     v_MyChar VARCHAR2(20) := 'test';
 3:     v_NUMBER NUMBER;
 4:     v_Date DATE := SYSDATE;
 5:     v_counter INTEGER;
 6: BEGIN
 7:     DBMS_OUTPUT.PUT_LINE('This is a Test');
 8:     DBMS_OUTPUT.PUT_LINE('Of Syntax Error Debugging');
 9:     For v_COUNTER IN 1..5 LOOP
10:         DBMS_OUTPUT.PUT_LINE('You are in loop: '
11:                              || v_counter);
12:     END LOOP;
13: END;
14: /
```

OUTPUT

```
This is a Test
Of Syntax Error Debugging
You are in loop: 1
You are in loop: 2
You are in loop: 3
You are in loop: 4
You are in loop: 5

PL/SQL procedure successfully completed.
```

Finally, you get some good results. The purpose of this example is to demonstrate the following:

- One syntax error sometimes masks others. Fixing that one will bring the others to light.
- The line number that Oracle flags as containing the error might not necessarily be the location of the true error.
- Taking the time to type in your code carefully saves a lot of time during program testing.

You can see from the number of iterations that we went through with this one piece of code that you can save a lot of time by catching syntax errors as you write code. The next section gives you some tips to help you do just that.

Preventing Syntax Errors

It would be nice if it were possible to somehow prevent all syntax errors from occurring. Unfortunately, you are a human being, humans do make mistakes, and nothing you do will ever change that. There are, however, some things that you can do to reduce your chances of ever writing syntax errors into your code.

13

One thing you can do is become familiar with the most common types of errors. I've found that the list of common syntax errors includes

- Using = where := belongs
- Leaving off the semicolon at the end of a statement
- Using ELSEIF when ELSIF is correct
- Using double quotes (") for strings instead of single quotes (')

Keep these common errors in mind as you write code. Also, determine what your personal list of common mistakes is, and keep that in mind as well. Just the act of being consciously aware of these potential mistakes will lessen the chance that you will make one of them.

The following are some other things you can do that you might find helpful:

- Format your code. Indent constructs such as loops and IF statements so that you can easily follow the logic flow, and so that you can easily spot missing END IFs, ENDs, LOOP statements, and so forth.
- Double-check expressions containing parentheses immediately after you write them. The number of left parentheses should match the number of right parentheses.
- If you are coding an IF statement, start by writing the IF and ENDIF lines. That way, you know that you have the beginning and ending of the statement written correctly. Then back up and insert the needed code between those two lines.
- Do the same thing when coding loops as when coding IF statements. Write the beginning and ending lines first.

You can also use an editor that recognizes PL/SQL syntax, or that at least can check for mismatched parentheses and quotation marks.

> One programmer's editor that I find very helpful in this regard is MultiEdit. MultiEdit matches parentheses for you, highlights quoted strings, and boldfaces many SQL and PL/SQL keywords. You can find out more about MultiEdit by visiting http://www.multiedit.com.

Handling Logic Errors

 Unlike syntax errors, logic errors do not stop a program from compiling. *Logic errors* are those that are caused when you misunderstand the problem at hand, or when you misunderstand the solution. They are mistakes that you make in the logical flow of a program, not in the syntax of the code that you write. After a program is compiled and tested, logic errors can still occur. Possible logic errors include the following:

- Not using proper order of operations
- Using the wrong calculation
- Using loops that never terminate

Logic errors are the hardest errors to debug, primarily because the compiler can't even begin to tell you where such an error occurs. You are totally on your own when it comes to finding and fixing logic bugs. The main steps in debugging logic errors are to identify the problem, narrow down the location of the problem, and then fix the problem.

The next few sections talk about problems that can occur because the order of operations is not understood, or because of loops that aren't coded correctly. Following that, you'll find a section talking about things you can do to help debug logic errors.

Order of Operations

NEW TERM Remember when students would ask if there are any real-world applications of math? Well, understanding the order of operations is critical, not only in algebra, but in PL/SQL and every programming language, database, and spreadsheet package you might use. The *order of operations* states the order of precedence each operator is given. Table 13.1 covers just a few of these levels, with the top level being the highest-priority order. Day 3, "Writing PL/SQL Expressions" covers this topic in detail.

TABLE 13.1 Simple Order of Operations, from Highest to Lowest

Operator	Description
( )	Parentheses
*, /	Multiplication, division
+, -	Addition, subtraction

13

If two or more operators are on the same priority level, then the expression is evaluated from left to right. Take the following equation, which looks as if it should add two numbers and multiply 9 by the result:

$$5 + 3 * 9$$

Whenever I ask this question in the classroom, at least one quarter of the class tells me the answer is 72. However, the order of operations tells you that multiplication should come first. In this case, 3 * 9 = 27, and when you add 5, you get the correct answer, 32. What if you wanted to arrive at 72? You would use parentheses around the expression you want to evaluate first:

(5 + 3) * 9 = 72

Misunderstanding the order of operations is a very common problem in areas of business, finance, statistics, and scientific application programming. On Day 3, you learned a great deal about this issue of operator precedence.

Nonterminating Loops

Another common logic problem is loops that never terminate. As an example, take a look at the code in Listing 13.2.

INPUT   **LISTING 13.2**   An Example of an Infinite Loop

```
 1: DECLARE
 2:     v_MyNumber NUMBER := 0;
 3: BEGIN
 4:     LOOP
 5:       IF v_MyNumber = 7 THEN
 6:             EXIT;
 7:       END IF;
 8:       v_MyNumber := v_MyNumber + 2;
 9:     END LOOP;
10: END;
11: /
```

ANALYSIS   As you can see, this loop will never exit because v_MyNumber will never evaluate to 7. Since it starts at zero, and is incremented by two each time, it will go from 6 to 8 - - skipping 7. To fix this, you could rewrite line 5 so that it looks like this:

```
IF v_MyNumber >= 7 THEN
```

This is a much safer way to terminate a loop, because it doesn't matter whether the v_MyNumber value is an exact match or not. It won't matter if the increment in line 8 is a 2 or a 3 or a 1. Whenever the value becomes greater than or equal to 7, the loop will terminate.

Debugging Approaches for Logic Errors

When you find that you have a logic error somewhere in your code, there are several things you can do to find it:

- Set up a test environment
- Set up some realistic test data
- Narrow down the scope of the problem until you find it

The first two items are things you should do before you even begin development. As for the third item, finding the exact location of a bug is often easier said than done. However, there are some techniques that you can use to better enable yourself to do that. The following sections describe these three items in more detail.

Setting Up a Test Environment

Although testing might seem like common sense, you would not believe how many major corporations either don't have test environments for all their applications or simply put code into production without thoroughly testing the code in a test environment. This problem occurred at one firm that used a program to calculate the raises for employees. The managers would enter a percentage such as .05. Unfortunately, the code took the current pay rate multiplied by the percentage of the raise and assigned this to the new value of the hourly rate. So people with a 5% raise on $10.00 per hour now were making 50 cents per hour! The formula should have been `pay_rate * (1+raise)`. Imagine being the IT manager trying to explain this "glitch" to your coworkers.

Unfortunately, this problem is more common than it might seem. Another case concerns code that that works fine when initially placed in production, but it affects code in later production processes. Whenever possible, you should set up a test environment and test extensively. It's best to have someone else actually do the testing. Programmers often prefer to test by themselves due to an often unspoken fear that a third party will find more bugs. Well, that's often true! Take advantage of it.

Setting Up Test Data

After you have set up your test environment, you need to test the code with sample data. One method to determine test data is to come up with a spreadsheet with a list of all possible values, or ranges of values, and then manually calculate the output. The whole purpose of programming is to work with the inputs, and output the *desired* results. Use test data that might not be used currently in the system, but that could possibly be entered by the user, and so on. For example, if a program uses only positive numbers, enter a negative number as test data. In addition to testing the unusual cases, your test environment should also include a reasonable volume of typical production data.

Setting up test data and testing all possible outcomes is critical in debugging any application. A major advantage of having a predefined test environment is that it allows you to document a series of tests and repeat them each time you modify your code. Taking a little extra time to do thorough testing will benefit you greatly down the road.

13

Narrowing Down the Location of a Bug

Suppose you encounter a case in which outputs do not match the desired output. What steps do you take next? No matter what, you need to narrow down the search area, especially because large-scale applications have millions of lines of code. The steps I would take to troubleshoot for a logic error bug are as follows:

1. Determine the overall process.
2. Determine where, when, and how frequently the error occurs.
3. Determine what outputs are invalid.
4. Determine what inputs and calculations make up those outputs.
5. Determine what does work. (This question can help in determining the cause.)
6. Define the problem.
7. Trace inputs, intermediate computations, and outputs.
8. Step away from the problem.
9. Ask for help. Software bugs have been discovered this way!
10. Document the solution.

The next few sections talk briefly about each of these steps.

Determining the Overall Process

Before you can troubleshoot, you should have some idea of the overall process and how it relates to the business. If you have no reinsurance knowledge, it will make troubleshooting a reinsurance application much more difficult. If you have been called in to troubleshoot someone else's problem, take time to learn the nature of the processes involved. Often that can help you more quickly focus on the specific module of code that is causing the trouble.

Determining Where, When, and How Frequently the Error Occurs

You should know where in the system the problem is occurring. What forms are involved? What data is involved? When does the problem occur and how frequently? Every time a user clicks the Send button? Every time a form is saved and the data is inserted into the table? Only when uniform #23 is inserted into the basketball database? Finding the answers to all these questions will help to determine the root problem.

Determining What Outputs Are Invalid

When attempting to define the problem, if it is not a systems crash but an error on output, attempt to define all outputs that are invalid. Such questions for a banking industry could be: Which accounts get a service fee when they are not supposed to? How much is the service fee? (You can use this information to see which variable references this value in a table.) How often does the error occur? What was the last transaction that occurred before the service fee? (Perhaps a trigger is causing the problem when updating the table.) What date does the error occur? (If the date is fixed, this will help to narrow down the problem area.) In reality, there should be no random problems, even though the problems might initially seem random. You should eventually see a pattern evolve, which will lead you to the problem.

Determining What Inputs and Calculations Make Up Those Outputs

If you know a bank fee is accessed, for example, you should begin researching the modules, programs, triggers, procedures, and so on that are involved with processing that fee. What tables do your inputs come from? Knowing the specific program elements involved can help you trace the problem more effectively.

Determining What Does Work

Asking the question "What does work?" might seem like an odd idea, but believe it or not, it is very effective. If you suspect that a procedure is bad, because the data you pass to the procedure is not processing properly, check the other modules that access this procedure. If they all have the same problem, it is the module. If all of them process properly, and you pass the same number of parameters, maybe it is something in your module. If the range of values you pass is different than that of the other modules accessing the procedure, it could be an out-of-range error in the procedure.

Defining the Problem

Usually, defining the problem is the most difficult part. If you have worked your way through proper troubleshooting and the asking of questions, you should now be able to determine the root cause of the problem, and where to start your search to fix the problem. Many people try to define the problem first, and take away the symptoms with "workaround" coding rather than find the true root cause, which could resurface at any time.

Tracing Inputs, Intermediate Computations, and Outputs

To help narrow down a problem to a specific module, and then to specific lines of code within that module, you can use the DBMS_OUTPUT package to output the values of key variables as the code executes. You can also write a debugging package—as you'll see later in this lesson—to log this information to a text file or a database table. Writing debug output to a file eliminates the problem of having it scroll off the screen too quickly, and also prevents display forms from being overwritten.

13

Stepping Away from the Problem

Have you ever had the solution to the problem stare you in the face but you did not see it? All too often, we get so involved in trying to find and eliminate the bug that we get too frustrated and start to repeat steps that we have already eliminated.

When faced with a situation like this, it often helps to take a break and get away from the problem. If whatever you're doing now isn't working, your whole approach to the problem may be flawed. You may need to give your subconscious mind some time to come up with a fresh approach. So instead of working late, beating your head against the wall, and frustrating yourself, go home. In the morning, you may find that you've thought up a fresh approach, or you may even "see" the solution that you missed the night before.

Asking for Help

If after you examine the code, it appears that you have followed all punctuation and syntax rules, and you have a complete understanding of the function package, procedure, and so on, don't be afraid to ask another consultant or programmer for help. Sometimes an extra set of eyes can pinpoint the problem. In addition, you might learn some new tips and tricks to speed up development or troubleshooting the next time around.

Documenting the Solution

You should document the solution, on paper, in the program (if possible), and ideally in an Oracle database of troubleshooting solutions. This will help you if the problem reoccurs and you can't remember what you did to fix it. Also, if you do this, you are on your way to building an expert system that might be of some value to other clients or end users. This is probably one of the most important processes you should complete after you have solved the problem. If you're too busy to document right after solving the problem, you might live to regret the decision if a similar error occurs and you have to spend more time trying to solve the problem again. Make the time!

Using Tools to Help in Debugging a Program

Tools can be an invaluable debugging aid, especially if you have access to a source code debugger. Historically, this has not been one of PL/SQL's strong points. Oracle doesn't supply a debugger at all for server-level stored procedures and triggers. Developer 2000, a client-side development tool, does include debugging capabilities. There are also some third-party tools on the market, many of which are mentioned on Day 1, "Learning the Basics of PL/SQL."

A good debugging tool will allow you to step through the execution of a procedure or a function one line at a time, examining variables as you go. This enables you to quickly pinpoint most problems. If you don't have a debugging tool available, there are still a couple things you can do. The DBMS_OUTPUT package can often be used to good effect. You can use it to display the values of key variables as a procedure executes. If you want to get a bit more involved, you can create a simple debugging package to log debugging messages to a disk file.

Using DBMS_OUTPUT as a Debugging Tool

The DBMS_OUTPUT package is described in great detail on Day 17, "Writing to Files and the Display." This package will either pass information to a buffer that can be retrieved, or it can display information to the screen. (When debugging a process, if I use DBMS_OUTPUT, I almost always output to the screen.)

The primary use for DBMS_OUTPUT when debugging is to display the values of key variables as a procedure or function executes. This is a time-honored approach to debugging. The key is to display information that will allow you to narrow down the focus of your search. For example, if you display a critical variable before and after a function call, and the value was correct before the call but incorrect afterward, you should focus your future efforts on the code that you called.

If you are using SQL*Plus to compile procedures in the database, you must issue the following command in order to see any output:

INPUT   SET SERVEROUTPUT ON

To disable sending output to the screen, you would turn off SERVEROUTPUT, like this:

INPUT   SET SERVEROUTPUT OFF

If you use DBMS_OUTPUT as a debugging tool, and you are debugging server code by using SQL*Plus, don't forget to turn on SERVEROUTPUT.

Writing a DEBUG Package

DBMS_OUTPUT is nice if you are debugging a procedure or function that you can invoke from SQL*Plus. However, if you need to run a client-side program in order to debug the interaction between that program and the stored procedure, you won't be able to use SQL*Plus to view the output. In such a case, you might want to consider creating a simple debugging package to log debug messages to a file. One such implementation is shown in Listings 13.3 and 13.4. This DEBUG package allows you to do just two things:

- Take the system date and time, comments, and the contents of a variable, and write these to a file while the program executes.

- Reset the file (erase the file) to start a new debugging run.

13

The statement in Listing 13.3 creates the package header, which defines the procedures available within the package.

LISTING 13.3 Defining the DEBUG Package Components

```
 1: CREATE OR REPLACE PACKAGE DEBUG AS
 2:     /* Procedure OUT is used to output a comment of your
 3:     choice, along with the contents of the variable. The
 4:     Procedure OUT statement defines the format of the function */
 5:     PROCEDURE OUT(p_Comments IN VARCHAR2, p_Variable IN VARCHAR2);
 6:
 7:     /* Procedure Erase is used to erase the contents of the file.
 8:     Used to start a new debugging process. Good idea to call
 9:     this function first. */
10:     PROCEDURE Erase;
11: END DEBUG; -- End Definition of package DEBUG
12: /
```

Package Created

After creating the package header, you can now enter and execute the package body as shown in Listing 13.4.

Note

This version of the package body assumes that the UTL_FILE_DIR initialization parameter is pointing to a directory named c:\a. The directory used for the debug.txt file must be one that UTL_FILE_DIR points to. You need to adjust the directory name in this procedure to match the UTL_FILE_DIR setting in your environment. See Day 17 for more information on using the UTL_FILE package.

LISTING 13.4 Creating the DEBUG Package Components

```
 1: CREATE OR REPLACE PACKAGE BODY DEBUG AS
 2:     PROCEDURE OUT(p_Comments IN VARCHAR2,p_Variable IN VARCHAR2) IS
 3:         v_MyFHOUT UTL_FILE.FILE_TYPE; -- Declare File Handle
 4: BEGIN
 5: /* Use A to append all output being sent to the file */
 6:
 7:     v_MyFHOUT := UTL_FILE.FOPEN('c:\a','debug.txt','a');
 8:
 9: /* Display System Time and Date as MM-DD-YY HH:MM:SS
10:     followed by comments and the contents of the
11:     variables. Each element is surrounded by quotation marks and
12:     separated by a comma to create a comma separated value file */
13:
14:     UTL_FILE.PUT_LINE(v_MyFHOUT,'"'||
```

```
15:              TO_CHAR(SYSDATE,'mm-dd-yy HH:MM:SS AM')
16:              || '","Comment: ' || p_Comments ||
17:              '","' || p_Variable || '"');
18:
19: /* Close the file handle which points to debug.txt */
20:     UTL_FILE.FCLOSE(v_MyFHOUT);
21:
22: EXCEPTION
23: /* Create Exception to simply display error code and message */
24:     WHEN OTHERS THEN
25:         DBMS_OUTPUT.PUT_LINE
26:             ('ERROR ' || to_char(SQLCODE) || SQLERRM);
27:         NULL; -- Do Nothing
28:     END OUT; -- End Execution of Procedure OUT
29:
30:
31:     PROCEDURE Erase IS
32:         v_MyFH UTL_FILE.FILE_TYPE; -- Create File Handle
33:     BEGIN
34: /* Open file to overwrite current file contents.  Doing this
35:    erases the contents of the original file completely */
36:
37:     v_MyFH := UTL_FILE.FOPEN('c:\a','debug.txt','w');
38:
39: -- Close the file handle which points to debug.txt
40:     UTL_FILE.FCLOSE(v_MyFH);
41:
42:     EXCEPTION
43: -- Create Exception to simply display error code and message
44:         WHEN OTHERS THEN
45:             DBMS_OUTPUT.PUT_LINE
46:                 ('ERROR ' || to_char(SQLCODE) || SQLERRM);
47:             NULL;
48:     END Erase; -- End Procedure Erase
49:
50: BEGIN
51:     Erase; -- Erase contents of the file
52:
53: END DEBUG; -- End procedure DEBUG
54:/
```

OUTPUT   Package body created.

You can now examine the components of the newly created DEBUG package.

The DEBUG.OUT Procedure

The DEBUG.OUT procedure enables you to log debugging messages to a file called debug.txt. The procedure automatically includes the system date and time with each message. The procedure accepts two parameters: a debug message and the variable you are tracking. Each time you call it, DEBUG_OUT appends the message and the value of the variable to the file named debug.txt.

The DEBUG.ERASE Procedure

The DEBUG.ERASE procedure erases the contents of the debug.txt file by opening a handle to the file in replace mode ('W') and then closing the file. This process creates an empty file. You should make at least one call to DEBUG_ERASE at the start of each debugging run to ensure that you start with a clean file.

An Example of Using the DEBUG Package

One possible use for the DEBUG package is to log the inputs and outputs from a function that you are testing. Listing 13.5 shows a function representing a variation on Oracle's built-in ADD_MONTHS function. This function is named ADD_MON, and includes calls to DEBUG.OUT to log both the input date and the date that it returns.

INPUT   **LISTING 13.5**   The ADD_MON Function, with Calls to the DEBUG Package

```
 1: CREATE OR REPLACE FUNCTION add_mon (date_in DATE,
 2:                                 months_to_add NUMBER)
 3: RETURN DATE AS
 4:     /*Similar to the built-in ADD_MONTHS, but this function
 5:     leaves the date alone as much as possible. The day is only
 6:     adjusted if it is out of range for the new month.*/
 7: day_in VARCHAR2(3);
 8: day_work VARCHAR2(3);
 9: date_out DATE;
10: date_work DATE;
11: BEGIN
12: debug.out ('DATE_IN = ',
13:             TO_CHAR(date_in,'yyyy mm dd hh mi ss'));
14:
15: --Grab the input day.
16: day_in := TO_NUMBER(TO_CHAR(date_in,'dd'));
17:
18: --Now, add the number of months requested by the caller
19: date_work := ADD_MONTHS(date_in, months_to_add);
20:
21: --Get the day of the month for the new date.
22: day_work := TO_NUMBER(TO_CHAR(date_work,'dd'));
23:
24: --If the day is unchanged, we are golden.  If it was
25: --adjusted downward, that's because the new month didn't
26: --have as many days. If it was ajdusted upwards, we
27: --want to set it back to where it was.
28: IF day_in = day_work THEN
```

```
29:     date_out := date_work;
30: ELSIF day_work < day_in THEN
31:     date_out := date_work;
32: ELSE
33:     date_out := date_work - (day_work - day_in);
34: END IF;
35:
36: --Return the new date to the caller.
37: debug.out ('DATE_OUT = ',
38:              TO_CHAR(date_out,'yyyy mm dd hh mi ss'));
39: RETURN date_out;
40: END;
41: /
```

ANALYSIS Unlike the built-in ADD_MONTHS function, ADD_MON does not change the day of the month unless it is forced to. The only situation where that occurs is if the new month has fewer days than the starting month. To help in debugging this function, two calls to DEBUG.OUT have been added. The first call logs the date coming in, and the second call logs the date going out. After executing the function a few times, you can look in the log to verify that the results are what you expect.

Listing 13.6 shows a test run being made on the ADD_MON function.

INPUT/OUTPUT **LISTING 13.6** Testing the ADD_MON Function

```
 1: SQL> EXECUTE debug.erase;
 2:
 3: PL/SQL procedure successfully completed.
 4:
 5: SQL>
 6: SQL> --The built-in ADD_MONTHS function keeps the date at
 7: SQL> --the end of the month when it is there to begin with.
 8: SQL> SELECT TO_CHAR(
 9:   2      ADD_MONTHS(TO_DATE('29-FEB-2000','DD-MON-YYYY'),1),
10:   3                  'DD-MON-YYYY')
11:   4  FROM dual;
12:
13: TO_CHAR(ADD
14: -----------
15: 31-MAR-2000
16:
17: SQL>
18: SQL> --The ADD_MON function preserves the date as it is, except
19: SQL> --when it is out of range for the new month.
20: SQL> SELECT TO_CHAR(
21:   2                  ADD_MON(TO_DATE('29-FEB-2000','DD-MON-YYYY'),1),
22:   3                  'DD-MON-YYYY')
```

13

continues

LISTING 13.6   continued

```
23:    4  FROM dual;
24:
25: TO_CHAR(ADD
26: - - - - - - - - - - -
27: 29-MAR-2000
28:
29: SQL>
30: SQL> SELECT TO_CHAR(
31:    2              ADD_MON(TO_DATE('15-FEB-2000','DD-MON-YYYY'),1),
32:    3              'DD-MON-YYYY')
33:    4  FROM dual;
34:
35: TO_CHAR(ADD
36: - - - - - - - - - - -
37: 15-MAR-2000
38:
39: SQL>
40: SQL> SELECT TO_CHAR(
41:    2              ADD_MON(TO_DATE('31-JAN-2000','DD-MON-YYYY'),1),
42:    3              'DD-MON-YYYY')
43:    4  FROM dual;
44:
45: TO_CHAR(ADD
46: - - - - - - - - - - -
47: 29-FEB-2000
```

ANALYSIS   Line 1 contains a crucial call to DEBUG.ERASE. This call creates an empty
debug.txt file for use by subsequent calls to DEBUG.OUT. Lines 6–15 demonstrate
how the built-in ADD_MONTHS function operates. Because the input date 29-Feb represented the last day of the month, the output date was adjusted so that it also represented the
last day of the month. Instead of returning 29-Mar, ADD_MONTHS returned 31-Mar. Lines
18–27 demonstrate how ADD_MON's behavior is different. ADD_MON adds one month, but
preserves the day, resulting in the value 29-Mar. The remaining lines test some other
cases that ADD_MON must handle correctly.

Having executed these tests, you'll find that the debug.txt file contains these entries:

```
"09-12-99 12:09:40 PM","Comment: DATE_IN = ","2000 02 29 12 00 00"
"09-12-99 12:09:40 PM","Comment: DATE_OUT = ","2000 03 29 12 00 00"
"09-12-99 12:09:40 PM","Comment: DATE_IN = ","2000 02 15 12 00 00"
"09-12-99 12:09:40 PM","Comment: DATE_OUT = ","2000 03 15 12 00 00"
"09-12-99 12:09:41 PM","Comment: DATE_IN = ","2000 01 31 12 00 00"
"09-12-99 12:09:41 PM","Comment: DATE_OUT = ","2000 02 29 12 00 00"
```

These entries allow you to verify that the ADD_MON function is operating as expected.

Preventing Errors and Planning for Debugging in the Future

If your code needs to be debugged in the future, you can plan ahead of time to make it easier through the use of liberal commenting and properly formatted code. To reduce the probability of errors, you should approach the design phase by checking for all possible scenarios and outcomes. In addition, you should design your code in modules, not only to reduce the amount of code to sort through when a problem occurs, but to be able to reuse those modules in the future.

Defining Requirements and Planning Projects

When you develop a new application, you should spend a significant amount of time defining the requirements of the users. Not only does this require some knowledge of the business, but it should cover all possible input and desired output scenarios. Someone knowledgeable in the industry should verify all calculations. What do you gain by sitting with the end users and verifying the application? You begin to understand the business and its needs, and you might be able to make suggestions that could aid in decision-making processes, reduce work time for manual processing, improve productivity, and so on. Not only that, it is easier to troubleshoot the system and identify problems before the application is placed in production. I can't stress enough how important it is to understand and plan for the application in the beginning: Doing so will save you a lot of time and aggravation at the tail end of the project.

 Tip

Always verify your understanding of the requirements with the business users of the system. Tell them what you think you heard them say in the first place. Make sure that they agree that you have a correct understanding of the problem at hand.

13

There is one pitfall in obtaining user requirements, which I found out the hard way. I coded an application that I felt met the user requirements for a financial department. After reviewing the application with the end user, and discussing the outputs and how the calculations worked, I wound up redesigning the application to meet the new perceived needs. Unfortunately, due to a language barrier, I had the application coded correctly the first time, and the new changes were wrong. Not only should you relay back to the end user what you perceive their requirements are, but if possible, you should try to verify the process you are about to code with at least one other knowledgeable resource. The next time I ran into a similar problem, by working with two resources, I was able to resolve any issues about what should be coded.

Using a Modular Approach to Coding

When developing your applications, you should take a modular approach to make debugging easier. This also gives you the added benefit of creating reusable code. For instance, in a payroll application, you could design modules to do the following:

- Calculate gross wage
- Calculate FICA
- Calculate federal withholdings
- Calculate state withholdings
- Withhold for benefits such as flexible spending or insurance

If a problem occurs that is related to gross wages, you can easily narrow down which procedure(s) is broken and then fix the bug. In addition, modules have another important aspect: You can test the modules independently of one another.

Commenting Code

One of the greatest benefits you can provide for yourself and other Oracle developers is to liberally comment your code. Although you could provide documentation manuals, in practice these manuals tend to get "misplaced" in almost every environment. Adding comments to your code will help, whether you are trying to debug the application or simply modifying the application to meet new requirements.

Proper labeling of variables is also important. Poorly worded variables confuse the developer and waste valuable time for people who are trying to follow the logic of the program. Listing 13.7 reflects code that can be very confusing at first glance.

INPUT   **LISTING 13.7**   Poorly Commented Code

```
 1: CREATE OR REPLACE FUNCTION RAISE(
 2:         p1 INTEGER,
 3:         p2 NUMBER)
 4:     RETURN NUMBER IS
 5:     p3 NUMBER;
 6: BEGIN
 7:     IF p1 = 1 THEN
 8:         p3 := p2 * 1.10;
 9:     ELSIF p1 = 2 THEN
10:         p3 := p2 * 1.05;
11:     ELSIF p1 = 3 THEN
12:         p3 := p2 * 1.04;
13:     ELSIF p1 = 4 THEN
14:         p3 := p2 * 1.03;
15: ELSIF p1 = 5 THEN
16:         p3 := p2 ;
```

```
17:      ELSE
18:         p3 := p2 * 1.02;
19:      END IF;
20:      RETURN p3; --
21: END RAISE;
22: /
```

ANALYSIS A quick glance at this code shows that there are no comments, and that the variable names are not mnemonic. In order to follow the code, you would have to first determine what p1, p2, and p3 are. You also do not know what the function raises: An hourly pay rate? The cost of benefits? Someone's GPA? The elevation of a building under construction?

Raise can mean many things, so a clarification is very important. The same code is provided again in Listing 13.8, with comments that easily clarify the function.

INPUT   **LISTING 13.8**   Proper Commenting and Naming of Variables

```
 1: CREATE OR REPLACE FUNCTION RAISE(
 2:          p_paylevel INTEGER, -- parameter for input of raise level
 3:          p_payrate NUMBER)   -- parameter for input of pay rate
 4: /* The purpose of this function is to calculate ANNUAL raises
 5:    for all of the hourly employees, based upon their raise level
 6:    values 1-4 and all others.  */
 7:
 8: /* On June 24, 1997, added feature to eliminate consultant raise,
 9:    which is pay level 5 */
10:
11:      RETURN NUMBER IS
12:      v_newrate NUMBER; -- New Hourly Rate After Raise
13: BEGIN
14:      IF p_paylevel = 1 THEN
15:          v_newrate := p_payrate * 1.10; -- Promotion Raise
16:      ELSIF p_paylevel = 2 THEN
17:          v_newrate := p_payrate * 1.05; -- Exceeds Rate
18:      ELSIF p_paylevel = 3 THEN
19:          v_newrate := p_payrate * 1.04; -- Hi Meets Rate
20:      ELSIF p_paylevel = 4 THEN
21:          v_newrate := p_payrate * 1.03; -- Meets Rate
22: ELSIF p_paylevel = 5 THEN
23:          v_newrate := p_payrate ; -- Consultants who get no raise
24:      ELSE
25:          v_newrate := p_payrate * 1.02; -- All Others
26:      END IF;
27:      RETURN v_newrate; -- Returns new paylevel rate to procedure
28: END RAISE;
29: /
```

13

ANALYSIS You can now follow the function, its purpose, what the variables are, and any modifications made at a later date. What a difference commenting and proper naming of variables makes!

Writing Assertions into Code

NEW TERM An *assertion*, in programming terms, is a test for a fact that should be true. Assertions serve several functions. Their primary function is to prevent errors from propagating further downstream in a process. Say you had a function that was never supposed to return a negative value. You could actually place a check in your function to be sure that a negative value is never accidentally returned. Listing 13.9 shows one approach that you might take to this problem.

INPUT **LISTING 13.9** A Function That Should Never Return a Negative Value

```
 1: CREATE OR REPLACE FUNCTION do_calc
 2: RETURN NUMBER AS
 3:     return_value NUMBER;
 4: BEGIN
 5:     ...
 6:     ...
 7:     IF return_value < 0 THEN
 8:         RAISE_APPLICATION_ERROR (
 9:             -20000,'DO_CALC: Negative value returned.');
10:     END IF;
11:
12:     RETURN return_value;
13: END;
14: /
```

ANALYSIS Lines 5–6 represent whatever computations are performed by this function. Lines 7–10 check the result immediately before the function returns the value that it computed. If the value is negative, instead of returning the erroneous value, the function raises an error.

A test like the one shown in Listing 13.9 is an assertion. Should you make a mistake coding the DO_CALC function, or should some future maintenance programmer induce an error, the assertion would fire, and you would immediately be alerted to the problem. Assertions also, in a manner of speaking, serve as a form of documentation to future maintenance programmers. They are like a comment, but with a loaded gun.

Coding assertions as shown in Listing 13.9 isn't too practical. You don't have any central control over whether they fire, and you can't make global changes to their behavior. A more robust approach is to create a procedure such as the one shown in listing 13.10.

INPUT   **LISTING 13.10**   An ASSERT Function

```
1: CREATE OR REPLACE PROCEDURE ASSERT (
2:     condition IN BOOLEAN,
3:     message IN VARCHAR2) AS
4: BEGIN
5:     IF NOT condition THEN
6:         RAISE_APPLICATION_ERROR (-20000,message);
7:     END IF;
8: END;
9: /
```

ANALYSIS   This ASSERT procedure evaluates any condition passed to it, and raises an error if that condition is not true. Listing 13.11 shows how you could apply this to the DO_CALC function in Listing 13.9.

INPUT   **LISTING 13.11**   Using the ASSERT Procedure in the DO_CALC Function

```
1: CREATE OR REPLACE FUNCTION do_calc
2: RETURN NUMBER AS
3:     return_value NUMBER;
4: BEGIN
5:     ...
6:     ...
7:     ASSERT (return_value >= 0,'DO_CALC: Return value is negative.');
8:     RETURN return_value;
9: END;
10: /
```

ANALYSIS   The three-line IF statement from Listing 13.10 has been replaced by a one-line call to ASSERT. The readability of the code is improved—you know what a call to ASSERT means, and centralizing the assertion logic in one procedure gives you a place where you can turn it off when you don't need it.

Formatting Code

Another ounce of error prevention is the proper formatting of code. Here are some formatting suggestions that you can either adopt or modify for your specific environment:

- For each new block of code, indent two to five spaces.
- Use uppercase for keywords.
- Use mixed case for variable names.
- Precede variable names with a v_ for variable, p_ for parameters, and so on.
- Use one statement per line.

13

Using Proper Indentation

Every time you start a new block of code, such as a loop, an IF statement, or a nested block, you should indent to make the code more readable. Listing 13.12 shows an example of poorly indented code.

INPUT   **LISTING 13.12**   Code with No Indentations

```
 1: DECLARE
 2: v_MyNumber NUMBER := 0;
 3: BEGIN
 4: LOOP
 5: IF v_MyNumber > 7 THEN
 6: EXIT;
 7: v_MyNumber := v_MyNumber + 2;
 8: END LOOP;
 9: END;
10: /
```

ANALYSIS   This code is very difficult to follow. At a glance, you cannot easily discern where the declarations begin and end, where the loop ends, or where the IF statement terminates.

If you reformat the code as shown in Listing 13.13, you can follow the program more easily.

INPUT   **LISTING 13.13**   Code with Proper Indentation

```
 1: DECLARE
 2:     v_MyNumber NUMBER := 0;
 3: BEGIN
 4:     LOOP
 5:         IF v_MyNumber > 7 THEN
 6:             EXIT;
 7:         v_MyNumber := v_MyNumber + 2;
 8:     END LOOP;
 9: END;
10: /
```

ANALYSIS   Not only is the code now easier to read, but the indentation makes it obvious that an ENDIF statement is missing after line 6.

Using Uppercase for Keywords

Using uppercase for reserved words or functions helps to distinguish between regular code and Oracle-provided code. If a keyword is misspelled, you can easily spot the problem. All the listings that you have seen in this book have capitalized SQL and PL/SQL keywords. The code in Listing 13.14 shows how less readable code can become if you don't do this.

INPUT   **LISTING 13.14**   Code with Keywords Not Capitalized

```
 1: declare
 2:      v_mynumber number := 0;
 3: begin
 4:      loop
 5:          if v_mynumber > 7 then
 6:              exit;
 7:          end if;
 8:          v_mynumber := v_mynumber + 2;
 9:      end loop;
10: end;
11: /
```

ANALYSIS   In this code it is difficult to pick out the datatypes of the variables. It is also difficult to see at a glance what type of statements exist in the block.

Using Mixed Case for Variable Names

To identify code, output, keywords, or variable names, you can easily distinguish variable names by using mixed case. By using MyVariable, for example, you can pick the variable name out faster than you could pick out myvariable or MYVARIABLE.

Preceding Variable Names with v_ or p_

By preceding variables with a first letter and an underscore, you can quickly identify variables and their type. One possible scheme is to use v_ for regular variables, p_ for parameters, and so forth. That way, you know at glance whether you are dealing with a regular variable, a parameter, or another specific kind of variable.

13

Using One Statement per Line

Because the semicolon (;) is used to terminate a statement, you could easily have multiple statements on one line. For instance, you could code something like this:

```
y := ''; x :=1;
LOOP x := x+1; y := y+' '; if x=10 THEN EXIT; END IF; END LOOP;
```

Although this code is syntactically correct and will execute, you'll run into trouble if you try to troubleshoot it or comment out a statement that might be causing the error. The code would be much easier to follow if you formatted it like this:

```
y := '';
x :=1;
LOOP
    x := x+1;
    y := y+' ';
    if x=10 THEN
        EXIT;
    END IF;
END LOOP;
```

Notice how the indentation makes it obvious which statements are part of the loop, and which are part of the IF statement. This code will execute just as fast, but it's a lot easier to read, understand, and maintain.

Summary

Today's lesson discusses the methodology of debugging an application. When debugging, you must deal with two kinds of errors: logic errors and syntax errors. Syntax errors are a result of improper formatting, missing punctuation, misspelled keywords, and so on. Logic errors do not cause your program to stop execution (usually); they allow the code to compile, but provide for the wrong type of processing. Common problem areas that cause logic errors are improper order of operations when performing calculations and infinite loops. Oracle does not feature any built-in debugging package, at least not with the database, although Developer 2000 includes a debugger. Proper commenting and formatting of code enables you to review and understand code much faster than you could otherwise.

Q&A

Q What debugging packages does Oracle provide with the standard relational database package?

A Currently, none are provided, although you can purchase tools from Oracle or other third-party vendors.

Q What can I use to debug applications?

A Using DBMS_OUTPUT to display the values of key variables is one method of debugging. You can also create your own debugging package to log debugging messages to a file.

Q If all operations are on the same level, how does Oracle know which calculations to process first?

A If all calculations are at the same level, the order of evaluation is from left to right.

Q What simple punctuation can easily override the natural order of operations?

A Parentheses ( ). Operations in parentheses are evaluated first, and the results are used in the rest of the expression.

Q Are comments needed in an application if you have sufficient separate documentation?

A Yes, absolutely. Documentation tends to get misplaced or never gets updated when a coding change is made. You should document not only what each procedure, function, and trigger does, but also document changes and updates as they occur.

Q Must we really document solutions to problems?

A Documenting solutions to problems helps you troubleshoot similar problems that occur in the future.

Q Why does proper formatting help in debugging code?

A Proper formatting allows you to view code quickly and assess what the code is doing. If you do not line up END IF statements when you are nesting IF...THEN clauses, it is difficult to see when the first statement ends, the second ends, and so forth.

Workshop

You can use this to test your comprehension of this lesson and put what you've learned into practice. You'll find the answers to the quiz and exercises in Appendix A, "Answers."

Quiz

1. True or False: Logic errors are easier to debug than syntax errors.
2. Missing a semicolon is what type of an error?
3. Provide the answer to the calculation 6 + 4 / 2 = ?.
4. True or False: Commenting code is a waste of time.
5. True or False: Formatting code is not necessary.

13

Exercises

The DEBUG package in this lesson always writes debugging messages to the file named debug.txt. That will cause problems if multiple developers use the package at once. Modify the DEBUG package as follows:

- Modify the ERASE procedure to accept a filename. This filename will be used by subsequent calls to the OUT procedure.

- Modify both the OUT and ERASE procedures so that if no filename is passed, or if ERASE is never called, no file is created and no messages get written.

For extra credit, add an ASSERT procedure to the DEBUG package, and build in a flag so that you can enable and disable assertions at will.

DAY **14**

Leveraging Large Object Types

by Tom Luers

Many new advanced features were added with the release of Oracle8i. This lesson covers several of these features, including locators, large objects, and the `DBMS_LOB` package. Today's lesson focuses on the following topics:

- Defining large objects
- Using the `DBMS_LOB` package with external files
- Understanding locators
- Using the `DBMS_LOB` package with internal files

Exploring Large Object Datatypes

The LOB, or large object, datatypes let you store blocks of unstructured data (such as text, graphic images, video clips, and sound waveforms) up to four gigabytes in size.

Oracle8i added four large object datatypes, which allows for efficient, random, and precise data access. These datatypes are summarized in Table 14.1.

TABLE 14.1   Large Object Datatypes

Object	Location	Description
CLOB	Internal	Character large object—Holds up to 4GB of single-byte characters that corresponds to the database's current character set.
NCLOB	Internal	National character large object—Holds up to 4GB of single-byte characters or multibyte characters that conform to the national character set defined by the Oracle database.
BLOB	Internal	Binary large object—Holds up to 4GB of raw, or unstructured, binary data.
BFILE	External	Binary file—Stored as a file accessible by the operating system that Oracle can access and manipulate. These files can reside on a variety of storage devices, including DVD-ROM, CD-ROM, and disk drives.

All the datatypes in previous table can store up to 4GB of unstructured data, which is more than enough to accommodate such items as sound, pictures, and video in databases. Of the available large object datatypes, three of them are internal to Oracle, and one is external. *External* refers to a physical file, for which Oracle stores the filename and file location. *Internal* objects store a locator in the large object column of the table, which points to the actual location of the data in the table. Therefore, when you retrieve a LOB datatype, only the data locator is returned, and not the actual data item. The Internal LOBs can also be either temporary in duration or more persistent in nature: persistent in that the LOB is present during the entire session duration.

Limitations of LOBs

Although they sound invincible, LOBs do have some limitations, such as the following:

- LOBs cannot be used in advanced Oracle table storage techniques such as clustering.
- LOBs are not allowed in GROUP BY, ORDER BY, SELECT DISTINCT, and JOIN statements, or in aggregates. However, LOBs are allowed in statements that use UNION ALL.

- Distributed LOBs are not permitted.
- LOBs are not allowed in VARRYs.

LOB Versus LONG Datatypes

Oracle introduced the LOB datatypes in the early release of Oracle8, to compensate for some of the limitations of the LONG datatypes. LONG datatypes certainly have their place in the world, but they have limitations when working with certain applications such as multimedia. LOBs are similar to LONG and LONG RAW types, but differ in the following ways:

- You can store multiple LOBs in a single row, but you can store only one LONG or LONG RAW per row.
- LOBs can be attributes of user-defined datatypes, but this is not possible with either a LONG or LONG RAW.
- Only the LOB locator is stored in the table column; BLOB and CLOB data can be stored in separate tablespaces, and BFILE data is stored as an external file. In the case of a LONG or LONG RAW, the entire value is stored in the table column. If the LOB is less than 3964 bytes in size, then the entire LOB is stored in the table column.
- When you access a LOB column, the locator is returned. When you access a LONG or LONG RAW, the entire value is returned.
- A LOB can be up to 4GB in size. The BFILE maximum depends on the operating system, but still cannot exceed 4GB. The valid accessible range is 1 to $(2^{32}-1)$. By contrast, a LONG or LONG RAW is limited to 2GB.
- There is greater flexibility in manipulating data in a random, precise manner with LOBs than there is with LONG or LONG RAW data. LOBs can be accessed at random offsets, whereas LONGs must be accessed from the beginning to the desired location.
- You can replicate LOBs in both local and distributed environments, but this is not possible with LONGs or LONG RAWs.

> **Note**
>
> You can convert existing LONG columns to LOBs by using the TO_LOB function. This function is covered a little later in this lesson.

14

Converting LONGs to LOBs

The TO_LOB function allows you to convert LONG or LONG RAW datatype values to LOB datatype values. This function can only be used to a LONG or LONG RAW column and can be used in a SELECT list of a subquery in an INSERT statement. The syntax for the TO_LOB function can be seen in the following example.

```
TO_LOB (long value)
```

In this syntax *long value* is the value of the data item you wish to convert to a LOB datatype.

The following example illustrates the use of the TO_LOB function:

```
INSERT INTO lob_table
    SELECT n, TO_LOB(long_col) FROM long_table;
```

ANALYSIS In this example, the INSERT INTO statement converts the value in the column long_col from the long_ table. The net result is that the long_col value is transformed into a LOB datatype.

Using External Files in an Oracle8i Database

The BFILE datatype is a large binary object that is external to Oracle. (*External* means that the file is accessible to the operating system and not stored within the Oracle database.) To access an external object, you need the directory object and the filename, and you need to have all the privileges associated with accessing the directories and files. The following sections discuss the creation of the BFILE datatype.

Creating the Directory Object

Before you can access external files, you need to create a directory object. This directory object maps a name to a path specified in the CREATE statement. The directory object name can be up to 30 characters, and the filename can be up to 2,000 characters. The syntax for creating a directory object is as follows.

```
CREATE (OR REPLACE) DIRECTORY Directory_Name AS Path
```

In this syntax the parameters are as follows:

- *Directory_Name* is the name of the directory object you are associating with the path. Oracle calls this directory name rather than specifying the actual path.

- *Path* is the physical path on the system of any secondary storage devices such as DVD or tape.

Note

In the next several sections, you will need to create a path called books somewhere on a hard drive to which you have access. Copy all the files from the books subdirectory from the Web site into this subdirectory. You will have a total of nine files in the books subdirectory after the copy process has ended.

Before you can try several of the examples in this book, you need to create a directory object called books. This object will hold the data and descriptions of future or current books required for purchase by your organization. To create the directory object, execute the code in Listing 14.1. Be sure that your operating system, such as NT or Unix, has granted your user Id the appropriate privileges to create directories and files on the system.

INPUT   **LISTING 14.1**   Creating the Directory Object books

```
CREATE OR REPLACE DIRECTORY books_Dir AS 'C:\BOOKS'
/
```

Note

Change the last parameter of the path to correspond to the actual path specified by your operating system, such as /home/users/Atwood/books for UNIX users, which you created and copied the nine files to this path.

After you have executed the SQL statement, you should see output stating that the directory was created.

Limitations of BFILE

The BFILE datatype does not offer transactional support for COMMIT or ROLLBACK. Also, files are opened as read-only, so you can't write or alter these external files in any manner. Another problem that could occur is a too many files open error. To avoid this error, you need to edit the INIT.ORA file and change the statement SESSION_MAX_OPEN_FILES=20 to the value you require (the default is 10). Also keep in mind any operating system requirements. When you open files, make sure that you close them; otherwise, they are tracked as opened files even when not in use, and you might get the message too many files open when you really are accessing under the limit. This mostly occurs when programs terminate abnormally and there is nothing in place to close all files when the error occurs.

14

Using the DBMS_LOB Package with BFILE

Oracle's DBMS_LOB package allows you to manipulate all types of LOBs. Because the BFILE datatype is the only external datatype, Oracle provides functions used solely for external LOBs. These are summarized in Table 14.2.

TABLE 14.2 Functions and Procedures Used with BFILE

Function or Procedure	Accessed By	Description
BFILENAME	BFILE	Creates a pointer (locator) in the PL/SQL block, or in the table to the location of the file.
COMPARE	All LOBs	Compares all or part of two LOBs.
FILECLOSE	BFILE	Closes files associated with the BFILE locator.
FILECLOSEALL	BFILE	Closes all open BFILEs.
FILEEXISTS	BFILE	Checks whether the file exists where the locator says the file should be located.
FILEGETNAME	BFILE	Returns the directory object and path of the BFILE.
FILEISOPEN	BFILE	Checks to see if the file is already open.
FILEOPEN	BFILE	Actually opens the file.
GETLENGTH	All LOBs	Returns the actual length of the LOB.
INSTR	All LOBs	Searches for matching patterns in a LOB with the string of characters specified.
READ	All LOBs	Reads a specific amount of a LOB into the buffer.
SUBSTR	All LOBs	Returns part or all of the LOB specified by the parameters.

The following sections will describe these functions in more detail and give examples of their syntax.

The BFILENAME Function

When working with external files or inserting locators for BFILEs into a table, you need to call the BFILENAME function, which creates the locator to the external file. The syntax for the BFILENAME function is as shown below.

SYNTAX

```
FUNCTION BFILENAME(Directory_Object IN VARCHAR2,
                             Filename IN VARCHAR2);
RETURN BFILE_Locator;
```

In this syntax the parameters are as follows:

- *Directory_Object* is a previously created object that stores the path of the file.

- *Filename* is the actual name of the file.

The function then returns a locator to the file, so that Oracle knows how to access the file. This value can be used in PL/SQL blocks, or it can be inserted into a table with a column of type BFILE.

Note

> If a file is deleted or moved, and Oracle still has a locator pointing to where this file used to reside, Oracle raises an error when attempting to open the file. Oracle does not automatically update or delete the locator if the file is erased or moved. Although this typically does not affect anonymous PL/SQL blocks, it does affect locators stored in a table.

The COMPARE Function

If you need to compare all or part of a LOB, you can use the COMPARE function. One useful purpose of this function is to check to see if you have two external files that are exactly identical. You could write a maintenance program to check for duplicate files and then remove the duplicate files because these large files can waste a lot of hard drive space. The following syntax box demonstrates the COMPARE function.

SYNTAX

```
FUNCTION COMPARE(
                 Lob1 IN BFILE,
                 Lob2 IN BFILE,
                 Number_Bytes_to_Compare IN INTEGER,
                 Origin_Lob1   IN INTEGER := 1,
                 Origin_Lob2   IN INTEGER := 1)
RETURN Compare_Result_Integer;
```

In this syntax the parameters are as follows:

- *Lob1* is the first LOB you are comparing.

- *Lob2* is the second LOB you are comparing.

- *Number_Bytes_to_Compare* is the total number of bytes you want to compare from *Lob1* to *Lob2*.

14

- *Origin_Lob1* is the starting location in the file where you want to compare. You could use the value 1 to start from the beginning of the LOB, or you could enter 100 to start comparing from the 100th byte.

- *Origin_Lob2* is the starting location of the second LOB you want to compare. The value returned is 0 if the data is identical, nonzero if the data is not identical, or NULL if any of the parameters are invalid, such as an incorrect starting origin, comparing bytes past the end of the LOB, or any other invalid parameter.

The FILECLOSE Procedure

When you have finished reading a BFILE, you should always close the file, not only to free up resources, but also so that you don't exceed the maximum number of allowable files that can be open. The FILECLOSE procedure closes a single file that is open.

```
PROCEDURE FILECLOSE(BFILE_Locator);
```

In this syntax the parameter *BFILE_Locator* is the BFILE locator assigned to the file from the BFILENAME function.

The FILECLOSEALL Procedure

If you are done processing all BFILEs and you want to end a session, you can use the procedure FILECLOSEALL to close every open BFILE.

```
PROCEDURE FILECLOSEALL;
```

Tip

When writing error-handling routines, it is always a good idea to automatically code the FILECLOSEALL procedure to properly close all the files and free up resources.

The FILEEXISTS Function

As stated previously, Oracle does not know if a file has been moved, deleted, or changed in size. Therefore, it is always good coding practice to see if the file exists before performing any operations on the file. Oracle provides the function FILEEXISTS to see if the file is physically at the location specified by the directory object and the filename.

▼ SYNTAX

```
FUNCTION FILEEXISTS (BFILE_Locator)
     RETURN Status_Integer;
```

In this syntax the parameter *BFILE_Locator* is the BFILE locator assigned to the file from the BFILENAME function. The function returns an INTEGER with one of the following values:

- 1 if the file exists at that specific location
- 0 if the file does not exist
- NULL if there is an operating system error, if you lack the privileges to access that file or path, or if the value of the locator is NULL

▲

The FILEGETNAME Procedure

Although you will probably never use FILEGETNAME in an anonymous block of PL/SQL, because you define the directory object and the filename, this is a useful procedure for BFILE locators stored in a table. The FILEGETNAME procedure returns the directory object and the filename associated with the locator. The directory object has a maximum size of 30 characters, and the filename has a maximum size of 2,000 characters.

▼ SYNTAX

```
PROCEDURE FILEGETNAME(BFILE_Locator,
                      Directory_Object OUT VARCHAR2,
                      Filename OUT VARCHAR2);
```

In this syntax the parameters are as follows:

- *BFILE_Locator* is the BFILE locator assigned to the file from the BFILENAME function.
- *Directory_Object* is the directory object associated with the path created with the CREATE DIRECTORY command.
- *Filename* is the name of the file associated with the BFILE locator.

▲

The FILEISOPEN Function

Before opening a BFILE, you should check to make sure that the file is not already open by using the FILEISOPEN function.

14

The Syntax for the FILEISOPEN Function

```
FUNCTION FILEISOPEN (BFILE_Locator)
    RETURN Status_Integer;
```

In this syntax the parameter *BFILE_Locator* is the BFILE locator assigned to the file from the BFILENAME function. The function returns an INTEGER with the value 1 if the file is open or any other integer value if the file is closed. An exception is raised if the file doesn't exist, if you have insufficient privileges, or the directory does not exist.

The FILEOPEN Procedure

Before you can access an external file, you need to first open the file by using the FILEOPEN procedure.

```
PROCEDURE FILEOPEN(BFILE_Locator,
                   DBMS_LOB.FILE_READONLY);
```

In this syntax the parameter *BFILE_Locator* is the BFILE locator assigned to the file from the BFILENAME function. The second parameter, DBMS_LOB.FILE_READONLY, is currently the only mode available to open files.

The GETLENGTH Function

The GETLENGTH function returns the actual length of the objects in bytes.

```
FUNCTION GETLENGTH (BFILE_Locator)
    RETURN Length_Integer;
```

In this syntax the parameter *BFILE_Locator* is the BFILE locator assigned to the file from the BFILENAME function. The function returns an INTEGER of the length of the file, or the value NULL if the following conditions exist: The locator is null, the file is not open, there is an operating system error, or you do not have the appropriate privileges to access the file.

The INSTR Function

The INSTR function allows you to match a pattern against the *n*th occurrence in the LOB, starting from the offset specified.

```
FUNCTION INSTR(BFILE_Locator,
               Pattern IN RAW,
               Starting Location IN INTEGER := 1,
               Nth_Occurrence IN INTEGER := 1)
RETURN Status_Integer;
```

In this syntax the parameters are as follows:

- *BFILE_Locator* is the BFILE locator assigned to the file from the BFILENAME function.

▼
- *Pattern* of type RAW is the pattern you want to match.
- *Starting_Location* is the position in the file where you want to start the search for a match.
- *Nth_Occurrence* is the *n*th time a match has been made. The function returns a value of 0 if the pattern is not found. It returns the offset from the start of the file where the match was found, or it returns a value of NULL if any of the parameters

▲   are null or invalid.

The READ Procedure

The READ procedure allows you to read part or all of a file into your machine's local memory.

▲ SYNTAX
▼

```
PROCEDURE READ(BFILE_Locator,
                   Read_Amount IN BINARY_INTEGER,
                   Starting_Location IN INTEGER,
                   Buffer OUT RAW);
```

In this syntax the parameters are as follows:

- *BFILE_Locator* is the BFILE locator assigned to the file from the BFILENAME function.
- *Read_Amount* is the number of bytes you read from the file into the buffer.
- *Starting_Location* is the location you want to start reading from in the file. For instance, you could read up to 32,768 bytes at a time from a file, and then store these in a BLOB in the Oracle database, and change the starting location by 32,768 each time you read the file.
▲
- *Buffer* is the location to store the contents of the file just read.

The VALUE_ERROR exception is raised if any of the parameters are NULL. The INVALID_ARGVAL exception is raised if any of the arguments are invalid. NO_DATA_FOUND is raised if you have reached the end of the file. If the file has not been opened, you get an UNOPENED_FILE exception.

The SUBSTR Function

The SUBSTR function allows you to extract a specified number of bytes from a file. This is often used when only a portion of the file is needed. For example you may only want part of the file for Quality Assurance testing.

14

▶ SYNTAX

```
FUNCTION SUBSTR(BFILE_Locator,
                        Read_Amount IN BINARY_INTEGER,
                        Starting_Location IN INTEGER := 1)
RETURN RAW;
```

In this syntax the parameters are as follows:

- *BFILE_Locator* is the BFILE locator assigned to the file from the BFILENAME function.

- *Read_Amount* is the number of bytes you want to extract from the file.

- *Starting_Location* is the position in the file where you want to start your extraction. The function returns a RAW value if successful.

▲

Exploring BFILE Examples, Using the DBMS_LOB Package

You can test all these functions and procedures with an anonymous PL/SQL block in the next several examples in this section. The functions and procedures common to internal and external LOBs, such as INSTR and SUBSTR, are demonstrated later in this lesson, in the section "Exploring Internal LOB Examples, Using the DBMS_LOB Package."

Accessing BFILEs

This first example demonstrates how to open files, close files, and do some minor error checking. Before you run any of these examples, make sure you have entered SET SERVEROUTPUT ON at the SQL*Plus prompt so you can see that the examples are working as they execute. Execute the code in Listing 14.2.

INPUT   **LISTING 14.2**   BFILE File Operations

```
 1: DECLARE
 2:
 3: /* This Anonymous PL/SQL block will demonstrate how to
 4:    open a BFILE, close the BFILE, and do some error checking
 5:    with FILEEXISTS, FILEISOPEN, and retrieve the Directory
 6:    Object and Path with GETFILENAME  */
 7:
 8:    v_BOOKFILE BFILE; -- BFILE to access
 9:    v_DIRNAME VARCHAR2(30); -- Holds Directory Object for FILEGETNAME
10:    v_LOCATION VARCHAR2(2000); -- Holds filename for FILEGETNAME
11:    v_FILEISOPEN INTEGER; -- Holds status to check if the file is open
12:    v_FILEEXISTS INTEGER; -- Holds status if the file actually exists
13:
14: BEGIN
```

```
15:        v_BOOKFILE := BFILENAME('BOOKS_DIR','BOOK1.GIF'); -- Create Locator
16:        v_FILEISOPEN := DBMS_LOB.FILEISOPEN(v_BOOKFILE);-- Check if file open
17:
       v_FILEEXISTS := DBMS_LOB.FILEEXISTS(v_BOOKFILE);
18:
19:        IF v_FILEEXISTS = 1 THEN
20:              DBMS_OUTPUT.PUT_LINE('The file exists');
21:        ELSE
22:              DBMS_OUTPUT.PUT_LINE('The file cannot be found');
23:        END IF;
24:
25:        IF v_FILEISOPEN = 1 THEN  --Determine actions if file is opened
26:              DBMS_OUTPUT.PUT_LINE('The file is open');
27:        ELSE
28:              DBMS_OUTPUT.PUT_LINE('Opening the file');
29:              DBMS_LOB.FILEOPEN(v_BOOKFILE);
30:        END IF;
31:        DBMS_LOB.FILEGETNAME(v_BOOKFILE,v_DIRNAME,v_LOCATION);
32:        DBMS_OUTPUT.PUT_LINE('The Directory Object is: ' || v_DIRNAME ||
33:              ' The File Name is: ' || v_LOCATION);
34:
35:        DBMS_LOB.FILECLOSE(v_BOOKFILE); -- Close the BFILE
36:
37: END;
```

After executing the code in Listing 14.4, your output will appear as

INPUT
```
The file exists
Opening the file
The Directory Object is: BOOKS_DIR The File Name is: BOOK1.GIF
```

ANALYSIS In the DECLARE section, a BFILE locator is defined as v_BOOKFILE. The v_DIRNAME and v_LOCATION variables hold the results of the FILEGETNAME function. The v_FILEISOPEN and v_FILEEXISTS variables hold the status if the file is open and if the file exists. The first step in the execution is to create the BFILE locator to the BOOKS_DIR path with the filename BOOK1.GIF. Both v_FILEISOPEN and v_FILEEXISTS are assigned values to see if the file is open and if the file exists. Because the FILEOPEN procedure was not called, this value will be 0. If you have created the path and copied the files to the BOOKS directory, you should receive a value of 1, which states that the file does exist, and you should see output stating that the file exists.

Because the FILEOPEN procedure returns the value 0, the file is not open. A message Opening the file is then displayed, and then the FILEOPEN procedure executes and opens the file for access from Oracle. Next, the FILEGETNAME procedure returns the directory object and the filename. Finally, the file is closed, and the execution ends.

14

Comparing Files

You can now practice comparing files and also getting the length of these files by executing the code in Listing 14.3.

INPUT **LISTING 14.3** BFILE Comparisons

```
 1: DECLARE
 2:
 3: /* The purpose of this anonymous PL/SQl block is to compare
 4:    the contents of three files completely.  The size of the
 5:    files is determined by the GETLENGTH function */
 6:
 7:     v_FILE1 BFILE;
 8:     v_FILE2 BFILE;
 9:     v_FILE3 BFILE;
10:     v_GETLENGTH1 INTEGER; -- Hold length of the file
11:     v_GETLENGTH2 INTEGER; -- Hold length of the file
12:     v_GETLENGTH3 INTEGER; -- Hold length of the file
13:     v_COMPARELENGTH INTEGER; -- Holds smallest of two values
14:     v_COMPARERESULT INTEGER; -- Hold result of comparing files
15:
16: BEGIN
17:
18: -- Create three locators for each of the files to compare
19:
20:     v_FILE1 := BFILENAME('BOOKS_DIR','BOOK1.GIF');
21:     v_FILE2 := BFILENAME('BOOKS_DIR','BOOK2.GIF');
22:     v_FILE3 := BFILENAME('BOOKS_DIR','BOOK5.GIF');
23:
24: -- Open the files for access
25:
26:     DBMS_LOB.FILEOPEN(v_FILE1);
27:     DBMS_LOB.FILEOPEN(v_FILE2);
28:     DBMS_LOB.FILEOPEN(v_FILE3);
29:
30:     v_GETLENGTH1 := DBMS_LOB.GETLENGTH(v_FILE1);
31:     v_GETLENGTH2 := DBMS_LOB.GETLENGTH(v_FILE2);
32:     v_GETLENGTH3 := DBMS_LOB.GETLENGTH(v_FILE3);
33:
34: -- Compare 1st and 2nd File
35:     IF v_GETLENGTH1 < v_GETLENGTH2 THEN
36:         v_COMPARELENGTH := v_GETLENGTH1;
37:     ELSE
38:         v_COMPARELENGTH := v_GETLENGTH2;
39:     END IF;
40:
41:     v_COMPARERESULT := DBMS_LOB.COMPARE(v_FILE1,v_FILE2,
42:         v_COMPARELENGTH,1,1);
```

```
43:
44:         IF v_COMPARERESULT = 0 THEN
45:             DBMS_OUTPUT.PUT_LINE('Both Files Are Identical');
46:         ELSE
47:             DBMS_OUTPUT.PUT_LINE('Both Files Are Different');
48:         END IF;
49:
50: -- Compare 1st and 3rd file
51:         IF v_GETLENGTH1 < v_GETLENGTH3 THEN
52:             v_COMPARELENGTH := v_GETLENGTH1;
53:         ELSE
54:             v_COMPARELENGTH := v_GETLENGTH3;
55:         END IF;
56:
57:         v_COMPARERESULT := DBMS_LOB.COMPARE(v_FILE1,v_FILE3,
58:             v_COMPARELENGTH,1,1);
59:
60:         IF v_COMPARERESULT = 0 THEN
61:             DBMS_OUTPUT.PUT_LINE('Both Files Are Identical');
62:         ELSE
63:             DBMS_OUTPUT.PUT_LINE('Both Files Are Different');
64:         END IF;
65:
66:         DBMS_LOB.FILECLOSEALL;
67:
68: END;
```

OUTPUT
```
Both Files Are Different
Both Files Are Identical
```

ANALYSIS First, you define several variables for each of the three files to be compared. Three locators are defined as v_FILE1, v_FILE2, and v_FILE3. The file lengths of each of these files are stored in v_GETLENGTH1, v_GETLENGTH2, and v_GETLENGTH3. Both v_COMPARERESULT and v_COMPARELENGTH are used for storing the length of the files.

When the code starts to execute, the three locators are assigned values of three files. These three files are then opened, and the length of each is retrieved. The lengths of the first two files are compared. The smallest value is stored in v_COMPARELENGTH. If the length to compare was used for the larger file, an exception would be raised because you would attempt to compare the smaller file after the end of the file has been reached. The variable v_COMPARERESULT is assigned the result of comparing the first two files. These files are not identical, and the output correctly states this. The process is repeated for the first and third files, which are identical. The FILECLOSEALL procedure is executed to close all three files and free up the resources.

14

Working with Locators

Locators are stored in the large object column and point to the location of where the actual data is stored. It is important for you to understand what occurs at a transactional level when using Oracle locators. When copying LOBs from one row to the next, a new locator is created, and all the data is copied and stored from the source row. This is necessary because if you were to delete one row and you did not copy the entire contents to the new row, all the data of the LOB would be lost. When deleting internal LOBs, the locator and the contents of the LOB are both deleted. If you're deleting external BFILEs, the file remains but the locator is deleted. When adding internal LOBs to a table, you need to create the locator either by assigning data to the LOB column or using the function EMPTY_BLOB or EMPTY_CLOB. When adding a BFILE to the table, you would use BFILENAME to assign a locator to the column. The last issue applies to internal LOBs only. It is a good idea to lock the LOB when working with it to prevent other users from accessing the LOB.

Using the DBMS_LOB Package with Internal LOBs

Oracle's DBMS_LOB package allows you to manipulate all types of LOBs. Because the BFILE datatype is of type RAW, additional files work with the database character set. Table 14.3 summarizes the functions and procedures that work with internal LOBs.

TABLE 14.3   Functions and Procedures Used with Internal LOBs

Function or Procedure	Accessed By	Description
APPEND	Internal LOBs	Appends one LOB to another LOB.
COMPARE	All LOBs	Compares all or part of two LOBs.
COPY	Internal LOBs	Copies a LOB from one row to another.
EMPTY_BLOB	BLOB	Creates a locator in a BLOB column.
EMPTY_CLOB	CLOB	Creates a locator in a CLOB column.
ERASE	Internal LOBs	Erases all or part of an internal LOB.
GETLENGTH	All LOBs	Returns the length of the LOB.
INSTR	All LOBs	Searches for matching patterns in a LOB, with the string of characters specified.
READ	All LOBs	Reads a specific amount of a LOB into the buffer.
SUBSTR	All LOBs	Returns the part or all of the LOB specified by the parameters.
TRIM	Internal LOBs	Reduces a LOB to the length specified.
WRITE	Internal LOBs	Writes data to a LOB.

The following sections describe each of these functions in more detail and show you examples of the syntax of each.

The APPEND Procedure

The APPEND procedure allows you to append one LOB to another LOB. The syntax for the APPEND procedure is as follows.

```
PROCEDURE APPEND(Dest_Locator IN OUT BLOB,
                Source_Locator  IN BLOB);


PROCEDURE APPEND(Dest_Locator IN OUT CLOB CHARACTER SET Set_Desired,
                Source_Locator  IN CLOB CHARACTER SET Dest_Locator%CHARSET);
```

In this syntax the parameters are as follows:

- *Dest_Locator* is the locator for the destination LOB that is appended by the source LOB.

- *Source_Locator* identifies the source LOB.

▲

- *Set_Desired* is used, when working with CLOBs, to specify the character set.

The COMPARE Function

If you need to compare all or part of a LOB, you can use the COMPARE function. An example of the syntax for the COMPARE function can be seen below.

```
FUNCTION COMPARE(
                Lob1 IN BLOB,
                Lob2 IN BLOB,
                Number_Bytes_to_Compare IN INTEGER,
                Origin_Lob1    IN INTEGER := 1,
                Origin_Lob2    IN INTEGER := 1)
RETURN Compare_Result_Integer;

FUNCTION COMPARE(
                Lob1 IN CLOB CHARACTER SET Set_Desired,
                Lob2 IN CLOB CHARACTER SET LOB1%CHARSET,,
                Number_Bytes_to_Compare IN INTEGER,
                Origin_Lob1    IN INTEGER := 1,
                Origin_Lob2    IN INTEGER := 1)
RETURN Compare_Result_Integer;
```

In this syntax the parameters are as follows:

- *Lob1* is the first LOB you are comparing.

- *Lob2* is the second LOB you are comparing.

- *Set_Desired* is the character set you want to use. If no character set is specified, the Oracle server's character set is used.

▼

14

▼

- *Number_Bytes_to_Compare* is the total number of bytes you want to compare from *Lob1* to *Lob2*.

- *Origin_Lob1* is the starting location in the LOB where you want to compare. You could use the value 1 to start from the beginning of the LOB, or you could enter 100 to start comparing from the 100th byte.

- *Origin_Lob2* is the starting location of the second LOB you want to compare. The value returned is either 0 if the data is identical, nonzero if the data is not identical, or NULL if any of the parameters are invalid, such as an incorrect starting origin, comparing bytes past the end of the LOB, or any other invalid parameter.

▲

The COPY Procedure

The COPY procedure allows you to copy all or part of a LOB from one row to another. The entire LOB is copied with a new locator entered into the table, which points to the copy of the original LOB.

▼ SYNTAX

```
PROCEDURE COPY(Dest_Locator IN OUT BLOB,
              Source_Locator  IN BLOB,
              Amount IN OUT INTEGER,
              Dest_Start_Position IN INTEGER := 1,
              Source_Start_Position IN INTEGER := 1);


PROCEDURE APPEND(Dest_Locator IN OUT CLOB CHARACTER SET Set_Desired,
              Source_Locator  IN CLOB CHARACTER SET Dest_Locator%CHARSET,
              Amount IN OUT INTEGER,
              Dest_Start_Position IN INTEGER := 1,
              Source_Start_Position IN INTEGER := 1);
```

In this syntax the parameters are as follows:

- *Dest_Locator* is the locator for the destination LOB that is being copied.

- *Set_Desired* is the character set you want to use. If no character set is specified, the Oracle server's character set is used.

- *Source_Locator* is the locator of the source LOB being copied.

- *Amount* is how much of the LOB you intend to copy.

- *Dest_Start_Position* and *Source_Start_Position* are the locations in the LOB to copy from and to. The value 1 indicates the starting position of the LOB.

▲

The EMPTY_BLOB Function

To add a BLOB to a table, you need to assign a locator to the BLOB by using the EMPTY_BLOB function.

SYNTAX

```
FUNCTION EMPTY_BLOB();
    RETURN Locator;
```

In this syntax *Locator* is the locator for the BLOB returned by the function.

The EMPTY_CLOB Function

To add a CLOB to a table, you need to assign a locator to the CLOB with the EMPTY_CLOB function.

SYNTAX

```
FUNCTION EMPTY_CLOB();
    RETURN Locator;
```

This function returns a locator for the CLOB, defined in the syntax as *Locator*.

The ERASE Procedure

The ERASE procedure allows you to erase all or part of a LOB.

▼ SYNTAX

```
PROCEDURE ERASE(BLOB_Locator IN OUT BLOB,
                    Amount IN OUT INTEGER,
                    Start_Position IN INTEGER := 1);


PROCEDURE APPEND(CLOB_Locator IN OUT CLOB ,
                    Amount IN OUT INTEGER,
                    Start_Position IN INTEGER := 1);
```

In this syntax the parameters are as follows:

- *BLOB_Locator* and *CLOB_Locator* indicate the locator assigned to the LOB.
- *Amount* is how much of the LOB you want to erase. You could use the GETLENGTH function to return the length and specify this as the amount in order to erase the contents of the entire LOB.
- *Start_Position* is the starting position from which you want to erase part or all of the LOB. The value 1 is the beginning of the LOB.

▲

14

The GETLENGTH Function

The GETLENGTH function returns the length of an object in bytes. The syntax for the
GETLENGTH function follows.

▼ SYNTAX

```
FUNCTION GETLENGTH (BLOB_Locator)
    RETURN Length_Integer;

FUNCTION GETLENGTH (CLOB_Locator CHARACTER SET Set_Desired)
    RETURN Length_Integer;
```

In this syntax the parameters are as follows:

- *BLOB_Locator* and *CLOB_Locator* indicate the locator assigned to the LOB.

- *Set_Desired* is the Oracle character set you want to use. The function returns an
  INTEGER of the length of the LOB or NULL if the locator is null.

The INSTR Function

The INSTR function allows you to match a pattern against the *n*th occurrence in the LOB,
starting from the offset specified.

▼ SYNTAX

```
FUNCTION INSTR(BLOB_Locator,
               Pattern IN RAW,
               Starting Location IN INTEGER := 1,
               Nth_Occurrence IN INTEGER := 1)
RETURN Status_Integer;

FUNCTION INSTR(CLOB_Locator CHARACTER SET Set_Desired,
                Pattern IN VARCHAR2 CHARACTER SET CLOB_Locator%CHARSET,
               Starting Location IN INTEGER := 1,
               Nth_Occurrence IN INTEGER := 1)
RETURN Status_Integer;
```

In this syntax the parameters are as follows:

- *BLOB_Locator* and *CLOB_Locator* indicate the BFILE locator assigned to the LOB.

- *Set_Desired* is the character set you want to use. If it is not specified, the character set used for the Oracle database will be used.

- The *Pattern* of type RAW or VARCHAR2 is the pattern you want to match in the LOB.

- *Starting_Location* is the position in the LOB where you want to start the search
  for a match.

- *Nth_Occurrence* is the *n*th time a match has been made in the LOB. The function
  returns 0 if the pattern is not found. It returns the offset from the start of the LOB
  where the match was found, or it returns NULL if any of the parameters are null or
  invalid.

The READ Procedure

The READ procedure allows you to read part or all of a LOB into the memory of your system. The following syntax box will show the proper usage for the READ procedure .

SYNTAX

```
PROCEDURE READ(BLOB_Locator,
               Read_Amount IN BINARY_INTEGER,
               Starting_Location IN INTEGER,
               Buffer OUT RAW);

PROCEDURE READ(CLOB_Locator CHARACTER SET Set_Desired,
               Read_Amount IN BINARY_INTEGER,
               Starting_Location IN INTEGER,
               Buffer OUT VARCHAR2 CHARACTER SET CLOB_Locator%CHARSET);
```

In this syntax the parameters are as follows:

- *BLOB_Locator* and *CLOB_Locator* indicate the locator assigned to the LOB.
- *Set_Desired* is the character set you want to use. If no character set is specified, the Oracle server's character set is used.
- *Read_Amount* is the number of bytes to read from the LOB into the buffer.
- *Buffer* stores the data from the READ procedure.
- *Starting_Location* is the location where you want to start reading from the LOB. The VALUE_ERROR exception is raised if any of the parameters are null. The INVALID_ARGVAL exception is raised if any of the arguments are invalid. NO_DATA_FOUND is raised if you have reached the end of the LOB.

The SUBSTR Function

The SUBSTR function allows you to extract a specified number of bytes from a LOB. There could be a variety of reasons why you would only want a portion of the LOB. For example, you may only want the last portion of the LOB to ensure all of the LOB was loaded correctly.

SYNTAX

```
FUNCTION SUBSTR(BLOB_Locator,
                Read_Amount IN BINARY_INTEGER,
                Starting_Location IN INTEGER := 1)
RETURN RAW;

FUNCTION SUBSTR(CLOB_Locator CHARACTER SET Set_Desired,
                Read_Amount IN BINARY_INTEGER,
                Starting_Location IN INTEGER := 1)
RETURN VARCHAR2 CHARACTER SET CLOB_Locator%CHARSET;
```

14

▼ In this syntax the parameters are as follows:

- *BLOB_Locator* and *CLOB_Locator* indicate the locator assigned to the LOB.

- *Set_Desired* is the character set you want to use. If no character set is specified, the Oracle server's character set is used.

- *Read_Amount* is the number of bytes you want to extract from the LOB.

- *Starting_Location* is the position in the LOB where you want to start the extrac-
▲   tion. The function returns a RAW value if successful for a BLOB, or VARCHAR2 for a
     CLOB.

The TRIM Procedure

The TRIM procedure allows you to reduce the LOB to the length specified.

```
PROCEDURE TRIM(BLOB_Locator,New_Length IN INTEGER);
```

```
PROCEDURE TRIM(CLOB_Locator,New_Length IN INTEGER);
```

In this syntax the variables and parameters are as follows:

- *BLOB_Locator* and *CLOB_Locator* indicate the locators assigned to the LOB.

- *New_Length* is the new length desired for the LOB.

The WRITE Procedure

If you can read a LOB, you should be able to write to a LOB. The WRITE procedure allows you to write to a LOB.

```
PROCEDURE WRITE(BLOB_Locator,
                Amount IN OUT INTEGER,
                Starting_Position IN INTEGER,
                Buffer IN RAW);
```

```
PROCEDURE WRITE(CLOB_Locator CHARACTER SET Set_Desired,
                Amount IN OUT INTEGER,
                Starting_Position IN INTEGER,
                Buffer IN VARCHAR2 CHARACTER SET CLOB_Locator%CHARSET);
```

In this syntax the parameters are as follows:

- *BLOB_Locator* and *CLOB_Locator* indicate the locator assigned.

- *Set_Desired* is the character set you want to use. If no character set is specified, the Oracle server's character set is used.

- *Amount* is how many bytes to write to the LOB.

- *Starting_Position* is the position you want to write in the LOB.

- *Buffer* is the buffer of the data to write to the LOB.

Exploring Internal LOB Examples, Using the DBMS_LOB Package

You can now test these previously described LOB functions and procedures using an anonymous PL/SQL block in the next several examples for internal LOBs. These examples will walk you through the steps necessary to create and use LOBs.

Creating a Table

Before you can work with LOBs, you first need to create and populate a table. Before you run any of these examples, make sure that you have entered SET SERVEROUTPUT ON at the SQL*Plus prompt so that you can see that the examples are working as they execute. Execute the code in Listing 14.4 to create the table called LOBS.

INPUT **LISTING 14.4** Creating an Internal LOB Table

```
CREATE TABLE LOBS(
    lob_index INTEGER,
    CLOB_Locator CLOB)
/
```

OUTPUT Table created.

ANALYSIS After the code has executed, the output should say Table Created. You just created a table with two columns. The first column, lob_index, stores an integer value that identifies the LOB. The second column is where the locator is stored for the CLOB datatype.

Adding Data to the Table

You can now add data of type CLOB to the table. Execute the code in Listing 14.5 to populate the LOBS table with some preliminary data.

INPUT **LISTING 14.5** Populating the CLOB Table

```
1: INSERT INTO LOBS VALUES(1,'Teach Yourself Oracle8i in 21 Days')
/
2: INSERT INTO LOBS VALUES(2,'Oracle Data Warehousing Unleashed')
/
3: INSERT INTO LOBS VALUES(3,'Teach Yourself Database Development With
    Oracle in 21 Days')
/
```

14

continues

LISTING **14.5**   continued

```
4: INSERT INTO LOBS VALUES(4,'Oracle Unleashed 2E')
/
5: INSERT INTO LOBS VALUES(5,EMPTY_CLOB())
/
6: INSERT INTO LOBS VALUES(6,EMPTY_CLOB())
/
```

ANALYSIS Lines 5 and 6 initialize a locator with no data. To verify that the LOBS table was populated, at the SQL prompt enter

INPUT   `SELECT * FROM LOBS;`

OUTPUT

```
LOB_INDEX CLOB_LOCATOR
--------- ----------------------------------------------------------------
        1 Teach Yourself Oracle8i in 21 Days
        2 Oracle Data Warehousing Unleashed
        3 Teach Yourself Database Development With Oracle in 21 Days
        4 Oracle Unleashed 2E
        5
        6
```

Populating the LOBS Table with the COPY Procedure

Listing 14.6 contains an example with internal LOBs, which uses the procedure COPY to copy two rows where no data exists.

INPUT   LISTING **14.6**   Copying Internal LOBs

```
 1: DECLARE
 2:    Source_Lob   CLOB;
 3:    Dest_Lob   CLOB;
 4:    Copy_Amount INTEGER;
 5: BEGIN
 6:    SELECT CLOB_LOCATOR into Dest_LOB
 7:        FROM LOBS
 8:        WHERE LOB_INDEX = 5 FOR UPDATE; -- FOR UPDATE locks the ROW
 9:    SELECT CLOB_LOCATOR into Source_LOB
10:        FROM LOBS
11:        WHERE LOB_INDEX = 1;
12:    Copy_Amount := DBMS_LOB.GETLENGTH(Source_Lob);
13:    DBMS_LOB.COPY(Dest_LOB, Source_LOB,Copy_Amount);
14:    COMMIT;
15: -- Start second copy process
16:    SELECT CLOB_LOCATOR into Dest_LOB
17:        FROM LOBS
18:        WHERE LOB_INDEX = 6 FOR UPDATE;
19:    SELECT CLOB_LOCATOR into Source_LOB
```

```
20:        FROM LOBS
21:        WHERE LOB_INDEX = 2;
22:    Copy_Amount := DBMS_LOB.GETLENGTH(Source_Lob);
23:    DBMS_LOB.COPY(Dest_LOB, Source_LOB,Copy_Amount);
24:    COMMIT;
25: END;
```

To verify that the COPY procedure worked, at the SQL prompt type

INPUT

```
SELECT * FROM LOBS;
```

OUTPUT

```
LOB_INDEX CLOB_LOCATOR
--------- ---------------------------------------------------------------
--
        1 Teach Yourself Oracle8i in 21 Days
        2 Oracle Data Warehousing Unleashed
        3 Teach Yourself Database Development With Oracle in 21 Days
        4 Oracle Unleashed 2E
        5 Teach Yourself Oracle8 in 21 Days
        6 Oracle Data Warehousing Unleashed
```

ANALYSIS Two LOBs are defined as type CLOB, which stores the locator for the source and destination LOBs. The Copy_Amount variable stores how much of the Source_Lob is to be copied. In this case, you assign this value to the length of the Source_Lob by using the GETLENGTH function. The locators are then read into Source_Lob and Dest_Lob. The COPY procedure then copies from the source to the destination LOB, and then commits the transaction.

Manipulating Internal LOBs by Using APPEND and WRITE

Next, you can practice appending from one LOB to another, and even writing to a LOB. In this example you will append row 1 to row 5 and then write a text value to row 6. Execute the code in Listing 14.7.

INPUT **LISTING 14.7** Appending and Writing to LOBs

```
1: DECLARE
2: /* This appends the contents of Row 1 to the contents of Row 5.
3:    In addition, it writes text at the end of the values in
4:    Row 6.  */
5:
6:    Source_Lob    CLOB;
7:    Dest_Lob    CLOB;
8:    Write_Amount INTEGER := 10;
9:    Writing_Position INTEGER ;
```

continues

14

LISTING 14.7 continued

```
10:      Buffer VARCHAR2(10) := 'Added Text';
11: BEGIN
12: -- Append from Row 1 to Row 5
13:      SELECT CLOB_LOCATOR into Dest_LOB
14:          FROM LOBS
15:          WHERE LOB_INDEX = 5 FOR UPDATE; -- Locks Row for Update
16:      SELECT CLOB_LOCATOR into Source_LOB
17:          FROM LOBS
18:          WHERE LOB_INDEX = 1;
19:      DBMS_LOB.APPEND(Dest_LOB, Source_LOB);
20:      COMMIT;
21: -- Write to a LOB
22:      SELECT CLOB_LOCATOR into Source_LOB
23:          FROM LOBS
24:          WHERE LOB_INDEX = 6 FOR UPDATE;   -- Locks Row for Update
25:
26:      Writing_Position := DBMS_LOB.GETLENGTH(Source_Lob) + 1;
27:      DBMS_LOB.WRITE(Source_LOB,Write_Amount,Writing_Position,Buffer);
28:      COMMIT;
29: END;
```

To verify that the WRITE and APPEND procedures from the previous example worked, at the SQL prompt type

INPUT

```
SELECT * FROM LOBS;
```

OUTPUT

```
LOB_INDEX CLOB_LOCATOR
--------- -----------------------------------------------------------------
        1 Teach Yourself Oracle8 in 21 Days
        2 Oracle Data Warehousing Unleashed
        3 Teach Yourself Database Development With Oracle in 21 Days
        4 Oracle Unleashed 2E
        5 Teach Yourself Oracle8 in 21 DaysTe
          ach Yourself Oracl
          e 8 in 21 Days
        6 Oracle Data Warehousing UnleashedAdded Text
```

ANALYSIS As you can see from the output, you appended Row 1 to Row 5, and you also added text to Row 6. For the purposes of the APPEND procedure, two variables of type CLOB are created for the source and destination location. For the WRITE procedure, three additional variables are created to hold how much data to write (stored in Write_Amount), where to start writing in the CLOB (stored in Writing_Position), and the text to write to the CLOB (stored in the Buffer variable). The procedure copies the source and destination locators into the corresponding variables and calls the APPEND procedure. The transaction is then committed.

The second part of the procedure selects the row where text will be added, locks the row for updating, assigns the starting position to the length of the contents + 1 (so no data is overwritten), and calls the WRITE procedure. This transaction is then committed.

Analyzing the Contents of an Internal LOB

In this section, you can analyze the contents of an internal LOB by working with the functions INSTR and SUBSTR. Execute the code in Listing 14.8, and make sure that you have entered SET SERVEROUTPUT ON at the SQL*Plus prompt so you can see output as the program executes.

INPUT   **LISTING 14.8**   Extracting and Matching Data Inside CLOBs

```
 1: DECLARE
 2: /* This PL/SQL block finds patterns in a CLOB.  It also
 3:    extracts part of the data from a CLOB with SUBSTR */
 4:
 5:     Source_Lob   CLOB;
 6:     v_Pattern VARCHAR2(6) := 'Oracle';
 7:     v_Starting_Location INTEGER := 1;
 8:     v_Nth_Occurrence INTEGER := 1;
 9:     v_Position INTEGER ;
10:     v_Extract_Amount INTEGER;
11:     v_Buffer VARCHAR2(100) ;
12: BEGIN
13: -- Search for 1st Occurrence of Oracle in Row 5
14:     SELECT CLOB_LOCATOR into Source_LOB
15:         FROM LOBS
16:         WHERE LOB_INDEX = 5;
17:     v_Position := DBMS_LOB.INSTR(Source_LOB,v_Pattern,
18:         v_Starting_Location,v_Nth_Occurrence);
19:     DBMS_OUTPUT.PUT_LINE('The first occurrence starts at position: '
20:         ¦¦ v_Position);
21:
22: -- Search for 2nd Occurrence of Oracle in Row 5
23:
24:     v_Nth_Occurrence := 2;
25:
26:     SELECT CLOB_LOCATOR into Source_LOB
27:         FROM LOBS
28:         WHERE LOB_INDEX = 5;
29:     v_Position := DBMS_LOB.INSTR(Source_LOB,v_Pattern,
30:         v_Starting_Location,v_Nth_Occurrence);
31:     DBMS_OUTPUT.PUT_LINE('The second occurrence starts at position: '
32:         ¦¦ v_Position);
33:
34: -- Extract part of the data from a CLOB
```

continues

14

LISTING **14.8**   continued

```
35:     SELECT CLOB_LOCATOR into Source_LOB
36:         FROM LOBS
37:             WHERE LOB_INDEX = 6;
38:     v_Buffer := DBMS_LOB.SUBSTR(Source_LOB,11,v_Starting_Location);
39:     DBMS_OUTPUT.PUT_LINE('The substring extracted is: '  || v_Buffer);
40:
41: END;
42:
```

OUTPUT
The first occurrence starts at position: 16
The second occurrence starts at position: 49
The substring extracted is: Oracle Data

ANALYSIS The procedure begins by selecting the data from Row 5, and reading the locator into the Source_Lob variable. Using the INSTR function, the pattern 'Oracle', assigned to the v_Pattern variable, is searched for the first occurrence, specified by the v_Nth_Occurrence variable. The Starting Location is defaulted to the first position in the CLOB, stored in the v_Starting_Location variable. The process is repeated, except that you are now searching for the second occurrence of 'Oracle' in the CLOB.

The last part of the procedure extracts 11 characters from Row 6, and stores them in v_Buffer, which is then displayed to the screen.

Using TRIM and ERASE to Edit CLOBs

This sections demonstrates the use of the TRIM and ERASE procedures. Execute the code in Listing 14.9.

INPUT   LISTING **14.9**   Reducing Data in CLOBs

```
 1: DECLARE
 2: /* This erases the data in Row 6, and trims the data in
 3:    row 5 to one occurrence of the book title. */
 4:
 5:     Source_Lob    CLOB;
 6:     Erase_Amount INTEGER;
 7:     Trim_Amount INTEGER;
 8:
 9: BEGIN
10: -- Erase the data completely in Row 6
11:
12:     SELECT CLOB_LOCATOR into Source_LOB
13:         FROM LOBS
14:             WHERE LOB_INDEX = 6 FOR UPDATE; -- Locks Row for Update
15:     Erase_Amount :=DBMS_LOB.GETLENGTH(Source_LOB);
```

```
16:       DBMS_LOB.ERASE(Source_LOB,Erase_Amount,1);
17:
18: --Reduce Data in Row 5 to one instance of Book Title
19:       SELECT CLOB_LOCATOR into Source_LOB
20:           FROM LOBS
21:           WHERE LOB_INDEX = 5 FOR UPDATE;
22:
23:       TRIM_AMOUNT := DBMS_LOB.GETLENGTH(Source_LOB) / 2;
24:       DBMS_LOB.TRIM(Source_LOB, TRIM_AMOUNT);
25:       COMMIT;
26:
27: END;
```

To verify that the ERASE and TRIM procedures worked, at the SQL prompt type

INPUT

```
SELECT * FROM LOBS;
```

OUTPUT

```
LOB_INDEX CLOB_LOCATOR
......... ...............................................................
        1 Teach Yourself Oracle8 in 21 Days
        2 Oracle Data Warehousing Unleashed
        3 Teach Yourself Database Development With Oracle in 21 Days
        4 Oracle Unleashed 2E
        5 Teach Yourself Oracle8 in 21 Days
        6
```

ANALYSIS Three variables are declared:

- Source_Lob holds the locator for the CLOBs you will alter.

- Erase_Amount holds the number of bytes to erase from Row 6.

- Trim_Amount stores the number of bytes that should remain in Row 5.

The procedure starts by reading the locator for the CLOB into the variable Source_Lob. Erase_Amount is assigned the value of the length of the data in Row 6 by using the GETLENGTH function. The ERASE procedure is called and passes the CLOB locator, the total bytes to erase, and the starting position for erasing the data, which is hard-coded to the value 1 in this example.

The second half of the block reduces the data in Row 5 by half. The locator for the CLOB in Row 5 is read into the variable Source_Lob. The Amount of data to remain is calculated by taking the total length of the data by using the GETLENGTH function, and dividing this value by 2. The TRIM procedure is called, passing the locator and the amount of bytes to remain. The transactions are then committed.

14

Temporary LOBs

Oracle8i introduced *temporary LOBs*, which are synonymous with local variables and do not exist permanently in the database. The most common usage of temporary LOBs is for performing transformations on LOB data. By default their life span is the duration of the session.

One of the biggest advantages of temporary LOBs is their ability to improve performance over the usage of persistent LOBs. By default LOBs are persistent in nature unless otherwise defined. This improved performance is gained because there are no redo records of logging occurring when temporary LOBs are used. Likewise, you can explicitly remove a temporary LOB, thereby freeing up additional memory and tablespace.

PL/SQL operates on temporary LOBs through locators in the same way as for persistent LOBs. Because temporary LOBs are never part of any table, you cannot use SQL Data Manipulation Language (DML) to operate on them. You must manipulated them by using the DBMS_LOB package as you would with persistent LOBs. Security is provided through the LOB locator. Only the user who created the temporary LOB can access it. Locators are not designed to be passed from one user's session to another.

 Note

> When you copy a persistent LOB into a temporary LOB locator, the temporary LOB locator points to the persistent LOB. The persistent LOB is not copied into the temporary LOB—only the locators are affected.

Managing Temporary LOBs

All temporary LOBs are recorded in the v$temporary_LOBS view. A simple selection on this view will display all temporary LOBs currently valid for that session. This is a great place to monitor for unwanted overhead of unnecessary temporary LOBs.

Creating Temporary LOBs

To create temporary LOBs, you use the procedure CREATETEMPORARY, which resides in the DBMS_LOB package. The Syntax for calling this procedure is as follows.

▼ SYNTAX

```
DBMS_LOB.CREATETEMPORARY (lob_loc, cache, dur);
```

In this syntax the parameters are as follows:

- *lob_loc* is the location of the LOB.

- *cache* specifies whether the LOB should be read into the database buffer.

- *dur* is one of two predefined duration values (SESSION or CALL), which specifies
  whether the temporary LOB is cleaned up at the end of the session or call. The
  default value for this parameter is duration.

▲

The following example illustrates the creation of a temporary LOB:

INPUT
```
begin
DBMS_LOB.CREATETEMPORARY
(Dest_Loc,
TRUE,
DBMS_LOB.SESSION);
End;
```

ANALYSIS In this example a temporary LOB is created that will be loaded into the buffer and
remain in existence for the duration of the current session. After this session is
completed, the temporary LOB will disappear, and all memory and tablespace allocated to
it will be returned.

Summary

In this lesson you have learned how Oracle handles large objects, referred to as LOBs. The
two types of LOBs are internal and external LOBs. Internal LOBs can be persistent or temporary. External LOBs, called BFILEs, are files accessible to the operating system, rather
than data stored in a table. Internal LOBs can also be binary, character, multicharacter, and
fixed width. These have full transactional support and can be committed or rolled back.
LOBs can have a maximum size of 4GB, or the size of an unsigned LONG integer.

Q&A

Q **What is the difference between an external and an internal LOB?**

A Internal LOBs are stored within the Oracle database. External LOBs are stored and
maintained by the operating system.

Q **What possible uses are there for LOBs?**

A You can use LOBs to easily store and track pictures, large text files, and sound files,
which can then be used by front-end systems to display or play back the data.

14

Q How are paths accessed by Oracle?

A A path is defined as a directory object, which you create by using the SQL statement `CREATE DIRECTORY`.

Workshop

You can use this to test your comprehension of this lesson and put what you've learned into practice. You'll find the answers to the quiz and exercises in Appendix A, "Answers."

Quiz

1. What are the two types of internal LOBs?
2. What is the maximum size of a LOB?
3. Can you write to external files?
4. When copying LOBs from one row to another, is a new locator copied?

Exercise

Create a temporary LOB that is of BLOB datatype, that will not be stored in the buffer, and that will be limited to the current call.

WEEK 2

In Review

8

You have finished your second week of learning how to program in PL/SQL. The week started with learning about SQL, creating and using tables, and working with stored procedures and packages. You know all about encapsulation and grouping similar procedures and functions together in packages. You have also learned how to plan for and react to certain runtime errors that can arise in PL/SQL code. This includes how to write exception-handling routines to handle internal and user-defined PL/SQL processing errors.

9

On Day 9 you learned how to manipulate data with PL/SQL cursors. Cursors are wonderful constructs in that they enable you to process a multiple-row query result set one row at a time. You also learned how to pass arguments into cursors and how to use cursors as variables.

10

You have also, on Day 10, learned about the various PL/SQL collection types. On Day 11, you learned how to use triggers, which are automatically executed in response to certain SQL statements and database events. On Day 12, you were introduced to Oracle8i's object features.

11

12

On Day 13, you learned how to prepare for errors and write error-handling routines to help prevent unwanted termination of your PL/SQL programs' execution. Finally, the week ended on Day 14 with you learning how to use the Oracle 8i large object datatypes.

13

14

WEEK 3

15

At a Glance

16

At this point, you should have mastered the basics of Oracle's PL/SQL language, from functions to procedures to cursors. With this knowledge, you can now master the packages supplied by Oracle, which offer some additional advanced features. Each chapter guides you through a package or concept and demonstrates its topic through an actual example you can try.

17

Where You Are Going

18

Day 15 covers advanced topics such as managing transactions and locks. You will then continue with the topics of dynamically creating SQL and writing to external files. Next you are exposed to the Oracle-provided package DBMS_JOB. Later in the week, you will see how sessions communicate using the DBMS_PIPE package and learn how to manage alerts by using the DBMS_ALERT package. Toward the end of the week you will learn about the Java engine, which is a new feature of Oracle 8i. You'll see how Java classes can be loaded into the database, and you'll learn how you can interface your PL/SQL code to Java methods. Finally, the week ends with a discussion on how to use Oracle8i's Advanced Queuing features.

19

20

This is your last week reading this book. It's the week with the toughest and most challenging topics, but they are also the most interesting topics. So forge ahead, and good luck!

21

WEEK 2

DAY 15

Managing Transactions and Locks

by Tom Luers

Today you will cover transactions and locks, plus the benefits you can gain by controlling them. Managing transactions provides the user of the Oracle server, the application developer, or the database administrator the capability of guaranteeing data consistency and data concurrency. Data consistency provides the user a consistent view of data, which consists of data committed by other users as well as changes made by the user. Data concurrency provides the user access to data concurrently used by many other users. Without transactions coordinating data concurrency and data consistency, the user of the server would experience inconsistent data reads, lost updates, and nonrepeatable reads. In today's transaction and locks lesson you will learn:

- Starting and stopping transactions
- Implementing two-phase commits
- Using savepoints
- Using locks

Types of Transactions

NEW TERM A *transaction* is a logical unit of work that is composed of one or more Data Manipulation Language (DML) or Data Definition Language (DDL) statements. For every transaction in Oracle, two situations can occur. If the statements in a transaction complete normally, then the effects of the transaction are made permanent in the database. This is called *committing* the transactions. The other situation occurs when any one of the statements is unable to complete for whatever reason. In this case, the effects of the transaction are removed from the database and the transaction ends. This removal of the effects of a transaction is called *rolling back* the transaction.

NEW TERM Oracle provides two general types of transactions: read-only and read-write transactions. The *read-only* transaction specifies that the queried data and all queries within the same transaction will not be affected by any other transactions that take place in the database. In other words, any subsequent query can only read changes committed prior to the beginning of the current transaction. The *read-write* transaction guarantees that data returned by a query is consistent with respect to the time the query began.

The read-only transaction enforces transaction-level read consistency. This type of transaction can contain only queries and cannot contain any DML statements. In this situation, only data committed prior to the start of the transaction is available to the query. Thus, a query can be executed multiple times and return the same results each time.

The read-write transaction provides for statement-level read consistency. This type of transaction will never see any of the changes made by transactions that commit during the course of a query execution.

Starting a Transaction

A transaction begins with the first SQL statement being executed and ends when the effects of the transaction are saved or backed out. The SET TRANSACTION command also initiates a transaction.

The SET TRANSACTION command is an integral part of transaction management. This command performs one of these operations on the current transaction:

- Establishes the transaction as either a read-only or a read-write transaction.
- Assigns your current read-write transaction to a specified rollback segment.

15

▼ SYNTAX

```
SET TRANSACTION parameter
```

In this syntax, *parameter* can be one of the following values:

- `READ ONLY`—Establishes transaction-level read consistency.

- `READ WRITE`—Establishes statement-level read consistency.

- `ISOLATION LEVEL`—Establishes how DML transactions are handled. You have two options here: `SERIALIZABLE` and `READ COMMITTED`. The `SERIALIZABLE` options causes any DML transaction to fail if it attempts to manipulate any data object that has been modified and not committed. The `READ COMMITTED` causes the same DML transaction to wait for the previous DML lock to disappear. This is the default nature of Oracle.

▲   - `USE ROLLBACK SEGMENT`—Defines the appropriate rollback segment to be used.

The read-only transaction is the default mode of all transactions. With this mode, you do not have a rollback segment assigned. Additionally, you cannot perform an `INSERT`, a `DELETE`, an `UPDATE`, or a `SELECT FOR UPDATE` clause command during this transaction. The read-write transaction mode provides no restrictions on the DML statements allowed in the transaction.

The `SET TRANSACTION` command allows you to explicitly assign a particular rollback segment to the read-write transaction. This rollback segment is used to undo any changes made by the current transaction should a rollback be executed. If you do not specify a rollback segment, Oracle assigns one to the transaction.

The following example of the `SET TRANSACTION` command would allow the user to run this script every weekend without worrying about any other users who might be modifying data:

```
COMMIT;
SET TRANSACTION read only;
execute_emp_change_2;
COMMIT;
```

Ending a Transaction

Ending a transaction means that either the changes made by the transaction are saved or that all changes are backed out. As you learned previously in this lesson, saving all pending changes to the database is known as committing the transaction. Backing out is accomplished through the `ROLLBACK` statement or when there is abnormal termination in the transaction. The `ROLLBACK` statement is discussed further in the next section, "Canceling a Transaction."

Committing occurs when the user either explicitly or implicitly saves the transaction changes to the database permanently. Until you perform a commit, the following principles characterize the state of your transaction:

- DML operations affect only the database buffer. Because the changes have only affected the buffer, these changes can be backed out.
- A rollback segment buffer is created in the server.
- The owner of the transaction can view the effects of the transaction by using the SELECT statement.
- Other users of the database cannot see the effects of the transaction.
- The affected rows are locked and other users cannot change the data within the affected rows.

After the commit is executed, the following occurs:

1. Locks held on the affected rows are released.
2. The transaction is marked as complete.
3. The internal transaction table of the server generates a system change number, assigns this number to the transaction, and saves them both in the table.

You use the COMMIT statement to explicitly make permanent the changes from a transaction. The following example shows a simple transaction being executed, with a COMMIT being issued after the transaction is executed:

```
SQL>INSERT INTO TABLE employee VALUES
SQL>(emp_id, emp_name)
SQL>VALUES (5, "Jacks Sharon")
1 row created
SQL> COMMIT;
Commit completed
```

You can use the COMMENT clause with the COMMIT statement to place a text string in the data dictionary, along with the transaction ID. You can view this information in the dba_2pc_pending data dictionary view. Usually you use this view to obtain additional information about a transaction that has a questionable status in a distributed environment.

To make an explicit commit by issuing the appropriate commands, you must have the force transaction system privilege. To manually commit a distributed transaction that was originated by another user, you must have the force any transaction system privilege. Oracle performs an implicit commit before and after every DDL command. Oracle does this implicit commit automatically without the user having to issue any commands.

Canceling a Transaction

15

Rolling back a transaction means undoing any change that the current transaction has made. To execute a rollback of the entire transaction, you issue the ROLLBACK command. The following example illustrates the use of the ROLLBACK command to undo the effects of the UPDATE command:

```
UPDATE TABLE employee
(set pay_rate = pay_rate * 1.25
WHERE pay_type = 'S';
ROLLBACK;
```

Alternatively, you can roll back a portion of a transaction by using the ROLLBACK TO SAVEPOINT command. Savepoints are discussed later in this lesson, in the section "Creating Bookmarks with Savepoints."

When you roll back an entire transaction, the following occurs:

1. All changes made by the current transaction are undone, using the corresponding rollback segment.

2. All locks on the rows caused by the transaction are released.

3. The transaction is ended.

When you roll back a transaction to a savepoint, the following occurs:

- Only the SQL statements executed after the last savepoint are rolled back.

- The specified savepoint in the ROLLBACK command is preserved, but all other savepoints after that savepoint are removed from the database.

- All locks established since the specified savepoint are released.

- The transaction is still active and can continue.

No privileges are required to roll back your own transaction. Oracle requires that you have the force transaction system privilege to roll back any in-doubt distributed transaction you own. If the distributed transaction is owned by someone else, then you are required to have the force any transaction system privilege.

Oracle performs an implicit rollback if a severe failure occurs with the host computer or in the application program.

Exploring the Two-Phase Commit

Oracle manages the commits and rollbacks of distributed transactions and maintains data integrity for all the distributed databases participating in the distributed transaction. Oracle performs these tasks by a mechanism known as *two-phase commit*.

NEW TERM A *two-phase commit* is a mechanism which guarantees that all database servers participating in a distributed transaction either all commit or all roll back the statements in the transaction. A two-phase commit mechanism also protects implicit DML operations performed by integrity constraints, remote procedure calls, and triggers.

In a nondistributed environment, all transactions are either committed or rolled back as a unit. However, in a distributed environment, commits and rollbacks of a distributed transaction must be coordinated over a network so that the participating databases either all commit or roll back the transaction. This must hold true even if the network fails during the distributed transaction. The two-phase commit guarantees that the nodes participating in the transaction either commit or roll back the transaction, thus maintaining complete data integrity of the global database.

All implicit DML operations performed by integrity constraints, remote procedure calls, and triggers are protected by Oracle's two-phase commit.

Creating Bookmarks with Savepoints

A savepoint is like a bookmark in the transaction. You explicitly place this bookmark for reference at a later time. Savepoints are used to break a large transaction up into smaller pieces. This allows you to roll back your work to intermediate points in the transaction rather than roll back the entire transaction. For example, if you are performing a large number of updates and an error occurs, you only have to roll back to the last savepoint; you would not need to reprocess every statement.

The following code creates the savepoint named `master_credit`:

```
SAVEPOINT master_credit
```

Savepoint names must be unique within a given transaction. If you create a second savepoint named the same as an earlier savepoint, the previous savepoint is erased.

The following is an example of rolling back a transaction to the `employee_1` savepoint:

INPUT
```
INSERT INTO employee VALUES
(6,'Tom Brandon',3,1000.00,'S');
SAVEPOINT employee_1;
INSERT INTO employee VALUES
(7,'Catherine Ann',2,2000.00,'S');
ROLLBACK TO SAVEPOINT employee_1;
```

ANALYSIS In this example, the insertion of the employee Catherine Ann is removed from the transaction. At the point of the rollback to the savepoint, the insertion of Tom is the pending data in the current transaction.

Using Release Option

Typically when your program ends successfully, all locks, cursors, and some memory are released back to the system. However, if your program terminates abnormally, some of these locks and cursors might remain active for a period of time. This causes unwanted overhead in the database, until the database recognizes the termination and then cleans up the mess.

The following example illustrates the use of the RELEASE option with the COMMIT and the ROLLBACK commands:

INPUT

```
EXEC SQL COMMIT RELEASE;
or
EXEC SQL ROLLBACK RELEASE;
```

ANALYSIS

In this example, you are forcing the program to terminate cleanly. This causes the locks, memory, and cursors to be freed up. Without the release option, you may incur some unwanted overhead in the database for a short period of time.

Using Locking

The Oracle database uses locks to give the user temporary ownership and control of a data object such as a table or row. Oracle automatically locks a row on behalf of a transaction to prevent other transactions from acquiring a lock on the same row. You don't want simultaneous row manipulations by two separate transactions. Data locks prevent destructive interference of simultaneous conflicting DDL and DML statements. For example, Oracle prevents a table from being dropped if there are uncommitted transactions on that table. These data locks are automatically released when the transaction completes by a commit or rollback.

Oracle generates what's known as a *read-consistent* view of data when you query data and while at the same time the data is being manipulated by another user. When a query is active, the results of the query do not change, regardless of any update manipulations that occur. If the query is reexecuted, the data returned reflects any updates executed. The next two sections examine two types of data locking: table and row.

Locking Tables

DML operations can obtain data locks for specific rows and for specific tables. These locks are used to protect the data in the table when the table is being accessed concurrently by multiple users.

A transaction acquires a table lock when a table is modified by the following DML statements: INSERT, UPDATE, DELETE, SELECT with the UPDATE option, and LOCK TABLE. The table lock is specifically in place to ensure that the current transaction has access to the data and to prevent any conflicting DDL operations that might happen.

Note	Note that placing a table lock does prevent other transactions acquiring a lock (row or table) on the same table.

The table lock can be executed in five different modes:

- row share—This table lock is the least restrictive of the table locks. It allows for other concurrent transactions to query, insert, update, delete, and lock rows in the same table. The row share table lock does not allow exclusive write access to the same table.

- row exclusive—This lock occurs when several rows in a table have been updated. This lock still allows other transactions to query, insert, update, delete, or lock rows in the same table. The row exclusive lock does not prevent any manual locking or exclusive read and writes on the same table.

- share lock—The share lock table lock allows for other transactions to only query and lock specific rows. This lock prevents all updates, inserts, and deletes from the same table.

- share row exclusive—This table lock is accomplished only through the lock table with the share row exclusive parameter. This lock only permits queries and selects for UPDATE statements.

- exclusive—This lock allows the transaction write access to a table. This lock means that other transactions can only query the table.

Implicit data locking occurs automatically for all SQL statements, so users of the database do not have to explicitly lock any rows. By default, Oracle locks resources at the lowest level possible.

In a multiuser database, locks have two different levels:

- exclusive—This prohibits the sharing of the associated resource. The first transaction that acquires the resource is the only transaction that can alter the resource until the lock is released.

- share—This lock allows the associated resource to be shared, depending on the operations involved. Several transactions can acquire share locks on the same resource. Share locks provide a greater degree of data concurrency than do exclusive locks.

15

Locking Rows

Row locks are acquired automatically by the transactions when a row is modified by the following commands: INSERT, DELETE, UPDATE, and SELECT with the FOR UPDATE clause.

The following example of the SELECT command places a row lock on the employee table:

INPUT
```
SELECT emp_id, pay_rate
FROM employee
WHERE pay_type = 'H'
FOR UPDATE;
```

ANALYSIS These row locks stay in effect until the transaction is completed or rolled back. The row lock is always exclusive, which prohibits other transactions from modifying the same row. When the row lock is issued, a corresponding table lock is also issued to prevent any conflicting DDL statements from taking effect.

Explicit Locks

A transaction explicitly acquires the specified table locks when a LOCK TABLE statement is executed and overrides the default locking mechanisms. When a LOCK TABLE statement is issued on a view, the underlying base tables are locked. The syntax for the LOCK TABLE statement is as follows.

```
LOCK TABLE table_name IN lock_mode MODE NOWAITE;
```

In this syntax the parameters are as follows:

- table_name is the name of the table you want to lock.
- lock_mode is the mode you want. See a full listing of the lock modes earlier in this lesson, in the section called "Locking Tables."
- NOWAIT is optional. If it is specified, then control is immediately returned to the transaction if there is already a lock on the data object. If NOWAIT is omitted, then the transaction waits for the existing lock to be lifted, and then locks the data object for itself and executes the transaction.

The following example illustrates the use of the LOCK TABLE statement:

INPUT
```
LOCK TABLE employee, department
IN EXCLUSIVE MODE;
```

ANALYSIS This example creates a table lock on the tables employee and department. The lock acquires exclusive table locks for the transaction. Because the NOWAIT option is omitted, the transaction will wait, if necessary, for any preexisting locks to diminish before continuing processing.

The DBMS_LOCK Package

Oracle supplies a package with the database to assist you in managing the database locks. This Oracle-supplied package is named DBMS_LOCK. Through this package, you can request a lock of a specific mode, give it a unique name recognizable in another procedure in the same or another instance, change the lock mode, and release the lock.

The following functions are included in the DBMS_LOCK package: ALLOCATE_UNIQUE, REQUEST, CONVERT, RELEASE, and SLEEP. They are described in more detail in the following sections.

The ALLOCATE UNIQUE Function

The ALLOCATE_UNIQUE function allocates a unique lock identifier (in the range of 1073741824 to 1999999999), given a lock name. Lock identifiers are used to enable applications to coordinate their use of locks. The ALLOCATE UNIQUE function is provided because in some cases it might be easier for applications to coordinate their use of locks based on lock names rather than lock numbers.

If you choose to identify locks by name, you can use ALLOCATE_UNIQUE to generate a unique lock identification number for these named locks.

The first session to call ALLOCATE_UNIQUE with a new lock name causes a unique lock ID to be generated and stored in the DBMS_LOCK_ALLOCATED table. Subsequent calls (usually by other sessions) return the lock ID previously generated. The syntax for the ALLOCATE_UNIQUE function is as follows

```
DBMS_LOCK.ALLOCATE_UNIQUE (
lockname IN VARCHAR2,
lockhandle OUT VARCHAR2,
expiration_secs IN INTEGER DEFAULT 864000);
```

▼ SYNTAX

In this syntax the parameters are as follows:

- *lockname* is the name of the lock for which you want to generate a unique ID.

- *lockhandle* returns the lock identifier for the unique identifier generated by the procedure.

- *expiration secs* is the number of seconds to wait after the last ALLOCATE_UNIQUE has been performed on a given lock, before permitting that lock to be deleted from the DBMS_LOCK_ALLOCATED table.

▲

Exploring the REQUEST Function

The REQUEST function, as the name implies, requests a lock with a given mode. The syntax for the REQUEST function is as follows.

15

```
DBMS_LOCK.REQUEST(
    id                  IN  INTEGER ||
    lockhandle          IN  VARCHAR2,
    lockmode            IN  INTEGER DEFAULT X_MODE,
    timeout             IN  INTEGER DEFAULT MAXWAIT,
    release_on_commit   IN  BOOLEAN DEFAULT FALSE,
    RETURN INTEGER;
```

In this syntax the parameters are as follows:

- *id* is the user assigned lock identifier or the `lockhandle` returned by the `ALLOCATE_LOCK` procedure.

- *lockmode* is the mode for the lock requested. The possible values are

  - 1—Null mode
  - 2—Row-share mode
  - 3—Row-exclusive mode
  - 4—Share mode
  - 5—Share-row-exclusive mode
  - 6—Exclusive mode

- *timeout* is the number of seconds a lock grant should try before it times out with an error.

▲
- *release on commit* is a Boolean which states that the lock is released when a commit or rollback is executed. The default is `true`.

Once the function is executed, it will return a value depending on the outcome of processing. The possible return values are as follows:

Return Value	Description
0	Success
1	Timeout failure
2	Deadlock detection
3	Syntax or parameter error
4	You already own the specified lock id or handle
5	An illegal lock handle

The CONVERT Function

The CONVERT function converts a lock from one mode to another mode. The following displays the syntax for the CONVERT function.

SYNTAX ▼

```
DBMS_LOCK.CONVERT(
    id          IN INTEGER ¦¦
    lockhandle  IN VARCHAR2,
    lockmode    IN INTEGER,
    timeout     IN NUMBER DEFAULT MAXWAIT)
  RETURN INTEGER;
```

In this syntax the parameters are as follows:

- *id* is the user-assigned lock identifier or the `lockhandle` returned by the `ALLOCATE_LOCK` procedure.

- *lockmode* is the new mode you want for the lock. The possible values are

  - 1—Null mode

  - 2—Row-share mode

  - 3—Row-exclusive mode

  - 4—Share mode

  - 5—Share-row-exclusive mode

  - 6—Exclusive mode

▲
- *timeout* is the number of seconds a lock grant should try before it times out with an error.

Once the function is executed, it will return a value depending on the outcome of processing. The possible return values are as follows:

Return Value	Description
0	Function success
1	Function timeout
2	Deadlock detection
3	Parameter error
4	You do not own the specified lock
5	An illegal lock handle or ID

The RELEASE Function

The RELEASE function is used to release a lock that was explicitly acquired via the REQUEST function.

```
DBMS_LOCK.RELEASE (
id IN INTEGER or lockhandle IN VARCHAR2
) RETURN INTEGER;
```

▲ In this syntax, *id* is the lock identifier or *lockhandle* for the lock to be released.

Once the function is executed, it will return a value depending on the outcome of processing. The possible return values are as follows:

Return Value	Description
0	Success
3	Parameter error
4	You do not own the specified lock
5	An ID or lockhandle error

The SLEEP Function

This procedure will suspend the current session for a specified period of time.

```
DBMS_LOCK.SLEEP (
    seconds  IN NUMBER);
```

In this syntax *seconds* is the number of seconds the session will be suspended.

Using Other Locks

Oracle provides a variety of other minor locks. I call them minor not because of their importance, but because most users don't generally interact with them directly. The following are the most common minor locks:

- *Dictionary locks* are used to protect the database objects from changing during a transaction. This type of lock is automatically acquired by Oracle when a DDL statement requires it. Like the locks mentioned in the previous section, the dictionary lock can be either exclusive or shared.

- *Internal locks* protect the internal components of the database and memory. These components are inaccessible by end users. For example, locks can be placed on log files, control files, data dictionary cache files, and archive files.

- *Distributed locks* ensure data consistency across multiple instances. Oracle automatically creates these locks as needed.

Monitoring Locks

Oracle provides several ways to monitor what locks are in place within the database. For example, examining the V$LOCK database view will list information about a lock, such as the system ID of the process holding the lock and the type of lock held. Additionally, the DBA_DDL_LOCKS, DBA_DML_LOCKS, and DBA_LOCKS tables display similar data about locks.

Likewise, you can use the Oracle tool SQL*DBA. In SQL*DBA, the Lock Monitor screen gives similar information from the V$Lock database view.

Summary

Transactions are logical groups of SQL statements that begin when the statements are executed and end with either a commit or rollback. Transactions provide database users the guarantee of data concurrency and data consistency. This guarantee holds true for distributed and nondistributed databases. Locks provide a means to ensure data integrity and concurrence when data manipulations occur.

Q&A

Q Why do DML statements need to be committed?

A Committing a DML statement accomplishes several things: The transaction is ended, which in turn releases any locks the transaction might have created.

Q Do I have to roll back an entire transaction if something does not process completely?

A The rollback can be issued to remove all effects of the current transaction. Additionally, you can roll back to an intermediate point in the transaction known as a savepoint.

Q What are the two types of transactions?

A The two main types of transactions are read-only and read-write transactions.

Workshop

You can use this workshop to test your comprehension of this lesson and put what you've learned into practice. You'll find the answers to the quiz and exercise in Appendix A, "Answers."

Quiz

1. How is a transaction ended?
2. What is the difference between row locking and table locking?
3. What is the purpose of a savepoint?
4. What is the purpose of the two-phase commit?
5. What is the typical return value when the DBMS_LOCK function ran successfully?

Exercise

Write a PL/SQL block that establishes a savepoint, inserts a single record into the employee table, commits the data if the new record does not replicate an existing record, or rolls back the data if the new record insert fails.

DAY **16**

Generating Dynamic SQL

by Timothy Atwood and Jonathan Gennick

Dynamic SQL is SQL, or PL/SQL, that is generated by a program when the program runs. You use dynamic SQL when you need to write generic software. For example, if you were developing a report generator, you wouldn't know ahead of time the reports that people would develop using that generator. You would need to make your code flexible and generic enough to allow users to execute any query they might want. You obviously can't do that by hard-coding SQL statements in your code. Your code would need to build the SQL statements on the fly.

Today you will learn how to do the following:

- Use Oracle's built-in DBMS_SQL package to execute dynamic SQL
- Use the new native dynamic SQL feature in Oracle8i

What Is Dynamic SQL and Why Use It?

 Dynamic SQL is SQL that is generated by software at runtime, and then executed. The statements to be executed may not be known at all when the code is being written. Consider the following PL/SQL block:

```
BEGIN
   DELETE FROM employee;
END
```

 The SQL statement in that block is a static SQL statement. A *static SQL* statement is one that you know about when you write the code and that does not change after the code has been compiled.

What would happen if you didn't really want to delete all the records in the table? What if you wanted to write a procedure that took a WHERE clause as an argument? Then a user could call your procedure and pass in conditions that identified the records to be deleted, and your procedure would delete them. You might try to use this code:

```
PROCEDURE delete_employees (where_clause IN VARCHAR2) IS
BEGIN
   DELETE FROM employee WHERE ¦¦ where_clause;
END;
```

Well, you might try that, but it wouldn't work. It is, however, an attempt at a dynamic SQL statement. In this example, you only know half the story when you are writing the code. You only know that you are going to delete employee records, but you don't know which ones. You need to be able to construct the entire DELETE statement on the fly when the procedure is invoked. That's what dynamic SQL is all about.

 Note

> With Oracle, dynamic SQL allows you to execute Data Definition Language (DDL) statements, such as CREATE TABLE and GRANT, from within PL/SQL. Regardless of whether you know the entire text of a DDL statement at compile time, dynamic SQL represents the only way to execute such a statement from within a stored procedure, function, or package.

Two Approaches to Dynamic SQL

There used to be only one way to execute dynamic SQL, and that was to use a package named DBMS_SQL. That package is a bit difficult to use, especially if you are executing dynamic queries and you want to retrieve the data for those queries. For example, to execute a GRANT command by using DBMS_SQL, you need to do something like this:

```
DECLARE
    cursor_id NUMBER;
    ret_val NUMBER;
BEGIN
    cursor_id := DBMS_SQL.OPEN_CURSOR;
    DBMS_SQL.PARSE (cursor_id, 'GRANT SELECT ON employee TO scott',
DBMS_SQL.NATIVE);
    ret_val := DBMS_SQL.EXECUTE (cursor_id);
    DBMS_SQL.CLOSE_CURSOR (cursor_id);
END;
/
```

16

That's four lines of code just to execute one simple GRANT statement. It gets much worse when you are executing a dynamic SELECT query because you need to make one DBMS_SQL.COLUMN_VALUE call for each column that your query returns. You also need to bind the query columns to PL/SQL variables. It can get pretty hairy. Native dynamic SQL makes things much simpler. Using it, you can rewrite the previous GRANT example, using just one line of executable code:

```
BEGIN
    EXECUTE IMMEDIATE 'GRANT SELECT ON employee TO scott';
END;
/
```

You can't get much simpler than that.

Using the DBMS_SQL Package

This section shows you how to use the DBMS_SQL package. There are three types of statements you can dynamically build and execute:

- Non-query DDL and Data Manipulation Language (DML) statements (that is, everything except SELECT)
- SELECT statements
- PL/SQL blocks

You'll see examples of each of these types in this section. Executing SELECT statements by using DBMS_SQL entails the greatest amount of complexity. You'll certainly come to appreciate the new native dynamic SQL after you've used DBMS_SQL to build dynamic queries.

Using the DBMS_SQL Package with Non-Query DDL and DML Statements

DDL statements are those such as CREATE, ALTER, and DROP that you can use to define and manage objects in a database. DML consists of the INSERT, UPDATE, and DELETE statements. You can use DBMS_SQL to execute both DDL and DML statements. These are the steps you use to do that:

1. Open a cursor.
2. Parse the statement you want to execute.
3. Bind any input variables that might be required.
4. Execute the statement.
5. Close the cursor.

The next few sections describe each step in detail.

Opening the Cursor

Whenever you execute a SQL statement inside a PL/SQL block, a cursor is opened. If you just write an INSERT or a DELETE statement into the code, the associated cursor is implicit, and is opened and closed behind the scenes without your ever being aware of it. When creating dynamic SQL, however, you have to open a cursor yourself, by making a call to the DBMS_SQL.OPEN_CURSOR function. The header for that function looks like this:

```
FUNCTION OPEN_CURSOR RETURN INTEGER;
```

The OPEN_CURSOR function returns an integer, which is the cursor ID. The cursor ID should be retained until the cursor is closed. After you have an open cursor, you can use it to execute as many statements as desired.

Parsing a Statement

After you have a cursor opened, you need to call DBMS_PARSE to parse the statement you want to execute. The parsing stage is when Oracle looks at the syntax of the statement, determines which database objects are involved, and determines how to optimize the execution of the statement.

The Syntax for the PARSE Procedure

▲ SYNTAX

```
PROCEDURE PARSE(c IN INTEGER,
                statement IN VARCHAR2,
                language_flag IN VARCHAR2);
```

In this syntax the parameters are as follows:

- c is the cursor returned by the OPEN_CURSOR statement.
- statement is the SQL statement you want to parse.

▼

- language_flag indicates the version of the database you are running against.

▼   The following versions are allowed for the `language_flag` argument:

   - `NATIVE`—Native handling for the server
   - `V6`—Handling for Oracle version 6.*x*
▲   - `V7`—Handling for Oracle version 7.*x*

The version can be expressed as `DBMS_SQL.NATIVE`, `DBMS_SQL.V7`, and so on. `DBMS_SQL.NATIVE` is usually the best choice.

16

Binding Input Variables

NEW TERM   *Binding* enables you to associate a specific variable to a placeholder in your SQL statement. This allows you to write a SQL statement like this:

```
DELETE FROM employee WHERE emp_id = :1
```

The placeholder is identified by a colon, and represents a value that you supply when the statement is executed. The advantage of this is that after you parse such a statement, you can execute it repeatedly by using different values for the bind variables, without having to reparse it each time.

The `DBMS_SQL.BIND_VARIABLE` procedure is used to bind variables to placeholders. The procedure is overloaded in order to allow it to bind variables of all different types. The syntax header for the `NUMBER BIND_VARIABLE` procedure is as follows.

▼ **SYNTAX**

```
PROCEDURE BIND_VARIABLE(c IN INTEGER,
                        name IN VARCHAR2,
                        value IN datatype);

PROCEDURE BIND_VARIABLE_CHAR(c IN INTEGER,
                        name IN VARCHAR2,
                        value IN CHAR,
                        out_value_size IN INTEGER);
```

In this syntax the parameters are as follows:

   - *c* is the cursor ID returned from `OPEN_CURSOR`.
   - *name* is the name of the placeholder, which is the variable in the SQL statement that is preceded by a colon.
   - *value* is the PL/SQL variable to be bound to the placeholder variable.
   - *datatype* can be any of the following: `NUMBER`, `DATE`, `VARCHAR2`, `BLOB`, `CLOB`, or `BFILE`. The `BIND_VARIABLE_CHAR` procedure is used to bind variables of type `CHAR` and `NCHAR`.
▲   - *out_value_size* is used with the `BIND_VARIABLE_CHAR` procedure as an optional parameter that represents the maximum expected size of the bound character string.

> **Note**
>
> Some variations of BIND_VARIABLE are used for ROWIDs and variables of type RAW. Their procedure names are BIND_VARIABLE_ROWID and BIND_VARIABLE_RAW, respectively. Their declarations look just like that of BIND_VARIABLE_CHAR.

Executing the Statement

After you have parsed the statement and bound any variables, you are ready to execute the statement by using the function DBMS_SQL.EXECUTE.

The Syntax for the EXECUTE Function

```
FUNCTION EXECUTE (c IN INTEGER) RETURN INTEGER;
```

In this syntax, c represents the cursor assigned by the OPEN_CURSOR call. The value returned by the EXECUTE function represents the number of rows affected by the statement that was executed. It is valid only when statements have been executed and should

 be ignored for DDL statements.

Closing the Cursor

After all processing has been completed, you should close the cursor by using the CLOSE_CURSOR procedure to free up resources.

The Syntax for the CLOSE_CURSOR Procedure

```
PROCEDURE CLOSE_CURSOR (c IN OUT INTEGER);
```

In this syntax, c is the cursor ID originally returned by the OPEN_CURSOR call. After the call to CLOSE_CURSOR has completed, the value of the c parameter is NULL.

Using DBMS_SQL to Create a Table

Now that you've seen several of the DBMS_SQL procedures defined, let's take a look at an example of dynamic SQL. In this case, we'll use it to create a table from within a PL/SQL block. Although the DDL in this example is still fixed, in the sense that it has been hard-coded into the code, it serves to demonstrate how DBMS_SQL is used.

INPUT   **LISTING 16.1**   Creating the Table mytable from a PL/SQL Block

```
1: DECLARE
2: /* The purpose of this PL/SQL block is to create a table
3:    called MyTable, which has two columns of type INTEGER and
4:    the second column of type VARCHAR2(50).  This uses the
5:    DBMS_SQL package to execute DDL statements */
```

```
 6:
 7:        v_CursorID  NUMBER;
 8:        v_CreateTableString  VARCHAR2(500); --  SQL string
 9:        v_NUMRows  INTEGER; --  Number of rows processed - of no use
10:
11: BEGIN
12:        v_CursorID := DBMS_SQL.OPEN_CURSOR; --  Get the Cursor ID
13:        v_CreateTableString := 'CREATE TABLE MyTable(
14:            MyRow INTEGER,
15:            MyDesc VARCHAR2(50))'; --  Write SQL code to create table
16:
17:        DBMS_SQL.PARSE(v_CursorID,v_CreateTableString,DBMS_SQL.V7);
18:            /* Perform syntax error checking */
19:        v_NumRows := DBMS_SQL.EXECUTE(v_CursorID);
20:            /* Execute the SQL code  */
21:
22: EXCEPTION
23:        WHEN OTHERS THEN
24:            IF SQLCODE != -955 THEN --  955 is error that table exists
25:                RAISE; --  raise if some other unknown error
26:            ELSE
27:                DBMS_OUTPUT.PUT_LINE('Table Already Exists!');
28:            END IF;
29:        DBMS_SQL.CLOSE_CURSOR(v_CursorID); --  Close the cursor
30: END; --  End PL/SQL block
31: /
```

OUTPUT   PL/SQL procedure successfully completed.

ANALYSIS   You have just created a table called MyTable. The code in Listing 16.1 sets up three variables:

- v_CursorID   Holds the cursor ID returned by the call to OPEN_CURSOR. This variable is set up in line 7.

- v_CreateTableString   Holds the SQL code required to create the table. This variable is set up in line 8.

Note

It's important that the SQL code used to create the table, or any SQL code used with the DBMS_SQL package, not end with a semicolon. The semicolon is only necessary when typing SQL statements into a PL/SQL program, so that Oracle can tell when the end of the statement has been reached. It's not necessary or valid to pass the semicolon to the DBMS_SQL package.

16

- v_NUMRows   Holds the number of rows processed, which is meaningless with DDL statements. Here it's used because the EXECUTE procedure returns a value anyway, and we need a place to store that value. This variable is set up in line 9.

Next, in line 12, v_CursorID is assigned the cursor ID returned by OPEN_CURSOR. In line 13, v_CreateTableString is assigned the necessary SQL code to create the table. Again, it is very important that the SQL code you execute not end in a semicolon. The statement is parsed for syntax errors in line 17. No variables need to be bound in this PL/SQL code. The dynamic SQL statement is then executed in line 19, and the cursor is then closed.

The exception handler traps error 955, which is raised if the table to be created already exists. In that case, the program displays a message telling you that the table exists, and then the program exits. This exception-handling routine is in lines 22–28. After making sure to enter SET SERVEROUTPUT ON, go ahead and execute the code in Listing 16.1 again. You will then see the message that the table already exists. If any other error occurs, the RAISE statement passes it up to the caller to be handled there.

Using DML to Add Records to the Table

Now that you have created a table, you can add some records by using DML statements. You can finally see how many rows were processed. The code in this example adds a total of five records. The fifth record does not need to be bound because it takes the default values of the previous bind, which effectively duplicates the fourth record. Go ahead and execute the code in Listing 16.2.

INPUT   **LISTING 16.2**   Using INSERT to Add Records to the Table

```
 1: DECLARE
 2: /* The purpose of this PL/SQL block is to demonstrate the use
 3:    of DML statements by adding a total of four records. This will
 4:    illustrate the use of binding variables and the multiple use
 5:    of accessing the Cursor ID */
 6:
 7:     v_CursorID  NUMBER;
 8:     v_InsertRecords  VARCHAR2(500); -- SQL string
 9:     v_NUMRows  INTEGER; -- Number of rows processed - of no use
10:
11: BEGIN
12:     v_CursorID := DBMS_SQL.OPEN_CURSOR; -- Get the Cursor ID
13:     v_InsertRecords := 'INSERT INTO MyTable(MyRow,MyDesc)
14:         VALUES (:mynum,:mytext)'; -- Write SQL to insert records
15:
16: /* Define and Insert the First Record */
17:
18:     DBMS_SQL.PARSE(v_CursorID,v_InsertRecords,DBMS_SQL.V7);
```

```
19:                /* Perform syntax error checking */
20:        DBMS_SQL.BIND_VARIABLE(v_CursorID, ':mynum',1);
21:        DBMS_SQL.BIND_VARIABLE(v_CursorID, ':mytext','One');
22:        v_NumRows := DBMS_SQL.EXECUTE(v_CursorID);
23:                /* Execute the SQL code  */
24:        DBMS_OUTPUT.PUT_LINE('The number of records just processed is: '
25:                ¦¦ v_NUMRows);
26:
27: /*  Define and Insert the Second Record */
28:
29:        DBMS_SQL.BIND_VARIABLE(v_CursorID, ':mynum',2);
30:        DBMS_SQL.BIND_VARIABLE(v_CursorID, ':mytext','Two');
31:        v_NumRows := DBMS_SQL.EXECUTE(v_CursorID);
32:                /* Execute the SQL code  */
33:        DBMS_OUTPUT.PUT_LINE('The number of records just processed is: '
34:                ¦¦ v_NUMRows);
35:
36: /*  Define and Insert the Third Record */
37:
38:        DBMS_SQL.BIND_VARIABLE(v_CursorID, ':mynum',3);
39:        DBMS_SQL.BIND_VARIABLE(v_CursorID, ':mytext','Three');
40:        v_NumRows := DBMS_SQL.EXECUTE(v_CursorID);
41:                /* Execute the SQL code  */
42:        DBMS_OUTPUT.PUT_LINE('The number of records just processed is: '
43:              - ¦¦ v_NUMRows);
44:
45: /*  Define and Insert the Fourth Record */
46:
47:        DBMS_SQL.BIND_VARIABLE(v_CursorID, ':mynum',4);
48:        DBMS_SQL.BIND_VARIABLE(v_CursorID, ':mytext','Four');
49:        v_NumRows := DBMS_SQL.EXECUTE(v_CursorID);
50:                /* Execute the SQL code  */
51:        DBMS_OUTPUT.PUT_LINE('The number of records just processed is: '
52:                ¦¦ v_NUMRows);
53:
54: /* Duplicate the Fourth Entry! */
55:
56:        v_NumRows := DBMS_SQL.EXECUTE(v_CursorID);
57:                /* Execute the SQL code  */
58:        DBMS_OUTPUT.PUT_LINE('The number of records just processed is: '
59:                ¦¦ v_NUMRows);
60:
61: EXCEPTION
62:        WHEN OTHERS THEN
63:                   RAISE; -- raise if some other unknown error
64:
65:        DBMS_SQL.CLOSE_CURSOR(v_CursorID); -- Close the cursor
66:        COMMIT;
67: END; -- End PL/SQL block
68: /
```

16

The number of records just processed is: 1
The number of records just processed is: 1
The number of records just processed is: 1
The number of records just processed is: 1
The number of records just processed is: 1

ANALYSIS You have just inserted five complete records, duplicating the fourth record. Notice that because a DML statement was being executed, the return value from EXECUTE is valid. In each case EXECUTE returns the value 1, telling us that one row had been inserted into the table.

Now review the steps for DML statements. In line 12, you first open the cursor by using OPEN_CURSOR. You then assign the value of v_InsertRecords to the SQL required to insert the records in line 13. Notice the placeholder variables as identified by the colon in front of the placeholder names in line 14. The next step is to parse the statement for syntax error checking, as shown in line 18. After parsing the statement, you need to bind the placeholder variables, as in lines 20–21. You are ready to execute the statement in line 22, and then to close the cursor in line 65, after all records are inserted.

The same process is repeated four more times to add four more records. Again, if you were to create a stored function or procedure, you should be able to pass as the parameter simply the record to insert, which could be variable names, for true dynamic SQL. Creating this type of function demonstrates the practicality of dynamic SQL with the DBMS_SQL package.

Using the DBMS_SQL Package with Queries

This section demonstrates how to execute queries by using the DBMS_SQL package. The processing method is very similar to DDL and DML processing. The following steps are required:

1. Open the cursor.
2. Parse the statement.
3. Bind the input variables (if required).
4. Define the output variables.
5. Execute the statement.
6. Fetch the rows.
7. Store the results from fetching the rows in PL/SQL variables.
8. Close the cursor.

Although the overall process is much the same as the process for using DBMS_SQL with DDL and DML, steps 6 and 7 increase the amount of code that you need to write. Step 7 is especially painful because you have to call `DBMS_SQL` once for each column returned by the query.

Opening a Cursor for Executing Queries

The process of opening a cursor is identical to that used in the previous examples. You simply declare a variable of type `NUMBER`, make a call to `DBMS_SQL.OPEN_CURSOR`, and store the result in the variable. You can then use that cursor to execute SQL queries.

Parsing Statements for Queries

Parsing queries is almost identical to parsing DDL and DML statements. They use the same syntax and both have the requirement that no semicolon should appear at the end of the SQL code. However, there are a couple additional requirements when executing queries:

- The `SELECT` statement can't be embedded in PL/SQL. There should be only one `SELECT` statement.
- The query should not contain an `INTO` statement.

Binding Variables for Queries

There is no difference between binding variables for queries and binding variables for DML statements. If you want to supply values to a query when you execute it, use placeholders in the `SELECT` statement, and bind those placeholders to PL/SQL variables. Then, before executing the query, make sure you store the desired values in those PL/SQL variables.

Defining Output Variables for Queries

The difference between processing DML and DDL statements and processing queries occurs at this point. DML and DDL statements simply execute, and then the cursor is closed. However, you are now writing a query that returns output. You need to have a way to receive this output. You have to define each column of output by using the `DEFINE_COLUMN` procedure. First, you declare PL/SQL variables with datatypes and lengths that match the columns returned by the query. You can then call `DEFINE_COLUMN` to match each PL/SQL variable to an output column. Because you can define several datatypes, the procedure `DEFINE_COLUMN` is overloaded.

The Syntax for Defining Output Variables

The header for the `NUMBER` version of `DEFINE_COLUMN` is

```
PROCEDURE DEFINE_COLUMN (c IN INTEGER,
                        position IN INTEGER,
                        column IN NUMBER);
```

▼ The header for the VARCHAR2 version of DEFINE_COLUMN is

```
PROCEDURE DEFINE_COLUMN (c IN INTEGER,
                         position IN INTEGER,
                         column IN VARCHAR2,
                         column_size IN INTEGER);
```

The header for the CHAR version of DEFINE_COLUMN is

```
PROCEDURE DEFINE_COLUMN (c IN INTEGER,
                         position IN INTEGER,
                         column IN CHAR,
                         column_size IN INTEGER);
```

The header for the DATE version of DEFINE_COLUMN is

```
PROCEDURE DEFINE_COLUMN (c IN INTEGER,
                         position IN INTEGER,
                         column IN DATE);
```

The header for the RAW version of DEFINE_COLUMN is

```
PROCEDURE DEFINE_COLUMN (c IN INTEGER,
                         position IN INTEGER,
                         column IN RAW,
                         column_size IN INTEGER);
```

The header for the ROWID version of DEFINE_COLUMN is

```
PROCEDURE DEFINE_COLUMN (c IN INTEGER,
                         position IN INTEGER,
                         column IN ROWID);
```

The header for the MLSLABEL version of DEFINE_COLUMN in Trusted Oracle is

```
PROCEDURE DEFINE_COLUMN (c IN INTEGER,
                         position IN INTEGER,
                         column IN MLSLABEL);
```

In this syntax the parameters are as follows:

- *c* is the cursor assigned by the OPEN_CURSOR statement.
- *position* identifies the position of the column in the output. The first column listed after the SELECT keyword is column 1, the next is column 2, and so forth.
- *column* is the variable defined in the declaration that is associated with the column in the table.
- *column_size* is an optional parameter that allows you to specify the size of the column; otherwise, the size used is the size defined for the variable itself. Not all datatypes allow a size to be specified.

Executing Queries

The procedure for executing a query is identical to that for DDL and DML statements. After you have defined the columns, you are ready to execute the query by using the EXECUTE function. The syntax for the EXECUTE function is shown earlier in this lesson in the section titled "Using the DBMS_SQL Package with Non-Query DDL and DML Statements."

16

▼ SYNTAX

Fetching the Rows into the Buffer with Queries

After the query is executed, you need to retrieve the results. You do this by retrieving one row at a time, using the FETCH_ROWS function. This function returns the number of rows stored into the buffer. You can then error-check or process based upon %FOUND or %NOTFOUND. The syntax header for the FETCH_ROWS function is as follows.

▲
```
FUNCTION FETCH_ROWS (c IN INTEGER) RETURN INTEGER;
```

Using EXECUTE_AND_FETCH to Retrieve the First Set of Rows

Instead of first running EXECUTE and then executing FETCH_ROWS, you can do the initial execution and fetching in one step with the use of the EXECUTE_AND_FETCH function.

SYNTAX

```
FUNCTION EXECUTE_AND_FETCH (c IN INTEGER,
                      exact IN BOOLEAN DEFAULT FALSE)
RETURN INTEGER;
```

The only difference between EXECUTE_AND_FETCH and EXECUTE is the added parameter exact. The value returns true if more than one row has been fetched.

Using COLUMN_VALUE to Read the Results into PL/SQL Variables

After fetching a row, you need to read the data from DBMS_SQL's buffer into some PL/SQL variables. You do this by making calls to the COLUMN_VALUE procedure, which is overloaded, allowing it to handle various datatypes. The syntax for the COLUMN_VALUE procedure is as follows.

▼ SYNTAX

There are two versions of COLUMN_VALUE used for NUMBER columns. The headers for those two versions are

```
PROCEDURE COLUMN_VALUE (c IN INTEGER,
                      position IN INTEGER,
                      value OUT NUMBER);
```

and

```
PROCEDURE COLUMN_VALUE (c IN INTEGER,
                      position IN INTEGER,
                      value OUT NUMBER,
                      column_error OUT NUMBER,
                      actual_length OUT INTEGER);
```

▼

▼ The headers for VARCHAR2 values are

```
PROCEDURE COLUMN_VALUE (c IN INTEGER,
                       position IN INTEGER,
                       value OUT VARCHAR2);
```

and

```
PROCEDURE COLUMN_VALUE (c IN INTEGER,
                       position IN INTEGER,
                       value OUT VARCHAR2,
                       column_error OUT NUMBER,
                       actual_length OUT INTEGER);
```

The headers for CHAR values are

```
PROCEDURE COLUMN_VALUE (c IN INTEGER,
                       position IN INTEGER,
                       value OUT CHAR);
```

and

```
PROCEDURE COLUMN_VALUE (c IN INTEGER,
                       position IN INTEGER,
                       value OUT CHAR,
                       column_error OUT NUMBER,
                       actual_length OUT INTEGER);
```

The formats for DATE values are

```
PROCEDURE COLUMN_VALUE (c IN INTEGER,
                       position IN INTEGER,
                       value OUT DATE);
```

and

```
PROCEDURE COLUMN_VALUE (c IN INTEGER,
                       position IN INTEGER,
                       value OUT DATE,
                       column_error OUT NUMBER,
                       actual_length OUT INTEGER);
```

The formats for RAW values are

```
PROCEDURE COLUMN_VALUE (c IN INTEGER,
                       position IN INTEGER,
                       value OUT RAW);
```

and

```
PROCEDURE COLUMN_VALUE (c IN INTEGER,
                       position IN INTEGER,
                       value OUT RAW,
                       column_error OUT NUMBER,
                       actual_length OUT INTEGER);
```
▼

▼ The formats for ROWID values are

```
PROCEDURE COLUMN_VALUE (c IN INTEGER,
                       position IN INTEGER,
                       value OUT ROWID);
```

and

```
PROCEDURE COLUMN_VALUE (c IN INTEGER,
                       position IN INTEGER,
                       value OUT ROWID,
                       column_error OUT NUMBER,
                       actual_length OUT INTEGER) ;
```

The formats for MLSLABEL values in Trusted Oracle are

```
PROCEDURE COLUMN_VALUE (c IN INTEGER,
                       position IN INTEGER,
                       value OUT MLSLABEL) ;
```

and

```
PROCEDURE COLUMN_VALUE (c IN INTEGER,
                       position IN INTEGER,
                       value OUT MLSLABEL,
                       column_error OUT NUMBER,
                       actual_length OUT INTEGER) ;
```

In this syntax the parameters are as follows:

- c represents the cursor ID assigned by OPEN_CURSOR.

- position represents the order of the column in the SELECT list.

- value is the PL/SQL variable that you declared to hold the results returned for the column.

- column_error is an optional parameter that enables you to determine if a column caused an error. When you retrieve the value for a column, the column_error parameter will normally be set to zero. A non-zero value means that the column value couldn't be retrieved.

- actual_length returns the length of the variable in the buffer before it is placed into the associated PL/SQL variable. This parameter is useful when the column's value in the table may be longer than the PL/SQL variable you have defined allows it to be. By comparing the actual length with the size of the PL/SQL variable, you
▲   can tell if a column's value has been truncated.

Closing the Cursor for Queries

After you've fetched all the data returned by a SELECT statement, or at least all that you wanted to look at, you should close the cursor by making a call to CLOSE_CURSOR. The

CLOSE_CURSOR call is made the same way for queries as it is for any other type of statement.

Using Queries with the DBMS_SQL Package

This section provides an example showing how to execute queries by using the DBMS_SQL package. The code in Listing 16.3 uses dynamic SQL to query the table you created earlier and then retrieve the five rows that you inserted earlier. These five rows are then displayed onscreen (if you are using SQL*Plus). You should execute the code in Listing 16.3, after making sure that you have entered SET SERVEROUTPUT ON at the SQL*Plus prompt.

INPUT **LISTING 16.3** Using SELECT to Verify Inserted Records

```
 1: DECLARE
 2: /* The purpose of this PL/SQL block is to demonstrate
 3:    executing queries within PL/SQL through the use of the
 4:    DBMS_SQL package.  We will simply display the output to
 5:    screen with the DBMS_OUTPUT package */
 6:
 7:     v_CursorID  NUMBER;
 8:     v_SelectRecords  VARCHAR2(500); --  SQL string
 9:     v_NUMRows  INTEGER; --  Number of rows processed - of no use
10:     v_MyNum INTEGER;
11:     v_MyText VARCHAR2(50);
12:
13: BEGIN
14:     v_CursorID := DBMS_SQL.OPEN_CURSOR; --  Get the Cursor ID
15:     v_SelectRecords := 'SELECT * from MyTable'; --  SQL to view records
16:
17:
18:     DBMS_SQL.PARSE(v_CursorID,v_SelectRecords,DBMS_SQL.V7);
19:         /* Perform syntax error checking */
20:
21:     DBMS_SQL.DEFINE_COLUMN(v_CursorID,1,v_MyNum);
22:     DBMS_SQL.DEFINE_COLUMN(v_CursorID,2,v_MyText,50);
23:
24:     v_NumRows := DBMS_SQL.EXECUTE(v_CursorID);
25:         /* Execute the SQL code  */
26: LOOP
27:     IF DBMS_SQL.FETCH_ROWS(v_CursorID) = 0 THEN
28:         EXIT;
29:     END IF;
30:
31:     DBMS_SQL.COLUMN_VALUE(v_CursorId,1,v_MyNum);
32:     DBMS_SQL.COLUMN_VALUE(v_CursorId,2,v_MyText);
33:
34:     DBMS_OUTPUT.PUT_LINE(v_MyNum ¦¦ ' ' ¦¦ v_MyText);
```

```
35:
36: END LOOP;
37:
38: EXCEPTION
39:     WHEN OTHERS THEN
40:                 RAISE; --  raise if some other unknown error
41:
42:     DBMS_SQL.CLOSE_CURSOR(v_CursorID); --  Close the cursor
43:
44: END; --  End PL/SQL block
45: /
```

16

After you have executed the block, you should see

 OUTPUT

```
1 One
2 Two
3 Three
4 Four
4 Four
```

ANALYSIS
You can see that it takes some work to execute a SELECT statement by using DBMS_SQL. First, you have to open the cursor with OPEN_CURSOR in line 14. Then, v_SelectRecords is assigned the string for the SQL query to select all records from MyTable in line 15. That SQL statement is parsed in line 18. No input variables need to be bound in this example, but if your query has a WHERE clause, you could use binding. In lines 21 and 22, the two output variables v_MyNum and v_MyText are defined. These are used to hold values from the two columns returned by the query. The query is then executed with DBMS_SQL.EXECUTE in line 24. In line 26, the code enters a loop that fetches each row, retrieves the values for the row by making calls to COLUMN_VALUES, and then passes those values to DBMS_OUTPUT. The EXIT statement in line 28 is executed when no more rows are found, causing the loop to terminate. Finally, the cursor is properly closed in line 42.

Using the DBMS_SQL Package with Anonymous PL/SQL Blocks

This section demonstrates how to execute anonymous PL/SQL blocks by using the DBMS_SQL package. The processing method is much the same as that used for processing queries and executing DDL or DML statements. The following steps are required:

1. Open the cursor.
2. Parse the statement.
3. Bind the input variables (if required).

4. Execute the statement.

5. Retrieve the results into variables.

6. Close the cursor.

Step 5 is the only place that you will see a difference between the processing required to execute a SQL statement dynamically and the process required to execute a PL/SQL statement dynamically. To retrieve the results, you will use a function named VARIABLE_VALUE, which is described next.

Retrieving Values with Anonymous Blocks

The major difference between executing a PL/SQL block and executing a query or DML statement is that you might need to retrieve the values of bind variables that have been modified by the block. For example, the dynamic PL/SQL block might call a procedure using several OUT parameters. You need a way to get at the values of those parameters. Using DBMS_SQL, you get those values by making calls to the VARIABLE_VALUE procedure, which is an overloaded procedure that has versions for several datatypes.

The Syntax for the VARIABLE_VALUE Procedures

▼ SYNTAX

The header for NUMBER values is

```
PROCEDURE VARIABLE VALUE(c IN INTEGER
                    name IN VARCHAR2,
                    value OUT NUMBER);
```

The header for VARCHAR2 values is

```
PROCEDURE VARIABLE VALUE(c IN INTEGER
                    name IN VARCHAR2,
                    value OUT VARCHAR2);
```

The header for CHAR values is

```
PROCEDURE VARIABLE VALUE(c IN INTEGER
                    name IN VARCHAR2,
                    value OUT CHAR);
```

The header for DATE values is

```
PROCEDURE VARIABLE VALUE(c IN INTEGER
                    name IN VARCHAR2,
                    value OUT DATE);
```

The header for RAW values is

```
PROCEDURE VARIABLE VALUE(c IN INTEGER
                    name IN VARCHAR2,
                    value OUT RAW);
```

▼

▼ The header for ROWID values is

```
PROCEDURE VARIABLE VALUE(c IN INTEGER
                        name IN VARCHAR2,
                        value OUT ROWID);
```

The syntax for MLSLABEL values in Trusted Oracle is

```
PROCEDURE VARIABLE VALUE(c IN INTEGER
                        name IN VARCHAR2,
                        value OUT MLSLABEL);
```

16

In this syntax the parameters are as follows:

- *c* is the cursor ID returned from OPEN_CURSOR.

- *name* is the name of the placeholder. Don't forget to include the preceding colon when passing these to VARIABLE_VALUE. For example, use :marker, not marker.

▲ - *value* is the PL/SQL variable used to hold the output.

Executing an Anonymous PL/SQL Block Using DBMS_SQL

This section demonstrates the process of executing an anonymous PL/SQL block by using the DBMS_SQL package. The block to be executed in this example retrieves just one row from the table named mytable that you created earlier. Make sure you have entered SET SERVEROUTPUT ON at the SQL*Plus prompt, and execute the code in Listing 16.4.

INPUT   **LISTING 16.4**   Using Anonymous Blocks

```
1: DECLARE
2: /* This procedure calls an anonymous block which performs a
3:    query to lookup the description for the row id value = 2.
4:    This demonstrates the use of an anonymous PL/SQL block
5:    within PL/SQL */
6:
7:     v_CursorID  NUMBER;
8:     v_MatchRecord  VARCHAR2(500); -- SQL string
9:     v_NUMRows  INTEGER; --  Number of rows processed - of no use
10:    v_MyNum INTEGER;
11:    v_MyText VARCHAR2(50);
12:
13: BEGIN
14:    v_CursorID := DBMS_SQL.OPEN_CURSOR; --  Get the Cursor ID
15:    v_MatchRecord := 'BEGIN --  Start of Anonymous PL/SQL Block
16:                         SELECT MyRow,MyDesc
17:                             INTO :MyRow, :MyText FROM MyTable
18:                             WHERE MyRow = 2;
```

continues

LISTING 16.4 continued

```
19:                            END;'; -- End of Anonymous PL/SQL Block
20:
21:         DBMS_SQL.PARSE(v_CursorID,v_MatchRecord,DBMS_SQL.V7);
22:             /* Perform syntax error checking */
23:
24:         DBMS_SQL.BIND_VARIABLE(v_CursorID, ':MyRow',v_MyNum);
25:         DBMS_SQL.BIND_VARIABLE(v_CursorID, ':MyText',v_MyText,50);
26:
27:         v_NumRows := DBMS_SQL.EXECUTE(v_CursorID);
28:             /* Execute the SQL code  */
29:
30:
31:         DBMS_SQL.VARIABLE_VALUE(v_CursorId,':MyRow',v_MyNum);
32:         DBMS_SQL.VARIABLE_VALUE(v_CursorId,':MyText',v_MyText);
33:         /* Defines variables to hold output */
34:
35:         DBMS_OUTPUT.PUT_LINE(v_MyNum || ' ' || v_MyText);
36:
37:
38: EXCEPTION
39:     WHEN OTHERS THEN
40:             RAISE; -- raise if some other unknown error
41:
42:         DBMS_SQL.CLOSE_CURSOR(v_CursorID); -- Close the cursor
43:
44: END; -- End PL/SQL block
45: /
```

After you have executed the block, you should see the following:

OUTPUT 2 Two

ANALYSIS The code first uses OPEN_CURSOR in line 14 to open a cursor. It then assigns the anonymous PL/SQL block to the variable v_MatchRecord in line 15. This string codes the PL/SQL block with proper syntax. Note that the block is terminated by a semicolon. When using DBMS_SQL to execute a PL/SQL block, you must terminate that block with a semicolon because the semicolon is proper PL/SQL syntax. The next step is to call DBMS_SQL.PARSE, as in line 21. After binding the appropriate variables in lines 24 and 25, the anonymous PL/SQL block is executed in line 27. The SQL statement executed by the block uses a SELECT...INTO statement to retrieve one row from the table. The values for that row are stored in the bind variables. To retrieve those values, you call DBMS_SQL.VARIABLE_VALUE, which the code does in lines 31 and 32. The output is displayed in line 35, after making a call to DBMS_OUTPUT.PUT_LINE. Finally, after the entire process has completed, line 42 makes a call to CLOSE_CURSOR to close the cursor.

DBMS_SQL Error Handling

The DBMS_SQL package provides many ways to avoid errors that would otherwise cause exceptions to be thrown. You can check to see if the cursor is open by using IS_OPEN. You can also check to see information provided by the DBMS_SQL package concerning the last set of rows retrieved by using the FETCH_ROWS function with the functions LAST_ROW_COUNT and LAST_ROW_ID. Other functions that provide information on errors are LAST_ERROR_POSITION and LAST_SQL_FUNCTION_CODE.

Using IS_OPEN

The IS_OPEN function enables you to see whether or not a cursor is open. One possible use for this is to check for an open cursor, and if it is still open, close the cursor.

The Syntax for the IS_OPEN Function

```
FUNCTION IS_OPEN(c IN INTEGER) RETURN BOOLEAN;
```

In this syntax c is the cursor ID originally returned by the OPEN_CURSOR function. If the cursor is open, it returns true; otherwise, if the cursor is closed, it returns false.

Using LAST_ROW_COUNT

The LAST_ROW_COUNT function passes the total number of rows fetched from the cursor to date. This should be called immediately after FETCH_ROWS in order to receive accurate results.

The Syntax for the LAST_ROW_COUNT Function

```
FUNCTION LAST_ROW_COUNT RETURN INTEGER;
```

If the call is made before FETCH_ROWS, you receive the value 0.

Using LAST_ROW_ID

The LAST_ROW_ID function returns the ROWID of the last row processed. Again, this should be called immediately after FETCH_ROWS in order for it to return correct results. The syntax for the LAST_ROW_ID function is as follows:

```
FUNCTION LAST_ROW_ID RETURN ROWID;
```

 Note If you are executing a SELECT statement, the LAST_ROW_ID function returns correct results only when the FOR UPDATE clause is used.

Testing LAST_ROW_ID and LAST_ROW_COUNT

Enter and execute the code in Listing 16.5 to test the LAST_ROW_ID and LAST_ROW_COUNT functions. Make sure that you have entered SET SERVEROUTPUT ON at the SQL*Plus prompt. Notice that the SELECT statement in line 18 includes the FOR UPDATE clause. That's done so that the LAST_ROW_ID function will return correct results.

INPUT   **LISTING 16.5**   Checking the Progress of Fetched Rows

```
 1: DECLARE
 2: /* The purpose of this PL/SQL block is to demonstrate
 3: executing queries within PL/SQL through the use of the
 4: DBMS_SQL package.  We will simply display the output to
 5: screen with the DBMS_OUTPUT package.  We also demonstrate
 6: the use of tracking the progress of fetching rows*/
 7:
 8:     v_CursorID  NUMBER;
 9:     v_SelectRecords  VARCHAR2(500); --  SQL string
10:     v_NUMRows  INTEGER; --  Number of rows processed - of no use
11:     v_MyNum INTEGER;
12:     v_MyText VARCHAR2(50);
13:     v_MyROWID ROWID;
14:     v_TotRow INTEGER;
15:
16: BEGIN
17:     v_CursorID := DBMS_SQL.OPEN_CURSOR; --  Get the Cursor ID
18:     v_SelectRecords := 'SELECT * from MyTable FOR UPDATE';
19:
20
21:     DBMS_SQL.PARSE(v_CursorID,v_SelectRecords,DBMS_SQL.V7);
22:         /* Perform syntax error checking */
23:
24:
25:     DBMS_SQL.DEFINE_COLUMN(v_CursorID,1,v_MyNum);
26:     DBMS_SQL.DEFINE_COLUMN(v_CursorID,2,v_MyText,50);
27:
28:     v_NumRows := DBMS_SQL.EXECUTE(v_CursorID);
29:         /* Execute the SQL code  */
30: LOOP
31:     IF DBMS_SQL.FETCH_ROWS(v_CursorID) = 0 THEN
32:         EXIT;
33:     END IF;
34:
35: /*  The next four rows are used for seeing the progress for
36:     fetching rows  */
37:
38:     v_TOTROW := DBMS_SQL.LAST_ROW_COUNT;
39:     v_MyROWID := DBMS_SQL.LAST_ROW_ID;
40:     DBMS_OUTPUT.PUT_LINE('The last row count is: ' ¦¦
```

```
41:            v_TOTROW || ' The last ROWID is: ' || v_MyROWID);
42:
43:     DBMS_SQL.COLUMN_VALUE(v_CursorId,1,v_MyNum);
44:     DBMS_SQL.COLUMN_VALUE(v_CursorId,2,v_MyText);
45:
46:     DBMS_OUTPUT.PUT_LINE(v_MyNum || ' ' || v_MyText);
47:
48: END LOOP;
49:
50: EXCEPTION
51:    WHEN OTHERS THEN
52:            RAISE; --  raise if some other unknown error
53:
54:     DBMS_SQL.CLOSE_CURSOR(v_CursorID); --  Close the cursor
55:
56: END; --  End PL/SQL block
57: /
```

OUTPUT

```
The last row count is: 1 The last ROWID is: AAADZ4AAHAAACtSAAA
1 One
The last row count is: 2 The last ROWID is: AAADZ4AAHAAACtSAAB
2 Two
The last row count is: 3 The last ROWID is: AAADZ4AAHAAACtSAAC
3 Three
The last row count is: 4 The last ROWID is: AAADZ4AAHAAACtSAAD
4 Four
The last row count is: 5 The last ROWID is: AAADZ4AAHAAACtSAAE
4 Four
```

ANALYSIS As you can see, both functions worked as expected. The row counter increased with each row fetched, and the ROWID was displayed for each row. Had the SELECT statement not included the FOR UPDATE clause (line 18), the row count would still be correct, but the ROWIDs would not. You must use FOR UPDATE in order for the LAST_ROW_ID function to work.

Note Selecting FOR UPDATE entails some overhead, and interferes with concurrent access to the data by other users. FOR UPDATE is used here to demonstrate the use of the LAST_ROW_ID function. In real life, you are better off not using FOR UPDATE unless you really intend to update the rows that you are selecting.

Using `LAST_ERROR_POSITION`

The `LAST_ROW_POSITION` function returns the location in an SQL statement where an error occurred. This is useful only if the `PARSE` call was unsuccessful. The syntax for the `LAST_ROW_POSITION` Function is as follows:

▲ `FUNCTION LAST_ROW_POSITION RETURN INTEGER;`

Using Native Dynamic SQL

 With the release of Oracle8i, Oracle extended the PL/SQL language to support dynamic SQL directly. For most purposes, you no longer need to use `DBMS_SQL` to write dynamic SQL. Instead, you can use the new features, which are referred to collectively as *native dynamic SQL*.

> **Note**
> You will need Oracle8i in order to execute the examples pertaining to native dynamic SQL in the remaining part of this lesson.

Executing DML and DDL

Executing DML and DDL statements is quite easy using native dynamic SQL. Instead of making all those calls to `DBMS_SQL`, you can simply issue a PL/SQL `EXECUTE IMMEDIATE` statement.

```
EXECUTE IMMEDIATE string
    [INTO {variable[, variable]... ¦ record}]
    [USING [IN ¦ OUT ¦ IN OUT] bind
        [, [IN ¦ OUT ¦ IN OUT] bind]...];
```

In this syntax the parameters are as follows:

- *string* is a variable or literal that contains the SQL statement you want to execute.

- *variable* is a PL/SQL variable. If you are executing a `SELECT...INTO` statement, you can supply a list of variables in which you want the results to be placed.

- *record* is a PL/SQL record. Instead of supplying a list of variables for a `SELECT...INTO` statement, you can supply a record instead. The results of the `SELECT` are placed in the record. The fields of the record must match the columns being selected.

- *bind* is a bind variable. You use these to pass parameters to a dynamic SQL statement. The parameter markers are numbered, and must be `:1`, `:2`, and so on. The first bind variable becomes the value `:1`, the second bind variable becomes the value `:2`, and so forth.

Executing a DDL Statement

Listing 16.6 demonstrates the use of EXECUTE IMMEDIATE in creating a table.

INPUT   **LISTING 16.6**   Creating a Table by Using EXECUTE IMMEDIATE

```
1: BEGIN
2:    EXECUTE IMMEDIATE 'CREATE TABLE YOURTABLE ('
3:                   || 'YOURROW NUMBER, '
4:                   || 'YOURDESC VARCHAR2(50))';
5: END;
6: /
```

ANALYSIS   This is a very simple block of code. The EXECUTE IMMEDIATE statement is in lines 2–4. The string to be executed is concatenated together from three smaller strings because the whole thing would be too long to fit on the page. When you execute the block, the EXECUTE IMMEDIATE statement in turn executes the CREATE TABLE statement, and you have a new table named yourtable.

Using Bind Variables

Bind variables allow you to pass values to a SQL statement that you are executing. They are much easier to use with native dynamic SQL than with the DBMS_SQL package.

Listing 16.7 shows a PL/SQL block that dynamically generates an INSERT statement, and then uses it to insert data into the table yourtable, created in Listing 16.6.

INPUT   **LISTING 16.7**   Using Bind Variables with Native Dynamic SQL

```
 1: DECLARE
 2:    v_YourNum   NUMBER;
 3:    v_YourDesc  VARCHAR2(50);
 4:    v_INSERT_stmt VARCHAR2(100);
 5: BEGIN
 6:    -- Generate an INSERT statement.
 7:    v_INSERT_stmt := 'INSERT INTO yourtable VALUES (:1, :2)';
 8:
 9:    -- Insert the first row
10:    v_YourNum := 1;
11:    v_YourDesc := 'One';
12:    EXECUTE IMMEDIATE v_INSERT_stmt
13:        USING v_YourNum, v_YourDesc;
14:
15:    -- Insert the second row
16:    v_YourNum := 2;
```

continues

16

LISTING **16.7** continued

```
17:     v_YourDesc := 'Two';
18:     EXECUTE IMMEDIATE v_INSERT_stmt
19:         USING v_YourNum, v_YourDesc;
20:
21:     -- Insert the third row
22:     v_YourNum := 3;
23:     v_YourDesc := 'Three';
24:     EXECUTE IMMEDIATE v_INSERT_stmt
25:         USING v_YourNum, v_YourDesc;
26:
27:     -- Insert the fourth row
28:     v_YourNum := 4;
29:     v_YourDesc := 'Four';
30:     EXECUTE IMMEDIATE v_INSERT_stmt
31:         USING v_YourNum, v_YourDesc;
32:
33:     -- Insert the fifth row
34:     v_YourNum := 5;
35:     v_YourDesc := 'Five';
36:     EXECUTE IMMEDIATE v_INSERT_stmt
37:         USING v_YourNum, v_YourDesc;
38: END;
39: /
```

ANALYSIS The INSERT statement to be executed is built in line 7. (In this case, it's not really very dynamic, but it serves to illustrate how this all works.) The two variables v_YourNum and v_YourDesc, declared in lines 2–4, are used as bind variables. They hold the values that we want to insert. In preparation for the first insert, these are set to 1 and 'One', respectively (lines 10 and 11). The EXECUTE statement in line 12–13 lists these variables in the USING clause. The order in which they are listed in the USING clause controls how they are bound to the numeric parameter markers in the SQL statement. The variable v_YourNum is listed first, so it becomes :1. The variable v_YourDesc is listed next, so it is used in place of :2. The INSERT statement is executed five times, with different values in the bind variables each time, in order to insert five rows in the table.

Executing SQL Queries

To execute a SELECT statement by using native dynamic SQL, you need to do three things:

1. Open a cursor by using a new form of the OPEN statement.
2. Fetch values from the cursor by using the FETCH statement.
3. Close the cursor.

Of those three steps, only the first step represents a difference from what you would do to process a static SELECT statement by using PL/SQL.

SYNTAX

The Syntax for the OPEN...FOR Statement

```
OPEN cursor
FOR string
[USING bind[, bind]...];
```

In this syntax the parameters are as follows:

16

- *cursor* is the cursor that you want to open. This is actually a pointer to a cursor, and must be a REF CURSOR variable.

- *string* is a variable or literal that contains the SQL statement you want to execute.

- *bind* is a bind variable. You use these to pass parameters to the dynamic SQL statement. The parameter markers are numbered, and must be :1, :2, and so on. The first bind variable becomes the value :1, the second bind variable becomes the value :2, and so forth.

The cursor that you declare and use with the OPEN...FOR statements must be a REF CURSOR. You can declare a REF CURSOR like this:

```
TYPE ref_cursor_type IS REF CURSOR;
your_cursor ref_cursor_type;
```

Listing 16.8 shows OPEN...FOR being used to open a cursor on a dynamic SQL statement. The rows returned by that statement are then fetched into a PL/SQL record, and from there they are displayed by using DBMS_OUTPUT.

INPUT   LISTING 16.8   Executing a SELECT by Using Native Dynamic SQL

```
 1: DECLARE
 2:     TYPE your_cursor_type IS REF CURSOR;
 3:     your_cursor  your_cursor_type;
 4:
 5:     -- Declare a record type for the output
 6:     TYPE dyn_record IS RECORD (
 7:         yourrow    yourtable.yourrow%TYPE,
 8:         yourdesc   yourtable.yourdesc%TYPE
 9:         );
10:
11:     -- Note, could also use:
12:     --     dyn_rec yourtable%ROWTYPE;
13:     --
14:     dyn_rec dyn_record;
15:
```

continues

LISTING **16.8** continued

```
16:        dynamic_select_stmt VARCHAR2(100);
17:  BEGIN
18:        -- Generate the dynamic SELECT statement.
19:        dynamic_select_stmt :=
20:            'SELECT yourrow, yourdesc FROM yourtable';
21:        dynamic_select_stmt := dynamic_select_stmt ||
22:            ' ORDER BY yourrow DESC';
23:
24:        -- Open a cursor on the dynamic statement.
25:        OPEN your_cursor FOR dynamic_select_stmt;
26:
27:        -- Loop through and display all the data.
28:        LOOP
29:            -- Fetch the next row, exit the loop when
30:            -- no more data is left.
31:            FETCH your_cursor
32:                INTO dyn_rec;
33:            EXIT WHEN your_cursor%NOTFOUND;
34:
35:            -- Display the data using DBMS_OUTPUT
36:            DBMS_OUTPUT.PUT_LINE(dyn_rec.yourrow ||
37:                             ' ' || dyn_rec.yourdesc);
38:        END LOOP;
39:
40:        -- Close the cursor.
41:        CLOSE your_cursor;
42:
43:  END;
44:  /
```

OUTPUT
```
5 Five
4 Four
3 Three
2 Two
1 One

PL/SQL procedure successfully completed.
```

ANALYSIS The REF CURSER variable used with the OPEN statement is declared in lines 2–3. Lines 18–20 build on the initial SELECT statement, and the next two lines (21–22) add an ORDER BY clause. The cursor is opened in line 25, through the use of the OPEN...FOR statement. Note that OPEN FOR references the VARCHAR2 variable containing the SELECT statement. From here on out, it's just normal everyday PL/SQL cursor processing. The FETCH in lines 31–32 fetches the data from the cursor into a record. You could also fetch the data into a list of variables. The DBMS_OUTPUT call in line 36–37 allow SQL*Plus to display the data, and the CLOSE statement in line 41 closes the cursor after all the data has been processed.

Executing PL/SQL Blocks

You can execute PL/SQL blocks by using native dynamic SQL through the use of the EXECUTE IMMEDIATE statement. Listing 16.9 shows the native dynamic SQL version of Listing 16.4.

INPUT **LISTING 16.9** Executing a PL/SQL Block Using Native Dynamic SQL

16

```
 1: DECLARE
 2:     block_to_execute VARCHAR2(200) :=
 3:         'BEGIN
 4:             SELECT YourRow,YourDesc
 5:             INTO :1, :2 FROM YourTable
 6:             WHERE YourRow = 2;
 7:         END;';
 8:
 9:     YourRow NUMBER;
10:     YourDesc VARCHAR2(100);
11: BEGIN
12:     EXECUTE IMMEDIATE block_to_execute
13:         USING OUT YourRow, OUT YourDesc;
14:
15:     DBMS_OUTPUT.PUT_LINE(YourRow || ' ' || YourDesc);
16: END;
17: /
```

ANALYSIS You can see that this code is a lot simpler to understand than the Listing 16.4 version. The block_to_execute variable, declared in lines 2–7, contains the PL/SQL block to be executed. The EXECUTE IMMEDIATE statement in lines 12–13 is used to execute the block. The crucial thing to note here is that the bind variables listed in the USING clause both have the keyword OUT in front of them. This allows them to receive values back from the PL/SQL block. So the PL/SQL block issues a SELECT...INTO statement that places values into these variables, and because they are OUT bind variables, those values are returned to you.

Caution This code fails if there are two rows in YOURTABLE with a value of 2 for the YOURROW column. If you ran Listing 16.7 more than once, that might be the case.

Summary

Today's lesson covers Oracle's DBMS_SQL package, as well as the new native dynamic SQL features included with Oracle8i. Both let you dynamically build and execute SQL statements from within PL/SQL. DBMS_SQL is the way to go if your code must run on releases of Oracle prior to the 8i release. Otherwise, you should use native dynamic SQL if you can. You'll find it much easier to deal with, and the resulting code will be more easily understood.

With DBMS_SQL, you have to open a cursor for each statement, define bind variables, fetch rows returned by queries, and get each column one at a time. Quite a lot of code is needed to do all that, and that code is rather tedious to write. Native Dynamic SQL simplifies things. Using Native Dynamic SQL, as with DBMS_SQL, you open a cursor for a dynamically generated SQL statement. However, unlike with DBMS_SQL, you can then treat that cursor as an ordinary PL/SQL cursor. Fetching the data then becomes a very easy task.

Q&A

Q Now that native dynamic SQL has arrived, is there any reason I would ever use DBMS_SQL?

A There probably are some reasons, but there sure aren't many. One thing that DBMS_SQL can handle that native dynamic SQL can't, at least not easily, is the situation where you know absolutely nothing about the tables and columns that you will be querying. DBMS_SQL allows you to issue a query, and then dynamically discover how many columns the query returns, as well as what the datatypes are. That's a fairly advanced use, but if you need to be able to do it, then you need to use DBMS_SQL.

Q What three types of statements can be executed dynamically?

A Using dynamic SQL, you can execute non-query DDL and DML statements, SQL queries, and anonymous PL/SQL blocks.

Q Should dynamically executed queries be written with trailing semicolons?

A No! This is a very common mistake to make. Do not include a trailing semicolon with any dynamic SQL statement. The reason is that strictly speaking, the semicolon is not part of the SQL syntax. You need it when you write a static SQL statement, because Oracle needs to know where the SQL statement ends. However, when you are writing dynamic SQL, you are only working with one statement at a time, so a terminator is not needed.

Q **What are the general steps for using DBMS_SQL?**

A You need to open a cursor, parse the statements to be executed, bind any variables that are necessary, define columns if you are executing a SELECT statement, execute the query, retrieve the data (if there is any) into some PL/SQL variables, and close the cursor.

Workshop

16

You can use this to test your comprehension of this lesson and put what you've learned into practice. You'll find the answers to the quiz and exercises in Appendix A, "Answers."

Quiz

1. For DML and DDL statements, and also for queries, what punctuation must not be included at the end of the query?
2. What is meant by the term *dynamic SQL*?
3. What is Oracle's term for the new version of dynamic SQL?
4. When using native dynamic SQL, what new form of the OPEN statement is used to open a cursor on a dynamic SQL statement?

Exercise

Write a stored procedure to take a username as an argument, and create a version of mytable in that user's schema.

WEEK 3

DAY 17

Writing to Files and the Display

by Timothy Atwood and Jonathan Gennick

The PL/SQL language itself does not have any mechanism for performing either file or screen output. However, Oracle supplies a number of built-in packages that allow you to perform I/O, and that can be called from PL/SQL. Today's lesson talks about the following:

- The DBMS_OUTPUT package
- The UTL_FILE package
- The TEXT_IO package

You've already seen DBMS_OUTPUT used throughout this book as a way to display output on the screen, using SQL*Plus. It has some other capabilities, too, which you'll learn about today. The UTL_FILE and TEXT_IO packages allow you to read and write text files. UTL_FILE is a server-side built-in package that allows you to read and write files on the database server. TEXT_IO is an Oracle Developer package that allows you to do file input/output (I/O) on the client.

Exploring the DBMS_OUTPUT Package

Looking at many of the examples in this book might lead you to believe that DBMS_OUTPUT's only function is to allow you to display PL/SQL output using SQL*Plus. That's only part of the story, though. DBMS_OUTPUT is actually designed to let you write output to a buffer in memory, and then read that output back again. Figure 17.1 illustrates this, and also shows how SQL*Plus fits into the picture.

FIGURE 17.1

DBMS_OUTPUT *allows you to read and write data to and from a buffer in memory.*

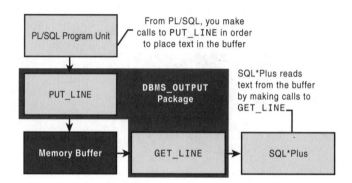

The usefulness of DBMS_OUTPUT becomes apparent when you realize that the procedure that reads data from the buffer does not have to be the same procedure that wrote it there in the first place. Any procedure can read the data. When you issue the command SET SERVEROUTPUT ON in SQL*Plus, you are really telling SQL*Plus to check the buffer for data after each statement executes, fetch any data that's found, and display it for you to see. In its most generic sense, DBMS_OUTPUT can be used to communicate data between any two PL/SQL procedures.

Note

DBMS_OUTPUT allows you to communicate between two program units that are part of the same session. To communicate across sessions, you need to use the DBMS_PIPE package. You'll learn about that on Day 19, "Alerting and Communicating with Other Procedures: The DBMS_ALERT and DBMS_PIPE Packages."

Enabling the DBMS_OUTPUT Package

Before you can use DBMS_OUTPUT, you need to call the initialization procedure DBMS_OUTPUT.ENABLE. SQL*Plus does this for you automatically whenever you issue a SET SERVEROUTPUT ON command. However, you might want to do it yourself. The main reason that you might want to call DBMS_OUTPUT.ENABLE yourself is to allocate a buffer larger than the default of 20,000 characters. Another reason to call DBMS_OUTPUT.ENABLE yourself would be if SQL*Plus isn't the destination for your messages.

The Syntax for the DBMS_OUTPUT.ENABLE Procedure

DBMS_OUTPUT.ENABLE (*buffer_size* IN INTEGER DEFAULT 20000);

The *buffer_size* parameter controls the size of the buffer, and can be any value between 2,000 and 1,000,000. The default is 20,000.

The following PL/SQL block shows a call to enable the DBMS_OUTPUT package:

```
BEGIN
  DBMS_OUTPUT.ENABLE (1000000);
END;
```

If you are using DBMS_OUTPUT to send a lot of data to SQL*Plus, keep in mind that SQL*Plus can't begin reading until all the data is sent. Therefore, your buffer must be large enough to contain all the output. Also bear in mind that SQL*Plus release 8.0 and above allows you to specify the buffer size as an argument to the SET SERVEROUTPUT ON command. For example, the following command also enables DBMS_OUTPUT, and with a buffer size of 1,000,000 bytes:

```
SET SERVEROUTPUT ON SIZE 1000000
```

After you enable the package, you can use it to write data to the buffer, and to read it back again.

Disabling the DBMS_OUTPUT Package

When you're done using DBMS_OUPUT, you can disable the package by making a call to DBMS_OUTPUT.DISABLE. This has the effect of purging the buffer of any remaining information.

The Syntax for the DBMS_OUTPUT.DISABLE Procedure

DBMS_OUTPUT.DISABLE;

There are no parameters to the DISABLE procedure. The following PL/SQL block shows how it is called:

```
BEGIN
  DBMS_OUTPUT.DISABLE;
END;
```

SQL*Plus calls DBMS_OUTPUT.DISABLE for you whenever you issue a SET SERVEROUTPUT OFF command. After output has been disabled, any further calls to DBMS_OUTPUT.PUT_LINE, DBMS_OUTPUT.GET_LINE, and so forth are ignored.

SYNTAX

17

Writing Data to the Buffer

You write data to the DBMS_OUTPUT buffer by using a combination of the PUT_LINE, PUT, and NEW_LINE procedures. PUT_LINE writes a line of text, followed by a newline character. PUT writes text, but doesn't follow that text with a newline. The NEW_LINE procedure writes one newline character.

The Syntax for the DBMS_OUTPUT.PUT_LINE, DBMS_OUTPUT.PUT, and DBMS_OUTPUT.NEW_LINE Procedures

```
DBMS_OUTPUT.PUT_LINE (item IN NUMBER);
DBMS_OUTPUT.PUT_LINE (item IN VARCHAR2);
DBMS_OUTPUT.PUT_LINE (item IN DATE);

DBMS_OUTPUT.PUT       (item IN NUMBER);
DBMS_OUTPUT.PUT       (item IN VARCHAR2);
DBMS_OUTPUT.PUT       (item IN DATE);

DBMS_OUTPUT.NEW_LINE;
```

In this syntax *item* is the value written to the buffer. Items of type DATE and NUMBER are always converted to text before being written.

The PUT and PUT_LINE procedures each take one argument. The procedures are overloaded in order to allow you to pass in dates, numbers, and text. If you pass in text, it is written to the buffer. If you pass in a date or a number, it is converted to text, and then written to the buffer. It's usually best to convert things to text yourself, so that you can control the output format.

The following example, in Listing 17.1, shows DBMS_OUTPUT being enabled, and some data being written to the buffer. SQL*Plus has been used to execute the block and capture the output.

INPUT   **LISTING 17.1**   Using DBMS_OUTPUT to Place Data in the Buffer

```
 1: SET SERVEROUTPUT ON
 2:
 3: BEGIN
 4: --We only need a small buffer for this example.
 5: DBMS_OUTPUT.ENABLE (2000);
 6:
 7: DBMS_OUTPUT.PUT_LINE('Three names will be written.');
 8: DBMS_OUTPUT.PUT('Jenny');
 9: DBMS_OUTPUT.NEW_LINE;
10: DBMS_OUTPUT.PUT('Shirley');
11: DBMS_OUTPUT.NEW_LINE;
12: DBMS_OUTPUT.PUT('Tina');
```

```
13: DBMS_OUTPUT.NEW_LINE;
14: END;
15: /
```

OUTPUT

```
Three names will be written.
Jenny
Shirley
Tina

PL/SQL procedure successfully completed.
```

ANALYSIS This PL/SQL block writes one line into the buffer by using the PUT_LINE procedure (line 5). It then writes three more lines using a combination of the PUT and NEW_LINE procedures (lines 6–11). Because SERVEROUTPUT had been turned on, SQL*Plus reads the data from the buffer and displays it onscreen.

The PUT and PUT_LINE procedures only handle lines up to 255 characters long. If you attempt to write a line longer than that, you get an error. You also get an error if you attempt to write more data into the buffer than it will hold.

Reading Data from the Buffer

Two procedures, GET_LINE and GET_LINES, allow you to read from the buffer. GET_LINE allows you to read one line at a time, and GET_LINES allows you to read several lines into an array.

The Syntax for GET_LINE and GET_LINES

```
DBMS_OUTPUT.GET_LINE (
    line    OUT VARCHAR2,
    status OUT INTEGER);

DBMS_OUTPUT.GET_LINES (
    lines       OUT   CHARARR,
    numlines IN OUT   INTEGER);
```

In this syntax the parameters are as follows:

- *line* is the line retrieved by GET_LINE.
- *status* indicates whether a line was retrieved. A status of 1 means that the line parameter contains a line retrieved from the buffer. A status of 0 means that the buffer was empty[md]that is, nothing was retrieved.
- *lines* is a table of VARCHAR2(255). You can declare this table by using the type DBMS_OUTPUT.CHARARR. See Listing 17.2 for an example.
- *numlines* is both an input and an output. When calling GET_LINES, you should set this to the number of lines that you want to retrieve. GET_LINES replaces that value with the number of lines that were actually retrieved.

The example in Listing 17.2 is an extension of Listing 17.1. It shows GET_LINE being used to retrieve the three names from the buffer. It also demonstrates that the buffer contents are maintained across PL/SQL blocks.

> **Note**
>
> This listing should be executed from SQL*Plus.

LISTING 17.2   Using GET_LINE to Retrieve Data From the Buffer

```
 1: SET SERVEROUTPUT OFF
 2:
 3: BEGIN
 4:    --We only need a small buffer for this example.
 5:    DBMS_OUTPUT.ENABLE (2000);
 6:
 7:    DBMS_OUTPUT.PUT_LINE('Three names will be written.');
 8:    DBMS_OUTPUT.PUT('Jenny');
 9:    DBMS_OUTPUT.NEW_LINE;
10:    DBMS_OUTPUT.PUT('Shirley');
11:    DBMS_OUTPUT.NEW_LINE;
12:    DBMS_OUTPUT.PUT('Tina');
13:    DBMS_OUTPUT.NEW_LINE;
14: END;
15: /
16:
17: PL/SQL procedure successfully completed.
18:
19:
20: SET SERVEROUTPUT ON
21: DECLARE
22:    throw_away VARCHAR2(50);
23:    name1 VARCHAR2(10);
24:    name2 VARCHAR2(10);
25:    name3 VARCHAR2(10);
26:    status NUMBER;
27: BEGIN
28: --The first line in the buffer is a throw away.
29: DBMS_OUTPUT.GET_LINE(throw_away, status);
30:
31:    --The next three lines will be the three names.
32:    DBMS_OUTPUT.GET_LINE(name1, status);
33:    DBMS_OUTPUT.GET_LINE(name2, status);
34:    DBMS_OUTPUT.GET_LINE(name3, status);
35:
36:    --Now that we have the names, write them out
37:    --on one line. SQL*Plus will pick this up and
38:    --display it.
39:    DBMS_OUTPUT.PUT_LINE(name1 || ' and ' ||
40:                         name2 || ' and ' || name3);
```

```
41: END;
42: /
```

```
Jenny and Shirley and Tina

PL/SQL procedure successfully completed.
```

ANALYSIS The first PL/SQL block (lines 3–14) writes three names into the buffer, one name to a line. Because this example is executed from SQL*Plus, the SERVEROUTPUT setting is turned off (line 1) to prevent SQL*Plus from reading and displaying the names. Instead, the names remain in the buffer, where they can be accessed by the second block. The second PL/SQL block (lines 21–41) reads the first line and throws it away (line 28–29). Then it reads each of the three names (lines 32–34). Finally, it concatenates those three names together in one line, and writes that line back out to the buffer (lines 36–40). Because the SERVEROUTPUT setting has been turned on for the second block, SQL*Plus reads the results and displays them onscreen.

17

Note

> The buffer is a first-in, first-out (FIFO) buffer. The first line to be written is also the first to be read.

If you need to retrieve several lines at once from the buffer, you can use the GET_LINES procedure. It accepts a PL/SQL table (the equivalent of an array) as an argument, and retrieves as many lines as you request into that array. By modifying the code shown in Listing 17.2 to use GET_LINES instead of GET_LINE, you can retrieve all three names by using only one procedure call, as shown in Listing 17.3.

INPUT/ OUTPUT

LISTING 17.3   Using GET_LINES to Retrieve Three Lines from the Buffer with One Procedure Call

```
 1: SET SERVEROUTPUT OFF
 2:
 3: BEGIN
 4:     --We only need a small buffer for this example.
 5:     DBMS_OUTPUT.ENABLE (2000);
 6:
 7:     DBMS_OUTPUT.PUT_LINE('Three names will be written.');
 8:     DBMS_OUTPUT.PUT('Jenny');
 9:     DBMS_OUTPUT.NEW_LINE;
10:     DBMS_OUTPUT.PUT('Shirley');
11:     DBMS_OUTPUT.NEW_LINE;
12:     DBMS_OUTPUT.PUT('Tina');
```

continues

LISTING **17.3** continued

```
13:    DBMS_OUTPUT.NEW_LINE;
14: END;
15: /
16:
17: PL/SQL procedure successfully completed.
18:
19:
20: SET SERVEROUTPUT ON
21: DECLARE
22:    throw_away VARCHAR2(50);
23:    names DBMS_OUTPUT.CHARARR;
24:    lines_to_get NUMBER;
25:    inx1 NUMBER;
26:    combined_names VARCHAR2(80);
27:    status NUMBER;
28: BEGIN
29:    --The first line in the buffer is a throw away.
30:    DBMS_OUTPUT.GET_LINE(throw_away, status);
31:
32:    --The next three lines will be the three names.
33:    lines_to_get := 3;
34:    DBMS_OUTPUT.GET_LINES(names, lines_to_get);
35:
36:    --Now that we have the names, write them out
37:    --on one line. SQL*Plus will pick this up and
38:    --display it.
39:    combined_names := '';
40:    FOR inx1 IN 1 .. lines_to_get LOOP
41:      IF inx1 > 1 THEN
42:        combined_names := combined_names || ' and ';
43:      END IF;
44:
45:      combined_names := combined_names || names(inx1);
46:    END LOOP;
47:    DBMS_OUTPUT.PUT_LINE(combined_names);
48: END;
49: /
```

```
Jenny and Shirley and Tina

PL/SQL procedure successfully completed.
```

ANALYSIS The use of GET_LINES actually makes this version of the code more complex.
Line 23, in the second block, is where the table of type DBMS_OUTPUT.CHARARR is
declared. That table is eventually used to hold the results. Lines 29–30 are the same as in
Listing 17.2, and simply serve to throw away the first line in the buffer. The call to

GET_LINES occurs in lines 32–34. The lines_to_get parameter contains the value 3, telling GET_LINES to return all three names. The loop in line 40–43 then uses the value that GET_LINES passes back to iterate through the array the proper number of times. If GET_LINES returned more than three lines, or fewer than three lines, the value of lines_to_get would be set appropriately, and the loop would concatenate all the lines together.

Exceptions Raised from the DBMS_OUTPUT Package

There are two exceptions you have to worry about when using the DBMS_OUTPUT package. These are described in Table 17.1, along with the actions required to fix the problems.

TABLE 17.1   Exceptions Raised by DBMS_OUTPUT

Exception Code	Error Description	Corrective Action
ORU-10027	Buffer overflow	Increase the buffer size if possible. Otherwise, find a way to write less data.
ORU-10028	Line length overflow, limit of 255 characters per line	Make sure that all calls made to PUT and PUT_LINE have fewer than 255 characters.

Now that you know the exceptions, you can trap errors as they occur.

Reading and Writing Files with the UTL_FILE Package

The UTL_FILE package enables you to read and write files on the database server. There are two prerequisites to using UTL_FILE:

- You must be granted execute privileges on the UTL_FILE package.
- Your database administrator must set a database initialization parameter named UTL_FILE_DIR.

Granting access to the package is easy. If you don't already have execute privileges on UTL_FILE, your database administrator can grant it by logging on as the user SYS, and issuing a command like this:

INPUT   GRANT EXECUTE ON utl_file TO *username*;

The matter of the UTL_FILE_DIR parameter is a bit more difficult to explain. You can't just read and write files in any directory on the server. When you make calls to UTL_FILE_DIR, Oracle is really reading and writing the files for you. On most systems, the Oracle software runs in privileged mode, giving it access to *all* the files. Needless to say, that presents a security risk. To mitigate that risk, before UTL_FILE can be used, your database administrator must set the UTL_FILE_DIR parameter to point to a specific list of directories. All file I/O done by UTL_FILE must be done in one of those directories. The examples in this book assume the following setting:

```
UTL_FILE_DIR = c:\a
```

If you're experimenting with UTL_FILE on a workstation, you need to add this line to the database parameter file. You also need to stop and restart the database afterward, in order for the new setting to take effect.

When UTL_FILE_DIR is set, and you have been granted EXECUTE access to the UTL_FILE package, you are ready to read and write files.

File Input

Using UTL_FILE, the overall process to read (or write) a file is as follows:

1. Declare a file handle variable to use in identifying the file when you make calls to the various UTL_FILE routines. You can use the type UTL_FILE.FILE_TYPE for this purpose.

2. Declare a string of type VARCHAR2 to act as a buffer for reading in the file one line at a time.

3. Make a call to UTL_FILE.FOPEN to open the file. When you open a file, you need to specify whether you want to read the file or write to the file. You can't do both.

4. If you're reading the file, make calls to UTL_FILE.GET_LINE. If you're writing, make calls to UTL_FILE.PUT_LINE.

5. When you're done, call UTL_FILE.FCLOSE to close the file.

The next section talks briefly about the various UTL_FILE procedures and functions, and shows the syntax information for each. Following that is a section with an example showing UTL_FILE being used to write data to a file.

Using `UTL_FILE` Procedures and Functions

The `UTL_FILE` package implements the following procedures and functions:

Procedure or Function	Description
FCLOSE	Closes a file.
FCLOSE_ALL	Closes all the files.
FFLUSH	Flushes any buffered data to be written out to disk immediately.
FOPEN	Opens a file.
GET_LINE	Reads one line from a file.
IS_OPEN	Checks whether a file is open.
NEW_LINE	Writes a newline character out to a file.
PUT	Writes a string of characters to a file, but doesn't follow that with a newline.
PUT_LINE	Writes one line to a file.
PUTF	Formats and writes output. This is a crude imitation of C's `printf()` procedure.

Many of the procedure names in the `UTL_FILE` package are named identically to corresponding procedures in `DBMS_OUTPUT`. For example, `GET_LINE` and `PUT_LINE` are used in both packages to read and write lines. The difference is in whether that I/O is done to and from a file or to and from a memory buffer.

The `FCLOSE` Procedure

The `FCLOSE` procedure closes a file. If the buffer for the file being closed is not empty, it is flushed to disk before the file is closed.

The Syntax for the `FCLOSE` Procedure

```
PROCEDURE FCLOSE(file IN OUT file_type);
```

The `file` parameter is the file handle returned from `FOPEN` when the file was originally opened. Table 17.2 shows a list of possible exceptions raised by `FCLOSE`.

TABLE 17.2   Exceptions Raised by `FCLOSE` and `FCLOSE_ALL`

Exception Raised	Description of Error
`UTL_FILE.INVALID_FILEHANDLE`	You passed a file handle that didn't represent an open file.
`UTL_FILE.WRITE_ERROR`	The operating system was unable to write to the file.
`UTL_FILE.INTERNAL_ERROR`	An internal error occurred.

The first exception in the list, that of an invalid file handle, is one that you can easily prevent simply by being careful to write good code. Make sure you open a file before you use it, and that you keep track of which variable has the file handle in it. Write errors can occur if the disk is full, or if some other error prevents Oracle from writing the data for you. An internal error indicates that Oracle itself is messed up.

The `FCLOSE_ALL` Procedure

The `FCLOSE_ALL` procedure closes all the files at once, flushing any buffers that are not empty.

The Syntax for the `FCLOSE_ALL` Procedure

```
PROCEDURE FCLOSEALL;
```

Refer to Table 17.2 for a list of possible exceptions raised by `FCLOSE_ALL`. You should be aware that although `FCLOSE_ALL` does close all files, it does not mark the files as closed. Future calls to `IS_OPEN` still indicate that they are open, even though in reality they are not.

The `FOPEN` Procedure

`FOPEN` opens a file for reading, or for writing. `FOPEN` is a function, and it returns a file handle pointing to the file that was opened. There are two versions of `FOPEN`. One allows you to specify a maximum line size, and the other does not.

The Syntax for the `FOPEN` Procedure

```
FUNCTION FOPEN(location IN VARCHAR2,
               filename IN VARCHAR2,
               openmode IN VARCHAR2)
RETURN FILE_TYPE;

FUNCTION FOPEN(location IN VARCHAR2,
               filename IN VARCHAR2,
               openmode IN VARCHAR2,
               max_linesize IN BINARY_INTEGER)
RETURN FILE_TYPE;
```

The parameters are as follows:

- *location* is the name of the directory containing the file. This must match one of the directories listed for the UTL_FILE_DIR parameter.
- *filename* is the name of the file. The name can include an extension.
- *openmode* is the mode in which you are opening the file. Valid values are R, W, and A. Use R to read a file, W to write to a file, and A to append to an existing file.
- *max_linesize* allows you to specify the maximum line size. The allowed range is 1 through 32,767. If you omit this parameter, then the default, 1023, is used.

Note	The ability to specify a line size in the FOPEN call is a new feature in Oracle8i. With releases of Oracle prior to 8.1.5, you are limited to a line size of 1023 bytes or less. If you open a file for write, and a file with the same name exists already, that file is overwritten. If you append to a file that does not exist, a new file is created.

17

After the file has been successfully opened, the FOPEN function returns a file handle. You must use that handle for all further operations on the file. FOPEN can raise several exceptions, which are listed in Table 17.3.

TABLE 17.3 Exceptions Raised by FOPEN

Exception Raised	Description of Error
UTL_FILE.INVALID_PATH	The directory is not valid. You should check it against UTL_FILE_DIR.
UTL_FILE.INVALID_MODE	An invalid mode was specified. The open mode must be either R, W, or A.
UTL_FILE.INVALID_OPERATION	The file could not be opened for some other reason. Verify that the Oracle software owner has access to the directory (it could be a permissions issue) and contact your database administrator for help.
UTL_FILE.INTERNAL_ERROR	An internal error occurred.

If you get the invalid path exception, you need to check your directory path against your database's UTL_FILE_DIR parameter setting. Remember, you can only write to the specific directories listed for that parameter. The invalid mode exception implies a coding error. To correct it, just modify your code to use one of the valid modes. If you get an invalid operation error, then there is some sort of operating system related reason why you can't open the file. Unfortunately, PL/SQL won't give you any details about what that problem is. The internal error is something you should never get, and indicates that Oracle is not functioning properly.

The GET_LINE Function

When performing file input, in order to read data from the file into the buffer, you use the GET_LINE function.

The Syntax for the GET_LINE Function

```
PROCEDURE GET_LINE(file IN FILE_TYPE,
                   buffer OUT VARCHAR2);
```

The parameters are as follows:

- *file* is the file handle returned from the FOPEN function when the file was originally opened.

- *buffer* is where the data is placed after it is read from the file. This must be of type VARCHAR2. Possible errors that could arise are shown in Table 17.4.

TABLE 17.4 Exceptions Raised by GET_LINE

Exception Raised	Description of Error
UTL_FILE.INVALID_FILEHANDLE	You passed an invalid file handle. Possibly you forgot to open the file first.
UTL_FILE.INVALID_OPERATION	The file is not open for reading (R mode), or there are problems with file permissions.
UTL_FILE.VALUE_ERROR	The buffer is not long enough to hold the line being read from the file. Increase the size of the buffer.
UTL_FILE.NO_DATA_FOUND	The end of file has been reached.
UTL_FILE.INTERNAL_ERROR	An error internal to the UTL_FILE system occurred.
UTL_FILE.READ_ERROR	An operating system error occurred while reading from the file.

When you use GET_LINE to read a file, the maximum line length that it can handle is the one specified when you opened the file. This defaults to 1023 bytes, not including the newline character. The newline characters are stripped out, and aren't returned to you.

The IS_OPEN Function

The IS_OPEN function tests to see if a file is open. You can use it before you attempt to open a file to be sure that it's not already open. You can also test to make sure a file is open before you attempt to close it.

SYNTAX
The Syntax for the IS_OPEN Function

```
FUNCTION IS_OPEN(file IN FILE_TYPE)
RETURN BOOLEAN;
```

If the file is open, the value true is returned; otherwise, false is returned. The *file* parameter is the file handle for the file that you are checking.

The NEW_LINE Procedure

The NEW_LINE procedure writes one or more newline characters to a file. The file must be open for output (mode A or W). You can't write newlines to a file that you are reading. This procedure would be used to add a newline character after you have made one or more calls to the PUT procedure.

▼ SYNTAX
The Syntax for the NEW_LINE Procedure

```
PROCEDURE NEW_LINE(file IN FILE_TYPE,
                   lines IN NATURAL :=1);
```

In this syntax the parameters are as follows:

- *file* is the file handle returned from FOPEN when the file was originally opened.

- *lines* is the total number of newline characters you want to write to the file. The default is to write one newline. This is an optional argument.

▲ The same exceptions can be raised for NEW_LINE as are raised with PUT. Table 17.5 shows a list of these.

The PUT Procedure

The PUT procedure writes the string to the output file, but without adding a newline character to the end.

▼ SYNTAX
The Syntax for the PUT Procedure

```
PROCEDURE PUT(file IN FILE_TYPE,
             buffer IN VARCHAR2);
```

In this syntax the parameters are as follows:

- *file* is the file handle as returned from FOPEN.

- *buffer* contains the text you want written to the file. The maximum number of
▲ characters that you can write using one call is limited to the line size you specified in the FOPEN call for the file, and defaults to 1023.

Table 17.5 lists the exceptions that can be raised by PUT.

17

TABLE 17.5 Exceptions Raised by PUT, PUT_LINE, PUTF, and FFLUSH

Exception Raised	Description of Error
UTL_FILE.INVALID_FILEHANDLE	You used an invalid file handle. This exception might be raised if you forgot to open the file.
UTL_FILE.INVALID_OPERATION	You attempted to write to a file that was not open for writing (modes W or A).
UTL_FILE.WRITE_ERROR	An operating system error occurred, such as a disk full error, while attempting to write to the file.
UTL_FILE.INTERNAL_ERROR	An internal error occurred.

Most of these exceptions have already been described earlier in this chapter. Invalid file handle and invalid operation exceptions represent coding errors. Make sure that you keep track of your file handles, and don't try to write to a file that was only opened for reading. Write errors represent operating system errors. Check for available disk space. You may have filled up the disk. Internal errors indicate a problem with the database software itself.

The PUT_LINE Procedure

The PUT_LINE procedure writes a string to a file, followed by a newline character. PUT_LINE basically combines PUT and NEW_LINE into one procedure.

The Syntax for the PUT_LINE Procedure

The procedure header for PUT_LINE looks like this:

```
PROCEDURE PUT_LINE(file IN FILE_TYPE,
                   buffer IN VARCHAR2);
```

In this syntax the parameters are as follows:

- *file* is the file handle as returned from FOPEN.

- *buffer* contains the text you want written to the file. The maximum number of characters you can write by using one call is limited to the line size you specified in the FOPEN call and defaults to 1023.

PUT_LINE is by far the most commonly used of the PUT procedures and can raise the same errors as PUT (refer to Table 17.5).

The PUTF Procedure

The PUTF procedure provides formatted output capabilities similar to those provided by the C language's printf() function. However, PUTF's capabilities pale in comparison to printf().

The Syntax for the PUTF Procedure

```
PROCEDURE PUTF(file IN FILE_TYPE,
              format IN VARCHAR2,
              arg1 IN VARCHAR2 DEFAULT NULL,
              arg2 IN VARCHAR2 DEFAULT NULL,
              arg3 IN VARCHAR2 DEFAULT NULL,
              arg4 IN VARCHAR2 DEFAULT NULL,
              arg5 IN VARCHAR2 DEFAULT NULL);
```

In this syntax the parameters are as follows:

- *file* is the file handle as returned from FOPEN.

- *format* represents the string you want written to the file. You can include two special format characters in this string. You use %S to indicate where the values of *arg1* through *arg5* should be placed. You use \n to indicate where newline characters should be placed.

- *arg1...arg5* are optional arguments containing values that are substituted into the format string before it is written to the file. The first %S found in the format string is replaced by the value of *arg1*, the second %S by the value of *arg2*, and so forth.

▲ PUTF can raise the same exceptions as PUT (refer to Table 17.5).

Understanding argument substitution is the key to understanding PUTF. The arguments represented by *arg1* through *arg5* are substituted for occurrences of %S in the *format* string. This substitution is done based on the order in which the arguments are listed. The value for *arg1* replaces the first use of %S. The value for *arg2* replaces the second use of %S, and so on. Here are some examples:

Call:	UTL_FILE.PUTF(handle, 'The argument is here: %S','1');
Results:	The argument is here: 1
Call:	UTL_FILE.PUTF(handle,[sr] 'Arg1 = %S, arg2 = %S, arg3 = %S', '1','2','3');
Results:	Arg1 = 1, arg2 = 2, arg3 = 3

The call represents a possible call to the PUTF procedures. The results show what would actually be written to the file.

17

> **Tip**
>
> If you need to output more than five arguments, just call the PUTF statement as many times in a row as necessary.

The PUTF function does not automatically write a newline character. If you want a newline written, you must indicate that by placing \n at the end of the *format* string. Alternatively, you could make a separate call to UTL_FILE.NEW_LINE.

The FFLUSH Procedure

When you use any of the PUT commands, the data is stored in the UTL_FILE package's buffer until the buffer is full, and then the contents are written to the file. If you need to flush the contents of the buffer immediately, you can call the FFLUSH procedure.

The Syntax for the FFLUSH Procedure

```
PROCEDURE FFLUSH(file IN FILE_TYPE);
```

The *file* parameter is the file handle returned from FOPEN when the file was originally opened. Refer to Table 17.5 for a list of possible exceptions raised by FFLUSH.

An Example of Using UTL_FILE

Suppose you wanted to generate a file that contains employee ID numbers and names, and that you want that data in comma-delimited format. You can do that by using UTL_FILE in conjunction with some PL/SQL code of your own.

The first step in writing such a procedure is to declare a file handle to use in identifying the file.

The Syntax for Creating a File Handle

```
DECLARE
     handle_name UTL_FILE.FILE_TYPE;
BEGIN
```

The type UTL_FILE.FILE_TYPE is a PL/SQL record defined by the UTL_FILE package. It contains information that UTL_FILE needs to know about the file. The variable *handle_name* is referred to as a file handle. Replace *handle_name* with a variable name of your choosing. The file handle needs to be passed to every UTL_FILE routine that operates on the file.

After declaring the file handle, your next step might be to code the open and close logic, as well as the error handling. Listing 17.4 shows what this might look like.

> **Note**
>
> This listing, and all the others related to UTL_FILE, use the c:\a directory.
> You either need to create that directory, or change the code to reference a
> directory that exists in your environment. You also need to be sure that the
> UTL_FILE_DIR parameter setting lists the directory that you are using.

INPUT   **LISTING 17.4**   The Core File-Handling Logic

```
 1: DECLARE
 2:     emp_data UTL_FILE.FILE_TYPE;
 3: BEGIN
 4:     --Open the file
 5:     emp_data := UTL_FILE.FOPEN ('c:\a','empdata.csv','W');
 6:
 7:     --Close the file
 8:     UTL_FILE.FCLOSE (emp_data);
 9:
10: EXCEPTION
11:     WHEN UTL_FILE.internal_error THEN
12:         DBMS_OUTPUT.PUT_LINE
13:             ('UTL_FILE: An internal error occurred.');
14:         UTL_FILE.FCLOSE_ALL;
15:     WHEN UTL_FILE.invalid_filehandle THEN
16:         DBMS_OUTPUT.PUT_LINE
17:             ('UTL_FILE: The file handle was invalid.');
18:         UTL_FILE.FCLOSE_ALL;
19:     WHEN UTL_FILE.invalid_mode THEN
20:         DBMS_OUTPUT.PUT_LINE
21:             ('UTL_FILE: An invalid open mode was given.');
22:         UTL_FILE.FCLOSE_ALL;
23:     WHEN UTL_FILE.invalid_operation THEN
24:         DBMS_OUTPUT.PUT_LINE
25:             ('UTL_FILE: An invalid operation was attempted.');
26:         UTL_FILE.FCLOSE_ALL;
27:     WHEN UTL_FILE.invalid_path THEN
28:         DBMS_OUTPUT.PUT_LINE
29:             ('UTL_FILE: An invalid path was give for the file.');
30:         UTL_FILE.FCLOSE_ALL;
31:     WHEN UTL_FILE.read_error THEN
32:         DBMS_OUTPUT.PUT_LINE
33:             ('UTL_FILE: A read error occurred.');
34:         UTL_FILE.FCLOSE_ALL;
35:     WHEN UTL_FILE.write_error THEN
36:         DBMS_OUTPUT.PUT_LINE
37:             ('UTL_FILE: A write error occurred.');
38:         UTL_FILE.FCLOSE_ALL;
```

continues

LISTING 17.4 continued

```
39:     WHEN others THEN
40:         DBMS_OUTPUT.PUT_LINE ('Some other error occurred.');
41:         UTL_FILE.FCLOSE_ALL;
42: END;
43: /
```

ANALYSIS The file handle is declared in line 2. The file is opened for write in line 5, and closed in line 8. Opening and closing a file like this, without writing any data, results in an empty file being created.

Error handling is especially important when you're working with files. It's common to have problems getting the FOPEN call just right. If you don't trap each specific UTL_FILE error, then you won't have any information to work with when a failure occurs. In Listing 17.4, the bulk of the code is in the exception handler, where each possible error is trapped separately. Trapping each error separately allows you to write a message that precisely identifies the error.

Notice the calls to UTL_FILE.FCLOSE_ALL in each of the error handler's WHEN clauses. This is an insurance call. If any files happen to be open when an error occurs, you want to be sure that they get closed. The FCLOSE_ALL procedure does that for you.

Tip

> This would be a good time to test the procedure. You should be able to run it and see that a new file is successfully created.

After you get the file to open and close correctly, the last step would be to add the code to select data from the employee table, and write it to the file. Listing 17.5 shows the finished routine.

INPUT **LISTING 17.5** A PL/SQL Block to Generate a Comma-Delimited File of Employee Information

```
1: DECLARE
2:      emp_data UTL_FILE.FILE_TYPE;
3: BEGIN
4:      --Open the file
5:      emp_data := UTL_FILE.FOPEN ('c:\a','empdata.csv','W');
6:
7:      --Write out a list of employee IDs and names
8:      FOR emp IN (
9:      SELECT emp_id, emp_name
10:     FROM employee) LOOP
```

```
11:          UTL_FILE.PUT_LINE (emp_data, TO_CHAR(emp.emp_id)
12:                          || ',"' || emp.emp_name || '"');
13:      END LOOP;
14:
15:      --Close the file
16:      UTL_FILE.FCLOSE (emp_data);
17:
18:  EXCEPTION
19:      WHEN UTL_FILE.internal_error THEN
20:          DBMS_OUTPUT.PUT_LINE
21:              ('UTL_FILE: An internal error occurred.');
22:          UTL_FILE.FCLOSE_ALL;
23:      WHEN UTL_FILE.invalid_filehandle THEN
24:          DBMS_OUTPUT.PUT_LINE
25:              ('UTL_FILE: The file handle was invalid.');
26:          UTL_FILE.FCLOSE_ALL;
27:      WHEN UTL_FILE.invalid_mode THEN
28:          DBMS_OUTPUT.PUT_LINE
29:              ('UTL_FILE: An invalid open mode was given.');
30:          UTL_FILE.FCLOSE_ALL;
31:      WHEN UTL_FILE.invalid_operation THEN
32:          DBMS_OUTPUT.PUT_LINE
33:              ('UTL_FILE: An invalid operation was attempted.');
34:          UTL_FILE.FCLOSE_ALL;
35:      WHEN UTL_FILE.invalid_path THEN
36:          DBMS_OUTPUT.PUT_LINE
37:              ('UTL_FILE: An invalid path was give for the file.');
38:          UTL_FILE.FCLOSE_ALL;
39:      WHEN UTL_FILE.read_error THEN
40:          DBMS_OUTPUT.PUT_LINE
41:              ('UTL_FILE: A read error occurred.');
42:          UTL_FILE.FCLOSE_ALL;
43:      WHEN UTL_FILE.write_error THEN
44:          DBMS_OUTPUT.PUT_LINE
45:              ('UTL_FILE: A write error occurred.');
46:          UTL_FILE.FCLOSE_ALL;
47:      WHEN others THEN
48:          DBMS_OUTPUT.PUT_LINE ('Some other error occurred.');
49:          UTL_FILE.FCLOSE_ALL;
50:  END;
51:  /
```

17

OUTPUT

```
502,"Kim Beanie"
511,"Jeffrey Beaner"
513,"Herman D. Terman"
514,"Egan Dryup"
401,"Harvey Wallbanger"
501,"Ashley Nue"
402,"Scarlet Tanninger"
403,"Freddie Fisher"
```

```
404,"Charlie Tuna"
597,"Matthew Higgenbottom"
598,"Raymond Gennick"
```

ANALYSIS   This listing is the same as Listing 17.4, except for the addition of a cursor FOR loop in lines 8–13. This loop selects the employee ID number and name for each employee, converts the number to text, and writes the information in comma-delimited format. Single quotes are placed around the name field in case the name contains any embedded comments.

With the data in a comma-delimited format like this, you can easily open it in Microsoft Excel, or any other program that accepts comma-delimited data.

The process of reading from a file is very similar to that of writing. The only difference is that you need to use GET_LINE instead of PUT_LINE, and you need to test for the end of file so that you know when to stop. You test for the end of file by trapping the NO_DATA_FOUND exception.

Exploring TEXT_IO with Client Files

The TEXT_IO package is similar to UTL_FILE, but it allows you to read and write files on the client rather than the server. TEXT_IO is not part of the Oracle database software. It comes with Oracle Developer, which used to be called Developer 2000.

The procedures in TEXT_IO are a combination of those found in UTL_FILE and DBMS_OUTPUT. The TEXT_IO package can be used to write both to the display and to a file. The procedure and function syntax are the same as for UTL_FILE and DBMS_OUTPUT, so they are not repeated here. Listing 17.6 shows a PL/SQL procedure that makes several calls to TEXT_IO.

INPUT   **LISTING 17.6**   Using TEXT_IO to Write Both to a File and to the Display

```
 1: PROCEDURE write_name IS
 2:     text_file TEXT_IO.FILE_TYPE;
 3: BEGIN
 4:     --Display a message to the user.
 5:     TEXT_IO.PUT_LINE
 6:         ('I am about to open a file named c:\name.txt');
 7:
 8:     --Open the file
 9:     text_file := TEXT_IO.FOPEN ('c:\name.txt','W');
10:
11:     TEXT_IO.PUT_LINE
12:         ('I have opened the file.');
13:
```

```
14:     TEXT_IO.PUT_LINE (text_file, 'Justin Nue');
15:
16:     TEXT_IO.PUT_LINE
17:        ('I wrote some data to the file.');
18:
19:     TEXT_IO.FCLOSE (text_file);
20:
21:     TEXT_IO.PUT_LINE ('The file has been closed.');
22:
23: EXCEPTION
24:     WHEN others THEN
25:         TEXT_IO.PUT_LINE ('Some other error occurred.');
26: END;
```

ANALYSIS This procedure uses TEXT_IO in two different ways. There are several calls to TEXT_IO that do not include a file handle. Line 6 contains one example. These calls do not result in file I/O. Because no file handle is used, the results are written to the display. Lines 9, 14, and 19 contain procedure calls to open a file, write one line of text to the file, and then close the file.

Figure 17.2 shows the Oracle Developer screen after a run of the write_name procedure from Listing 17.5. Notice the screen output at the bottom of the PL/SQL Interpreter window.

FIGURE 17.2

Executing the write_name *procedure from Oracle Developer.*

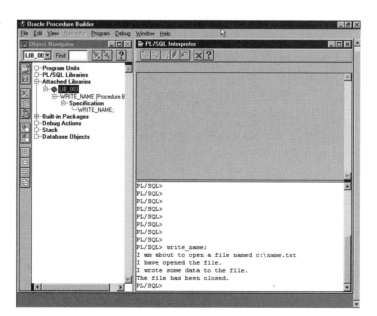

The contents of the `name.txt` file, after `name_write` is run, should be this one line:

```
Justin Nue
```

Despite the procedure and function names being the same as those in `UTL_FILE`, there are a few differences between the two that you should be aware of. First, there are no exceptions defined for `TEXT_IO`. That means you can't use code to detect different types of errors, and it's why the exception handler in Listing 17.6 is so short. In addition, `TEXT_IO` does not implement the `FFLUSH` and `FCLOSE_ALL` procedures that you find in `UTL_FILE`.

Summary

Today you have learned about three methods of performing I/O with Oracle. The `DBMS_OUTPUT` package, which you used earlier this week without much in-depth discussion, enables you to read and write information to and from a buffer in memory. When you execute PL/SQL code from SQL*Plus, SQL*Plus automatically reads the buffer and displays the data onscreen for you to see. `DBMS_OUTPUT` is primarily used as a debugging tool. The `UTL_FILE` package enables you to read and write files on the database server. The `TEXT_IO` package is part of the Oracle Developer software, and allows you to read and write files on the PC. The entry points for `TEXT_IO` are named the same as those for `UTL_FILE` and `DBMS_OUTPUT`.

Q&A

Q When working with `UTL_FILE`, can you access a file for reading and writing simultaneously?

A No. You can choose only one method of operation on a file. If you attempt to write to a file that is read-only, an exception is raised.

Q What is one major purpose for the `UTL_FILE` package?

A It provides a slick way to import and export data from one application to another. For example, you can use `UTL_FILE` to generate comma-delimited files for import into Microsoft Excel.

Q What is the difference between the `UTL_FILE` package and the `DBMS_OUTPUT` package?

A The `UTL_FILE` package allows you to read and write files, whereas you use `DBMS_OUTPUT` to write data to a memory buffer and read it back again.

Q **What happens if I use DBMS_OUTPUT and try to write more than 255 characters in a line?**

A An exception is raised. See Table 17.1 for definitions of the errors.

Workshop

You can use this workshop to test your comprehension of this chapter and put what you've learned into practice. You'll find the answers to the quiz and exercises in Appendix A, "Answers."

Quiz

1. What is the difference between PUT and PUT_LINE?

2. Assuming that you use the version of FOPEN where no line size is specified, what is the maximum number of bytes that can be read by using GET_LINE?

3. What is the maximum line size that you can specify with the FOPEN call?

4. What does FCLOSE_ALL do to the file open flag referenced by IS_OPEN?

5. What is the maximum number of characters that can possibly be allocated to the buffer when using DBMS_OUTPUT?

Exercise

Listing 17.5 shows how to write comma-delimited data to a file. Using GET_LINE instead of PUT_LINE, modify that code to read the data back and display it by using DBMS_OUTPUT.

17

DAY **18**

Managing Database Jobs

by Tom Luers

Like other production systems, Oracle provides a way to handle jobs: the
DBMS_JOB package. This package enables you to schedule jobs immediately or
schedule them at a precise time and day, which could be monthly, weekly, and
so on. This lesson describes the DBMS_JOB package, as well as how to communicate between multiple processes. Today's lesson focuses on

- The DBMS_JOB package
- Running a job in the background
- Running a job immediately
- Viewing jobs
- Managing jobs

Submitting Jobs by Using the DBMS_JOB Package

 The DBMS_JOB package enables you to submit jobs to a job queue. A *job* is a stored program, which is scheduled to run at a specific time or after a specific event. A *job queue* is simply a holding place for these scheduled jobs.

From the job queue, you can schedule these jobs to execute immediately, or you can specify when to run the jobs and how often to run them. In addition, you can find information on currently executing jobs, broken jobs, the scheduling of jobs, or any other piece of job information. The DBMS_JOB package requires PL/SQL 2.2 or higher. You also need the appropriate privileges to access the DBMS_JOB package. Table 18.1 describes each of the procedures provided in the DBMS_JOB package.

TABLE 18.1   DBMS_JOB Procedures

Procedure Name	Description
BROKEN	Disables job execution. Oracle does not execute the code if it is marked as broken.
CHANGE	Alters specified job particulars, such as job description, the time at which the job will be run, or the interval between executions of the job.
INTERVAL	Alters the interval between executions for a specified job.
NEXT_DATE	Alters the next execution time for a specified job.
REMOVE	Removes a specified job from the job queue.
RUN	Forces a specified job to run.
SUBMIT	Submits a job to the job queue.
WHAT	Alters the job description for a specified job.

Using Background Processes

Instead of utilizing a lot of resources by running the same multiple programs for each user to schedule or run a job, Oracle provides SNP (Snapshot Refresh Process) background processes. These processes share common functions and code, which allows them to monitor Oracle processes for possible parallel execution. One key feature of SNP is that if a job fails, it does not bring down the database as other processes would. In addition, SNP processes monitor jobs at user-specified intervals, start any jobs that need to be executed, and then wait for the next interval. You could liken this to grocers monitoring for expired food in the freezer or refrigerator. At night, after close (the specific time interval), the background process looks for jobs to execute (the employees scan for expired food), and if found (the expired food is found), the job executes (the food is discarded), and the process waits to be repeated again (the employees go home and will repeat the same process tomorrow).

Oracle provides up to 10 SNP processes, identified as SNP0 through SNP9. The three parameters defined in the INIT.ORA file are listed in Table 18.2. The INIT.ORA file is loaded automatically with the Oracle database. It is typically located in your Oracle directory. Depending on the operating system your database is loaded on, this file may be named INITORCL.ORA or INITDW.ORA. These parameters manage the SNP job processes for the database.

TABLE 18.2   SNP Parameters

Parameter	Value Range	Default Value	Description
JOB_QUEUE_ PROCESSES	0–10	0	Determines the number of background processes to start for each instance.
JOB_QUEUE_ INTERVAL	1–3600 (seconds)	60	The interval, in seconds, for when the SNP process searches for jobs to execute.
JOB_QUEUE_KEEP_ CONNECTIONS	true, false	false	If true, all database connections are kept open until the job completes. Otherwise, connections are opened and closed as needed.

Each job uses one process; therefore, you cannot have one job executing across multiple processes.

Note

If the JOB_QUEUE_PROCESSES parameter is set to 0 (the default), no jobs execute. Make sure you have defined this in your INIT.ORA configuration file. I always set this value to 10, which on today's systems does not greatly affect performance.

Executing Jobs

There are two methods of job execution—timed by submitting to a job queue and immediate execution. This section focuses first on submitting jobs on a timed basis to a job
queue through the use of the SUBMIT procedure or the ISUBMIT procedure.

Submitting Jobs to the Job Queue by Using SUBMIT

SUBMIT is used to submit jobs to the job queue. The syntax for the SUBMIT procedure can
be seen in the following example.

```
PROCEDURE SUBMIT(job_number OUT BINARY_INTEGER,
    job_to_submit IN VARCHAR2,
    next_run IN DATE DEFAULT SYSDATE,
    interval IN VARCHAR2 DEFAULT NULL,
    job_parsing IN BOOLEAN DEFAULT false,
    instance IN BINARY_INTEGER DEFAULT any_instance,
    force IN BOOLEAN DEFAULT FALSE);
```

In this syntax the parameters are as follows:

- *job_number* is the job number assigned to the process. The job number remains the
  same as long as the job exists. Only one job number can be assigned to a process.

- *job_to_submit* is the PL/SQL code to submit.

- *next_run* is the date when the job will next run.

- *interval* is the time when the job will next run.

- *job_parsing* is a parameter that, if set to false, causes Oracle to parse the job,
  making sure all objects exist. If the objects do not yet exist, such as tables that you
  will create later, set the value to true. The job is then parsed upon execution, and
  if the tables still do not exist, it becomes a broken job.

- *instance* specifies which instance can run the job.

- *force* is a parameter that, if true, causes any positive integer to be acceptable as
  the job instance. If it is false (the default), then the specified instance must be
  running; otherwise, the routine raises an exception.

> **Note**
> These parameter definitions are the same for the other functions and para-
> meters described throughout the remainder of this chapter.

Exploring SUBMIT Examples

Take a look at some sample listings for submitting jobs. The first, Listing 18.1, is a basic
submittal of a procedure HELLO. This procedure is a stored procedure that does not
include any arguments. We will create the HELLO procedure first, then execute it.

Note

Listing 18.1 is only a sample procedure—it won't execute.

INPUT **LISTING 18.1** A Simple Procedure with SUBMIT

```
1: CREATE OR REPLACE PROCEDURE HELLO AS
2: BEGIN
3: DBMS_OUTPUT.PUT_LINE ('Hello World! ' ||
4:    TO_CHAR(SYSDATE,'MM-DD-YY HH:MM:SS AM'));
5: END;
6: /

7: DECLARE
8:      v_JobNum  BINARY_INTEGER;
9: BEGIN
10:       DBMS_JOB.SUBMIT(v_JobNum,'HELLO;',SYSDATE,
11:             'SYSDATE + (1/(24*60*60))');
12: END;
```

ANALYSIS First, the program declares a variable of type BINARY_INTEGER in line 2 to hold the value of the job number assigned to the job. Then it submits the job in line 4 by passing the job number assigned, the PL/SQL code to execute (HELLO), the next date to execute (system date), and the interval (system date executing every minute). You can compute this by multiplying 24 hours in the day by 60 minutes/hour by 60 seconds/minute, and then taking the inverse.

The next example calls a stored procedure, which passes three parameters with the values maintenance, 1000, and Friday, and occurs every Friday night at 10:00 p.m. This procedure launches several jobs for maintenance, and then backs up the system. This procedure is shown in Listing 18.2.

INPUT **LISTING 18.2** A More Complex Approach Using SUBMIT

```
1: DECLARE
2:      v_JobNum  BINARY_INTEGER;
3: BEGIN
4:       DBMS_JOB.SUBMIT(v_JobNum,'WEEKLY(''maintenance'',1000,
5:             ''Friday'');',SYSDATE,
6:             'NEXT_DAY(TRUNC(SYSDATE),''FRIDAY'') + 22/24');
7: END;
```

18

ANALYSIS This process submits a stored procedure called WEEKLY (line 4), which requires three parameters.

> **Note**
>
> A requirement for the DBMS_JOB package is that all parameters that regularly require a single quote must have two single quotes around each string (see lines 4 and 5). When the string is parsed, one set of single quotes is removed and then sent to the process for handling.

Another parameter is the interval specified in line 6. These settings guarantee that the job will always run on Friday at precisely 22/24, or 10:00 p.m.

> **Note**
>
> You could not realistically use SYSDATE + 7 when executing the initial job on Friday to run every Friday. The way SNP processes work is that if the system or network goes down, when the system is brought back up, any jobs that should have executed and didn't are then processed. So if the network went down on the weekend, the first occurrence would be Monday, and it would always execute every subsequent Monday until the next disturbance occurred.

Using RUN to Execute Jobs Immediately

You can execute jobs immediately after they have been sent to the job queue by using the RUN procedure. The syntax for the RUN procedure is as follows.

SYNTAX

```
PROCEDURE RUN(job_number_specified IN BINARY_INTEGER);
```

In order to use the RUN procedure, you must know the job number assigned to the job you want to execute. When the process executes, the next date for the job is reset. The time interval occurs after the run date and time when the job was executed. Again, if you had initially run the job on Friday with a SYSDATE + 7 time interval and you expect the job to run every Friday, and if you now immediately execute this on Thursday, the job runs every Thursday. Listing 18.5 shows the original submission of the job, and Listing 18.6 shows an example of using RUN.

INPUT   **LISTING 18.5**   Using DBMS_OUTPUT to See the Assigned Job Number

```
1: DECLARE
2:      v_jobnum BINARY_INTEGER;
3: BEGIN
4:      DBMS_JOB.SUBMIT(v_jobnum,'HELLO;',SYSDATE,
```

```
5:              'SYSDATE + (1/(24*60*60))');
6:         DBMS_OUTPUT.ENABLE;
7:         DBMS_OUTPUT.PUT_LINE('Your Job Number assigned is: ' ¦¦ v_jobnum);
8: END;
```

ANALYSIS Lines 6 and 7 allow you to see what job number is assigned to the process you just submitted for execution. In this case, the sample output is

OUTPUT `Your Job Number assigned is: 13`

You can now run the job from Listing 18.6.

INPUT **LISTING 18.6** Using RUN to Execute the Job in the Queue Immediately

```
1: BEGIN
2:     DBMS_JOB.RUN(13);
3: END;
```

ANALYSIS This code immediately executes job 13.

Exploring the Job Environment

When you submit a job, the following variables are stored in Oracle:

- The current user.
- The user submitting or altering the job.
- Current job schemas, such as the job number assigned. You'll learn more about this later in this lesson, in the section "Viewing Jobs."
- NLS_(National Language Support) LANGUAGE
- NLS_CURRENCY
- NLS_ISO_CURRENCY
- NLS_NUMERIC_CHARACTERS
- NLS_DATE_FORMAT
- NLS_DATE_LANGUAGE
- NLS_SORT

After a job is executed, the NLS parameters are restored. You can change these characteristics by using the ALTER procedure discussed later in this lesson, in the section "Altering a Job."

18

The Job Owner

As soon as you submit a job, Oracle records and assigns ownership of the job to the user who submitted the job. Only the owner can change the job, execute the job on demand, and remove the job from the queue.

The Job Number

As discussed earlier in this lesson, Oracle assigns the next sequential job number from the stored value SYS.JOBSEQ. This job number can't be changed or assigned to a different process until the job is removed. You can always specify your own job number with ISUBMIT, but if the job number already exists, your job does not execute. The error you receive if you attempt to use the same job number is as follows:

```
ERROR at line 1:
ORA-00001: unique constraint (SYS.I_JOB_JOB) violated
ORA-06512: at "SYS.DBMS_JOB", line 105
ORA-06512: at line 2
```

The Job Definition

The *job definition* is the identifier to the PL/SQL code you want executed via the DBS_JOB.SUBMIT package. This is usually—but not always—a stored procedure. Any parameters that must have the single quote with normal PL/SQL parameters must now be enclosed by two single quotes; otherwise, when Oracle removes the single quotes when processing the job, you get an invalid parameter. Table 18.3 lists some additional special parameters recognized by Oracle.

TABLE 18.3 Special Job Definition Parameters

Parameter	Mode	Description
job	IN	The current job number.
next_date	IN/OUT	The next date for the job to execute. If not specified, the default is SYSDATE.
broken	IN/OUT	Job status: The IN value is always false, and the OUT value is true if the job is broken and false if it is not.

> **Note**
>
> The IN mode indicates that you pass this parameter to the called package. The OUT mode indicates that the called parameter will return this parameter back to the calling program. The IN/OUT mode allows you to pass parameters to the called package and return a return value from the called package.

The following are some examples of the job definition when submitting a job:

```
'HELLO;'
'paycheck(''FRIDAY'',SYSDATE);'
'sample(''String1'',100,20,''String2'');'
'final_try(''good'',next_date_broken);'
'dbms_job.remove(job);'
```

In the above examples, each line represents the PL/SQL identifier you would use in the DBMS_JOB.SUBMIT statement. The first example is simply asking the SUBMIT procedure to execute the HELLO procedure. The remaining examples execute procedures, but they also are passing parameters relevant to the called procedure or to the SUBMIT procedure. Remember that the double single quotes indicate that that parameter is directed toward the SUBMIT procedure and not the called procedure.

Viewing Jobs

To obtain any information about jobs, you can use queries against the database. The three Oracle-provided views that display information about jobs in the job queue are shown in Table 18.4. A *view* is a collection of information, like a table, about a specific topic of information.

TABLE 18.4 Data Dictionary Views for Jobs

View	Description
DBA_JOBS	Shows all jobs in the database.
DBA_JOBS_RUNNING	Shows all jobs currently running.
USER_JOBS	Shows all jobs owned by the user. PRIV_USER is your user ID.

The view for USER_JOBS and DBA_JOBS has the same structure. At any time, you could type

```
SELECT * from USER_JOBS:
```

This command enables you to view all the possible columns. Refer to Table 18.5 for some of the possible columns and meanings.

Note You will most likely have to reduce your array size by typing SET ARRAYSIZE 10 for all the columns to appear on the screen without getting a size or memory error.

TABLE 18.5 Columns Used in the DBA_JOBS and DBA_USERS Views

Column Name	Description
JOB	The job number
LOG_USER	The user associated with the job
PRIV_USER	The user who submitted and owns the job
LAST_DATE	The date of the last successful execution
LAST_SEC	The time of the last successful execution
THIS_DATE	The date the currently executing job started
THIS_SEC	The time the currently executing job started
NEXT_DATE	The next date the job is scheduled to run
NEXT_SEC	The next time the job is scheduled to run
TOTAL_TIME	The total time it took to execute the job, in seconds
BROKEN	The indicator of whether the job is broken; shows Y if it is
WHAT	The WHAT parameter supplied with SUBMIT or ISUBMIT
INTERVAL	The time interval between jobs
FAILURES	The number of times the job has started and failed since the last successful completion

To see all the available columns (and all jobs currently running), you would type

SELECT * from DBA_JOBS_RUNNING;

The available columns and descriptions are shown in Table 18.6.

TABLE 18.6 Columns Used in the DBA_JOBS_RUNNING View

Column Name	Description
JOB	The job number
SID	A list of the processes executing the job
LAST_DATE	The date of the last successful execution
LAST_SEC	The time of the last successful execution
THIS_SEC	The time the currently executing job started
FAILURES	The number of times the job has started and failed since the last successful completion

Samples for Viewing Jobs

This section gives some more examples of how to view jobs. The first example, in Listing 18.7, displays all the jobs that are currently executing.

INPUT   **LISTING 18.7**   Viewing Executing Jobs

```
SELECT SID,JOB,THIS_SEC,FAILURES from DBA_JOBS_RUNNING;
```

OUTPUT
```
SID   JOB   LOG_USER   THIS_DATE   THIS_SEC
.......... .......... .......... .......... ..........
12    14144  JFEE       21-APR-94   17:21:24
25    8536   SCOTT      03-MAY-94   16:45:12
2 rows selected.
```

ANALYSIS   The output from your query reveals all those jobs that are currently running. It also displays the System ID number (SID), the job number, owner of the job, and the start time and date of when the job was started.

If you want to view information on jobs that you own, use the code in Listing 18.8 to view the process name, the job number, and the date when the job will next execute.

INPUT   **LISTING 18.8**   Viewing Your Own Jobs

```
SELECT JOB,WHAT,NEXT_DATE, NEXT_SEC, FAILURES,BROKEN from USER_JOBS;
```

OUTPUT
```
JOB         NEXT_DATE NEXT_SEC FAILURES   B
.......... .......... ........ .......... .
  9125     10-MAR-98 00:00:00    4         N
 14144     03-OCT-99 16:35:35    0         N
 41762     29-SEP-00 00:00:00   16         Y
3 rows selected.
```

ANALYSIS   As you can see from the output, there are currently three jobs in the database. This output shows you the job number, the next date and time the job will run, the number of failures, and the broken status. In this case only job number 41762 is broken.

Exploring Job Management

So far, this lesson has focused on creating and viewing jobs. Now, you will learn about a major responsibility of a systems administrator—performing job management. Job management can include removing a job, altering a job, importing and exporting jobs from

18

one database to another, and even fixing broken jobs. You might also need to manage how long a job runs: If a job starts taking too long, you might have to review the procedure and either fine-tune it or delegate this task to another Oracle expert.

Removing a Job

If you can submit jobs, you should be able to remove them. Oracle provides the REMOVE procedure, which enables you to remove only jobs that you own.

```
PROCEDURE REMOVE(job_number IN BINARY_INTEGER);
```

> **Note**
>
> You cannot remove a job if the job has started executing. You have to wait for the job to complete before removing it from the job queue.

Listing 18.9 shows an example of removing a job whose assigned number is 109.

INPUT   **LISTING 18.9**   Removing a Job

```
1: BEGIN
2:     DBMS_JOBS.REMOVE(109);
3: END;
```

ANALYSIS   After you execute the code, if the job isn't running, job 109 is removed permanently from the job queue.

Altering a Job

After a job has been submitted, you can change the parameters of the job by using the CHANGE procedure. If you want to alter specific parameters of the job, you use WHAT, NEXT_DATE, or INTERVAL. Again, you can only change jobs that you own; otherwise, there would be utter chaos!

Several possible formats can be used to change job parameters. The first uses the CHANGE procedure:

```
PROCEDURE CHANGE(job_number IN BINARY_INTEGER,
                 process_name IN VARCHAR2,
                 next_run IN DATE,
                 interval IN VARCHAR2,
                 instance IN BINARY_INTEGER DEFAULT any_instance,
                 force IN BOOLEAN DEFAULT FALSE);
```

▼   The second format uses the WHAT procedure:

```
PROCEDURE WHAT(job_number in BINARY_INTEGER,
                            process_name IN VARCHAR2);
```

The third format uses the NEXT_DATE procedure:

```
PROCEDURE NEXT_DATE(job_number IN BINARY_INTEGER,
                            next_run IN DATE);
```

The fourth format uses the INTERVAL procedure:

```
PROCEDURE INTERVAL(job_number IN BINARY_INTEGER,
                            interval IN VARCHAR2 );
```

The CHANGE procedure alters all the job parameters, whereas WHAT, NEXT_DATE, and
▲   INTERVAL alter only those specific parameters.

Importing and Exporting Jobs

A nice feature that is provided in the DBMS_JOB package is the ability to import and
export jobs from one database to another. However, the job number assigned from the
source database becomes the job number in the destination database. This becomes a
problem only if the destination database already has a job with the same job number. If
there is a conflict between job numbers, simply resubmit the job in the source database
by using ISUBMIT, and assign it a job number not used in the destination database, export
the job, and delete the extra job in the source database.

The Syntax for the USER_EXPORT Procedure

```
PROCEDURE USER_EXPORT(job_number IN BINARY_INTEGER,
                            Destination_database OUT VARCHAR2);
```

Handling Broken Jobs

A broken job is a job that has failed to execute 16 times in a row. Oracle marks this job
with a flag in the BROKEN column and stores the value true in the column. The only way
this job will execute is if you

  • Use DBMS_JOB.RUN to execute the job.

  • Change the flag in the BROKEN column to the status Fixed, where BROKEN is equal
    to false.

You learned how to run a job earlier in this lesson, in the section "Using RUN to Execute
Jobs Immediately."

To mark a job as fixed with the BROKEN procedure, the syntax is

```
PROCEDURE BROKEN(job_number IN BINARY_INTEGER,
                            broken_status IN BOOLEAN,
                            next_date IN DATE DEFAULT SYSDATE);
```

▲ You use this format to mark a job as fixed.

Listing 18.10 shows how to make a broken job start running.

INPUT   **LISTING 18.10**   Starting a Broken Job

```
1: BEGIN
2:     DBMS_JOBS.BROKEN(109,false,SYSDATE + 7);
3: END;
```

ANALYSIS   This job is now set to execute in one week. You could also mark a valid job as broken, by using the code in Listing 18.11.

INPUT   **LISTING 18.11**   Creating a Broken Job

```
1:BEGIN
2:     DBMS_JOBS.BROKEN(109,true)
3: END;
```

Hands-on Practice in Job Management

Next, we'll run through a long exercise that demonstrates some of the concepts learned today. You can practice creating a few procedures, submitting the jobs, immediately executing jobs, viewing jobs, altering a job, and removing a job.

Creating Procedures to Submit as Jobs

Before you can really get started, you must enter and then execute the three procedures in Listings 20.12 through 20.14. After creating these procedures, you can submit them as jobs to test the DBMS_JOB package. The procedure in Listing 18.12 displays Hello World! to the screen. Listing 18.13 writes Hello World! to a file and adds the current system time and date when the procedure executes. Listing 18.14 accesses the same file as Listing 18.13, adds Hello Again for the Second Time!, and adds the current system time and date when the procedure executes.

INPUT   **LISTING 18.12**   Displaying Hello World! to the Screen

```
1: CREATE OR REPLACE PROCEDURE HELLO AS
2: BEGIN
```

```
3:        DBMS_OUTPUT.PUT_LINE('Hello World! ' ||
4:             TO_CHAR(SYSDATE,'MM-DD-YY HH:MI:SS AM'));
5: END;
```

INPUT   **LISTING 18.13**   Writing Hello World! to a File

```
 1: CREATE OR REPLACE PROCEDURE HELLOFLE IS
 2:
 3: --DECLARE
 4:-- Create a file handle of type UTL_FILE.FILE_TYPE
 5:     v_MyFileHandle UTL_FILE.FILE_TYPE;
 6:BEGIN
 7:-- Open the file to write.
 8:     v_MyFileHandle := UTL_FILE.FOPEN('C:\','HELLO.TXT','a');
 9:     UTL_FILE.PUT_LINE(v_MyFileHandle,
10:            'Hello World! ' || TO_CHAR(SYSDATE,'MM-DD-YY HH:MI:SS AM'));
11:
12:-- Close the file handle which points to myout.txt
13:     UTL_FILE.FCLOSE(v_MyFileHandle);
14:EXCEPTION
15: -- Create Exception to simply display error code and message
16:     WHEN OTHERS THEN
17:         DBMS_OUTPUT.PUT_LINE
18:             ('ERROR ' || TO_CHAR(SQLCODE) || SQLERRM);
19:         NULL;
20: END;
```

18

INPUT   **LISTING 18.14**   Another Process for Accessing the Same File

```
 1: CREATE OR REPLACE PROCEDURE SHAREFLE IS
 2:
 3: --DECLARE
 4: -- Create a file handle of type UTL_FILE.FILE_TYPE
 5:     v_MyFileHandle UTL_FILE.FILE_TYPE;
 6: BEGIN
 7: -- Open the file to write.
 8:     v_MyFileHandle := UTL_FILE.FOPEN('C:\','HELLO.TXT','a');
 9:     UTL_FILE.PUT_LINE(v_MyFileHandle,
10:         'Hello Again for the Second Time! ' ||
11:             TO_CHAR(SYSDATE,'MM-DD-YY HH:MI:SS AM'));
12: -- Close the file handle which points to myout.txt
13:     UTL_FILE.FCLOSE(v_MyFileHandle);
14: EXCEPTION
15: -- Create Exception to simply display error code and message
16:     WHEN OTHERS THEN
17:         DBMS_OUTPUT.PUT_LINE
18:             ('ERROR ' || TO_CHAR(SQLCODE) || SQLERRM);
19:         NULL;
20: END;
```

Caution Make sure in the INIT.ORA file that utl_file_dir is set to *;; otherwise, you will get a USER_EXCEPTION error.

Submitting All Jobs to the Job Queue

You can submit all three jobs at once to the job queue with the code in Listing 18.15.

INPUT **LISTING 18.15** Submitting All Three Jobs at Once

```
 1: DECLARE
 2:     v_jobnum BINARY_INTEGER;
 3: BEGIN
 4:     DBMS_JOB.SUBMIT(v_JobNum,'HELLO;',SYSDATE,
 5:         'SYSDATE + (1/(24*60*60))');
 6:     DBMS_OUTPUT.ENABLE;
 7:     DBMS_OUTPUT.PUT_LINE('Your Job Number assigned to hello is: '
 8:         ||v_jobnum);
 9:     DBMS_JOB.SUBMIT(v_JobNum,'hellofle;',SYSDATE,
10:         'SYSDATE + (1/(24*60))');
11:     DBMS_OUTPUT.PUT_LINE('Your Job Number assigned to hellofle is: '
12:         ||v_jobnum);
13:     DBMS_JOB.ISUBMIT(109,'sharefle;',SYSDATE,'SYSDATE +
14:         (1/(24*60))');
15:     DBMS_OUTPUT.PUT_LINE('Your Job Number assigned to
16:         sharefle is: 109');
17: END;
```

OUTPUT Your Job Number assigned to hello is: 24
Your Job Number assigned to hellofle is: 25
Your Job Number assigned to sharefle is: 109

Running All Three Jobs Immediately

There may be times when you want to submit more than one job at a time. As an example of this, let's submit all three jobs immediately from Listing 18.16. Before you execute the code, make sure that you have typed SET SERVEROUTPUT ON and pressed Enter at the SQL*Plus prompt.

INPUT **LISTING 18.16** Alternate Method to Submitting Three Jobs at Once

```
 1: BEGIN
 2: --Make sure you enter the job numbers assigned for the first two jobs
 3:     DBMS_JOB.RUN(24);
 4:     DBMS_JOB.RUN(25);
 5:     DBMS_JOB.RUN(109);
 6: END;
```

Your output should look similar to

OUTPUT   Hello World! 06-22-99 09:37:42 PM

Viewing Information About the Jobs

You can view information about your jobs by using the code in Listing 18.17.

INPUT   **LISTING 18.17**   Viewing Information on Your Jobs

```
SELECT JOB,WHAT,LAST_SEC,INTERVAL from USER_JOBS;
```

OUTPUT
```
JOB
----------
WHAT
------------------------------
LAST_SEC
---------
INTERVAL
------------------------------
        24
HELLO;
21:57:43
SYSDATE + (1/(24*60*60))

        25
hellofle;
21:57:43
SYSDATE + (1/(24*60*60))

       109
sharefle;
21:57:43
SYSDATE + (1/(24*60*60))
```

Altering the Job by Running the HELLO Job

Listing 18.18 demonstrates modifying the HELLO job to execute from once every minute to once per week from the current date. Remember that if it's a background process, you will see Hello World! on the screen, but the job is still running and you can verify it by running the query against USER_JOBS.

18

INPUT **LISTING 18.18** Altering the HELLO Process to Run Once per Week

```
1: BEGIN
2: -- Enter your job number assigned!
3:    DBMS_JOB.INTERVAL(24,'SYSDATE + 7');
4: END;
```

OUTPUT

```
JOB
----------
WHAT
------------------------------
LAST_SEC
----------
INTERVAL
------------------------------
        24
HELLO;
21:57:43
SYSDATE + 7

        25
hellofle;
21:57:43
SYSDATE + (1/(24*60*60))

       109
sharefle;
21:57:43
SYSDATE + (1/(24*60*60))
```

ANALYSIS Notice that the HELLO job's time interval reflects SYSDATE + 7. You have success-fully altered the interval.

Removing the Hello Job

Listing 18.19 demonstrates removing the HELLO job.

INPUT **LISTING 18.19** Removing the HELLO Job from the Queue

```
1: BEGIN
2: -- Enter your job number assigned!
3:    DBMS_JOB.REMOVE(24);
4: END;
```

To verify it, execute the code in Listing 18.20.

INPUT **LISTING 18.20** Verifying the Job Removal

```
SELECT JOB from USER_JOBS;
```

OUTPUT
```
JOB
----------
        25
       109
```

ANALYSIS You now have only two jobs. And the file C:\HELLO.TXT should look similar to this:

OUTPUT
```
Hello World! 06-22-97 09:37:42 PM
Hello Again for the Second Time! 06-22-97 09:37:42 PM
Hello World! 06-22-97 09:38:35 PM
Hello Again for the Second Time! 06-22-97 09:38:35 PM
Hello World! 06-22-97 09:38:36 PM
Hello Again for the Second Time! 06-22-97 09:38:36 PM
Hello World! 06-22-97 09:39:36 PM
Hello Again for the Second Time! 06-22-97 09:39:36 PM
Hello World! 06-22-97 09:39:37 PM
Hello Again for the Second Time! 06-22-97 09:39:37 PM
Hello World! 06-22-97 09:40:38 PM
Hello Again for the Second Time! 06-22-97 09:40:38 PM
Hello World! 06-22-97 09:40:38 PM
Hello Again for the Second Time! 06-22-97 09:40:38 PM
Hello World! 06-22-97 09:41:38 PM
Hello Again for the Second Time! 06-22-97 09:41:38 PM
Hello World! 06-22-97 09:41:38 PM
Hello Again for the Second Time! 06-22-97 09:41:38 PM
Hello World! 06-22-97 09:42:39 PM
Hello Again for the Second Time! 06-22-97 09:42:39 PM
Hello World! 06-22-97 09:42:39 PM
Hello Again for the Second Time! 06-22-97 09:42:39 PM
Hello World! 06-22-97 09:43:40 PM
Hello Again for the Second Time! 06-22-97 09:43:40 PM
Hello World! 06-22-97 09:43:40 PM
Hello Again for the Second Time! 06-22-97 09:43:40 PM
Hello World! 06-22-97 09:44:40 PM
```

18

Your output might be a lot longer, depending on when you view this file. Notice that the two procedures HELLOFLE and SHAREFLE are appending to HELLO.TXT the phrase and the date and time every minute.

Summary

Today you have learned how to work with the DBMS_JOB package in Oracle8i. This package handles all jobs by using background processes to check for jobs to execute at a specific interval, and then places them in job queues. To submit a job for processing, you must submit the job to the queue first. After a job is submitted, if you are the owner, you can change the parameters. You can also fix any of your broken jobs, as well as remove your own jobs from the queue. This chapter also covered the techniques used to run a job immediately. You can also import and export jobs from one database to another. Always remember that the job number is unique, and any attempt to use the same job number will result in a failure of the job to execute.

Q&A

Q Can jobs be executed immediately, without being sent to the job queue?

A No. All jobs must be submitted to a job queue, and then you can use DBMS_JOB.RUN to execute a given job immediately. The job then returns to executing at its scheduled time interval.

Q What is the difference between SUBMIT and ISUBMIT?

A ISUBMIT enables you to assign job numbers, provided that the job number is not being used in the system.

Q Which parameters can be altered in the job?

A All the parameters can be altered in a job. You can use CHANGE to alter them all immediately or use specific procedures such as WHAT, NEXT_DATE, and INTERVAL.

Q Who can remove or alter a job?

A Only the owner of the job can alter or remove the job.

Q What can be done about a broken job?

A You could either use RUN to execute the job immediately or use the BROKEN procedure to reschedule the job. If needed, you could also delete the job by using REMOVE.

Q When submitting a job, what punctuation should be used around regular procedure parameters?

A Any parameters that normally are surrounded by a single quote (') must be surrounded by two single quotes (' '); otherwise, the job never executes.

Workshop

You can use this workshop to test your comprehension of this chapter and put what you've learned into practice. You'll find the answers to the quiz and exercises in Appendix A, "Answers."

Quiz

1. If the server goes down for two days (Monday to Tuesday), and a job with an execution of SYSDATE + 7 was supposed to run when the server went down (Tuesday), will the job always run on the original day of the week (that is, run every Tuesday)?

2. Why must you use two single quotes around parameters specified in SUBMIT, when you used to need only one set of single quotes?

3. Can you alter someone else's job?

4. How do you assign your own job number to a job?

5. What interval would you use to run a procedure every hour on the hour, starting from the current date?

Exercises

1. Write the code to submit a procedure called PAYDAY, where the parameters are FRIDAY, Bi_Monthly, and 6. The job should always execute at 4 a.m. Saturday.

2. Write the code to view the JOB, last-second run, and WHAT from USER_JOBS.

3. Write the code to submit job 200 once per day, starting from SYSDATE for the procedure EASY, which has no parameters.

4. Write the code to alter job 200 to execute once per week for the interval SYSDATE + 7.

5. Write the code to remove job 200.

18

DAY 19

Alerting and Communicating with Other Procedures: The DBMS_ALERT and DBMS_PIPE Packages

by Tom Luers

Oracle provides two packages to assist the developer with creating applications: DBMS_PIPE establishes communications within sessions, and DBMS_ALERT notifies about events from other procedures. Both packages help make your applications more robust and powerful within the Oracle database.

Both packages come with your Oracle database. They are automatically installed when the database is created and the `CATPROC.SQL` procedure is executed.

In today's lesson, you will learn to

- Work with the `DBMS_ALERT` package
- Send and register an alert
- Wait for an alert and remove an alert
- Execute polling and events
- Use `DBMS_PIPE`
- Recognize the differences between public and private pipes
- Use pipe messages
- Know the differences between alerts and pipes

The DBMS_ALERT Package

As the name suggests, you can use alerts to notify you about an event for informational purposes. The DBMS_ALERT package is typically a one-way asynchronous communication that is triggered when a transaction commits. Unless a transaction commits, no information is sent to the alert. This means that a waiting procedure or application remains idle until the desired transaction commits. Because alerts provide one-way communication, they have limited usage. Consider these examples of how you can use alerts: An insurance company agent can be alerted to natural disasters so that she can dispatch a team of experts to aid the survivors. You can also be alerted if a trigger fails, which can corrupt your database.

 Note

> Because the DBMS_ALERT package uses COMMIT, you cannot use this package in Oracle Forms.

Because the DBMS_ALERT package is transaction-based, any ROLLBACK removes any waiting alerts. The order for setting up an alert is

- Use REGISTER to record your interest in a particular alert.
- Issue the WAITONE procedure to wait for a specific alert.
- Issue the WAITANY procedure to wait for any of your registered alerts.
- Use SIGNAL when the condition for the alert is met and the transaction has been committed.

> **Note**
>
> To work with the DBMS_ALERT package, you must have the package installed, and you must have the EXECUTE permission for the package.

Using SIGNAL to Issue an Alert

When you want to send an alert, you need to use the SIGNAL procedure. As mentioned earlier, this procedure only executes when a COMMIT is issued.

▼ SYNTAX

The Syntax for the SIGNAL Procedure

```
PROCEDURE SIGNAL(alert_name IN VARCHAR2,
                 message_sent IN VARCHAR2);
```

alert_name can be a maximum of 30 characters, and it is not case sensitive. In addition, the name must not start with ORA$, which is reserved for use with Oracle. *message_sent* can be up to 1,800 characters, which allows for a generous concatenation of text, variable names, and so on. This message is sent to the waiting session.

▲

It is common for multiple sessions to concurrently issue signals on the same alert. In this case, as each session issues the alert, it blocks all other concurrent sessions until it commits. The net effect of this behavior is that alerts can cause transactions to become serialized.

After the alert is sent, Oracle changes the state of the alert from not signaled to signaled. This information is recorded in the DBMS_ALERT_INFO data dictionary. Because there is only one record for each alert, any other sessions attempting to send an alert are blocked until the alert has been received.

If no sessions have registered the alert, the alert remains signaled until the session has registered the alert. If multiple sessions have registered for the alert, after the alert has been signaled, all sessions receive the alert, and the alert returns to the nonsignaled state.

Registering for an Alert

Before you can even search for an alert, you must register the alert you want to monitor, which adds you to the master registration list. You take this first step by using the REGISTER procedure.

19

The Syntax for the REGISTER Procedure

```
PROCEDURE REGISTER(alert_name IN VARCHAR2);
```

In this syntax, *alert_name* is the name of the alert to monitor. A session can register interest in an unlimited number of alerts. You can monitor as many alerts as you are registered for. You can remove yourself from the master registration list through the REMOVE or REMOVEALL procedures.

> **Note**
>
> Simply registering an alert does not block the session from executing; rather, it simply records an interest in the alert. Only the WAITONE and WAITANY commands can block the session from executing. Although you can benefit from registering for all possible alerts and then checking for the alert later in a procedure, you are using valuable resources to monitor the registration. Use REGISTER only when necessary.

Waiting for a Specific Alert

If you want to monitor one alert, use the WAITONE procedure.

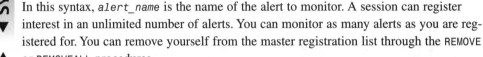

The Syntax for the WAITONE Procedure

```
PROCEDURE WAITONE(alert_name    IN VARCHAR2,
                  alert_message  OUT VARCHAR2,
                  alert_status   OUT INTEGER,
                  timeout        IN NUMBER DEFAULT maxwait);
```

Again, *alert_name* is the name of the alert you are monitoring. *alert_message* is the message that you receive when the alert has been signaled. This message is sent via the SIGNAL call. The *alert_status* parameter has two possible values: 0 if the alert is signaled before the timeout or 1 if the timeout occurs before any alert has been received. *timeout* is how long you will wait (in seconds) for the alert before the procedure continues executing if no alert is received. The default time period for maxwait is 1,000 days.

> **Tip**
>
> When testing a DBMS_ALERT procedure, it is a good idea to make maxwait no longer than five minutes; otherwise, you could be at the keyboard for 1,000 days!

If the *alert_name* specified has not been registered, you receive an error message:

```
ORA-20000, ORU-10024:  there are no alerts registered.
```

Waiting for Any Registered Alert

The WAITANY procedure allows you to constantly monitor for any alert for which you have registered in the current session.

The Syntax for the WAITANY Procedure

```
PROCEDURE WAITANY(alert_name OUT VARCHAR2,
                  alert_message OUT VARCHAR2,
                  alert_status OUT INTEGER,
                  timeout IN NUMBER DEFAULT maxwait);
```

alert_name is an OUT parameter of type VARCHAR2 instead of type IN VARCHAR2. Instead of specifying *alert_name* as an input, you receive the *alert_name* of the first registered alert that was sent. *alert_message* is the message that you receive when the specific alert is signaled. This message is provided via the SIGNAL call. The *alert_status* parameter has two possible values: 0 if any alert is signaled before the timeout or 1 if the timeout occurs before any alert is received. *timeout* is how long you will wait (in seconds) for the alert before the procedure continues executing. Again, the default for maxwait is 1,000 days. You receive the same error message as you do with WAITONE if you do not register the alert before trying to wait for it.

Removing One Alert

To remove only one specific alert from the registration list, use the REMOVE procedure.

The Syntax for the REMOVE Procedure

```
PROCEDURE REMOVE(alert_name IN VARCHAR2);
```

alert_name is the alert you want to remove from the registration list. After you no longer need to wait for an alert, you should use REMOVE to remove the registration instead of using up valuable resources. Whether you wait for an alert or not, once registered, the alert attempts to signal all registered procedures. Not only does the system waste resources attempting to send an alert to what it believes is a waiting process, but also it takes longer for the system to process through the registration list when it contains alerts you no longer need.

19

Removing All Alerts

You can remove all registered alerts from the current session by placing a call to the procedure REMOVEALL. The format for the REMOVEALL procedure is as follows:

```
PROCEDURE REMOVEALL;
```

After the procedure is executed, all registered alerts are deleted. An implicit COMMIT is executed with this call.

Polling and Events with the SET_DEFAULTS Procedure

As an Oracle event occurs, it is picked up in the system and processed. You see this happen in the walkthrough example, Listing 19.3, of the DBMS_ALERT package using the WAITONE procedure. The WAITONE procedure waits for the specific event to occur and either alerts you when the alert occurs or eventually times out. On the other hand, some situations require polling or specifically searching for an alert:

- When shared instances of a database can issue an alert, you need to poll for an alert for any of the shared instances.
- When using the WAITANY procedure, you need to search for a specific alert. The WAITANY procedure enters a looping poll mode to search for any registered alerts. When WAITANY enters a sleep mode after polling for alerts, it picks up only the most recently signaled alert if three alerts are signaled during the sleep period. The default poll starts at 1 second and increases exponentially to 30 seconds.

Because two possibilities[md]using shared instances or using WAITANY—can result in missed alerts, you can change the polling time in seconds using SET_DEFAULTS.

The Syntax for the SET_DEFAULTS Procedure

```
PROCEDURE SET_DEFAULTS(polling_interval IN NUMBER);
```

You specify the interval between polling in seconds. The default interval for this procedure is 5 seconds.

Demonstrating the DBMS_ALERT Package

The best way to understand alerts is to use the DBMS_ALERT package. Your goal is to solve a security problem. Suppose that some employees gained access to the payroll database and had some fun changing around pay rates. The IS director has empowered you to devise an alert, which security will constantly monitor, to detect any changes in the payroll database.

To meet this goal, you have decided to create a copy of the payroll database, along with who has changed what data at what time. In addition, because human resources can legitimately change data in the database, you need to add a Verified field, which security will change to Y for yes after the change is approved. You have to create the following:

- A backup database called security, which will hold the old and new values, the user who changed the information, the date the user changed the information, and whether the information has been verified

- A trigger based upon the insert, update, or delete performed on a row, which will then issue an alert

- A program to monitor for the security alert

Creating the Backup Database

As with any type of audit trail, you will create a database that will hold a copy of the old and new information, the date, time, and user for the changed data, and whether the data was verified by security. To create the database, enter and execute the code in Listing 19.1.

INPUT　　**LISTING 19.1**　Creating the Backup Security Database

```
 1: CREATE TABLE security(
 2: /* This database holds the original and new data archived from
 3:    the payroll database to look for any violations of pay rate,
 4:    name changes, and so on by internal employees or external hackers */
 5:
 6: /*  Store the original values */
 7:     OLD_Emp_Id INTEGER,
 8:     OLD_Emp_Name VARCHAR2(32),
 9:     OLD_Supervised_By INTEGER,
10:     OLD_Pay_Rate NUMBER(9,2),
11:     OLD_Pay_Type CHAR,
12:     OLD_Emp_Dept_Id INTEGER,
13: /* Store the changed values */
14:     NEW_Emp_Id INTEGER,
15:     NEW_Emp_Name VARCHAR2(32),
16:     NEW_Supervised_By INTEGER,
17:     NEW_Pay_Rate NUMBER(9,2),
18:     NEW_Pay_Type CHAR,
19:     NEW_Emp_Dept_Id INTEGER,
20: /* Flag to retain status if security has verified the change (Y/N) */
21:     Verified CHAR(1),
22: /* Store Date and who made the changes */
23:     Changed_By VARCHAR2(8),
24:     Time_Changed DATE)
25: /
```

19

This code is based on the original table called employee, which you created on Day 8, "Using SQL." After you execute the code, the following message should appear at the prompt:

`Table Created`

You can now create the trigger that will occur whenever anyone alters the employee table.

Creating the Trigger to Signal an Alert

It's time to create the trigger that will signal an alert when any changes are made to the employee table. Enter and execute the code in Listing 19.2.

INPUT   **LISTING 19.2**   Creating the Trigger to Signal the Alert

```
 1: CREATE or REPLACE TRIGGER security
 2:
 3: /* This trigger package will send an alert called emp_change when
 4:     a row has been inserted, deleted, or updated. It will also send
 5:     a message with the old Employee ID, the New Employee ID, the old
 6:     Pay Rate and the new Pay Rate  */
 7:
 8: BEFORE INSERT OR UPDATE OR DELETE ON employee
 9: FOR EACH ROW
10: BEGIN
11:
12: /* Send the Alert emp_change with the old and new values from the
13:     row being updated, changed, or deleted. Notice the use of :OLD
14:     for the contents of the original data and :NEW for the contents
15:     of the new data  */
16:
17:     DBMS_ALERT.SIGNAL('emp_change','NOTICE:  OLD ID: ' || :OLD.emp_id
18:         || ' NEW ID: ' || :NEW.emp_id || ' OLD Pay Rate: '
19:         || :OLD.pay_rate || ' NEW Pay Rate:  ' || :NEW.pay_rate);
20:
21: /* Insert all of the values into the security table */
22:     INSERT INTO security
23:         (OLD_emp_id,OLD_emp_name,OLD_supervised_by,
24:          OLD_pay_rate,OLD_pay_type,OLD_emp_dept_id,
25:          NEW_emp_id,NEW_emp_name,NEW_supervised_by,
26:          NEW_pay_rate,NEW_pay_type,NEW_emp_dept_id,
27:          verified,changed_by,time_changed)
28:     VALUES
29:         (:OLD.emp_id,:OLD.emp_name,:OLD.supervised_by,
30:          :OLD.pay_rate,:OLD.pay_type,:OLD.emp_dept_id,
31:          :NEW.emp_id,:NEW.emp_name,:NEW.supervised_by,
32:          :NEW.pay_rate,:NEW.pay_type,:NEW.emp_dept_id,
33:          'N',USER,SYSDATE);
34:
35: END security; -- End of the Trigger Security
```

ANALYSIS Because you are looking at values being altered in a row, you base the trigger on FOR EACH ROW, only when the values of the row have been inserted, updated, or deleted from the table employee. The occurrence of any of those conditions signals an alert called emp_change, which passes the following in the message:

- The original employee ID
- The new employee ID
- The original employee pay rate
- The new employee pay rate

All of these items are concatenated into a VARCHAR2 string using the concatenation operator (¦¦). The total length of the information is well under the message limit of 1,800 characters.

The trigger then performs an INSERT on the security table to add all the original data, the new data, who changed the data, the date the data was changed, and whether the data has been verified by security. At any point in time, you can run a query against this table for Security.Verified = 'N' when no one has been watching the screen, waiting for the alert to occur.

Waiting for the Alert

The next step is to wait for an alert and then finally cause an alert to happen. Because you are going to practice inserting, deleting, and updating, I recommend that *before* you do anything else, you enter the code in Listings 19.3 through 19.6. Listing 19.3 registers the alert and then waits for the alert. The other three listings practice, in order, an insert, an update, and a delete. At the SQL*Plus prompt, type **SET SERVEROUTPUT ON** and press Enter to see output to the screen.

19

INPUT **LISTING 19.3** Registering and Waiting for an Alert

```
1: DECLARE
2:     message VARCHAR2(1800); -- Display Incoming Message from Alert
3:     status INTEGER; -- Holds Status 0 if success, 1 if timed out
4: BEGIN
5:     DBMS_ALERT.REGISTER('emp_change'); -- Registers for Alert emp_change
6:     DBMS_ALERT.WAITONE('emp_change',message,status,60); -- Wait for alert
7:     DBMS_OUTPUT.PUT_LINE(message);  -- Display Message
8:     DBMS_ALERT.REMOVE('emp_change'); -- Remove Registration for Alert
9: END;
```

ANALYSIS You first create two variables, one called `message` to hold the message sent by the alert and the other called `status` to hold the status of the procedure `WAITONE`. You begin by registering for the alert `emp_change`. You then wait for the alert for 60 seconds. For these examples, I recommend that you set this to `600` to wait for the alert. This value gives you enough time to execute this procedure in one window and then execute the insert, update, and delete in another window. If the alert is signaled before your time limit expires, the `DBMS_OUTPUT` package displays the message to the screen. Then, remove the alert from the registration. The wait time will change, depending upon the circumstance.

Using INSERT to Signal the Alert

You can practice inserting a record into the employee database. This practice requires two open sessions. In the first session, execute the code in Listing 19.3. Make sure that you have first typed **SET SERVEROUTPUT ON** and pressed Enter. Before you execute the code, make sure that you have changed the time to wait to 600 seconds if you need the time to enter the SQL code in Listing 19.4.

INPUT   **LISTING 19.4**   Inserting a Record to Trigger an Alert

```
1: INSERT INTO employee
2:     (emp_id, emp_name,supervised_by,pay_rate,pay_type,emp_dept_id)
3:     VALUES(9109,'Benjamin Franklin',209,20.50,'H',10);
4: COMMIT;
```

Without the final `COMMIT` statement, the alert never triggers. When you execute the code from Listing 19.4, on the screen where you perform the insert, your output should be

OUTPUT   `1 row created`

After the `COMMIT` is executed, you should see

`Commit complete`

On the other screen that is monitoring the alert, your output should look like

`NOTICE:  OLD ID:  NEW ID: 9109 OLD Pay Rate:  NEW Pay Rate:  20.5`

`PL/SQL procedure successfully completed.`

If the procedure ends without output, make sure that you have entered SET SERVEROUTPUT ON. The other possibility is that the `INSERT` command did not complete before the time to wait for the alert elapsed.

Because this is a new record, as you expect, there is no data in the `OLD` values.

Using UPDATE to Signal the Alert

With your two sessions still open, execute in one of the SQL*Plus screens the code in Listing 19.3. On the other screen, execute the code in Listing 19.5 to practice updating a record. Before you execute the code from Listing 19.3, make sure you change the time to wait to 600 seconds if you need the time to enter the SQL code in Listing 19.5.

INPUT   **LISTING 19.5**   Updating a Record to Trigger an Alert

```
1: UPDATE employee
2:    SET pay_rate = 75
3:    WHERE emp_id = 9109;
4: COMMIT;
```

When you execute the code in Listing 19.5, on the screen where you perform the update, your output should be

OUTPUT   1 row updated

After the COMMIT is executed, you should see

```
Commit complete
```

On the other screen that is monitoring the alert, your output should look like

```
NOTICE:  OLD ID: 9109 NEW ID: 9109 OLD Pay Rate: 20.5 NEW Pay Rate:  75
PL/SQL procedure successfully completed.
```

If the procedure ends without output, make sure that you have entered SET SERVEROUTPUT ON. The other possibilities are that the UPDATE command did not complete before the time to wait for the alert elapsed or that you forgot to commit the transaction.

Look at this! You notice an employee's pay rate change from $20.50 per hour to $75.00 per hour. This scheme is reminiscent of the *Superman* movie where Richard Pryor gives himself a huge raise after breaking into the payroll computer. This change definitely bears investigation.

Using DELETE to Signal the Alert

With your two sessions still open, execute in one of the SQL*Plus screens the code in Listing 19.3. On the other screen, execute the code in Listing 19.6 to practice deleting a record. Before you execute the code from Listing 19.3, make sure that you have changed the time to wait to 600 seconds if you need the time to enter the SQL code in Listing 19.6.

19

INPUT **LISTING 19.6**   Deleting a Record to Trigger an Alert

```
1: DELETE from employee
2:    WHERE emp_id = 9109;
3: COMMIT;
```

When you execute the code in Listing 19.6, on the screen where you perform the delete, your output should be

OUTPUT   `1 row deleted`

After the COMMIT is executed, you should see

`Commit complete`

On the other screen that is monitoring the alert, your output should look like

```
NOTICE: OLD ID: 9109 NEW ID: OLD Pay Rate: 75 NEW Pay Rate:
PL/SQL procedure successfully completed.
```

If the procedure ends without output, make sure that you have entered SET SERVEROUTPUT ON. The other possibilities are that the UPDATE command did not complete before the time to wait for the alert elapsed or that you forgot to commit the transaction.

Security finally escorted the person who manipulated the payroll database out the door to the police waiting outside. Human resources then deleted his record from the system. There are no NEW values because you deleted this record. You can now run a query against the security database to show that the trigger did indeed work and place the data into the table security.

Viewing the Results of the Trigger in the Security Database

To see the three rows in the security database, execute the following code line:

`SELECT * from SECURITY;`

When you execute this code line, your output should look like

```
OLD_EMP_ID OLD_EMP_NAME        SUPERVISED_BY OLD_PAY_RATE O OLD_EMP_DEPT_ID
---------- ------------------- ------------- ------------ - ---------------
NEW_EMP_ID NEW_EMP_NAME        SUPERVISED_BY NEW_PAY_RATE N NEW_EMP_DEPT_ID V
---------- ------------------- ------------- ------------ - --------------- -
CHANGED_ TIME_CHANGED
-------- ----------
      9109 Benjamin Franklin   209                   20.5 H              10
      9109 Benjamin Franklin   209                     75 H              10 N
SCOTT    29-JUN-97
```

```
        9109 Benjamin Franklin  209                      75 H              10 N

SCOTT     29-JUN-97


        9109 Benjamin Franklin  209                      20.5 H            10 N
SCOTT     29-JUL-99
```

> **Note**   If you do not have to use alerts based on transactions, then using the Oracle
> DBMS_PIPE procedure is a useful alternative.

The DBMS_PIPE Package

The DBMS_PIPE package enables you to communicate between multiple sessions in the same database instance. You communicate by sending and receiving messages through the pipe. A message you send is a *writer*. A message you receive is a *reader*. Each pipe can have one or more writers and one or more readers. Anyone who has access to the database instance and can execute PL/SQL code can access a pipe.

One key feature of pipes is that they are asynchronous. You can access a pipe without having to use COMMIT. In addition, the ROLLBACK command does not work with pipes. This fact allows you to use pipes as a powerful debugging tool, as well as an audit trail. If you need transactional control for your communications, the DBMS_ALERT is a useful alternative.

> **Note**   When you are trying to work with pipes, error messages can mean one of
> two things. Either you do not have access to the DBMS_PIPE package, or the
> package has not been installed. If you need access, contact the system
> administrator, who can grant you permissions to the EXECUTE ANY PROCEDURE
> privilege. Personal Oracle 95 users must sign on as SYS with the password
> CHANGE_ON_INSTALL and then execute @c:\ORAWIN95\RDBS73\ADMIN\
> CATPROC.SQL to install the package.

Public Versus Private Pipes

PL/SQL version 2.2 or later provides private pipes. All earlier versions supported *public* pipes, which can be accessed by anyone in the database instance as long as the user knows the name of the pipe and has EXECUTE access to DBMS_PIPE. *Private* pipes can be accessed only by

- DBAs
- The creator of the pipe
- Any stored procedure created by the owner

You use private pipes, for example, when running three modules of a job simultaneously that need to share data without being interrupted. You can also use private pipes as an audit trail or debugging tool. Public pipes are useful for projects to which everyone needs access.

Using Pipes

The following steps demonstrate the order in which pipes operate:

1. If you are creating a private pipe, you first issue the CREATE_PIPE function. You can implicitly create a public pipe by referencing it the first time. This implicit pipe then disappears when it no longer contains data.

2. Whether the pipe is public or private, you send the data you want to transmit to a pipe to the message buffer by issuing the PACK_MESSAGE procedure. You are limited to 4,096 bytes in the message buffer area.

3. Before the buffer is overfilled, you issue the SEND_MESSAGE procedure to send the data to the pipe. If you are creating a public pipe, SEND_MESSAGE creates the pipe by default.

4. When you are ready to receive data, you first call the RECEIVE_MESSAGE procedure. Each time the procedure is called, it reads the first unread message in the pipe and dumps it into the message buffer. Every time you want to extract the next message, you need to call RECEIVE_MESSAGE. If you need to know the data type, because it could vary, you call the function NEXT_ITEM_TYPE.

5. You use UNPACK_MESSAGE to interpret the message.

Of course, at any time, multiple sessions can be writing to the same pipe, and multiple sessions can be reading from the same pipe. A great application use, especially for multiple processor servers (SMP), is an application for student registration. Two or more terminals can use the same form to send data to the same pipe to register different students. The pipe can be read by multiple sessions to then process the records as each one comes across the pipe to process the records much more quickly. In return, you can send triggers, which can also use pipes if the enrollment gets too large.

By default, pipes retain the information for up to 1,000 days. However, all data buffered in a pipe is lost when the instance is shut down. To define the duration of the retention period, use the PL/SQL constant `maxwait`. This constant is defined in Oracle as

```
maxwait CONSTANT INTEGER := 86400000;
```

The constant is expressed in seconds, so 60 seconds/minute × 60 minutes/hour × 24 hours/day × 1,000 days = 8,640,000 seconds. Of course, you can change the default to increase or decrease the time the pipe retains the data.

When naming a pipe, you must follow some conventions. Never begin pipes with `ORA$`, which is reserved for use by Oracle. The pipe name can be up to 128 characters. Also, make sure the pipe name is always unique. When in doubt, assign the name of the pipe to an Oracle-defined name by using the function `UNIQUE_SESSION_NAME`.

You can change the pipe size from the default of 8,192 bytes. Remember, you always have to deal with a 4,096-byte limitation on the message buffer.

Table 19.1 lists all functions and procedures for the `DBMS_PIPE` package.

TABLE 19.1   DBMS_PIPE Functions and Procedures

Name	Type	Description
CREATE_PIPE	Function	Primarily used to create a private pipe but can be used to create a public pipe.
NEXT_ITEM_TYPE	Function	Extracts the data type of the next item in the message buffer. Used primarily with unpacking the message received.
PACK_MESSAGE	Procedure	Sends data to the message buffer to eventually be sent to the pipe.
PURGE	Procedure	Removes all data from the pipe.
RECEIVE_MESSAGE	Function	Receives a message from the pipe and writes it to the message buffer.
REMOVE_PIPE	Function	Deletes the pipe from memory.
RESET_BUFFER	Procedure	Clears the data from the message buffer.
SEND_MESSAGE	Function	Sends all data from the message buffer to the pipe specified. If the pipe does not exist, it is created as a public pipe.
UNIQUE_SESSION_NAME	Function	Returns a unique session name.
UNPACK_MESSAGE	Procedure	Retrieves the next item from the message buffer.

19

The Functions and Procedures of `DBMS_PIPE`

This section discusses the functions and procedures in more detail, including the syntax and a hands-on example for passing data back and forth between pipes.

The `CREATE_PIPE` Function

As stated earlier, you need the CREATE_PIPE function to create private pipes.

The Syntax for the `CREATE_PIPE` Function

The syntax for the CREATE_PIPE function is

```
FUNCTION CREATE_PIPE(name_of_pipe IN VARCHAR2,
                     pipesize IN INTEGER DEFAULT 8192,
                     private IN BOOLEAN DEFAULT true)
RETURN INTEGER; -- Status on pipe creation
```

name_of_pipe is the name you assign to the pipe. The next parameter is *pipesize*, which is the maximum size of the pipe. The default is 8,192 bytes, which you can change. The last parameter simply states whether the pipe is private or public based upon the BOOLEAN value passed. The value is `false` for public and `true` for private. Remember, by calling SEND_MESSAGE, you do not have to use CREATE_PIPE to create a public pipe.

An example of creating a private pipe is

```
v_status := DBMS_PIPE.CREATE_PIPE('mypipe');
```

This code creates a pipe with a maximum size of 8,192 bytes, which is also private (the default of `true`). Remember, this is a function with a return type of `status`.

To create the public pipe, the code looks similar to

```
v_status := DBMS_PIPE.CREATE_PIPE('itpublic',8192,false);
```

You now have a public pipe called `itpublic` with a size of 8,192 bytes.

If the return value (this example uses the variable v_status) is zero, the pipe was successfully created. If the user does not have access rights to create a pipe, or the pipe name already exists, the ORA-23322 exception is raised.

The `PACK_MESSAGE` Procedure

After a pipe is created (or will be created with SEND_MESSAGE for public pipes), you can send data to the message buffer for later transmittal to the pipe using the PACK_MESSAGE procedure. Because the function is overloaded, you can send a data type of VARCHAR2, DATE, or NUMBER.

The Syntax for the PACK_MESSAGE Procedure

SYNTAX

The format for PACK_MESSAGE is

```
PROCEDURE PACK_MESSAGE(data IN VARCHAR2);
PROCEDURE PACK_MESSAGE(data IN DATE);
PROCEDURE PACK_MESSAGE(data IN NUMBER);
```

data is the data that you are sending to the buffer. Remember that the buffer has only 4,096 bytes available for use. If you go over this limit, you receive the following error:

OUTPUT
```
ORA-06558 buffer in DBMS_PIPE package is full.
No more items allowed.
```

Using the SEND_MESSAGE Function

Before you overfill your message buffer, you should send the data to the pipe with the SEND_MESSAGE function. This function moves the data in the message buffer to the pipe specified from the function call.

The Syntax for the SEND_MESSAGE Function

SYNTAX

The format for the function SEND_MESSAGE is

```
FUNCTION SEND_MESSAGE(name_of_pipe IN VARCHAR2,
                      timeout IN INTEGER DEFAULT maxwait
                      pipesize IN INTEGER DEFAULT 8192)
RETURN INTEGER;
```

▲ name_of_pipe is the name of the pipe already in existence, whether private or public. If no pipe of this name exists, Oracle creates one upon successful execution of SEND_MESSAGE. timeout is how long Oracle attempts to place the message in the pipe in seconds. The default is 1,000 days. Finally, because you can create a public pipe on execution, you control the size of the pipe with pipesize, which you indicate in bytes.

The SEND_MESSAGE values are listed in Table 19.2.

TABLE 19.2 Return Values from SEND_MESSAGE

Return Code	Meaning
0	The message was sent successfully.
1	The maximum wait time has been exceeded while waiting for some room to clear from the pipe from the RECEIVE_MESSAGE function.
3	The message being sent was interrupted.

Use these return codes for proper error checking and error handling.

19

Using the RECEIVE_MESSAGE Function

The RECEIVE_MESSAGE function moves a message from the pipe to the message buffer. Then, you can identify the data type with NEXT_ITEM_TYPE or use UNPACK_MESSAGE to read the message buffer and use it in your process.

The Syntax for the RECEIVE_MESSAGE Function

The format for RECEIVE MESSAGE is

```
FUNCTION RECEIVE_MESSAGE(name_of_pipe IN VARCHAR2,
                timeout IN INTEGER DEFAULT maxwait);
RETURN INTEGER;
```

name_of_pipe is the name of the pipe already in existence. timeout is how long Oracle attempts to read the next line from the pipe if there are no current messages in the pipe. ▲ The possible return codes are listed in Table 19.3.

TABLE 19.3 Return Values from RECEIVE_MESSAGE

Return Code	Meaning
0	The message was received successfully.
1	The maximum wait time has been exceeded while waiting for a message to be sent to the pipe.
2	The message in the pipe is too large for the message buffer. You should never see this code because both the SEND_MESSAGE and RECEIVE_MESSAGE buffers are limited to the same length of 4,096 bytes.
3	The message being received was interrupted.

The UNPACK_MESSAGE Procedure

After you have received a message in the buffer, you need to move the message from the buffer into a variable with the UNPACK_MESSAGE procedure. As with the PACK_MESSAGE procedure, the UNPACK_MESSAGE procedure is overloaded and can accept such data types as VARCHAR2, DATE, and NUMBER.

The Syntax for the UNPACK_MESSAGE Procedure

The syntax of the procedure is

```
PROCEDURE UNPACK_MESSAGE(data OUT VARCHAR2);
PROCEDURE UNPACK_MESSAGE(data OUT DATE);
PROCEDURE UNPACK_MESSAGE(data OUT NUMBER);
```

data is the data that you are receiving from the message buffer. You can receive two possible errors when trying to unpack the message:

```
ORA-06556 the pipe is empty, cannot fulfill the UNPACK_MESSAGE request
ORA-06559 wrong datatype requested, datatype, actual datatype is datatype
```

You can address both of these errors through error-message handlers. The first error tries to read the message buffer, which is empty. The second error message says that the data type you are requesting is a different data type from the one stored in the pipe. You will most likely not encounter this problem if the data type in the pipe is always the same, but if it can vary, you use the NEXT_ITEM_TYPE function to determine the data type of the next item in the buffer before you retrieve it.

The format for NEXT_ITEM_TYPE function is

```
FUNCTION NEXT_ITEM_TYPE RETURN INTEGER;
```

No parameters are required for the function. It returns the value of the data type, which is described in Table 19.4.

TABLE **19.4** Return Data Type Definitions from NEXT_ITEM_TYPE

Return Code	Description
0	No more items
6	NUMBER
9	VARCHAR2
11	ROWID
12	DATE
23	RAW

You can use the NEXT_ITEM_TYPE function for exception handling for no data in the pipe, as well as for determining the type of data being passed to you from the message buffer. You can easily implement a NEXT_ITEM_TYPE test with a series of IF...ELSIF statements.

The REMOVE_PIPE Function

After you no longer need a pipe, you can either wait for the system to eventually delete the pipe, or you can use the REMOVE_PIPE function.

19

The Syntax for the REMOVE_PIPE Function

The syntax for the function is

```
FUNCTION REMOVE_PIPE(name_of_pipe IN VARCHAR2);
RETURN INTEGER; -- Status on pipe deletion
```

The return value is 0 whether the pipe exists or not. The only exception you will receive is ORA-23322, which means that you don't have access to remove the pipe. When a pipe is removed, all messages stored in the pipe are also deleted.

An Example of Using Pipes

This section demonstrates the use of pipes by creating both a public and private pipe and then extracting the data from both pipes and displaying it onscreen.

Creating Public and Private Pipes

To create the public and private pipes, enter and execute the code in Listing 19.7. Before you execute the code, make sure that you type **SET SERVEROUTPUT ON** to see output from the DBMS_OUTPUT package.

INPUT   **LISTING 19.7**   Creating Pipes

```
 1: DECLARE
 2:      v_statpipe1 integer; -- Status for private pipe
 3:      v_statpipe2 integer; -- Status for public pipe created on the fly
 4:      v_pubchar VARCHAR2(100) := 'This is a text string';
 5:      v_pubdate DATE := SYSDATE;
 6:      v_pubnum NUMBER := 109;
 7: BEGIN
 8: -- Creates Private Pipe
 9:      v_statpipe1 := DBMS_PIPE.CREATE_PIPE('myprivatepipe');
10: -- If the pipe was successfully created
11:      IF (v_statpipe1 = 0) THEN
12:          DBMS_PIPE.PACK_MESSAGE('privateline1');
13:          DBMS_PIPE.PACK_MESSAGE('privateline2');
14: -- Send Message Buffer to Private Pipe
15:          v_statpipe1 := DBMS_PIPE.SEND_MESSAGE('myprivatepipe');
16:      END IF;
17:
18:      DBMS_PIPE.PACK_MESSAGE(v_pubchar); -- sends data type VARCHAR2
19:      DBMS_PIPE.PACK_MESSAGE(v_pubdate); -- sends data type DATE
20:      DBMS_PIPE.PACK_MESSAGE(v_pubnum);  -- sends data type NUMBER
21: -- Creates public pipe and sends message buffer to the pipe
22:      v_statpipe2 := DBMS_PIPE.SEND_MESSAGE('mypublicpipe');
23: -- Check status of both pipes to make sure they're 0 (created properly)
24:      DBMS_OUTPUT.PUT_LINE('The Status of your Private Pipe is: ' ||
25:          v_statpipe1 );
```

```
26:      DBMS_OUTPUT.PUT_LINE('The Status of your Public Pipe is: ' ||
27:           v_statpipe2 );
28:
29: END;
```

After the code has executed, if you have all the permissions to the DBMS_PIPE package, then you should see the following output:

OUTPUT
```
The Status of your Private Pipe is: 0
The Status of your Public Pipe is: 0
```

ANALYSIS In this example, the program first creates a private pipe called myprivatepipe in line 9. It then sends two messages of type VARCHAR2 to the message buffer and uses SEND_MESSAGE in line 15 to output the buffer to the pipe. The only error checking here is making sure that the private pipe is created properly in line 11. Ideally, you should check for overflows of the message buffer and whether the data was sent to the pipe (pipe not full and so on).

The program sends more data to the message buffer of type VARCHAR2, DATE, and NUMBER in lines 18 through 20, and then it creates upon execution of SEND_MESSAGE in line 22 the public pipe mypublicpipe. The DBMS_OUTPUT package displays the status of the newly created pipes in lines 24 through 27.

Reading Data from the Pipes

You can now prepare to read data from both pipes. Enter and execute the code in Listing 19.8. Again, make sure that you have typed **SET SERVEROUTPUT ON** for proof that the pipes work.

19

INPUT **LISTING 19.8** Reading Data from the Private and Public Pipe

```
1: DECLARE
2:      v_statpipe1 integer; -- status of private pipe
3:      v_statpipe2 integer; -- status of public pipe
4:      v_holdtype INTEGER; -- holds status of next item type
5:      v_holdchar VARCHAR2(100);
6:      v_holddate DATE;
7:      v_holdnum NUMBER;
8: BEGIN
9: -- start procedure of getting message from private pipe
10:      v_statpipe1 := DBMS_PIPE.RECEIVE_MESSAGE('myprivatepipe',15);
11:      DBMS_PIPE.UNPACK_MESSAGE(v_holdchar);
12:      DBMS_OUTPUT.PUT_LINE(v_holdchar); -- display 1st data type from msg
13:      DBMS_PIPE.UNPACK_MESSAGE(v_holdchar);
14:      DBMS_OUTPUT.PUT_LINE(v_holdchar); -- display 2nd data type from msg
15:
```

continues

LISTING 19.8 continued

```
16: -- start procedure of getting message from public pipe
17:     v_statpipe2 := DBMS_PIPE.RECEIVE_MESSAGE('mypublicpipe',10);
18:     LOOP
19:         v_holdtype := DBMS_PIPE.NEXT_ITEM_TYPE;
20:         IF v_holdtype = 0 THEN EXIT;
21:         ELSIF v_holdtype = 6 THEN
22:             DBMS_PIPE.UNPACK_MESSAGE(v_holdnum);
23:         ELSIF v_holdtype = 9 THEN
24:             DBMS_PIPE.UNPACK_MESSAGE(v_holdchar);
25:         ELSIF v_holdtype = 12 THEN
26:             DBMS_PIPE.UNPACK_MESSAGE(v_holddate);
27:         END IF;
28:     END LOOP;
29: -- display all three types of data
30:     DBMS_OUTPUT.PUT_LINE(v_holdchar || ' ' || v_holddate || ' '
31:         || v_holdnum);
32: END;
```

If the code executes with no errors, your output looks similar to

OUTPUT
```
privateline1
privateline2
This is a text string 24-JUN-97 109
```

 ANALYSIS   This example shows how you can write different code that performs the same function. Because you know that the private pipe has only two lines in the message buffer, you can use two UNPACK_MESSAGE statements in a row to retrieve the information. Because only one variable is holding the data, you use DBMS_OUTPUT to display the information to the screen before it is overwritten.

You can now retrieve the information from the public pipe. However, I am assuming that you do not know what data type or how many items are in the buffer. (I do make an assumption improperly when displaying the final results with DBMS_OUTPUT when I display only one of each data type because I sent to the pipe one of each data type. Proper coding would correct this.) First, read the message from the pipe and store it into the message buffer. Then, execute a continuous loop until no more data is found in the pipe (NEXT_ITEM_TYPE = 0). I use IF...ELSIF to assign the appropriate data type to the appropriate variable[md]no guesswork here:

- If the return type is 6, it is of type NUMBER.
- If the return type is 9, it is of type VARCHAR2.
- If the return type is 12, it is of type DATE.
- If the return type is 0, EXIT because there is no more data.

The loop ends and prints to the screen the three data types initially sent on the CREATE procedure.

| Note | One more point I want to make concerns the use of parameters with both RECEIVE_MESSAGE statements. I wait 10 to 15 seconds for a response before I give up. I do not want to tie up resources for the default of 1,000 days! |

Removing the Pipe

You can free resources by removing the pipes. Enter and execute the code in Listing 19.9.

INPUT **LISTING 19.9** Removing Both Pipes

```
 1: DECLARE
 2:     v_stat NUMBER ;
 3: BEGIN
 4:     v_stat := dbms_pipe.remove_pipe('myprivatepipe');
 5:     DBMS_OUTPUT.PUT_LINE('The status for removing the
 6:          private pipe is: ' ¦¦ v_stat);
 7:     v_stat := dbms_pipe.remove_pipe('mypublicpipe');
 8:     DBMS_OUTPUT.PUT_LINE('The status for removing the
 9:          public pipe is: '¦¦ v_stat);
10: END;
```

Your output should look similar to

OUTPUT
```
The status for removing the private pipe is: 0
The status for removing the public pipe is: 0
```

19

Other Pipe Functions and Procedures

Several other functions and procedures are available for the DBMS_PIPE package. These functions and procedures include PACK_MESSAGE_RAW, PACK_MESSAGE_ROW_ID, UNPACK_MESSAGE_RAW, UNPACK_MESSAGE_ROW_ID, RESET_BUFFER, PURGE, and UNIQUE_SESSION_NAME.

PACK_MESSAGE_RAW

For writing data to the message buffer, the PACK_MESSAGE_RAW function enables you to process RAW data.

The Syntax for the PACK_MESSAGE_RAW Procedure

The format for the procedure is

```
PROCEDURE PACK_MESSAGE_RAW(data IN VARCHAR2);
```

You still have the limit of 4,096 bytes for the message buffer size; therefore, you cannot use the LONG RAW data type.

UNPACK_MESSAGE_RAW

Because you can send the RAW data type, you use UNPACK_MESSAGE_RAW to decode the RAW data type from the message buffer.

The Syntax for the UNPACK_MESSAGE_RAW Procedure

The syntax for the procedure is

```
PROCEDURE UNPACK_MESSAGE_RAW(data OUT VARCHAR2);
```

PACK_MESSAGE_ROWID

You can send the ROWID data type to the message buffer, which ultimately gets sent to the pipe by the PACK_MESSAGE_ROWID procedure.

The Syntax for the PACK_MESSAGE_ROWID Procedure

The syntax of the procedure is

```
PROCEDURE PACK_MESSAGE_ROWID(data IN VARCHAR2);
```

Don't forget the 4,096-byte message buffer limit.

UNPACK_MESSAGE_ROWID

To decode the information from the pipe, you use the UNPACK_MESSAGE_ROWID procedure.

The Syntax for the UNPACK_MESSAGE_ROWID Procedure

The format for the UNPACK_MESSAGE_ROWID procedure is

```
PROCEDURE UNPACK_MESSAGE_ROWID(data OUT VARCHAR2);
```

RESET_BUFFER

If you ever need to clear the message buffer, such as when an exception is raised, you use the RESET_BUFFER procedure. The format of the RESET_BUFFER procedure is as follows:

```
PROCEDURE RESET_BUFFER;
```

PURGE

PURGE enables you to remove all data in the pipe specified, which is useful if you need to clear the pipes before processing data. It's also useful if an error occurs and you need to reset the pipes.

SYNTAX

The Syntax for the PURGE Procedure

The format for the procedure is

```
PROCEDURE PURGE(name_of_pipe IN VARCHAR2);
```

UNIQUE_SESSION_NAME

If you are worried that the name of a pipe might already exist, you can always assign the name of the pipe to the function UNIQUE_SESSION_NAME, which provides a name that is not already used in Oracle. The format for the UNIQUE_SESSION_NAME function is as follows:

```
FUNCTION UNIQUE_SESSION_NAME RETURN VARCHAR2;
```

The function returns a unique name with a length up to 30 bytes.

Other Uses for Pipes

Although you can use pipes for parallel processing in multiple processor environments, use pipes for an audit trail, or just use pipes to debug processes, you can also use third-generation languages to communicate with database procedures through pipes.

Refer to the *Oracle Server Applications Guide* in the documentation for some examples of C code communicating with Oracle pipes.

Alerts Versus Pipes

By now, you should see many similarities and differences between pipes and alerts. The similarities can be summarized as follows:

- Both use asynchronous communication.
- Both send messages between sessions of the same instance.
- Both can signal the execution of a C program.
- Both are PL/SQL packages.

19

The differences between alerts and pipes are

- The DBMS_ALERT package uses COMMIT, whereas DBMS_PIPE does not. Because alerts are transaction-based and use commits, a ROLLBACK can remove any waiting alert that has not been received. With pipes, after the message has been sent, there is no way to recall the message.

- Alerts are generally used for one-way communication, whereas pipes are usually used for two-way communications.

- Not only does the DBMS_ALERT package allow multiple sessions to wait for an alert, but also all sessions receive the alert after it has been signaled. This is similar to broadcasting a message in networking. With the DBMS_PIPE package, if more than one session is waiting for a message from the pipe, only one of the sessions receives the message and then clears the pipe.

- Alerts can only send a string of characters, whereas pipes can send STRING, DATE, and NUMBER data types.

Summary

Today, you learned how to use two of Oracle's packages, DBMS_ALERT and DBMS_PIPE. To receive an alert, you must first register the alert. You can then wait for one specific alert with WAITONE or poll for any registered alert with WAITANY. The procedure is blocked until the wait time has expired, which returns a status of 1, or an alert is signaled, which returns a status of 0. Alerts are asynchronous and can generally only communicate one way. The DBMS_PIPE package handles all jobs by using background processes to check for jobs, which are placed in job queues, to execute at a specific interval. To submit a job for processing, you must submit the job to the queue first. After a job is submitted, the owner can only change the parameters. The owner can also fix any broken jobs as well as remove only her own jobs from the queue.

Q&A

Q What is required to check for an alert?

A You must first register the alert and then use WAITONE or WAITANY to wait for the alert to occur.

Q What is the difference between WAITONE and WAITANY?

A WAITONE waits for one specific alert to occur as an event, whereas WAITANY polls for all alerts that are registered to that session.

Q Do you need to remove the alert after the session ends?

A Removing the alert is highly recommended to clean up the registration table and also to recover resources used by the alert process.

Q Why use alerts instead of pipes?

A Alerts offer you the ability to broadcast a message to all sessions monitoring the alert. The DBMS_PIPE package only sends the message to the first session that reads the pipe. In addition, pipes do not offer ROLLBACK to remove the message waiting for pickup.

Q What are the steps to send data to the pipe?

A Create the pipe (if private), then send the data to the message buffer with PACK_MESSAGE, and finally, send the message buffer to the pipe with SEND_MESSAGE.

Q What are the steps to receive data from the pipe?

A Retrieve the message from the pipe into the message buffer with RETREICE_MESSAGE. Then, use UNPACK_MESSAGE to retrieve all data from the message you just received.

Workshop

Use the following workshop to test your comprehension of this lesson and put what you've learned into practice. You'll find the answers to the quiz and exercises in Appendix A, "Answers."

Quiz

19

1. What is the maximum length of an alert name?

2. What is the maximum length of the message?

3. What data type is the message sent as?

4. If 20 sessions are monitoring for an alert and the alert is sent, how many of those sessions receive the signaled alert?

5. Alerts require a _____ because you are working on a transactional level, whereas pipes do not.

6. What interval do you use to run a procedure every hour on the hour starting from the current date?

7. If you send a message to a full pipe, how long will you wait before you abort the process?

8. What is the maximum length of the message buffer?

Exercises

1. Change the code in Listing 19.3 to wait for any alert and also register for two more alerts called 'my_test' and 'extra_alert'. Store the name of the alert that is signaled in a variable titled alert_name of type VARCHAR2(30). After the alert has been handled, remove all registered alerts.

2. Write a loop that continually executes until the value of FIRE equals 1, which will then trigger the alert called 'a_fire', which passes the message 'A Fire has Broken Out'.

3. Write the code to submit a procedure called PAYDAY, where the parameters are FRIDAY, Bi_Monthly, and 6. The job should always execute at 4 a.m. on Saturday.

4. Write the code to view the JOB, the last second it was run, and WHAT from USER_JOBS.

5. Write the code to submit job 200 once per day starting from SYSDATE for the procedure EASY, which has no parameters.

6. Write the code to remove job 200.

DAY **20**

PL/SQL and Java

by Jonathan Gennick

The addition of a Java engine to the Oracle database is one of the most exciting features in the Oracle8i release. When developing server-side code, you now have a choice: You can use PL/SQL, or you can use Java. In fact, you can even mix the two together. If you're a PL/SQL programmer, you're probably wondering about the impact of all this. You're also probably wondering how this Java thing works, and how you can interface your PL/SQL code to it.

In today's lesson you will learn about Oracle's Java support, and you'll learn a little about how the various pieces fit together. When you are done, you'll be able to do the following:

- Load Java classes and source code into the database
- Call Java code from PL/SQL
- Call PL/SQL code from Java

One thing this lesson can't do is teach you how to program in Java. We would need another 21 days for that, at least. In fact, you might look at Laura Lemay's and Rogers Cadenhead's book *Sams Teach Yourself Java 2 in 21 Days* by Sams Publishing. The Java examples in this lesson are simple enough, however, that if you've had any exposure at all to Java, you shouldn't have any trouble following along.

Using Oracle's Java Engine

NEW TERM Oracle uses the name *JServer* for the Java-enabled Oracle8i database. So when you see references to JServer, or hear people talking about it, don't be confused. They are really referring to the Oracle8i database from the perspective of Java. JServer includes the following components:

- A Java virtual machine (JVM)
- Java Database Connectivity (JDBC) support
- SQLJ runtime support
- A SQLJ translator

Oracle's name for its JVM is Aurora. You'll see references to that from time to time. If you look closely at a newly created Oracle8i database, you'll see that it has a user named AURORAORBUNAUTHENTICATED. That user is used for connections to the ORB.

All the JServer components run in the same memory space as PL/SQL and SQL, which makes for a tight integration with the database. Figure 20.1 illustrates how the various components fit together.

FIGURE 20.1

JServer components.

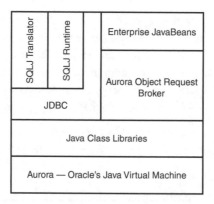

Oracle's JServer is written entirely in C, and the JVM has passed Sun's Java Compatibility Kit (JCK) version 1.1.6 tests. The only exception is that Oracle did not run the JCK tests for java.awt and other libraries related to instantiating a graphical user interface (GUI). Because JServer's JVM runs within the context of a database server, a

GUI doesn't make sense. Oracle does support the GUI libraries in the sense that you can write them into code, but any attempt at actually instantiating a GUI interface within the server results in an exception being thrown.

Will PL/SQL Go Away?

Will Java replace PL/SQL as the preferred programming language to use within the server? Will PL/SQL die off? Should you throw out this book, and buy one on Java? Almost every PL/SQL programmer had these questions when support for Java was announced.

Oracle's official position on this is that both PL/SQL and Java will continue to be supported, and that they will receive equal treatment. PL/SQL is more tightly integrated with SQL, and is the recommended choice for developing data-intensive applications. Java, on the other hand, is the recommended choice for use when developing object-oriented applications.

Note

> I believe that the market will rule on this issue. If everyone jumps ship to Java, and stops writing PL/SQL, then PL/SQL will almost certainly die off. If people continue to program in both environments, then both will continue to exist. In any case, I think there's little likelihood of PL/SQL going away in the near future. Too many sites have a considerable amount invested in it, and several of Oracle's tools depend on it as well. Will PL/SQL be around in five years? I believe so. Will it be around in 10? That I couldn't say.

Creating a Java Procedure

Oracle8i allows you to load a Java class into the database, and then use that class from PL/SQL. In order to do that, you must do the following:

1. Write and debug the Java class or classes.
2. Load the class or classes into the Oracle8i database.
3. Publish the Java class methods that you want to expose for use by PL/SQL routines.

The rest of this section gives you an example of how these three things are done.

Prerequisites Needed

You need Oracle8i in order to run the examples in this lesson. You also need to have the Java option installed. SQL*Plus tells you if both are true when you connect to a database. If you get a message like the following when connecting with SQL*Plus, you should have everything you need to follow along with these examples

Oracle8i Enterprise Edition Release 8.1.5.0.0 - Production
With the Partitioning and Java options
PL/SQL Release 8.1.5.0.0 - Production

If you're running PL/SQL release 8.1.5 under Windows NT, you should check your CLASSPATH environment variable before proceeding. The 8.1.5 install does not set CLASSPATH, and the result is that you get errors when you try to use the loadjava program (described later in this lesson) to load Java source code into your database.

To check your CLASSPATH variable, right-click the My Computer icon, and select Properties. A System Properties window should open, similar to that shown in Figure 20.2. Click the Environment tab to see your environment variable settings.

FIGURE 20.2

CLASSPATH *variable set so that* loadjava *will work.*

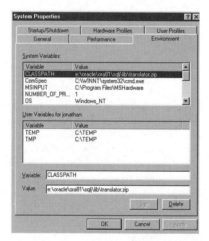

Check to see if you have a CLASSPATH variable set. If you have a CLASSPATH variable, make sure that it includes the following path:

```
$ORACLE_HOME\sqlj\lib\translator.zip
```

Replace $ORACLE_HOME with the top-level Oracle directory on your machine. If you do not have a CLASSPATH variable, you should create one, by typing the information into the Variable and Value fields on the bottom of the screen, and clicking the Set button. Figure 20.2 shows this being done.

The SS_CONSTANTS Class

Way back on Day 1, "Learning the Basics of PL/SQL," you were introduced to a simple PL/SQL function named SS_THRESH. That function returns one number, the Social Security contribution and benefit base for tax year 1999. Social Security taxes aren't withheld on income in excess of that threshold. We're going to use that same function for our first Java example in this lesson. Listing 20.1 shows a Java version of SS_THRESH. This time it's a Java method named SSThresh that is part of a class named SSConstants.

Note   You can find this listing in the file named SSConstants.java. You can find that file on the Sams Web site created for this book.

INPUT   **LISTING 20.1**   The SSThresh Function Implemented in Java

```
1: public class SSConstants {
2:   public static int SSThresh ()
3:     {
4:     return 65400;
5:     }
6: }
```

ANALYSIS   Line 1 defines a class named SSConstants. Java methods are always defined in the context of a class. A Java class can have any combination of methods or variables, but in this case there is only one method: SSThresh. The SSThresh method is declared in line 2 as a `public static` function. That means that you can call the function without first instantiating an instance of the class. The actual method code is in line 4, and simply returns the value 65400.

Java is very picky about filenames. The source file for a Java class must be named to match the class. In this case, if you want to work with the code in Listing 20.1, you must place it in a text file named SSConstants.java. Java is also very picky about case. The case of the class must match letter for letter the case used for the filename.

Loading the Class

Oracle allows you to load a class into JServer by either loading in the source code or by loading in the .class file created when you compile the code. For developing and debugging Java classes, you're much better off using a PC-based Java development environment such as Oracle's JDeveloper than you are trying to compile and debug your code using JServer's built-in compiler. It's not that there's anything wrong with JServer's compiler, it's just that you'll get much better diagnostic messages using an Integrated Development Environment (IDE). When you are sure that the code is correct, you can load it into Oracle.

To load a Java class file, or a source file, into the Oracle8i database, you need to use the loadjava command. The syntax for the loadjava command can be seen in the following syntax.

20

```
loadjava {-user ¦ -u} username/password[@database]
         [-option [-option ...]]
         filename [ filename...]
```

In this syntax the parameters are as follows:

- {-user ¦ -u} username/password[@database] specifies the database username and password. The Java objects are loaded into this user's schema.

- option is one of the following options:

  {andresolve¦a}—Compiles source files and resolves each class as it is loaded. This should not normally be used.

  debug—Generates debug information.

  {definer¦d}—Specifies that classes execute with the definer's rights. Otherwise, they execute with the invoker's rights.

  {encoding¦e}encoding_schema—Specifies a standard JDK encoding scheme. The encoding scheme must match that used in the file. The default is latin1.

  {force¦f}—Forces Java class files to be loaded, even if they have been loaded before.

  {grant¦g}{username¦rolename}[{username¦rolename}...]—Grants execute privileges on the classes being loaded to the users and roles listed.

  {help¦h}—Generates a short help screen that explains all these options.

  {oci8¦o}—Tells loadjava to use the Oracle Call Interface (OCI)-based JDBC driver, as opposed to the thin drivers, when communicating to Oracle.

  oracleresolver—Resolves object references first by looking in the user's schema, and then by looking at public objects.

  {resolve¦r}—Resolves all external references for classes that were loaded. Otherwise, the resolving doesn't happen until runtime.

  {resolver¦R}"resolver_spec"—Allows you to specify your own resolver specification, controlling how references to other classes are resolved.

  {schema¦S}schema—Loads objects into the specified schema. By default, objects are loaded into the user's own schema.

  {synonym¦s}—Creates public synonyms for classes that are loaded. You must hold the CREATE PUBLIC SYNONYM privilege in order to use this option.

  {thin¦t}—Tells loadjava to use the thin JDBC driver to connect to the database.

▼

  {verbose¦v}—Tells loadjava to display progress messages as files are loaded.

- • *filename* is the name of a Java class file (.class), a Java source file (.java), or an SQLJ file (.sqlj). You can load multiple files by using one loadjava command.

Despite the fact that so many options are available, you can often get away with specifying just your username and password, together with the list of files you want to load.

Listing 20.2 shows the loadjava command being used to load the SSConstants class into the database. The -verbose option is used to give a better picture of what is happening.

> **Tip**
>
> If you get a java.lang.NoClassDefFoundError exception while executing the loadjava command shown in Listing 20.2, the likely cause is that your CLASSPATH variable is not pointing to the translator.zip file.

INPUT/OUTPUT **LISTING 20.2** Loading the SSConstants Class

```
1: $loadjava -user jeff/jeff -verbose SSConstants.java
2: initialization complete
3: loading  : SSConstants
4: creating : SSConstants
```

ANALYSIS The loadjava command in line 1 causes the SSConstants class to be loaded. In line 3, loadjava reports that it is loading the file. In line 4, loadjava reports that it has created the class.

Publishing the SSThresh Method

After loading the class, the next thing to do is to publish the methods that you want to call from PL/SQL. Java classes typically contain large numbers of methods. In many cases, only a small handful need to be exposed to PL/SQL.

NEW TERM You publish a method by using a special form of the CREATE FUNCTION and CREATE PROCEDURE commands to write what Oracle refers to as a call spec. A *call spec* looks like a PL/SQL function or procedure header, and specifies how that PL/SQL header should be mapped onto the Java method being invoked.

You'll learn more about call specs later in this lesson. For now, though, you can use the CREATE FUNCTION command shown in Listing 20.3 to expose the SSConstant class's SSThresh function to PL/SQL.

20

INPUT/
OUTPUT **LISTING 20.3**   Publishing the SSThresh Method

```
1: SQL> CREATE OR REPLACE FUNCTION SS_THRESH RETURN NUMBER AS
2:  LANGUAGE JAVA NAME 'SSConstants.SSThresh() return int';
3:  /
```

Function created.

ANALYSIS   The first part of the CREATE OR REPLACE command, shown in the first line of this
listing, looks just like what you would use to create any PL/SQL function. Line 2
is where things become different. The keywords LANGUAGE JAVA tell Oracle that the function SS_THRESH is being mapped onto a Java method. The NAME keyword introduces the
method name, which must be within single quotes. In this case, the PL/SQL function
SS_THRESH is being associated with the Java method SSConstants.SSThresh(). The last
part of the NAME string identifies the return type of the SSThresh method. A Java type
must be used here, and in this case it's an int. The forward slash in line 3 terminates the
command. It's easy to forget that when there's no PL/SQL block associated with the
command, but you do need it.

> **Note**   The PL/SQL name of a function does not need to match the Java method
> name. In this case, as far as PL/SQL is concerned, the function is named
> SS_THRESH. In the Java world, the name is still SSThresh.

After the SSThresh method has been published, you can use it just as you would any
other function. Just be sure to use the published name—in this case, SS_THRESH.

Calling SS_THRESH from SQL*Plus

There are two ways you can invoke the SS_THRESH method from SQL*Plus. You can
SELECT it's value from DUAL, as you might any other function, or you can use the new
SQL*Plus CALL statement. Listing 20.4 shows both methods being used.

INPUT/
OUTPUT **LISTING 20.4**   Invoking SS_THRESH from SQL*Plus

```
1: SQL> SELECT ss_thresh FROM dual;
2:
3: SS_THRESH
4: ---------
5:     65400
6:
```

```
 7: SQL>
 8: SQL> VARIABLE threshold NUMBER
 9: SQL> CALL ss_thresh() INTO :threshold;
10:
11: Call completed.
12:
13: SQL> PRINT threshold
14:
15: THRESHOLD
16: ---------
17:     65400
```

ANALYSIS   Lines 1–5 show the method of selecting the value of the function from the DUAL
table. This is commonly done from SQL*Plus, and you saw the technique used
on Day 1 to experiment with the SS_THRESH function. The second method of invoking the
function involves the use of the SQL*Plus CALL command. The CALL command allows
you to invoke a function directly from SQL*Plus, and to return the results in a SQL*Plus
bind variable. To that end, a bind variable named threshold is declared in line 8. The
CALL command is issued in line 9, and the INTO clause is used to specify that the result of
the SS_THRESH function should be placed into the bind variable named threshold.
Finally, in line 13, the SQL*Plus PRINT command is used to display the results.

Calling SS_THRESH from PL/SQL

Published Java methods look just like any regular PL/SQL function, and can be used that
way in PL/SQL blocks. The block shown in Listing 20.5 invokes the SSThresh method
by calling the published name SS_THRESH.

Note   Be sure to execute SET SERVEROUTPUT ON before executing this block from
SQL*Plus.

20

INPUT   **LISTING 20.5**   Invoking SS_THRESH from a PL/SQL Block

```
1: DECLARE
2:     threshold NUMBER;
3: BEGIN
4:     threshold := ss_thresh;
5:     DBMS_OUTPUT.PUT_LINE('The threshold is ' ¦¦ threshold);
6: END;
7: /
```

ANALYSIS This short block calls the SS_THRESH function, gets the result, and then makes a call to DBMS_OUTPUT in order to display the result. As you can see from the call in line 4, even though SS_THRESH is really a Java method, you can treat it as if it were a PL/SQL function.

Dropping the SSConstants Class

After you get a Java class into your database, how do you get it out again? In the case of SS_THRESH, you can drop the published interface easily, just by using a normal DROP FUNCTION command, like this:

```
DROP FUNCTION SS_THRESH;
```

Note, however, that the DROP command only drops the published interface that you created earlier by using the CREATE OR REPLACE FUNCTION command. The SSConstants class still exists in your schema. To drop the class, you can use the dropjava command.

▼ SYNTAX

```
dropjava {-user ¦ -u} username/password[@database]
         [-option [-option ...]]
         filename [ filename...]
```

In this syntax the parameters are as follows:

* {-user ¦ -u} username/password[@database] specifies the database username and password. The Java objects represented by the listed files are dropped from this user's schema.

* option is one of the following options:

  {help¦h}—Generates a short help screen that explains all these options.

  {oci8¦o}—Tells dropjava to use the OCI-based JDBC driver, as opposed to the thin drivers, when communicating to Oracle.

  {schema¦S}schema—Drops objects from the specified schema. By default, objects are dropped from the user's own schema.

  {thin¦t}—Tells dropjava to use the thin JDBC driver to connect to the database.

  {verbose¦v}—Tells dropjava to display progress messages as classes are dropped.

* filename is the name of a Java class file (.class), a Java source file (.java), or an SQLJ file (.sqlj). The dropjava utility figures out what classes are represented by these files, and drops those from your database. The files themselves are not touched.

▼

▼ Despite the fact that so many options are available, you can often get away with specifying just your username and password, together with the list of files containing classes
▲ that you want to drop.

Listing 20.6 shows the dropjava command being used to remove the SSConstants class
from the user Jeff's schema.

 LISTING 20.6 Dropping the SSConstants Class

```
1: $dropjava -user jeff/jeff -verbose SSConstants.java
2: dropping source   : SSConstants
```

ANALYSIS Except for the fact that dropjava is used instead of loadjava, this command is
identical to the command used in Listing 20.2 to load the SSConstants class. In
this case, the class is dropped from the database.

The dropjava command is somewhat counterintuitive in that you supply it with a list of
filenames rather than with a list of classes you want to drop. You have to think of it as
being the opposite of loadjava. To undo a loadjava operation, just invoke dropjava
with the same list of files that you originally provided to loadjava. Remember that the
files themselves are not deleted. Only the classes defined in the files are deleted, and then
only from the database.

Calling Java from PL/SQL

As you saw in the previous section, the key to being able to call Java from PL/SQL is to
publish the methods you want to call. You also need to know how to pass arguments back
and forth. The SSThresh method in the previous section has no input arguments,
although it returns a result. In this section, you will learn how to pass arguments to a
Java method. You'll learn which Java and PL/SQL datatypes are compatible, and you will
learn more about the syntax used to publish a Java method.

20

The Employee Class

The examples in this section showing how to call Java from PL/SQL are built around the
Java Employee class, shown in Listing 20.7.

 Note   You can find this listing in the file Employee.sqlj, which you can download
from the Web site for this book.

```
 1: import sqlj.runtime.*;
 2: import sqlj.runtime.ref.*;
 3:
 4: #sql iterator EmpSuper (String empName);
 5:
 6: public class Employee {
 7:
 8: public static String getSuperName(int empID) throws Exception {
 9:
10:     /* Declare an iterator (cursor) to return
11:     the results of the query to get the supervisor */
12:     EmpSuper iterEmpSuper;
13:
14:     /* SELECT the name of the employee's supervisor */
15:     int empIDb;
16:     empIDb = empID;
17:
18:     #sql iterEmpSuper={ SELECT emp_name AS empName
19:                         FROM employee
20:                         WHERE emp_id IN (
21:                                 SELECT supervised_by
22:                                 FROM employee
23:                                 WHERE emp_id = :empIDb) };
24:
25:     /* Return the supervisor's name to the caller */
26:     if (iterEmpSuper.next())
27:     {
28:     return iterEmpSuper.empName();
29:     }
30:     else
31:     {
32:     return "None";
33:     }
34: }
35: }
```

ANALYSIS   Without trying to provide a full explanation of Java and SQLJ, here's a brief
explanation of what's going on in this class. Lines 6–35 represent the Employee
class definition. The class has one method, named getSuperName, which is declared in
line 8. The getSuperName class is a static method, which means you can call it without
having to instantiate an instance of the class. The method takes one argument—an
employee ID number—and uses that to retrieve the name of the employee's supervisor.
An iterator type is defined in line 4, and a corresponding iterator variable is defined in
line 12. An iterator could be thought of as somewhat analogous to a cursor. Lines 18–23

contain the SELECT statement executed by this function. They also set the iterator so that it points to the results returned by the SQL statement. Note that the names listed in the iterator type's definition (line 4) must match the names of the columns returned by the SELECT (line 18). A call to the iterator's next method is made in line 26. This actually gets us to the *first* record returned by the SELECT statement. Line 28 then uses the empName column, which is the supervisor's name, as the return value for the getSuperName method.

Publishing a Java Method

The Java engine sort of represents its own little world within the Oracle database. You can create all the classes and methods you want, but they won't be visible to PL/SQL or to SQL until you publish them. Figure 20.3 illustrates this.

FIGURE 20.3

Java running in its own little world.

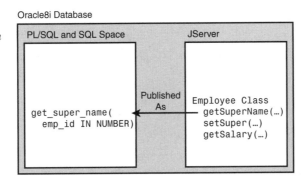

To publish a class, a special form of function or procedure definition is used. Let's use the CREATE FUNCTION statement to illustrate that. The key part of the syntax to focus on here begins with the keyword LANGUAGE.

```
CREATE [OR REPLACE] FUNCTION function_name [(function_parameter_list)]
RETURN datatype
[AUTHID {CURRENT_USER|DEFINER}]
[PARALLEL_ENABLE] [DETERMINISTIC] {IS|AS}
LANGUAGE JAVA NAME 'class.method ([java_type[, java_type...]]) return
java_type';
/
```

▼ SYNTAX

20

Most of this syntax is the same as that used to declare any PL/SQL function. The differences start at the LANGUAGE keyword, and the remaining parameters are as follows here:

- LANGUAGE JAVA tells Oracle that you are publishing a Java method.
- NAME introduces the string that contains the definition for the Java method being published.

▼

▼
- *class.method* identifies the specific method being published.
- *java_type[, java_type...]* represents the Java method parameters. The PL/SQL parameters are positionally mapped onto these. That is, the first PL/SQL parameter is used as the first Java parameter. The second PL/SQL parameter is used as the second method parameter, and so forth.

Note

Java datatype names must be fully qualified. For example, if the datatype is String, you must always use the fully qualified java.lang.String.

- return *java_type* identifies the return type of the method. This must be a Java type. It should be compatible with the PL/SQL return type.

Tip

It's very important for the keyword return inside the NAME string to be lowercase. Java is case sensitive. If you uppercase the word return by mistake, you get back a rather unintuitive error message telling you that your declaration is incomplete or malformed.

If you are publishing a Java method of type void—that is, one that doesn't return a value—then you should use CREATE PROCEDURE instead of CREATE FUNCTION. You might also use the LANGUAGE clause for functions and procedures declared within a PL/SQL
▲ package.

Listing 20.8 shows the CREATE FUNCTION statement used to publish the getSuperName method for the Employee class.

INPUT **LISTING 20.8** Publishing the getSuperName Method

```
1: CREATE OR REPLACE FUNCTION get_super_name (
2:     emp_id IN NUMBER )
3:  RETURN VARCHAR2
4:  AS LANGUAGE JAVA
5:  NAME 'Employee.getSuperName(int) return java.lang.String';
6:  /
```

OUTPUT Function created.

ANALYSIS In line 1, the name get_super_name is the one given to the Java method in the PL/SQL world. Line 4 begins the Java-specific portion of the function declaration. LANGUAGE JAVA tells Oracle that you are publishing a Java method. In line 5, the method is identified as Employee.getSupername(int). The parameter list (int) indicates that the method takes one parameter, which must be an integer. It is not necessary to name the parameter, you just need to tell Oracle the type so that it can properly convert the NUMBER value that you pass from PL/SQL to the Java type expected by the method. The last portion of line 5 identifies the Java return type, which in this case is java.lang.String. Now, when you call get_super_name from PL/SQL, Oracle will do the following:

1. Convert the emp_id value from a PL/SQL NUMBER to a Java int.
2. Call the Employee.getSuperName method, passing the int value from step 1 as the parameter.
3. Convert the method's return value from a Java String value to a PL/SQL VARCHAR2 value.
4. Return the resulting VARCHAR2 value as the result of the PL/SQL function.

The PL/SQL block in Listing 20.9 uses the now-published getSuperName method.

Note
This listing should be executed from SQL*Plus, and you should execute the SET SERVEROUTPUT ON command first.

INPUT   **LISTING 20.9**   Calling getSuperName from PL/SQL

```
1: SQL> DECLARE
2:        super_name VARCHAR2(30);
3:    BEGIN
4:        super_name := get_super_name(514);
5:        DBMS_OUTPUT.PUT_LINE('514''s supervisor is ' || super_name);
6:
7:        super_name := get_super_name(999);
8:        DBMS_OUTPUT.PUT_LINE('999''s supervisor is ' || super_name);
9:    END;
10: /
```

20

OUTPUT
```
514's supervisor is Ashley Nue
999's supervisor is None
```

ANALYSIS   The PL/SQL block in this listing is executed from SQL*Plus. Lines 4–5 called get_super_name in order to get the supervisor's name for employee 514. A name is found, returned, and displayed, using DBMS_OUTPUT.PUT_LINE. Lines 7–8 do the same thing, but for an employee that doesn't exist. In this case, the Java method simply returns the value None, which is also displayed by using DBMS_OUTPUT.PUT_LINE.

Note If you don't already have employees 514 and 501 in your database, download and execute the `preload.sql` script from the Web site for this book.

Datatype Compatibility

A key part of what Oracle does when you invoke a Java method from PL/SQL is to automatically convert between the datatypes used in the different environments. Your job is to make sure that the datatypes you are using are compatible with each other. Table 20.1 lists PL/SQL types, along with their compatible Java types.

TABLE 20.1   PL/SQL and Java Datatype Compatibility

PL/SQL Type	Compatible Java Type or Class
NUMBER	oracle.sql.NUMBER
	byte
	short
	int
	long
	float
	double
	java.lang.Byte
	java.lang.Short
	java.lang.Integer
	java.lang.Long
	java.lang.Float
	java.lang.Double
	java.math.BigDecimal
VARCHAR2	oracle.sql.CHAR
CHAR	java.lang.String
NVARCHAR2	java.sql.Date
NCHAR	java.sql.Time
LONG	java.sql.Timestamp
	byte
	short
	int
	long
	float
	double
	java.lang.Byte
	java.lang.Short

PL/SQL Type	Compatible Java Type or Class
	java.lang.Integer
	java.lang.Long
	java.lang.Float
	java.lang.Double
	java.math.BigDecimal
DATE	oracle.sql.DATE
	java.sql.Date
	java.sql.Time
	java.sql.Timestamp
	java.lang.String
ROWID	oracle.sql.CHAR
	oracle.sql.ROWID
	java.lang.String
BFILE	oracle.sql.BFILE
BLOB	oracle.sql.BLOB
	oracle.jdbc2.Blob
CLOB, NCLOB	oracle.sql.CLOB
	oracle.jdbc2.Clob
OBJECT	oracle.sql.STRUCT
	oracle.SqljData
	oracle.jdbc2.Struct
REF	oracle.sql.REF
	oracle.jdbc2.Ref
TABLE, VARRAY	oracle.sql.ARRAY
	oracle.jdbc2.Array

To publish a Java method to PL/SQL, you should make sure that the method arguments and return types are listed Table 20.1, and that the corresponding Java and PL/SQL types are compatible with each other.

Using the OUT and IN OUT Arguments

PL/SQL allows you to modify arguments passed to a procedure or function. All you need to do is to declare the arguments that you want to modify as OUT or IN OUT. Java, on the other hand, does not allow function parameters to be modified because they are always passed by value, never by reference. The exception to this is that Java passes arrays by reference. If you feel that you must write a Java method that appears to PL/SQL as if it had OUT or IN OUT parameters, you can do that by passing all the parameters as single-element arrays. Take a look at Listing 20.10.

20

INPUT   **LISTING 20.10**   The Employee2 Class

```
 1: import sqlj.runtime.*;
 2: import sqlj.runtime.ref.*;
 3:
 4: #sql iterator EmpSuper (String empName);
 5:
 6: public class Employee2 {
 7:
 8: public static void getSuperName(
 9:         int empID, String[] empName) throws Exception {
10:
11:     /* Declare an iterator (cursor) to return
12:     the results of the query to get the supervisor */
13:     EmpSuper iterEmpSuper;
14:
15:     /* SELECT the name of the employee's supervisor */
16:     int empIDb;
17:     empIDb = empID;
18:
19:     #sql iterEmpSuper={ SELECT emp_name AS empName
20:                         FROM employee
21:                         WHERE emp_id IN (
22:                                 SELECT supervised_by
23:                                 FROM employee
24:                                 WHERE emp_id = :empIDb) };
25:
26:     /* Return the supervisor's name to the caller */
27:     if (iterEmpSuper.next())
28:     {
29:     empName[0] = iterEmpSuper.empName();
30:     }
31:     else
32:     {
33:     empName[0] = "None";
34:     }
35: }
36: }
```

ANALYSIS   This is a variation on the Employee class. The difference here is that getSuperName method accepts an array of type String as its second argument (line 9), and passes back the supervisor name as the first element of that string (line 29). You can make this method useable from PL/SQL by publishing it with the CREATE PROCEDURE statement shown in Listing 20.11.

INPUT **LISTING 20.11**   Publishing a Java Method with an OUT Argument

```
1: CREATE OR REPLACE PROCEDURE get_super_name2 (
2:     emp_id IN NUMBER,
3:     emp_name OUT VARCHAR2)
4: AS LANGUAGE JAVA
5: NAME 'Employee2.getSuperName(int, java.lang.String[])';
6: /
```

ANALYSIS   In line 3 the emp_name argument is declared as an OUT argument. If you look at the last part of line 5, you'll see that the corresponding method parameter is an array. Oracle looks at this situation and assumes that element 0 (the first element) of that array is going to contain the output value. When you call this procedure, after the Java method completes, Oracle takes element 0 of the String array, and places it into the variable used for the emp_name parameter. Note that because the Java method has a void return type, it was published as a procedure (line 1) and not as a function.

Listing 20.12 shows the get_super_name2 procedure, which you just published in Listing 20.11, being executed from SQL*Plus.

INPUT/ OUTPUT   **LISTING 20.12**   Invoking get_super_name2 from SQL*Plus

```
 1: SQL> VARIABLE emp_id NUMBER
 2: SQL> VARIABLE emp_name VARCHAR2(30)
 3: SQL> EXECUTE :emp_id := 514;
 4:
 5: PL/SQL procedure successfully completed.
 6:
 7: SQL> EXECUTE get_super_name2(:emp_id,:emp_name);
 8:
 9: PL/SQL procedure successfully completed.
10:
11: SQL> PRINT emp_id
12:
13: EMP_ID
14: ---------
15:      514
16:
17: SQL> PRINT emp_name
18:
19: EMP_NAME
20: ------------------------------
21: Ashley Nue
```

20

ANALYSIS The statements in lines 1 and 2 declare two SQL*Plus bind variables for use when calling the published function. A bind variable is necessary for the output variable because you need a place for PL/SQL to store the output. The EXECUTE statement in line 3 sets the value of the emp_id bind variable to 514. This is the input to the Java method. The EXECUTE statement in line 7 calls the Java method by using the interface published in Listing 20.11. Lines 11–15 show the value of the emp_id variable being displayed. It's still unchanged, at 514. Lines 17–21 show the contents of the emp_name variable being displayed, which you can see now contains the supervisor's name.

Calling PL/SQL from Java Using SQLJ

Just as you can call Java methods from PL/SQL, you can also call PL/SQL procedures and functions from Java. An easy way to do that is by using SQLJ, which is a precompiler that converts SQL statements, PL/SQL blocks, and the like into a series of JDBC method calls. You've already seen SQLJ at work in some of the earlier listings in this chapter. For example, it is used in Listing 20.7 to code the SELECT statement required to retrieve the name of an employee's supervisor.

Using SQLJ to Execute an Anonymous PL/SQL Block

As far as SQLJ is concerned, a PL/SQL block is just like an SQL statement—it needs to be sent to the database and executed. You can use SQLJ to execute an anonymous PL/SQL block using the syntax shown here.

▼ SYNTAX
```
SQL# { [DECLARE
         declarations]
       BEGIN
         code
       [EXCEPTION]
         exception_handlers
       END
     }
```

The contents of the curly braces must be a PL/SQL anonymous block, just like the ones that you have been using throughout this book. The parameters above have the following meanings:

- *declarations* refers to any PL/SQL variable definitions that you need in your PL/SQL block.
- *code* refers to the PL/SQL code in the block that you are executing.
- *exception_handlers* refers to any exception handlers (WHEN statements) in the PL/SQL block.

The syntax for each of these elements is exactly what you have been learning throughout
▲ this book.

You can refer to Java variables within the block by prefacing their variable names with colons. Listing 20.13 shows a relatively simple example of a Java method using SQLJ to call a PL/SQL function. Notice the use of a colon to identify the variable named `timeNow` as a Java variable.

> **Note** You can find this listing in the file CallAnon.sqlj, which you can download from Macmillan's Web site for this book.

INPUT **LISTING 20.13** Executing a PL/SQL Block from Java

```
 1: import sqlj.runtime.*;
 2: import sqlj.runtime.ref.*;
 3:
 4: public class CallAnon {
 5:
 6: public static java.sql.Timestamp getSysdate() throws Exception {
 7:
 8:     java.sql.Timestamp timeNow;
 9:
10:     #sql { BEGIN
11:                 :timeNow := sysdate;
12:           END
13:         };
14:
15:     return timeNow;
16: }
17: }
```

ANALYSIS The two imports in lines 1 and 2 are necessary whenever you are using SQLJ. The class name in this example is `CallAnon` (line 4), and the only method is `getSysdate` (line 6). The PL/SQL block in lines 10–13 makes a call to Oracle's built-in `SYSDATE` function to get the date and time. That value is then stored in the `timeNow` variable, which is a Java variable. The value is finally returned to the method caller in line 15.

Using SQLJ to Call a PL/SQL Procedure or Function

To call a PL/SQL procedure or function from within Java, you can use the SQLJ `CALL` statement. There are two slightly different forms of `CALL`: one for calling procedures and one for calling functions.

20

▼ SYNTAX

```
sql# {CALL procedure_name (
{:in¦:out¦:inout} param[, {:in¦:out¦:inout} param...]
};

sql# {VALUES (function_name (
{:in¦:out¦:inout} param[, {:in¦:out¦:inout} param...]
)};
```

In this syntax the parameters are as follows:

- *procedure_name* is the name of the PL/SQL procedure you want to call.
- *function_name* is the name of the PL/SQL function you want to call.
- *param* is a Java variable.
- :in indicates that the parameter is an input parameter. This is the default, and :in can be omitted.
- :out indicates that the parameter is an output parameter.

▲
- :inout indicates that the parameter is both an input and an output.

As an example of calling PL/SQL from Java, you are going to see a slightly modified version of the Employee class shown earlier in Listing 20.7. This version is named Employeeb, and makes use of the PL/SQL function to retrieve the name for any given employee number. This function is named EMPNAME, and is shown in Listing 20.14.

INPUT   **LISTING 20.14**   The PL/SQL EMPNAME Function

```
 1: CREATE OR REPLACE FUNCTION empname(empid IN NUMBER)
 2: RETURN VARCHAR2 AS
 3: empname  VARCHAR2(30);
 4: BEGIN
 5: SELECT emp_name INTO empname
 6: FROM employee
 7: WHERE emp_id = empid;
 8:
 9: return empname;
10: EXCEPTION
11: WHEN OTHERS THEN
12:     return 'No name found';
13: END;
14: /
```

ANALYSIS   This is really a simple function. It takes one argument, an employee ID number, and retrieves that employee's name from the database. The SELECT statement is contained in lines 5–7. Line 9 returns the name, if one is found. If any type of error occurs, the assumption is that the employee number was not valid. Line 12 in the exception handling section returns a message to that effect.

Listing 20.15 shows the Employeeb class. The getSuperName method has been modified to use the PL/SQL EMPNAME function to retrieve the supervisor's name.

Note You can find this listing in the file Employeeb.sqlj. You can download this file from the Web site for this book.

INPUT **LISTING 20.15** The Employeeb Class

```
 1: import sqlj.runtime.*;
 2: import sqlj.runtime.ref.*;
 3:
 4: #sql iterator EmpSuper (int superID);
 5:
 6: public class Employeeb {
 7:
 8: public static String getSuperName(int empID) throws Exception {
 9:
10:     /* Declare an iterator (cursor) to return
11:     the results of the query to get the supervisor */
12:     EmpSuper iterEmpSuper;
13:
14:     /* SELECT the name of the employee's supervisor */
15:     int empIDb;
16:     empIDb = empID;
17:
18:     #sql iterEmpSuper={ SELECT supervised_by AS superID
19:                         FROM employee
20:                         WHERE emp_id = :empIDb };
21:
22:     /* Return the supervisor's name to the caller */
23:     if (iterEmpSuper.next())
24:     {
25:     java.lang.String superName;
26:     int superID;
27:     superID = iterEmpSuper.superID();
28:     #sql superName = {VALUES(empname(:superID))};
29:     return superName;
30:     }
31:     else
32:     {
33:     return "None";
34:     }
35: }
36: }
```

20

ANALYSIS   The `getSuperName` method here is only a bit different from that shown in Listing 20.7. There's still a `SELECT` statement (lines 18–20), but this time it gets only the supervisor's ID number, not the supervisor's name. That ID number is then passed as a parameter to the PL/SQL `EMPNAME` function (line 28). The PL/SQL function returns the supervisor's name to the Java method, which in turn returns the value to its caller in line 29.

To test this, you can publish the `Employeeb.getSuperName` method to PL/SQL, and call the method from SQL*Plus. Listing 20.16 does both.

INPUT/OUTPUT   **LISTING 20.16**   Testing the `Employeeb.getSuperName` Method

```
1:  CREATE OR REPLACE FUNCTION get_super_nameb (
2:      emp_id IN NUMBER )
3:  RETURN VARCHAR2
4:  AS LANGUAGE JAVA
5:  NAME 'Employeeb.getSuperName(int) return java.lang.String';
6:  /


Function created.

1:  SELECT get_super_nameb(514)
2:  FROM dual;

GET_SUPER_NAMEB(514)
----------------------------------------------------------------
Ashley Nue
```

ANALYSIS   The `CREATE OR REPLACE FUNCTION` statement in the first part of this listing publishes the `Employeeb.getSuperName` method. The following `SELECT` statement uses this method to return the name of employee 514's supervisor. You end up with a SQL statement calling a published Java method, which then calls a PL/SQL function, which in turn executes a SQL statement.

Summary

In today's lesson you have learned how PL/SQL and Java interoperate. You've seen how to publish Java methods so that they can be called from PL/SQL, and you've seen how to use SQLJ to call PL/SQL methods from Java. You've probably even picked up a sense of how SQLJ operates from reading the listings in this lesson. SQLJ is just one of the tools you can use to interact with an Oracle database from Java. JDBC is another option—in fact, SQLJ is translated to JDBC, as is CORBA.

Q&A

Q **Now that Java is available in the database, will PL/SQL go away?**

A Oracle maintains that the answer to this question is no. I tend to agree that PL/SQL is likely to be around for years in the future. Ultimately, though, the marketplace will decide whether there is room for both PL/SQL and Java.

Q **What is SQLJ? How does it compare to JDBC?**

A SQLJ is a precompiler. It translates SQL statements and PL/SQL blocks into JDBC method calls. Precompilers have been around for years, and there's really no difference between what SQLJ does and what PRO*C or PRO*COBOL do.

Q **When you publish a Java method, does the PL/SQL name need to match the Java name?**

A No. Because the PL/SQL and Java naming rules are different, that probably couldn't be the case anyway. For example, Java names are case-sensitive, and PL/SQL names are not. In Java, `getSuperName`, `GETSUPERNAME`, and `getsupername` are all different names. In PL/SQL, they are the same.

Q **What does it mean to *publish* a method?**

A Normally, Java methods are not visible from the PL/SQL world. When you *publish* a method, you give it a PL/SQL-compatible interface and you make it visible to PL/SQL code.

Q **When working with Java, is it necessary for the filename to match the name of the class defined within the file?**

A Generally, yes. Both names are case-sensitive and must match exactly.

Q **I want to drop a class from my database. Should I really use `dropjava`? Won't it delete my source file, too?**

A No, the `dropjava` command will not delete any disk files. It reads files, figures out what classes they define, and removes those classes from the database.

20

Workshop

You can use this to test your comprehension of this lesson and put what you've learned into practice. You'll find the answers to the quiz and exercises in Appendix A, "Answers."

Quiz

1. What does Oracle use for the collective Java capabilities of Orcale8i?
2. What is the name of Oracle's Java engine?
3. What command-line utility can you use to load Java source code, SQLJ source code, and Java classes into an Oracle8i database?
4. When publishing a Java method, what determines whether you should publish it as a procedure or as a function?

Exercise

Revisit the Employee class shown in Listing 20.7, and create a PL/SQL function that publishes the getSuperName method. This time, though, make that PL/SQL function part of a package.

DAY 21

Advanced Queuing

by Jonathan Gennick

Advanced Queuing (AQ) is a relatively new PL/SQL feature. First introduced with Oracle8, it has been significantly enhanced for Oracle8i. Advanced Queuing is a message-oriented subsystem that provides a robust and reliable way to communicate between applications, even if those applications run on different databases. Although you can't learn everything there is to know about AQ in one day, you can learn the fundamentals. Today you will learn how to do the following:

- Enable AQ on a database
- Create a queue
- Post messages to the queue
- Retrieve messages from a queue

What Is AQ?

Advanced Queuing, or AQ, as it is often called, is a messaging system. Rather than transmit messages from one application to another as DBMS_PIPE allows you to do, AQ uses message *queues* as the basis for message transmission. Processes that generate messages are termed *producers*. Processes that receive messages are termed *consumers*. Queues hold the messages between the time that they are posted by a producer and the time that they are received by a consumer. Figure 21.1 illustrates this process.

FIGURE 21.1

AQ relies on queues for the transmission of messages.

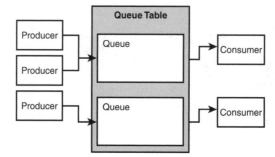

As you can see from Figure 21.1, more than one producer can write messages to a queue, and more than one consumer can receive those messages.

AQ's features are exposed to PL/SQL through two packages. One package, DBMS_AQADM, is used for administrative tasks such as creating queue tables, creating queues, granting access to queues, scheduling propagation, and so forth. The operational interface is contained in the DBMS_AQ package, and contains entry points allowing you to send and receive messages.

 Note To use AQ as described in this chapter, you need to have Oracle8i Enterprise Edition with the Objects option.

Removing Some of the Mystery from AQ

Oracle has built up a whole new terminology around the subject of advanced queuing. It's a bit intimidating when you first encounter all those new terms. Table 21.1 defines some of the terms that you will encounter, and attempts to explain them in clear English.

TABLE 21.1   Advanced Queuing Terminology

AQ Term	Explanation
Agent	A producer or a consumer.
Consumer	A program or process that retrieves messages from a queue.
Control data	Data elements in a message that Oracle uses to keep track of what it's doing.
Deferred messaging	The same as *disconnected messaging*.
Dequeue	To receive a message.
Disconnected messaging	The ability to post messages to a queue, even when the intended receiver process is not running, and the ability to receive messages long after the posting process has stopped running.
Enqueue	To post a message.
Message	Data that you want transmit to another application. In practical terms, you would most often define an Oracle object type containing the data elements you wanted to transmit, and then pass objects of that type back and forth.
Message Delay	The delay between the time a message is posted and when it becomes available for retrieval.
Message Expiration	The automatic deletion of messages that haven't been retrieved within a specified time period.
Payload	The portion of the message that has meaning to the producer and consumer. In this lesson, Oracle8 objects are used as payloads.
Producer	A program or process that posts messages to a queue.
Propagation	The transmission of messages from one queue to another. Note that the queues may be in different databases.
Queue	A place where messages are held. Queues are implemented as database tables.

The bottom line is that to send a message, you would typically create an Oracle8 object, store data in the attributes of that object, and post the object to a queue. The queue is implemented in a table, and one column of that table is an object column. Each message that you post ends up as a row in the table, and the message is stored in that object column. Oracle handles all the details of then getting that message to the intended recipient.

Key Features of AQ

A number of key features distinguish AQ from the DBMS_PIPE package and combine to make it a very serious messaging product. Some of these features include the following:

21

- Message repository—The queues serve as a message repository. Producers and consumers don't need to be online at the same time. Queues preserve messages until they can be consumed.

- Transparency—A message producer does not need to know anything about the ultimate recipient. Producers only need to know which queue to use when posting a message. Consumers only need to know which queue to use when retrieving. The AQ administrator defines the links between queues, which may not even be on the same machine.

- Transaction support—Enqueued messages participate in transactions. If you roll back a transaction, any messages posted as part of that transaction are rolled back as well.

- Support for prioritizing—AQ allows you to define queues such that messages are retrieved based on their priority, the time that they were enqueued, or a combination of both.

- Propagation—Queues can be defined such that messages posted to one queue are automatically forwarded to one or more other queues. The propagation can be instantaneous, or it can be scheduled. The queues do not need to be in the same database.

- Publishing/subscribing—Consumers can subscribe to receive messages from a queue. Rule-based subscriptions allow consumers to define specific types of messages that they will service.

- Automatic notification—Consumers can register to be automatically notified when messages of interest are posted to a queue.

All these features together make AQ a much better messaging solution than DBMS_PIPE, especially if you need to communicate in a distributed environment where different agents are on different computers, are not all attached to the same database, or aren't all online at the same time.

Configuring Your Server to Use AQ

Configuring a database to use AQ requires that you set two or three initialization parameters. You also should identify one or more users who will serve as AQ administrators. To use the AQ features, you need to have Oracle8i Enterprise Edition. To use queues with objects, as this lesson does, you need to also have the Objects option installed.

You need to check several initialization parameters:

- aq_tm_processes
- job_queue_processes
- job_queue_interval

The aq_tm_processes parameter controls the number of queue monitoring processes that will be created. These processes implement some of AQ's time-based features such as message delay and message expiration. If you are not using those features, you don't need to set this parameter. You can have up to 10 queue monitor processes.

 Note For the examples in this lesson, you do not need to set the aq_tm_processes parameter.

AQ uses the DBMS_JOBS package to schedule message propagation between queues. If you're doing any type of automated propagation, you should set the job_queue_processes parameter to at least 1.

Related to job_queue_processes is job_queue_interval. The job_queue_interval parameter tells Oracle how frequently it should check for jobs in the job queues. This value is in seconds. The default is 60, which causes Oracle to check the job queues every 60 seconds.

The following three parameter settings in the initialization file will result in one queue monitor process, one job queue process, and a job queue interval of 60 seconds:

```
aq_tm_processes = 1
job_queue_processes = 1
job_queue_interval = 1
```

Aside from setting these parameters, the only other thing you need to do is to grant the AQ_ADMINISTRATOR_ROLE role to the user who will be administering the queues for your database. By default, the SYS and SYSTEM users already have this role. If you are the database administrator, you can just log in as SYSTEM to manage the queues. If you want to delegate that work to someone else, grant the role to that person.

21

Exploring an AQ Scenario

To help you understand how AQ works, and how you can use it from PL/SQL, this lesson works through the following scenario:

- Your company has decided that all salary changes must be reviewed by upper management before being saved in the employee table.

- Your payroll clerk, who is the second cousin of the company president's nephew, has declared that it is taking way too long to make department changes for employees. You have traced the problem to the time it takes the trigger on the employee table to update the employee count in the department table.

- Relative to both of the preceding issues, especially the department issue, you have determined that a small delay is acceptable between the time that a change is made and the time that it is reflected in the database. This is because payroll is run late at night, well after any changes have been made.

Because you're a forward-looking person, always eager to implement the latest Oracle technology, you decide to use the new AQ features to address the challenges presented here. Specifically, you decide to do the following:

- Record salary changes as messages in a queue. A management application then retrieves those messages, allows management to review the changes, and records those changes in the database.

- Department changes are also queued. You believe it will be faster to write one message to a queue than it is to update an employee record and wait while all the employee table triggers fire. A background process retrieves and processes the department changes, allowing the payroll clerk to get on with his work.

Because both messages contain employee information, you decide to create just one queue. Both types of messages will be written to the queue, but they will be retrieved by different applications: Department change messages will be retrieved by a background process, and salary change messages will be retrieved by the management application. Figure 21.2 illustrates the planned implementation.

The examples in the rest of this lesson take you through the following steps to implement this scenario:

1. Creating a message queue
2. Starting a message queue
3. Placing messages into a queue
4. Retrieving messages from a queue

FIGURE 21.2

An AQ solution for department and salary changes.

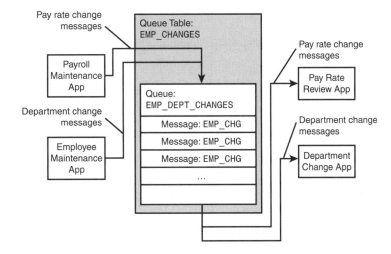

Creating a Message Queue

The first step in this scenario will be to implement the message queue. Doing that involves three steps:

1. Define an object type that contains the data (the payload) for the messages that are to be sent.

2. Create a queue table.

3. Create a queue.

In order to do these things, you need to hold the role named AQ_ADMINISTRATOR_ROLE. You can log in as SYSTEM if you don't want to grant this role to another user. The SYSTEM user is assigned the role AQ_ADMINISTRATOR_ROLE by default.

Defining a Type for the Payload

You define the payload for a message in terms of an Oracle8i object type. You define that object type by using the CREATE TYPE command that you learned about on Day 12, "Using Oracle8i Objects for Object-Oriented Programming." You need to create the type first, because it's used when creating the queue table.

Because we are dealing with employee salary and department changes, you need to create a type with that information. Listing 21.1 shows one approach that you could take. The type is named EMP_CHG.

21

LISTING 21.1 Creating the EMP_CHG Type

```
1: CREATE OR REPLACE TYPE emp_chg AS OBJECT (
2:     emp_id NUMBER,
3:     pay_rate NUMBER(9,2),
4:     pay_type CHAR(1),
5:     leave_dept NUMBER,
6:     join_dept NUMBER
7:     );
8: /
```

The EMP_CHG type has five attributes. The first three are used when an employee's salary or hourly rate changes. The last two are used when a department change is made. Because most department changes are transfers, we should record both the department that the employee is leaving (LEAVE_DEPT) and the one the employee is joining (JOIN_DEPT). If necessary, one or the other department attribute will be null.

Creating the Queue Table

Now that we have defined an object type to use for the message payload, the next step is to create a queue table. For that, you make a call to DBMS_AQADM.CREATE_QUEUE_TABLE. Based on information you pass as parameters to the procedure, DBMS_AQADM.CREATE_QUEUE_TABLE creates the queue table for you.

The procedure header for the CREATE_QUEUE_TABLE procedure in the DBMS_AQADM package looks like this:

```
PROCEDURE create_queue_table (
    queue_table IN VARCHAR2,
    queue_payload_TYPE IN VARCHAR2,
    storage_clause IN VARCHAR2 DEFAULT NULL,
    sort_list IN VARCHAR2 DEFAULT NULL,
    multiple_consumers IN BOOLEAN DEFAULT FALSE,
    message_grouping IN BINARY_INTEGER DEFAULT none,
    comment IN VARCHAR2 DEFAULT NULL,
    auto_commit IN BOOLEAN DEFAULT TRUE,
    primary_instance IN BINARY_INTEGER DEFAULT 0,
    secondary_instance IN BINARY_INTEGER DEFAULT 0,
    compatible IN VARCHAR2 DEFAULT NULL
    );
```
▼

Note
Parameters with default values, identified by the keyword DEFAULT, are optional.

In this syntax the parameters are as follows:

- QUEUE_TABLE is the name you want to give the table. You can specify a schema name, if you want, by using the standard *schema.table_name* notation. If you don't specify a schema name, then the table is created in your schema.

- QUEUE_PAYLOAD is the datatype of the messages that this queue table can handle. This is where we will pass the name of the object type.

- STORAGE_CLAUSE is a text string containing any of the following standard CREATE TABLE clauses: STORAGE, INITRANS, MAXTRANS, TABLESPACE, and LOB. This string is appended to the end of the CREATE TABLE statement that CREATE_QUEUE_TABLE procedure executes.

- SORT_LIST allows you to specify a sort order for the queue. You can sort on any combination of priority or enqueue time, using the keywords PRIORITY and ENQ_TIME, respectively. For example, to sort first on priority and then on time of enqueue, specify PRIORITY,ENQ_TIME for this parameter.

- MULTIPLE_CONSUMERS tells Oracle whether to create the table with support for multiple consumers. Specifying FALSE results in a single-consumer queue. Specifying TRUE results in a queue that can support many consumers.

- MESSAGE_GROUPING can be either DBMS_AQADM.NONE or DBMS_AQADM.TRANSACTIONAL. Making a queue transactional causes enqueued messages to be grouped by transaction. All messages enqueued in one transaction must be dequeued together by the same consumer.

- COMMENT is a comment that is recorded in the data dictionary. You can put something here to remind yourself why you created the queue.

- AUTO_COMMIT, if TRUE, causes CREATE_QUEUE_TABLE to commit the current transaction before creating the table. If FALSE, it prevents CREATE_QUEUE_TABLE from issuing a commit.

- PRIMARY_INSTANCE applies to Oracle Parallel Server (OPS) only, and specifies the instance that should normally manage the queue.

- SECONDARY_INSTANCE specifies the instance that should take over when the primary instance fails.

- COMPATIBLE specifies whether a release 8.0 or 8.1-compatible queue is created. Oracle recommends using 8.1-compatible queues. Valid values are 8.0 and 8.1.

21

Many of these parameters are optional, and most can be left at their default settings unless you have a specific reason to change them. The one parameter that you should change for this scenario is the MULTIPLE_CONSUMERS parameter. The queue needs to pass messages to a management program and to a background process. That's two consumers right there, so a multiple-consumer queue is needed.

Listing 21.2 shows how you would call DBMS_AQADM.CREATE_QUEUE_TABLE to create a queue named EMP_CHANGES. The payload type is EMP_CHG, the same type created earlier, in Listing 21.1, and the queue table is defined to support multiple consumers. The compatible parameter is set to 8.1 in order to make this an Oracle 8.1-compatible queue table.

INPUT   **LISTING 21.2**   Creating the EMP_CHANGES Queue Table

```
 1: BEGIN
 2:     DBMS_AQADM.CREATE_QUEUE_TABLE (
 3:         'EMP_CHANGES',
 4:         'EMP_CHG',
 5:         NULL,
 6:         'priority,enq_time',
 7:         TRUE,
 8:         DBMS_AQADM.NONE,
 9:         'For pay rate and department changes.',
10:         TRUE,0,0,
11:         '8.1'
12:         );
13: END;
14: /
```

ANALYSIS   The queue table is named EMP_CHANGES (line 3). Because no schema was explicit-
ly specified, the table is stored in the schema of the user who executed this block. The payload type is EMP_CHG (line 4), and refers to the object type that was created earlier. No storage clause is supplied (line 5), so all the defaults are taken for the user and tablespace in question. The sort order has been specified as 'priority,enq_time' (line 6). That means that higher-priority messages jump to the front of the line to be retrieved first. Messages of equal priority are retrieved in the order in which they were enqueued. Line 7 specifies TRUE for the MULTIPLE_CONSUMERS parameter, making this a multiple-consumer queue table. No transactional grouping is needed, hence the DBMS_AQADM.NONE in line 8. The text supplied in line 9 is commentary, and shows up in the DBA_QUEUE_TABLES data dictionary view.

Two items in Listing 21.2 deserve special mention. First is the use of DBMS_AQADM.NONE in line 8. The DBMS_AQADM package defines several constants that are used in procedure calls like this. NONE and TRANSACTIONAL are two of them. Whenever you reference those constants from outside the package, as we are doing here, you must qualify the constant name with the package name, using dot notation (for example, DBMS_AQADM.NONE).

The other thing to notice is that by specifying DBMS_AQADM.NONE for the MESSAGE_GROUPING parameter, we are not requiring that all messages from one transaction be retrieved by the same consumer. In the scenario in this lesson, it's likely that multiple messages from a transaction would need to go to different consumers. A pay rate change and a department change at the same time, for example, would require two messages: one to the management application and one to the background job.

> **Note**
>
> Even though grouping of messages by transaction has not been requested, normal transaction semantics still apply. Messages enqueued during a transaction are rolled back if the transaction itself is rolled back.

Creating the Queue

The final step, now that the type and queue table have been created, is to create the queue itself. To do that, you make another call to a DBMS_AQADM procedure. This time you are calling the procedure CREATE QUEUE. The Header for DBMS_AQADM.CREATE_QUEUE is as follows.

SYNTAX

The procedure header for the CREATE_QUEUE procedure in the DBMS_AQADM package looks like this:

```
PROCEDURE create_queue (
    queue_name IN VARCHAR2,
    queue_table IN VARCHAR2,
    queue_type IN BINARY_INTEGER DEFAULT normal_queue,
    max_retries IN NUMBER DEFAULT 5,
    retry_delay IN NUMBER DEFAULT 0,
    retention_time IN NUMBER DEFAULT 0,
    comment IN VARCHAR2 DEFAULT NULL,
    auto_commit IN BOOLEAN DEFAULT TRUE
);
```

> **Note**
>
> Parameters with default values, identified by the keyword DEFAULT, are optional.

21

▼ In this syntax the parameters are as follows:

- QUEUE_NAME is the name that you want to give the table. Note that the queue name must be unique within the schema. No two queues in the same schema, even if they are in different tables, can have the same name.

- QUEUE_TABLE is the name of the queue table in which you want to store the queue you are creating.

- QUEUE_TYPE can be either NORMAL_QUEUE or EXCEPTION_QUEUE. Remember to preface your choice with DBMS_AQADM.

- MAX_RETRIES limits the number of attempts that can be made to dequeue a message from the queue. A dequeue—which is an attempt to retrieve a message, followed by a rollback—constitutes a failed attempt. Messages are moved to an exception queue after the specified number of failures occur.

- RETRY_DELAY specifies the amount of time that must pass between successive attempts to retrieve an object. This value is in seconds. The default is 0, meaning that no delay is required.

- RETENTION_TIME specifies the length of time that messages will be retained in the queue after they have been dequeued. This time is in seconds. The default is 0, which means messages will be removed immediately after a successful dequeue. If you specify a value of 10, then messages will be retained after dequeue for 10 seconds. A value of DBMS_AQADM.INFINITE results in messages being retained in the queue indefinitely.

- COMMENT is a comment that is made visible in the DBA_QUEUES data dictionary view.

- AUTO_COMMIT has the same effect as the AUTO_COMMIT parameter to the CREATE_QUEUE_TABLE procedure. If it is TRUE, which is the default, any outstanding transaction is committed prior to the queue being created.

▲

For purposes of our scenario, we need a normal queue, and we can take all the default settings. Listing 21.3 shows the code needed to create the queue, which is named EMP_DEPT_CHANGES.

INPUT   **LISTING 21.3**   Creating the EMP_DEPT_CHANGES Queue

```
1: BEGIN
2:     DBMS_AQADM.CREATE_QUEUE (
3:         'EMP_DEPT_CHANGES',
4:         'EMP_CHANGES');
5: END;
6: /
```

ANALYSIS The call to `DBMS_AQADM.CREATE_QUEUE` specifies the queue name and the queue table, and takes the defaults for the remaining arguments. The queue name, `EMP_DEPT_CHANGES`, is specified in line 3. The queue table, `EMP_CHANGES`, is named in line 4.

Starting and Stopping a Queue

As if all your work so far—creating the payload type, the queue table, and the queue itself—weren't enough, you need to perform one more step before you can actually use the queue: You need to start the queue. You use the `DBMS_AQADM.START_QUEUE` procedure to start a queue, and the `DBMS_AQADM.STOP_QUEUE` procedure to stop it again.

▼SYNTAX

The procedure headers for the `START_QUEUE` and `STOP_QUEUE` procedures in the `DBMS_AQADM` package look like this:

```
PROCEDURE start_queue (
    queue_name IN VARCHAR2,
    enqueue IN BOOLEAN DEFAULT TRUE,
    dequeue IN BOOLEAN DEFAULT TRUE
);

PROCEDURE stop_queue (
    queue_name IN VARCHAR2,
    enqueue IN BOOLEAN DEFAULT TRUE,
    dequeue IN BOOLEAN DEFAULT TRUE,
    wait IN BOOLEAN DEFAULT TRUE
);
```

Note | Parameters with default values, identified by the keyword `DEFAULT`, are optional.

In this syntax the parameters are as follows:

- `QUEUE_NAME` is the name of the queue that you want to start or stop.
- `ENQUEUE` can be either `TRUE` or `FALSE`, and indicates whether the start or stop operation should be applied to the enqueue functionality.
- `DEQUEUE` can be either `TRUE` or `FALSE`, and indicates whether the start or stop operation should be applied to the queue's dequeue functionality.
- `WAIT` can be either `TRUE` or `FALSE`, and applies only to `STOP_QUEUE`. If this is `TRUE`, the queue is not stopped until all pending transactions complete. If `wait` is `FALSE`, then the queue is stopped immediately.

▲

21

The ENQUEUE and DEQUEUE parameters default to TRUE, so by default when you start a queue, you can both enqueue and dequeue from that queue. When you stop a queue, the default behavior is to stop both functions. You could, if you liked, call STOP_QUEUE with enqueue=TRUE and dequeue=FALSE. This would stop producer processes from adding to the queue, while allowing the queue's consumers to finish out what was already there.

The code in Listing 21.4 starts the EMP_DEPT_CHANGES queue that you just created.

 LISTING 21.4   Starting the EMP_DEPT_CHANGES Queue

```
1: BEGIN
2:    DBMS_AQADM.START_QUEUE('EMP_DEPT_CHANGES');
3: END;
4: /
```

 The call to DBMS_AQADM.START_QUEUE, shown in line 2, specifies only the queue name. Therefore, the default value, TRUE, is used for the other parameters. The queue is started, and both enqueuing and dequeuing are enabled.

Placing Messages in a Queue

After creating and starting a queue, you place messages in the queue by enqueuing them. Enqueuing a message involves these steps:

1. Instantiate (that is, create) an object of the payload type.
2. Instantiate objects for the enqueue options object, and the message properties object. Set any options or properties that you deem necessary.
3. Call the DBMS_AQ.ENQUEUE procedure.

> **Note**
>
> The operational interface to AQ is implemented by the DBMS_AQ package. The administrative interface is implemented by DBMS_AQADM.

Two of the parameters you pass to DBMS_AQ.ENQUEUE are records. They, in turn, contain elements that are also records. The next two sections describe these record types, and then describe the code needed to enqueue the two message types supported by our scenario: one to change an employee's salary, and one to change an employee's department.

SYNTAX

Enqueue-Related Record Types

You need to be aware of four record types in order to use the enqueue and dequeue interfaces:

- MESSAGE_PROPERTIES_T
- ENQUEUE_OPTIONS_T
- AQ$_AGENT
- AQ$_RECIPIENT_LIST_T

Each of these types are described in the following sections.

Each message has an associated message properties record that contains information used by Oracle AQ to manage the message. The record looks like this:

```
TYPE message_properties_t IS RECORD (
    priority BINARY_INTEGER DEFAULT 1,
    delay BINARY_INTEGER DEFAULT no_delay,
    expiration BINARY_INTEGER DEFAULT never,
    correlation VARCHAR2(128) DEFAULT NULL,
    attempts BINARY_INTEGER,
    recipient_list aq$_recipient_list_t,
    exception_queue VARCHAR2(51) DEFAULT NULL,
    enqueue_time DATE,
    state BINARY_INTEGER,
    sender_id aq$_agent DEFAULT NULL,
    original_msgid RAW(16) DEFAULT NULL
);
```

In this definition the record elements are as follows:

- PRIORITY indicates the priority of the message. This can be any integer, and can be negative. Lower values indicate higher priority.

- DELAY indicates the number of seconds to wait after the message has been enqueued before it is made available for dequeuing. The default value is NO_DELAY, which results in the message being made available immediately.

- EXPIRATION indicates the number of seconds that the message is to remain available for dequeuing. When that time is up, the message will be moved to the exception queue. NEVER, the default value, allows messages to remain in the queue indefinitely.

- CORRELATION is a field you can use for application-specific identifiers.

- ATTEMPTS has meaning only when a message is dequeued, and returns the number of dequeues that were attempted.

21

▼
- RECIPIENT_LIST specifies a list of recipients for the message.

- EXCEPTION_QUEUE provides the name of the exception queue in which to place this message if it cannot be processed before it expires, or if there are too many unsuccessful dequeue attempts.

- ENQUEUE_TIME returns the time at which a message was enqueued. This has meaning only when a message is dequeued. You can't set this parameter. The system sets it for you.

- STATE returns the state of a message when it is dequeued, and has meaning only when you are dequeuing a message. The state is one of the following:

    0—The message is ready to be processed.

    1—The message delay has not yet been reached.

    2—The message has been processed and is retained.

    3—The message has been moved to the exception queue.

- SENDER_ID identifies the application sending the message.

▲
- ORIGINAL_MSGID is used internally by the Oracle AQ feature.

The ENQUEUE_OPTIONS_T Record

▼ SYNTAX

When you enqueue a message, there are some options that you can specify. These are passed to the enqueue procedure using the ENQUEUE_OPTIONS_T record, which looks like this:

```
TYPE enqueue_options_t IS RECORD (
    visibility BINARY_INTEGER DEFAULT ON_COMMIT,
    relative_msgid RAW(16) DEFAULT NULL,
    sequence_deviation BINARY_INTEGER DEFAULT NULL
);
```

In this record the elements are as follows:

- VISIBILITY controls when the message becomes visible in the queue. ON_COMMIT is the default, and results in the message becoming visible only when the current transaction is committed. IMMEDIATE can be used to make the message visible immediately, and also serves to make the message independent of the current transaction.

- RELATIVE_MSGID is used with the SEQUENCE_DEVIATION parameter to arbitrarily position the message within the queue.

- SEQUENCE_DEVIATION controls where in the queue the message is placed. NULL is the default value, and results in the default behavior. BEFORE works in conjunction with RELATIVE_MSGID, and causes the message to be placed ahead of the message specified by that field. TOP causes the message to be added to the head of the

▲
queue.

▲ SYNTAX

The AQ$_AGENT Object Type

AQ$_AGENT actually represents an object type owned by the user SYS, not a record type
It's used to identify either the producer or consumer of a message. In our scenario, we
will use this type to specify the target consumer for the messages that we place in the
EMP_DEPT_CHANGES queue. The type definition looks like this:

```
CREATE TYPE sys.aq$_agent IS OBJECT (
    name VARCHAR2(30),
    address VARCHAR2(1024),
    protocol NUMBER
);
```

In this object type definition the elements are as follows:

- NAME is the name of a producer or consumer.

- ADDRESS is the address of the producer or consumer. Currently, this must be in the
  form [schema.]queue[@dblink].

- protocol identifies the protocol associated with the address. The only currently
  supported value is 0. The value of the protocol attribute controls how the address
  attribute is interpreted. Currently, only one protocol, and thus only one address
  interpretation, is supported. In the future, it's likely that other protocols will be
  added.

▲

▲ SYNTAX

The AQ$_AGENT Object Type

AQ$_AGENT actually represents an object type owned by the user SYS, not a record type.
It's used to identify either the producer or consumer of a message. In our scenario, we
will use this type to specify the target consumer for the messages that we place in the
EMP_DEPT_CHANGES queue. The type definition looks like this:

```
CREATE TYPE sys.aq$_agent IS OBJECT (
    name VARCHAR2(30),
    address VARCHAR2(1024),
    protocol NUMBER
);
```

In this object type definition the elements are as follows:

- NAME is the name of a producer or consumer.

- ADDRESS is the address of the producer or consumer. Currently, this must be in the
  form [schema.]queue[@dblink].

- protocol identifies the protocol associated with the address. The only currently
  supported value is 0. The value of the PROTOCOL attribute controls how the address
  attribute is interpreted. Currently, only one protocol, and thus only one address
  interpretation, is supported. In the future, it's likely that other protocols will be
  added.

▲

21

▼ SYNTAX
The AQ$_RECIPIENT_LIST_T Object Type

This type is a table of aq$_agent objects. The type definition looks like this:

```
TYPE aq$_recipient_list_t IS TABLE OF sys.aq$_agent
    INDEX BY BINARY_INTEGER;
```

The message properties record contains a variable of this type, which is used to specify a list of recipients for the message being enqueued.

Enqueuing a Message

You enqueue a message by creating a payload object, setting properties and options, and calling DBMS_AQ.ENQUEUE. For the sake of this example, the listings in this section create two stored procedures. The first, SALARY_CHANGE, posts a salary change message to the queue. It can be called by the program that is used to maintain wage data. The second procedure, DEPT_CHANGE, posts a department change message to the queue. Both procedures make use of DBMS_AQ.ENQUEUE.

The header for the DBMS_AQ.ENQUEUE procedure looks like this:

```
PROCEDURE ENQUEUE (
    queue_name IN VARCHAR2,
    enqueue_options IN enqueue_options_t,
    message_properties IN message_properties_t,
    payload IN object,
    msgid OUT RAW);
```

The parameters for this procedure are as follows:

- QUEUE_NAME is the name of the queue to which you want to post the message.

- ENQUEUE_OPTIONS is a record you can use to set various enqueue options. See the description for ENQUEUE_OPTIONS_T earlier in this lesson.

- MESSAGE_PROPERTIES is a record that you can use to set various message properties. See the description for MESSAGE_PROPERTIES_T earlier in this lesson.

- PAYLOAD is the payload object. This argument accepts any valid object type.

- MSGID is an output variable that returns the message ID of the enqueued message.

Enqueuing Salary Change Messages

Listing 21.5 shows the code for a procedure that enqueues salary changes for later review by management.

INPUT   **LISTING 21.5**   The SALARY_CHANGE Procedure

```
 1: CREATE OR REPLACE PROCEDURE salary_change (
 2:      emp_id   OUT NUMBER,
 3:      new_pay_rate OUT NUMBER,
 4:      new_pay_type OUT CHAR
 5: ) AS
 6:      enq_options dbms_aq.enqueue_options_t;
 7:      enq_mess_properties dbms_aq.message_properties_t;
 8:      recipients dbms_aq.aq$_recipient_list_t;
 9:      payload emp_chg;
10:      queued_message_id RAW(16);
11: BEGIN
12:      --Setup the payload
13:      payload := emp_chg(emp_id, new_pay_rate, new_pay_type
14:                    ,NULL,NULL);
15:
16:      --The recipient for salary changes is SALCHG.
17:      --Since we aren't crossing databases or queues, we
18:      --only need to specify a name, no protocol or address
19:      --is needed.
20:      recipients(1) := sys.aq$_agent('SALCHG',NULL,NULL);
21:      enq_mess_properties.recipient_list := recipients;
22:
23:      dbms_aq.enqueue('EMP_DEPT_CHANGES',
24:                    enq_options,
25:                    enq_mess_properties,
26:                    payload,
27:                    queued_message_id);
28: END;
29: /
```

ANALYSIS   This procedure takes three arguments (lines 2–4): emp_id, new_pay_rate, and new_pay_type. These are the relevant values for changing an employee's pay. Several records and objects are needed in order to call the enqueue procedure. These are defined in lines 6–10. Lines 6–7 declare a queue options record and a message properties record. These records are later passed as parameters to DBMS_AQ.ENQUEUE. A recipients list is declared in line 8. This record ultimately becomes a part of the message properties record. The payload object is declared in line 9. Notice that the object type used here is EMP_CHG—the same type that was used back when the queue table was created. Finally, a message ID variable is declared in line 10. This variable receives the message ID back from the DBMS_AQ.ENQUEUE.

21

The first thing this procedure does is to create an object of type EMP_CHG, which is done by calling the object's constructor and passing in the required values (lines 13–14). The salary-related values are the only ones set. The others are null because they don't apply here.

The next step is to specify a recipient for the message. This is actually an optional step. You could allow the message to be sent to the default recipients, known as *subscribers*, but for this example we won't do that. The recipients variable is a table of aq$_agent objects, so once again, in line 20, we call an object constructor. Because we are sending messages to another process attached to the same database, we only need to supply a name. The name used here is 'SALCHG', and is an entirely arbitrary choice—you just need to be sure that your receiving process uses the same name.

Finally, in lines 23–27, the DBMS_AQ.ENQUEUE procedure is called. All the parameters that you have set up are passed to the procedure, and it enqueues your message for you.

 Note   After enqueuing a message, unless you've set the visibility option to DBMS_AQ.IMMEDIATE, you have to commit your current transaction in order for that message to show up in the queue.

After you enqueue a message and commit the transaction, you can rest assured that the message will be delivered. In this example, because all the default enqueue options and message properties are used, there is no expiration time. The messages stay around in the queue until they are eventually retrieved.

Retrieving Messages from a Queue

To retrieve a message from a queue, you make a call to the DBMS_AQ.DEQUEUE procedure. Just as you have options when enqueuing a message, you also have options that you can set when dequeuing. A dequeue options record is used for this. When a message is dequeued, Oracle returns both the message and the message properties. The message properties are returned in the same MESSAGE_PROPERTIES_T record that you use with the enqueue procedure.

Dequeue-Related Record Types

The DBMS_AQ.DEQUEUE procedure uses the following record types:

- DEQUEUE_OPTIONS_T
- MESSAGE_PROPERTIES_T

You learned about the message properties record earlier in this chapter, in the section titled "Placing Messages in a Queue." The only new record here is the dequeue options record.

The DEQUEUE_OPTIONS_T Record

The definition of the dequeue options record looks like this:

```
TYPE dequeue_options_t IS RECORD (
    consumer_name VARCHAR2(30) DEFAULT NULL,
    dequeue_mode BINARY_INTEGER DEFAULT remove,
    navigation BINARY_INTEGER DEFAULT next_message,
    visibility BINARY_INTEGER DEFAULT on_commit,
    wait BINARY_INTEGER DEFAULT forever,
    msgid RAW(16) DEFAULT NULL,
    correlation VARCHAR2(128) DEFAULT NULL
);
```

In this record the elements are as follows:

- CONSUMER-NAME is for multiple-consumer queues to specify a recipient name. DBMS_AQ.DEQUEUE then returns the next message for the specified recipient.

- DEQUEUE_MODE can be either BROWSE, LOCKED, or REMOVE. The default is REMOVE, which means that messages are removed from the queue after they are dequeued. The BROWSE setting allows you to dequeue a message just to look at it. The message remains in the queue after the dequeue, and can be dequeued by other users. The LOCKED setting locks the message that is retrieved. The message remains in the queue, but no one else can touch it until your transaction completes.

- NAVIGATION specifies the position from which to retrieve a message. The default is NEXT_MESSAGE, which results in messages being retrieved in the normal order specified by the sort_list parameter used when you created the queue table. FIRST_MESSAGE resets your position to the beginning of the queue, and retrieves the first message matching your search criteria. NEXT_TRANSACTION can be used only when message grouping has been enabled, and skips forward to the first message of the next transaction.

- VISIBILITY controls whether dequeuing is done as part of the current transaction. The default is ON_COMMIT, which means that the dequeue is not final until your transaction commits. Use IMMEDIATE if you don't want the dequeue to be dependent on your transaction.

- WAIT specifies how long, in seconds, to wait before returning without a message. The default is FOREVER, which means that the dequeue procedure waits until a message becomes available. You can use NO_WAIT if you don't want to wait at all. Otherwise, specify a wait time in seconds.

Tip

In practice, I've noticed that even when there are messages available in the queue, they aren't retrieved when NO_WAIT is specified. If this happens to you, then specify a one-second wait time.

- MSGID is for passing the ID if you want to dequeue a specific message and you know the message ID (perhaps from browsing it earlier).
- CORRELATION specifies a correlation string. This is a user-defined string that you can set when messages are enqueued. You can then match on that string when dequeuing. The SQL LIKE operator is used when comparing on this, so you can use the percent sign (%) and underscore (_) wildcard operators here.

Dequeuing a Message

The DBMS_AQ.DEQUEUE procedure is used to retrieve a message from a queue. The syntax for DBMS_AQ.DEQUEUE can be seen in the syntax box below.

SYNTAX

The header for the DBMS_AQ.DEQUEUE procedure looks like this:

```
PROCEDURE DEQUEUE (
    queue_name IN VARCHAR2,
    dequeue_options IN dequeue_options_t,
    message_properties OUT message_properties_t,
    payload OUT object,
    msgid OUT RAW
);
```

The parameters in this procedure are as follows:

- QUEUE_NAME is the name of the queue from which you want to retrieve a message.
- DEQUEUE_OPTIONS is a record of type DEQUEUE_OPTIONS_T in which you specify any desired dequeuing options.
- MESSAGE_PROPERTIES is where DEQUEUE returns the message properties.
- PAYLOAD is where DEQUEUE returns the message payload.
- MSGID is where DEQUEUE returns the ID of the message that was dequeued.

Dequeuing Change Messages

In our scenario, we want to do two things when dequeuing a message. We want to dequeue only messages for a specific recipient—SALCHG. The second thing we want to do is to place a limit on the amount of time that the dequeuing procedure will wait. Presumably the management application used to review salary changes will be an online application. Having it wait forever to dequeue a message could make it appear hung to the user.

The procedure in Listing 21.6 can be used to dequeue salary change messages. It could be called by any program that needed to review these changes.

INPUT   **LISTING 21.6**   The GET_SALARY_CHANGE Procedure

```
 1: CREATE OR REPLACE PROCEDURE get_salary_change (
 2:      emp_id  OUT NUMBER,
 3:      new_pay_rate OUT NUMBER,
 4:      new_pay_type OUT CHAR
 5: ) AS
 6:      deq_options dbms_aq.dequeue_options_t;
 7:      deq_mess_properties dbms_aq.message_properties_t;
 8:      payload emp_chg;
 9:      dequeued_message_id RAW(16);
10: BEGIN
11:      --Specify our consumer name
12:      deq_options.consumer_name := 'SALCHG';
13:
14:      --Specify the time that we will wait.
15:      --In this case, we won't wait at all.
16:      deq_options.wait := 2;
17:
18:      --Perform the dequeue
19:      BEGIN
20:          dbms_aq.dequeue('EMP_DEPT_CHANGES',
21:                              deq_options,
22:                              deq_mess_properties,
23:                              payload,
24:                              dequeued_message_id);
25:      EXCEPTION
26:          WHEN OTHERS THEN
27:              emp_id := NULL;
28:              new_pay_rate := NULL;
29:              new_pay_type := NULL;
30:              RETURN;
31:      END;
32:
33:      --Return the information that was dequeued.
34:      emp_id := payload.emp_id;
35:      new_pay_rate := payload.pay_rate;
36:      new_pay_type := payload.pay_type;
37: END;
38: /
```

21

ANALYSIS   This procedure dequeues one message from the EMP_DEPT_CHANGES queue, and returns the results through the three output parameters declared in lines 2–4. A dequeue options variable is declared in line 6. In line 12, the consumer field is set to SALCHG so that only messages for SALCHG are retrieved. (Another procedure handles the

DEPTCHG messages.) A two-second wait time is specified in line 16. If there are no messages in the queue for SALCHG, DBMS_AQ.DEQUEUE waits two seconds for some to appear before giving up.

The actual call to DBMS_AQ.DEQUEUE is made in lines 20–24, and is inside a nested PL/SQL block. This is because the dequeue procedure throws an error if no message could be dequeued. The exception handler (lines 25–30) for the nested block traps this error, and sets all the return values to null. Otherwise, control passes to lines 34–36, where the dequeued values are placed into the output variables.

When the calling program has these values, they can be displayed for review. If the pay rate change is accepted, the employee table can be updated with the new rate. Otherwise, if the pay change is rejected, the message is thrown away, and no changes are ever made to the employee's record.

Using Other AQ Procedures

There are a few other AQ procedures you should know about. In addition to creating queue tables and queues, you can also drop them. The DBMS_AQADM package contains procedures to drop both tables and queues. You might also want to allow other users to use queues that you have defined. To do that, you must grant access to those queues. That's also done by calling procedures in the DBMS_AQADM package.

Dropping a Queue

The DBMS_AQADM.DROP_QUEUE procedure is used to drop a queue. Before you can drop a queue, you must first stop the queue. Refer to the section "Starting and Stopping a Queue" earlier in this lesson for details on how to do that.

The procedure header for DBMS_AQADM.DROP_QUEUE looks like this:

```
PROCEDURE dbms_aqadm.drop_queue (
    queue_name IN VARCHAR2,
    auto_commit IN BOOLEAN DEFAULT TRUE
);
```

For this procedure the parameters are as follows:

- QUEUE_NAME is the name of the queue you want to drop.
- AUTO_COMMIT can be either TRUE or FALSE, and determines whether the current transaction is committed before dropping the queue.

Dropping a Queue Table

When all the queues in a table are dropped, you can drop the table itself. The `DBMS_AQADM.DROP_QUEUE_TABLE` procedure is used for that purpose.

▼ SYNTAX

The procedure header for `DBMS_AQADM.DROP_QUEUE_TABLE` looks like this:

```
PROCEDURE dbms_aqadm.drop_queue_table (
    queue_table IN VARCHAR2,
    force IN BOOLEAN DEFAULT FALSE,
    auto_commit IN BOOLEAN DEFAULT TRUE
);
```

For this procedure the parameters are as follows:

- `QUEUE_TABLE` is the name of the queue table you want to drop.

- `FORCE` controls whether the presence of queues in the table prevents the table from being dropped. The default is `FALSE`, which prevents the table from being dropped while queues are still present. The value `TRUE` allows you to drop a table and all its queues together.

▲

- `AUTO_COMMIT` can be either `TRUE` or `FALSE`, and determines whether the current transaction is committed before dropping the queue table.

Granting and Revoking Access to a Queue

You can grant other users access to your queues by using the `DBMS_AQADM.GRANT_QUEUE_PRIVILEGE` procedure. You can also revoke those privileges by using `DBMS_AQADM.REVOKE_QUEUE_PRIVILEGE`.

▼ SYNTAX

The header for the `DBMS_AQADM.GRANT_QUEUE_PRIVILEGE` procedure looks like this:

```
PROCEDURE grant_queue_privilege (
    privilege VARCHAR2,
    queue_name VARCHAR2,
    grantee VARCHAR2,
    grant_option BOOLEAN DEFAULT FALSE
);
```

In this syntax the parameters are as follows:

- `PRIVILEGE` is the privilege that you want to grant. You can choose from the following:

  `ENQUEUE_ANY`—The user can place messages into the queue.

  `DEQUEUE_ANY`— The user can retrieve messages from the queue.

  `ALL`—The user both places messages into the queue and retrieves them from the queue.

▼

21

▼

- QUEUE_NAME is the name of the queue on which you are granting the privilege.

- GRANTEE is the name of the user or role to which you are granting the privileges. You can also use the keyword PUBLIC here, to make the queue accessible to everyone.

- grant_option indicates whether the grantee can in turn grant access to others. FALSE is the default, and means that he or she can't. TRUE means that he or she can.

▲

The Syntax for DBMS_AQADM.REVOKE_QUEUE_PRIVILEGE

The header for the DBMS_AQADM.REVOKE_QUEUE_PRIVILEGE procedure looks like this:

```
PROCEDURE revoke_queue_privilege (
    privilege VARCHAR2,
    queue_name VARCHAR2,
    grantee VARCHAR2,
);
```

In this syntax the parameters are as follows:

- PRIVILEGE is the privilege you want to revoke. You can choose from ENQUEUE_ANY, DEQUEUE_ANY, and ALL.

- QUEUE_NAME is the name of the queue for which you are revoking the privilege.

- GRANTEE is the name of the user or role from which you are revoking the privilege. If that user was able to grant the privilege to other users, and did so, then the privilege is also revoked from those other users.

▲

Summary

In today's lesson, you have learned how to do the following:

- Create and drop queue tables
- Create and drop queues
- Stop and start queues
- Enqueue and dequeue messages
- Address queue messages to a specific recipient

What you have seen here is just a small fraction of what AQ is capable of. Using AQ, you can automatically propagate messages from one queue to another. You can funnel messages from many queues into one, and you can fan them out from one queue to several. Messages can even be routed between queues in two different databases. All this can be done transparently to the applications using those queues. If you are writing C code, and using Oracle's OCI interface, you can even define callback functions so that you can be notified in real-time when a message is available.

Oracle AQ is a robust, secure, and reliable messaging mechanism. If you're thinking of implementing an application using DBMS_PIPE or DBMS_ALERT, consider using AQ instead.

Q&A

Q Can you give me a short, bottom-line description of AQ?

A Yes. Oracle AQ is a messaging system. It's reliable, it's robust, and it participates fully in database transactions. Using AQ, you can send messages between applications connected to the same database, or between applications in a distributed database environment.

Q Where does Oracle keep AQ messages between the time they are enqueued and the time that they are dequeued?

A The messages are kept in database tables. Each queue is associated with a queue table. A queue table is like any other database table.

Q Does each queue get its own queue table?

A It can, but queue tables can hold more than one queue. The only restriction is that the payload type must be the same for all queues in the table.

Workshop

You can use this to test your comprehension of this chapter and put what you've learned into practice. You'll find the answers to the quiz and exercises in Appendix A, "Answers."

Quiz

1. What are the terms that Oracle AQ uses to describe the acts of placing messages into queues and retrieving them again?

2. What three initialization parameters should you check when implementing AQ on a database?

3. What database role must you grant AQ administrators?

4. After creating a queue, and before you can place messages into it, what must you do?

5. What are the two Oracle packages used with AQ?

21

Exercises

1. The procedure in Listing 21.5 enqueues salary change messages into the EMP_DEPT_CHANGES queue. Write a similar procedure to enqueue department change messages.

2. Write a procedure to dequeue department change messages. Your result should be similar to Listing 21.6. However, this time the procedure should block. In other words, it should always wait until a message can be retrieved before returning.

WEEK 3

In Review

This week you started off learning about how to manage transactions by locking a record as it is processed. That prevents another user from accessing the same record and thus helps prevent data corruption. You learned about the use of the COMMIT and ROLLBACK commands. On Day 16, you worked with the DBMS_SQL package, which offers the capability to create dynamic SQL from within PL/SQL. It also allows you to use DDL from within PL/SQL.

On Day 17, you were able to write and read files with the UTL_FILE package, which is an excellent way to import and export data in any format for any application. Day 18 covered the use of the DBMS_JOBS package, which you can use to schedule jobs that need to be on a recurring basis. On Day 19, you learned how to handle the communications between sessions by using the DBMS_PIPE package. This day also includes a lesson on the DBMS_ALERT package, which you can use to alert users to a specific event.

On Day 20 you learned about the Oracle 8i Java engine and its interaction with PL/SQL. Finally, on Day 21, you learned about Advanced Queuing in PL/SQL.

Congratulations on finishing this book! We, the authors, as well as all the editors at Sams, hope that you've enjoyed your three-week excursion into PL/SQL. You've certainly had a chance to see the power, and the wide-ranging capabilities that PL/SQL offers. As you continue to work with Oracle, you will have many chances to put this newfound knowledge to good use. A solid knowledge of PL/SQL will enhance the career of any Oracle professional.

APPENDIX

Answers

Day 1, "Learning the Basics of PL/SQL"

1. What tells SQL*Plus to send your PL/SQL code to the Oracle database for execution?

   Typing the slash character (/) on a line by itself immediately following the end of the PL/SQL block.

2. What is the fundamental basis of all PL/SQL code?

   The PL/SQL block.

3. List an advantage of pushing program logic up to the server level.

   There are at least two advantages:

   - It gives a central point of control.
   - Intermediate data does not have to be brought down to the client.

4. Name three Oracle products that use PL/SQL.

   There are several that execute PL/SQL:

   - Developer/2000
   - Oracle Forms
   - Oracle Reports
   - The Oracle database itself
   - Procedure Builder

   And several that recognize it:

   - SQL*Plus
   - SQL*DBA
   - Server Manager

5. What command tells SQL*Plus to display PL/SQL output?

   ```
   SET SERVEROUTPUT ON
   ```

6. Name at least two options for managing your PL/SQL source code.

   The three options described in the chapter are as follows:

   - Cut and paste from Notepad.
   - Execute a text file using the SQL*Plus @ command.
   - Use the SQL*Plus EDIT command.

Exercises

1. If you didn't encounter any errors when compiling your first function, try putting some in on purpose. Then try out the SHOW ERRORS command.

   I'll leave the task of generating errors up to you.

2. Try each of the three ways mentioned in the chapter for managing your source code. Become familiar with the SQL*Plus EDIT command. Try using the @ command or the START command to execute your PL/SQL code from a text file.

   You should be able to type any PL/SQL block into SQL*Plus, execute it, and then use the EDIT command to bring up Notepad so that you can change it.

   As for executing a PL/SQL block from a file, one possible solution is to create a file with these lines and call it test.sql:

   ```
   SET SERVEROUTPUT ON
   BEGIN
     dbms_output.put_line('Hello there!');
   END;
   /
   ```

You can then execute the file from SQL*Plus using the command
`@test`

Day 2, "Writing Declarations and Blocks"

Quiz

1. What are three benefits of using functions and procedures?

    Procedures and functions hide complexity, promote modularity, and allow for reuse of code.

2. What values can a variable declared as NUMBER(6,2) hold? What will be the maximum value?

    A declaration of number(6,2) allows you to store values such as 1234.56, -2333.99, and so on. The maximum value you could store is 9999.99.

3. What values can a variable declared as NUMBER(2,2) hold? Where will rounding occur?

    A declaration of number(2,2) allows you to store values such as 0.01, 0.02, up through 0.99. All values are rounded to the nearest hundredth.

4. What is the maximum length of a VARCHAR2 variable in PL/SQL? In the Oracle database?

    The maximum length of a varchar2 in PL/SQL is 32,767 bytes. In an Oracle database, the maximum length is 2,000 bytes.

5. What can you do to ignore the time portion of a DATE variable?

    The trunc() function may be used to truncate a date so that it no longer contains a time element.

6. When comparing a VARCHAR2 and a CHAR variable, how can you eliminate any trailing spaces?

    The rtrim() function may be used to eliminate trailing spaces from both char and varchar2 strings.

Exercises

1. Try writing an anonymous block that declares a variable and displays the value. Then add a nested block that declares a variable of the same name and displays its value. What happens and why?

Here is one solution:

```
set serveroutput on
declare
  state_name  varchar2(30);

begin
  state_name := 'Michigan';

  --Now code a nested block which declares and prints
  --a variable of the same name.
  declare
    state_name  varchar2(30);
  begin
    state_name := 'Tennessee';
    dbms_output.put_line(state_name);
  end;

  --Now print the state_name variable's value in the outer block.
  dbms_output.put_line (state_name);
end;
/

Tennessee
Michigan

PL/SQL procedure successfully completed.
```

The inner block will print the value assigned to state_name within that block. However, the value of state_name in the outer block is undisturbed because the scope of the inner block's state_name declaration is limited to that block.

2. Write a function that computes a person's age in years. Hint: To get started on this, look at Listing 2.2.

Here is a PL/SQL block containing a function named "age_as_of," which is one possible solution to the exercise of coding an age calculation function.

```
set serveroutput on
set echo on
declare
  age    binary_integer;

  birth_date    date := to_date('11-15-1961','mm-dd-yyyy');
  current_date  date;

  function age_as_of (birth_date in date, as_of_date in date)
  return positive is
    as_of_year  natural;    --a year of 00 is valid.
    as_of_month positive;
    as_of_day   positive;
```

A

```
      birth_year    natural;  --a year of 00 is valid.
      birth_month   positive;
      birth_day     positive;

      age    positive;
   begin
      --Get the various parts of the dates needed to determine age.
      as_of_year := to_number(to_char(as_of_date,'yyyy'));
      as_of_month := to_number(to_char(as_of_date,'mm'));
      as_of_day := to_number(to_char(as_of_date,'dd'));

      birth_year := to_number(to_char(birth_date,'yyyy'));
      birth_month := to_number(to_char(birth_date,'mm'));
      birth_day := to_number(to_char(birth_date,'dd'));

      --Now make the actual computation.
      if as_of_month > birth_month then
         age := as_of_year - birth_year;
      elsif (as_of_month = birth_month) and (as_of_day >= birth_day) then
         age := as_of_year - birth_year;
      else
         age := as_of_year - birth_year - 1;
      end if;

      return age;
   end;
begin
   --Let's test each of the cases that the age
   --function needs to consider.
   dbms_output.put_line('Age as of 11-13-1997');
   current_date := to_date('11-13-1997','mm-dd-yyyy');
   age := age_as_of (birth_date, current_date);
   dbms_output.put_line(age);

   dbms_output.put_line('Age as of 11-15-1997');
   current_date := to_date('11-15-1997','mm-dd-yyyy');
   age := age_as_of (birth_date, current_date);
   dbms_output.put_line(age);

   dbms_output.put_line('Age as of 12-13-1997');
   current_date := to_date('12-13-1997','mm-dd-yyyy');
   age := age_as_of (birth_date, current_date);
   dbms_output.put_line(age);

   dbms_output.put_line('Age as of 5-13-1997');
   current_date := to_date('5-13-1997','mm-dd-yyyy');
   age := age_as_of (birth_date, current_date);
   dbms_output.put_line(age);

end;
/
```

```
Age as of 11-13-1997
35
Age as of 11-15-1997
36
Age as of 12-13-1997
36
Age as of 5-13-1997
35

PL/SQL procedure successfully completed.
```

Day 3, "Writing PL/SQL Expressions"

Quiz

1. What is the difference between a unary operator and a binary operator?

   A unary operator works on only one value. An example is the negation operator, which is often used to write negative numbers. Binary operators work on two values. Examples are the addition and multiplication operators.

2. What are the results of each of the following expressions?

   a. `(5-4)-(3-1)`

   b. `4*2**3-2`

   c. `4*2**(3-2)`

   d. `4=4 AND 5=6 or 3=3`

   The expressions evaluate as follows:

   a. (5-4)-(3-1) evaluates to -1.

   b. 4*2**3-2 evaluates to 30.

   c. 4*2**(3-2) evaluates to 8.

   d. 4=4 AND 5=6 or 3=3 evaluates to TRUE.

3. Using the NOT operator, write equivalent expressions for each of the following:

   a. `A <> B`

   b. `A < B`

   c. `(A <= B) AND (B <= C)`

   The equivalents are:

   a. not (A = B)

   b. not (A >= B)

   c. not ((B < A) or (B > C))

A

4. Match the patterns and strings shown following. Hint: Not every string or pattern has a match, and one pattern matches more than one string.

`'123-45-6789'` `'___-__-____'`

`'Boom'` `'John%'`

`'Johnson'` `'_oo_'`

`'517-555-1212'`

`'Broom'`

`'Jonson'`

`'Johnston'`

The patterns and strings match as follows:

'John%' matches 'Johnson' and "Johnston'. '_oo_' matches 'Boom'. '___-__-____' matches '123-45-6789'. The remaining strings and patterns don't match at all.

5. When does PL/SQL not pad strings with spaces, in order to make them of equal length, when doing comparisons?

Anytime a `varchar2` string is involved.

Exercise

Write a function to compute wages based on an hourly rate and the number of hours worked. Have it use a minimum wage of $5 per hour if the rate is unknown. Have it also use the minimum wage if the rate is too low.

Here is one solution:

```
set serveroutput on
declare
function wage_calculate (
  hours_worked in number,
  hourly_rate in number) return number is

hourly_rate_to_use  number;
minimum_wage  number := 5;
begin
  if (hourly_rate is null) or (hourly_rate < minimum_wage) then
    hourly_rate_to_use := minimum_wage;
  else
    hourly_rate_to_use := hourly_rate;
  end if;

  return hours_worked * hourly_rate_to_use;
end;
begin
```

```
      dbms_output.put_line(wage_calculate(40,10));
      dbms_output.put_line(wage_calculate(40,2));
      dbms_output.put_line(wage_calculate(40,null));
   end;
   /
   400
   200
   200

   PL/SQL procedure successfully completed.
```

Day 4, "Using Functions, IF Statements, and Loops"

Quiz

1. What parts of the function are required for coding?

   The required parts of the function are the function keyword and name, the RETURN statement and type, and BEGIN and END statements with the function name at the end of the END statement.

2. If a function takes parameters, is it always necessary to pass these parameters from the calling statement?

   It is not always necessary to pass values, even if the function allows for this. To compensate, make sure that you have a DEFAULT for the parameter if nothing is passed.

3. If an error occurs, and you have not coded the EXCEPTION statement, what gets returned from the function?

   The function causes an error and returns no value.

4. Is there a way to return more than one value from a function?

   You can return more than one parameter by using the optional MODE of OUT or IN OUT. However, using MODE is not a recommended programming practice.

5. If you code an IF...ELSE statement, and you do not have any conditions to execute if the statement is false, how would you code the ELSE statement?

   After the ELSE statement, code a NULL;.

6. What are some of the common pitfalls in coding IF statements?

   Some common errors are forgetting to put a space between END and IF; forgetting the semicolon after the END IF; missing an END IF statement, especially in nested IFs; and misspelling ELSIF as ELSEIF.

A

7. How can I determine what is wrong with my code when it compiles?

From your command prompt, type **SHOW ERRORS** and then troubleshoot. Remember, a program can compile and still be incorrect due to logic errors.

8. When coding a loop in reverse, how must you code the beginning and ending values?

Even though you are adding the REVERSE keyword, you must still code the starting and ending values from lowest value to highest value.

Exercises

1. Rewrite the Grade example from Listing 4.12 as a stored function that passes the parameter of the score and returns a value of a grade letter.

Here's one solution:

```
CREATE OR REPLACE FUNCTION mygrade(p_score NUMBER)
     RETURN CHAR IS
BEGIN
IF p_Score >= 90 THEN
     RETURN 'A';
ELSIF p_Score >= 80 THEN
     RETURN 'B';
ELSIF p_Score >= 70 THEN
     RETURN 'C';
ELSIF p_Score >= 60 THEN
     RETURN 'D';
ELSE
     RETURN 'E';
END IF;
END;
```

2. Rewrite the Grade example from Listing 4.12 and use between for the ranges. Make sure that there is no overlapping of ranges.

Here's one solution:

```
DECLARE
v_Score Number := 85; --Percentage
v_LetterGrade Char(1);
BEGIN
IF v_Score between 90 and 100 THEN
     v_LetterGrade := 'A';
ELSIF v_Score between 80 and 89 THEN
     v_LetterGrade := 'B';
ELSIF v_Score between 70 and 79 THEN
     v_LetterGrade := 'C';
ELSIF v_Score between 60 and 69 THEN
     v_LetterGrade := 'D';
ELSE
```

```
        v_LetterGrade := 'E';
    END IF;
        DBMS_OUTPUT.PUT_LINE('Your Letter Grade is: ' ¦¦ v_LetterGrade);
    END;
    /
```

3. Write a loop that increments by a value of 3 and then multiplies this counter by the returned value of the function mypi. The range should be 1 to 9. Output the values with DBMS_OUTPUT. Make sure that you enter SET SERVEROUTPUT ON to see the output.

Here's one solution:

```
BEGIN
    FOR v_loopcounter IN 1..9 LOOP
        IF MOD(v_loopcounter,3) = 0 THEN
            DBMS_OUTPUT.PUT_LINE('The counter * pi is ' ¦¦
                v_loopcounter * mypi );
        END IF; -- End execution of statements for even counter
    END LOOP;
END;
```

4. Write a loop to calculate a factorial. In other words, 6! is 6 * 5 * 4 * 3 * 2 * 1. Allow the high boundary to be a variable that can change. Use an initial value of 3 for testing.

Here's one solution:

```
DECLARE
    v_factorial NUMBER := 1;
BEGIN
    FOR v_loopcounter IN REVERSE 1..4 LOOP
        v_factorial := v_factorial * v_loopcounter;
            DBMS_OUTPUT.PUT_LINE('Your factorial value is now ' ¦¦
                v_factorial);
    END LOOP;
END;
```

Day 5, "Implementing Loops and GOTOs"

Quiz

1. True or False: The label name must be within the same PL/SQL block of code as the GOTO statement calling the label name.

   True. This is one of many reasons why you probably will never need to use the GOTO statement.

2. When should you use GOTO?

The GOTO statement is typically used in emergency situations that require you to respond immediately. The situation could be something as simple as a server going down or as complex as an incoming nuclear warhead. Otherwise, it is not good coding practice to use the GOTO statement.

3. WHILE loops must end with a(n) _____ statement.

END LOOP;

4. Can you potentially write a WHILE loop that never ends?

Yes. As long as the condition never evaluates to true, the same code repeats over and over again.

5. What statement(s) allow you to abort the processing of a loop?

The EXIT and EXIT WHEN statements allow you to break out of the execution of a loop.

6. To change the execution of nested loops, you can use the EXIT and EXIT WHEN statement in conjunction with _____.

label names for loops

7. Must you have EXIT or EXIT WHEN as part of a simple LOOP?

This is not required as part of the syntax. However, you should make it mandatory as a part of good programming practice instead of writing infinite loops!

8. Does Oracle have a REPEAT...UNTIL loop?

No. You can simulate it by using the simple LOOP with the EXIT or EXIT WHEN statement.

9. In a simple LOOP, where is the best location for the EXIT or EXIT WHEN statements?

These statements should appear at the beginning or at the end of the LOOP body to avoid potential logic errors.

Exercises

1. Create an example using GOTO that checks some variable for a value of 10 and then branches off to a NULL statement.

Here is one solution:

```
DECLARE
    v_GOTOVARIABLE NUMBER := 0;
BEGIN
    v_GOTOVARIABLE := 10;
    IF v_GOTOVARIABLE = 10 THEN
        GOTO nullstatement;
    ELSE
        NULL;
```

```
    END IF;
<<nullstatement>>
    NULL;
END;
/
```

2. Create a WHILE loop to calculate a factorial. In other words, 6! is 6 * 5 * 4 * 3 * 2 * 1. Use an initial value of 4! for testing. Make sure to issue the command SET SERVEROUTPUT ON and use DBMS_OUTPUT.

Here is one solution:

```
DECLARE
    v_factorial NUMBER := 1;
    v_factorial_counter NUMBER := 4;
BEGIN
    WHILE v_factorial_counter != 1 LOOP
        v_factorial := v_factorial * v_factorial_counter;
        DBMS_OUTPUT.PUT_LINE('Your factorial value is now '
            || v_factorial);
        v_factorial_counter := v_factorial_counter - 1;
    END LOOP;
END;
/
```

3. Create the same factorial calculation as you do in Exercise 2, but use the simple LOOP statement instead.

Here is one solution:

```
DECLARE
    v_factorial NUMBER := 1;
    v_factorial_counter NUMBER := 4;
BEGIN
    LOOP
        v_factorial := v_factorial * v_factorial_counter;
        DBMS_OUTPUT.PUT_LINE('Your factorial value is now '
            || v_factorial);
        v_factorial_counter := v_factorial_counter - 1;
        EXIT WHEN v_factorial_counter = 1;
    END LOOP;
END;
/
```

Day 6, "Using Oracle's Built-In Functions"

Quiz

1. True or False: All functions are accessible within PL/SQL.

   False. There are many SQL-only commands, which perform calculations on rows, such as AVG, MIN, MAX, and so on.

2. What function do I use to combine two strings together?

   You use the CONCAT function; however, you can still rely on ¦¦ to concatenate strings.

3. What function converts '11/28/99' to an Oracle DATE?

   The TO_DATE function gives you this flexibility.

4. In a VARCHAR2 string, each string can be a variable length. What function do you use to determine the length so that you can search through the entire string?

   By using the LENGTH function, you can determine the actual length of VARCHAR2. If the value is NULL, NULL is returned. If you are using type CHAR, it includes the padded spaces in the count.

5. How do you get rid of padded spaces to the right of a string in Oracle?

   By using RTRIM and specifying the space as a character, you can trim any padded spaces in a string.

6. To determine the remainder, you use the _____ function.

   MOD

7. To determine how many months a customer is delinquent, you can use the _____ function.

   MONTHS_BETWEEN

8. You can use the TRUNC and ROUND functions with what data types?

   Both NUMBER and DATE include the ROUND and TRUNC functions.

Exercises

1. Create a PL/SQL block that reads in the month of a date and displays the month in a Roman numeral format. Use a date of 06/11/67. This allows you to practice the TO_CHAR function. When printing the Roman numeral equivalent, use LTRIM to remove any spaces padded to the left of the Roman numeral. If you are really ambitious, on your own you can create the same RM-type function by using IF...THEN...ELSE statements for practice from Day 4. Remember, practice helps to solidify your knowledge through repetition and understanding.

   Here is one solution:

```
DECLARE
    v_Hold_Month Number;
BEGIN
    v_Hold_Month := TO_NUMBER(TO_CHAR(TO_DATE('11-JUN-67'),'MM'));
    DBMS_OUTPUT.PUT_LINE(v_Hold_Month);
    DBMS_OUTPUT.PUT_LINE('Converted to Roman Numeral ' ¦¦
        LTRIM(TO_CHAR(v_Hold_Month,'RM'),' '));
```

```
END;
/
```

Your output is

```
6
Converted to Roman Numeral VI
```

2. Use the TRUNC function on the SYSDATE to round to the nearest century.

The answer is

```
SELECT TO_CHAR(TRUNC(SYSDATE,'CC'),'MM/DD/YYYY HH:MI:SS AM')
      "Today's Date and Time"
 from DUAL
```

The output is similar to

```
Today's Date and Time
------------------------
01/01/1900 12:00:00 AM
```

3. Use CONCAT to link two strings together. Repeat the same line by using ¦¦ instead of CONCAT.

Here is one solution:

```
DECLARE
     v_String1 VARCHAR2(60) := CONCAT('Connect String1 to',
                                        ' String2');
     v_String2 VARCHAR2(60) := 'Connect String1 to' ¦¦ ' String2';
BEGIN
     DBMS_OUTPUT.PUT_LINE(v_String1);
     DBMS_OUTPUT.PUT_LINE(v_String2);
END;
/
```

Your output looks similar to

```
Connect String1 to String2
Connect String1 to String2
```

4. Calculate the number of days between 01/01/97 to 03/31/97. Remember to use the TRUNC function to eliminate the TIME dependency.

The answer is

```
SELECT TRUNC(TO_DATE('03/31/97','MM/DD/YY')) -
     TRUNC(TO_DATE('01/01/97','MM/DD/YY')) "Days_Subtracted"
     from DUAL;
```

Your output is

```
Days_Subtracted
---------------
             89
```

5. Convert the CHARACTER string `'06/11/67'` to a date, and subtract from 06/11/97 to see how old your author is (and holding).

The answer is

```
SELECT (TO_DATE('06/11/97','MM/DD/YY') -
    TO_DATE('06/11/67','MM/DD/YY'))/365 "Years Old"
    from DUAL;
```

Your output is

```
Years Old
---------
30.021918
```

6. Calculate how many months are between 05/15/97 and 08/22/97.

The answer is

```
SELECT MONTHS_BETWEEN('22-AUG-97','15-MAY-97') "Fractional"
    from DUAL;
```

Your output is

```
Fractional
----------
 3.2258065
```

7. Round the SYSDATE to the nearest century.

The answer is

```
SELECT TO_CHAR(ROUND(SYSDATE,'CC'),'MM/DD/YYYY HH:MI:SS AM')
    "Today's Date and Time"
  from DUAL;
```

Your output is similar to

```
Today's Date and Time
----------------------
01/01/2000 12:00:00 AM
```

8. Calculate the time in Newfoundland from Central Standard Time from 02-22-97, 05:00 AM.

Here is one solution:

```
SELECT TO_CHAR(NEW_TIME(TO_DATE('02-22-97 05:00:00 AM',
        'MM-DD-YY HH:MI:SS AM'),
        'CST','NST'), 'DD-MON-YY HH:MI:SS AM')
            "Central to Newfoundland"
    from DUAL;
```

Your output is

```
Central to Newfoundland
-----------------------
22-FEB-97 07:30:00 AM
```

9. From Listing 6.22, subtract one month and explain the answer.

Several possible answers are

```
SELECT ADD_MONTHS(TO_DATE('31-MAR-97'),-1) from DUAL;
SELECT ADD_MONTHS(TO_DATE('31-MAR-97'),-1.5) from DUAL;
SELECT ADD_MONTHS(-1,TO_DATE('31-MAR-97')) from DUAL;
```

The output, of course, is the end of February because February has fewer than 30 days:

```
ADD_MONTH
---------
28-FEB-97
```

10. Calculate the number of days until Christmas from the last day of the month of today's date. (We don't get paid until the end of the month!)

Here is one solution:

```
SELECT LAST_DAY(SYSDATE) "Last_Day",
        TO_DATE('25-DEC-97') - LAST_DAY(SYSDATE) "Shopping Days"
    from DUAL;
```

The output is similar to

```
Last_Day   Shopping Days
---------  -------------
30-JUN-97      177.67266
```

Day 7, "Procedures, Packages, Errors, and Exceptions"

Quiz

1. What statement do you use to recompile a procedure?

   You use the CREATE OR REPLACE PROCEDURE command to recompile a procedure.

2. How do you invoke a procedure?

   You use the execute command if you want to explicitly and manually call a procedure. From within a package or another PL/SQL construct, you simply list the procedure name in the code, and the call to it is made automatically.

3. Name at least four predefined Oracle exception errors.

   There are many Oracle predefined exceptions, including no_data_found, too_many_rows, invalid_cursor, value_error, invalid_number, zero_divide, cursor_already_open, and login_denied.

4. How do you call a module of a package?

To call a specific procedure within a package, you use dot notation, as shown in the following example:

```
package_name.procedure_name
```

Exercises

1. Write a package specification for the functions written in previous lessons. Additionally, include in the specification one or two of the procedures used in this lesson.

Package specifications contain public declarations of the name of the package and its functions and procedures. The following is an example and might differ slightly from your answer:

```
CREATE PACKAGE day_8_package_spec as                          --
➥package
name declaration
FUNCTION  inv_count (qty number, part_nbr varchar2(25))      -- function
declaration return number;
PROCEDURE pay_salary (emp_id number);                         --
➥procedure
declaration
PROCEDURE hire_employee (emp_name, pay_date number, pay_type char)); --
➥procedure
declaration
END day_8_package_spec;
```

2. Write an exception-handling piece of code to trap the error of receiving more rows than you expected as well as an unknown error.

One possible way to write this exception handler is

```
exception
WHEN too_many_rows THEN
    ...             -- code to be executed when a SELECT returns
                    -- too many rows
END;
WHEN others THEN
    ...             -- code to be executed when an exception is
                    -- encountered which is not the too_many_rows
```

Day 8, "Using SQL to Manipulate Data and Control Transactions"

Quiz

1. Name some of the database objects that you can base a variable declaration on.

   PL/SQL variables can be based on database table columns, other variables, constants, and cursors.

2. Name at least two of the exception types discussed in this chapter.

   There are many exceptions that a programmer can prepare for while coding. Some of the most common are `no_data_found`, `too_many_rows`, `invalid_cursor`, and `when_others`.

3. Do you need to list the table column names while inserting data into that table?

   No. If you elect to omit the column names during an insert statement, Oracle will automatically align the input data with the columns of the data. The first piece of data is inserted into the first column, the second piece of data will be inserted into the second column, and so on.

4. What are the four SQL DML statements permitted in a PL/SQL block?

   The four DML statements that are supported within a PL/SQL block are `INSERT`, `DELETE`, `UPDATE`, and `SELECT`.

Exercises

Evaluate each of the following three declarations and determine which ones are legal or not legal. Explain your answer for those that are not legal.

1. Legal or not legal:

   ```
   DECLARE
   emp_rec          emp_rec_type;
   ```

   This is an invalid declaration because `emp_rec_type` must be declared prior to this declaration. A proper declaration would be

   ```
   DECLARE
   TYPE emp_rec_type IS record
         (id       INTEGER,
          name     VARCHAR2(35));
   emp_rec          emp_rec_type;
   ```

2. Legal or not legal:

   ```
   DECLARE
   emp_last_name            %type;
   ```

This is an invalid declaration. The proper declaration would have to include a table and column reference such as

```
emp_last_name          emp.l_name%type;
```

3. Legal or not legal:

```
DECLARE
TYPE   emp_table_type is table of VARCHAR2(55);
emp_dept_table   emp_table_type;
```

This declaration is incorrect because the INDEX BY clause is missing. This declaration should look like

```
DECLARE
TYPE   emp_table_type is table of VARCHAR2(55)
INDEX BY BINARY_INTEGER;
emp_dept_table   emp_table_type;
```

Day 9, "Manipulating Data with Cursors"

Quiz

1. What are the cursor attributes and what is their purpose?

   The implicit and explicit cursors each have four attributes, which provide useful information about the cursor. These attributes are %isopen, %found, %notfound, and %rowcount.

2. How many cursors can you use at a time?

   There are no predefined limits on the number of cursors a session can have. The only constraint that limits the number of cursors is the availability of memory to manage them.

3. Where is the cursor pointer when the cursor is first opened?

   The cursor pointer is pointing to immediately prior to the first row when the cursor is first opened.

4. Name the different cursor variable parameter modes and their purpose.

   The cursor variable argument can have one of three different modes:

   IN—The program can have read-only abilities with the parameter. In other words, the cursor argument is passed only to the procedure or function.

   OUT—The program can return values to the calling PL/SQL block.

   IN OUT—The program can read and write to the variable.

Exercise

Create a PL/SQL block that determines the top five highest paid employees from your Employee table. Be sure to incorporate the usage of the appropriate cursor attributes. Print these five employees to the screen.

This exercise can be solved in several different ways. Your solution can include exception handling as well as other methods of processing the data. I have chosen the following method as my solution:

```
DECLARE
c_emp_name              VARCHAR2(32);
c_sal                   NUMBER(9,2);

CURSOR  emp_cursor is                     -- cursor declaration
SELECT emp_name, pay_type
from employee
ORDER BY pay_rate desc;      -- key to getting top 5 highest paid employees

BEGIN

OPEN emp_cursor;
FETCH emp_cursor
INTO c_emp_name, c_sal;    --fetch into variables for later use
WHILE emp_cursor%rowcount<=5 and          -- only fetch top 5 employees
    emp_cursor%found                      -- be sure there is data
LOOP
DBMS_OUTPUT (c_emp_name || ' is paid ' || c_sal );
                         -- prints results to screen
FETCH emp_cursor INTO c_emp_name, c_sal;
END LOOP;
CLOSE emp_cursor;                         -- closes the cursor
END;
```

Day 10, "Collections"

Quiz

1. Name the three collection types PL/SQL supports.

   The three collection types PL/SQL supports are index-by tables, nested tables, and varrays.

2. What declaration would you use to declare a variable named emp_name with a datatype and size that exactly match the definition of the employee.emp_name column in the database?

   In this case, the declaration would be emp_name employee.emp_name%type.

3. What declaration would you use to declare a record named `emp` that matches the definition of a row in the `employee` table?

   To declare `emp` to match the `employee` table, use `emp employee%rowtype`.

4. What method can you call on to be sure that a collection element really exists?

   The `exists` method can be used to determine whether a given element exists.

5. What must you be sure to do before you can add data to a nested table or to a varray?

   Before you can do anything with a nested table or a varray, you must initialize it with the value returned by its constructor function.

Exercise

Write the code necessary to generate a PL/SQL nested table with 10 new department IDs and names. Use department ID numbers that are not currently being used in the database. Make up the department names. Next, write a FORALL statement that inserts all the records by using a bulk bind.

Here is one possible solution to the exercise:

```
1: DECLARE
2:     --Define a nested table type for department IDs and names.
3:     TYPE dept_id IS TABLE OF department.dept_id%TYPE;
4:     TYPE dept_name IS TABLE OF department.dept_name%TYPE;
5:
6:     --Declare a nested table variable for each type.
7:     dept_ids dept_id;
8:     dept_names dept_name;
9:     inx1 PLS_INTEGER;
10: BEGIN
11:     --Initialize the collections
12:     dept_ids := dept_id();
13:     dept_names := dept_name();
14:
15:     --Extend once, outside the loop for better performance.
16:     dept_ids.extend(10);
17:     dept_names.extend(10);
18:
19:     --Generate 10 new departments, numbered from
20:     --1101-1110.
21:     FOR inx1 IN 1..10 LOOP
22:         dept_ids(inx1) := inx1 + 1100;
23:         dept_names(inx1) := 'Dept #' || TO_CHAR(inx1+1100);
24:     END LOOP;
25:
26:     FORALL x IN dept_ids.first..dept_ids.last
27:     INSERT INTO department (dept_id, dept_name)
28:     VALUES (dept_ids(x), dept_names(x));
```

```
29: END;
30: /
```

ANALYSIS The nested tables types are declared in lines 3–4. The corresponding variables are declared in lines 7–8. The tables are initialized by calling their constructor methods in lines 12–13. Because we know that we are going to deal with only 10 elements, only one call to extend is made for each table. These calls occur in lines 16–17, and they extend each table by 10 entries. The loop in lines 21–24 generates 10 new departments, numbered from 1101 through 1110. The FORALL statement in lines 26–28 inserts these 10 rows into the department table.

Day 11, "Writing Database Triggers"

Quiz

1. Which data manipulation statements can support triggers?

   INSERT, UPDATE, and DELETE.

2. What are the four basic parts of a trigger?

   The event that fires the trigger, the database table on which the trigger is defined, the optional WHEN clause, and the PL/SQL block containing the code to be executed.

3. In a trigger, what are the correlation names :OLD and :NEW used for?

   :OLD is used to refer to the values in a row before it is changed. :NEW is used to refer to the values after the row is changed.

4. What is the name of the system view that can be used to retrieve trigger definitions?

   The USER_TRIGGERS view shows all triggers you own. In addition, you might want to look at the ALL_TRIGGERS view and the DBA_TRIGGERS view. The ALL_TRIGGERS view adds triggers that others own but which are defined on your tables. If you have database administrator privileges, the DBA_TRIGGERS view lists all triggers defined in the database.

5. What is a mutating table?

   A mutating table is one that is in the process of being modified by the SQL statement which fired a trigger. Because the table is being changed it is not in a consistent state and Oracle does not allow queries against it.

6. Name some possible uses for triggers.

   Some possible uses for triggers are enforcing a business rule, enforcing security, logging changes, replicating data, and calculating column values.

Exercises

1. Write a set of triggers to maintain the emp_name and dept_name fields redundantly in the emp_dept relation so that you do not have to join the employee and department tables just to get a simple department listing.

Here is one solution:

```
CREATE OR REPLACE TRIGGER emp_dept_names
  BEFORE INSERT OR UPDATE OF emp_id, dept_id ON emp_dept
  FOR EACH ROW
DECLARE
  redundant_dept_name      department.dept_name%TYPE;
  redundant_emp_name       employee.emp_name%TYPE;
BEGIN
  --Get the employee's name
  BEGIN
    SELECT emp_name INTO redundant_emp_name
      FROM employee
     WHERE employee.emp_id = :NEW.emp_id;
  EXCEPTION
    --the employee record may not exist.
    WHEN OTHERS THEN
      redundant_emp_name := '';
  END;

  --Get the department name
  BEGIN
    SELECT dept_name INTO redundant_dept_name
      FROM department
     WHERE department.dept_id = :NEW.dept_id;
  EXCEPTION
    --the department record may not exist.
    WHEN OTHERS THEN
      redundant_dept_name := '';
  END;

  --Store the employee and department names in the emp_dept record.
  :NEW.dept_name := redundant_dept_name;
  :NEW.emp_name := redundant_emp_name;
END;
/
Trigger created.
CREATE OR REPLACE TRIGGER department_emp_dept
  AFTER UPDATE OF dept_name ON department
  FOR EACH ROW
BEGIN
  UPDATE emp_dept
     SET emp_dept.dept_name = :NEW.dept_name
   WHERE emp_dept.dept_id = :NEW.dept_id;
END;
```

```
/
Trigger created.
CREATE OR REPLACE TRIGGER employee_emp_dept
  AFTER UPDATE OF emp_name ON employee
  FOR EACH ROW
BEGIN
  UPDATE emp_dept
    SET emp_dept.emp_name = :NEW.emp_name
  WHERE emp_dept.emp_id = :NEW.emp_id;
END;
/
Trigger created.
```

ANALYSIS The first trigger, emp_dept_name, handles inserts and updates on the emp_dept table itself. Whenever a new record is inserted or an existing record updated, the current employee and department names are retrieved from their respective tables and stored with the emp_dept record. The second trigger, department_emp_dept, ensures that any changes to a department's name are propagated to all the related records in the emp_dept table. The third trigger does the same thing for changes to employee names.

Writing these triggers almost leads to a mutation problem. Recall the emp_dept_upd trigger shown in Listing 11.3. It is defined to fire only when the dept_id field is updated. In other words, it is defined as AFTER UPDATE OF dept_id ON emp_dept. Removing the words OF dept_id would cause it to fire whenever an emp_dept record was changed. In that case, a change to a department name would fire department_emp_dept, which would issue an update against the emp_dept table. That would in turn fire the emp_dept_upd trigger, which would issue an update against the department table, which in turn would mutate because the SQL statement that started all this was an update against that table.

2. Write the SQL statements necessary to populate the emp_name and dept_name fields for any existing emp_dept records.

   This could be done as either one or two updates. Here is a solution done with one UPDATE statement:

```
UPDATE emp_dept ed
  SET emp_name = (SELECT emp_name
                    FROM employee e
                   WHERE e.emp_id = ed.emp_id),
      dept_name = (SELECT dept_name
                     FROM department d
                    WHERE d.dept_id = ed.dept_id);
```

Day 12, "Using Oracle8i Objects for Object-Oriented Programming"

Quiz

1. What is the difference between a class and an object?

    A class, or an *object type,* as it is called by Oracle, serves as the blueprint for one or more objects. It is just a design, and you might compare it to a table definition. An object, on the other hand, represents an instance of a class. You can create many objects of a given type, just as you can create many records in a table.

2. What are the allowed return values for an ORDER function?

    The allowed return values for an ORDER function are 0, 1, and -1. A 0 value means that the two objects being compared are equal. A value of -1 means that the object whose method was called is less than the other object. A value of 1 means that the object whose method was called is greater than the other object.

3. An object table has one column for each attribute of an object, plus one additional column. What is this additional column used for?

    The extra column in an object table is used to store the *object identifier*, which uniquely identifies that object in the database. It is an Oracle-generated value, and is automatically assigned to each object when it is first stored in the table.

4. How is an object reference different from an object?

    An object reference functions similarly to a pointer in a language such as C. It is used to store a reference from one object to another. It is only a pointer, and in order to access the referenced object, you must use that pointer in a query to retrieve the specified object.

5. How many attributes must an object have? How many methods?

    An object must have at least one attribute. It does not, however, have to have any methods.

6. What datatypes are allowed for the return value of a MAP function?

    A MAP function can return values only of type NUMBER, VARCHAR2, or DATE.

7. What are accessor and mutator methods?

    Accessor methods are member functions that exist primarily to enable you to retrieve specific attribute values from an object. *Mutator methods* are member procedures that enable you to set the value of a specific attribute or set of attributes. Using accessor and mutator methods helps insulate your code from changes to an object's underlying implementation.

Exercises

1. Write a stored function that creates and returns an object of type building. This function should accept as parameters the building's name, its address, and the manager's employee number. Have the function check the database before creating the new building object, to be sure that another building with the same name does not already exist. If another building with the same name does exist, the function should return null.

Here is one solution:

INPUT

```
 1: CREATE OR REPLACE FUNCTION CreateBuilding (
 2:    --This is an example of how you can work around the
 3:    --fact that you can't write your own "constructor" for
 4:    --the building object. This stored function serves
 5:    --as a psuedo-constructor. Note however, that Oracle can't
 6:    --force you to call this.
 7:    inBldgName         VARCHAR2,
 8:    inBldgStreet       VARCHAR2,
 9:    inBldgCity         VARCHAR2,
10:    inBldgStateAbbr    VARCHAR2,
11:    inBldgZip          VARCHAR2,
12:    inBldgMgr          employee.emp_id%TYPE
13:    ) RETURN building AS
14: TheNewBldg     building;
15: NoFlag         integer;
16: BEGIN
17:    --Check to see if this building already exists.
18:    SELECT count(*) INTO NoFlag
19:      FROM buildings
20:     WHERE BldgName = inBldgName;
21:
22:    IF NoFlag > 0 THEN
23:      RETURN null;
24:    END IF;
25:
26:    --Check to see if the manager employee id is valid.
27:    SELECT count(*) INTO NoFlag
28:      FROM employee
29:     WHERE emp_id = inBldgMgr;
30:
31:    IF NoFlag = 0 THEN
32:      RETURN null;
33:    END IF;
34:
35:    --All validation checks have been passed, create the new
36:    --building object.
37:    TheNewBldg := building (inBldgName
38:                           ,address (inBldgStreet
39:                                    ,'' --no second addr line
```

```
40:                                              ,inBldgCity
41:                                              ,inBldgStateAbbr
42:                                              ,inBldgZip
43:                                              ,'') --no phone number
44:                              ,inBldgMgr);
45:
46:    RETURN TheNewBldg;
47: END;
48: /

Function created.

49: --Create some building objects
50: DECLARE
51:    a_building     building;
52: BEGIN
53:        --This will succeed
54:        a_building := CreateBuilding('The Red Barn',
55:                                    '101 Pasture Lane',
56:                                    'Mio','MI','48826',599);
57:        dbms_output.put_line('Created: ' ¦¦ a_building.BldgName);
58:
59:        --This will fail because the building exists.
60:        a_building := CreateBuilding('East Storage Shed',
61:                                    '101 Pasture Lane',
62:                                    'Mio','MI','48826',599);
63:        dbms_output.put_line('Created: ' ¦¦
64:                            nvl(a_building.BldgName,'Nothing'));
65:
66:        --This will fail because the manager does not exist.
67:        a_building := CreateBuilding('The Blue Barn',
68:                                    '101 Pasture Lane',
69:                                    'Mio','MI','48826',999);
70:        dbms_output.put_line('Created: ' ¦¦
71:                            nvl(a_building.BldgName,'Nothing'));
72:
73:    END;
74: /

Created: The Red Barn
Created: Nothing
Created: Nothing

PL/SQL procedure successfully completed.
```

ANALYSIS The CreateBuilding function takes five arguments: a building name, street address, city, state abbreviation, and manager ID. It returns an object of type building. The SELECT statement in lines 18–20 first checks to see if a building with the same name already exists. Then the SELECT statement in lines 27–29 checks to be sure that the manager ID is a valid employee ID. If everything checks out, the building constructor is called in lines 37–44 to actually create the building object, which is then returned to the calling program (see line 46).

The PL/SQL block at the end of the listing (lines 50–74) shows the results of three attempts to create building objects. The first succeeds. The second fails because a building with the same name already exists. The third also fails, but this time because the building manager ID does not represent a valid employee ID.

2. Modify the building object type definition to use a MAP function, instead of an ORDER function, for comparisons.

   Here is one solution:

INPUT

```
 1: CREATE OR REPLACE TYPE building AS OBJECT (
 2:    BldgName           VARCHAR2(40),
 3:    BldgAddress        address,
 4:    BldgMgr            INTEGER,
 5:    MEMBER PROCEDURE   ChangeMgr (NewMgr IN INTEGER),
 6:    MAP MEMBER FUNCTION Compare
 7:        RETURN VARCHAR2
 8:    );
 9:
10: Type created.
11:
12: CREATE OR REPLACE TYPE BODY building AS
13:    MEMBER PROCEDURE   ChangeMgr(NewMgr IN INTEGER) IS
14:       BEGIN
15:          BldgMgr := NewMgr;
16:       END;
17:
18:    MAP MEMBER FUNCTION Compare
19:    RETURN VARCHAR2 IS
20:       BEGIN
21:          RETURN BldgName;
22:       END;
23: END;
24: /
```

Type body created.

ANALYSIS This version of the building object is much the same as the one you first created from Listing 12.7, except that it has a MAP function defined instead of an ORDER function. This MAP function, declared in lines 6–7 and defined in lines 18–22 of the second segment, simply returns the building name. When comparing objects of type building, Oracle will call this function and base the comparison on the values returned.

Day 13, "Debugging Your Code and Preventing Errors"

Quiz

1. True or False: Logic errors are easier to debug than syntax errors.

   False. Because the compiler doesn't point them out, logic errors are almost always more difficult to debug than syntax errors.

2. Missing a semicolon is what type of an error?

   A syntax error.

3. Provide the answer to the calculation 6 + 4 / 2 = ?.

   The expression 6 + 4 / 2 evaluates to 8. The division takes precedence over the addition, so it is done first.

4. True or False: Commenting code is a waste of time.

   False. Comments improve the readability of code and clarify the intent of the application programmer.

5. True or False: Formatting code is not necessary.

   False. If you don't format your code, it will be difficult to read, increasing the likelihood of making a mistake.

Exercise

The DEBUG package in this lesson always writes debugging messages to the file named debug.txt. That will cause problems if multiple developers use the package at once. Modify the DEBUG package as follows:

- Modify the ERASE procedure to accept a filename. This filename will be used by subsequent calls to the OUT procedure.

- Modify both the OUT and ERASE procedures so that if no filename is passed, or if ERASE is never called, no file is created and no messages get written.

For extra credit, add an ASSERT procedure to the DEBUG package, and build in a flag so that you can enable and disable assertions at will.

In one possible solution to the exercise, the modified DEBUG package would look like this:

```
 1: CREATE OR REPLACE PACKAGE DEBUG AS
 2:     /* Procedure OUT is used to output a comment of your
 3:     choice, along with the contents of the variable.  The
 4:     Procedure OUT statement defines the function.*/
 5:     PROCEDURE OUT(p_Comments IN VARCHAR2,
 6:                   p_Variable IN VARCHAR2);
 7:
 8:     /* Procedure Erase begins a new file.
 9:     Used to start a new debugging process.  Good idea to call
10:     this function first.  */
11:     PROCEDURE Erase (p_filename IN VARCHAR2);
12:
13:     /*Procedure ASSERT tests a condition, and raises an error
14:     if that condition is not true. */
15:     PROCEDURE assert (
16:         p_condition IN BOOLEAN,
17:         p_message IN VARCHAR2);
18: END DEBUG; -- End Definition of package DEBUG
19: /
20:
21: CREATE OR REPLACE PACKAGE BODY DEBUG AS
22:     log_filename VARCHAR2(30) := '';
23:
24: PROCEDURE OUT(p_Comments IN VARCHAR2,
25:               p_Variable IN VARCHAR2) IS
26:         v_MyFHOUT UTL_FILE.FILE_TYPE; -- Declare File Handle
27:
28: BEGIN
29:     /* Exit if no filename has been specified. */
30:     IF log_filename = '' THEN
31:         RETURN;
32:     END IF;
33:
34:     /* Use A to append all output being sent to the file */
35:     v_MyFHOUT := UTL_FILE.FOPEN('c:\a',log_filename,'a');
36:
37:     /* This outputs the Time and Date as MM-DD-YY HH:MM:SS
38:     followed by comments, and then by the contents of the
39:     variables. Each element is surrounded by quotation marks,
40:     and separated by a comma.*/
41:
42:     UTL_FILE.PUT_LINE(v_MyFHOUT,'"'||
43:         TO_CHAR(SYSDATE,'mm-dd-yy HH:MM:SS AM')
44:         || '","Comment: ' || p_Comments ||
45:             '","Variable Contents: ' || p_Variable || '"');
46:
47:     /* Close the file handle which points to debug.txt */
48:     UTL_FILE.FCLOSE(v_MyFHOUT);
49: EXCEPTION
50:     /* Create Exception to display error code and message */
51:     WHEN OTHERS THEN
```

```
52:             DBMS_OUTPUT.PUT_LINE
53:                 ('ERROR ' || to_char(SQLCODE) || SQLERRM);
54:             NULL; -- Do Nothing
55: END OUT; -- End Execution of Procedure OUT
56:
57:
58: PROCEDURE Erase (p_filename IN VARCHAR2) IS
59:             v_MyFH UTL_FILE.FILE_TYPE; -- Create File Handle
60: BEGIN
61:     /* Save the filename, then check to see if it is blank.
62:     If the filename is blank, then do not do anything more. */
63:     log_filename := p_filename;
64:     IF log_filename = '' THEN
65:         RETURN;
66:     END IF;
67:
68:     /* Open file to overwrite current file contents.
69:     This erases the original file.*/
70:
71:     v_MyFH := UTL_FILE.FOPEN('c:\a',log_filename,'w');
72:
73:     -- Close the file handle which points to debug.txt
74:     UTL_FILE.FCLOSE(v_MyFH);
75:
76: EXCEPTION
77:     -- Create Exception to display error code and message
78:         WHEN OTHERS THEN
79:             DBMS_OUTPUT.PUT_LINE
80:                 ('ERROR ' || to_char(SQLCODE) || SQLERRM);
81:             NULL;
82: END Erase; -- End Procedure Erase
83:
84: PROCEDURE ASSERT (
85:         p_condition IN BOOLEAN,
86:         p_message IN VARCHAR2) AS
87: BEGIN
88:     IF NOT p_condition THEN
89:         RAISE_APPLICATION_ERROR (-20000,p_message);
90:     END IF;
91: END ASSERT;
92:
93: BEGIN
94:     Erase('debug.txt'); -- Erase contents of the file
95: END DEBUG; -- End procedure DEBUG
96: /
```

As you can see, the ASSERT procedure has been added to this package. The procedure header is in lines 15–17, and the procedure body is in lines 84–91. Further, the ERASE procedure has been modified to accept a filename as an argument (lines 11 and 58). If the filename is blank, the ERASE procedure stores it and quits (lines

63–66). The OUT procedure has also been modified. The first thing it does, in lines 29–31, is check the filename. If the filename is blank, OUT returns without logging any debugging information. So not only can you now write debugging information to any file you like, but you can also turn the feature off.

Day 14, "Leveraging Large Object Types"

Quiz

1. What are the two types of internal LOBs?

   The two types of internal LOBs are the persistent and the temporary LOBs.

2. What is the maximum size of a LOB?

   4GB.

3. Can you write to external files?

   Currently, you can only read from external files, not write to them.

4. When copying LOBs from one row to another, is a new locator copied?

   Not only is a new locator created, but the entire LOB from the row is copied. If you have some 4GB objects, this table can eat up storage space fast!

Exercise

Create a temporary LOB that is of BLOB datatype, that will not be stored in the buffer, and that will be limited to the current call.

Your solution should look similar to this:

INPUT
```
begin
DBMS_LOB.CREATETEMPORARY
( blob_lob_loc,
FALSE,
DBMS_LOB.CALL);
End;
```

ANALYSIS In this solution, you have created a temporary LOB of the BLOB datatype. You have specified that it will not be stored in memory and will disappear after the current Oracle8i call.

Day 15, "Managing Transactions and Locks"

Quiz

1. How is a transaction ended?

   A transaction is ended when it is committed or rolled back.

2. What is the difference between row locking and table locking?

Row locks are enabled when a specific row is being modified by a DML statement. Table locks are acquired either explicitly or implicitly when either a row or a table is being modified.

3. What is the purpose of a savepoint?

Savepoints are like bookmarks within a transaction: They facilitate the rollback of a transaction to some intermediate point, which is defined by the placement of the savepoint.

4. What is the purpose of the two-phase commit?

Oracle's two-phase commit mechanism guarantees that all database servers participating in a distributed transaction either all commit or all roll back the statements in the transaction.

5. What is the typical return value for when the DBMS_LOCK function ran successfully?

The typical returned value from the DBMS_LOCK function will be 0 when it ran successfully.

Exercise

Write a PL/SQL block that establishes a savepoint, inserts a single record into the employee table, commits the data if the new record does not replicate an existing record, or rolls back the data if the new record insert fails.

Here is one solution:

INPUT

```
SAVEPOINT exercise;            -- use this to roll back to
INSERT INTO employee VALUES (10, 'Loraine Williams',2,4000.00,'S');
COMMIT;      -- saves the data if insert was successful
             -- this is not executed if there is an exception
EXCEPTION
WHEN DUP_VAL_ON_INDEX THEN   -- exception handler
ROLLBACK;                    -- back out data from insert
```

Day 16, "Generating Dynamic SQL"

Quiz

1. For DML and DDL statements, and also for queries, what punctuation must not be included at the end of the query?

You must not end queries, DDL statements, or DML statements with a semicolon.

2. What is meant by the term *dynamic SQL*?

   A dynamic SQL statement is one that a program generates when it is running. It is dynamic because it can change from one run to the next. A static SQL statement, on the other hand, is written directly into your program code, and never changes.

3. What is Oracle's term for the new version of dynamic SQL?

   Oracle uses the term *native dynamic SQL* to describe the new dynamic SQL features released with Oracle8i.

4. When using native dynamic SQL, what new form of the OPEN statement is used to open a cursor on a dynamic SQL statement?

   The OPEN...FOR statement is used to open a cursor on a dynamic SQL statement.

Exercise

Write a stored procedure to take a username as an argument, and create a version of mytable in that user's schema.

The following is one possible solution to this problem:

INPUT

```
 1: CREATE OR REPLACE PROCEDURE make_mytable (
 2:     username IN VARCHAR2
 3: ) AS
 4:     create_stmt     VARCHAR2(200);
 5: BEGIN
 6:     --Build up the CREATE TABLE statement.
 7:     create_stmt := 'CREATE TABLE '
 8:                 || username || '.mytable'
 9:                 || '(myrow NUMBER, mydesc VARCHAR2(50))';
10:
11:     --Execute the statement just built.
12:     EXECUTE IMMEDIATE create_stmt;
13: END;
14: /
```

ANALYSIS The variable create_stmt, declared in line 4, will ultimately contain the CREATE TABLE statement that this procedure builds. Lines 7–9 build that statement, and the username parameter is referenced in line 8 to specify that user's schema as the scheme in which the table is to be created. Line 12 contains the EXECUTE IMMEDIATE statement that executes the SQL statement in the create_stmt variable, thus creating the table.

Day 17, "Writing to Files and the Display"

Quiz

1. What is the difference between PUT and PUT_LINE?

   PUT_LINE adds a newline after the text that you write, and PUT does not.

2. Assuming that you use the version of FOPEN where no line size is specified, what is the maximum number of bytes that can be read by using GET_LINE?

   The default maximum line size is 1,023 bytes.

3. What is the maximum line size that you can specify with the FOPEN call?

   The maximum line size you can specify in an FOPEN call is 32,767 bytes.

4. What does FCLOSE_ALL do to the file open flag referenced by IS_OPEN?

   Nothing. If you close files by using FCLOSE_ALL, the IS_OPEN function still reports them as being open.

5. What is the maximum number of characters that can possibly be allocated to the buffer when using DBMS_OUTPUT?

   One million. The buffer size can range from 2,000 to 1,000,000.

Exercise

Listing 17.5 shows how to write comma-delimited data to a file. Using GET_LINE instead of PUT_LINE, modify that code to read the data back and display it by using DBMS_OUTPUT.

The following is one possible solution to the exercise:

INPUT

```
SQL> SET SERVEROUTPUT ON
SQL>
SQL> DECLARE
  2      emp_data UTL_FILE.FILE_TYPE;
  3      end_of_file_flag BOOLEAN;
  4      emp_data_line VARCHAR2(80);
  5  BEGIN
  6      --Open the file
  7      emp_data := UTL_FILE.FOPEN ('c:\a','empdata.csv','R');
  8
  9      --Read all the data from the file
 10      end_of_file_flag := FALSE;
 11      LOOP
 12          BEGIN
```

```
13              UTL_FILE.GET_LINE(emp_data, emp_data_line);
14          EXCEPTION
15              WHEN NO_DATA_FOUND THEN
16                  end_of_file_flag := TRUE;
17              WHEN OTHERS THEN
18                  raise;
19          END;
20
21          IF NOT end_of_file_flag THEN
22              --Display the line for SQL*Plus users to see.
23              DBMS_OUTPUT.PUT_LINE (emp_data_line);
24          ELSE
25              EXIT;
26          END IF;
27      END LOOP;
28
29      --Close the file
30      UTL_FILE.FCLOSE (emp_data);
31
32  EXCEPTION
33      WHEN UTL_FILE.internal_error THEN
34          DBMS_OUTPUT.PUT_LINE
35              ('UTL_FILE: An internal error occurred.');
36          UTL_FILE.FCLOSE_ALL;
37      WHEN UTL_FILE.invalid_filehandle THEN
38          DBMS_OUTPUT.PUT_LINE
39              ('UTL_FILE: The file handle was invalid.');
40          UTL_FILE.FCLOSE_ALL;
41      WHEN UTL_FILE.invalid_mode THEN
42          DBMS_OUTPUT.PUT_LINE
43              ('UTL_FILE: An invalid open mode was given.');
44          UTL_FILE.FCLOSE_ALL;
45      WHEN UTL_FILE.invalid_operation THEN
46          DBMS_OUTPUT.PUT_LINE
47              ('UTL_FILE: An invalid operation was attempted.');
48          UTL_FILE.FCLOSE_ALL;
49      WHEN UTL_FILE.invalid_path THEN
50          DBMS_OUTPUT.PUT_LINE
51              ('UTL_FILE: An invalid path was give for the file.');
52          UTL_FILE.FCLOSE_ALL;
53      WHEN UTL_FILE.read_error THEN
54          DBMS_OUTPUT.PUT_LINE
55              ('UTL_FILE: A read error occurred.');
56          UTL_FILE.FCLOSE_ALL;
57      WHEN UTL_FILE.write_error THEN
58          DBMS_OUTPUT.PUT_LINE
59              ('UTL_FILE: A write error occurred.');
60          UTL_FILE.FCLOSE_ALL;
61      WHEN others THEN
62          DBMS_OUTPUT.PUT_LINE ('Some other error occurred.');
63          UTL_FILE.FCLOSE_ALL;
64  END;
65  /
```

OUTPUT
```
502,"Kim Beanie"
511,"Jeffrey Beaner"
512,"junk"
513,"Herman D. Terman"
514,"Egan Dryup"
401,"Harvey Wallbanger"
501,"Ashley Nue"
402,"Scarlet Tanninger"
403,"Freddie Fisher"
404,"Charlie Tuna"
597,"Matthew Higgenbottom"
598,"Raymond Gennick"

PL/SQL procedure successfully completed.
```

ANALYSIS Lines 11–27 contain the read loop. Here, each line is read from the file and displayed by using DBMS_OUTPUT. The actual read is embedded within a nested PL/SQL block (lines 12–19) because of the need to detect the end-of-file. Encountering an end-of-file will result in a NO_DATA_FOUND exception being raised. This is trapped in lines 15–16, where the end-of-file flag is set to TRUE. When the flag becomes true, the loop exits.

Day 18, "Managing Database Jobs"

Quiz

1. If the server goes down for two days (Monday to Tuesday), and a job with an execution of SYSDATE + 7 was supposed to run when the server went down (Tuesday), will the job always run on the original day of the week (that is, run every Tuesday)?

   No, because the new SYSDATE is assigned when the server is restored (Wednesday), the job will now be running every Wednesday until the job is altered or removed, or another problem occurs.

2. Why must you use two single quotes around parameters specified in SUBMIT, when you used to need only one set of single quotes?

   When Oracle parses the data and removes the quotes, any part that does not have two sets of single quotes and is a string parameter is stripped down to no single quotes and thus causes the job to fail.

3. Can you alter someone else's job?

   Only if you know the owner's login and password and sign on as that person. In other words…no!

4. How do you assign your own job number to a job?

   Use ISUBMIT.

5. What interval would you use to run a procedure every hour on the hour, starting from the current date?

   You would use SYSDATE + 1/24.

Exercises

1. Write the code to submit a procedure called PAYDAY, where the parameters are FRI-DAY, Bi_Monthly, and 6. The job should always execute at 4 a.m. Saturday.

   One possible answer to this exercise is

   INPUT
   ```
   DECLARE
        v_JobNum  BINARY_INTEGER;
   BEGIN

   DBMS_JOB.SUBMIT(v_JobNum,'PAYDAY(''FRIDAY'',''BI_Monthly,6);',SYSDATE,
            'NEXT_DAY(TRUNC(SYSDATE),''SATURDAY'') + 4/24');
   END;
   ```

   ANALYSIS In this exercise, the solution submits a procedure named PAYDAY. This command passes to the procedure PAYDAY these three parameters:FRIDAY, Bi_Monthly, and 6. Finally, this job will be executed on Saturday at 4am.

2. Write the code to view the JOB, last-second run, and WHAT from USER_JOBS.

   One possible answer to this exercise is

   INPUT
   ```
   SELECT JOB,LAST_SEC,WHAT from USER_JOBS;
   ```

   ANALYSIS This statement simply selects several columns from the USER_JOBS table. These columns describe the current jobs and when they last where executed.

3. Write the code to submit job 200 once per day, starting from SYSDATE for the procedure EASY, which has no parameters.

   One possible answer to this exercise is

   INPUT
   ```
   DECLARE
   BEGIN
        DBMS_JOB.ISUBMIT(200,'EASY;',SYSDATE,'SYSDATE + 1');
   END;
   ```

   ANALYSIS This statement will execute the procedure named EASY and it will run every day beginning today.

4. Write the code to alter job 200 to execute once per week for the interval SYSDATE + 7.

One possible answer to this exercise is

INPUT

```
BEGIN
    DBMS_JOB.INTERVAL(200,'SYSDATE+7');
END;
```

ANALYSIS This statement will define the frequency that job number 200 will run. In this example, the statement defines that job 200 will run once a week.

5. Write the code to remove job 200.

One possible answer to this exercise is

INPUT

```
BEGIN
    DBMS_JOB.REMOVE(200);
END;
```

ANALYSIS This statement deletes job number 200 from the system. You will have to re-create this job if you desire to run it again in the future.

Day 19, "Alerting and Communicating with Other Procedures: The DBMS_ALERT and DBMS_PIPE Packages"

Quiz

1. What is the maximum length of an alert name?

The maximum length of the alert name is 30 bytes. The name is not case sensitive. In addition, the name cannot begin with any reserved word or phrase such as ORA$.

2. What is the maximum length of the message?

The alert message can be up to 1,800 bytes in length.

3. What data type is the message sent as?

The alert message is sent as the data type VARCHAR2 (1800).

4. If 20 sessions are monitoring for an alert and the alert is sent, how many of those sessions receive the signaled alert?

All 20 sessions receive the alert. One of the differences between alerts and pipes is that only one of the pipes would get the message in this scenario.

5. Alerts require a _____ because you are working on a transactional level, whereas pipes do not.

Commit. Alerts can also be rolled back if necessary.

6. What interval do you use to run a procedure every hour on the hour starting from the current date?

SYSDATE + 1/24 causes the procedure to run every hour.

7. If you send a message to a full pipe, how long will you wait before you abort the process?

The answer is a very long time. By default, the maxwait period is set to 1,000 days.

8. What is the maximum length of the message buffer?

The message buffer can be up to 4,096 bytes in length.

Exercises

No answers are provided for the four exercises in Day 19, but the exercises are listed below.

1. Change the code in Listing 19.3 to wait for any alert and also register for two more alerts called 'my_test' and 'extra_alert'. Store the name of the alert that is signaled in a variable entitled alert_name of type VARCHAR2(30). After the alert has been handled, remove all registered alerts.

2. Write a loop that continually executes until the value of FIRE equals 1, which will then trigger the alert called 'a_fire', which passes the message 'A Fire has Broken Out'.

3. Write the code to submit a procedure called PAYDAY, where the parameters are FRIDAY, Bi_Monthly, and 6. The job should always execute at 4 AM on Saturday.

4. Write the code to view the JOB, the last second it was run, and WHAT from USER_JOBS.

Day 20, "PL/SQL and Java"

Quiz

1. What does Oracle use for the collective Java capabilities of Orcale8i?

Oracle uses the name JServer to refer to the Oracle8i database and all its Java-related functionality.

2. What is the name of Oracle's Java engine?

Aurora is the name of Oracle's Java engine.

3. What command-line utility can you use to load Java source code, SQLJ source code, and Java classes into an Oracle8i database?

The loadjava command can do all these things. The dropjava command does the reverse, and deletes Java classes from a database.

4. When publishing a Java method, what determines whether you should publish it as a procedure or as a function?

If the method returns a value, you should publish it as a function. If the method is of type void, you should publish it as a procedure.

Exercise

Revisit the Employee class shown in Listing 20.7, and create a PL/SQL function that publishes the getSuperName method. This time, though, make that PL/SQL function part of a package.

The following is one possible solution to this exercise:

INPUT

```
1: CREATE OR REPLACE PACKAGE emp AS
2:     FUNCTION get_super_name (emp_id IN NUMBER)
3:     RETURN VARCHAR2
4:     AS LANGUAGE JAVA
5:     NAME 'Employee.getSuperName(int) return java.lang.String';
6: END emp;
7: /
```

ANALYSIS The actual declaration to publish the Java function is the same regardless of whether that function is published as part of a package. Compare these results with those in Listing 20.8. The function declaration is identical, except that here it is not a standalone function. Here, the function is part of the package named emp.

Day 21, "Advanced Queuing"

Quiz

1. What are the terms that Oracle AQ uses to describe the acts of placing messages into queues and retrieving them again?

When you place a message into a queue, you are said to be enqueuing it. When you retrieve the message again, you are said to be dequeuing it.

2. What three initialization parameters should you check when implementing AQ on a database?

You should check the AQ_TM_PROCESSES parameter, which controls the number of queue monitoring processes. You should also check the JOB_QUEUE_PROCESSES and JOB_QUEUE_INTERVAL parameters, which control the number of job queues and the frequency at which Oracle checks to see if jobs are ready to run.

3. What database role must you grant AQ administrators?

   AQ administrators need to hold the role AQ_ADMINISTRATOR_ROLE.

4. After creating a queue, and before you can place messages into it, what must you do?

   You must start a queue, after creating it, before you can enqueue and dequeue messages.

5. What are the two Oracle packages used with AQ?

   The two packages used with AQ are DBMS_AQADM and DBMS_AQ. DBMS_AQADM implements the management interface, which includes all the procedures used to create and manage queues. DBMS_AQ implements the operational interface, which encompasses the procedures used for enqueuing and dequeuing.

Exercises

1. The procedure in Listing 21.5 enqueues salary change messages into the EMP_DEPT_CHANGES queue. Write a similar procedure to enqueue department change messages.

   The following is one possible implementation of a DEPT_CHANGE procedure:

INPUT

```
 1: CREATE OR REPLACE PROCEDURE dept_change (
 2:     emp_id  IN NUMBER,
 3:     old_dept IN NUMBER,
 4:     new_dept IN NUMBER
 5: ) AS
 6:     enq_options dbms_aq.enqueue_options_t;
 7:     enq_mess_properties dbms_aq.message_properties_t;
 8:     recipients dbms_aq.aq$_recipient_list_t;
 9:     payload emp_chg;
10:     queued_message_id RAW(16);
11: BEGIN
12:     --Setup the payload
13:     payload := emp_chg(NULL,NULL,NULL
14:                      ,old_dept,new_dept);
15:
16:     --The recipient for salary changes is DEPTCHG.
17:     --Since we aren't crossing databases or queues, we
18:     --only need to specify a name, no protocol or address
19:     --is needed.
20:     recipients(1) := sys.aq$_agent('DEPTCHG',NULL,NULL);
21:     enq_mess_properties.recipient_list := recipients;
22:
23:     dbms_aq.enqueue('EMP_DEPT_CHANGES',
24:                     enq_options,
25:                     enq_mess_properties,
26:                     payload,
```

```
27:                          queued_message_id);
28: END;
29: /
```

ANALYSIS Compare this listing with 21.5, and you'll see that the code is almost identical. There are only two differences. The first is that this time the department related fields in the payload object are set, and the salary fields are left null. The other difference is that the recipient list specifies the recipient as DEPTCHG.

2. Write a procedure to dequeue department change messages. Your result should be similar to Listing 21.6. However, this time the procedure should block. In other words it should always wait until a message can be retrieved before returning.

The following is one possible implementation of a GET_DEPT_CHANGE procedure:

INPUT

```
1: CREATE OR REPLACE PROCEDURE get_dept_change (
2:     emp_id   OUT NUMBER,
3:     old_dept OUT NUMBER,
4:     new_dept OUT NUMBER
5: ) AS
6:     deq_options dbms_aq.dequeue_options_t;
7:     deq_mess_properties dbms_aq.message_properties_t;
8:     payload emp_chg;
9:     dequeued_message_id RAW(16);
10: BEGIN
11:     --Specify our consumer name
12:     deq_options.consumer_name := 'DEPTCHG';
13:
14:     --Specify the time that we will wait.
15:     --In this case, we won't wait at all.
16:     deq_options.wait := dbms_aq.forever;
17:     deq_options.navigation := dbms_aq.first_message;
18:
19:     --Perform the dequeue
20:     dbms_aq.dequeue('EMP_DEPT_CHANGES',
21:                         deq_options,
22:                         deq_mess_properties,
23:                         payload,
24:                         dequeued_message_id);
25:
26:     --Return the information that was dequeued.
27:     emp_id := payload.emp_id;
28:     old_dept := payload.leave_dept;
29:     new_dept := payload.join_dept;
30: END;
31: /
```

ANALYSIS The code in this listing is very similar to that in Listing 21.6. However, there are some differences worth noting. First, the dbms_aq.forever constant is used in line 16 to prevent the dequeue procedure from returning without a message. If no message is available, the procedure will wait until one does become available. Another item of note is in line 17, where the navigation option has been set to dbms_aq.first_message. This is added only because you are probably running both procedures from the same database session. After you use dequeue once, and identify yourself as SALCHG, you can't switch names (to DEPTCHG in this case) without also navigating to the first message. In a real-life production environment, these procedures would be used from different sessions, and there would be no need for line 17.

Another major difference between this listing and Listing 21.6 is that this listing does not enclose the dequeue call within a nested block. It doesn't need to because no dequeue wait limit was specified. The call always returns a message, unless a real error occurs. In that case, the error is propagated to the caller of GET_DEPT_CHANGE. The last difference between this listing and Listing 21.6 is that this listing accesses and returns the department related fields (lines 27–29), not the salary-related fields.

INDEX

Symbols

! (inequality operator), 68
% (percent sign), wildcard character, 70
%found attribute
    explicit cursors, 252
    implicit cursors, 255
%isopen attribute
    explicit cursors, 251
    implicit cursors, 255
%isopen attribute (explicit cursors), 249
%notfound attribute
    explicit cursors, 252
    implicit cursors, 255-256
%rowcount attribute
    explicit cursors, 252
    implicit cursors, 256
%ROWTYPE attribute, 236
%TYPE attribute, 235-236
( ) (parentheses), operator precedence, 85
* (asterisk), multiplication operator, 65

** (exponentiation operator), 65-66
+ (plus sign)
    addition operator, 65
    identity operator, 65, 67
- (minus sign)
    negation operator, 65, 67
    subtraction operator, 65
/ (slash), division operator, 65
< (less than operator), 68
<= (less than/equal to operator), 68
= (equals sign), equality operator, 68
@ command, SQL*Plus, 18-19

A

ABS function, 158
absolute values (numbers), returning, 158
accessor methods, 342
ACOS function, 158
active sets, 246
adding data to varrays, 283-284
ADD_MONTHS function, 159, 178-179
    syntax, 178
Advanced Queuing, *see* AQ
after triggers, 296
agents, AQ (Advanced Queuing), 587
alerts
    monitoring any, 535
    monitoring one, 534-535
    polling (setting time interval), 536
    registering, 533-534

D

data
concurrency, 437
consistency, 437
data dictionary views
DBA_JOBS, 517
columns, 518
DBA_JOBS_RUNNING, 517
columns, 518
stored procedures, 195
USER_JOBS, 517
columns, 518
data integrity (triggers), 300-304
delete trigger, 301
insert trigger, 301
listing, 302
update trigger, 301
data locks, 443-444, 449
dictionary locking, 449
distributed locking, 449
internal locking, 449
monitoring, 449
row locking, 445
table locking, 443-444
exclusive mode, 444
row exclusive mode, 444
row share mode, 444
share lock mode, 444
shr rw exclusv md, 444
databases
connecting to (Procedure Builder), 27-28
external files, 404-405
accessing, 412-413
checking for, 408-409
comparing, 407-408, 414-415
creating pointer to, 406-407

determining if open, 409-410
extracting from, 412
getting length, 410
getting name, 409
matching patterns in, 410-411
opening, 410
reading into buffers, 411
Oracle, obtaining for exercises, 12
Privileges (exercise completion requirements), 12
removing classes from (SSConstants), 568-569
triggers, 294
syntax, 298-300
datatypes, 34-35, 37, 39
BINARY_INTEGER, 41
subtypes, 41-43
syntax, 41
CHAR, 36
listing, 38
maximum length, 37
syntax, 36-37
VARIABLE_VALUE procedure, 468
Compatibility, calling Java from PL/SQL, 574-575
converting, 64, 92, 94
explicitly, 94-95
implicitly, 92-94
DATE (VARIABLE_VALUE procedure), 468
LOBs, 402
appending to one another, 417, 425-427
BFILE, 402
BLOB, 402
CLOB, 402
comparing, 417-418
copying, 418, 424-425

erasing, 419, 429
extracting from, 422, 427-428
matching patterns in, 420, 427-428
NCLOB, 402
reading into buffers, 421
returning length, 420
trimming, 422, 428-429
writing to, 422, 425-427
MLSLABEL (VARIABLE_VALUE procedure), 469
NUMBER (VARIABLE_VALUE procedure), 468
RAW (VARIABLE_VALUE procedure), 468
ROWID (VARIABLE_VALUE procedure), 469
string comparisons, 79-81
padding, 79
subtypes, 35
VARCHAR2, 35
subtypes, 36
syntax, 35-36
VARIABLE_VALUE procedure, 468
see also variables
DATE datatype
defining output variables, 462
syntax, 44-45
VARIABLE_VALUE procedure, 468
date functions, 159, 175-178, 180-185
ADD_MONTHS, 159, 178-179
syntax, 178

Other Related Titles

Oracle Development Unleashed, Third Edition
0-672-31575-0
Advanced Information Systems, Inc., and Dan Hotka
$49.99 USA/$74.95 CAN

SQL Unleashed, Second Edition
0-672-31709-5
Sakhr Youness, et al.
$49.99 USA/$74.95 CAN

Sams Teach Yourself Java 2 in 21 Days
0-672-31638-2
Laura Lemay
$29.99 USA/$44.95 CAN

Sams Teach Yourself SQL in 24 Hours
0-672-31245-X
Ryan Stephens
$24.99 USA/$35.95 CAN

Oracle Datatbase Construction Kit
0-672-1419-1
John Palinski
$49.99 USA/$70.95 CAN

Sams Teach Yourself SQL in 21 Days, Third Edition
0-672-31974-9
Ryan Stephens and Ronald Plew
$34.99 USA/$59.95 CAN

Sams Teach Yourself Oracle 8 Database Development in 21 Days
0-672-31078-3
David Lockman
$49.99 USA/$70.95 CAN

Sams Teach Yourself Oracle 8 in 21 Days
0-672-3115-9
Ed Whalen
$39.99 USA/$56.95 CAN

Developing Client/Server Applications with Oracle Developer 2000
0-672-30852-5
Paul Hipskey
$49.99 USA/$68.95 CAN

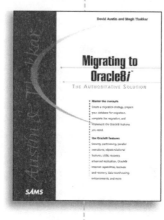

Migrating to Oracle 8i
0-672-31577-7
David Austin
$29.99 USA/$44.95 CAN

Sams Teach Yourself Oracle 8i on Windows NT in 24 Hours
0-672-31578-5
Meghraj Thakkar
$24.99 USA/$37.95 CAN

SAMS
www.samspublishing.com

All prices are subject to change.